THESE
FISTS
BREAK
BRICKS

Copyright © 2025 by Grady Hendrix and Chris Poggiali
Cover illustration copyright © 2025 by Pedro Correa
Cover copyright © 2025 by Hachette Book Group, Inc.

Hachette Book Group supports the right to free expression and the value of copyright. The purpose of copyright is to encourage writers and artists to produce the creative works that enrich our culture.

The scanning, uploading, and distribution of this book without permission is a theft of the authors' intellectual property. If you would like permission to use material from the book (other than for review purposes), please contact permissions@hbgusa.com. Thank you for your support of the authors' rights.

Running Press
Hachette Book Group
1290 Avenue of the Americas, New York, NY 10104
www.runningpress.com
@Running_Press

Previously published edition: © 2021 Grady Hendrix and Chris Poggiali
First Running Press Edition: May 2025

Published by Running Press, an imprint of Hachette Book Group, Inc.
The Running Press name and logo are trademarks of Hachette Book Group, Inc.

The Hachette Speakers Bureau provides a wide range of authors for speaking events.
To find out more, go to www.hachettespeakersbureau.com or email HachetteSpeakers@hbgusa.com.

Running Press books may be purchased in bulk for business, educational, or promotional use. For more information, please contact your local bookseller or the Hachette Book Group Special Markets Department at Special.Markets@hbgusa.com.

The publisher is not responsible for websites (or their content) that are not owned by the publisher.

Print book cover design by Amanda Richmond
Print book interior design by Kelli McAdams

Library of Congress Control Number: 2024944048

ISBNs: 978-0-7624-8948-0 (hardcover), 978-0-7624-8950-3 (ebook)

Printed in Malaysia

PCF

10 9 8 7 6 5 4 3 2 1

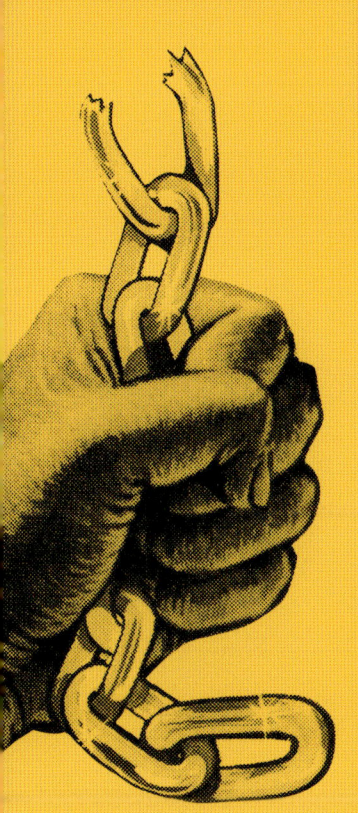

GRADY HENDRIX

THESE FISTS BREAK BRICKS

HOW KUNG FU MOVIES SWEPT AMERICA AND CHANGED THE WORLD

REVISED AND EXPANDED EDITION

CHRIS POGGIALI

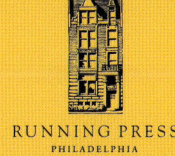

RUNNING PRESS
PHILADELPHIA

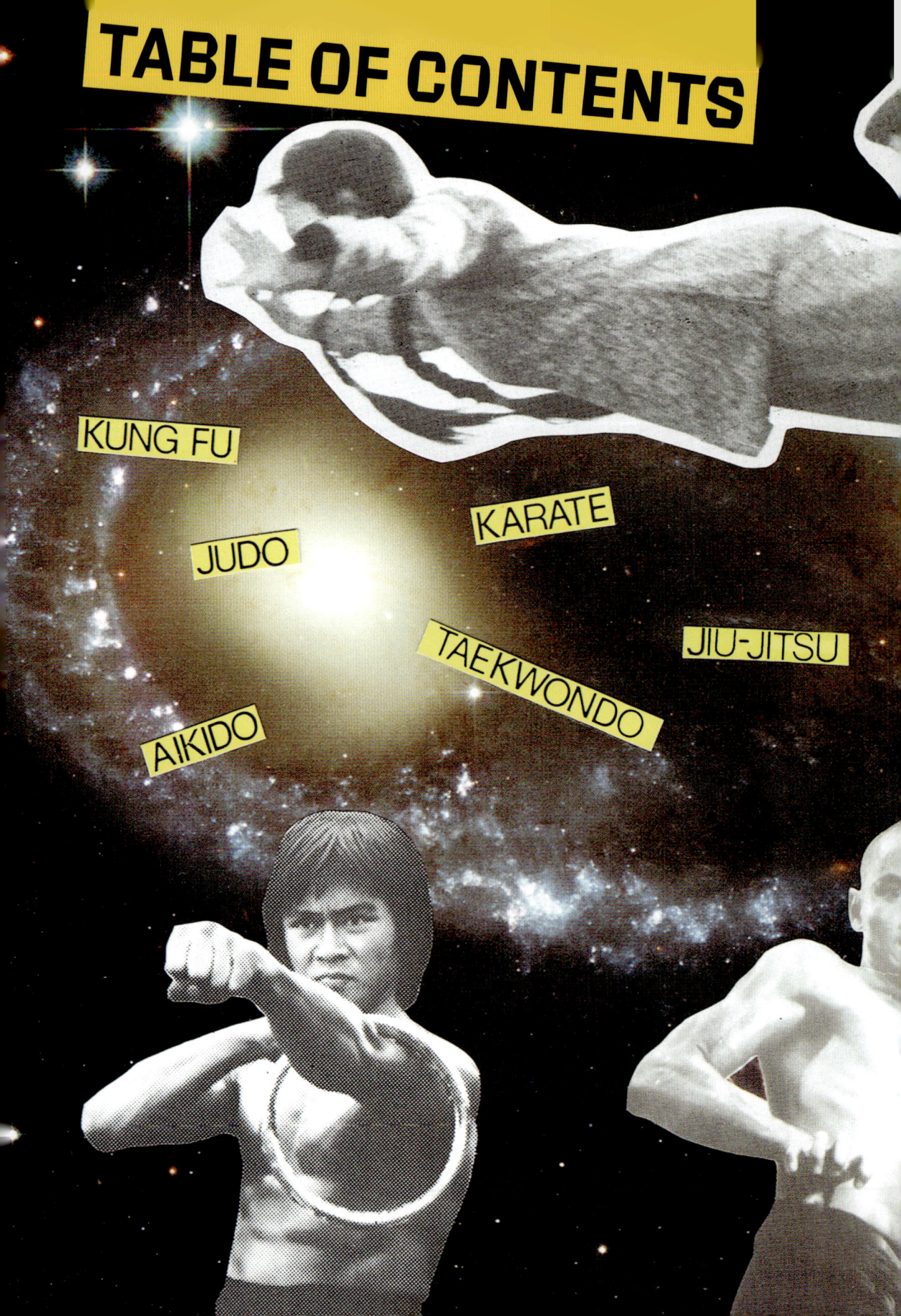

vi	*Foreword by RZA*
viii	*Introduction*
1	**IN THE BEGINNING**
30	*Karate: The Hand of Death*
35	*Billy Jack*
37	**THE SEVENTIES**
64	Hey, Kids! It's Kung Fu
81	Enter the Merch
84	The Paperback Connection
88	Comic Books That Kill!
92	**BRUCEPLOITATION**
124	The Bruce Directory
166	Directory of Distributors
198	Martial Music
232	Nunchuks
244	**THE EIGHTIES**
252	Flyover Fighters
271	Creepy Fu
274	Master of Masters
276	Heroes of the 3rd Dimension
294	Raw Farce
317	Dog of the Week
330	Fast and Furious
342	Video Companies
348	Digital Dojo
360	Enter the Video Kid
372	*Acknowledgments*
373	*Image Credits*
374	*About the Authors*

FOREWORD

ONLY IN THE CITY THAT never sleeps can a place with a name like Times Square be the location where past, present, and future all shared the same ambiguous reality. The place where the sirens of police, ambulances, and fire trucks screeched in sync with the breakbeat blasting out of a 90-watt boom box as street dancers and verbal assaulters displayed their skills for the hopes of fame . . . or to earn a few dollars to buy some weed. Hats or cardboard boxes on the ground awaiting tips as businessmen, local pedestrians, tourists, and junkies all passed by in a sea of lights and grime.

While some kids hustled to buy liquor, dope, or coke, I was on a different high. I was just out to make a couple of bucks to gain entry into a grindhouse theater to stimulate my brain with a triple feature of kung fu madness. Inside that theater, away from the noise, cold, and business of outside, I found myself in an audience of like-minded fans allowing ourselves to be transported from the slums of NYC to the hillsides of China and Japan; from the modern-day cityscape to the feudal towns and temples of the martial world.

Even though the reality was that we were packed in a smoke-filled fire hazard room with sticky floors, ripped seats, and an occasional rodent skittering around our feet, we were hypnotized by the flickering light of the films along with their scratches and disordered reels—probably because the projectionist was as high as the patrons. The cinematic battles kept us spellbound for hours before leaving, acting out the scenes on the subway train home, then returning again the next weekend to do it all again.

The violence of the NYC streets in its own unique way reflected in the violence on screen. The treacherous nature of the antagonist vs. the heroic nature of the protagonist, with the uncertainty of who would be the victor, kept audiences coming back for more.

Looking for stories that reflected their own struggles, audiences could role-change at any moment, inspired by the characters they watched.

Who can forget *Fist of Fury*, retitled *The Chinese Connection* in the US, probably following the success of *The French Connection* and in line with grindhouses and distributors renaming Asian films to resonate with their market. When Bruce Lee defied oppression and Japanese lawlessness to his fellow countrymen, he ignited the audience to cheer him on and travel the road of vengeance with him. Yet, after his victory over his enemy using his hands, feet, and nunchucks, he's met with an array of bullets from the rifles of law enforcement, leaving the audience with an insatiable desire for more of Bruce and the types of characters played by him and other martial greats.

Or on the opposite side of the spectrum, we had films like *Fists of the White Lotus*, starring Lo Lieh as the titular villain using "100 Pace Palm," leaving every kung fu buff hungry for movies with a grey-haired old master causing mayhem in the countryside.

I'll never forget the first time I watched *The Mystery of Chess Boxing* and hearing the entire cinema roar each time Ghost Face Killer (played by Mark Long) appeared on the screen. He was a villain killing off his enemies—in some cases in front of their wives and children—yet we walked out the theater wanting to be him, the baddest motherfucker on the screen. Wong Fei, Phillip Ko, and Tommy Lee all demanded similar respect as they played recurring villain roles. When you saw them on the screen, you knew you were in for an incredible final showdown.

Another great aspect of these films and their audience was the multicultural and gender-inclusive perspective. I would see guys in the theater with their girlfriends cheering, booing, and even making out to these films. Such titles as *The Tattoo Connection*, *Hong Kong Godfather*, *Bruce Lee in New Guinea*, or even the Shaw Brothers' *Shaolin Handlock* weren't afraid to show cleavage . . . which for a kid under 12 years old (who had to sneak his way in) was an extra treat. But even more important was watching various female heroines dominating the screen, destroying their bullying male counterparts. Films like *Come Drink with Me*, *Golden Swallow*, and *14 Amazons* laid the foundation for later films following the Bruce Lee explosion. Angela Mao in *Sting of the Dragon Master* or Kara Hui in *My Young Auntie*, or one of my independent favorites *8 Strikes of the Wildcat*—all had female leads and each had the audience raving for more.

In the following pages of *These Fists Break Bricks*, we will travel down that path of yesterday, where grindhouse theaters and the films they displayed inspired the filmmakers of today and the sound of the world's most popular music. May this book's history and the culture it revisits inspire future generations to come.

RZA
Wu-Tang Clan

INTRODUCTION

IN MARCH 1973, THE WORLD changed. Kung fu movies came roaring out of Hong Kong, landed in American movie theaters, and blew everyone's minds, leaving dropped jaws on sticky floors and launching a tidal wave of martial arts movies that swamped grindhouse theaters across the country for 15 years, started fashion trends, influenced music, and put a shirtless Bruce Lee on the wall of every kid's bedroom.

Before 1973, no one knew a nunchuk from a ninja, but over the next decade and a half, kung fu movies would influence the birth of hip hop and breakdancing, sell millions of albums, win Emmy awards, earn millions at the box office, sell hundreds of thousands of videocassettes, and introduce America to the biggest non-white stars to hit the silver screen. The Thelma to this revolution's Louise, the Jim Kelly to its Bruce Lee, the *Power Man* to its *Iron Fist* arrived simultaneously in August 1973 when DJ Kool Herc started spinning at a party in a Bronx rec room, kickstarting hip hop, whose beats, graffiti, fashion, and b-boying became America's dominant cultural force of the '80s and '90s.

March and August 1973 sparked genuine revolutions. Kung fu movies came from the Hong Kong streets, surging with anti-colonial protests. Hip hop came from Herc's beats, born in a busted borough written off as a no-hope neighborhood that would never produce anything but poverty and crime. Hip hop and kung fu turned that story around.

This is the story of the remix. It's about people who took what they were given and turned it into something new. It's about Koreans teaching karate to Black students in Washington, DC. About movies from Hong Kong featuring Taiwanese stars playing in Los Angeles movie theaters and inspiring Latino kids. About forms that aren't karate or kung fu but combine the best of both. It's a never-ending mixing, remixing, spinning, spitting, spraying, styling, strutting, smashing, that blurs racial identities, blends nationalities, takes it to the streets, and mixes it into sick beats.

It's not just a story about movies and music, it's about politics and poverty, martial arts mysteries and black histories. A lot of the facts we found are hotly contested by people immersed far deeper in these scenes than we'll ever be. Someone can contradict everything in this book by citing an earlier example or a more obscure Hung Gar teacher, but to tell this story we've had to focus our narrative on certain people and places, and that comes at the expense of others. We made choices. They may not be the right ones, but they're ours. No fact appears in this book that we couldn't verify from at least two sources, although there are a small handful of stories that were just too good to leave out.

But relax. This book isn't the final word, it's a starting position. It should inspire readers to put their feet on the streets and discover their own version of events. Did Vic Moore block Bruce Lee's unblockable punches? He says he did and that's how it looks on film but you might interpret it differently. Did Chuck McNeil actually make *Disco-Dynomite* or was it all a scam? We can't find any evidence that his movie ever existed, but someone else might. We don't own this history, we're just passing it along. This history belongs to the people who made it.

Angela Mao, DJ Kool Herc, Bruce Lee, Grandmaster Flash, Ron Van Clief, TAKI 183, Sha-Rock—they broke boundaries, broke limits, broke conventions, broke chains. They raised their fists against a world that wanted to define them by what they weren't: not white, not rich, not famous, not acceptable. They used their bodies and their voices to forge something out of nothing. They used their fists and their feet to transform themselves into legends. And they used those legends to change the world.

"**ME JIU-JITSU," A JAPANESE HOUSEBOY** says, tripping Cary Grant and sending him into a somersault.

"Is that so?" Grant asks, picking himself up off the floor.

He takes the houseboy by the hand and sends him flying.

"Me jiu-jitsu, too."

The year is 1937, the movie is *The Awful Truth*, and the actor playing the houseboy is Miki Morita, one of four Japanese character actors then working in Hollywood. That year he appeared in 12 other movies, playing a houseboy, a servant, a cook, a valet, a spy, a human trafficker, another houseboy, a house guest, a dinner guest, a gardener, and a houseboy again. With *The Awful Truth* he became the first Asian actor to perform martial arts on American movie screens. With one exception, he'd be the last until 1964.

Hollywood first put martial arts onscreen in 1935's surprise hit, *G-Men*, during a two-minute scene of Jimmy Cagney, patron saint of Hollywood judo, getting slammed all over the gym while his instructor wets his pants laughing. Then came Mr. Moto. Star of three books before making the leap to the big screen, the Japanese detective's judo and jiu-jitsu skills were amped up for Hollywood, where he was played by Peter Lorre in yellowface.

His first film, *Think Fast, Mr. Moto* (1937), appeared two months before *The Awful Truth*, and featured Lorre applying judo to a cop, an antique store owner, two posh swells, and a nefarious ship's steward before the end credits rolled. Or, rather, Lorre's stunt double, Harvey Parry, applied the judo. Parry doubled for "all the little guys,"

Created as a replacement for Charlie Chan, Mr. Moto appeared in 9 movies and 23 radio shows, always played by a white actor either in yellowface or putting on an "Oriental" accent.

as he called them, like Lorre, Edward G. Robinson, and Cagney.

Jimmy Cagney loved judo, and he delivered a three-minute judo throwdown versus an evil Japanese military officer in *Blood on the Sun* (1945), but his opponent was a disgraced, 6'2" LAPD cop in yellowface named Jack Sergel. (More about him later.) A boxer beat the tar out of a judo fighter played by Ukrainian-born actor Mike Mazurki in *Behind the Rising Sun* (1943), and Republic serials saw lady crimefighters like the Tiger Woman and Dolores Quantero trounce male opponents with judo throws, courtesy of stuntwomen Helen Thurston and Babe DeFreest.

The '60s kicked off a karate craze, but even when newspaper ads for *The Manchurian Candidate* (1962) ballyhooed "Karate!" Sinatra's opponent was Henry Silva, a New York native in yellowface playing a Korean.

Edmond O'Brien judo tosses one of James Cagney's thugs in *White Heat* (1949) and a one-armed Spencer Tracy used judo to mop up a diner with Ernest Borgnine's face in *Bad Day at Black Rock* (1955), but they were all Anglo.

The one exception to this whites-only policy occured in Humphrey Bogart's *Tokyo Joe* (1949), a cynical noir with Bogart essentially reprising his role as Rick from *Casablanca*, only this time in post-war Tokyo. The production searched high and low for Japanese actors, a rare commodity after World War II, and finally found Teru Shimada, one of the four original Japanese character actors who worked alongside Miki Morita, to play Bogart's friend, Ito. It's the first movie Shimada made after his release from Arizona's Poston internment camp in 1943 and, in the movie, Bogie and Shimada celebrate their reunion with a few bouts of roughhouse judo. For years after, people on the street recognized Shimada as the guy who kicked Bogart's ass.

It wasn't until *A Shot in the Dark* (1964) that an actual Asian person did actual martial arts on the big screen again, and even then it was a full circle right back to 1937. Burt Kwouk, born in Britain and raised in Shanghai, played Cato Fong, Inspector Clouseau's houseboy, instructed to ambush the inspector at every opportunity to keep his martial arts skills sharp. Funny? Sure. But what's the difference between houseboy Miki Morita clumsily throwing Cary Grant to the floor and houseboy Burt Kwouk emerging screaming from freezers or dropping down from canopied beds on top of Peter Sellers for comic effect?

But white Americans needed to ridicule martial arts, because when they first arrived in this country, they were terrifying.

PEOPLE SAY BRUCE LEE PIONEERED multiple schools of martial arts into one super-technique, but mixing and remixing is the martial arts story. In 1882, Kano Jigoro forged an unbeatable combat combination when he mixed Tenjin Shin Yo–ryu jiu-jitsu with Kito-ryu jiu-jitsu, added a pinch of wrestling and a dash of sumo, and rebranded it as "judo." His super-regimented, ultrahierarchical school, the Kodokan, opened in Tokyo with a dozen students. By 1911 it had over a thousand.

Judo promised that one skilled judoka could defeat many opponents, no matter their size. One of Jigoro's students was the famed brawler Professor Yamashita, who once got in a fight in a restaurant. When the injured party returned with 14 friends, Yamashita "calmly sat at the head of the stairs," and as they came up, he "simply choked them in detail and hurled them back down again."

Brought over to America in 1902 to coach the sheltered son of a Seattle businessman, Professor Yamashita caught the eye of President Teddy Roosevelt, who poached him to be the White House's judo instructor instead. For years after, Roosevelt, now a brown belt, would challenge everyone who entered the Oval Office, shouting, "Do you boys understand jiu-jitsu?" before tackling them to the floor.

The President's enthusiasm, and tiny Japan's victory over mighty Russia in the Russo-Japanese War (1904–1905), caused the Department of War to appoint a committee to study whether all branches of the service should be required to study judo. Suddenly, Westerners wanted to learn about this so-called judo that let a small man—or country—beat the crap out of a larger one.

The first English-language judo instruction book came out in 1905, and it sent the judo craze global. In Germany, the Kaiser ordered all his military officers and mailmen to learn judo. Women in the United Kingdom learned judo "to make them better able to look after themselves when out late at night." Chicago policewomen were ordered to learn judo "to fit them for emergency encounters."

Newspapers reported on people being killed by judo before being brought back to life, also by judo. Arnold Henry Savage Landor claimed to be working on a flying machine based on the principles of jiu-jitsu (a word used interchangeably in the West with "judo"), although no one, including Arnold Henry Savage Landor, seemed to be able to describe exactly what that meant.

In pulp fiction, detective Nick Carter fought enemies like Princess Olga, tiger chief of the Russian Nihilists, alongside his pals, Talika the Geisha Girl and Ten-Ichi, the son of the Mikado, who was not only a judo expert but also nearly as good a detective as Carter himself.

America turned out to be the land of opportunity for fictional judoka but real-life Japanese judo experts struggled to survive. Souring on this foreign martial art, the Navy kicked Professor Yamashita to the curb as soon as his two-year contract expired, and on the West Coast the first judo dojo opened in the back of a candy store. Rafu Dojo (literally "Los Angeles Dojo") was founded in 1910 by Mogusa Nina, a hard-drinking, fun-loving couchsurfer who avoided starving to death thanks to the generosity of the owner of a local café and occasional odd jobs on various farms. In 1915, Rafu Dojo relocated to the back of a pool hall, then to Yamato Hall, a three-story building that also provided space for two Japanese newspapers, a Buddhist temple, and an underground casino that paid the LAPD to look the other way.

At the time, Catch Wrestling ("catch as catch can") was a favorite of strongmen in traveling carnivals, who would challenge locals to take them down for a cash prize. Combining a mishmash of techniques, it was backwoods MMA that attracted anyone who wanted to make a name for themselves or needed money. Professor Tokugoro Ito was both.

Arriving in Washington State around 1907, Professor Ito, a fourth-degree black belt, was the highest-ranked judoka in North America, but no one cared until he started Catch Wrestling. Between 1909 and 1912, he trashed one white wrestler after another: Eddie Robinson at the Seattle Grand Opera House ("Kind friends held Eddie's head while he heaved up everything but his Adam's apple," according to reporters), George Braun at the Seattle Theater ("After a lot of slapping and kneading, Braun's eyelids finally fluttered, and in a half gasp he wanted to know if many were killed when the roof fell in"), and Joe Acton ("Ito threw his opponent . . . and choked him breathless in three minutes"). Appalled, the *Seattle Times* wrote that they were "scratching their heads trying to think of some white man who can beat him."

(opposite page) H. Irving Hancock, author of the first American book on judo, went out of his way to recommend judo to women, later publishing a book devoted to women's physical health. At a time when women were demanding equal rights, judo seemed like the great physical equalizer.

(above) Professor Ito in 1927, about 10 years after he arrived in the United States.

When the Russo-Japanese War broke out, Japan sent ambassadors around the world to present the country as a modern nation, not some "savage backwater." They were more successful than anyone anticipated, and Japanese culture, especially judo and jiu-jitsu, spread everywhere.

Enter Ad Santel, a massive German wrestler who hated the Kodokan for no good reason. He began taking down their judoka one by one, and in 1916, he bounced Professor Ito's head off the floor during a match in Seattle, winning by a knockout. Since Professor Ito claimed to be the Kodokan's best fighter, Santel immediately proclaimed himself the world's top judoka, which drove the Kodokan crazy. Their students traveled to the United States to take on Santel, who laid them out one after the other. After the Kodokan barred its students from fighting Santel, he went to Japan and took down all six Kodokan students who fought him in secret. (They were thrown out of the Kodokan for their trouble.) The splash Santel made in Japan is widely seen as the beginning of that country's fascination with professional wrestling, which continues to this day.

Professor Ito, meanwhile, decided he was done with Seattle, but before departing for Los Angeles he took on Santel in a rematch, hurling him "around the ring like a bag of sawdust" until Santel "gave a couple of gurgles, turned black in the face, and thumped the floor, signifying he had enough."

Honor avenged, Professor Ito took over LA's Rafu Dojo and kept taking down wrestlers, challenging the German-Russian Berne Brothers, who rented out the Shrine Auditorium for their match and drummed up publicity by touring Japanese athletic clubs, where they bent steel bars. Foolishly, Ito agreed to compete according to wrestling rules, not judo rules, which meant he had to pin his man to win. This was tricky, since each Berne Brother outweighed him by at least 100 pounds.

The night of the fight, Ito threw one Berne Brother 14 times but couldn't pin him down. In desperation, he finally put him in an arm lock and, as one of his students remembers, "harder and harder he applied the lock. Bonner [*sic*] was groaning from the pain, but he still wouldn't give up. Ito kept applying the lock, and finally, we could hear the noise in Bonner's arm. It sounded as if it were cracking. Bonner finally gave up. When he got up, he couldn't use the arm and it hung down by his side. It must have been broken."

Judoka kept arriving on the West Coast. Yasu Fujita, son of a millionaire, came on a student visa but was deported after being caught taking down American wrestlers with judo. Back in Japan, he became mayor of his hometown. George Yoshida brought judo to New York. Sego Murakami established the San Fernando Dojo, where he and his father had moved to open a plant nursery. By the mid-'20s there were 27 dojos in Los Angeles alone.

Everyone wanted to learn judo. The Chicago Police Department was the first to offer its officers judo instruction, followed by the New York Police Department in 1923. Eccentric Philadelphia socialite and wannabe concert singer Anthony J. Drexel Biddle wrote *Do or Die: A Supplementary Military Manual on Individual Combat* and taught judo to G-men. The San Francisco Police taught judo, the Army taught judo, even the Teamsters Union took up judo. "We aren't looking for a fight," said Dave Beck, international vice president of the union. "But if anybody else wants one, our boys will be able to take care of themselves." Even two-time Nobel Prize winner Madame Curie and her husband became judo instructors in Paris because "their salaries at the Radium Institute are inadequate."

Then came the War, and judo was its first casualty.

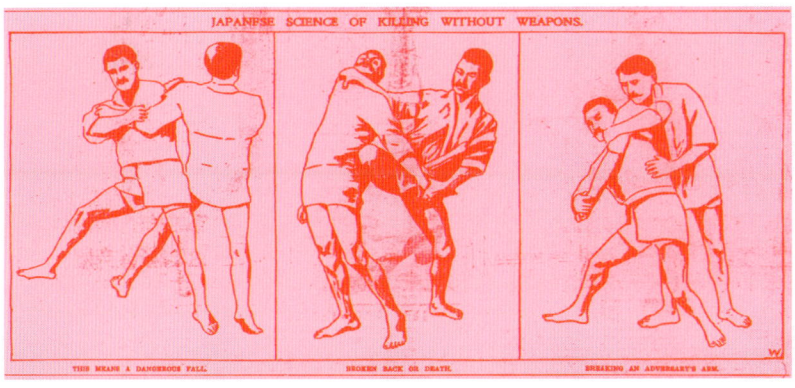

Three of the jiu-jitsu moves taught to law enforcement officers in Boston and New York in 1900 by John J. O'Brien, a Beantown cop who had traveled to Japan to study their "science of killing without weapons" and proved so proficient at it that he became chief of police in Nagasaki.

THIS IS A TOMBSTONE FOR a way of life wiped out by World War II.

"I started out as a child with a hostility toward all of mankind," begins the letter to *Black Belt* magazine. "Each time anyone came to town purporting to teach a method of mayhem . . . I would somehow wrangle the tuition fee. I learned a lot, even from some of the phonies under whom I studied. It was more a matter of good fortune than good management that they did not lock me up and throw away the key, for I felt the need to demonstrate my powers at the least provocation."

The writer is John "Jack" Sergel. An American citizen born in Buenos Aires, Sergel moved to Los Angeles, where he became an undertaker. An allergy to embalming fluid drove him to the Los Angeles Police Department, which might have been a better fit, since by then he was an expert at Argentine knife fighting, American catch-wrestling, and French savate, a kind of Euro-kickboxing.

> **Judo Tussle Takes Place in Home of Actor Jim Cagney**
>
> HOLLYWOOD (⑰)—There was a wild judo battle early today in the home of James Cagney but the movie tough guy, though quite handy at the sport, did not take part.
>
> Police said Kenneth Kuniyuki, 39, former butler at the Cagney home, called to see his estranged wife, Elizabeth, 29, a domestic for the actor. She expressed fears for her safety and sought aid of Jack Sergel, Cagney's bodyguard.
>
> The wife told police that Kuniyuki, a judo instructor, struck her and then Sergel went into action. He is a former police department judo instructor and soon restrained Kuniyuki.
>
> Police booked the ex-butler on battery charges.

Sergel heard about judo and barged into Sego Murakami's San Fernando Dojo demanding lessons. Confronted with this loud, angry, 6'2" American, Murakami refused. But Sergel kept coming back until, on May 9, 1933, Murakami accepted him as a probationary student.

Sergel had enormous energy (one student remembers him as "a big kid") and he was devoted to Murakami, bowing to him and calling him sensei, because, as he later wrote, judo gave him a sense of "humble pride . . . and fellowship. Since that time, I've been a very changed man." Sergel trained constantly, moving between the San Fernando Dojo, Rafu Dojo, and the Seinan Dojo in Southwestern LA, where classes were taught by Kenneth Kuniyuki, a third-degree black belt. In 1939, at the Grand Judo Championship in Los Angeles, Sergel threw five Japanese-American judoka in a row to earn his own black belt, and shortly after he joined the LAPD and began training fellow officers in judo.

Then came Executive Order 9066.

Passed barely two months after Japan's sneak attack on Pearl Harbor, it locked 112,000 Japanese Americans in concentration camps. Some, like Murakami, had migrated to the US. Others, like Kuniyuki, were born here. Didn't matter. They were Japanese? They went to prison, and they could only take what they could carry.

Murakami unloaded his nursery at a fire sale price to a white guy who immediately stuck an American flag out front next to a sign reading, "Now owned by White Americans." Japanese families sold their cars for a fraction of their value. White families moved into houses recently vacated by their Japanese neighbors.

In the midst of this mayhem, Sergel became the caretaker for the property of his Japanese friends, storing their heirlooms and valuables beneath his house and taking over Seinan Dojo at the request of Kuniyuki, who was sent to the Minidoka War Relocation Center in Idaho.

Only a teacher who'd achieved a certain belt level could advance a student to their next belt, but all the high-ranked teachers were imprisoned. For Sergel, the solution seemed obvious. Sego Murakami had been interned at Manzanar, at the base of the Sierra Nevada Mountains, a four-hour drive from LA. Sergel loaded up two cars with his students, pooled their gas rations, and headed for the prison camp.

At Manzanar, Murakami had kept teaching judo and his students had become unofficial camp peacekeepers. He'd even built a rickety dojo that shook so much in the wind his students named it Shindokan ("Shaking and Quaking") Dojo. Sergel's students, including teenagers and women, stayed for three days, competed with internees, and were examined by Murakami for their next belts.

When reporters called, Sergel gave interviews, naively thinking he'd done nothing wrong. The press went wild, painting a depraved picture of an LAPD officer forcing pure white Americans to mix with "Jap" traitors and bowing to pictures of the Emperor while innocent white women were groped by "Jap" prisoners. Public outrage reached a fever pitch and Police Commissioner Al Cohn ordered an investigation. It took this commission less than a week to clear Sergel, dismissing the bad press as a "tempest in

(left) Jack Sergel in uniform; (right) Sergel in costume and makeup as Captain Oshima in *Blood on the Sun*.

a teapot," but five days later Cohn announced that the LAPD would no longer teach judo to its officers, calling it "an art of treachery."

"Judo teaches a man to shake hands and then break the other fellow's arm or neck," he blustered. "It is typical of the Japanese and should not be allowed in any American institution."

The next blow came a few weeks later when Sergel asked for leave to work on a film. Jimmy Cagney had started observing classes at his dojo and the two men struck up a friendship. Forty-five years old, Cagney hadn't played an action role in almost five years, but his next picture would be his two-fisted comeback, *Blood on the Sun*, set in wartime Japan and featuring Cagney's passion: judo. His former coach had been Kuniyuki, but with Kuniyuki in the camps he needed an advisor and Sergel wanted the job. The LAPD gave Sergel a hard time about working on the movie, so Sergel quit, changed his name to John Halloran, and proceeded to throw Cagney around onscreen.

Blood on the Sun came out five months before Japan surrendered, at the same time a Supreme Court challenge shut down the internment camps. Uncle Sam kicked his former internees out with nothing but $25 in their pockets and a train ticket home. Murakami returned to his dojo and Kuniyuki took Seinan Dojo back from Sergel. He also took back his position with Cagney, moving into the actor's house with his wife, Elizabeth, who became Cagney's cook.

In 1949, Sergel, Murakami, and Kuniyuki presided as judges over the first official judo tournament in Southern California since the War. About 120 contestants showed up, from adults to eight-year-olds, competing before a crowd of 500. "Judo," Sergel told the papers, "makes the weak strong, the small man large."

That was November. By March of the following year Kuniyuki was getting a divorce from his wife, Sergel had become Cagney's coach again, and the two men were fighting on Cagney's front lawn. Kuniyuki went on to train the American Olympic judo team in the early '80s and Sergel appeared in over 70 films as John Halloran and

Sergel Quits Police Post

Police Sergeant John R. Sergel, revealed by the Examiner in August as having taken Los Angeles girls to Manzanar to wrestle judo-style with interned Japanese, resigned from the department yesterday.

The Police Commission, which following the Examiner's revelations condemned the officer's judo cult activities as "gross violation of official propriety," fixed November 13 as the effective date of the resignation. However, Sergel terminated his 12-year career with the department as of last night.

we'll never know why they started fighting that day in 1950. However, it's enough to know that in just a few years, Kuniyuki went from trusting Sergel enough to give him his dojo to hating him enough to take a swing at him on his boss's front lawn. A promise had been broken. Relationships between Japanese-Americans and Anglo-Americans were poisoned and wouldn't recover for decades.

Cohn Demands Ouster of Police Judo Expert

EXAMINER AUGUST 30

NOTICE CLEVER RETOUCHING JOB AROUND EYES — MOUTH ETC.

THE GUY DID ME A FAVOR I LOOK AS ORIENTAL AS OSHIMA!

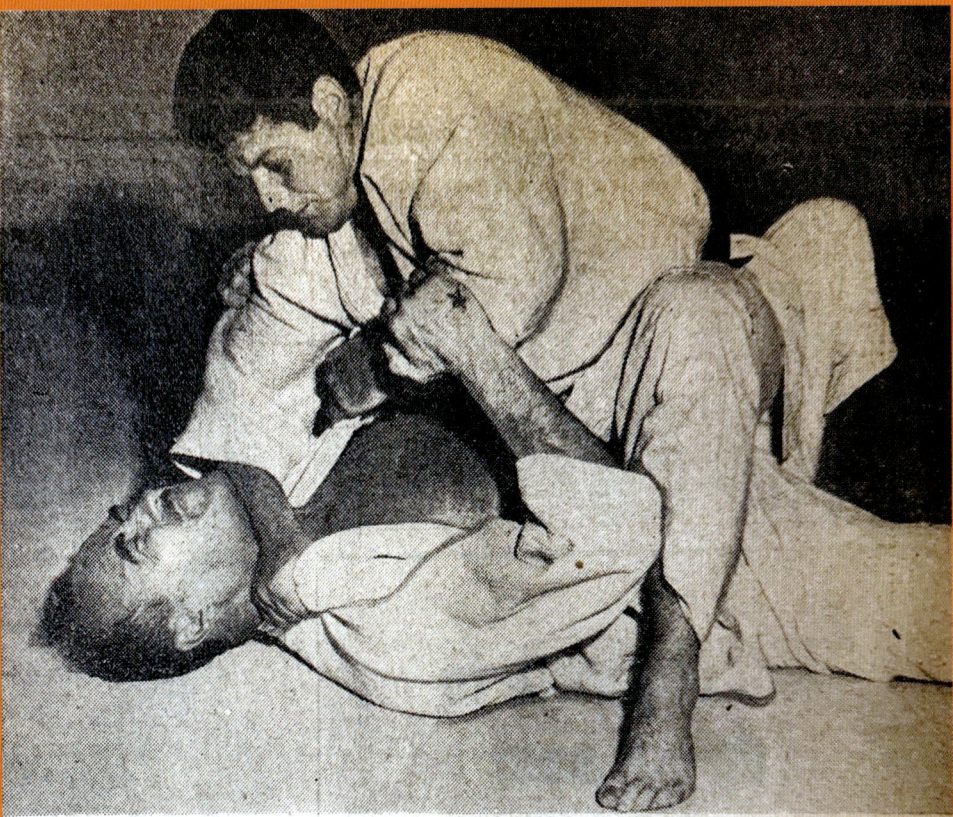

CONDEMNED—Police Officer John R. Sergel, here being choked by Eddie Heizman in a judo demonstration, yesterday was assailed by the Police Commission for "gross violation of official propriety" in taking Los Angeles girls to Manzanar for judo demonstrations with Jap men. Judo also was ordered eliminated from police instruction courses. (Story on Page 7.)

(top) A headline regarding Sergel's trip to Manzanar. In a handwritten note next to the clipping, Sergel points out the photographer's retouching job, turning an intended insult into what he regards as a compliment.

(bottom) News coverage such as this drove Jack Sergel out of law enforcement and into the entertainment industry.

WORLD WAR II CHANGED AMERICA'S feeling about fighting. Before the war, boxing ruled, but within a year of Pearl Harbor, half the boxing clubs in the country went out of business. America had a war to win and dancing around in a ring didn't help. Sportsmanship was out. Winning was in.

The Nazis and Japanese appeared unstoppable in the early days of the war, and the Allies realized victory required a new kind of combat: gutter fighting.

Dan Fairbairn joined the Shanghai Municipal Police in 1907. This unit of South Asians, Britons, Jewish refugees, Japanese expats, and Chinese cops patrolled an intense beat. Within three months of joining, Fairbairn was beaten and left for dead. He woke up in the hospital to find a business card on his chest reading, "Professor Okada, Jujutsu and Bone-setting." For the next three and a half years he studied jiu-jitsu with Professor Okada daily before blending it with wrestling techniques, savate, and "Chinese boxing," to create his very own style, Defendu.

In June 1940 the Germans broke the back of the British army at Dunkirk. Eleven days later, a triumphant German army entered Paris. Despite being in their late 50s and ready for retirement, Fairbairn and his friend on the force, Bill Sykes, returned to Great Britain and asked what they could do for their country. The answer: teach them how to fight dirty. Alongside an American, Major Rex Applegate, they created forms of knife-fighting, close combat, and firearms training that are still used today. As Fairbairn wrote in his 1942 book *Get Tough!* (he also wrote a sister book for women that year called *Hands Off!*), "We've got to be tough to win, and we've got to be ruthless . . . tougher and more ruthless than our enemies." Applegate liked to say, "Do unto others as they would do unto you, but do it first."

After the war, the State Department sent NYPD officers to Tokyo to train the Tokyo Police, only to discover the Tokyo police were better at physically subduing prisoners than they were. And so Air Force lieutenant general Curtis LeMay arranged for Japanese instructors to teach US servicemen aikido, judo, and karate on and off bases across the Pacific.

The American military produced an enormous number of Hispanic, Anglo, and African-American veterans who returned home knowing how to kill men with their bare hands. Robert Trias was a Navy

The same year he wrote *Get Tough!* Fairbairn wrote a companion book for women called *Hands Off!* His publisher took out a full-page ad in the *New York Times* for them in 1942, which infuriated the New York Police Department, who believed Fairbairn had revealed their secret combat systems to criminals. Fairbairn made it up to them, however, devoting a large part of his subsequent life to developing and personally testing bulletproof vests and riot shields.

welder and boxer who got his ass handed to him by a karate-dealing Chinese monk in the Solomon Islands and immediately became his student. In 1945 he came back to Arizona, joined the Highway Patrol, and started teaching karate in his backyard before opening a dojo in Phoenix. He helped build a network of karate instructors across the country, founding the United States Karate Association in 1948. He also got into repeated trouble with local law enforcement for his menagerie of elephants, monkeys, and a lion that constantly escaped and terrorized his suburban neighborhood.

But many of the veterans who came home and opened dojos were Black.

IN 1964, SOME SCHOOL KIDS swiped a few pieces of fruit from a street vendor's stand in Harlem, resulting in an outrageous police response. The incident became known as the Fruit Stand Riot, and the *New York Times* spread a rumor that a gang called the Blood Brothers had been on the scene, provoking mayhem. According to the *Times*, the Blood Brothers roamed the city, attacking white people, with a membership that ranged in size from 25 to 400, depending on how panicky the paper's editors felt that day. What made them especially dangerous? "In the six weeks since the riot, the Blood Brothers have intensified their training in karate and judo fighting methods."

It turned out that the Blood Brothers didn't actually exist, they were a complete fabrication. But Black people and martial arts? That's a made-in-America love match.

Wallace Fard Muhammad, the founder of the Nation of Islam, preached that Africans were actually Asians. W.E.B. Du Bois spent his 91st birthday in China, proclaiming in a radio broadcast, "China is colored, and knows to what the colored skin in this modern world subjects its owner." In a 1964 speech at the Audubon Ballroom, where he would be assassinated less than a year later, Malcolm X said, "If you're interested in freedom, you need some judo, you need some karate, you need all the things that will help you fight for freedom."

The Nation of Islam's security arm, the Fruit of Islam, didn't carry weapons, but, as a United Press International article pointed out in 1963, they were "trained in the Oriental fighting art of Karate." Martial arts' lessons of self-reliance, discipline, and strength were perfectly in tune with the times. After World War II, Europe's former colonies became independent nations, often through violent revolution. Kenya's bloody Mau Mau Uprising, the Angolan and Mozambican wars of independence, and the Cuban Revolution all confronted white Americans with images of strong non-white people who wanted equal rights and who were willing and capable of fighting for them.

> **"WHY DOES JUDO OR KARATE SUDDENLY GET SO OMINOUS BECAUSE BLACK MEN STUDY IT?"**
> —MALCOLM X

The United States had fought a civil war over slavery barely 100 years before, and since then they'd kept African-Americans down through an official program of institutional segregation and an unofficial program of racial violence. In less academic terms, the government crowded Black people into ghettos through redlining and kept them in place with segregation and, when that didn't work, lynching. For a lot of Black Americans, kung fu, karate, jiu-jitsu, what-have-you, looked like paths to empowerment.

Moses Powell, born in Norfolk, Virginia, moved to New York City as a kid, where he picked up boxing and met the visionary Professor Vee. Born to farmers in the Filipino province of Ilocos Norte, Florendo M. Visitacion started learning traditional martial arts at 10 years old and immigrated to the United States at 16.

Barely 5'2" and hardly 125 pounds, he absorbed multiple fighting styles as he chopped sugar cane in Hawaii and picked grapes in California. While serving as a medic in World War II the "by any means necessary" hand-to-hand combat training pioneered by Bill Sykes and Rex Applegate (see page 12) hit him like a lightning bolt. Professor Vee realized that the perfect martial art would be a remix of the best techniques from a library of styles. The second he got out of the Army, he headed to New York City and trained with teachers like Charles Nelson (unarmed combat), Kiyose Nakae (jiu-jitsu), and Jerome Mackey (judo). His wild style earned recognition from the American Judo and Jujitsu Federation as Vee-jitsu. Shortly thereafter, Professor Vee resigned from the American Judo and Jujitsu Federation because he thought their members lacked the courage to go beyond their own styles.

When he met Professor Vee in 1954, Moses Powell was just a 13-year-old kid learning how to box. The Professor opened his eyes to what real discipline could accomplish. By the time he was a green belt in Vee-jitsu, Powell was instructing the Professor's black belt students. By 1960, he was teaching his own system, eventually named Sanuces. He demonstrated it at the 1965 World's Fair, became the first martial artist to perform at the UN in 1971, and his numerous schools turned out major martial artists like Robert Crosson (one of the youngest black belts in the country) and Ron Van Clief, who would achieve onscreen fame as the Black Dragon (see page 211). He would become one of the teachers for the Fruit of Islam's combat training.

But he wasn't alone.

Victor Moore came out of Cincinnati, picking up moves from other kids before he saw Ronald "Grave Man" Williams practicing karate on a hill in his neighborhood.

Williams, who'd acquired his nickname thanks to his actual profession of digging graves and his karate skills thanks to his time as a military instructor, taught the barely adolescent Moore karate out in the woods. The first Black man admitted to Trias' United States Karate Association thanks to the intercession of John Keehan (see page 234), Moore also became the first Black man to win a national karate competition (1965's USKA Grand Nationals), no small thing in a segregated world where he sometimes wasn't even allowed in the whites-only venues where the competitions took place. Moore met Bruce Lee at the Long Beach International Karate Championships in 1967, where Lee was billed as the main event, demonstrating a punch that was "too fast to block." Trias volunteered Moore to block it, and, much to the audience's amusement, Moore blocked the first two "unblockable" punches. Frustrated, Lee doubled down, slinging a surprise punch at Moore's head that Moore missed. Bursting out laughing, Moore said, "I'll give you that one. See if you can stop mine." Then he tagged Lee twice in the chest. Moore would go on to defeat everyone in karate who could be defeated, from Bill "Superfoot" Wallace to Chuck Norris, and later taught martial arts in Fayetteville, North Carolina, with the occasional aid of Trudy, a chimpanzee whom he'd taught karate.

Sijo Saabir Quwi Muhammad (born Steve Sanders), a sheriff in LA for 20 years, served as a Marine Pathfinder in Vietnam, cleaned up on the karate tournament circuit, and, in 1969, founded the Black Karate Federation to combat a toxic atmosphere of racism in the tournament world. That's a polite way of saying some venues refused to allow Black competitors in their front doors, and once inside, some judges refused to call points in their favor. Muhammad counted Jim Kelly and Bruce Lee among his friends and cameoed in *Enter the Dragon* (1973). The karate school where Jim Kelly says goodbye to his teacher at the beginning of the film? It's the Black Karate Federation's famous 103rd Street School in LA.

(opposite page) Grandmaster Moses Powell (left); Sijo Saabir Quwi Muhammad (right).

(above) Logo of the Black Karate Federation.

SPREADING MARTIAL ARTS REQUIRED FACE time. Instructors attracted students with in-person demonstrations, and students learned new techniques by seeing other martial arts schools strut their styles at competitions. Robert Trias held his Arizona Karate Championships in 1955, followed by the 1st World Karate Tournament at the University of Chicago Fieldhouse in 1963. And early in 1964, Jhoon Rhee held the US National Karate Championships in Washington, DC.

A Korean immigrant, Rhee taught taekwondo, but, realizing white people wouldn't have a clue what that meant, he rebranded it "Korean karate." A born promoter, Rhee opened his Washington, DC, school on June 28, 1962, after conducting a letter-writing campaign to every diplomat he could find offering to teach their children for free. Two hundred people turned up on opening day, and by August he had 125 students. In 1965, after reading in the papers that New Hampshire congressman James Cleveland had been mugged, Rhee offered him free lessons. Cleveland thought that sounded like fun, and the US Congressional Tae Kwon Do Club was born in May 1965. Among its first students? Future president Joe Biden.

But Rhee's 1964 US National Karate Championship flopped hard. "If karate is to become a popular spectator sport," an annoyed attendee wrote *Black Belt* magazine, "much will have to be done to change the public's mind and erase the impression that was conveyed at the 1964 National Championship." Then again, Robert Trias' first World Karate Tournament at the University of Chicago Fieldhouse in 1963 hadn't fared much better, with one official calling the event "a real mess."

On August 2, 1964, Ed Parker would hold one of the most influential karate tournaments in America, and he was determined his tournament wouldn't face the same fate as those of his predecessors. A Hawaiian-born Mormon who claimed his powerful fingers came from ukulele playing, Parker had opened his Pasadena school in 1956 and quickly became the karate instructor to the stars, counting Natalie Wood, Warren Beatty, and George Hamilton among his students. A 1961 issue of *Time* magazine called Parker Hollywood's "High Priest" of karate, and he was the technical advisor on *The Case of the Dangerous Robin*, the first American TV show to feature karate (see page 31). Now, Parker thought it was time to use his show biz contacts to introduce karate to Hollywood in style.

The program book for the August 2, 1964, Long Beach International Karate Championships boasted congratulatory ads from Blake Edwards and Jack

Lemmon. Thousands showed up to see demonstrations from Tsutomu Ohshima, the first Japanese karate teacher in America, Master Jhoon Rhee, and an unknown 23-year-old kid from Oakland named Bruce Lee.

Born in San Francisco to a Chinese opera star, Lee grew up in Hong Kong and starred in 23 Cantonese movie melodramas before his parents sent him to America in 1959 to straighten him out. He became a waiter in a Chinese restaurant but was fascinated by kung fu. In Hong Kong he'd learned Wing Chun, a style founded by a Buddhist nun in the 18th century, but in America he began to remix it with multiple styles, picking up bits and pieces from other teachers and friends, just like Professor Vee. Now he had a chance to show his skills off in public.

With the air conditioner broken, the 8,000-seat auditorium had gotten swampy, and the audience was restless by the time Lee took the floor. He did his two-finger push-ups and his patented One-Inch Punch, then launched into a demonstration mocking the traditional styles of martial arts. "Teachers should never impose their favorite patterns on their students," he said while parodying their techniques. By the time he had finished, half the audience wanted to kick his ass, and the other half wanted to kiss it. Among the kissers was hairdresser and future Manson family victim Jay Sebring.

Months later, in January 1965, Sebring was doing William Dozier's hair and listening to Dozier complain. The producer of the upcoming *Batman* TV series, Dozier also wanted to make a show about Charlie Chan's son out to avenge his father's death called *Charlie Chan's Number One Son*, but he couldn't find an "Oriental actor who speaks English and can handle action." Sebring had the answer. Parker had filmed Bruce's demonstration and a few weeks later, Sebring and Parker were sitting in Dozier's office showing it to him. But Bruce Lee wouldn't become a star if it wasn't for what was about to happen at an artificial flower factory in Hong Kong.

(opposite page) Jhoon Rhee newspaper ad teaching "karate," which was actually taekwondo.

(above) Jhoon Rhee's "Nobody Bothers Me" earworm jingle was recorded by Nils Lofgren, member of Bruce Springsteen's E Street Band. His payment? Lifetime lessons. He says he hasn't taken them yet.

BEFORE 1967, THE BIGGEST STARS in Hong Kong movies were women. The most popular stars of the day were two teenaged girls, Connie Chan and Josephine Siao, whose fan clubs would occasionally rumble in the streets. Chan and Siao often starred in genteel, low-budget wu xia (heroic swordsman) pictures together, with Siao playing the heroine and Chan, cross-dressing, playing the hero. Although half of Hong Kong's population was under 15, Hong Kong movies felt like they were made by people in their 50s.

Because they were. In 1957, Run Run Shaw had just celebrated his 50th birthday when he got the call to come back to Hong Kong and take over his family's film studio. The Shaws had been making movies across Southeast Asia for decades, but their Hong Kong outpost had fallen into the doldrums under the stewardship of brother Runme, and their movies were regularly trounced at the box office by rival MP&GI (later known as Cathay).

Run Run's solution: build a motion picture Death Star in Clearwater Bay called Movietown. There, 12 soundstages shot day and night, filming scripts churned out by 15 staff scriptwriters and processing eight hours of film a day at its in-house labs. Shaw trained its stars, ran their fan clubs, and housed them in Movietown dormitories so that Run Run could "keep an eye on them."

Shaw made perky musicals, weepy melodramas, and expensive historical epics. Their wu xia movies resembled ballet more than bare-knuckled brawling, and they weren't doing that great. What made bank at the Hong Kong box office were stylish James Bond thrillers from Hollywood, nihilistic spaghetti westerns from Italy, and bloody samurai films from Japan. For true homegrown combat cinema, Hong Kong audiences had to turn to the independently produced Wong Fei-hung flicks, based on the exploits of a legendary Chinese folk hero. Shot on shoestring budgets and churned out in bulk (25 of them in 1956 alone), they'd starred the same lead actor since 1949: Kwan Tak-hing, now 60 years old.

So in 1965, Shaw's in-house magazine, *Southern Screen*, bragged that the studio was launching a color wu xia offensive.

左圖為位於清水灣的邵氏影城鳥瞰全貌，①大門口 ②辦公大樓 ③冲印室 ④音樂廳（第一錄音室）⑤第二錄音室 ⑥彩色冲印大樓 ⑦貨倉 ⑧道具間 ⑨第一廠 ⑩第二廠 ⑪第三廠 ⑫第四廠 ⑬第五廠 ⑭第六廠 ⑮第七廠 ⑯第八廠 ⑰第九廠 ⑱第十廠 ⑲露天佈景場 ⑳木工間 ㉑露天佈景場 ㉒演職員宿舍 ㉓新職員宿舍 ㉔固定佈景場 ㉕片倉 ㉖停車場。

Left photo is a panoramic view of sprawling Shaw's Movie Town located at Clear Water Bay, Kowloon. The celebrated studio occupies about 1,000,000 sq. ft. of ground. ①Main Gate ②Administration Building ③Film Processing Room ④Music Hall (1st Sound Recording Room) ⑤Second Sound Recording Room ⑥Color Film Processing Building ⑦Warehouse ⑧Storeroom ⑨1st Sound Stage ⑩2nd Sound Stage ⑪3rd Sound Stage ⑫4th Sound Stage ⑬5th Sound Stage ⑭6th Sound Stage ⑮7th Sound Stage ⑯8th Sound Stage ⑰9th Sound Stage ⑱10th Sound Stage ⑲Open-Air Set ⑳Carpentry Workshop ㉑Open-Air Set ㉒Staff Mess ㉓New Staff Dormitory ㉔Fixed Set ㉕Film Storeroom ㉖Car Park.

"Shaws will break with tradition," it proclaimed. "Creating a new vista for martial arts films. The fake, fantastical, and theatrical fighting and the so-called special effects of the past will be replaced by realistic action and fighting that immediately decides life or death."

The first movie, *Come Drink with Me* (1966) did well, but the next three flopped. It was called the "color wu xia offensive," but several of the films were shot in black-and-white to save money. No one cared about them.

Then came May 6, 1967.

The Hong Kong Artificial Flower Works in the crummy industrial neighborhood of San Po Kong needed to increase its profit margins, so owner Duncan Tong slashed wages and banned paid leave. The workers elected representatives to express their concerns and in response Tong fired 92 people, including most of the representatives. The remaining workers went on strike and Tong called the cops.

Being a colony, Hong Kongers saw the police as tools of British rule. When the fuzz arrived on Tai Yau Street, workers threw bottles. The cops arrested 21 people and,

---

(opposite page) The famous Shawscope logo heralded the start of yet another classy Shaw Brothers production with a blast of trumpets.

(above) A map of the Movietown studio in Clearwater Bay. It could house 1,500 workers on its 850,000-square-foot lot.

with temperatures in the 90s, they made sure the arrests weren't gentle. The next day, protesting police brutality and proclaiming worker solidarity, thousands of people took to the streets waving Chairman Mao's Little Red Book. The police fired tear gas, the protests became riots, and the riots spread. Six days later, Hong Kong declared martial law.

For the next 11 months, Hong Kong burned. Protestors waged a running battle with the cops. A bombing campaign saw almost 8,000 bomb threats called in around the city, with 1,100 of them turning out to be the real deal. Children had their arms blown off. Fifty-one people died, ten of them police officers. In the face of all this chaos, musicals about perky young starlets working in nightclubs felt terminally out of touch.

At Shaw Brothers, five men saw the future. First came Raymond Chow, then head of production, who'd lobbied Run Run Shaw to launch the color wu xia offensive in the first place. He convinced Shaw to give a directing job to his latest discovery, Chang Cheh. Fleeing Mainland China, Chang wound up writing film reviews in Hong Kong. Desperate to make action movies, he believed that "when a sword goes in, blood comes out."

He thought everyone was sick of seeing women onscreen, including women. Besotted with macho Hollywood stars like James Dean, he wanted to work with unknown actors who had bold looks and big attitudes. He found one in Jimmy Wong Yu, an egotistical Taiwanese contract actor whose face could convey an encyclopedia's worth of badassery with one glower. Three down, two to go.

The final two parts of the equation were found in the action choreography team of Lau Kar-leung and Tong Kai. The job of action choreographer didn't officially exist until 1961, and Lau and Tong were two of the first and best. They'd both started out working on the Wong Fei-hung series and were masters of multiple martial arts styles, allowing them to bust out whatever stance looked best in any given situation.

Chang Cheh's contribution to Shaw's color wu xia offensive was its seventh film, *The One-Armed Swordsman*. Jimmy Wong Yu plays the son of a servant of the Golden Blade sect, bullied by the wealthy students. The master's bratty teenaged daughter hacks off his arm in a snit fit, but instead of bleeding to death, Wong Yu teaches himself a one-armed fighting technique and returns just in time to save the Golden Blade sect

(left) It's David Chiang in the neckerchief, standing beside him is Chang Cheh, and next to Chang is the boss man himself, Sir Run Run Shaw; (right) Jimmy Wong Yu fondles his chin in a pose designed to set female hearts aflame.

from destruction. The movie hit screens in August 1967 right after Mainland soldiers machine-gunned five Hong Kong police officers to death on the border. People were angry. They wanted blood. Chang Cheh delivered plenty of it. The movie smashed box office records.

Before *The One-Armed Swordsman*, wu xia were about sophisticated swordsmen and women dressed in silk, wielding mystical weapons. *The One-Armed Swordsman* gave audiences a young, male, pissed-off working-class hero, stripped to the waist and smeared with gore, hacking out his future with a broken blade.

Utilizing an arsenal of slow-motion shots, sudden zooms, freeze frames, double exposures, and blood squibs, this Gang of Five repeated their success for Shaw with *The Assassin* (1967), *The Trail of the Broken Blade* (1967), *The Golden Swallow* (1968), *The Sword of Swords* (1968), and *The Return of the One-Armed Swordsman* (1969). By the time they were finished, actors were in, actresses were out, and Hong Kong cinema was dripping with blood.

But there was more to Chang Cheh's movies than violence. At heart, they were about hing dai, a Chinese term meaning brotherhood. Confucianism emphasized a vertical hierarchy: a son obeyed his parents, his parents obeyed the emperor. But hing dai was a blood bond with a brother that was stronger than family, stronger than country, stronger than death. Brothers would kill for each other, die for each other, seek revenge for each other, and stand shoulder to shoulder in the face of overwhelming odds together.

Movies about hing dai weren't just screened in Hong Kong, but throughout North America, where aspiring martial artists caught them early on the Chinatown circuit.

IN THE '50S AND '60S, New York City had Spanish movie theaters (The New Edison), Japanese movie theaters (Toho Cinema), Greek movie theaters (The Ditmars), and even Polish (The Chopin). But Chinatown was something different.

The Sun Sing opened in 1950, built into the foundations of the Manhattan Bridge, gently rocked by the passing F train. The Canal Street Cinema up the street had its walls and curtains dyed brown by ever-present clouds of cigarette smoke. The Pagoda proudly proclaimed its name on the facade right below a three-tiered pagoda rising from its rooftop. Selling lychee nuts and Chinese snacks in their lobbies, running a non-stop rotation of recent and repertory hits from Hong Kong with English subtitles, these movie houses would be joined by the Music Palace in 1973, part of the Shaw Brothers circuit, and the Rosemary in 1982, but this empire of Chinese-language movie theaters first kicked into high gear around 1964.

That year, in San Francisco, exhibitor Maury Schwartz needed more leverage to negotiate better deals with the studios, so he added five movie houses to his circuit, including the Bella Union, a dud on the border of Chinatown that couldn't even make a buck screening nudie flicks. He partnered with Frank Lee, producer of a local radio show called *Voice of Chinatown* to start programming Shaw Brothers movies there, and the cash came showering down. Soon, Lee was opening theaters in New York, LA, Vancouver, and Toronto, eventually booking a circuit of 50 Chinatown cinemas across the country.

In New York, Lee brought Shaw's posh period epics like *The Magnificent Concubine* (1962) and *The Last Woman of Shang* (1964) to midtown's 55th Street Playhouse.

The bonds between the Black and Chinese communities were so strong that for years Alan Lee's martial arts schools regularly advertised in New York's Black-owned newspapers.

America's Chinatown circuit turned out to be so lucrative that Shaw sent its stars to tour the States and Run Run Shaw himself considered shooting special versions of his movies for the American market.

Starting with Shaw's color wu xia offensive, these Chinatown theaters began attracting martial artists, particularly Black martial artists.

"We had one theater," Dennis Brown, a kung fu teacher in Washington, DC, said. "Run by Mr. and Mrs. Huang, called the American on 21st Street in Washington, DC. It only showed kung fu movies on Sunday morning, so at 11 o'clock on Sunday we'd all gather there and watch their movies like we were going to church."

Brown had started taking judo at Howard University and he, like kids across the country who wanted to learn kung fu but couldn't find a teacher or couldn't afford the fees, began to work out in a local park with friends. Every Friday Brown and his vagabond crew would drive five and a half hours to New York City's Chinatown to watch movies.

"We'd get there as early in the morning as possible, load up on bags of char siu bao, and watch the double feature at one theater, then run to the Canal Cinema to catch the next double feature, then run to the Pagoda, or the Sun Sing. We'd watch movies all day long and they'd sleep on the way home and I'd drive. Then we'd get up early on Sunday morning and go to Malcolm X Park and practice what we'd seen in the movies."

> "YOU CAN TAKE AWAY MY GUN, BUT YOU CAN'T TAKE AWAY MY KUNG FU."
> —WARRINGTON HUDLIN

If you were Black, and you had an interest in martial arts, the Chinatown circuit felt like home. One manager at New York City's Music Palace estimated that as much as 10% of his audience was Black.

"We would all go there because there were techniques in the movies we couldn't learn from our teachers," Warrington Hudlin said. "We were in a room with nothing but Chinese families and these Black guys, who were either from the Nation of Islam or the Black Panther Party, and we were these fish out of water but we just loved it."

Karate still ruled the martial arts schools, so Chinatown movie theaters were the only place to see kung fu. In 1969, when Dennis Brown wanted more than park workouts and something different than karate, he signed up for the only option on offer: taekwondo with Master Jhoon Rhee. But he kept learning kung fu on the side, which kept getting him into trouble. He'd drive hours to attend tournaments, but when he'd unleash his kung fu on a karate crowd, the judges would stand up and turn their backs on him. Sometimes they scored him all zeroes. But he kept showing up, and he kept going to the movies, and he kept practicing in the park.

This cold shoulder wasn't so different from the one the One-Armed Swordsman himself, Jimmy Wong Yu, got when he tried to convince Run Run Shaw to stop churning out so many wu xia pictures and try something new, like kung fu.

With its large Asian population, Hawaii was home to numerous Japanese-language movie theaters, with seven in Honolulu alone (many of these also screened Filipino films). In the '60s, however, Shaw started to take them over and turned them into showcases for movies like *The Last Woman of Shang* and *The Chinese Boxer*. *The Last Woman of Shang* came out shortly after the suicide of its star, Linda Lin Dai, and her fans showed up in droves to mourn, turning it into a massive hit.

"Run Run Shaw only had one answer: no," Wong Yu said in an interview. "Even when I was a box-office success."

Noticing that Japanese films were always pitting one martial art against another, he figured, "If you can make a film about judo against karate, why couldn't I make a film about Chinese iron fist against karate?" So he sat down and wrote a script and gave it to Run Run Shaw.

"I told him, this script will make you a lot of money, but he said no. He had no confidence in me . . . I showed it to Chang Cheh, and he didn't agree either. He said, 'No, no, Jimmy. Stay with swordplay. You're at the top in swordplay.'"

So Wong Yu threatened to quit Shaw Brothers. Desperate to hold on to his moneymaker, Shaw agreed: he could direct and star in *The Chinese Boxer* (1970). The story of a young guy (played by Wong Yu) whose teacher is killed by evil Japanese caricatures wearing cheap wigs, Wong Yu learns iron fist kung fu and kills them in enormous quantities while wearing a surgical mask. It was the first flick to exchange the wu xia sword for the kung fu fist, and it was another massive hit. Suddenly, all the studios in Hong Kong were unleashing kung fu.

The impact seeped over into the United States. Alan Lee advertised his "Chinese Kung-Fu, Wu-Su Ass'n" schools in Black newspapers like the *Amsterdam News*.

Kareem Abdul-Jabbar had started training in aikido after he saw a Japanese Zatoichi movie at the Kokusai on Crenshaw Boulevard in LA and realized that if he could get that kind of body control it'd step up his basketball game. But later, during his junior year at UCLA, he asked a friend at *Black Belt* magazine to recommend a teacher for this stuff he'd heard of called kung fu. They recommended a guy named Bruce Lee.

Fab 5 Freddy learned about kung fu films when he went to Barbados one summer to visit his grandparents and came back talking up movies like *The One-Armed Swordsman* (1967) and *The Bloody Fists* (1972) to his schoolyard friends.

But, for now, if you lived in America and you didn't make the trek down to your local Chinatown, the only place you saw martial arts was on TV, and most of it was karate.

BELLA UNION "ONE-ARMED SWORDSMAN"

Fantastic Sword Fighting
The One-Armed & One-Eyed Master Swordsman
A Frank Lee Int'l Release
All in Eastmancolor & Scope
CO-HIT: "MADAM WHITE SNAKE"

Kearny & Wash.
GA 1-4824

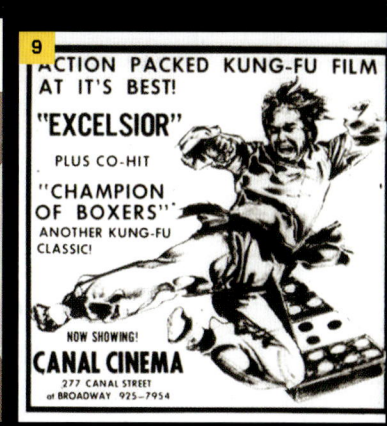

6 / San Francisco's World Theater was built on the site of the Liberty Theater, which was torn down in 1954. It screened foreign films, but focused on Chinese movies due to its location near Chinatown.

7 / New York's Pagoda opened in 1964 and was demolished in 1992. It is now the site of the Glory China Tower office building.

8 / Flyers like this one for the Sun Sing's run of *Tough Guy* (1978) were distributed

9 & 10 / The Canal Cinema was one of the first Chinatown theaters in New York City, although it was originally known as Cinema Giglio.

11 / The last all-Chinese movie theater in North America (San Francisco's 4 Star also showed Hollywood fare), the Music Palace opened in 1973 and finally closed in 2000.

12 / The Sun Sing had 900 seats and was located in the base of the Manhattan Bridge. It closed in 1993.

KARATE: THE HAND OF DEATH

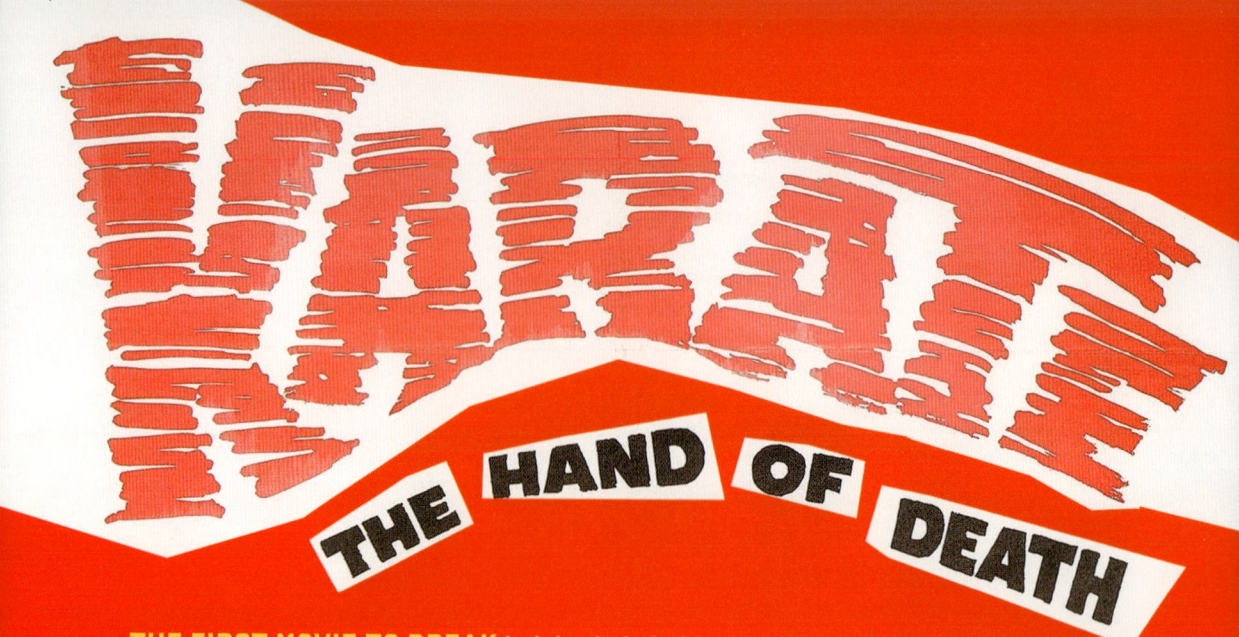

THE FIRST MOVIE TO BREAK judo's chokehold over Hollywood was a low-budget, independent, black-and-white film called *Karate, the Hand of Death* (1961). Produced, directed by, and starring Joel Holt, a storm window salesman and television chef on New York's WPIX, Channel 11, *Karate* was shot in Japan and tells the touching tale of an American raised in Japan who fought for the Allies during World War II and killed so many Japanese soldiers with his neck-shattering hands of death that he can't bring himself to karate chop anyone anymore. In postwar Tokyo, tracking down his childhood sweetheart, he gets embroiled in shenanigans involving murder, a gold coin, and secret troves of plutonium, but really it's just a showcase for karate. The hard-chopping martial arts action is reserved for the white guys, except for a clumsy, one minute and eleven second climactic karate showdown wherein the evil Japanese traitor is disposed of with a finger strike to the neck, and a 12-minute chunk in the middle showing a Japanese karate class strutting its stuff in what could generously be called padding.

The most fascinating aspect of this movie is that its producer was a spy. Robert Sandstrom (sometimes credited as Richard Sloan) was an undercover agent for the Army. He'd previously been part of Project Paperclip, which snuck Nazi rocket scientists into the American space program, but this time his mission was to root out post–World War II communist infiltration overseas. A series of strange decisions saw him start a production company in Tokyo that produced Holt's karate movie as a cover so that he could recruit spies in Japan's entertainment industry.

Instead of establishing a spy network, Sandstrom met his future wife on the set (she plays a nurse in the film), had a son, and returned to the States just in time to lead a reconnaissance mission over Cuba, taking photos of Soviet missile installations. These photos led directly to the Cuban Missile Crisis in October 1962. Distributor Joseph Brenner kept *Karate, the Hand of Death* in theatrical release for over a decade. Holt continued as a product pitchman and narrated sexploitation flicks like *Paris Topless* (1966), but Robert Sandstrom? He almost started a nuclear war.

The Green Hornet may not have been a ratings hit, but the studio still manufactured plenty of merch, like Green Hornet and Kato chewing gum.

AFTER BEING TAUNTED BY SOME leather-jacketed toughs while out for dinner with his wife, actor Rick Jason started taking karate with Ed Parker. When he got cast in the television show *The Case of the Dangerous Robin* (1960), he asked the producers if his insurance investigator character could use karate to take down the bad guys. Knowing a good gimmick when they heard one, they agreed.

They hired Parker as a technical advisor, and Jason did his own stunts, because, as he explained to a reporter, "There are no stuntmen who know karate, which is an ancient form of judo, but I do." Thirty minutes later, Jason was getting ten stitches in his hand after a stunt went wrong. "No loss," he rationalized over coffee to the same journalist. "The script called for blood on my shirt anyway."

The Case of the Dangerous Robin only ran for one season, but four years later, Robert Conrad broke open a can of karate on almost every first-season episode of *The Wild Wild West*, and Robert Loggia's series, *T.H.E. Cat*, saw his character go from being a cat burglar to a martial arts crimefighter. Victor Sen Yung, who got his start playing Charlie Chan's Number Two Son, occasionally showed off his karate skills on *Bonanza*, where he regularly played Chinese cook Hop Sing. But nothing did more for martial arts than eight minutes of black-and-white footage shot by William Dozier.

After viewing Ed Parker and Jay Sebring's Long Beach footage, Dozier ordered Bruce Lee to shoot a screen test. Lee wears a tight black suit, razor burn all over his neck, sitting uncomfortably on a living room set as an offscreen Dozier asks questions. He only loosens up when Dozier asks him to show some Chinese kung fu.

"Well," an embarrassed Lee shrugs, "it's hard to show it alone but, uh, I will try to do my best."

"Maybe one of the fellas will walk in," Dozier says, and a middle-aged, white-haired assistant director in a suit slouches onto set.

A newspaper ad for *The Case of the Dangerous Robin*.

The next four minutes are some of the most incredible footage ever filmed. Unused to playing for the camera, Lee's strikes and kicks are too fast to see. The air blurs as he lashes out at the assistant director's eyes, throat, and groin, the poor man flinching as Lee pulls his full-power blows fractions of an inch before contact, narrating what he's doing, cracking corny jokes, and reassuring the terrified man in a non-stop stream of patter. One thing becomes very clear: Bruce Lee was born to do this.

Dozier immediately signed Lee to an exclusive contract, got him a Hollywood agent, sent him the materials on the *Charlie Chan's Number One Son* project, then immediately informed him that it was on hold. ABC wanted Dozier to focus on *Batman*, his upcoming series with Adam West and Burt Ward (who'd karate-chopped a board in his audition), so Dozier strung Lee along until *Batman* premiered to great success, at which point ABC greenlit Dozier's *Green Hornet* project with Bruce playing the Hornet's sidekick, Kato.

If anyone thought Asians had arrived in Hollywood and would no longer be low-paid houseboys for the white stars, well, Kato was the Green Hornet's houseboy, and Van Williams, the star, got $2,000 per week while Bruce got $400.

Still, Lee's Kato electrified audiences. Dressed in his costume, he appeared before 8,000 attendees at Jhoon Rhee's 1967 karate tournament, and dojos saw their enrollment spike as kids, inspired by Lee's performance, signed up for classes, but *Hornet* never got *Batman*-level traction. ABC declined to renew it for a second season.

Unemployed, Lee became a kung fu coach to the stars, taking on students like Academy Award–winning screenwriter Stirling Silliphant (*In the Heat of the Night*) and tough-guy actors James Coburn and Steve McQueen. He also permanently injured his back and spent the rest of his life in excruciating pain.

On the wrong side of 30, over the hill for an aspiring actor who wanted to do action, Lee's career looked like a dead end. But a pair of joke writers for Phyllis Diller wrote a spec script called *The Way of the Tiger, the Sign of the Dragon*, which landed on the desk of a young agent, who took it to Warner Bros. at exactly the moment movies seemed to be getting their necks broken by TV.

In 1946, 78 million people bought movie tickets each week. By 1971, only around 16 million did. The business got so bad that Warner Bros. was sold cheap to Kinney National Company, which owned parking lots and cleaning services. Kinney dumped 18 of the studio's 21 top executives and replaced them with kids, the oldest being Fred Weintraub, then 41 and sporting a beard and a ponytail.

Weintraub's first big hit was *Woodstock* (1970), a documentary that kept the studio solvent. From his pot-scented office, Weintraub read *The Way of the Tiger, the Sign of the Dragon* treatment and paid for a script. The movie was about a Shaolin monk in the Old West, so he changed its name to *Kung Fu*, watched a ton of Shaw Brothers flicks to see what he could steal, and, after a student introduced him to Bruce Lee, decided Lee would be perfect as the lead. But when Zanuck and Brown took over Warner Bros. in 1970, they put the project on ice.

In the summer of 1971, Weintraub revived *Kung Fu* for television. ABC fell in love with the project, and on July 22, 1971, they announced it as a movie of the week, but, worried about Bruce's accent, they auditioned David Carradine.

Carradine had only heard the words "kung fu" twice before, but he needed the cash to finance his own project, an X-rated version of Herman Hesse's psychedelic novel, *Siddhartha*. His audition was the last time the producers say they saw the actor sober, but Warners liked the pilot so much they went to series in October 1972. It became a huge hit, and *Kung Fu* took kung fu mainstream.

Carradine told interviewers, "To me, Caine is a fool," but the rebroadcast of the pilot was interrupted to show live footage of President Nixon shaking Mao Tse-tung's hand on his groundbreaking visit to China, and suddenly *Kung Fu* felt like it captured a moment like nothing else on television. No fool he, Carradine changed his tune.

"I found myself getting caught up in the mystical, political importance of this thing," he started saying. "I caused the show to grow in that direction." Meanwhile, disappointed with Hollywood, Bruce retreated to Hong Kong. Weintraub still believed in him, but Bruce refused to sign a contract to develop his own project with Warners on their terms. Instead, he made a low-budget Hong Kong flick during the summer of 1971. He believed that when *The Big Boss* premiered, it would change his asking price.

Bruce was right. Kung fu was about to become the next big thing in American movies. But he wouldn't be the one who took it there.

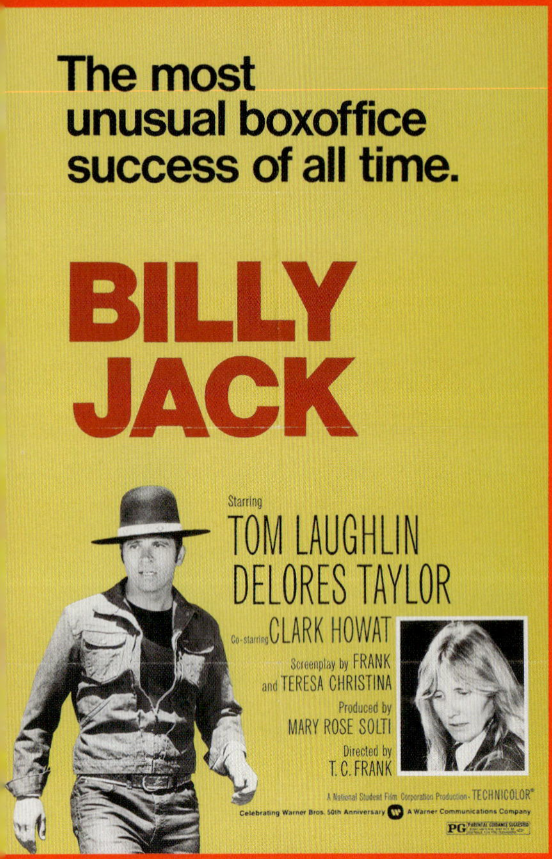

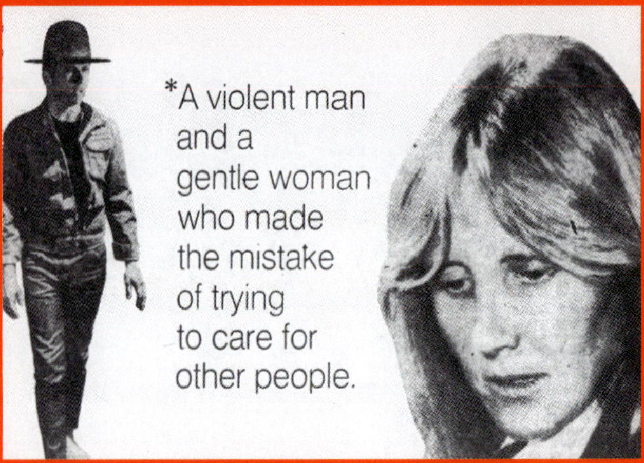

TOMORROW IS "BILLY JACK DAY" IN DAYTON

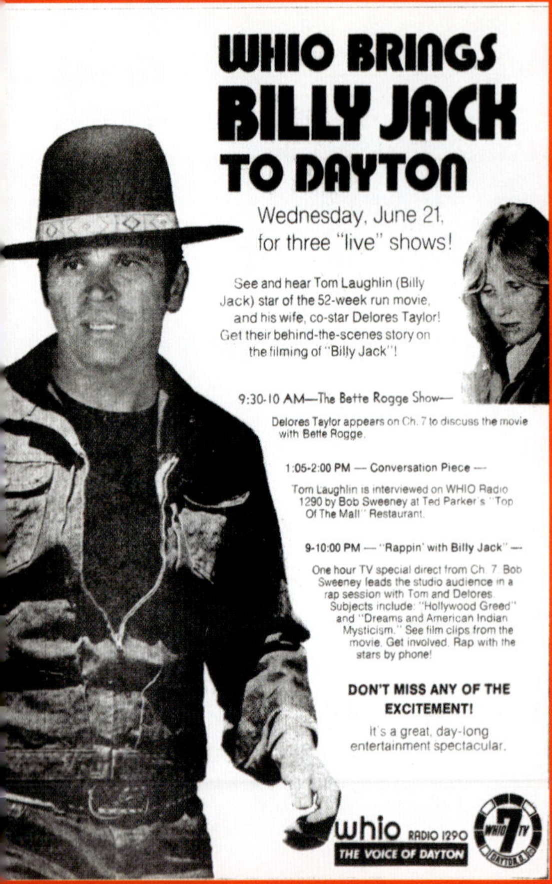

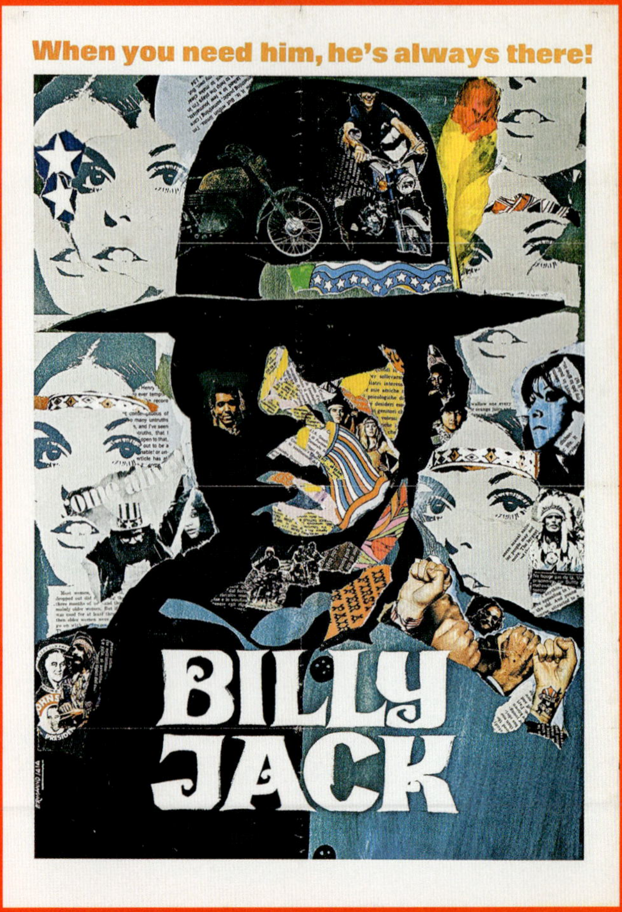

BILLY JACK

TOM LAUGHLIN SINGLEHANDEDLY CHANGED HOLLYWOOD forever. A hard-headed actor who starred in Robert Altman's *The Delinquent* (1957), he was rumored to be Stanley Kubrick's first pick for a lead role in *2001: A Space Odyssey* (1968) but he preferred to go his own way. And so, in 1967, he wrote, directed, and starred in *The Born Losers*, a biker flick that introduced Laughlin's Billy Jack character to audiences. A mysterious, half–Native American Vietnam veteran with sick hapkido skills, Billy Jack's countercultural cool made *Losers* a huge hit for exploitation powerhouse American International Pictures (AIP).

Laughlin's next film for AIP was *Billy Jack* (1971) but he irritated his producers so much AIP shut him down. Laughlin convinced 20th Century Fox to buy the film, but during post-production the studio's conservative head of production, Richard Zanuck, demanded Laughlin remove a line comparing President Nixon to Hitler. In protest, Laughlin stole the entire soundtrack and threatened to erase it unless Fox returned his film. Next stop: Warner Bros., whose Ted Ashley hated the movie but saw its potential for the youth market.

Billy Jack made $4 million and turned its theme song, "One Tin Soldier," into a radio hit, but that wasn't good enough for Laughlin. He slapped Warner Bros. with a $35 million lawsuit for mishandling the marketing. Two years later, they settled out of court and allowed Laughlin to distribute the movie himself. No theater wanted to book a two-year-old movie, so Laughlin four-walled it, renting it to movie theaters for a flat fee and keeping the box office.

Four-walling was a method of last resort for only the most desperate distributors, but when Laughlin unleashed his "bike riding, karate chopping, hip-shooting messenger of peace" onto hundreds of movie theaters at once, backed by a $7 million ad campaign, it earned a staggering $42 million. Laughlin's sequel, *The Trial of Billy Jack*, opened on 1,200 screens in November 1974 backed by millions in TV advertising. It made $32 million in its first month, thus paving the way for Hollywood's modern-day blockbuster release pattern, front-loading the opening weekend of a movie with its advertising and launching it on hundreds of screens at the same time. *Jaws* (1975) got credited with pioneering this practice, but the first person to prove it could work was Tom Laughlin and his jeans-wearing hapkido-hurling martial artist, Billy Jack.

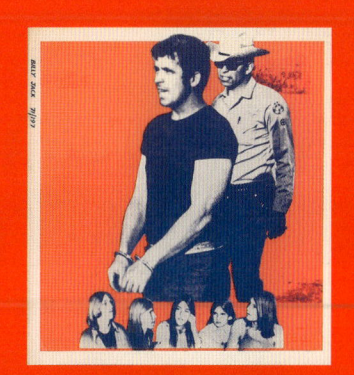

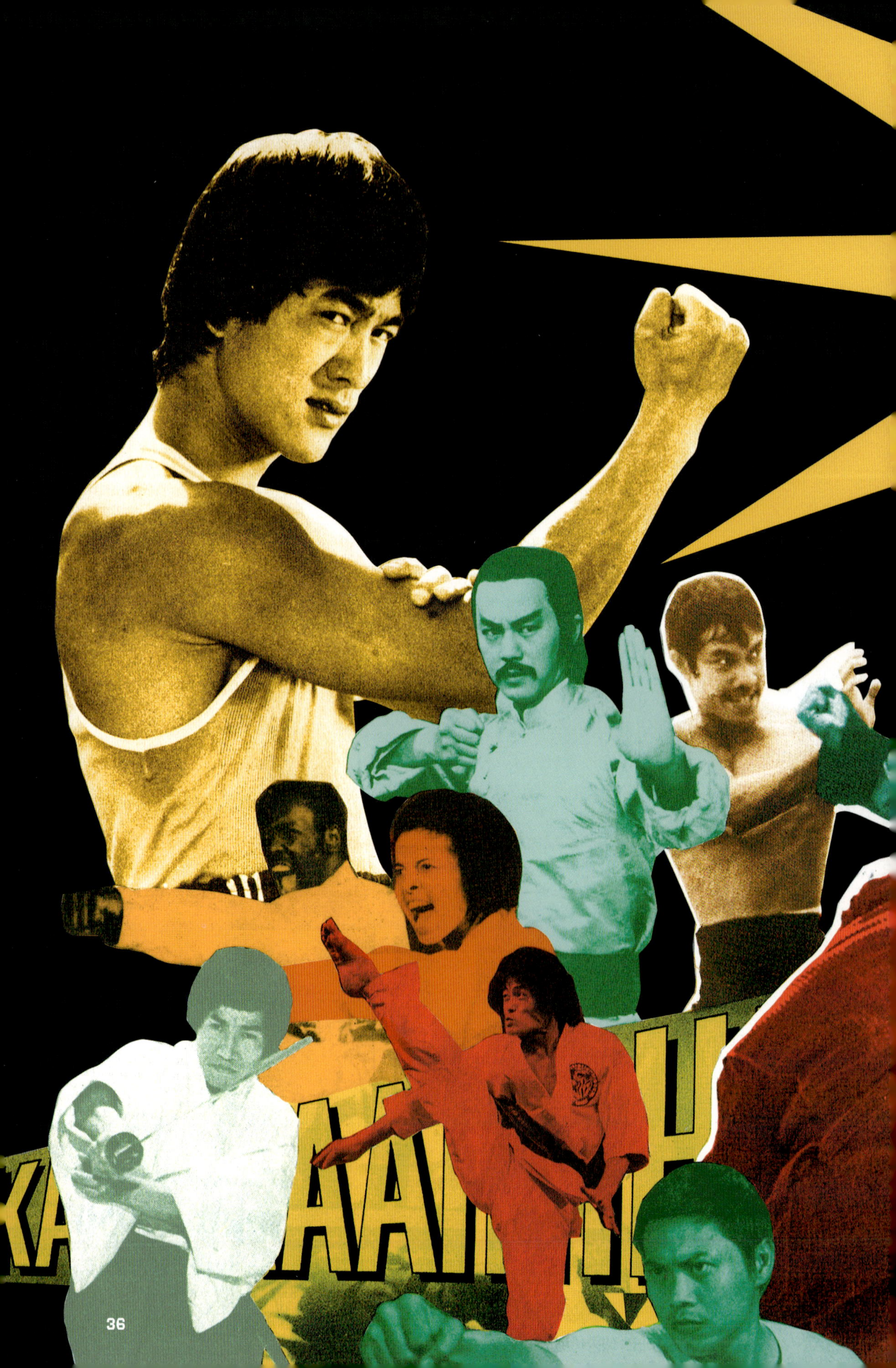

THE SEVENTIES

MORE KUNG FU ACTION THAN EVER!

THE FLYERS PROMISED "ONE INCREDIBLE onslaught after another!" in a "Martial Arts Masterpiece!" that's "Stunning the Entire World" but the Times Square audience had heard all that hype before. What drew them to the State Theater on a chilly Tuesday night in March wasn't the promise that they would "Pale before the forbidden ritual of the steel palm!" but the promise of free tickets.

The first show started at six, the second at eight, the third at ten, but by 6:30pm the line for the second screening stretched around the block. Warner Bros. had set up a table in the lobby and gone all out, stocking it with free posters, Day-Glo stickers, and a fake newspaper called the *Martial Art News* touting their film.

Exactly one year earlier, the State had hosted Henry Kissinger and Ali MacGraw at the star-studded world premiere of *The Godfather*. Tonight, on March 20, 1973, the crowd jamming the 1,100 seats were young, mostly Black and Latino, predominantly male, and they were cynical—the first few minutes would determine whether they'd get their kicks from watching the movie or mocking the movie. The lights went down, the streamlined 1970s Warner Bros. logo hit the bloodred screen, followed by the fast 'n' furious credits, and immediately a gang of young thugs surrounded an old man on a dark street, mayhem on their minds. Suddenly, the 63-year-old actor leapt into the air and kicked two of the kids in the skull at once before taking the gang apart with his bare hands. No one had ever seen anything like it. The crowd went wild, then sat, riveted. Fighters tore out eyes, smashed hands into bloody hamburger, and split foreheads with iron-hard fingers, sending bright red Shaw Brothers blood ejaculating across the screen. The fight scenes didn't pad out the running time, they were the reason the movie existed. As the hero stumbled off into the sunset in the final 15 seconds, bloody and scarred, with no one left to fight because everyone was dead, the audience erupted into applause, then rushed the merch table in the lobby and stripped it bare.

Word of mouth burned through the city. People went back to see it again and again. It was the first dubbed kung fu movie released in a mainstream movie theater and it changed the American film business forever. But its star wasn't Bruce Lee, it was Lo Lieh. And they called it . . . *Five Fingers of Death*.

Warner Bros. marketing muscle made *Five Fingers* a huge hit. It cost Shaw $23,000 to make. Warners picked it up for a percentage of the box office. On its opening weekend in three American cities it made $696,000 alone. In Italy it made $1.5 million. By May 1973 it had made around $10 million worldwide.

THE MARTIAL ARTS MASTERPIECE!
Sights and sounds like never before!

SEE one incredible Onslaught after another!

PALE before the forbidden ritual of the steel palm!

CHEER the young warrior who alone takes on the evil war-lords of martial arts!

COME PREPARED for the thrill of a lifetime!

LEARN THE SECRET OF THE 5 FINGERS OF DEATH

THE NEW MOVIE SENSATION THAT'S STUNNING THE ENTIRE WORLD!!

R — RESTRICTED

A SHAW BROS. PRODUCTION · IN EASTMANCOLOR®   Celebrating Warner Bros. 50th Anniversary   A Warner Communications Company

N 1967, RUN RUN SHAW summoned the director of the low-budget Korean movie *Special Agent X7* (1966) to his offices and demanded to know: How did a 39-year-old foreigner shoot so much footage on the streets of Hong Kong? Location shooting cost way too much money. The streets couldn't be controlled like a soundstage. As far as Shaw was concerned, it was impossible.

"We Koreans," director Chung Chang-Hwa told him, "we get it done."

Shaw signed him up. A stubborn hardass who sometimes shot at his actors with live ammunition ("No one got killed while working on my films," the Korean director always reminded interviewers), Chung had essentially invented the action genre in Korea, learning how to get the most out of the least, compensating for actors who couldn't fight with fast cutting, short takes, and multiple camera angles to send the action flying off the screen.

He made some decent wu xia films for Shaw, but by 1971 Jimmy Wong Yu's *Chinese Boxer* had stuffed swordplay flicks in the trash and Chung wanted to be part of the latest trend. After studying Chinese culture for a few months, he sold Shaw on his new movie, *King Boxer*. He hired essentially the same cast as *Chinese Boxer*, minus Jimmy Wong Yu, and elevated that movie's main baddie, Lo Lieh, to be his movie's star. Shaw wouldn't assign Chung a good action director, so he hired Lau Kar-leung's little brother, hoping his big bro would stop by to help out. Shaw assigned Lo Lieh to shoot another picture simultaneously. The studio swapped Chung's cinematographer every few days, depending on their availability, and Chung didn't have enough seniority to get on the soundstage schedule, sometimes going 20 days without filming a single shot because he couldn't book studio space.

Didn't matter. Lifting its iconic Iron Fist siren from Quincy Jones' soundtrack for *Ironside*, using spaghetti western slow zooms to build pre-fight tension, *King Boxer* is a gothic doom opera (one fight scene takes place entirely in the dark) about a young man (Lo Lieh) who suffers unbearable humiliations at the hands of a bunch of rich brats, before learning an unbeatable technique that lets him shatter their skulls with his iron fists. Enraged, they crush his hands, but he just trains harder and finally pounds them, and their hired Japanese bastards, into a thick, red paste.

The movie came out in Hong Kong and didn't even make that year's box office top 10, but Dick Ma, Warners' head of Far East distribution, picked it up because the studio had just signed a deal with Bruce Lee.

In late 1971, Golden Harvest founder, Raymond Chow, sent Fred Weintraub at Warners a print of Bruce Lee's first motion picture, *The Big Boss*, but never heard back. Annoyed, he sold it to a Chinatown distributor. Weintraub hadn't ignored his movie, however; instead, he'd used the print to convince his boss, Ted Ashley, that they needed to poach Bruce Lee from Chow. A canny Lee then spent months playing Warner Bros. and Golden Harvest against each other, and finally they both agreed to co-produce a Bruce Lee vehicle called *Blood & Steel*. It was based on a western script Weintraub had previously developed for Lee called *Kelsey* about a Black man, a white man, and a Chinese man brawling in tournaments on an island run by an evil Native American warlord. Warners had turned it down once, but now they didn't have any better ideas.

By early 1973, *Blood & Steel* had wrapped, but a nervous studio wanted to test the market, so Leo Greenfield, their savvy distribution manager, got the *King Boxer* print from Dick Ma and called one of his sub-distributors in New York City, the colorful exploitation genius Terry Levene (see page 166), to take a look.

"What do you think of it?" Greenfield asked after the movie.

"It . . ." Levene said, ". . . is nothing but money."

Warners retitled it *Five Fingers of Death*, opened it in Europe, where it did well, then on March 20, 1973, they previewed it in New York City. And the crowd went wild.

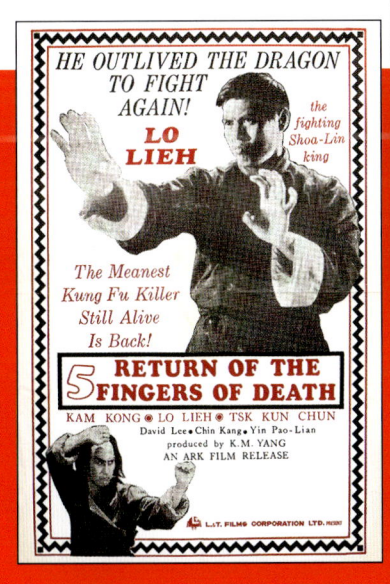

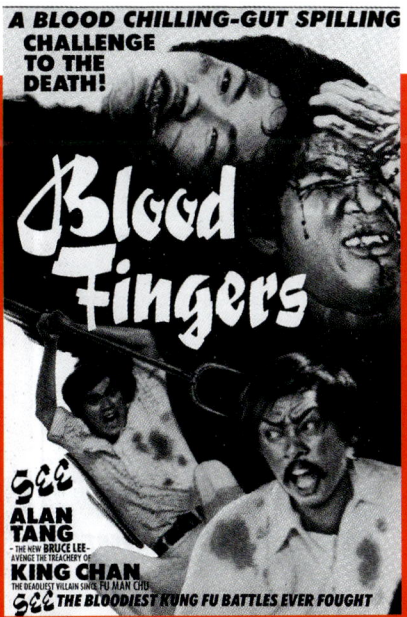

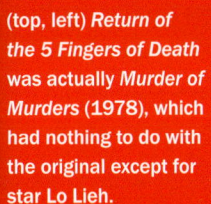

(top, left) *Return of the 5 Fingers of Death* was actually *Murder of Murders* (1978), which had nothing to do with the original except for star Lo Lieh.

(top, right) Fingers were the most lucrative body part of all, whether they were bloody (*Blood Fingers* aka *Brutal Boxer*, 1972), made of steel (*Ten Fingers of Steel* aka *Wang Yu, King of Boxers*, 1973), or belonged to Bruce Lee (*Bruce's Deadly Fingers*, 1976).

(bottom, left) Some movies, like *18 Bronzemen* (1976), simply lifted and tweaked *Five Fingers'* poster art.

(bottom, right) The more fingers the better as this poster for *10 Fingers of Death* (aka *The Escaper*, 1973) proves.

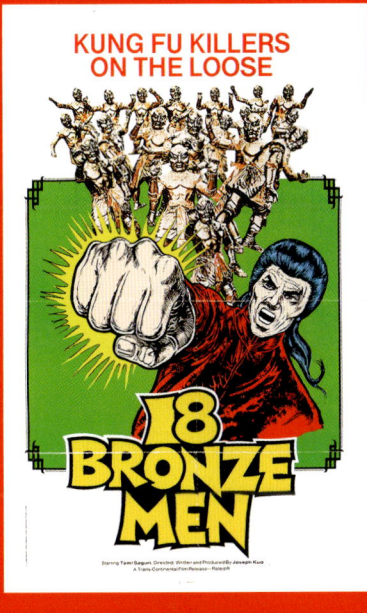

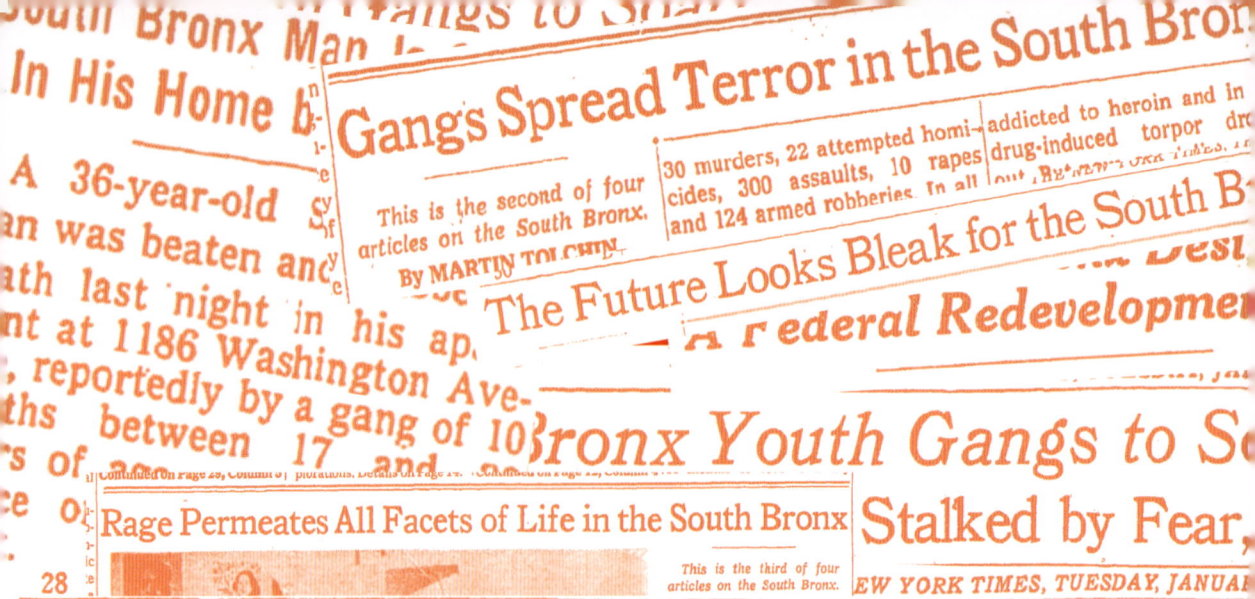

FIVE FINGERS OF DEATH TOUCHED a match to a powder keg. American audiences craved movies like this, but the studios weren't delivering. Blaxploitation movies had been good business in 1971 and 1972 but faced diminishing returns, in part due to opposition by the NAACP, who accused them of "cultural genocide." They had a point. Blaxploitation movies might be fun but too often they trafficked in racially charged images that sometimes shaded into plain old racism with their gun-toting drug dealers, ho-slapping pimps, and street-hustling hookers.

But kung fu movies offered audiences non-white heroes without the taint of America's racial baggage, starring in stories about young, working-class kids with nothing but their own two fists standing up to corrupt 1%-ers who paid off the cops and exploited workers. The hero would suffer their slings and arrows as long as he or she could, but finally fought back, throwing their body into the gears of the system, taking down as many of the bad guys as possible before they were inevitably killed in a tornado of blood.

Wounds were created, eyeballs denucleated, blood splattered, skulls shattered, arms broke, necks choked, fingers stabbed soft guts, women kicked dudes' butts, but the essential appeal was so much more than the gore. These movies sang a revolutionary song: young people, kept down by the older generation, finally fought back against corruption. They spoke to young, marginalized kids who felt left behind, exploited, and ripped off. And in the '70s, that meant everyone who wasn't white, and everyone who lived in a city.

In 1972, an election year, Richard Nixon had ordered federal programs to fund as many anti-poverty and urban renewal projects as possible, dumping money into the system to buy votes. The minute he got re-elected, he reversed course, vetoing appropriation bills and impounding funds already authorized by Congress. In New York City, Nixon clawed back Bronx housing subsidies and cut off promised cash for parks, water lines, and sewers. It shocked a system that couldn't take many more shocks.

In the late '60s, police brutality had sparked riots that left hundreds dead in Harlem, Watts, Detroit, and Alabama. Riots had rattled Rochester, Newark, Michigan, Toledo, Flint, Houston, Tucson, Milwaukee, Portland, and Minneapolis. In the early '70s, Boston's white population rioted over school integration. Cleveland defaulted on millions in debt and "lost" $50 million of city funds. In disgust, a judge removed Cleveland's entire waterworks from city control. Millions of people across the country fled the cities for the suburbs and the countryside.

New York became the poster child for urban decay. Between 1970 and 1980, one million white people fled the Big Apple, starving the tax base and leaving the most vulnerable citizens behind. With the city broke, services slashed, and the police at war with the mayor's office, car thefts doubled, rapes tripled, and robberies increased tenfold. Nowhere got hit harder than the South Bronx, home to 400,000 citizens, most of them Puerto Rican and Black.

Robert Moses, New York's all-powerful architect, had hacked the Bronx into a North and South when he jammed the Cross Bronx Expressway right down the middle of the borough between 1948 and 1963. This seven-mile highway evicted tens of thousands of residents and left some neighborhoods totally abandoned. Criminals, squatters, and addicts moved in and took decades to displace.

(opposite page) Headlines about the South Bronx were a constant chorus of despair.

(above) Distributors knew their audiences, and so they retitled and advertised kung fu movies using language that emphasized solidarity, urban slang, and sticking it to The Man.

"The whole atmosphere of the South Bronx is geared to crushing a person's spirit," said one politician.

At the start of the '70s, 60,000 Bronx buildings stood abandoned. Fire hydrants provided clean drinking water for 20% of the population. Only 20% of high school students read at grade level.

The head of a community medical clinic referred to the South Bronx as "a necropolis—a city of death." Reporters saw seven-year-olds drunk in the street and 12-year-olds with babies on their hips and needles in their arms. Fifteen-year-old hitmen stood trial for committing $30 contract murders. Teenagers hijacked city buses at gunpoint. No one went to the police because the police were part of the problem. As one prominent NYPD historian wrote, "Just about any and everything could be bought or done if you could find the right cop. And that went for every precinct in the city, bar none."

Many Black and Latino kids lived in a landscape with few luxuries. Like the martial arts world, which was divided into a rigid hierarchy of schools and clans, their world was divided into gangs. The South Bronx had 9,500 gang members who committed 30 murders, 300 assaults, and 124 armed robberies in 1973 alone. In response, that year the police made 1,500 gang-related arrests.

Gangs had ruled the '40s and '50s but were wiped out by heroin in the early '60s. They returned at the end of that decade with a militantly anti-drug agenda. Gangs patrolled their neighborhoods and drummed junkies off their blocks, but the cure could be as bad as the disease. In one instance, the Secret Bachelors murdered a dealer by shooting him six times and leaving his body in the middle of the street.

Gangs conducted urban combat with hand grenades and beer can bazookas, dynamite and tommy guns, but they could help as well as hurt. They held voter registration drives and block parties, where delinquents danced with detectives from the local precinct house. Members fed their families with food stolen from supermarket trucks. The Young Lords, a political Puerto Rican street gang, took over Lincoln Hospital, kicked out its administrator, fired doctors, and completely reformed its mental health services.

Gangs had chiefs and vice presidents and war counselors who conducted their business according to their whims. They negotiated truces and mapped turf. No matter who you were, there was a gang for you: the Golden Guineas (Italian), the Savage Skulls (Puerto Rican), the Flying Dragons (Hong Kong immigrants in Chinatown), the Enchanters (East Harlem), the Harlem Turks (from the General Grant projects on 125th Street).

With rival gangs rumbling in the streets, with authority either remote or corrupt, with no future they could see, inner-city kids dreamed of standing up to the people who kept them down, of making a place in the world with their bare hands. One place they could see that dream breathe? Kung fu movies. Suddenly, distributors were in a race to deliver them.

Poster for *The Dragon's Fatal Fist* (aka *Invincible Kung Fu Trio*, 1977).

AFRICAN ATTO

IN AUGUST 1973, READERS OF the Black entertainment magazine *Sepia* were confronted with a bizarre advertisement on page 15: a mail-order martial arts manual for an ancient African self-defense method called African Atto ("which means AFRICAN ATTACK!" the ad screamed) resurrected from white-suppressed obscurity by a Black militant author, historian, and martial artist known as Mohammad X. According to the order form, the company, which promised the secrets of "Black Power" for "less than the cost of a good pair of pants," was Black Products and operated out of a PO box in Denham Springs, Louisiana. A sharp-eyed reporter for the *Denham Springs and Livingston Parish News* recognized the box number as belonging to the local chapter of the Knights of the Ku Klux Klan and exposed the truth a few months later in a front-page article.

Louisiana State University student and Grand Dragon David Duke admitted to the reporter that the KKK was responsible for the ad and there really was no Mohammad X or martial art known as African Atto, but he refused to elaborate on why the ruse was perpetrated at all, except to say that the Klan had received valuable information from responses to the ad. It took another four years and Duke's failed bid for the Louisiana Senate before this story broke at the national level, when Wayne King of the *New York Times* News Service discovered the African Atto manual was copyrighted under the name C. E. Holdin, the maiden name of Duke's wife, Chloe. Duke denied being the author (it was probably Chloe, who also holds the copyright for *Finderskeepers*, a 1976 manual on "how to find, attract and keep the man you want"), but was more forthcoming regarding the impetus of the endeavor. "I believe very strongly that America is headed for a racial conflict," said the future Louisiana state representative. "What the book essentially did was get us the names of the most radical blacks in the United States, so when the time comes we will know where they are." Meanwhile, Freedom of Information Act documents available online today reveal that, thanks to informants, the FBI office in New Orleans knew about African Atto almost as soon as the issue of *Sepia* hit newsstands.

AFRICAN ATTO WILL SHOW YOU THE WAY TO BLACK POWER!

Do you want BLACK POWER?

AFRICAN ATTO will turn your Body into BLACK STEEL and show you how to use your new strength with the most powerful self-defense program known: AFRICAN ATTO.

AFRICA was the birthplace of man, and the birthplace of Hand-to-Hand COMBAT! Not China or Japan, AFRICA produced the best BODY BUILDING PROGRAM in the history of the world — and the most deadly FIGHTING METHODS. White history has denied you this fact.

Mohammed X is an expert in both SELF-DEFENSE and BLACK HISTORY. He resurrected the ancient African method of fighting and body-building — called AFRICAN ATTO -- which means AFRICAN ATTACK!

Deadlier than Karate, more powerful than boxing. AFRICAN ATTO is the most terrific way of fighting ever known.

BLACK STEEL

Are you FAT or SKINNY?   If you are FAT ——

AFRICAN ATTO will show you the easy natural AFRICAN way to take off pounds of ugly fat! A real BLACK MAN is not a jellyfish.   OR if you are SKINNY ——

AFRICAN ATTO will show you the natural-AFRICAN way to gain weight - added pounds of solid, virile, sexy, BLACK MUSCLE. The AFRICAN ATTO course even charts a diet of muscle-building soul foods.

BLACK POWER

FEAR NO MAN, BLACK OR WHITE.

AFRICAN ATTO will mold your body into a weapon more powerful than a gun.

AFRICAN ATTO is the only Self-Defense method developed strictly for Blacks.

AFRICAN ATTO requires very little practice or strenuous exercise. It uses simple normal body movements. You receive its power when you learn its secrets.

BLACK POWER = SEX POWER

Do you want to be the kind of man a real woman respects and wants?

AFRICAN ATTO will change your physical Body into Black steel and then show you how to use it as BLACK POWER!

AFRICAN ATTO will give your body power that translates to sex appeal! You will attract women, loving, beautiful women.

A GOOD PAIR OF PANTS?

How much is Your Body Worth?

For a very limited time the cost of the entire AFRICAN ATTO COURSE is only $9.95. That's less than the cost of a good pair of pants. Is your body worth that?

WHAT YOU GET

- BIG AFRICAN ATTO manual featuring over 100 illustrations and drawings.
- Easy to follow instructions on how to lose or gain weight the African way
- The best physical fitness course for Blacks in the world.
- The best BLACK SELF-DEFENSE method in the world.
- Complete physical training chart and soul food chart.

ON SELF DEFENSE

- STEP BY STEP ILLUSTRATED INSTRUCTIONS OF African ATTO self defense method.
- Complete chart of human body showing sensitive parts.

LEARN

- How to fight "Dirty"
- 100 secrets of fighting
- How to use weapons in self-defense
- How to make weapons for self-defense
- How to fight "Whitey"

CUT OUT HERE

BLACK PRODUCTS
BOX 1234
DENHAM SPRINGS, LA. 70726

☐ PLEASE RUSH ME THE COMPLETE AFRICAN ATTO COURSE. ENCLOSED IS $9.95.

☐ SEND C.O.D. ENCLOSED IS $1.00 DEPOSIT. I WILL PAY THE POSTMAN $8.95 AND POSTAL CHARGES.

NAME _____
(PLEASE PRINT)
ADDRESS _____
CITY _____
STATE _____ ZIP _____

BORN IN GREECE, SERAFIM KARALEXIS was a quick-witted film fan who'd run 16mm Andy Warhol movies for sold-out crowds while attending Boston University before getting into distribution with United International Pictures, a Boston outfit that mostly distributed European softcore porn. A staple for independent distributors, softcore didn't need fancy locations or special effects, just an actress willing to drop her top and simulate sex, but it came with big headaches. In 1969, Karalexis' latest acquisition, a Swedish sex flick called *I Am Curious (Yellow)*, got seized by Customs for obscenity, then released, then seized again by the cops on opening night. Karalexis argued his case all the way to the Supreme Court and won, but who needed the grief? He was 29, the youngest of three partners, and he ached to do something new.

The Sunday after *Five Fingers* opened, he called to check on his softcore movies' New York City grosses.

"What's going on, Howard?" he asked Howard Mahler (see page 168), his sub-distributor. "How's business?"

"Eh, it's okay," Howard said. "But nothing like that Chinese picture."

"What Chinese picture?"

"Some Chinese picture that's doing gangbusters," Howard said. "I can't believe it."

"What Chinese picture?" Karalexis repeated.

"I don't know what the hell it is! Probably some communist bullshit!"

The next day Karalexis spoke with a European distributor who told him it wasn't "some communist bullshit," it was a kung fu movie. And it wasn't playing Boston for another week. Impatiently waiting for it to open, Karalexis saw this unknown film's grosses shoot through the roof. Something big was going down.

Finally, *Five Fingers of Death* opened in Boston, at the Savoy, on a Sunday. No one opened a movie on a Sunday but the owners couldn't wait. Karalexis and one of his partners, Steve Prentoulis, got tickets for the last show of opening day. Even with no trailers, no publicity, and no ads, by 10pm that Sunday night all 1,500 seats had sold out.

"It just POPPED," Karalexis said. "You could feel the electricity in the audience."

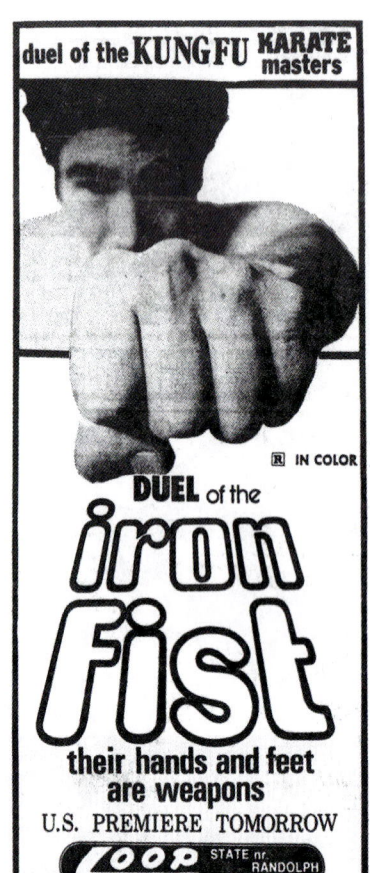

After it was over, Karalexis and Prentoulis debriefed at a nearby coffee shop. Prentoulis thought the movie wasn't very well made. Karalexis thought the movie was going to make a million dollars. It gave the audience exactly what it wanted.

"We have to get one of these pictures," he said. "If they made one, there have to be others."

"Okay," Prentoulis said. "But we don't even know where they made this one."

But Karalexis had sat through the end credits.

"Tomorrow," he said, "I'm going to Hong Kong."

He called TWA and asked for the first flight out. On Monday, April 2, at 9am, he boarded the plane and realized his mistake: he'd asked for the first, not the fastest, flight to Hong Kong. Thirty-four hours later, he stumbled through customs and into the Hong Kong Hilton.

Dazed with jet lag, Karalexis felt time running out. He'd lost a day crossing the international date line and for all he knew someone else had already released the second kung fu movie back in America. Even if he found a film and bought it, he had no time to get it dubbed. He had no time to develop an ad campaign. But he'd come this far. He opened the phone book and looked up movie studios. He didn't see any. He called the Hong Kong government and they told him to look under "cinematographers" and there he found a number for Shaw Brothers.

(opposite page) With the clock ticking and all the art with Karalexis, who was stuck on a flight home, his partners still needed to promote their movie. They found a Japanese cab driver who knew karate, dressed him in a kung fu outfit, and took pictures to use in this early newspaper ad.

(above) The one sheet for *Duel of the Iron Fist* bragged about its endorsement by Chang Ming Lee, "China's Grand Master of Kung Fu" which would be amazing if Chang actually existed. But the distributor was trying every trick to get people excited, including making up imaginary martial arts masters.

He called and told them he was Mr. Serafim Karalexis from New York City and he wanted to buy some movies. Run Run Shaw sent his chauffeured Rolls-Royce to pick him up. Then 66, Run Run Shaw turned him over to his nephew, Vee King Shaw, the same age as Karalexis.

"Put it there," Vee King said, sticking out his hand. "How much do you pay for films?"

Telling Vee King that it depended on what he had, Karalexis begged off the mandatory Movietown studio tour and went right to a screening room. He didn't have time to watch full movies, so Vee King ran trailer after trailer. After trailer. After trailer. Karalexis didn't want wu xia, he wanted kung fu. And he didn't want period costumes, he wanted something modern. But Vee King saw this as a chance to dump old inventory, so Karalexis watched trailers for wu xia and historical dramas; he watched everything Shaw had going back 10 years, and he started to lose hope.

Suddenly, he saw it. *The Duel* (1971) set in 1930s China, starring Ti Lung and David Chiang, directed by Chang Cheh, the actors in suits rather than robes, using guns alongside their kung fu. Even better, it was already dubbed into English. Vee King told him Shaw had never sold a movie for less than $100,000. Karalexis got him down to $50,000 and 35% of the gross, then he packed the negative and two prints in his suitcase, called his office long-distance, and told them they had a movie. *Five Fingers of Death* mentioned a "Book of the Iron Fist" so he decided to rename it *Duel of the Iron Fist*.

Karalexis had been gone for a week and already things were changing.

On the promotional circuit for her new movie, *Paper Moon*, a reporter asked ten-year-old Tatum O'Neal to name her favorite film.

"*Five Fingers of Death*!" she gleefully cheered.

The same day *Five Fingers of Death* opened, a shot-in-the-Philippines flick called *Wonder Women* debuted in El Paso, Texas, starring Nancy Kwan, a Chinese star who'd shot to Hollywood fame playing the title role in *The World of Suzie Wong* (1960). In *Wonder Women* she played a mad scientist kidnapping the world's top athletes so her rich clients could transplant their brains into these healthy young bodies. The only person who could stop her was an insurance investigator. "He tried to stop them," the ads screamed. "And they took him apart piece by piece!" Three weeks later, its ad campaign had changed its tune, claiming that the movie starred, "The most Lethal KUNG FU team on Earth."

Without even time to submit the movie to the MPAA for a rating, Karalexis booked *Duel of the Iron Fist* into the first theater he could find for the first date they had. Three weeks after he watched *Five Fingers of Death*, Serafim Karalexis' *Duel of the Iron Fist* opened at the Loop in Chicago on Easter Sunday, 1973. It blew the doors off, grossing $12,000 in a weekend, eventually raking in over $4 million. Karalexis' partners told him he was a genius.

Audiences agreed. When *Duel* finally arrived in Times Square it played the New Amsterdam, a grand old house now fallen on hard times, with bullet holes in the lobby ceiling and a men's room that doubled as a shooting gallery. About a week into its New York run, a member of the MPAA caught the film and knew it was too violent to have gotten an R rating as advertised. The theater had to play the movie without its fifth reel while the distributor cut the violence, but when the return crowd came back with their friends and saw the censored result, they rioted. The New Amsterdam's owner called sub-distributor Howard Mahler in a panic, and Mahler dispatched his editor Jim Markovic to the theater with an uncut print, with the reel five bloodbath intact. Markovic found the audience in full revolt and described walking through them on his way to the projection booth as "harrowing."

Hallmark Releasing, a Boston-based outfit known for their eye-catching ad campaigns (often involving vomit bags), released the next kung fu movie in America at the Paris Theater in Pittsfield, Pennsylvania. It starred a woman and so, in a classy move, they called it *Deep Thrust* to remind audiences of the previous year's hardcore porno hit, *Deep Throat*. To reinforce the connection, Angela Mao, its female lead, was billed as "mistress of the death blow." The movie was distributed nationally by American International Pictures, the former home of director Roger

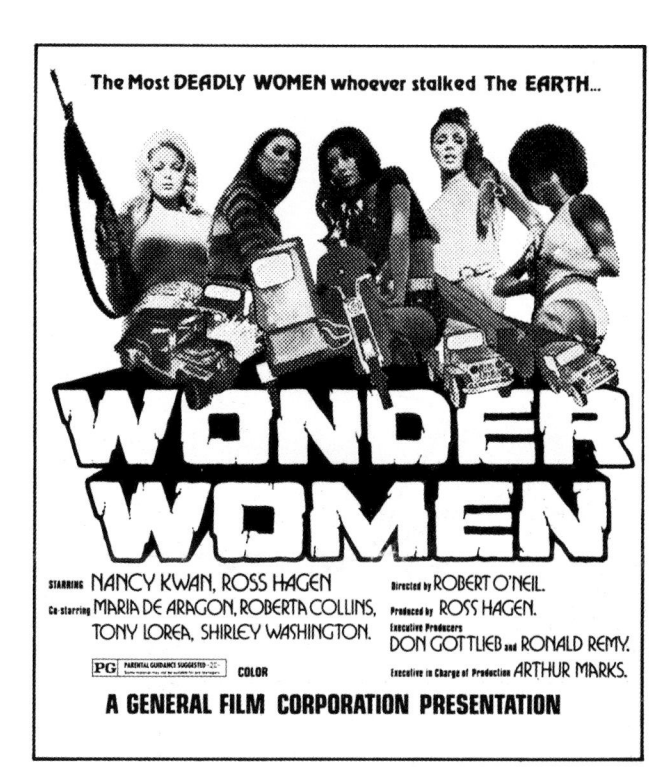

When it opened in El Paso, *Wonder Women* bragged that its lethal lady gang were "deadly women," but three weeks later the movie opened in Honolulu, Kansas City, and Shreveport, Louisiana, and its ad campaign called them a "lethal kung fu team." Other ads proclaimed: "KUNG-FU Killers of the Orient . . . DEADLY With Their Hands . . . DEADLIER With Their Bodies . . ."

Corman, whose New World Pictures also got in on the kung fu action. The first three entries in their R-rated nurse series—*The Student Nurses*, *Private Duty Nurses*, and *Night Call Nurses*—had done so well that Corman decided to expand his winning four-girl format. *The Student Teachers* featured a karate class taught by Chuck Norris, who ran six karate studios in the LA area. A proud Norris and his wife brought their two sons to the premiere, then spent most of the running time shielding their eyes from the rampant nudity and onscreen drug use.

"I was told it was going to be about teachers who break away from the traditional method of teaching," he complained.

Kung fu movies were big, but they were about to get bigger. On Wednesday, May 2, *Deep Thrust* opened in New York City, the same week as another movie, called *Fists of Fury*. It was actually a retitled version of a cheapass flick from Hong Kong called *The Big Boss*. All of a sudden, Bruce Lee was in the house.

(above) Roger Corman sent three starlets to the Philippines to star in a sexy stewardess comedy, but what came back was barely an hour of usable footage about dope smugglers and white slavers, so he enlisted Jonathan Demme and *Kung Fu*'s technical advisor, David Chow, to transform it into *Fly Me*.

(opposite page) The one sheet for *Deep Thrust*. Independent distributors had to get butts in seats any way they could. If that meant using as much suggestive language as possible and showing a lot of skin to promote Angela Mao's bone-breaker, why not?

MISTRESS OF THE DEATH-BLOW!

SEE... the Deadliest Woman in the world take on a dozen skilled fighters bare-handed.

DEEP THRUST

...the deadly stroke of Bare-Hand Combat!

A HALLMARK Presentation · Color by DeLuxe® · An AMERICAN INTERNATIONAL Release

N 1970, BRUCE LEE HAD touched down in Hong Kong for a family visit, a broke former child star with a washed-up television career and a crippling back injury. An invitation to appear on the massively popular variety show *Enjoy Yourself Tonight* revealed, however, that he had something new to offer. Most Hong Kong stars worked for Run Run Shaw, and the boss saw everything. In public appearances, they wore suits, showed respect, and acted like office workers. Bruce talked like a regular guy, cracked jokes, wore a leather jacket and jeans, and did kung fu at blistering speed.

Even better, he owed Shaw Brothers nothing.

After directing what would arguably be their most famous movie, *Five Fingers of Death*, Chung Chang-Hwa moved on to his next Shaw Brothers production. Arriving one morning, his jaw hit the floor when he saw his costumes cut off at the knees and the spears chopped from six feet to three.

Orders from the boss, wardrobe told him.

Mona Fong was that boss. A nightclub singer who'd caught Run Run Shaw's eye, she'd become his mistress and, later, his wife. That didn't bother Chung. But Shaw had also made her head of production, and to save money, she'd slashed the art department budget in half by literally slashing everything in half. The pissed-off director loaded the mini-robes and toothpick spears into his car, drove to Fong's office, threw them on her desk, and quit. When he got home, his phone was already ringing. It was Raymond Chow, Shaw Brothers' former head of production.

"Need a job?" he asked.

Another refugee from Mona Fong's regime, Chow thought Shaw was too slow to adapt to changing times, so he'd grabbed Leonard Ho, another Shaw employee, and bailed to form rival studio Golden Harvest. They had no stars, no infrastructure, and no money. What they did have were lawsuits.

They'd made a movie with the One-Armed Swordsman himself, Jimmy Wong Yu, whose recent contract dispute with Shaw meant he couldn't legally work in Hong Kong. Craftily, Raymond Chow shot their movie in Taiwan and Japan. Not-so-craftily, he called it *Zatoichi and the One-Armed Swordsman*. Shaw sued for copyright infringement, figuring it could bleed this upstart rival dry. So far, they were doing a pretty good job of it.

A few journeyman directors like Wong Fung and Lo Wei had also made the jump from Shaw to Golden Harvest, but scoring Chung Chang-Hwa was a coup. However, Golden Harvest still didn't have what mattered: a star. Shaw owned all of those.

Then Lo Wei's son saw Bruce Lee on *Enjoy Yourself Tonight*, and he made his dad watch, and his dad made Raymond Chow watch, and Raymond Chow sent Lo Wei's wife to LA to negotiate a deal because Bruce Lee had already returned to California. She arrived at almost the exact moment Lee realized he couldn't make his next mortgage payment. He signed her two-film contract.

Twenty days later, on July 18, 1971, Bruce arrived in Pak Chong, Thailand, 100 miles north of Bangkok, to film a janky, threadbare production called *The Big Boss*. The script was a three-page outline. The director was a former Shaw Brothers veteran, the fight choreographer was a former Cathay journeyman, and the star was a former Shaw Brothers contract actor named James Tien. Everyone hated Bruce Lee, and he hated them right back. He had to fight to shoot the action his way. He had to fight to get enough protein in his diet. He had to fight until Chow fired the director and replaced him with Lo Wei, who brought the movie in on time, and a midnight preview was set for Halloween weekend.

Bruce sat in the front of the theater with Linda Lee (his wife) and Bob Baker, a student from LA he'd invited to work on his next, and probably final, movie for Golden Harvest. Onscreen, Bruce awkwardly delivered his lines, playing a country bumpkin come to Thailand for work. When the first fight erupts, co-star James Tien tells him, "Stay out of this," and he does. Same with the next fight. And the next. Bruce Lee, the world's most famous fighter, doesn't lift a finger for the first hour and twenty minutes of the movie. Instead, the sneering, drug-smuggling factory boss makes him look like a jerk, gets him drunk, and turns his friends against him.

It was all part of the plan.

(opposite page) Raymond Chow, looking unworried.

(above) Before they landed Bruce Lee, Golden Harvest leveraged all the success they could muster to seduce American distributors and exhibitors. And their public association with former Shaw Brothers rival, Cathay Films, probably made the gods of Movietown extra salty.

Leonard Ho, Golden Harvest's quiet co-founder, believed that logic and realism didn't matter in a movie. What mattered was connecting to the audience on an emotional level. For *The Big Boss*, one colleague remembers, "He insisted that Bruce Lee's character should suppress his anger and rein in his emotions until the final, cathartic showdown at the end of the film."

Sitting in the audience, Lee wasn't so sure this strategy was working.

"As the movie progressed," he said, "we kept looking at the fans. They hardly made any noise."

Then, around minute 77, Lee unleashed the beast. The final back-to-back fight scenes lasted for 18 minutes. They ended when pretty much everyone onscreen was dead.

"There was about 10 seconds of silence," Mel Tobias, an audience member said. "They didn't know what hit them, and then they started roaring."

The Big Boss became the highest-grossing movie in Hong Kong history. Bruce Lee, over 30 years old and not getting any younger, who had barely been scraping by in Los Angeles as a kung fu coach for celebrities, who couldn't get cast in a Hollywood movie, who'd had to run back to Hong Kong for a job, who couldn't even get in the door of the prestige studio and had to sign with the second-tier team at Golden Harvest, was about to become one of the biggest movie stars in the world . . . except America.

In Lee's next film, *Fist of Fury* (1972), set in the 1930s, he plays an immigrant from overseas who returns home to Shanghai because his master has been killed by evil Japanese colonizers. This time, he's kicking butt by minute 15. When Bruce shatters a sign on a park gate proclaiming "No dogs or Chinese," it connected with immigrants of all races who felt like they'd been seeing similar signs all their lives. The movie made even more money than *The Big Boss*.

Finally in charge of his own career, Bruce went to Rome to direct his third film himself. *Way of the Dragon* (1972) stars Bruce as a Chinese superman exported overseas to save his uncle's restaurant from white thugs, which he does in spectacular fashion. For the final fight, he called up Chuck Norris and offered him the part.

"Who gets to win?" Norris asked.

And Bruce got to say a line he'd probably been practicing his entire life: "I'm the star."

Way earned almost twice as much as *The Big Boss*, but Bruce didn't think it was good enough to break him into Hollywood on his terms. Every day he fielded calls from Weintraub and Ted Ashley at Warners asking him to star in a movie, but he wanted to

---

(top) Americans knew karate better than this new-fangled kung fu, so National General hedged its bets and mashed them together in its trade ads announcing the premieres of its Bruce Lee flicks. They tested the market by releasing Lee's films down south before bringing them to the big cities.

(bottom) Before that, Bruce Lee's movies were such big hits that Chinatown cinemas ran English language ads to tempt Western audiences, but the curious ones who came were only a tiny preview of the massive crowds waiting for Lee's movies to be dubbed into English.

The new screen excitement is Karate-Kung Fu*...
and National General is flying high with the first two!

BRUCE LEE, every limb of his body is a lethal weapon in "FISTS OF FURY"

Pre-release Early April
Charlotte, Texas,
Oklahoma Territories...
National release April 28th

MAKE "FISTS" YOUR BIGGEST BOXOFFICE BELT...
WITH A SMASHING SEQUEL TO FOLLOW
from NATIONAL GENERAL PICTURES

*Reprint of the Sunday Jan. 14th Los Angeles Times Syndicated Feature, Available on Request.

BRUCE LI
T.V. PERSONALITY
CHINESE BOXING
MARTIAL ARTS
KING-FU

"THE BIG BOSS"
(WITH ENGLISH SUBTITLES)
SMASHED ALL BOX OFFICE
RECORDS IN THE FAR EAST

ALSO "ZATOICHI & THE ONE-ARMED SWORDSMAN"
STARRING SHINTARO KATSU
SEPT. 11-26

BOSS: 1:00, 4:00, 7:10, 10:20
ZATOICHI: 2:30, 5:35, 8:45

PALACE THEATRE
1741 POWELL ST., S.F.
TEL. 392-8526

write, direct, *and* star in his first Hollywood film. He thought his Hong Kong movies looked too cheap to impress Hollywood, so he started shooting an epic, philosophical kung fu flick aimed at the international audience, featuring American stars like Kareem Abdul-Jabbar.

Raymond Chow didn't share Lee's vision. He wanted cash. By late 1972, subtitled prints of *The Big Boss* and *Fist of Fury* had already played American Chinatowns, but outside of Chinese speakers, only the most hardcore kung fu cultists knew these theaters even existed. Raymond Chow thought the films would find a bigger audience dubbed into English, with English advertising campaigns and playing in mainstream movie houses, so he sold their theatrical rights again, this time to a dying distributor named National General. Chow credited Charles Boasberg, its head, as the first Westerner to smell money in Bruce Lee's films, and Boasberg was definitely desperate for hits. His National General had been acquired by the American Financial Corporation, a faceless corporate juggernaut that had already started chopping it up for parts. National's films mostly came through a deal with First Artists, a vanity studio founded by Barbra Streisand, Steve McQueen, and Dustin Hoffman to release their own pictures, but these megastars made movies too slowly, so National General looked for off-the-grid pick-ups to fill in the gaps. Which is where Bruce Lee came in.

National General dubbed *The Big Boss* and *Fist of Fury* into English and changed their titles. *The Big Boss* became the plural *Fists of Fury* and *Fist of Fury* became *The Chinese Connection* because there had already been a *French Connection* the previous year, so why not?

Bruce thought he needed something better than these low-budget movies to prove he deserved complete control of a Hollywood production, and he was furious Raymond Chow had exposed them to English-speaking audiences behind his back. To spite Chow, he signed with Warners to shoot *Blood & Steel*, inspired by Weintraub's old Western script, *Kelsey*. Chow had no choice: he could either play along or lose his star to an American studio. *Blood & Steel* became a Warner Bros. / Golden Harvest co-production, and in January 1973, it started shooting in Hong Kong.

"From the first, nothing went right," says Weintraub.

A nervous Bruce, paralyzed by pressure to perform, didn't show up for the first three weeks of shooting. He insisted they fire the screenwriter. He developed a facial twitch. He pulled a groin muscle. He banned Raymond Chow from the set. The Hollywood crew found the Golden Harvest facilities primitive. The Chinese crew found the Hollywood team arrogant. Warner Bros. didn't expect more than a modest exploitation flick, so they'd given the movie about a quarter of their average budget. At one point, Bruce stormed up to Robert Clouse, a small-time director making his first studio feature, and fumed, "There are only two people on this set who give a shit what this thing looks like—you and me." That sounded about right. *Blood & Steel* showed all the signs of becoming a flop.

(opposite page) *Lady Kung Fu* (*Hap Ki Do*, 1972) was the third of four Golden Harvest hits unleashed in the States by National General, arriving in theaters after *Fists of Fury* (*The Big Boss*) and *The Chinese Connection* (*Fist of Fury*) but ahead of *The Chinese Professionals* (*One-Armed Boxer*).

(above) National General ran an ad calling out *Deep Thrust* (left). AIP not only sued National General, but ran its own response ad (right).

HERE COMES THE UNBREAKABLE CHINA DOLL WHO GIVES YOU THE LICKING OF YOUR LIFE!

ANGELA MAO

"LADY KUNG FU"

National General Pictures presents Angela Mao as the "LADY KUNG FU!" Produced by Raymond Chow Directed by Huang Feng · Color · A National General Pictures Release

IT WAS A LONG, HOT SUMMER and the number one television show in America started broadcasting in May 1973, featuring a bunch of old white guys asking each other questions. PBS aired all 250 hours of the Senate's Watergate Hearings all day, every day, for the entire summer while kung fu movies blistered the big screen.

At the beginning of May 1973 National General's *Fists of Fury* hit New York, LA, Cincinnati, and St. Louis screens the same day *Deep Thrust* opened in New York City. Headlined by Angela Mao, a wispy 23-year-old, it picked up $459,000 in its opening week.

Fists of Fury didn't do so bad, either, raking in $651,000 that week alone, but the Catholic Church slapped both movies with a C for Condemned, which meant it became a mortal sin for Catholics to view either ("Viewers will gasp at the gore more than the hero's prowess," it gasped). Vincent Canby, writing for the *New York Times*, warned viewers away from kung fu films as if they were some kind of proletarian plague. "The two I've just seen," he sniffed, "*Fists of Fury* and *Deep Thrust*, make the worst Italian Westerns look like the most solemn and noble achievements of the early Soviet cinema." Apparently he didn't like Italian Westerns, either.

Didn't matter. As *Kung Fu* wrapped up its first season on TV, Serafim Karalexis' *Duel of the Iron Fist* continued to roll out across the country, as did *Five Fingers of Death*. For one beautiful week in May, *Fists of Fury*, *Deep Thrust*, and *Five Fingers of Death* held the #1, #2, and #3 positions at the country's box office.

Independent and low-budget movie distributors had been dying in the desert, so these kung fu movies weren't just a lifesaving oasis, they were a waterfall of cash, and distributors treated them with deadly seriousness. AIP filed a $5 million lawsuit in federal court against National General, claiming its ad campaign for *Fists of Fury* (see page 59) implied that *Deep Thrust* was an inferior film.

It was. But that didn't matter, because it starred Angela Mao, and she possessed supreme star power. Shot in the backyards, forests, hillsides, and shacks of Korea, *Deep Thrust* (aka *Lady Whirlwind*, 1972) got churned out fast and cheap while Mao was in Korea learning hapkido for her posh debut in *Hap Ki Do* (*Lady Kung Fu*, 1972). Mao had studied for eight years at Taiwan's Fu Hsing Dramatic Arts Academy, a tough Chinese Opera school, and become one of Taiwan's top wudan (a woman playing a male warrior role) before getting scouted by Golden Harvest director Huang Feng. She signed her Golden Harvest contract alongside their other new recruit, Nora Miao, and the two of them appeared in Golden Harvest's first film, *The Invincible Eight* (1971), a Lo Wei production starring James Tien. (Six months later, Lo Wei, James Tien, and Nora Miao would start shooting *The Big Boss* with Bruce Lee.)

The trailer for *Lady Kung Fu* (aka *Hap Ki Do*, 1972) featured the instrumental "Eruption" by Emerson, Lake & Palmer and narration that referred to the movie by its original US title, *Hong Kong Hellcat*.

Wednesday, May 16, 1973 — Variety — PICTURE GROSSES — 9

50 Top-Grossing Films
[WEEK ENDING MAY 9]
Compiled by Standard Data Corp., N.Y.

TITLE	DISTR	THIS WEEK $	RANK	LAST WEEK $	RANK	TOTALS CITIES	FIRST RUN	SHOW CASE	ROAD SHOW	THEATRES	WEEKS ON CHART	TOTAL TO DATE $
FISTS OF FURY	NGP	697,000	1	19,675		6	3	71		74	1	753,706
DEEP THRUST—THE HAND OF DEATH	AIP	459,000	2			2	1	45		46	1	459,000
FIVE FINGERS OF DEATH	WB	326,387	3	475,350	2	10	8	26		34	7	3,225,982
SLEUTH	FOX	306,619	4	136,300	15	10	10	34		44	21	2,947,588

Groomed to be one of Golden Harvest's big stars alongside Lee, Mao had a secret weapon: Sammo Hung (see page 258). This portly martial artist designed all the action in her early movies and turned her into a buttkicking machine.

In *Deep Thrust*, his opening gambit is a 15-against-1 brawl unleashed when Mao walks into a casino and smashes stools and fools before hurling hatchets into chumps' chests. Playing a woman out to avenge her sister by slaughtering the man who did her dirty, Mao barely gets half the screen time of her male co-star but steals the spotlight, delivering brutal beatdowns that make goons barf blood and die.

Deep Thrust became famous overseas, but in Hong Kong it was Mao's follow-up film, *Hap Ki Do*, that made her a star. A female version of Bruce Lee's *Fist of Fury*, it showcased Mao as a fist-slinging sister out to avenge her two brothers murdered by evil Japanese martial artists. Mao would play her most famous sister role in the upcoming *Enter the Dragon* (1973) as Bruce Lee's little sis, whose murder sparks Bruce's quest for revenge.

Mao kicked ass all over the world, fractured her spine on *Thunderbolt* (1973), shot lots of movies in Korea, and became wildly popular in Japan after *Enter the Dragon* finally got released there in 1974.

As Andre Morgan, a producer at Golden Harvest recalled, "I took Angela Mao to Australia and went on the local talk shows, and she's this little petite Chinese woman breaking boards and doing all of these things. The world just didn't know what to make of it."

In 1973, Angela Mao owned New York City's screens for a five-week period from mid-August to late September when three of her movies—*Enter the Dragon*, *Deadly China Doll*, and *Lady Kung Fu*—all hit the city one after the other like a bunch of fists smacking the audience right in the face.

(above) Validated by *Variety*! The industry's trade mag celebrates the week when kung fu ruled American screens.

(opposite page) "She's on a manhunt, and she's a man-eater!" Adolph Caesar growled in the trailer for *Deadly China Doll* (aka *The Opium Trail*, 1973), a major studio release and the first production credit for Andrew G. Vajna, who later founded Carolco and Cinergi Pictures.

VIOLENT!
UNSTOPPABLE!
UNBREAKABLE!
UNINHIBITED!
DANGEROUS!
DEVASTATING!
WICKED! DEADLY!
DELICIOUS!
MGM Presents
Angela Mao
as the
DEADLY CHINA DOLL
Produced by
ANDREW G. VAJNA
Directed by HUANG FENG
A Panasia Film
In Color
MGM
R
RESTRICTED
Under 17 requires accompanying Parent or Adult Guardian

HEY, KIDS! IT'S KUNG FU!

BETWEEN 1960 AND 1985, ADS touting martial arts training appeared in comic books everywhere.

One of the first and the biggest was Yubizawa. Emblazoned with all the colors of the rainbow, each ad came topped by a photo of Nelson J. "Mitch" Fleming, accompanied by a picture of his wife, Yoshie Imanami. Contemporary accounts indicate Fleming was a serious martial artist who intended to promote his style, Sosuishi-ryu jiu-jitsu, which he'd studied in Japan, where he also married Imanami, who shared the same training.

As the story goes, the publisher of Yubiwaza signed up at Fleming's New Jersey school for six months of private lessons back in 1960 and convinced Fleming to write a book about his techniques. Fleming did and got paid a measly $200.

Translated as "finger techniques," Yubizawa involves pressure point strikes with the fingers and thumbs. Calling Yubiwaza a martial art is akin to calling punching a martial art. What's more, learning to correctly employ it in combat takes years of training.

The ads made Fleming feel like a chump. Where he imagined a heftier book of 100 pages, the publisher slimmed it down to a mere 14. Yubiwaza was more intended for women, and Fleming received letters of thanks from women who claimed this or that Yubiwaza technique saved their purses, their honor, or their lives, but he disliked the trickery of it all.

Fleming, however, weathered the storm and enjoyed a respectable career as a teacher and American Sosuishi-ryu representative until he died in 1987.

A soldier for much of his life, Wallace Reumann trained in Chito-ryu karate under Sensei Hank Slomanski while stationed in Japan. Reumann's ads claimed he returned to the States with a fifth-degree black belt, opened a couple of karate schools in New Jersey, and founded the American Karate Federation.

No doubt Reumann was a competent karateka and instructor, but unlike Fleming's Yubiwaza ads—which seem almost like daily affirmations—Reumann's fear tactics are shameless, almost cruel in their chiding of the mark. He, or his marketers, went wild with Asian othering, drawing upon a purposeless Japanese Kabuki mask for a spot illustration and using such buzz words as "forbidden," "secret," and "outsiders." His ads also claim a Japanese wife—though, unlike Yoshie Imanami, she does not appear in the ads.

Reumann outlasted all the mail-order martial artists. His most persistent appeal, the half-page "I'LL MAKE YOU A MASTER OF KARATE" ad, showed up as late as 1982 in an issue of Marvel's *Daredevil*, recently taken over by Frank Miller.

—TEXT BY DAN KELLY

CHINESE MARTIAL ARTS SOCIETY, LTD.

8 movies of Secret Arts!
DEADLY KUNG FU DANCES
$19.95 PER REEL PLUS WRITTEN INSTRUCTIONS AND FREE CHART OF PRESSURE POINTS TO HELP YOU LEARN

ON HAND
HAND
EATH BY PALM & FINGERS!
OF DESTRUCTION & ELIMINATION
SHOWN TO YOU BY PROFESSIONAL
ORS ON FILM & PAPER
IN THE CONVENIENCE
OWN HOME.
SEND 25¢ FOR CATALOG

BECOME A REGISTERED BLACK BELT

THE DEADLIEST MEN ALIVE ARE AICONDO MEN

THE COMBAT SYSTEM THAT CAN CHANGE YOUR LIFE
DISTILLED FROM ANCIENT FIGHTING ARTS!
SOLD NATIONALLY AT $9.95. NOW ONLY $6.95.

AICONDO WILL TURN YOU INTO A DEADLY FIGHTING MACHINE.

KUNG-FU

Now you can learn the Worlds Most Effective self defense and attack method in the privacy of your own home. Our course teachs you to: kick, punch and throw, 1 or more opponents...as well as knife and gun defenses - Also learn Martial Arts Weapons! Free Brick Breaking Course! **EARN YOUR BLACK BELT!**
Send Coupon & 25¢ For Details

can Southwest Academy of Fighting Arts
Suite 804/M-58, Dept. MC
Franklin Blvd. S.-Chicago, Ill. 60606

e _____
ess _____
_____ Zip _____

Super KARATE made easy

LIMITED EDITION ~~$9.95~~
now only **$1.35**

WHAT IS KARATE?
Karate is the supreme art of self defense. It is more effective than boxing, wrestling, or judo, and offers lightning-swift defensive power against surprise attack. A puny man under 100 pounds can floor a powerful brute weighing over 220 with one swift, crippling thrust to any one of scores of pressure points and focal nerve centers.

So Simple — Anyone Can Learn Fast!
The author, Maja Rone, has done a superb job of condensation and simplification in this book. He has lifted the cloak of secrecy and mystery that surrounded this art for centuries. Ancient Japanese expressions have given way to fast-reading English words. Over 200 anatomical illustrations integrated in the text to make it easy, fast, and fun for any man, woman or teen-ager to learn.

Over 200 illustrations plus the author's all-new simplified method teach you how to ward off any attacker no matter how big, or how powerful. Your fingers, hands, feet and elbows become super weapons when you use Super Karate—the deadliest art of self defense known to mankind.

Essentials of a $250.00 Gym Course!
Too busy for a gym course on Karate? This book gives you all the essentials of a $250.00 course and allows you to train at home at your convenience. The principles and step-by-step instruction in this book are so easy to follow that in 3 short weeks, you will become "a Karate man" with super power! You will be supreme! You will fear NO MAN OR GIANT!

MAIL THIS COUPON TODAY!
STRATHMORE — DEPT. 78
P.O. BOX 397-ROCKVILLE CENTRE, N.Y. 11570
RUSH ME _____ KARATE(S) AT ONLY
$1.35 EACH. I ENCLOSE $ _____
NAME _____
ADDRESS _____
CITY _____ STATE _____ ZIP _____
CANADIAN AND FOREIGN ADD 25¢ INT'L MONEY ORDER

---

132 Nassau St Dept. ENT. N.Y. N.Y. 10038

KARATE
JUDO · SAVATE · JU-JITSU
ntastic Fighting Secrets GUARANTEED
E REPORT! Write Karate Box 16037 NC
Brent Sta Cincinnati Ohio 45217

HAT IS NINJA?
You can be told these deadly techniques!!! Ultimate in Self Defense!! $1 for more details. * Instant self defense system, $4.95. * Ninja Combat System, $6. * Ninja Throwing Star & Caltrop, $5. DEFENSE ARTS, INC., P.O. BOX 1828, SMYRNA, GA 30080.

Learn YOGA
The Art of SELF MASTERY
Practical Course—ONLY $5.95 Com
Yogism aids your self-confidence, will-p
self-control. Helps your personal effic
Points out time-tested methods for a ha
more successful life...based on modern
tific discoveries plus ancient Yoga Secre
releasing your deeper powers. Practical,
able for everyday use by busy, level-h
Americans. Send No Money. Pay postman
plus COD, or send $5.95 for postpaid ship

FEAR NO MAN with KUNG FU

GO ANYWHERE — ANYTIME with CONFIDENCE, SAFETY and DIGNITY —

Because you have mastered KUNG FU, The Ancient Oriental Art of defense handed down from father to son. Kung Fu's DEADLY POWER will atomize your attacker disarming and turning him into a helpless mush in seconds.

BECOME A NEW MAN — ABLE TO PROTECT YOUR FAMILY AND LOVED ONES —

GUARANTEED — 10 Day Trial — Money Back if you are not amazed at you new mighty power with "KUNG - FU." You OUGHT TO ACT NOW.

LEARN TO DEFEND YOURSELF WITH KETSUGO

DEFEND YOURSELF!
Be unbeatable in the art of Self-Defense!

By HANK ROBERT

Ketsugo combines all the fine points of Judo, Ate-Waza, Aikido, Yawara, Savate & Jiu-Jitsu. Fully illustrated, easy to learn.

Money Back Guarantee—No C.O.D.'s $1.00 Add 25¢ for mailing

KUNG-FU

©1973
We teach you what Kung-Fu should be! You will learn quickly and easily from a REGISTERED BLACK BELT SCHOOL the strange secrets of:
* PREYING MANTIS
* CHINESE HAND CONDITIONING
* HORIZONTAL & VERTICAL CIRCLE POWER
* SNAKE AND CRANE
* TIGER CLAW & IRON PALM
* POISON FINGER

CERTIFICATE & MEMBERSHIP
Home Study Course
FREE COLOR BROCHURE

EVERYONE HAD KUNG FU FEVER. Richard Ellman, an independent distributor whose company logo featured an MGM circle with himself, sporting a lush porn-stache and groovy aviator shades, roaring like a lion in the center, picked up a cheap wu xia picture full of rayon capes and homemade masks, and recruited his friend, Chinese-American actor James Hong (*Big Trouble in Little China, Everything Everywhere All at Once*), to dub it into English. Giving the characters comic book names like One Man Army and Solar Ray of Death, they retitled it *Fearless Fighters* and claimed it was shot in "Widescreen Chinascope," whatever that was. In the summer of '73, it briefly became the #4 movie in the nation.

James Hong himself directed an X-rated May release about telephone operators called *Hot Connections*, but now, as it hopped from drive-in to grindhouse over the sultry summer months, its ad campaign suddenly declared it "The first seX with karate" movie.

Bruce Lee's *The Chinese Connection* stormed across the country, held over for months in some theaters. In Los Angeles, Ted Ashley smelled money and approved an extra $300,000 to get famed composer Lalo Schifrin to compose the score for the upcoming *Blood & Steel*. Ashley also realized that Bruce Lee was about to become a superstar, so he finally caved to Bruce's demand and retitled *Blood & Steel*. Its new title? *Enter the Dragon*. He set its release date for August.

And then Bruce Lee died.

Everyone in Hong Kong remembers where they were when Bruce Lee died because the entire city stopped. Fifteen thousand people attended his funeral. At 32 years old, the biggest star in Asia, the one who stood up to power, who did it his own way, who embodied the dreams of every Chinese person working in an artificial flower factory or an office building, was gone.

As if the loss of Bruce removed any sense of shame, kung fu films got real trashy, real fast.

In Hong Kong, fly-by-night producers drowned in the cash thrown at them by hungry American distributors, who bought anything as long as it came on celluloid and ran roughly 90 minutes. Raymond Chow noted that almost every available kung

---

Only 82 minutes long, *Fearless Fighters* was re-edited, re-written, re-scored, and dubbed into English in a blistering three weeks. The soundtrack was patched together out of needle drops from other soundtrack albums and Ellman didn't even have time to show the movie to poster artist Chet Collom before the poor guy had to paint it.

YOU'VE SEEN THE REST... NOW SEE THE BEST!
ONE MAN ARMY
GOLDEN ARCHER
SOUL PICKER
SOLAR RAY OF DEATH
SEE 10 INCREDIBLE DEVIL WEAPONS USED BY KUNG FU MASTERS
DEVIL RIPPER
DRAGON RAZOR
FROM CHINA
ALL NEW FIERY ACTION
RICHARD ELLMAN PRESENTS
FEARLESS FIGHTERS
THE ULTIMATE IN ALL MARTIAL ARTS!
R
Starring: CHANG CHING · YEE YUANG · CHEN LIEH Directed by: WU MIN-HSIUNG
Produced by: SUN WAH MOTION PICTURE COMPANY
AN ELLMAN FILM ENTERPRISES RELEASE
WIDESCREEN CHINASCOPE
METROCOLOR

The Ultimate in Martial Arts Excitement and Adventure!

Starring
BRUCE LEE   JOHN SAXON
AHNA CAPRI   JIM KELLY

MAJOR STUDIO
SNEAK PREVIEW
TONIGHT 8:30 P.M.

MANN'S CHINESE
HOLLYWOOD BLVD • 464-8111 R

"MACKINTOSH MAN" SHOWN BEFORE AND AFTER SNEAK PREVIEW!

fu movie in Hong Kong had been purchased. Low-budget producers sold what they had from offices with a clothesline strung down the center, their business on one side, their family living on the other. When they needed music, they shamelessly grabbed tracks from American movies. *Deep Thrust* featured cues from Alfred Hitchcock's *Psycho* and *Diamonds Are Forever*, while Isaac Hayes' iconic "Theme from *Shaft*" can be heard in *Queen Boxer*, *Kung Fu—The Invisible Fist*, *The Rage of Wind*, and others.

In August, *Enter the Dragon* finally opened in high style at Mann's Chinese Theater, and despite its star being dead, it became a huge hit.

On the other hand, that same month, Serafim Karalexis released a movie called *Black Belt* that he called "probably the worst karate film ever made . . . this was real trash." But it grossed.

As summer shaded into fall, Spiro Agnew pleaded "no contest" to charges of tax evasion and stepped down from the vice presidency, President Richard Nixon delivered his infamous "I am not a crook" speech live from Disney World, and distributors kept dumping kung fu chum into the water to slake audiences' seemingly insatiable appetite for destruction. Cannon Films, run by two dudes in their late 20s, Dennis Friedland and Christopher C. Dewey, released *Fists of the Double K* (1973). Ghost-directed by John Woo and produced by Jimmy L. Pascual, son of a Filipino filmmaking family, the movie looked like the kind of thing someone shot over a long weekend where everyone got paid in beer. Nevertheless, it became one of the top 50 grossers of the year thanks to the hard-hitting action choreography of Yuen Wo-ping (*The Matrix*; *Crouching Tiger, Hidden Dragon*) and his brother.

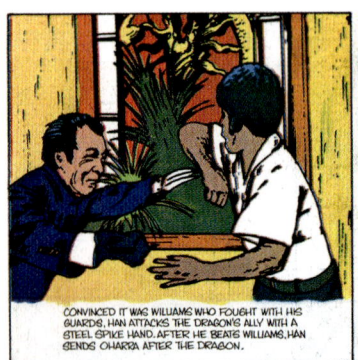

One distributor bundled bottom-of-the-barrel movies together and released them as "The First Annual Chop-Saki Show," and other distributors soon followed suit. *The Shanghai Killers* came out and so did *Slash—The Blade of Death*, which were actually the same movie under two different titles. Ads for sexploitation movies got kung fu taglines (*Fly Me*: "See stewardesses battle kung fu killers!"; *Superchick*: "Meet Tara B. True, mistress of kung fu!"), and teachers running dojos in Harlem complained to the *New York Times*, "They're bringing us in a lot of people, but the people come in with a very bad attitude . . . The newcomers want to be Bruce Lee overnight."

As *Kung Fu* kicked off its second season on ABC with even more guest stars (Tim Matheson! Slim Pickens! Tina Louise!), Cannon dumped its ultra-cheap *Godfathers of Hong Kong* in 44 New York–area theaters, where it easily scooped up $270,000. Quality didn't count. Only kung fu mattered.

If kung fu movies produced a male star to rival Bruce Lee, it was Jimmy Wong Yu, the One-Armed Swordsman himself. He'd kicked off the kung fu revolution at Shaw Brothers with *The Chinese Boxer* but despite its success, Wong Yu only made a few hundred extra dollars for wearing three hats on the production. As long as his eight-year contract was in effect, he was indentured to Shaw. When Raymond Chow left the company to start Golden Harvest, he asked Wong Yu to come with him.

"At Shaw Brothers, every time I needed help, Raymond Chow took care of me," Wong Yu said. "He was like an elder brother to me. [So when] he offered me a contract, I took it. He gave me much more money." This sparked a dispute with Shaw Brothers,

---

(opposite page, top) Ad for the sneak preview of *Enter the Dragon* at Mann's Chinese Theater on August 10, 1973.

(opposite page, bottom) An excerpt from a promotional comic book for *Enter the Dragon* that was part of a package sent to distributors to help them pump up audiences for the upcoming flick.

(above) By the end of the summer of '73, distributors were trying every trick, from ladies' nights to triple and quadruple features, to squeeze more cash out of kung fu films.

the details of which are still murky, but the outcome wasn't: Shaw Brothers tore up Wong Yu's contract if he agreed not to shoot any movies in Hong Kong for three years.

Instead, Wong Yu headed home to Taiwan, where he became director, producer, and star of his own movies, many of which were released by Golden Harvest and many of which were tweaks of Shaw Brothers films. He gleefully violated copyright in *Zatoichi and the One-Armed Swordsman* (1971), a Golden Harvest production shot in Kyoto that pitted Daiei's blind swordsman against Wong Yu's one-armed bladesman. Shot with two endings, in Japan, Zatoichi won; in Hong Kong, the One-Armed Swordsman claimed victory. *The One-Armed Swordsman* begat Wong Yu's *One-Armed Boxer* (1972) which hit American screens at the end of '73 as *The Chinese Professionals*.

Wong Yu's Taiwanese movies weren't exactly good, but they had a purity and outrageousness that can only be compared to early heavy metal: they're either ridiculous or thrilling, depending on how many beers you've had.

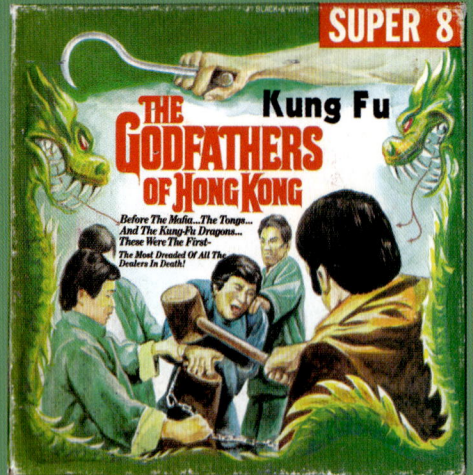

One more way for fans to get their kung fu fix before these movies hit the airwaves was to buy them as super-short 8mm reels. Four of the kung fu movies released by Cannon—*The Godfathers of Hong Kong*, *The Thunder Kick*, *The Hong Kong Connection*, and *Fists of the Double K*—were issued as Super 8 movies running seven and a half minutes each by Ken Films of Fort Lee, New Jersey, and sold in camera shops and Kmarts across the country.

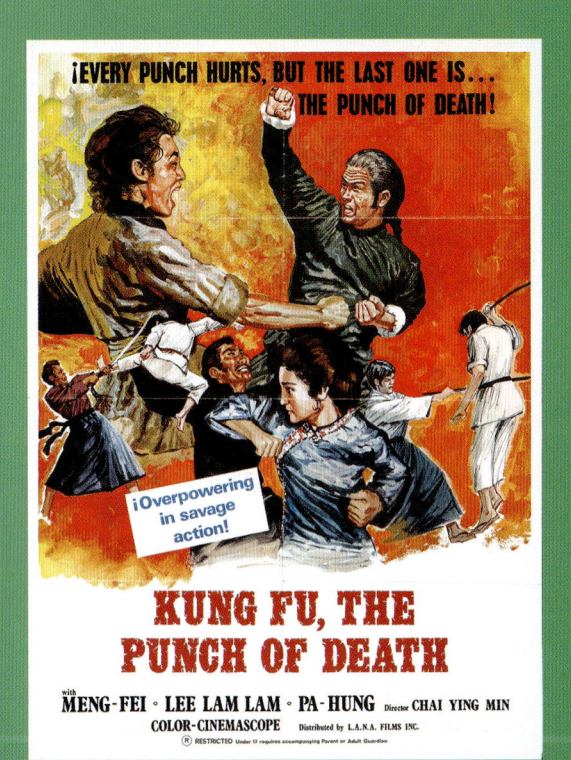

As the movies got cheaper, promo art got cheaper, too. The one exception pictured here is *Kung Fu, the Punch of Death*, released by L.A.N.A. out of Chicago. A partnership between James Gilette and Aquarius, it released Spanish-language versions of kung fu movies to great success. *Punch of Death* hit 18 theaters in the New York area and made $75,000 its opening week. *Black Belt*, on the other hand, was described by its own distributor as "real trash."

Over the summer, Wong Yu's *Chinese Boxer*—retitled *The Hammer of God*—opened at #1. AIP quickly picked up *Wang Yu, King of Boxers* (1973) and retitled it *Screaming Tiger*, proclaiming Wong Yu "The New King of Kung Fu-Karate" much as National General had advertised Bruce Lee.

That same summer, Wong Yu's 1971 movie *The Desperate Chase* was acquired by a music producer turned film distributor named Michael Thevis, who promoted Jimmy Wong Yu as "The Chinese Hercules" (to tie in with a brief fad for reissuing Steve Reeves' Hercules movies) and changed the picture's name to *Blood of the Dragon*. One of the few Hong Kong films directed by a woman (Kao Pao-shu, a Shaw Brothers actress turned producer and director), it's got Wong Yu at his scowling best, skewering the Emperor's soldiers with his silver spear before a bleak, nihilistic ending in which he stands alone in a field of slaughtered bad guys, having saved two adorable street urchins. They run up to hug him, only to find they're hugging the corpse of a man who's so tough he doesn't even lie down to die. The sound of their sobbing merges with the bleak wind howling on the soundtrack.

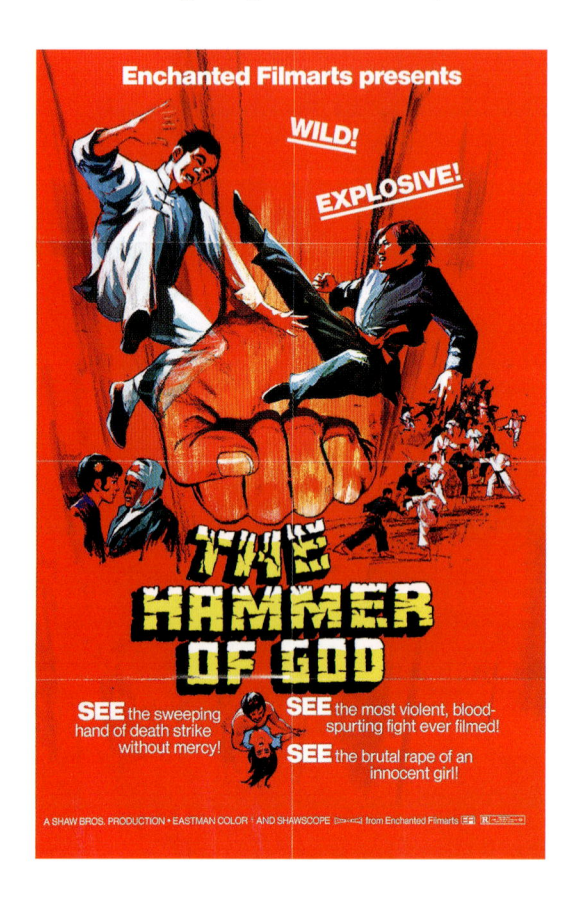

Georgia-based Thevis commissioned an English-language script for *Blood* from William Diehl, a local journalist, and for the soundtrack, he recruited Atlanta favorites Flood, a psychedelic outfit in the vein of Pink Floyd who seemed ready for the big time. He'd even signed them to his record label, GRC Records. The movie came out and did okay, even earning nice notices in *Variety* for Flood's music, which convinced Thevis to send them to Jamaica to record their first album. But as they boarded the plane, the FBI showed up and ushered them off. Turns out Thevis wasn't just a local businessman running a record label but the emperor of a porn empire, and he'd murdered a few people to keep it going. Like his mail-order fruit and cheese club, movies were an attempt to launder his money legitimately, but there wasn't anything else legitimate about him. The same month *Blood of the Dragon* opened, Thevis' former bodyguard died in a car bomb explosion. No one's saying Thevis

---

(above) Wong Yu's *Chinese Boxer* got retitled *The Hammer of God* for the American market.

(opposite page) The key art for *Blood of the Dragon* taken from the front cover of its press kit.

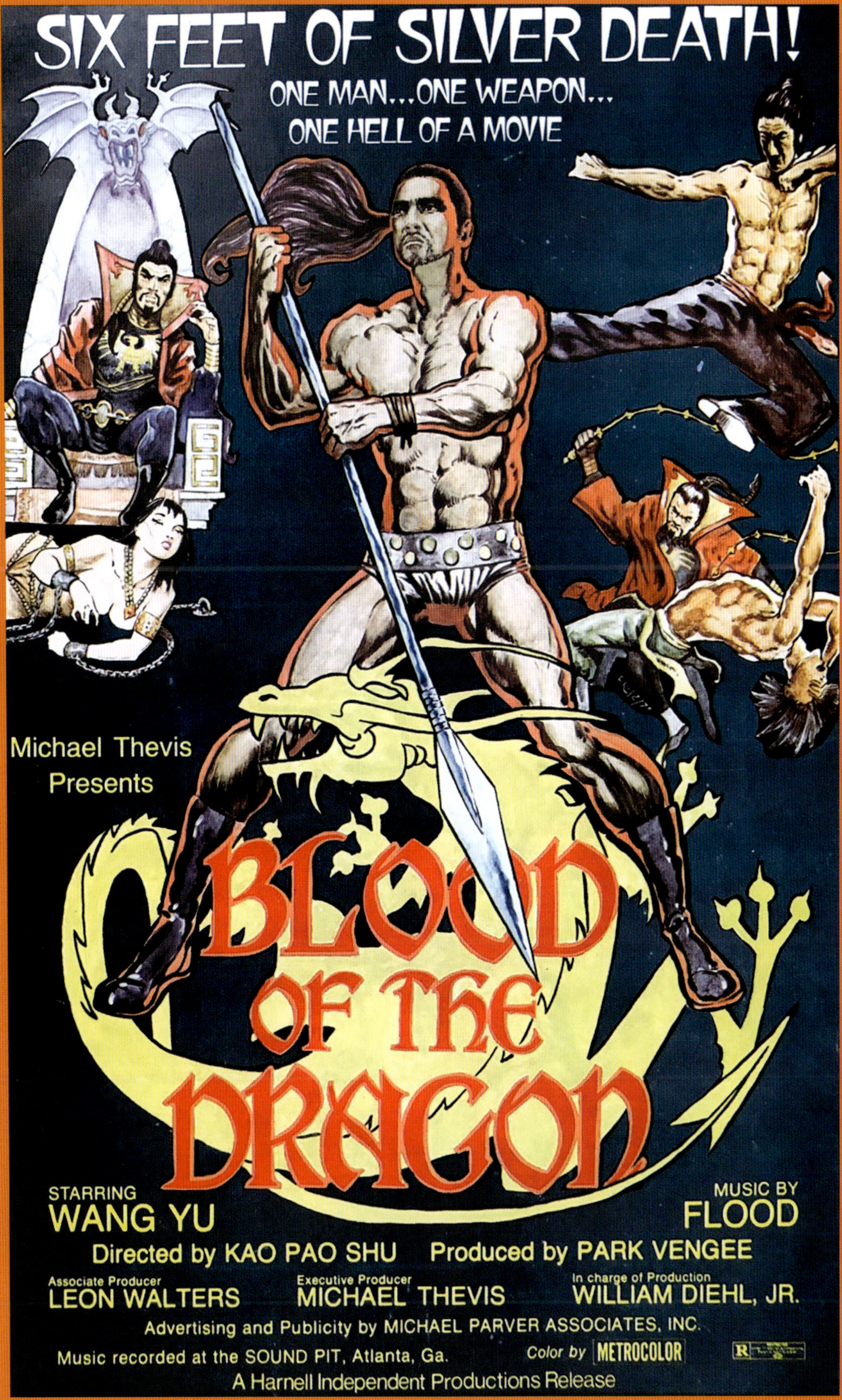
SIX FEET OF SILVER DEATH!
ONE MAN...ONE WEAPON...
ONE HELL OF A MOVIE
Michael Thevis
Presents
BLOOD OF THE DRAGON
STARRING
WANG YU
MUSIC BY
FLOOD
Directed by KAO PAO SHU
Produced by PARK VENGEE
Associate Producer
LEON WALTERS
Executive Producer
MICHAEL THEVIS
In charge of Production
WILLIAM DIEHL, JR.
Advertising and Publicity by MICHAEL PARVER ASSOCIATES, INC.
Music recorded at the SOUND PIT, Atlanta, Ga.
Color by METROCOLOR
R
A Harnell Independent Productions Release

Where each session is a happening
THE SOUND PIT
RECORDING STUDIOS
125 Simpson St. N.W., Atlanta, Ga. 30313 phone: (404) 522-8460
A Michael Thevis Enterprise

An ad for one of Michael Thevis' legit fronts, The Sound Pit recording studios.

hired someone to put a bomb in the guy's truck, but the former bodyguard in question was in the midst of setting up a rival porn empire, and Thevis discussed having some of his remains incorporated into a glass paperweight to keep on his desk, so those might be clues?

Thevis went to prison in 1974, and his empire crumbled, including all his big plans for Flood. Ever resourceful, he used his connections with President Jimmy Carter to engineer his transfer to a low-security Indiana prison, where in April 1978 he just walked right out the front door.

While at large, Thevis shotgun-murdered a former associate who planned to testify against him, landed on the FBI's 10 Most Wanted List, and got re-arrested about seven months later while cashing a $31,000 check. Awaiting trial, he tried to establish a macho prison rep by bragging about all the murders he'd committed on the outside, which got him convicted a dozen times over thanks to his fellow convicts who were eager to shave a few years off their own sentences. Thevis died in prison while serving life.

The indie producers making bank from dubbed kung fu movies were fast-talking hustlers, and sometimes actual criminals, whose ad campaigns were often the best part of the film. But they were definitely more interesting than the studio suits.

As the end of 1973 approached, kung fu movies poured into theaters faster and faster, because distributors had to get everything onscreen to write it off as a tax loss. Producers rushed subpar product into production hoping to grab some of that *Enter the Dragon* dough. ABC greenlit the made-for-TV movie *Men of the Dragon* about righteous white dudes smashing a human trafficking ring in Hong Kong, and in December 1973, they took their two potential leads, Jared Martin and Kurt Russell, neither of whom had any martial arts experience, to Griffith Park, where the first one to run to a tree and back got the part. Russell lost the race, and the movie aired in March 1974, by which time no one cared.

Shaw Brothers' pictures looked posher than the bargain-basement movies earning big bucks in America, which turned out to be a liability. Shaw sold Roger Corman's New World Pictures *The Water Margin* (1972), their prestige adaptation of one of China's literary classics, co-directed by three of their finest auteurs and featuring seven of their biggest stars. Corman knew his audience wanted exploitiation movies, not big-budget epics, so he hacked a half hour from the film, stuck in a sex scene, and sold it in America as *Seven Blows of the Dragon*. Learning its lesson, Shaw stopped selling movies to US distributors, and for the next five years, their American releases were few and far between.

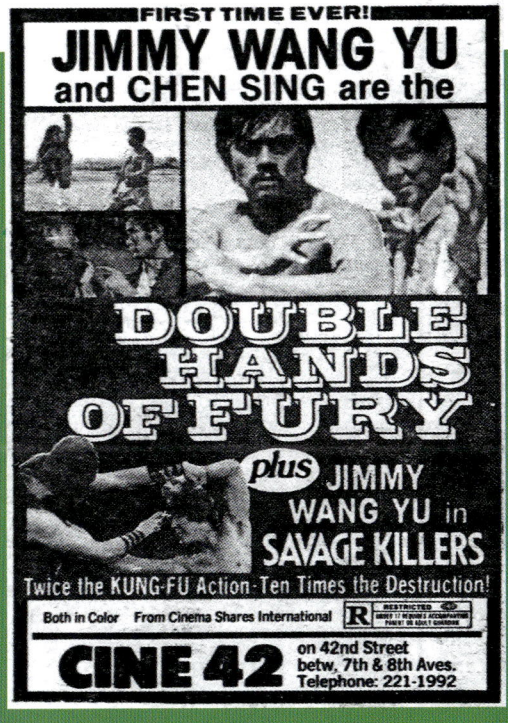

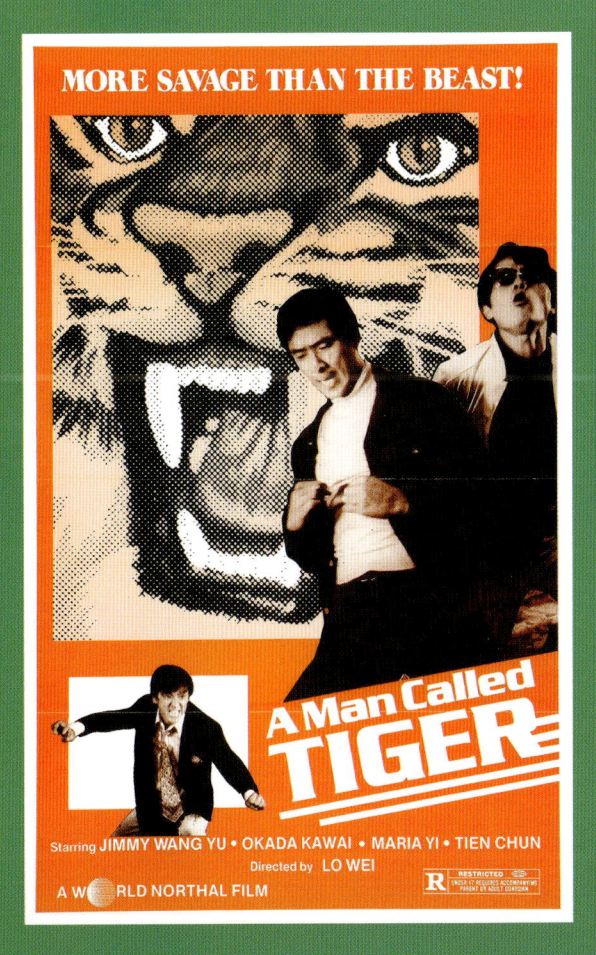

(above, left) Jimmy Wong Yu was often credited on posters as "Jimmy Wang Yu"; however, his business card read "Jimmy Wong Yu" and we won't argue with the man himself.

(above, right) Lo Wei was supposed to make *A Man Called Tiger* with Bruce Lee as *Yellow-Faced Tiger*, but Lee had no intention of working with Lo again once he got famous and so it wound up being a Jimmy Wong Yu vehicle.

(bottom, left) *Revolt of Kung Fu Lee* is really *The Iron Man* (1973) being sold as a "bionic" cash-in on the hit TV shows *The Six Million Dollar Man* and *The Bionic Woman*.

DYNAMITE BROTHERS

AT THE HEIGHT OF THE summer of '73, two music-industry talent managers and a former Chinese soccer player, none of whom knew the first thing about producing movies, decided they wanted to make a movie—a kung fu movie. They went to Samuel Sherman of Independent-International Pictures for help. Sherman's bread and butter was horror, sexploitation, and motorcycle movies for the drive-in market, but he knew that kung fu was popular with Black audiences, so he suggested they update Academy Award winner *The Defiant Ones* by replacing the "white prisoner handcuffed to a Black prisoner" dynamic with an Asian martial artist handcuffed to a Black man. He set it in Los Angeles so his West Coast partner, Al Adamson (*Black Samurai*), could direct in his usual budget-conscious style. Hong Kong actor Alan Tang and former Philadelphia Eagles running back Timothy Brown took the lead roles, with James Hong, Aldo Ray, and Carol Speed in the supporting cast. The music-industry guys enlisted jazz organist Charles Earland to compose a funky score, and the Chinese soccer player (an uncredited producer) pulled strings to get top-notch screen fighters flown in from Hong Kong to handle the action, including Phillip Ko, Phillip Kwok, Tony Liu, Dick Wei, Lung Chan, and Mars, a core member of Jackie Chan's stunt team. The result is one of Adamson's better efforts, even if he tried to pass off the RKO 40 Acres backlot (instantly recognizable as Mayberry in *The Andy Griffith Show*) as Watts in a couple of action scenes.

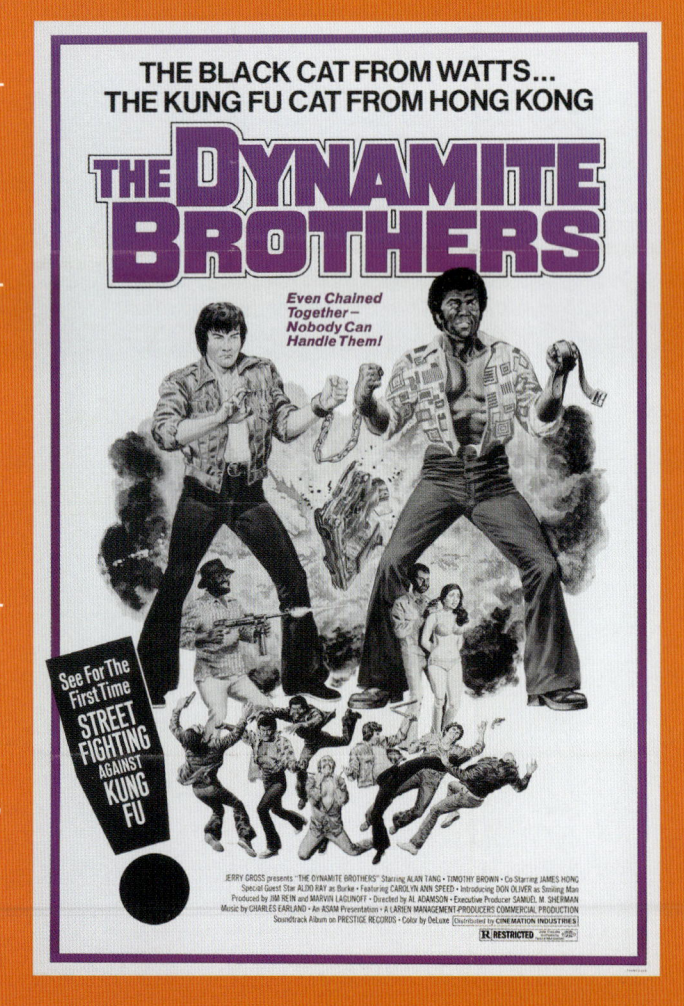

The film was announced in the trades as *Black Belt Brothers*, but Warner Bros. thought that sounded too much like their upcoming release *Black Belt Jones*, so the title was changed to *The Dynamite Brothers*. Jerry Gross, of Cinemation Industries, picked up the domestic distribution rights for $150,000 and released it in April 1974. When it failed to attract the shrinking kung fu crowd, Sherman changed the title to *Stud Brown* and tried to sell it as a Blaxploitation flick ("Stud Brown! He packs the biggest rod in town!"), but by then there was a bigger problem to contend with: Gross had only made one meager payment on the $150K advance and was dodging phone calls from everyone. Out of desperation, Sherman showed up at Gross's office with six Chinese friends of the soccer player and introduced them as Chinatown mobsters who had invested in the movie and were going to kill Gross if they didn't get their $150K. Gross paid up within 24 hours and filed for bankruptcy a few days later, which is when the soccer player confessed to Sherman that the money he had raised for the movie really *had* come from a Chinese crime organization, so it was a good thing they'd leaned on Gross when they did; otherwise all three of them might have been killed. Ever the pragmatist, Sherman grabbed *The Dynamite Brothers* at the Cinemation bankruptcy sale shortly thereafter and foisted it off on drive-in crowds as a sexploitation picture called *Main Street Women*.

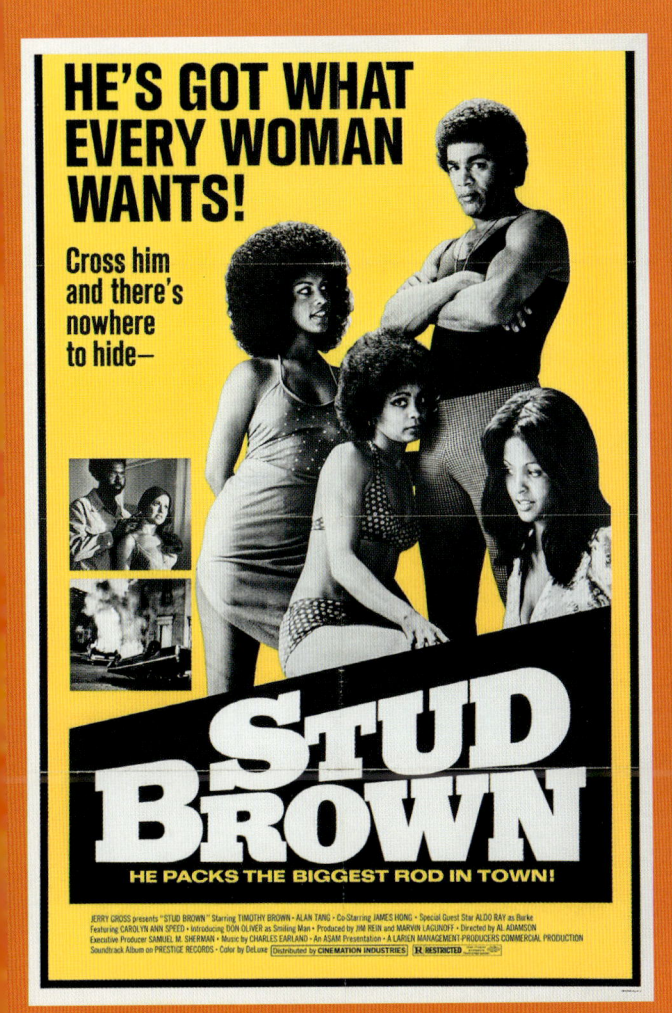

Comic book artist Gray Morrow illustrated many of his friend Sam Sherman's ad campaigns, including *The Dynamite Brothers* (opposite page) and its later incarnation as *Main Street Women* (above, right).

LIBERTY THEATRE
Ph. 536-6094
1179 NUUANU AVENUE

SPECIAL TIME SCHEDULE FOR THIS PICTURE ONLY.
MONDAY THRU FRIDAY 6:05 & 8:30 P.M.
SATURDAY & SUNDAY 1:30 P.M. CONTINUOUS

STARTS TODAY

PREMIERE SHOWING IN HAWAII...
Shaw Brothers' New Million Dollar Super Swordfight Epic!... With 43 TOP STARS!

"THE WATER MARGIN"

★ DAVID CHIANG ★ TI LUNG ★ CHEN KUAN TAI
★ YUEH HUA ★ KU FENG ★ LILY HO

...AND JAPANESE GUEST STARS:
★ TETSURO TAMBA
★ TOSHIO KUROZAWA
PLUS 35 OTHER TOP SUPPORTING STARS

THE ACTION-PACKED CHAPTERS FROM THE MOST FAMOUS OF THE CHINESE HISTORICAL CLASSICS; BROUGHT TO THE SILVER SCREEN BY SHAW BROS.
- A CAST OF 1000's
- MATCHLESS SWORD-FIGHTS!
- COLOSSAL BATTLES!
- STIRRING ADVENTURES!
- KUNG-FU TECHNIQUES!
- ACTION-FILLED SCENES!
- A TREAT YOU CAN'T AFFORD TO MISS!

SHAW SCOPE
IN EASTMAN COLOR—A CHINESE PICTURE WITH ENGLISH SUB-TITLES

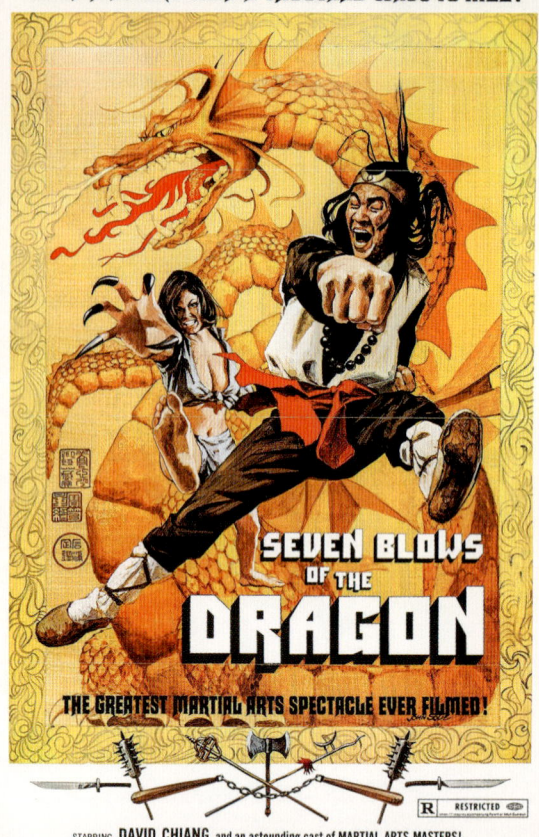

EMPRESS THEATRE
Ph. 538-1035
1190 NUUANU AVENUE
cr. Beretania & Nuuanu

STARTS TODAY!
PREMIERE U.S. SHOWING
MON.-FRI. 6:10 & 8:30 P.M.
SAT. & SUN. 1:50 P.M. CONT.

OUR **GRAND OPENING** FEATURE AT THE **EMPRESS THEATRE**
Shaw Brothers' Colossal Historical Sword fight Hit

"ALL MEN ARE BROTHERS"
...the action-packed sequel to "The Water Margin"...

★ DAVID CHIANG ★ TI LUNG
★ CHEN KUAN TAI ★ WANG CHUNG
★ AND A CAST OF HUNDREDS!
- COMBAT KUNG FU!
- FIERCE SWORD DUELS BY THE 108 HEROES OF "LIANG SHAN"

SHAW SCOPE IN EASTMAN COLOR
A CHINESE PICTURE WITH ENGLISH TITLES

SPECIAL GRAND OPENING CEREMONIES TODAY ONLY... FRI., FEB. 1 1974
- 5:45 P.M. ... LION DANCE BY LUNG KONG PHYSICAL CULTURE CLUB
- 6:00 P.M. ... FIREWORKS
- 6:10 P.M. ... PREVUES OF COMING ATTRACTIONS
- 6:24 P.M. ... "ALL MEN ARE BROTHERS"

SEVEN MASTERS WITH A THOUSAND WAYS TO KILL!

SEVEN BLOWS OF THE DRAGON

THE GREATEST MARTIAL ARTS SPECTACLE EVER FILMED!

STARRING DAVID CHIANG and an astounding cast of MARTIAL ARTS MASTERS!
In METROCOLOR · Produced by The SHAW BROTHERS · A NEW WORLD PICTURES RELEASE

IT SLASHES! IT SMASHES! IT RIPS YOU APART!
IT'S THE BLOODIEST WEAPON OF THE MARTIAL ARTS!

TRIPLE IRONS

Watch it outdo Kung-Fu!

NATIONAL GENERAL PICTURES PRESENTS "TRIPLE IRONS" STARRING DAVID CHIANG
A RUN RUN SHAW PRODUCTION · DIRECTED BY CHANG CHEH · COLOR
A NATIONAL GENERAL PICTURES RELEASE

AS 1973 CAME TO A CLOSE, American Financial Corp sold National General to Warner Bros., who couldn't care less about their Bruce Lee movies—they only bought it for their relationship with Barbra Streisand and Steve McQueen. Right after buying the company, they broke National General down for scrap.

In 1973, 21 kung fu flicks pulled in a collective $11.1 million at the box office, a figure *Variety* noted provided "a life-saving cash flow" for independent distributors and struggling movie theaters. On top of that there was the breakout success of Warner's *Enter the Dragon*. Bruce Lee's greatest dream had been for *Enter the Dragon* to outgross his frenemy Steve McQueen's picture *The Getaway*.

Final score:
The Getaway — $17.5 million
Enter the Dragon — $6.65 million*

But the big picture was, well, bigger.

Today few people celebrate *The Getaway*. It even suffered the indignity of a '90s remake starring Alec Baldwin and Kim Basinger. *Enter the Dragon* is considered one of the greatest action movies ever made, a copy is preserved in the Library of Congress, it's never been out of print on home video, and anyone suggesting it be remade with Alec Baldwin would immediately be murdered by a mob. It's not just a movie, it's a legend.

Bruce Lee was dead, but really? He had only just begun.

* Numbers taken from *Variety* grosses reported at the end of 1974.

(opposite page, top left & right) Shaw's classy *The Water Margin* vs. Corman's retitling as the crassy *Seven Blows of the Dragon*, which sounds like a skin flick for dragon fetishists.

(opposite page, bottom left) *All Men Are Brothers* (1973) was Shaw Brothers' follow-up film to *The Water Margin* and managed to be even bigger and better than its predecessor. But quality didn't count to American distributors, and it wouldn't get seen in the States until it aired on TV in the '80s as *7 Soldiers of Kung Fu*.

(opposite page, bottom right) Shaw attempted to replace Jimmy Wong Yu with David Chiang in *The New One-Armed Swordsman* (1971) and billed it as a reunion of the "Iron Triangle" of Chiang, co-star Ti Lung, and the original film's director, Chang Cheh. National General picked it up, misunderstood completely, and retitled it *Triple Irons*, thinking the promotional language must refer to a weapon.

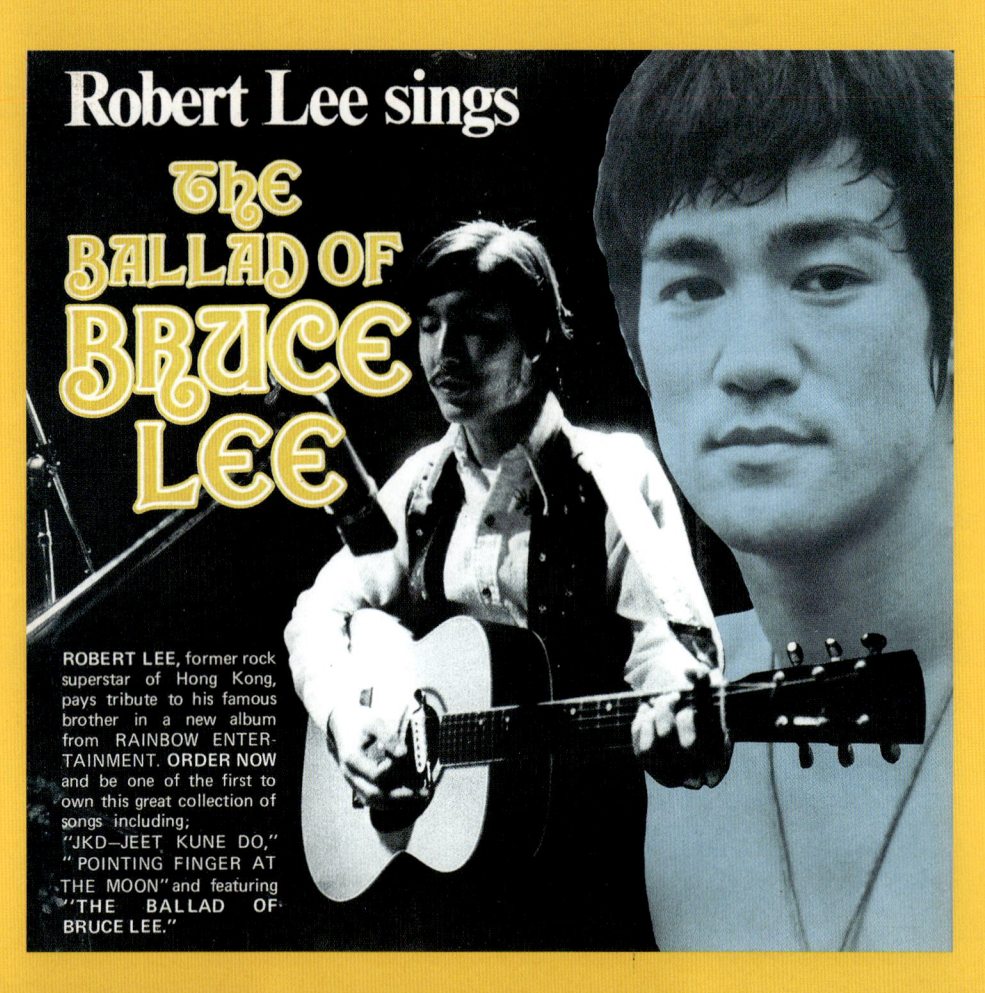

Robert Lee sings THE BALLAD OF BRUCE LEE

ROBERT LEE, former rock superstar of Hong Kong, pays tribute to his famous brother in a new album from RAINBOW ENTERTAINMENT. ORDER NOW and be one of the first to own this great collection of songs including: "JKD—JEET KUNE DO," "POINTING FINGER AT THE MOON" and featuring "THE BALLAD OF BRUCE LEE."

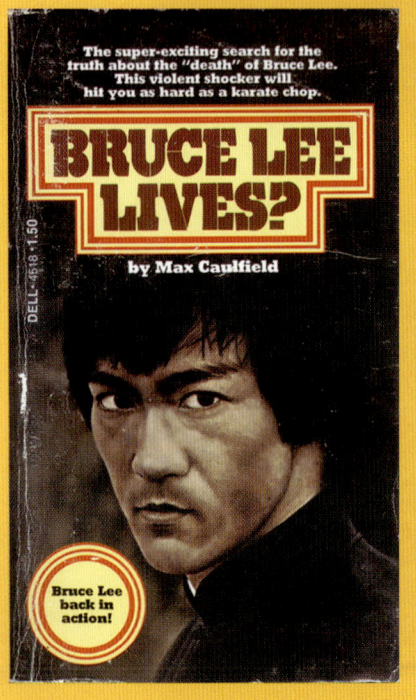

The super-exciting search for the truth about the "death" of Bruce Lee. This violent shocker will hit you as hard as a karate chop.

BRUCE LEE LIVES?
by Max Caulfield

Bruce Lee back in action!

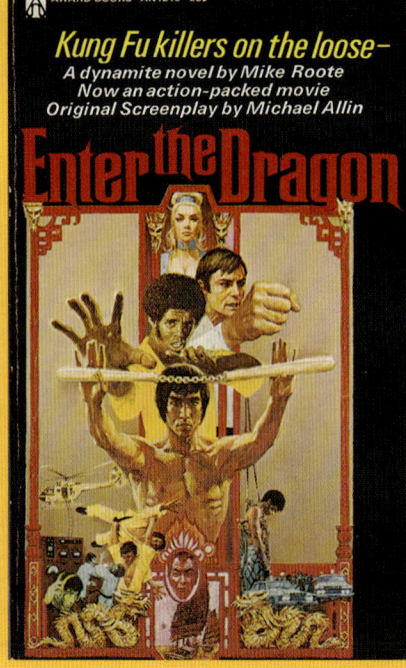

Kung Fu killers on the loose—
A dynamite novel by Mike Roote
Now an action-packed movie
Original Screenplay by Michael Allin

ENTER THE DRAGON

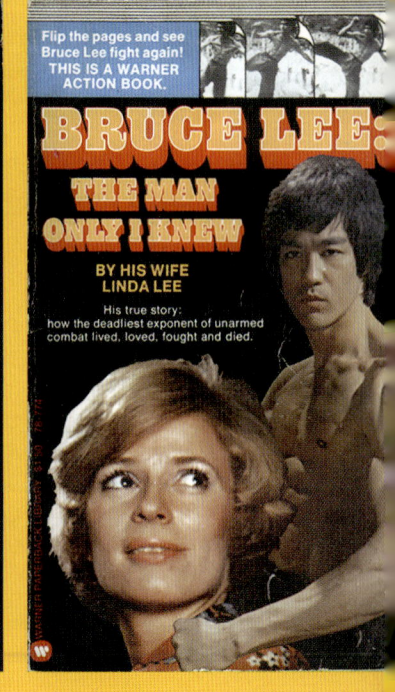

Flip the pages and see Bruce Lee fight again! THIS IS A WARNER ACTION BOOK.

BRUCE LEE: THE MAN ONLY I KNEW
BY HIS WIFE LINDA LEE

His true story: how the deadliest exponent of unarmed combat lived, loved, fought and died.

ENTER THE MERCH

EVERYONE REACTED TO BRUCE LEE'S death differently. In January 1974, the producers of *Kung Fu* changed David Carradine's costume color from brown to saffron to commemorate Lee's passing. That June, Aaron Banks took his Oriental World of Self-Defense convention (see page 203) to the main stage of Madison Square Garden for the first time, attempting to fill its 20,000 seats. He renamed it "Bruce Lee Day" and invited David Carradine and Linda Lee to receive a special award. Carradine showed up; Linda Lee didn't. Movie theaters also goosed their box office by holding "Bruce Lee Days."

Some people remembered Bruce Lee by selling tchotchkes with his face on them, but the merch helped make him as famous as the movies did. The iconic poster of a bare-chested Lee in *Enter the Dragon* is said to have been the second-highest-selling poster of the '70s after the famous poster of Farrah Fawcett in her red swimsuit. Linda Lee's memoir, *Bruce Lee: The Man Only I Knew*, came out from Warner Books, and soon the family struck a deal with Zebra, a low-rent paperback publisher, to release *Bruce Lee's Basic Kung-Fu Training Manual*, *Bruce Lee's My Martial Arts Training Manual*, and *Bruce Lee's Guide to Savage Street Fighting* (all 1976).

Max Caulfield wrote *Bruce Lee Lives?* (1974), a cheap paperback novel from Dell about a writer named Max Caulfield who discovers shocking evidence that Bruce Lee didn't die but instead went underground to wage war on the CAS (Chinese Asian Syndicate), single-handedly destroying their drug empire. Caulfield also added a sexy, young Asian junkie for himself to hook up with in his book that, as the cover blurb proclaims, "will hit you as hard as a karate chop."

A sexed-up novelization of *Enter the Dragon* emerged from the pen of Mike Roote, aka Leonore Fleischer, a mom who started churning out novelizations of everything from *Benji* to *Super Fly* under different pseudonyms after her 1969 divorce. A senior editor at Ballantine Books, she told an interviewer that she hid behind pen names because "I didn't want my bosses to see my name on every paperback rack and wonder what I was doing when I was supposed to be working." Fleischer put the "crank" in "cranking them out," telling *People* magazine in 1977, "When I had a full-time job, I would sit down on Friday night and take amphetamines. On Monday morning, I would topple over sideways with a completed manuscript."

LA's World of Bruce Lee Museum opened its doors in 1978, the passion project of Norman Borine, a middle-aged man whose life changed when he saw his first Bruce Lee movie. Guardian of an Aladdin's cave of oddball Lee memorabilia and Lee-inspired artwork, Borine befriended Lee's mother, hosted seminars with Lee's students, and screened Lee's movies almost every weekend. But he wildly overestimated the public's interest in artifacts like the life cast of Lee's face used to mold his Kato mask, and in November 1981, the World of Bruce Lee Museum turned off its lights and put its exhibits into storage.

In 1976, a tiny Hong Kong company released an animated fantasy feature, *The Story of Chinese Gods*, that *Variety* called "well-intentioned." Despite the film's Shang dynasty setting (1600–1046 BC), somebody someplace thought the three-eyed, nunchuk-wielding, armored warrior who appeared two-thirds of the way into the story looked an awful lot like you-know-who and made sure the dubbing team added very Bruce-like kung fu cries to the soundtrack. The result received a commercial release in the US in 1980, appearing in TV syndication packages as *Bruce Lee in Chinese Gods* and on tape from Video Gems as *Bruce Lee in Animation: Chinese Gods*.

In 1977, the *Los Angeles Times* syndicate approached famed cartoonist Milton Caniff (*Terry and the Pirates*, *Steve Canyon*) about creating a Bruce Lee comic strip for syndication. Irritated by their nitpicking, Caniff dropped out of the project, but by 1982, every single pop culture property had a licensed newspaper strip, from *Spider-Man* to *Dallas*, so with Linda Lee's blessing, the *Los Angeles Times* recruited Sharman DiVono, a taekwondo practitioner and writer of the *Star Trek* newspaper strip, to come up with a daily Bruce Lee strip. Out of the 1,400 newspapers that were approached, only five agreed to carry it, and nine months later, the strip got canceled.

There were Japanese photo magazines, a Bruce Lee coin distributed by Allied Artists for *The Dragon Dies Hard* (see page 97), *The Bruce Lee Times* newspaper printed by Larry Joachim for audiences who attended *Fury of the Dragon* (see page 102), T-shirts, posters, patches, black light posters, lunchboxes, and trading cards. Bruce Lee moved merch. And it wasn't just Lee. It was martial arts itself.

In 1967, Pfizer launched Hai Karate cologne for men, which became such a big seller that they launched Black Belt cologne the following year. Every package of Hai Karate came with a tiny booklet on self-defense because, buyers were warned, its scent would drive women into sexual frenzies, and men had to be prepared to fight them off. It also came in "Oriental Lime."

FREE! BRUCE LEE LUCKY COINS

IT'S A COIN... MAKE IT INTO A NECKLACE!

THE LEGEND OF BRUCE LEE
The first time anywhere! The sensational life and strange death of the King of Kung Fu
ALEX BEN BLOCK
With exclusive photos

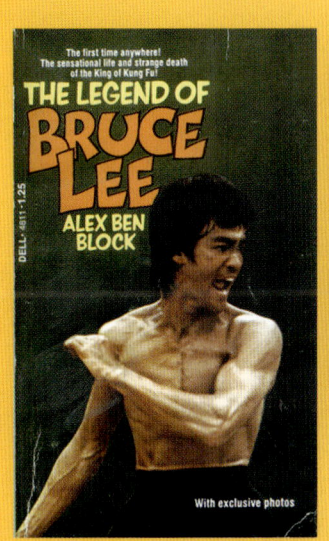

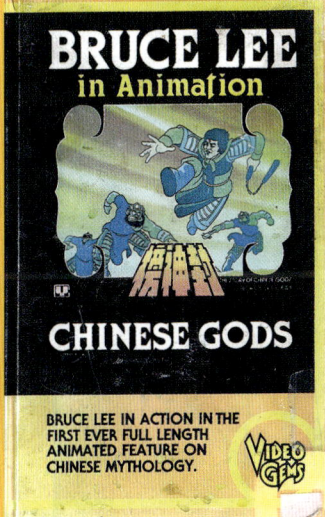

BRUCE LEE in Animation — CHINESE GODS
BRUCE LEE IN ACTION IN THE FIRST EVER FULL LENGTH ANIMATED FEATURE ON CHINESE MYTHOLOGY.
Video Gems

BRUCE LEE'S BASIC KUNG-FU TRAINING MANUAL
OVER 100 action diagrams! AN OFFICIAL BRUCE LEE MARTIAL ARTS MANUAL #1
by Claude St. Denise and Jacques Anton

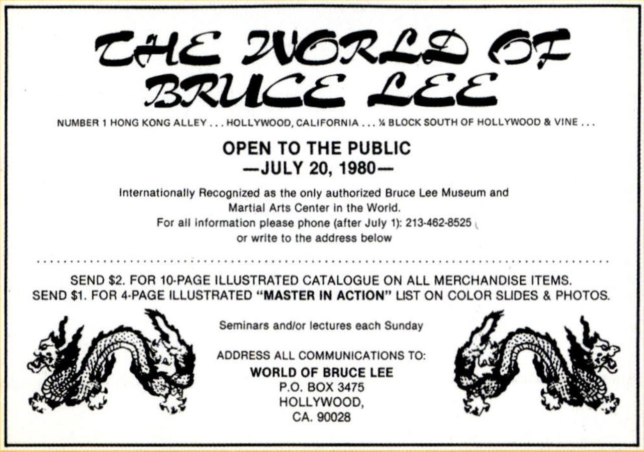

THE WORLD OF BRUCE LEE

NUMBER 1 HONG KONG ALLEY... HOLLYWOOD, CALIFORNIA... ¼ BLOCK SOUTH OF HOLLYWOOD & VINE...

OPEN TO THE PUBLIC — JULY 20, 1980 —

Internationally Recognized as the only authorized Bruce Lee Museum and Martial Arts Center in the World.
For all information please phone (after July 1): 213-462-8525 or write to the address below

SEND $2. FOR 10-PAGE ILLUSTRATED CATALOGUE ON ALL MERCHANDISE ITEMS.
SEND $1. FOR 4-PAGE ILLUSTRATED **"MASTER IN ACTION"** LIST ON COLOR SLIDES & PHOTOS.

Seminars and/or lectures each Sunday

ADDRESS ALL COMMUNICATIONS TO:
WORLD OF BRUCE LEE
P.O. BOX 3475
HOLLYWOOD,
CA. 90028

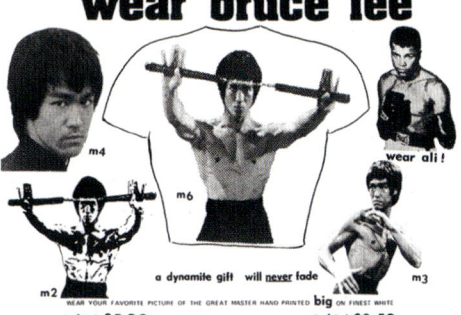

wear bruce lee

wear ali!

a dynamite gift will never fade

WEAR YOUR FAVORITE PICTURE OF THE GREAT MASTER HAND PRINTED **big** ON FINEST WHITE
t shirt $5.00 OR LONG SLEEVED WARM WHITE sweat shirt $8.50
ALL PICTURES AVAILABLE WITH OR WITHOUT THE MOTTO **bruce lee lives!** PLEASE SPECIFY
PLEASE SPECIFY DESIGN AND SIZE. 16, S, M, L
HAVE ANOTHER OF OUR GREAT PICTURES PRINTED ON THE BACK OF YOUR SHIRT $2.00 EXTRA

new! bruce lee tattoos! 5 DIFFERENT TATTOOS ONLY $1.00
to Soho Foto, 344 W 22 St NY, NY 10011

BRUCE LEE Page 2 — By DiVono and Matera

ON THE HOLLYWOOD SET OF BRUCE LEE'S LATEST PICTURE, "CLAW OF DEATH," THE CAMERAS ARE ROLLING...

BUT... HE CAME TOO CLOSE!

STOP THE SCENE, BENNY'S HURT!

THE PAPERBACK CONNECTION

IF YOU'VE READ ANY OF the 50-plus books in Ed McBain's 87th Precinct series, you probably know who Hal Willis is because he was there from the very first book, *Cop Hater*, published in 1956. At 5'8" Willis barely cleared the minimum height requirement for joining the police force. However, he'd found a way to level the playing field: he became a judo expert, possibly crime fiction's first.

But Hal Willis was a supporting character, so if you're looking for the first paperback *hero* who was trained in the martial arts, then private investigator Burns Bannion is your man. An American living in Japan after World War II, Bannion learned karate and started taking cases and kicking butt with the publication of *Kill Me in Tokyo* in 1958. Nine more Burns Bannion mysteries followed, all written by Norman Thomson under the pseudonym Earl Norman.

John Ball's *Judo Boy* is a 1964 young adult novel in which bullied middle schooler Rod Mitchell begins taking judo lessons at the suggestion of his new friend Mark Takahashi, the son of the Japanese gardener who works for Rod's parents. Real-life master Sego Murakami makes a cameo appearance as one of the judges of the big judo competition at the end. Ball was a member of the Judo Black Belt Federation, the All-American Karate Federation, and California Aiki Kai, and he dedicated the book to his 10-year-old son, also a student of judo, karate, and aikido.

Ball's next novel, *In the Heat of the Night*, won the Edgar Allan Poe Award of the Mystery Writers of America for best first novel of 1965. Two years later it was adapted into a film, which won five Academy Awards, including Best Picture, and later became a television series. In the book, Virgil Tibbs is a homicide detective for the Pasadena Police Department who has studied aikido and has a black belt in karate. Ball wrote six more novels and two short stories about Tibbs, none of which were adapted for the big screen or small.

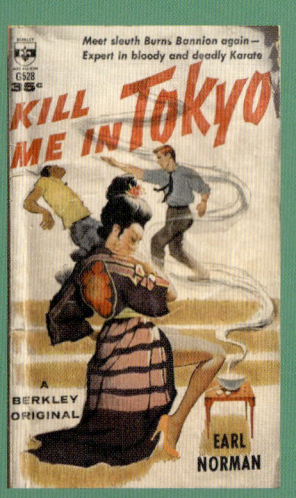

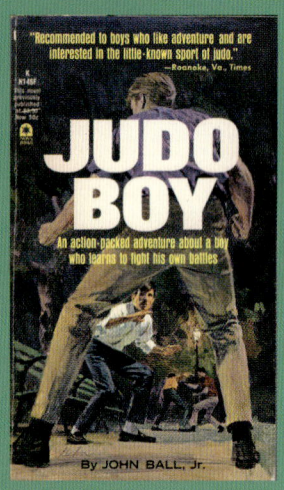

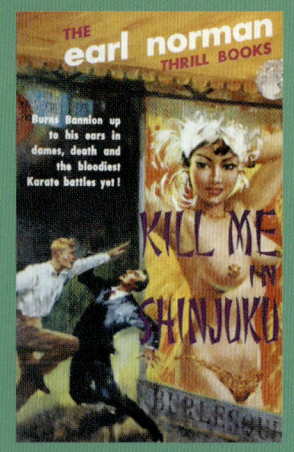

A Friendly Place to Die by Michael P. Faur, Jr. was published in 1966 and is about a martial arts expert named Cord, who spent a decade studying kung fu in a Chinese monastery with the monks who saved his life and is now trying to stop an assassination attempt on Fidel Castro. The book was sold as an espionage novel during the height of the James Bond craze, but no other Cord adventures were ever published.

His name was Remo Williams, and he was a patrolman for the Newark Police Department until he was framed for murder, sentenced to death, and executed in the electric chair. He awoke three days later to learn that he was being recruited as an enforcer for a secret crime-fighting organization called CURE and trained in an obscure style of martial arts called Sinanju by an elderly North Korean named Chiun. This is the premise of the long-running Destroyer series by Richard Sapir and Warren Murphy, introduced by Pinnacle Books in June 1971. Argentine-born artist Hector Garrido painted most of the covers.

In Harry Reed's *A Piece of Something Big*, published in 1972, a small-time crook named Kruger—the second deadliest man in the world, with black belts in karate, judo, kempo, and akido—is hired by a mobster to rough up a boxer who's dating his daughter. When the boxer turns up with his head caved in, Kruger realizes he's been set up—and the real killer is most likely Tomo Yobiyashi, the number one deadliest man in the world, who also blames Kruger for the death of his sister. The back cover promises "Soon to be a chilling motion picture!" but there's no evidence one was ever in the works.

The seven-book K'ing Kung Fu series chronicles the strange adventures of Chong Fei K'ing and his efforts to destroy the evil Red Circle cult and its leader, Kak Nan Tang, who killed K'ing's sensei Lin Fong in the first book, *Son of the Flying Tiger*. Author Marshall Macao was a house name used by at least two authors, Thaddeus Tuleja and Alexander Sidar III, for this series, which was published between September 1973 and spring 1974 by Freeway Press. If the books are remembered at all today, it's because of their cover art: comic book artist Barry Smith painted the first four installments, DC Comics stalwart Dick Giordano came in for numbers five and six, and the seventh—which copies a still from *Enter the Dragon*—was done by Chris Achilleos, who also painted the cover of the Richard Dragon novel *Dragon's Fist*.

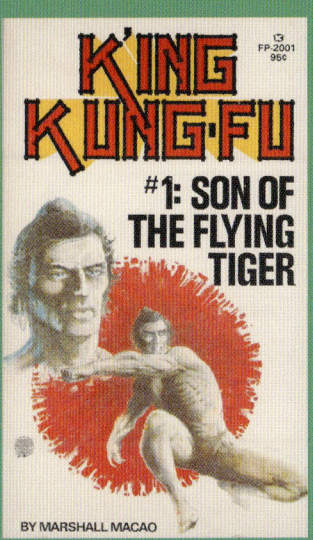

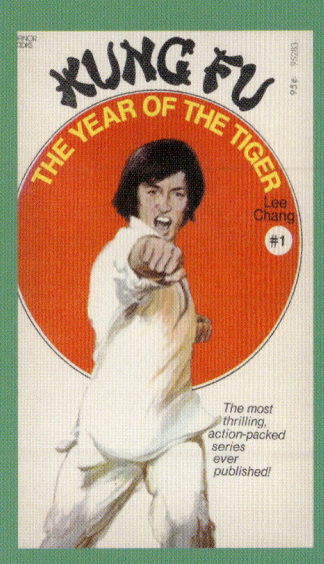

Also starting in September '73 was the Manor Books paperback series *Kung Fu*, which billed itself as "The *first* kung fu series in print!" It wasn't even the first kung fu series to call itself *Kung Fu*; Warner Paperback Library was about to publish the first of four *Kung Fu* tie-in novels based on the ABC television series, so, to avoid legal action, Manor changed the name of its series to *Kung Fu Featuring Mace*, beginning with the second novel, *The Year of the Snake*. "Mace" refers to Victor Mace, an Asian-American karate, kung fu, and ninjutsu expert who sometimes works for the CIA. The series ran for eight books, with the first six credited to Lee Chang, a house name used by Joseph Rosenberger, who also wrote the four-book ninja series Shadow Warrior, published by Dell in 1988.

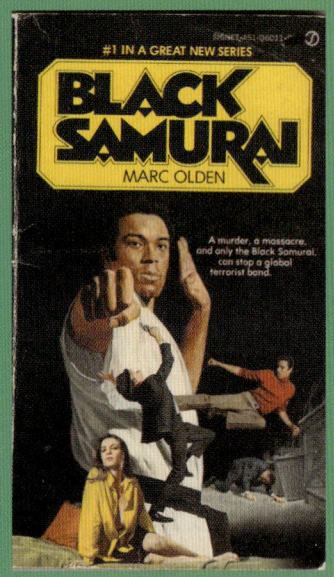

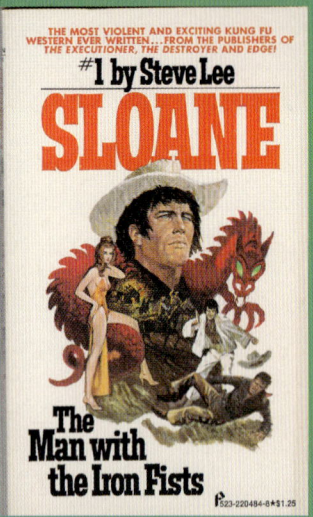

Jason Striker, Master of Martial Arts, made his debut in *Kiai!* in 1974 by Piers Anthony and Roberto Fuentes. After four more entries—*Mistress of Death*, *Bamboo Bloodbath*, *Ninja's Revenge*, and *Amazon Slaughter*—the series was canceled in 1976 by publisher Berkley Medallion before Anthony and Fuentes could complete the sixth novel, *Curse of the Ninja*. The unfinished manuscript was published twenty-five years later by Xlibris.

At the start of *Black Samurai* by Marc Olden, published in 1974, a platoon of military terrorists led by a psychotic US Army colonel descends upon Master Konuma's compound and kills the sensei and all but one of his students. Robert Sands, alias the Black Samurai, escapes and is recruited by The Baron, aka William Baron Clarke, former president of the United States and retired Texas millionaire philanthropist. Olden, who held advanced-degree black belts in karate and aikido, wrote eight Black Samurai adventures that were published by Signet concurrently with the nine Narc novels he penned under the pseudonym Robert Hawkes.

Advertised by Pinnacle Books as "the most violent and exciting kung fu western ever written," *Sloane: The Man with the Iron Fists* opens with a traveling troupe of demented carnival performers—led by a killer clown named Carmello—wiping out the whole Sloane family save for 12-year-old Tod, who is nursed back to health and raised by kung fu master Chang Fung and his wife and daughter. After a half dozen years of training ("Tiger Claw! Eagle form! Drunken Gods!"), Tod leaves the Fungs to track down the clown and his crew and kick some carny butt. *A Fistful of Hate* was the second and final Sloane adventure.

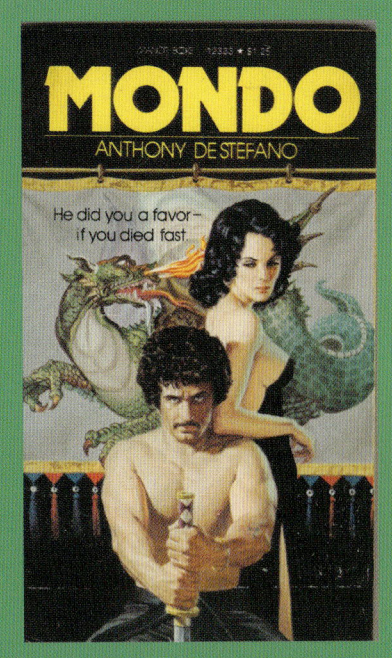

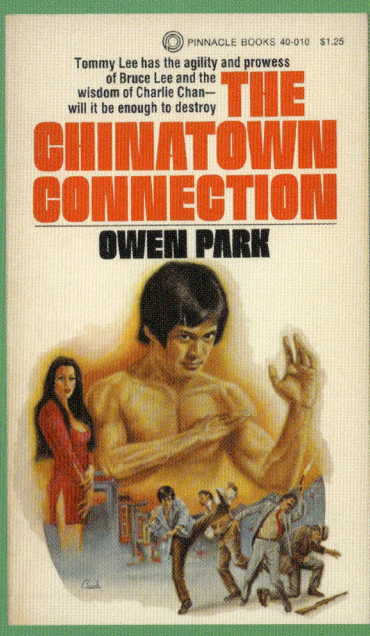

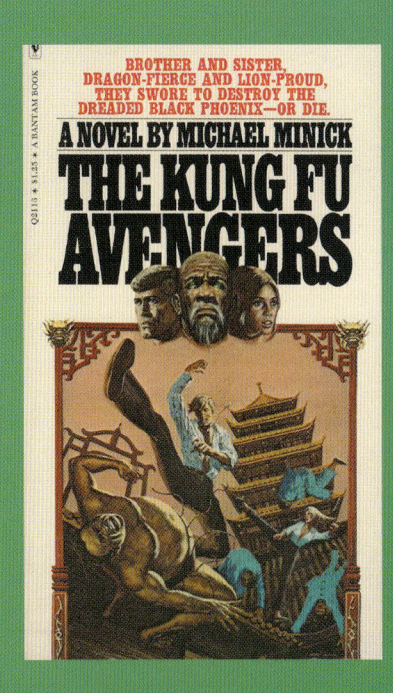

John Mondo, a thief with samurai fighting skills, goes after the mobsters who double-crossed him on his last heist and caused the death of his young son in *Mondo* by Anthony DeStefano, published in 1975. The mobsters respond by importing a Dim Mak "death touch" practitioner named Chan Ho Lee to kill Mondo before he can reach them. Two more Mondo books followed, *Cocaine Kill* and *A Minute to Pray, a Second to Die*, with Bob Larkin painting all three covers.

The Bruce Lee look-alike on the cover of *The Chinatown Connection* is Tommy Lee, the half-Chinese head of East-West Investigations, who takes on a case involving a Chinatown gang trying to move in on the Mafia's heroin operation. He uses as much gun fu as kung fu in this Pinnacle publication from 1977, a couple of years too late to cash in on the craze. *Kung Fu Avengers* (1975) is a young adult novel by Michael Minick, author of the nonfiction books *The Wisdom of Kung Fu* and *The Kung Fu Exercise Book*. The paperback cover art is by Ken Barr, a Scottish comic book artist who painted a few *Deadly Hands of Kung Fu* covers and the *Fearless Fighters* video box.

Vengeance Is His by Wade Barker, published in 1981, introduced readers to crime fighter Brett Wallace, Ninja Master! Stephen Smoke wrote the first book, and the remaining seven were penned by Ric Meyers, trading off with an unidentified third author. There's little or no continuity from one novel to the next. After the initial 1981–1983 run, Meyers continued the Ninja Master adventures in two additional series, Year of the Ninja Master (1985–1986) and War of the Ninja Master (1988), writing all four books in each.

COMIC BOOKS THAT KILL!

THE SIXTH OF PHIL SEULING'S New York Comic Art conventions was held at the Commodore Hotel on East 42nd Street on July 4th, 1973, right in the middle of America's Kung Fu Summer and just 16 days before Bruce Lee's death. There, its 5,000 attendees witnessed the unveiling of the cover of *Special Marvel Edition* #15 featuring "the most fantastic, most fascinating hero of this or any other year"—Shang-Chi, the Master of Kung Fu.

Shang-Chi creators, Steve Englehart and Jim Starlin, loved ABC's *Kung Fu* series and saw an opening in the comics market for something similar. They pitched Marvel editor-in-chief Roy Thomas, who had two caveats: one, the protagonist would have to be half-Chinese, half-Caucasian—like Kwai Chang Caine on *Kung Fu*. Two, the story would have to incorporate Sax Rohmer's infamous supervillain Fu Manchu because during the previous decade, Marvel had made a deal with Rohmer's agents to develop comics based on the novelist's creation, but they'd all stalled. The two agreed and went to work, but despite the promise of "Martial-arts action as you've never seen it before!!" this wasn't the first comic book to incorporate martial arts.

ENTER (AND EXIT) SARGE STEEL AND JUDOMASTER

First came poverty row publisher Charlton Comics, which sometimes paid its artists in free copies rather than cash. Trained in judo and jiu-jitsu, their Sarge Steel was a private detective and Vietnam veteran with a steel left hand to replace the one he'd lost in combat. *Sarge Steel* #1 hit the stands in December 1964, before jumping on the James Bond bandwagon to become *Sarge Steel—Special Agent*, then became *Secret Agent* with #9 before getting canceled one issue later in October 1967.

A three-page Sarge Steel feature in *Special War Series* called "Sport of Judo" introduced readers to Judomaster. Created, written, and drawn by Frank McLaughlin, a judo instructor at the Westport, Connecticut, YMCA, Judomaster was Sergeant Rip Jagger, given judo training and a Rising Sun–inspired superhero suit to wear while fighting the Japanese in the Pacific. Charlton editor Charlie Santangelo was a judoka like McLaughlin and the son of the company's founder, and he quietly canceled their western series *Gunmaster* and slipped *Judomaster* (June 1966) into its place when his dad wasn't looking. Charlton canceled their entire line of superhero titles at the end of 1967.

ENTER (AND EXIT) YANG

After Marvel's 1973 announcement, Charlton tapped South Korean artist Sanho Kim to create a Shang-Chi rival who'd hit newsstands first. He called his book *Wrong Country*, starring Kangho Chull, a Korean avenging his father's murder with taekwondo in the Wild West. Kim sent his penciled pages to Charlton, but they went missing in the mail and executive editor George Wildman enlisted Charlton stalwarts Joe Gill and artist Warren Sattler to come up with a rapid replacement. Their first issue of *Yang* appeared in November 1973, beating Shang-Chi to the stands by three days. Set in the Wild West, its lead character, Chung Hui, would be the only purely Asian martial artist to star in a comic book.

The *Wrong Country* pencils finally arrived at the Charlton offices in the middle of a paper shortage, so the editors postponed its publication. A year and a half later, with paper in abundance again, Charlton launched their second martial arts title, a tired *Yang* spin-off titled *House of Yang*, starring Yang's cousin. Sanho Kim's *Wrong Country* was finally published in 1975 as part of a "Special Kung-Fu Issue" of the unofficial Charlton fanzine *The Charlton Bullseye* (#3). Kim drew the first four issues of *House of Yang*, leaving in February 1976, and his fourth and final issue would be the only comic book featuring Asian characters to be written or drawn by an Asian artist until Larry Hama launched *G.I. Joe* at Marvel in 1982.

ENTER THE MASTER OF KUNG FU

In September, 1974, Shang-Chi's "iron-fisted first issue" opened with the Master of Kung Fu fighting a sumo wrestler who calls him a "half-breed fool" and sneers, "No matter how skillful you are, you will never reach my master—he who is called Fu Manchu!" Shang-Chi responds "You are the fool, Sumo—for I am Shang-Chi, and I am the son of—FU MANCHU!" By the end of the episode, Shang-Chi has turned his back on his dad and spends the next 118 issues fighting him.

One part James Bond, one part Bruce Lee, *Master of Kung Fu* became such a hot seller that the title went monthly and a black-and-white magazine called *The Deadly Hands of Kung Fu* appeared in April 1974. A runaway hit, at least Shang-Chi was actually half-Asian, because the next Marvel martial arts star would be all Caucasian.

ENTER THE IRON FIST

Roy Thomas and Gil Kane premiered Danny Rand, the Living Weapon, aka the Iron Fist in *Marvel Premiere* #15 (May 1974). With his name inspired by an Iron Fist ceremony Thomas had seen in a kung fu movie (probably *Five Fingers of Death* or *Duel of the Iron Fist*), Rand's an Anglo orphan, raised in the mystical city of K'un-Lun after his father gets pushed off a mountain by his business partner and his mother is eaten by wolves. Rand learns kung fu, attains the power of the Iron Fist, and leaves K'un-Lun to avenge his father's death. His solo book lasted for 15 issues, but rather than canceling the title outright, the editors did what movie bookers were already doing, and merged martial arts and blaxploitation, teaming Iron Fist with Luke Cage (aka Power Man), an African-American superhero and ex-con whose catchphrase was "Sweet Christmas!"

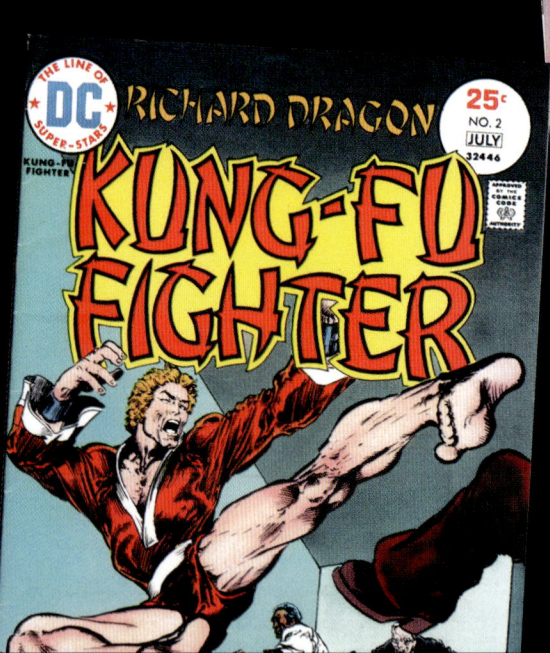

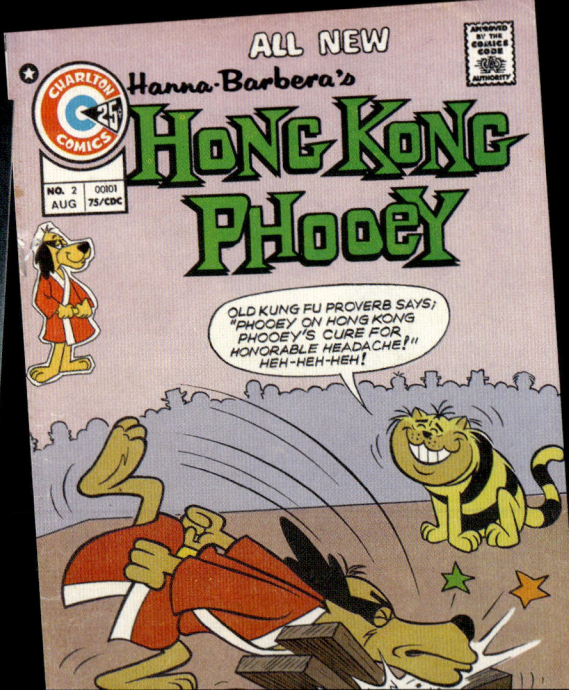

ENTER THE (RICHARD) DRAGON

Before he was the star of an 18-issue run from DC Comics, Richard Dragon was the main character in the paperback *Dragon's Fist*, published in July 1974 by Jim Dennis, a pseudonym of comic book writer Dennis O'Neil, and James R. Berry, who both had an interest in the martial arts going back to the '60s. A few months after *Dragon's Fist* came out, DC started searching for a martial arts comic to add to the company's roster and O'Neil had just the property: his own. *Richard Dragon, Kung-Fu Fighter* debuted in the spring of 1975, pairing the Anglo Richard Dragon with African-American martial artist Ben Turner (aka The Bronze Tiger). The two stuck together for 18 issues before getting canceled in December, 1977 the same month Danny Rand teamed up with Luke Cage.

ENTER THE (HANDS OF) THE DRAGON

When Marvel Comics founder Martin Goodman sold Marvel to the Cadence Corporation back in 1968, there'd been an unwritten agreement that Goodman's son, Charles "Chip" Goodman, would take over as publisher. Instead, Cadence put Stan Lee at the helm. Wanting revenge, the elder Goodman revived his former Atlas Comics imprint and hired Larry Lieber, Stan Lee's younger brother, to run it.

Atlas paid well, attracting top talent like Steve Ditko and Neal Adams, but it only existed from June 1974 to July 1975. They wanted to imitate Marvel's top titles, and so Lieber happily produced *Hands of the Dragon*, his knock-off of *Master of Kung Fu*. Its one and only issue appeared in June 1975. By that time, ABC had canceled *Kung Fu* and Hollywood had relegated martial arts movies to the drive-ins and inner-city action markets. *Yang* and *House of Yang* fell in May and June of 1976, respectively. Marvel ceased publication of their black-and-white spin-off magazine, *The Deadly Hands of Kung Fu*, in February 1977, and seven months later canceled *Iron Fist* as a solo title. Shang-Chi retired to become a fisherman in *Master of Kung Fu* #125, published in June 1983, and Iron Fist's death killed the title he shared with Luke Cage in September 1986.

BRUCEPL

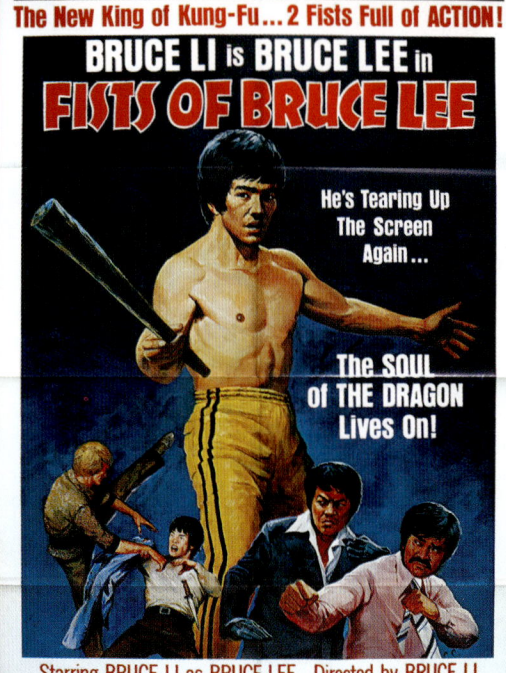

OITATION!

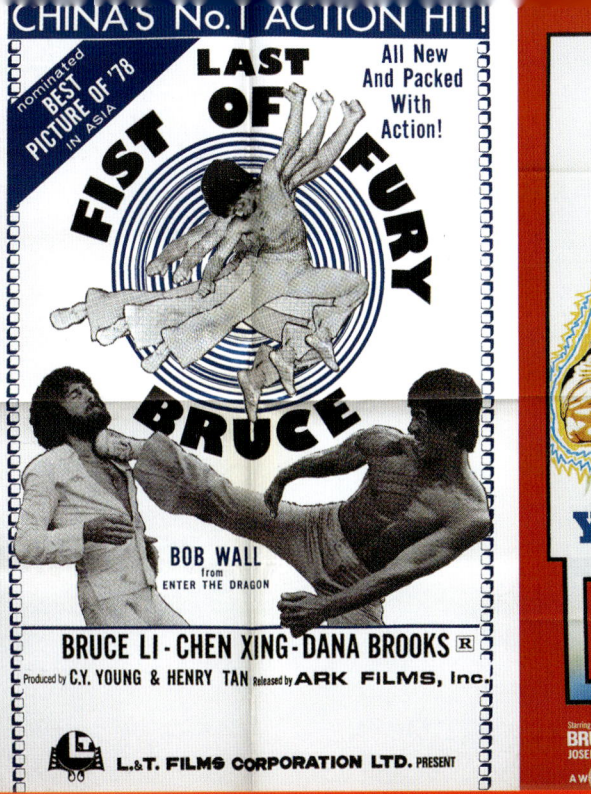

MARLON BRANDO IS DEAD. In the wake of his passing, imitators appear: Marlin Brando, Marlon Brandy, Brandon Brando, Marlon R. Method. Low-budget producers churn out sequels. Martin Brando stars in *Second to the Last Tango in Paris*. Brenda Brando stars in *The Godfather IV: Godmother's Revenge*. There's *Another Streetcar Named Desire*, *Return of a Streetcar Named Desire*, *Return of the Revenge of a New Streetcar Named Desire*.

Existing footage is duped and dubbed into a dizzying array of Brando exploitation flicks. Outtakes from *Superman* appear in *Marlon's Deadly Method*. Screen test footage from *One-Eyed Jacks* crops up in an unauthorized science fiction sequel, *Five-Eyed Jacks*. Frequent co-star Karl Malden appears in dozens of Brando exploitation movies, occasionally sporting a tiny Hitler mustache for reasons no one can quite explain. So many of these movies are made that eventually exploitation distributors can assemble entire movies by cutting and combining their pre-existing knock-offs.

Now, imagine that Marlon Brando is Bruce Lee and you have a snapshot of the Bruceploitation industry.

Never in motion picture history has the death of an actor unleashed so much greed. Whether it was Bruce Lee's home studio, Golden Harvest, or hole-in-the-wall distributors, everyone wanted to wring as much money as they could out of Bruce Lee's corpse. And nickle by dime, they did.

(right) *Revolt of the Dragon* (aka *The Brave Lion*, 1974) is a prisoner of war movie that has absolutely nothing to do with Bruce Lee.

(opposite page, top left) *Bruce Has Risen* (aka *Deadly Strike*, 1978) was also released as *Wanted! Bruce Li, Dead or Alive*.

(opposite page, top right) *Black Hornet* is actually *Bandits, Prostitutes and Silver* (1977) and has nothing to do with the Green Hornet.

(opposite page, bottom left) *Dragon Lee vs. The Five Brothers* is an early Dragon Lee period film, originally titled *The Five Disciples* (1978).

(opposite page, bottom right) Despite what the ad claims, neither Johnny Chang (credited) nor Bruce Li (pictured) appear in *The Bruce Lee Connection*, which is actually *Scorching Sun, Fierce Winds, Wild Fire* (1977).

Back From The Grave!
BRUCE HAS RISEN
AN ARK FILMS RELEASE
R
L.&T. FILMS CORPORATION LTD. PRESENT

Don't Let His Stinger Get You In A Ringer!
BLACK HORNET
Starring LO LIEH WASHINGTON LEE
WANG TAO ANGELA MAO
Directed by KAO PAO SHU Produced by VENGEE PARK
A PARK FILM (H.K.) LTD. picture release by CONDOR FILMS

Dragon Lee vs...
the 5 Brothers
Starring DRAGON LEE • KAN-CHIA FONG
Directed by YUEN-LIN LIU Produced by TOMMY LEE W.G.
R RESTRICTED UNDER 17 REQUIRES ACCOMPANYING PARENT OR ADULT GUARDIAN
Presented and Distrubuted by FURY FILMS DISTRIBUTION, LTD.
DRAGON LEE

They Fight Like the Dragon...
They Kill to Survive!
THE BRUCE LEE CONNECTION
Starring
JOHNNY CHANG
(Star of "Snake Fist vs. The Dragon")
With MAD YING • TAN TAD LIANG • LUO LIEH • CHANG YI
21st CENTURY
Released by 21st Century Distribution Corp.
• In Color
R RESTRICTED

RAYMOND CHOW ASSIGNED A GOLDEN HARVEST CAMERAMAN to shoot Lee's packed funeral, capturing plenty of footage of the celebrity attendees and Lee's body in its coffin. He also, according to some, made a deal with Linda Lee to pay for Lee's funerals in Hong Kong and Seattle if he could film them.

Three months after Bruce Lee's death, and less than three weeks after an inquest returned a verdict of "death by misadventure," Golden Harvest released *Bruce Lee, the Man and the Legend* (1973), a feature documentary that opens with his Hong Kong funeral and closes with his funeral in Seattle.

"Bruce Lee, recognized king of kung fu, is dead," the opening voiceover emphatically declares. "His wife, Linda, has taken him home to Seattle. As she sits in the plane on the long, lonely flight across the Pacific, a week after his tragic and untimely death, she reflects on the last few traumatic days in Hong Kong . . . and the biggest funeral Hong Kong had seen for years!"

Golden Harvest's script brags that "30,000 people" attended Lee's funeral, that his coffin was worth $100,000 to $200,000 Hong Kong dollars, and waxes orgasmic over the guest list, featuring a galaxy of guest stars ("Look! There's James Bond star, George Lazenby, who had just signed a contract to team up with Bruce only days before his death!") The funeral footage is made even more awkward by its constant close-ups of Lee's traumatized children, five-year-old Shannon and nine-year-old Brandon who pointedly turns his back on the camera.

Bruce Lee, the Man and the Legend created the playbook for Bruceploitation movies to come: close-ups of Lee's corpse in its coffin, footage of his co-stars (Nora Miao, Shek Kin), stolen music (from Alfred Hitchcock's *Vertigo* and Pink Floyd), and a line between fact and fiction so blurry you needed an extremely strong prescription to see it. Actual individuals from Lee's past are cast opposite a nameless Bruce Lee impersonator in re-enactments from his childhood. Footage of Lee in *Enter the Dragon* is spliced into the doc to make it seem as if Lee is watching home movies of himself along with the audience.

Existing footage of Lee had been repurposed before. Back in March 1973 Lee's childhood friend, Unicorn Chan, asked his famous buddy to help choreograph the action in his new movie, *Fist of Unicorn*. It wasn't until the premiere that Bruce realized footage of him working behind the scenes had been cut into the film and the distributors were selling it as a new Bruce Lee flick. As bad as that was, *Bruce Lee, the Man and the Legend* felt like a more shocking betrayal. Golden Harvest claimed to be Lee's home. Raymond Chow claimed to be his business partner. But once Lee died, all bets were off.

Linda Lee tried to stop the madness, filing at least two lawsuits against Allied Artists to block their Bruce Lee biopic, *The Dragon Dies Hard* (1974) starring Bruce Lee impersonator Bruce Li (see page 128). She sued them again when they released *Bruce Lee—Superdragon* also starring Li. But with Lee's estate in seemingly infinite probate she ultimately settled out of court. Everyone expected Golden Harvest would be the one to strike it rich off Lee's name, especially since they had his footage in the can for an unreleased movie he'd shot in the summer and fall of 1972, but it turned out that the first people to make a mint on Lee after his death would be an 11-year-old boy and his dad.

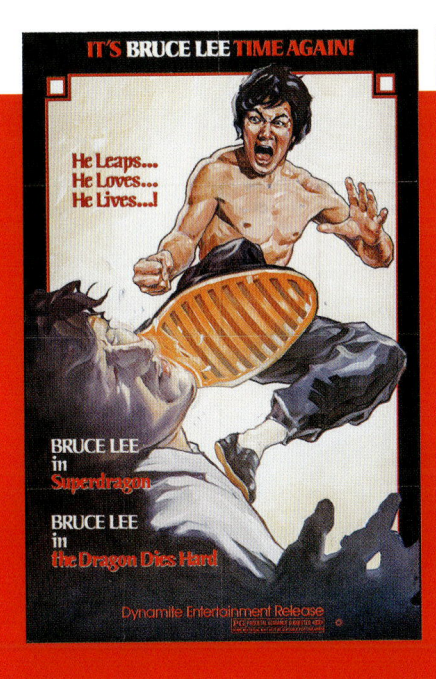

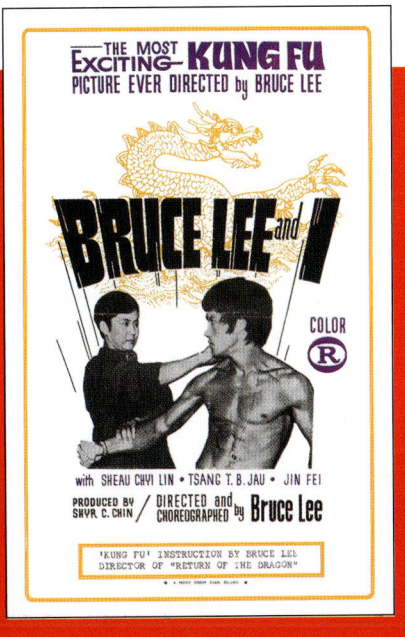

(opposite page) In 1976, after an outcry from angry fans, a Pennsylvania judge ordered that distributor Aquarius Releasing put a disclaimer on its ads for *Goodbye Bruce Lee: His Last Game of Death* (1975) and also post a notice at the box office stating that Bruce Lee did not actually appear in their film. When the movie played Pittsburgh, critic Edward L. Blank wrote that it was "such a ripoff you can just about hear the film tear."

(above, left) Poster for a double bill of *Superdragon* (1974) and *The Dragon Dies Hard* (1974). Confusingly, *The Dragon Dies Hard* would sometimes be called *Super Dragon*.

(above, right) *Bruce Lee & I* (aka *Fist of Unicorn*, 1973) saw one of Lee's childhood friends drop secretly shot footage of Lee into his own movie after asking Lee for help choreographing the action.

BRUCE LEE

the Green Hornet

BRUCE LEE • VAN WILLIAMS •
PRODUCED BY — Richard Bluel — Stanley Sheptner
EXEC PRODUCER — William Dozier   WRITTEN BY Jerry Thomas
DIRECTED BY Norman Foster — MUSIC by AL HIRT.

COPYRIGHT (C) 1974 LAWRENCE-ROBERT ENT. INC.

PG PARENTAL GUIDANCE SUGGESTED
Some material may not be suitable for pre-teenagers

74/269

AFTER WORKING AS A COMEDIAN and gag writer, Larry Joachim drifted into distribution, specializing in weekend kiddie matinees in the New York City area during the 1960s and early '70s. One of his biggest successes was *5 Big Happenings of Horror*, a spook show that promised appearances by Dracula and the Frankenstein monster at each theater. (They were actually ushers dressed in costumes Larry dropped off with the film prints the night before.)

Larry's ear for what the kids wanted was due to the fact that he had the perfect sounding board: Marco, his son with Tony Award–winning actress Barbara Loden.

"When I was two years old, my father and mother got divorced and I moved in with my mother and Elia Kazan," Marco reveals, "but I'd spend the weekends with my dad, who was around the block. He would ask me questions and listen to my suggestions because I was a kid and he figured I knew what would appeal to other kids."

When Marco saw a television ad for *Five Fingers of Death*, he insisted his dad take him to see it. Larry covered Marco's eyes every time the blood flew onscreen, but Marco fell in love with kung fu, which led to an obsession with Bruce Lee. Not long after Lee's death, Marco remembered that Larry had rented the 1966 *Batman* movie from 20th Century Fox a couple of years earlier for a very profitable weekend matinee.

"I told my dad that the producer of *Batman* had done another show, *The Green Hornet*, that Bruce Lee was in, and if he could buy that series we could make it into a movie. He didn't think he could get the rights, but I kept saying 'We can really make a lot of money.'"

Larry was a divorced dad running a business on tight margins.

"I was always worried about my father," Marco admits. "He was always hustling."

Larry had some connections at Fox, so after a few calls, he flew to LA and met with Fox executives, who had no idea what this East Coast crackpot saw in a seven-year-old, one-season TV series, but they were willing to take $5,000 off his hands for the US theatrical rights. As Larry was leaving, he turned back to the execs and asked nonchalantly, "Just out of curiosity . . . how much would it cost for the world rights?"

And that's how Larry Joachim bought the world for $15,000.

Back in Manhattan, episodes of *The Green Hornet* began arriving from Fox on 16mm reels. Larry turned the project over to Marco, who watched all of the episodes

---

(opposite page) The original poster for *The Green Hornet*, painted by a *New York Times* fashion illustrator. After the posters were printed and ready to ship, Marco worried they didn't work, so his Dad trashed them and commissioned new ones.

(above) Marco and Larry circa 1978, around the time they started their distribution company, Trans-Continental Film Corp.

while taking notes and selected three he thought would work best. He took their reels back to Kazan's brownstone and started cutting (on the same equipment that had been used to edit his mom's acclaimed film *Wanda*).

After watching the rough assembly, Marco decided there weren't enough fight scenes. Larry thought it wouldn't make sense if they included more but did it anyway, cutting in material from seven additional episodes.

"When we were finished, it was this whole jumble. My dad sent it back to Fox, and they edited it, made a master negative and fixed it up a bit, because obviously we weren't editors," Marco said. "Music was jumping in and out and all sorts of stuff was going on."

Then Larry and Marco turned their attention to the advertising campaign. The posters were already printed and ready to ship, but Marco had doubts that the artwork would appeal to the kung fu crowd. He had seen comic artist Jim Janes' rendering of Bruce Lee on the cover of *The Monster Times* and convinced Larry to hire Janes and the newspaper's publishers, Larry Brill and Les Waldstein, to design a new campaign. Father and son worked together with scissors and glue to create full-page ads for *Boxoffice* and *Variety*.

When the film came back from Fox in cleaned-up 35mm, Larry screened it for friends and family . . . and they hated it.

"Nobody liked it," Larry recalled in 2012. "I had a guy working for me, Ray Wells, he said, 'This isn't even good enough to sell as a kiddie matinee!'"

"They all put it down," Marco remembers, but his faith never wavered. He told his dad, "Don't worry, it's great. I love it."

When *Tales of the Green Hornet* premiered in Chicago, Bruce Lee photos were given out free to the first 2,000 patrons, which helped attract crowds.

Larry understood how *Variety* compiled their 50 Top-Grossing Films chart each week: it was a sample of roughly 700 theaters in 20 to 24 cities and represented only 7% of the overall number of cinemas.

Therefore, one strategically placed 35mm print could land a film midway up the chart, proving its profitability to exhibitors who might otherwise be wary of booking an old TV series as a first-run feature. Larry zeroed in on Chicago and Philadelphia as his first targets.

Tales of the Green Hornet premiered at the Oriental Theatre in the Chicago Loop on October 18, 1974. The film grossed $45,000 in five days, landing it at the #28 position in *Variety*. The following Wednesday, under a shortened title, *The Green Hornet* opened at the Fox Theater in Philadelphia. By the end of the third week the film was still on the chart, boasting a total gross of over $120,000 from just two theaters.

With the money he'd made so far, plus a chunk he borrowed from his mother, Larry ordered 100 more prints. On November 27—the day before Thanksgiving—*The Green Hornet* opened in the New York tri-state area on 40 screens, as well as in Cincinnati, Sacramento, Salinas, and San Francisco. It was the biggest gamble of Larry's career.

That night, he and Marco went to watch the movie with a Times Square audience.

"As we approached 42nd Street, we noticed a line that went around the block," Marco remembers. "I said to my dad, 'That can't be the line for this film!'

"We got closer and sure enough, the line started at the [New Amsterdam Theater] box office and went around the corner, and it was for *The Green Hornet*. We went inside and it was standing room only. People were cheering. It was incredible. It was like we had hit the lottery."

Larry's phone started ringing off the hook. He'd sometimes have two calls going at once, with a receiver in each ear—"You want Bruce Lee?" he'd ask one theater owner. "Yeah, we got *The Green Hornet*!" he'd answer the other. The movie made a mint all over the world, and Fox, still baffled, agreed

Larry acquired the rights to Bruce Lee's screen test and added it to the front of his films to boost their box office.

to a sequel. Larry thought they'd already mined all the best material, but Marco assured him there was enough for a second film. *Fury of the Dragon* (1976), an even crazier concoction, premiered in New York on November 24, 1976, and was also a hit, and the two Hornet films were default programmers for almost a decade, playing as part of double bills all the way to 1982.

Marco and Larry's *Green Hornet* movies deserve recognition as two of the earliest, and most widely distributed and financially successful, fan edits in history. They also paved the way for the Bruceploitation genre to go big. Seeing the *Green Hornet* grosses, distributors found the courage they needed to stop dipping their toes in the Bruceploitation pool. Now they stripped off their polyester suits and dove right in.

A line for *The Green Hornet* outside the New Amsterdam Theatre on 42nd Street, November 1974.

BRUCE LEE

FURY OF THE DRAGON

Starring BRUCE LEE - VAN WILLIAMS ☐ Produced By L.L. & J.M.J. ENTERPRISES
Executive Producer LAURENCE JOACHIM ☐ Directed By WILLIAM BEAUDINE ☐ Music By AL HIRT

FEW MOVIES MAKE AS LITTLE SENSE as a Bruceploitation movie. Cobbled together from footage of the real Bruce Lee that's been duped so many times it's little more than a pink blur, or starring actors who vaguely resemble Bruce Lee, or starring characters trying to solve the mystery of Bruce Lee's death, these movies are like snowflakes: no two are alike in their awfulness. Ungainly celluloid Frankenstein's monsters, reanimated by lightning bolts of pure greed, they follow a simple philosophy: who needs plots, characterization, budgets, or logic when you have Bruce Lee on your poster?

Dialogue becomes aggressively vague.

"Where do you want to go?" one character asks.

"Here. This place."

"All right."

Lives change at random, cause and effect are uncoupled. In *Bruce Lee Fights Back from the Grave* (1976) cops arrest Bruce K. L. Lea and shout at him for killing a man in a fight. Bruce tells them it was self-defense. They tell him he's about to get a big surprise and be sent to prison for the rest of his life.

"Nothing would surprise me," Bruce says. "I've learned to be philosophical about this kind of thing."

The police captain's phone rings. The captain listens to the caller, then tells Bruce that for reasons unknown he's being released.

"I'm not surprised," Bruce drawls.

According to Bruceploitation movies, life happens at random. You walk down the road in the middle of nowhere and men you've never met jump out of the bushes and attack you. You stop to change a flat tire and thugs move in, swinging chains. Ambulances race through cities, sirens wailing, taking patients we may never encounter again to hospitals we may never see. The only thing you can count on is that at some point the main character will strip to the waist, flex his ripped muscles, and utter a high-pitched, KIIIIIIIyaaaaaaaah! just like Bruce Lee. Or maybe the producers will dub in Bruce Lee's scream from one of his own movies.

Actors appear in sequels playing their own brothers from earlier movies in which they played characters previously played by Bruce Lee. Sometimes recycled footage of

---

(top left) *Final Fist of Fury* (aka *Snake Shadow, Lama Fist*, 1979) starts with *The Final Days of Bruce Lee*, a short film cobbled together from Bruce Lee funeral footage and attached to ghoulishly goose the box office gross.

(top right) *Fist Like Lee* (aka *Along Comes a Tiger*, 1977) was a star vehicle for Don Wong Tao that had absolutely nothing to do with Bruce Lee.

(bottom left) *Bruce Ali* (aka *Crippled Kung Fu Boxer*, 1981) doesn't feature any known Bruce Lee impersonator and looks more like a Jackie Chansploitation film (see page 265).

(bottom right) *Fist Like Lee Part II* is actually *Kung Fu of Seven Steps* (1979), a star vehicle for Ricky Cheng that had absolutely nothing to do with Don Wong Tao.

2 BIG HITS
FIGHTING KIN FROM
THE FIRST FAMILY OF FURY
Savage Force!
Black Belt Killers!
FINAL FIST OF FURY
Also
The Dragon's Last Fall!
"THE FINAL DAYS OF
BRUCE LEE"
STARRING BRUCE CHI KONG TAO DAVID YUEN
L & T FILMS CORP. LTD presents AN ARK FILM, INC. RELEASED

SMASH OUT!
FIST
TO FIST
HE FOUGHT
LIKE THE
KING
UNDER
THE
DRAGON'S
SHADOW
HE
LEARNED
KUNG FU
FIST LIKE LEE
THE QUICK-KILL PUNCHER
starring:
WONG TAO-BRUCE K. LING
CATHY F. LEE-BRYNN HSAN
directed by: T.N. HSO produced by: C.H. YANG
an ARK FILMS release

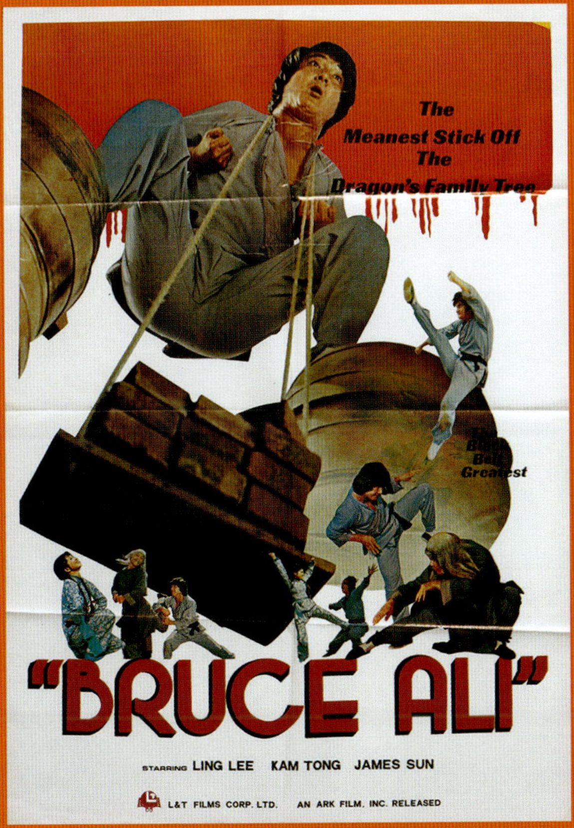
The
Meanest Stick Off
The
Dragon's Family Tree
"BRUCE ALI"
STARRING LING LEE KAM TONG JAMES SUN
L&T FILMS CORP. LTD. AN ARK FILM, INC. RELEASE

Fist
Like Lee
PART II
UNBEATABLE...
UNDEFEATED...
HE'S STILL
THE BEST!
STARRING DRAGON CHAN-TZU
WITH HA CHIA-KAI • CHAN LANG
Released by 21st Century Distribution Corp. • In Color

an early BRUCE LEE film found
in the Chinese film archives and never seen before
We Positively Guarantee the Real Bruce Lee
Serafim Karalexis presents
The Real Bruce Lee
IN COLOR
BRUCE LEE 14
BRUCE LEE 28
BRUCE LI
DRAGON LEE
starring
BRUCE LEE co-starring BRUCE LI
and introducing the new sensation
DRAGON LEE
Written by Serafim Karalexis & Lerry Dolchin Directed Edited by Jim Markovic
Produced by Serafim Karalexis
R RESTRICTED
A MADISON WORLD FILM A CINEMATIC RELEASE

Bruce Lee appears in these same sequels to inform viewers, via dubbed dialogue, that he's the brother of the actor previously playing Bruce Lee. It's a sprawling hall of funhouse mirrors, every single one of them reflecting Bruce.

Larry and Marco Joachim proved that the best way to make a Bruceploitation movie was to have footage of the real Bruce Lee. Serafim Karalexis had been co-producing movies with the Hong Kong producer Yeo Ban-yee of Yangtze Productions, with Yeo keeping the Asian rights and Karalexis distributing them in the US. It was a perfect partnership, the only bone of contention being that Yeo always wanted the Chinese hero to win in his market, and Karalexis needed the American hero to win in his. But during production of their movie, *Kung Fu Fever* (1979), Yeo died and Karalexis abandoned martial arts movies and got into music with *The Punk Rock Movie*. When that wasn't successful, he decided to give martial arts movies another try. Looking over the flooded kung fu marketplace, he knew he needed a great gimmick.

"I wanted to find some Bruce Lee footage," he said, so he turned to Dick Randall.

A one-time writer for Milton Berle and former theatrical impresario, Randall was reputedly barred from the United States after allegedly paying off a European film crew with counterfeit US dollars. Now living in Rome, he scoured continental film processing labs for Karalexis and found three of the movies Lee had made as a child in Hong Kong: *The Kid* (1950), *Thunderstorm* (1957), and *The Orphan* (1960).

Not sure what he could do with footage of Bruce Lee not doing kung fu, Karalexis took the Randall material and edited it into a half-hour documentary about Lee's life, then added a demo by Lee imitator Bruce Li (see page 128) and attached a film starring Korean Bruce Lee imitator Dragon Lee (see page 132). The ads promised, "We Positively Guarantee the Real Bruce Lee . . . An early BRUCE LEE film found in the Chinese film archives and never seen before!" *The Real Bruce Lee* (1979) made over half a million bucks in a single week, grossing more than $50,000 from one Philadelphia theater alone.

(opposite page) The theme song of *The Real Bruce Lee* is "Devil's Gun" by C. J. & Co., a #1 Disco/#2 R&B hit in 1977 and the first record played at the Studio 54 opening that same year.

(above) Independent distributors aggressively boasted about their box office grosses in ads they bought in trade magazines like *Variety* and *Boxoffice*. What better way to pimp their prints and lure bookings?

NEXT, EXPLOITATION GENIUS TERRY LEVENE decided that he needed his own Bruce Lee movie, too. Taking some of the same footage from some of the same movies, he gave it to his longtime director/editor/partner in crime, Matthew Mallinson, along with a Taiwanese wu xia film Aquarius had first released in 1974 called *Forced to Fight*. Mallinson shot footage of Aaron Banks' 1979 Oriental World of Self-Defense at Madison Square Garden, shot footage of martial arts star Ron Van Clief (see page 210) and blaxploitation legend Fred Williamson as themselves, and hired Levene's favorite voiceover artist, Academy Award nominee Adolph Caesar, to tie it all together.

When they showed up to shoot at Madison Square Garden, Mallinson's crew hit a roadblock because MSG was a union shop and Levene refused to pay union wages. In an inspired move, Levene disguised Mallinson's crew as a television news team, who were allowed to shoot at the Garden without being union.

Levene created as many problems as he solved, however, taking Caesar out for a liquid lunch where he got the actor so looped he couldn't remember his lines. Throughout the movie, Caesar appears to be giving commentary while looking down at a TV monitor showing the action in the ring, when in reality the sozzled actor was reading directly from his script.

The show's promoter, Aaron Banks (see page 203), encouraged a carnival atmosphere. Karate champion Bill Louie pretends to rip out an opponent's eyeballs and throws them into the cheering crowd. Another martial artist lays his arm on top of a stack of boards then has it pounded through them with a sledgehammer.

Supposedly the event is being held to determine who will become Bruce Lee's successor, although, as Fred Williamson asks, "Whoever heard of fighting for Bruce Lee's title that doesn't even exist?" After opening with Banks' dark warning about Bruce Lee

Adolph Caesar (left, standing with Fred Williamson) narrated the movie, as well as multiple other Aquarius trailers, but most audiences knew his voice from his television PSA for the United Negro College Fund in which he intoned the famous tagline, "Because a mind is a terrible thing to waste."

being murdered and shots of the Oriental World of Self-Defense, Mallinson edited in Bruce Lee's childhood films as a framing story showing young Bruce Lee's dreams, made up of footage from *Forced to Fight*.

"I could become more famous than my ancestors," a teenaged Lee sighs in dubbed English before Caesar intones that "Bruce's great-grandfather was one of China's great samurai master swordsmen of the 19th century" and even though there's not a single accurate word in that entire sentence, it provides a link to half an hour of footage from *Forced to Fight*. Ron Van Clief rescues a young woman from muggers, Bill Louie fights muggers while dressed as Kato, there's a fake interview between Bruce Lee and Aaron Banks in which Aaron asks questions of dubbed Bruce Lee close-ups taken from an episode of the TV series *Longstreet*. It all crashes back together at the end for eight minutes of a welterweight fight nobody cares about between Louis Neglia and John "Cyclone" Flood.

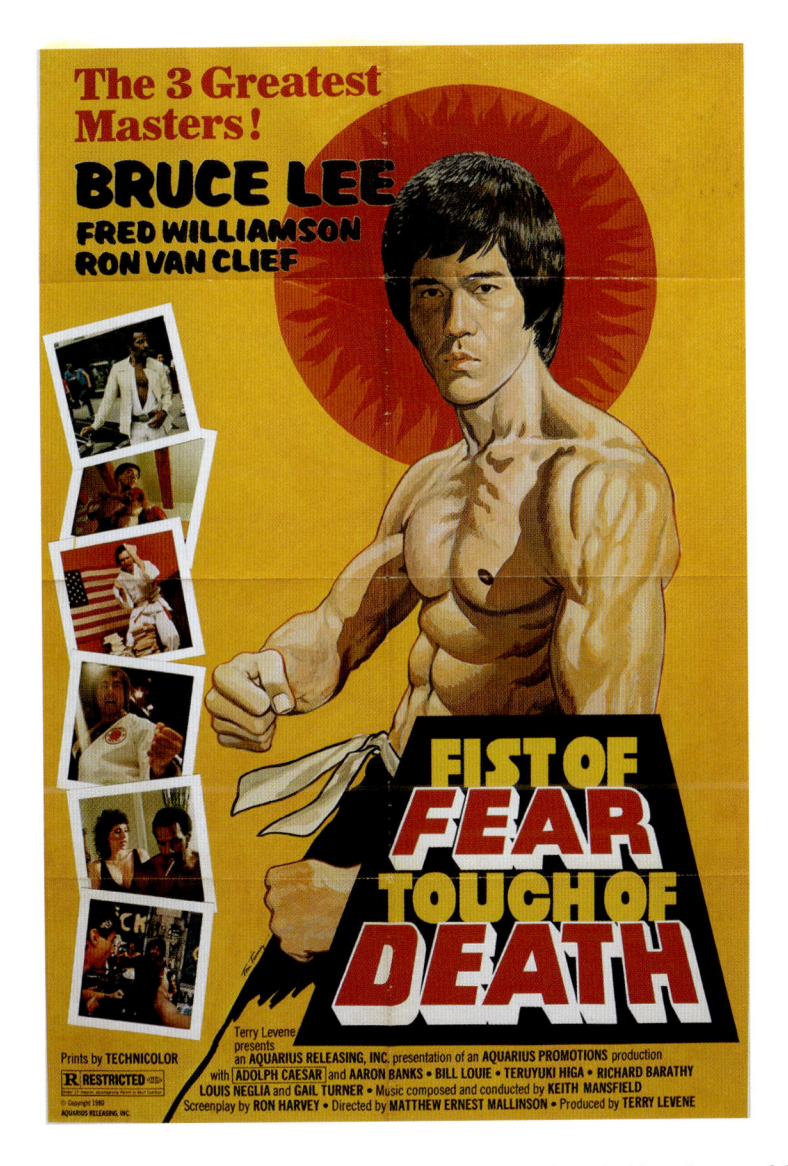

As Caesar sums up at the end:

"What have we discovered from all this? A new champion? Perhaps. A successor to Bruce Lee? I doubt it. You see, what most heir apparents to Bruce Lee seem to forget is that to be the best you must beat the best and Bruce Lee was the best and he can no longer be beaten so all else is just . . . speculation."

With a budget of about $122,000, Levene struck 33 prints, paid Van Clief to appear at the Selwyn Theatre for eight karate demonstrations on opening weekend, and cleaned up at the box office.

IF YOU DIDN'T HAVE FOOTAGE of Bruce Lee you could still stick to the Bruce Lee story by making a biopic like *Bruce Lee Superstar* (1976) or *Bruce Lee, We Miss You!* (1976).

The idea of a Bruce Lee biopic wasn't crazy. First Artists and Warner Bros. conducted a worldwide talent search in April 1975 to find an actor to star in their official bio based on Linda Lee's book, *Bruce Lee: The Man Only I Knew*. Applicants flooded the auditions, which were judged by Chuck Norris, Robert Lee (Bruce's brother), Linda Lee, and Barbra Streisand, a co-founder of First Artists and the mastermind behind this project. The auditions were a bust, but the producers eventually spotted a college student named Alex Kwon doing a *Black Belt* magazine photo shoot and hired him to play Bruce. Production kept getting pushed back, however, and when the Hong Kong–produced biopic, *Bruce Lee: The Man, the Myth* became a huge hit in 1977, First Artists quietly let their project die. But that didn't stop the madness.

Shaw Brothers studios, possibly annoyed they'd missed the Bruce Lee money train while he was alive, decided to piss all over his grave now that he was dead, hiring Betty Ting Pei, the woman whose bed he died in, to star in *Bruce Lee—His Last Days, His Last Nights* (1976). Danny Lee, a Shaw contract actor, portrays Bruce as an impetuous hothead who rescues Betty from some thugs, then starts drinking, which turns him into a horny playboy who screws dozens of women in his bachelor pad full of mirrors, massive pictures of himself, and a circular trampoline bed.

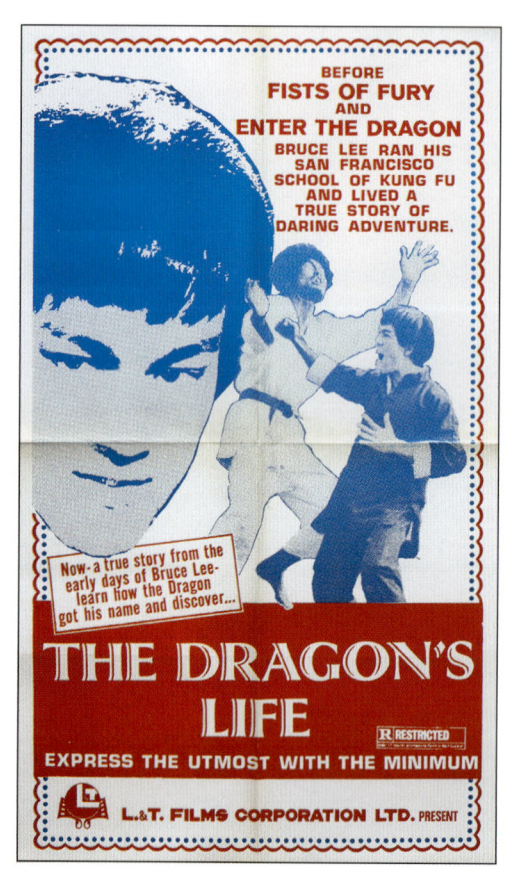

L&T/Ark Films released *The Story of the Dragon* (1976) as both *Bruce Lee's Secret* and *The Dragon's Life* in 1978. Three years later, 21st Century re-released it under the title *Bruce Lee's Deadly Kung Fu*.

Bruce's sacred mission in these biopics is not to become a star or make movies, but to demonstrate the supremacy of kung fu. Caucasian, Japanese, Italian, cowboy, and African-American fighters line up to dispute this claim. Sometimes the African-American fighters are, unfortunately, Chinese actors in blackface.

In *He's a Legend, He's a Hero* (1976), an actor playing *Green Hornet* producer William Dozier insists that Bruce wear ancient Chinese robes, for a part and when Bruce protests he screams, "You're not in Hong Kong anymore, you're in the United States, and if I want you to walk around with chopsticks shoved up your ass, you'll do it!"

But when Bruce wins the Long Beach Championships, reporters clamor to know about this new martial art of kung fu and plaster his face all over the covers of their magazines. "Chinese kung fu is really way out," a white studio executive chuckles, patting another on the back.

In the biopics, shoots for *The Big Boss* or *Way of the Dragon* are merely stages where Bruce takes on foreign fighters who mock kung fu. When Bruce inevitably wins these battles, the foreign fighters fall to their knees, begging, "Boss, you must teach me Jeet Kune Do."

Part of the legend of Bruce Lee is that he got screwed by The Man, so the Bruce Lee biopic's primal scene is a Faustian moment when Bruce signs a (one-sided) contract.

(top) The First Artists / Warner Bros. auditions being judged by a panel that included Robert Clouse, director of *Enter the Dragon*, Clouse's longtime stunt choreographer, Pat Johnson, and Linda Lee, Bruce Lee's widow.

(bottom left) Potential Bruce Lees wait to audition outside the Warner Bros. talent search.

(bottom right) Alex Kwon, who would be tapped to play Bruce Lee, with Linda Lee.

BRUCE LEE
'HIS' TRUE STORY
EXPLODES
ACROSS THE SCREEN!
ALL NEW ACTION!
THE DRAGON LIVES
HERMAN COHEN presents
"THE DRAGON LIVES"
Starring BRUCE LI • CARYN WHITE
BETTY CHEN • ERNEST 'CURT' CURTIS
Screenplay by SINGLOY WANG and YI KWAN
Produced by C.H. WONG • Directed by SINGLOY WANG
R RESTRICTED
UNDER 17 REQUIRES ACCOMPANYING PARENT OR ADULT GUARDIAN
Color By Deluxe ®
A FILM VENTURES INTERNATIONAL RELEASE
© FVI 1978

Subsequently, he gets equipped with a high-tech gym full of computers and pushes himself too hard ("Yes, I should rest, but life's too short. When I'm dead, then I'll rest") while uttering cryptic fortune cookie-isms ("The last game, the game of birth, the game of life, the whole thing is only a game, but still, I want to be winner of this game . . .") but all stations of the cross lead to Bruce's crucifixion in Betty Ting Pei's apartment, establishing the Betty Ting Pei character as an essential component of many, many Bruceploitation flicks.

At the end of *He's a Legend, He's a Hero* (1976) the theme song reminds us that "even a strong man must dieeeeee!" as Bruce hops into bed with Betty during a raging storm. The camera zooms into their lovemaking through a pot of percolating coffee before cutting away to an enormous framed picture of Betty looming over her bed, shots of her stuffed animals watching, then to a clearly fake dog licking Bruce's foot with a rubber tongue. As Betty climaxes, lightning flashes and Bruce laughs maniacally while holding her in his arms. A wall collapses. Framed pictures crash to the ground. Raymond Chow laughs like a lunatic. A hushed crowd watches. Lightning strikes a tree. The crowd rushes Bruce in the ring at the Long Beach International Karate Championships, cheering, lifting him on their shoulders as the screen cuts to headlines of his death, then to black, as a Caucasian actor howls "Bruuuuuuuuuuuccccce! Bruuuuuuuuuuuuucccccccce!" in utter despair.

Some of the biopics suggest that Bruce Lee isn't actually dead at all. In *Bruce Lee: The Man, the Myth* (1976), a fortune teller explains that Bruce will come to a bad end unless he fakes his death and walks away from his family, his friends, and his career. And so, the movie tells us, over a shot of Bruce walking into a forest, he isn't actually dead, just living in total seclusion until his planned return. In 1983.

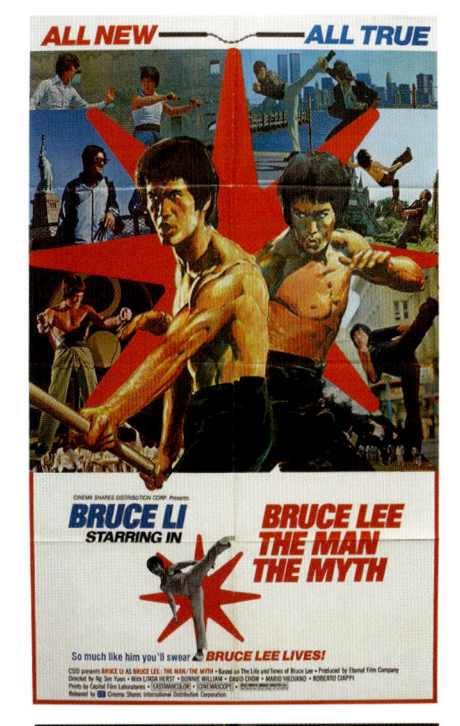

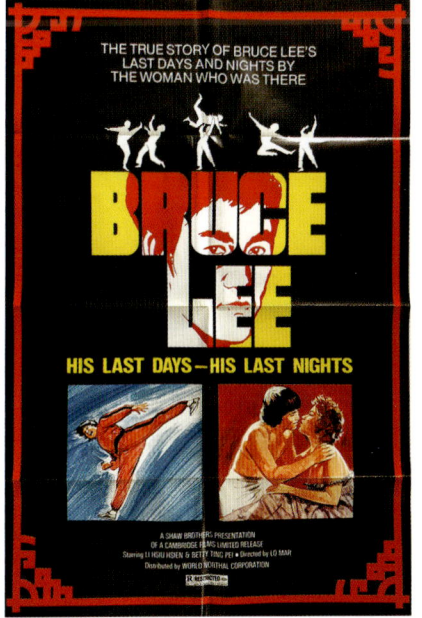

(opposite page) *Bruce Lee—His Last Days, His Last Nights* was unhinged, but *Bruce Lee—The Dragon Lives* (aka *He's a Legend, He's a Hero*, 1976) redefined insanity with its ultraviolence, a Japanese wrestler with a tiny Hitler mustache, and a Jim Kelly stand-in named Elton the Black Devil's Fist.

(above) *Bruce Lee: The Man, the Myth* (1976) was the highest-grossing Bruceploitation movie released in the States and the first one to air on TV. *Bruce Lee—His Last Days, His Last Nights* was Shaw's mean-spirited takedown of Bruce, depicting him as a petulant manchild who wasn't worthy of Betty Ting Pei.

THEN THERE ARE THE SPIN-OFFS wherein characters named Bruce Lee, or someone associated with Bruce Lee, have further adventures. Sometimes Bruce is an undercover cop infiltrating a gang (*Fists of Bruce Lee*, 1978), or busting a ring of international jewel thieves (*Image of Bruce Lee*, 1978), or looking for a stolen antique (*My Name Called Bruce*, 1978), or trying to rescue a scientist who's invented Topoleela, the first foodstuff made from petroleum (*Bruce Lee Against Supermen*, 1975). Sometimes Bruce is a secret agent who must battle an army of his own clones (*The Clones of Bruce Lee*, 1980).

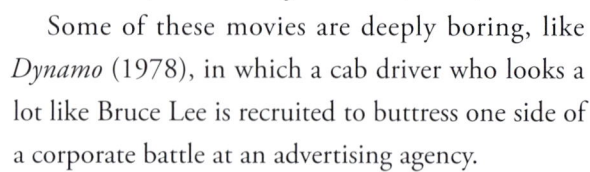

Some of these movies are deeply boring, like *Dynamo* (1978), in which a cab driver who looks a lot like Bruce Lee is recruited to buttress one side of a corporate battle at an advertising agency.

The spin-off subgenre reaches its zenith/nadir in *The Dragon Lives Again* (1977), the one Bruceploitation movie to rule them all, and the most famously berserk disaster-piece ever to come out of Hong Kong. Beginning with Bruce Lee's sheet-covered corpse popping an enormous boner in the morgue (yes, a posthumous erection plays a part in the Bruce Lee legend), it then follows Bruce to Hell, where the King of the Underworld tells him he can escape back to Earth but only if he fights an army of copyright infringing characters: Dracula! Clint Eastwood! James Bond! The Godfather! And Japan's blind swordsman, Zatoichi! There are also armies of skeletons.

Aiding Bruce are Popeye, the spinach-chugging sailorman (played by Hong Kong director and star, Eric Tsang), and Caine from the TV series *Kung Fu* (not played by David Carradine). Sexy ladies scream for Bruce ("When a man's endowed like Bruce," someone sighs, "the girls are bound to want him"), and things hit overdrive in a sexy subplot in which softcore starlet Hong Kong Emmanuelle tries to take over Hell by screwing the King of the Underworld to death.

Made less than three years after the real Bruce Lee passed away, *The Dragon Lives Again* is the brainchild of Goldig, a company best known for its sex films like *Jenny and Her Sexy Mother*, and directed by Law Kei, who would go on to shoot movies like

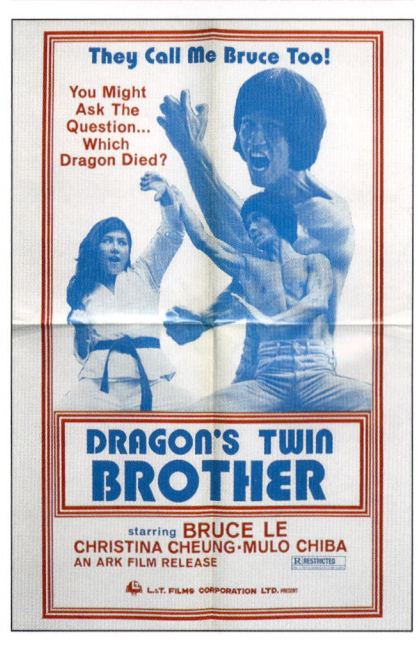

(top) It turned out to be his nunchuks, but not before *The Dragon Lives Again* restated the apocryphal legend that Bruce Lee died with a powerful posthumous erection.

(bottom) *Dragon's Twin Brother* (aka *My Name Called Bruce, 1978*) was another Joseph Velasco picture, written by a regular Bruceploitation scriptwriter who used the name "Zackey Chan."

Seven Sexual Maniacs. Bruce Leung (see page 134) plays Bruce Lee, and he reportedly hated making this movie with a passion. Even the part where he flies away at the end like a magical pixie as the entire cast waves "Goodbye!"

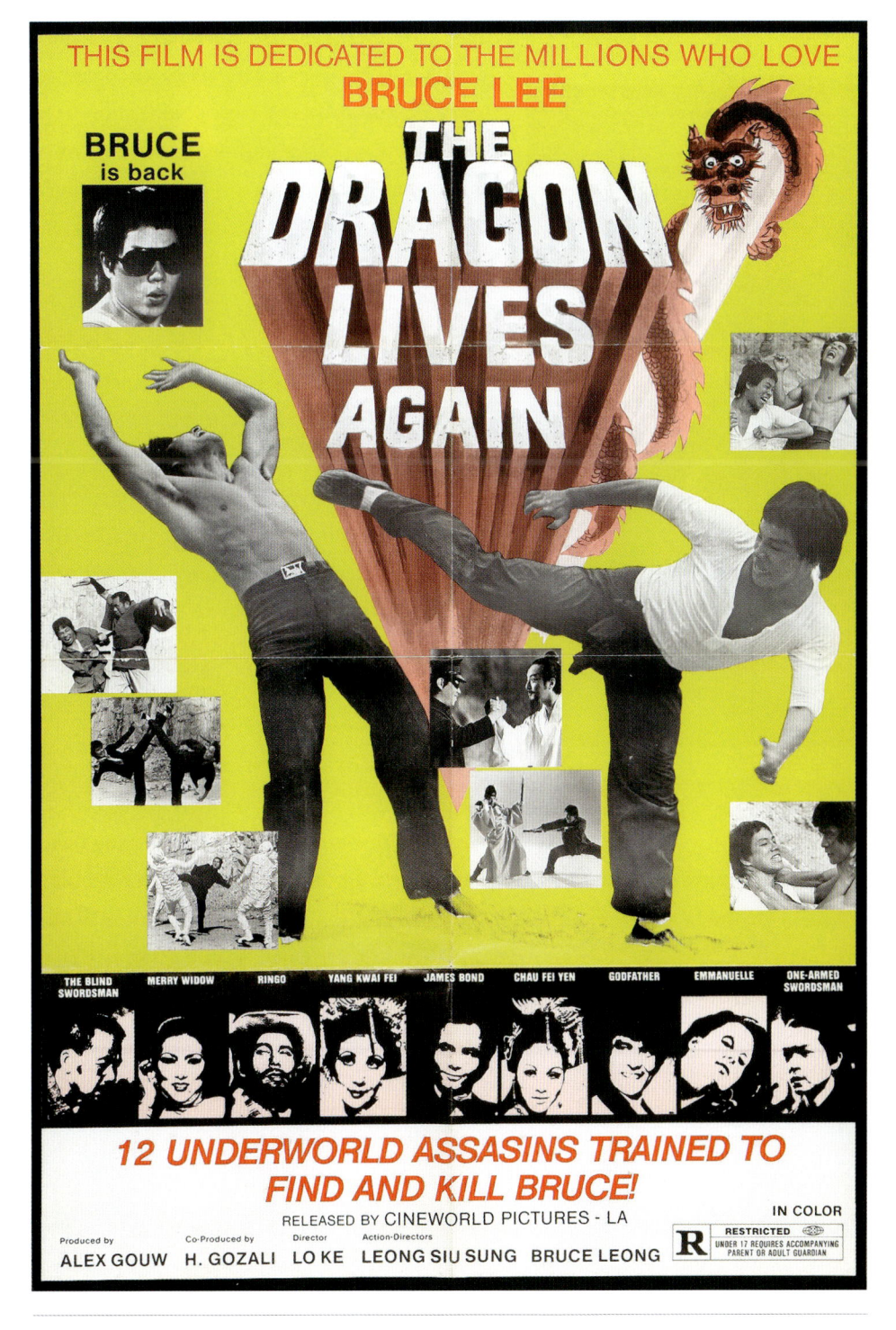

Among the team out to bedevil Bruce Lee in Hell are Yang Kwei Fei, a legendary beauty who once enraptured the Emperor of China, and someone named Ringo.

THE THIRD SUBGENRE OF BRUCEPLOITATION movies are the sequels, none of which bear any resemblance to their predecessors. *Enter the Panther* (1975) has zero to do with *Enter the Dragon*, and *Way of the Dragon 2* (aka *Bruce Le's Greatest Revenge*, 1978) actually plays more like a sequel to *Fist of Fury*, although there actually already was a *Fist of Fury 2* (1977), which sometimes gets retitled as *The Chinese Connection 2*. It's confusing. *Fist of Fury* was Bruce's most popular film from which to spin off unauthorized sequels, most prominently in the Shaolin Kung Fu Trilogy.

This trilogy begins with *Bruce and Shaolin Kung Fu* (1977), in which imitator Bruce Le (see page 130) plays Lee Ching-lung, the brother of the Chinese martial arts hero from the Ching Wu school who was shot like a dog by the evil Japanese at the end of *Fist of Fury*.

Now the Japanese occupiers want to close all the kung fu gyms, but Lee vows to keep them open, but then the Japanese hire five kung fu killers, one of whom sports a tiny Hitler mustache. The movie ends when Lee turns his back on a squad of Japanese soldiers in disgust and strides manfully into the sunset right before they gun him down.

That didn't kill him, apparently, because *Bruce and Shaolin Kung Fu Part 2* (1977) begins with Bruce Le as Lee Ching-lung being nursed back to health so he can fight the Japanese again, which means it's essentially a remake of the first movie, although—thanks to the vagaries of international film production—*Bruce and Shaolin Kung Fu Part 2* got released months before Part 1. The third movie, *Return of the Fist of Fury* (1978), stars Bruce Pak (see page 141) as Lee Ching-lung's brother, wandering the wilderness and eating random birds before stopping by a tavern where he Frisbees his hat through someone's skull and de-brains a guy with a pair of hurled chopsticks. Then he chain kicks one miscreant so many times their pants fall down.

He's come to get revenge on the Japanese creeps who killed his brother in Parts 1 and 2. Cut to the Japanese gym where assorted minions are mopping up after the last fight and complaining about their bad luck. They can't even go out drinking anymore without some guy showing up and cleaning their clocks with Chinese kung fu. Without warning, Bruce Pak crashes through the window and mops the gym up

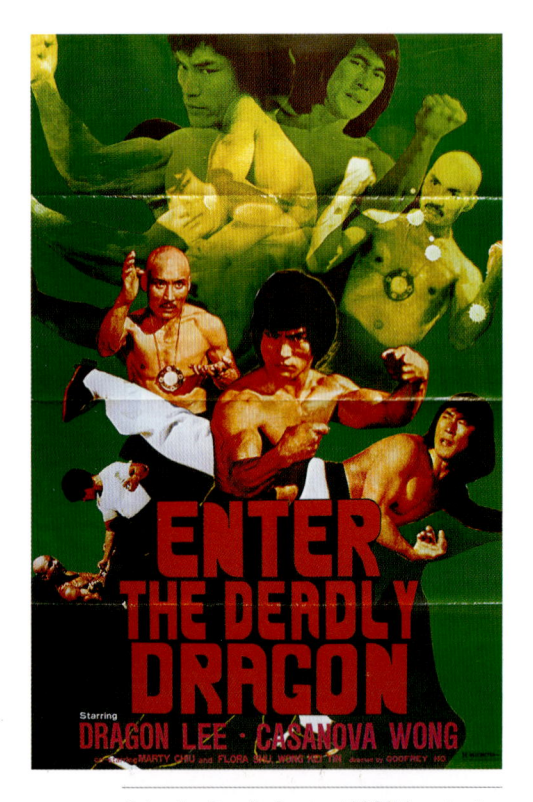

Enter the Deadly Dragon (1981) is actually *Enter the Invincible Hero*, an IFD production (see page 306).

with them in a nearly shot-for-shot remake of the dojo fight from *Fist of Fury*, except this time around the Japanese minions seem existentially resigned to their fate.

The Bruce Lee sequels all posit a future where every character Bruce ever played—Cheng Chiu-On from *The Big Boss*, Chen Zhen from *Fist of Fury*, Tang Lung from *Way of the Dragon*—continue forever, spawning brothers and look-alikes, running into co-stars and former enemies, history repeating itself endlessly, a Moebius strip of Bruces marching around in a loop, eternally.

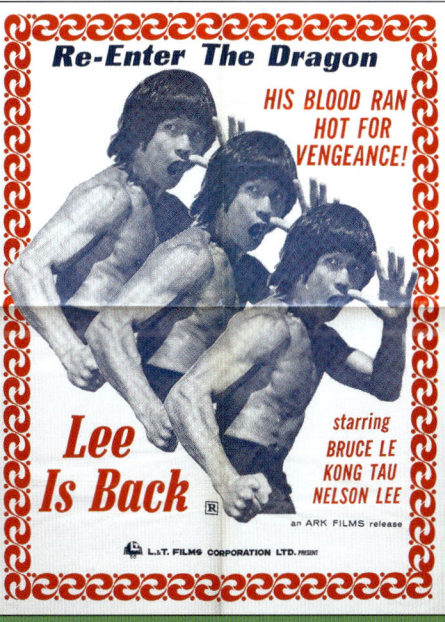

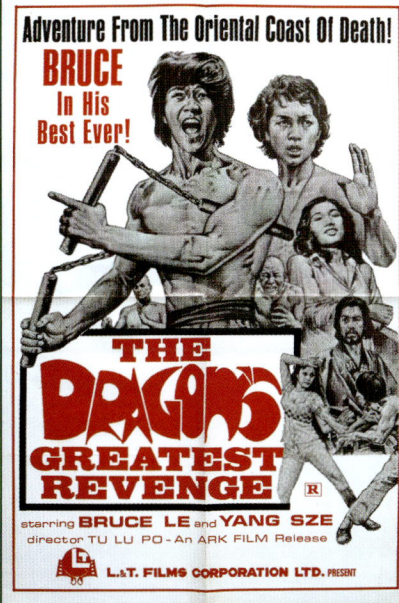

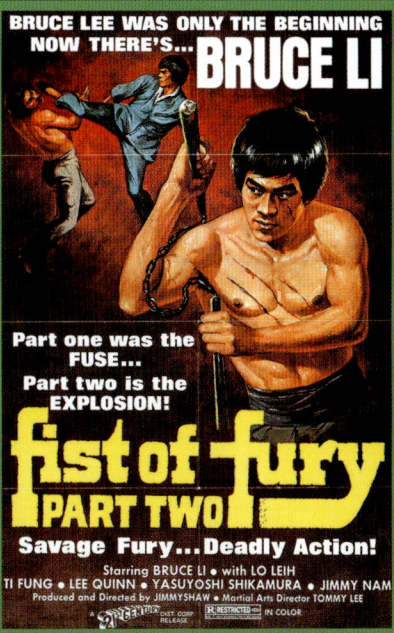

Bruce and Shaolin Kung Fu is also *Fist of Fury Part Two*; *Lee is Back* is actually *Bruce and Shaolin Kung Fu 2*; *The Dragon's Greatest Revenge* is *Bruce Le's Greatest Revenge*, also known as *The Chinese Connection 2* or *Fist of Fury Part Two*; and also here's *Fist of Fury Part Two*, which is sometimes called *The Chinese Connection 2*.

BRUCE LEE'S CO-STARS FLOCKED TO the spin-offs and sequels. Class acts like Shek Kin, who had already achieved widespread fame in the long-running Wong Fei-hung series before playing the villainous, one-handed Mr. Han in *Enter the Dragon*, found his connection to *Enter the Dragon* plastered across the posters of unrelated movies by their producers. Probably figuring if you can't beat them, join them, he reprised his role as Mr. Han opposite Bruce Le in *Bruce—King of Kung Fu* (1980). Nora Miao, Lee's co-star in *The Big Boss* and *Fist of Fury*, found herself in *Bruce's Fingers* (1976), then played opposite Lo Wei's latest discovery, Jackie Chan, whom Lo hoped would replace Bruce on the big screen, in *New Fist of Fury* (1976).

The massive, muscle-bound Bolo Yeung made an impression in *Enter the Dragon* and would go on to appear in no less than 16 Bruceploitation movies over 10 years, often sporting a tiny Hitler mustache, achieving his own kind of cut-rate stardom. He appeared front and center in the marketing materials for *Chinese Hercules* (aka *Freedom Strikes a Blow*, 1973) which National General picked up as their final film but wound up handing over to Bryanston Releasing when they went bankrupt, along with *Way of the Dragon*. Despite Bolo Yeung being portrayed as the lead in the movie, the actual star of *Chinese Hercules* is Michael Chan Wai-man, a veteran of dozens of Shaw Brothers movies who had spent years as a member of Hong Kong's criminal triads, shaking film crews down for protection money, before finding fame in front of the cameras. Bolo did star, however, in *Bolo the Brute* (1977) as the comedy lead opposite Jason Pai Pao. Later, he'd take on Jean-Claude Van Damme in *Bloodsport* (1988; see page 354), fight two Jean-Claude Van Dammes in *Double Impact* (1991), and reunite with the director of *Enter the Dragon*, Robert Clouse, for *Ironheart* (1992).

But no one rode the Bruce Lee train harder or longer than Jon Benn, who played Mr. Big in *Way of the Dragon*. The 6'4" Benn had run a fast-food franchise called World's Wurst Sandwich and Sausage and a chain of souvenir kiosks before moving to Hong Kong to see where all those knickknacks he sold came from. He met Raymond Chow at a cocktail party and wound up playing Mr. Big in *Way*, then parlayed that role into appearances in several Joseph Velasco Bruceploitation pictures: *Enter Three Dragons* (1979), *The Clones of Bruce Lee* (1980), and *Challenge of the Tiger* (1980). In 1998 he opened the Bruce Lee Café in Hong Kong, selling Lee souvenirs and serving up dishes like "Fish of Fury," "Satay of the Dragon," and "Bruce Juice." The last movie he shot before his death was *Space Ninjas* (2019), featuring Godfrey Ho (see page 306).

Whether he was billed as Sek Kin, Shih Kien, Shih Chien, or even as his character from *Enter the Dragon*, Mr. Han, as he is in this live appearance ad, Sek Kin reluctantly embraced exploiting his Bruce Lee connection.

U.S. & HONG KONG
UNITED KUNG-FU EXHIBITION
Featuring:
BRUCE LEE'S SPARRING PARTNER
FROM 'ENTER THE DRAGON'
SAT. & SUN.,
MAY 24, 25, 1975
7:00 P.M. TO
10:00 P.M.
(BOTH DAYS)
Program varies each day
MR. HAN
KEZAR PAVILION,
GOLDEN GATE PARK,
STANYAN ST.,
SAN FRANCISCO, CALIF.
HONG KONG & U.S. MASTERS
COVERING NORTHERN & SOUTHERN SYSTEMS
DEMONSTRATING FORMS, WEAPONS & OTHER SPECIALTIES
ALSO APPEARING
HUNG-GAR Y.C. Wong
HOP-GAR David Chin
NORTHERN PRAYING-MANTIS Peter Kwong
NORTHERN PRAYING-MANTIS Brendan Lai
WHITE CRANE William Siu
WING CHUN Chris Chan
TAI-MANTIS Simon Tam
EAGLE CLAW Jeannie Lau
FIVE ANCESTERS Gate Chan
BAK SILUM Lai Hung
MOK GAR Chuk Fung
Tickets: GENERAL ADMISSION, $5.00 RING SIDE SEATS, $7.50
DOWNTOWN BOX OFFICE
Macy's Department Store
325 Mason St./S.F. Ca. 775-2021
Y.C. WONG KUNG-FU STUDIO
729 A Clay St./S.F. Ca. 781-4682
BRENDAN LAI'S KUNG-FU STUDIO
2849 California St./S.F. Ca. 346-3724
WHITE CRANE SUPPLIES CO.
47 Golden Gate Ave./S.F. Ca. 861-6363
CHINATOWN PHOTOGRAPHY SERVICE
24 Ross Alley/S.F. Ca. 391-3616

THE FLYING KILLER OF KUNG FU
SHIH KIEN from ENTER THE DRAGON
THE BIONIC THUNDER KICK
CHEN KUAN TAI - CHEN XING - WO CHING
produced by C.J. KWOK - An Ark Film Release R

HIS WRATH HOLDS NO EQUAL!
STARRING BRUCE LEE'S DEADLIES ENEMY
SHIH KIEN from ENTER THE DRAGON
GOD WEARS A BLACK BELT
R
AN ARK FILMS RELEASE

From BRUCE LEE'S "ENTER THE DRAGON" COMES SHIH CHIEN in . . .
The Last Challenge of the Dragon
POWER-PACKED ACTION-DRAMA
The Most Exciting Fighting Scenes Ever filmed!
STARRING SHIH CHIEN • OU YANG SO FEI • KUAN SHAN AND STEVE CHAN
PRODUCED BY ALEX GOUW & CHOW HIAP HOU DIRECTED BY STEVE CHAN
SCREENPLAY BY STEVE CHAN & KUNG MING MUSIC BY FRANKIE CHAN • IN COLOR
RELEASED BY CINEWORLD PICTURES INTERNATIONAL
R RESTRICTED UNDER 17 REQUIRES ACCOMPANYING PARENT OR ADULT GUARDIAN

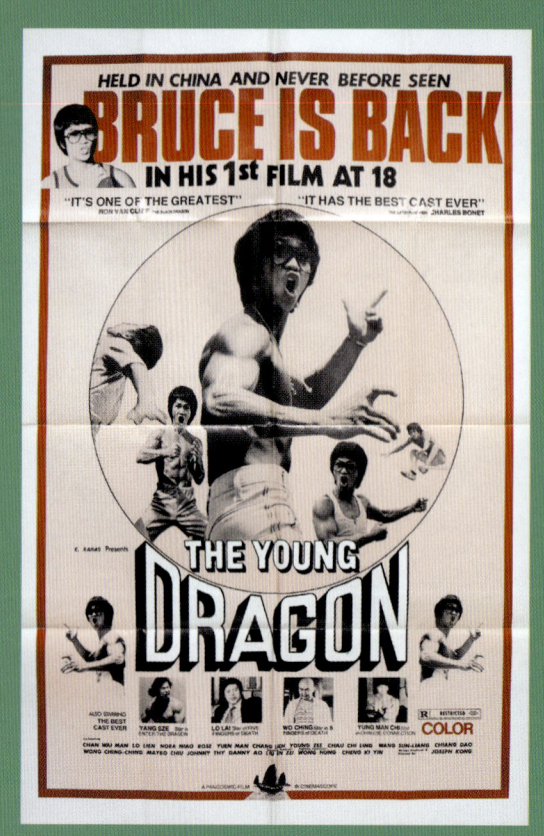

Bruce's Deadly Fingers was first released in the US by Serafim Karalexis as *The Young Dragon* (1977). Objectively terrible, *The Clones of Bruce Lee* stars Dragon Lee, Bruce Le, Bruce Lai, and the enigmatic Bruce Thai. But sometimes, as in this ad for *Bruce's Deadly Fingers*, a Bruce Lee impersonator like Bruce Le just co-starred "with."

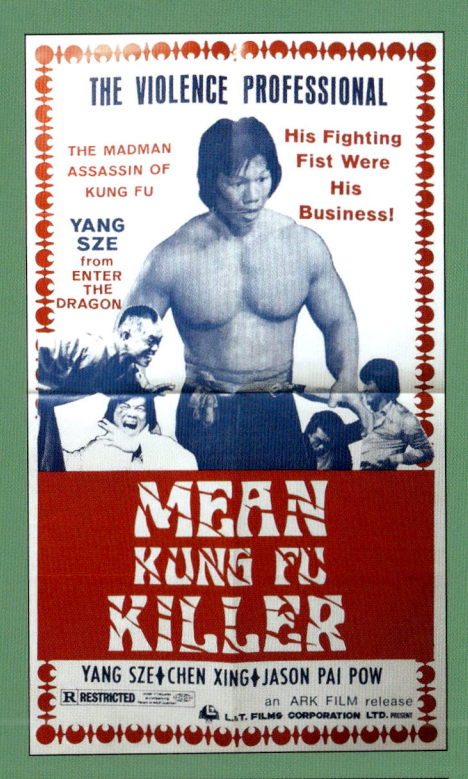

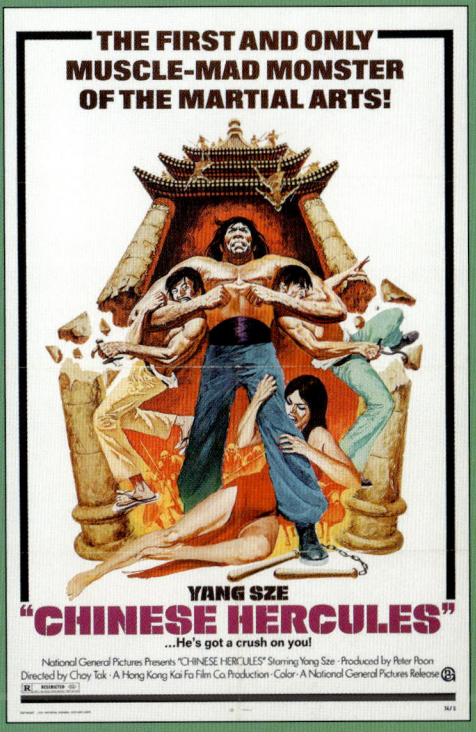

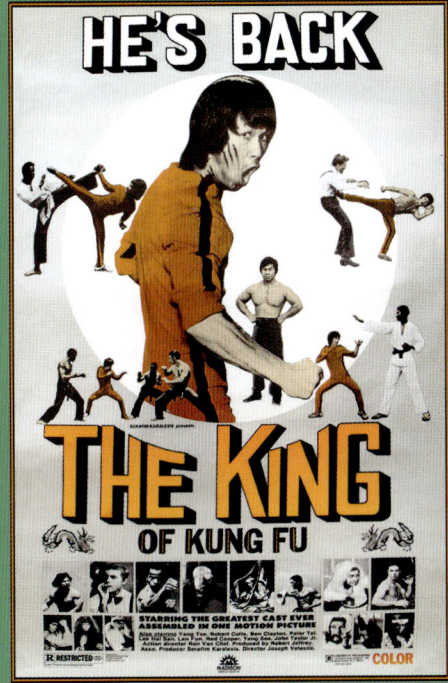

(top, left) *Mean Kung Fu Killer* is *Amsterdam Connection* (1978) and features Bolo Yeung in a supporting role. It was later re-released by Unifilm as *Big Bad Bolo*.

(top, right) *Chinese Hercules* actually starred Chan Wai-man, a friend of Bruce Lee's who had the same whipcord body. Chan couldn't strip off his shirt to reveal it, however, because he was covered with tattoos that advertised his triad connections.

(bottom, left) *The King of Kung Fu* (1978) brought all the co-stars together, from Bolo Yeung to Sek Kin.

(bottom, right) Bolo Yeung's favorite out of all of the movies he's appeared in is *Bolo the Brute* (1977), a kung fu comedy he also directed.

CHAINED RE-ACTION!
Smoking Fists And Blazing Feet!
He's High Flying! Hard Hitting!
DRAG-ON TOKER
THE KUNG FU SMOKER
R
Dealer Of Death In The Martial Arts

KICK ACE!
He Fought The Deadly Black Belt Ace Of Thieves And Won The Fortune Of The Dragon's Treasure!
ALL NEW
COLOR
R
DRAGON'S DEN OF THIEVES
THEATRE
L.&T. FILMS CORPORATION LTD. PRESENT

THE MAST
OF THE
MANTIS
DRAG
LUNG

HIS FAST FISTS AND WICKED
Vicious Black Dragon Killer
KICKS FOUGHT THE DEADLY BEST
DIRECTOR
CHARLES CHIU
STARRING
Allen Law
Thomas Tam
Rocky Wong
Tommy Kwan
Raymond Chiu
John Liu
Robert Tien

ALL NEW AND PACKED WITH ACTION!
THE VICIOUS KUNG FU DRAGON
STARRING
CHAN WAI MAN
DAVID TONG
MAU YING
DIRECTED BY
TANG WEI TZU
EXECUTIVE PRODUCER
LEE CHING
MARTIAL ART DIRECTOR
CHAN WAI MAN
SCREEN PLAY
TONY CHENG

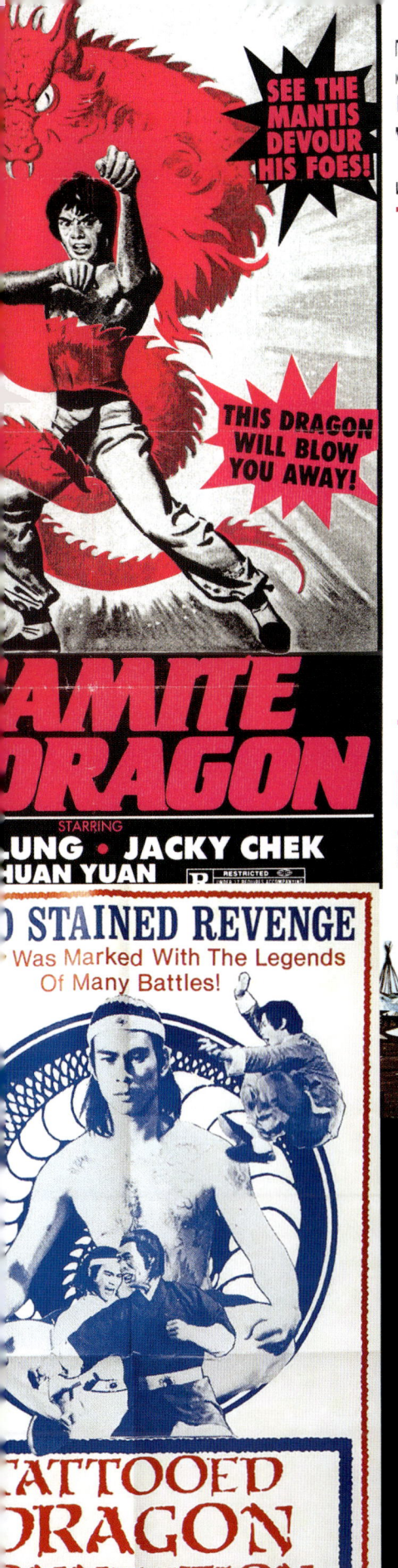

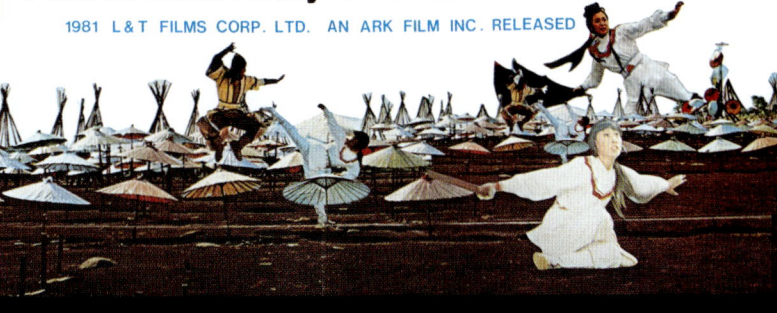

Bruce Lee had been known as the Dragon. He was born in the year of the Dragon (1940), and his Cantonese screen name, Lee Siu-lung, literally meant "Little Dragon." So the minute he died, distributors couldn't get enough dragons into their movies, especially after Enter the Dragon became the most famous kung fu movie in the world. Throughout the '70s it was Enter Five Dragons, then Six Dragons, then 6,000 Dragons . . .

THE BRUCE DIRECTORY

JUDY LEE

MARTY LEE

ROCKY LEE

JOHNNY YUNE

SHOU LUNG

BRUCE LO

ROBERT LEE

BRUCE CHEUNG

BRUCE LY

EVAN KIM

BRUCE LE

BRUCE LEI

BRUCE LI

MYRON BRUCE LEE

BRUCE K.L LEA

SNAPPER LEE

BRUCE LAI

BRONSON LEE

DRAGON LEE

BRUCE PAK

BRUCE LEUNG

SONNY BRUCE

BRUCE TAI

★ JUDY LEE (AKA CHIA LING)

Judy Lee has a legitimate claim to being the first Bruceploitation star. Her real name is Chia Ling, but her debut movie, *The Avenger* (1972), was purchased by Aquarius Releasing in 1973. Terry Levene, the head of Aquarius, was the evil genius of Times Square marketing and believed in advertising that was "like a two-by-four across the bridge of the nose." He thought *The Avenger* had great production values and wanted to design a campaign that depicted the heroine holding her hand out to the viewer with two eyeballs in the middle of her palm, dripping blood, since the movie featured a few eye gougings set to the sound of the *Shaft* soundtrack. He also changed Chia Ling's name, billing her as "Judy Lee, the female Bruce Lee." The film opened as *Queen Boxer* in October 1973, making it one of the first Bruceploitation pictures on the market. By the time the picture reached Philadelphia a couple of months later, Levene had changed his ads to read, "Judy Lee, the sister of Bruce Lee." Chia Ling would go on to have a long-lasting career in kung fu movies, but only after she apologized to the Lee family for that claim.

(above) *Queen Boxer* hit cinemas with typical Aquarius ballyhoo: karate demonstrations, triple features, and warnings that the movie was too violent for kids. No matter how tiny the ad, or under what name, all the promotions made sure to emphasize Judy Lee's Bruce Lee connection, even claiming she was Lee's little sister. They did not, however, show audiences Judy Lee. All the *Queen Boxer* ads and art features a nameless, non–Judy Lee model.

(opposite page) That *Kung Fu Exorcist* poster is no mistake, however; Kathy Leen, aka Lady Bruce Lee, was actually Judy Lee under another stage name.

The Fighting Shaolin A Holy Man Of Kung Fu Duels The Devil's Evil Power In A Blistering Assault Of Action!

Featuring
KATHY LEEN - Lady Bruce Lee

KUNG FU EXORCIST

YOU WILL LEARN THE 18 DEADLY PLAYS OF THE SHAOLIN MASTER... SEE HIM WALK ON WATER

R

★ BRUCE LI (HO TSUNG-TAO, aka LI SHAO-LUNG)

In 1949, Hong Kong boasted a thriving film industry, whereas Taiwan only had four shabby studios: one called the Agriculture Education Film Company, one run by the Defense Ministry, another run by the Education Ministry, and one inherited from the Japanese colonial government. However, a few decades of local filmmaking transformed this busted, bureaucratic graveyard into a bustling film biz thanks to the country's awesome locations, its movie-hungry population, and its deep well of talent due to the fact that its mandatory military service included training in martial arts. Taiwan became one of Hong Kong's most important markets and talent pools, with actors and directors moving freely between the two countries and co-productions facing few restrictions. Some of Hong Kong's biggest entertainers came from Taiwan, like Jimmy Wong Yu, Angela Mao, and Bruce Li.

Judy Lee may have been billed as the first faux Bruce Lee, but Ho Tsung-tao was the first Chinese actor to actually play the Little Dragon onscreen in *Super Dragon* (1974). A Taiwanese gymnast and physical education instructor who had actually taken some acting classes, Ho Tsung-tao was discovered by Taiwan's independent martial arts movie maestro, director Joseph Kuo, who gave him small roles in some of his first movies before Ho landed the Bruce Lee role in *Super Dragon* because of his resemblance to Lee—but only when viewed from the right side.

Between 1974 and 1982, the right side of Li's face starred in about 28 Bruceploitation movies, and strangely

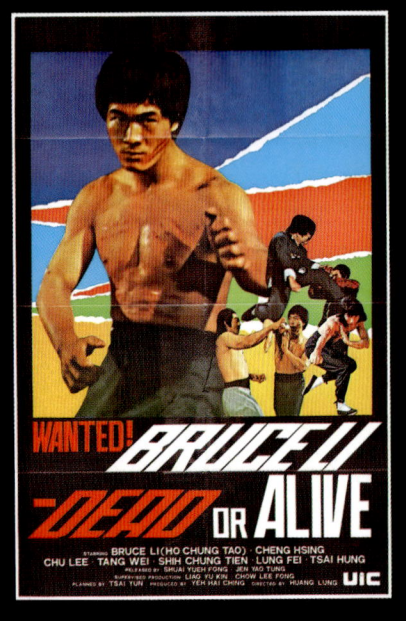

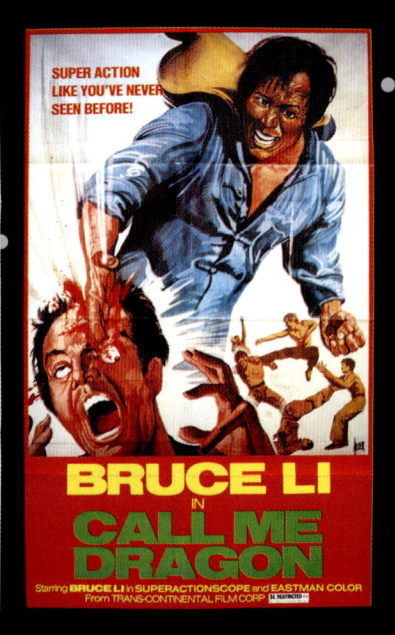

Bruce Li—Dead or Alive (aka *Deadly Strike*, 1978) is kind of a riff on *The Dirty Dozen* but is mostly terrible. Bruce Li's *Magnum Fist* (aka *The Great Hero*, 1978) is a wartime comedy co-starring Polly Shang-Kuan. *Call Me Dragon* was actually *Bruce Lee Against Supermen* (1975), which Larry Joachim picked up for American distribution and almost feels like a parody of his own *Green Hornet* movies.

he was the impersonator most respectful of Lee's legacy and the one least interested in being a celebrity. When Golden Harvest needed someone to play Bruce Lee in *Game of Death* (1978), they supposedly approached Li and offered him the role—or, rather, a part of it, since Lee would also be doubled by Yuen Biao for the action scenes. Li told the studio he'd be honored to take a year off and prepare for the role since he wanted "to do my best for Bruce Lee," but he would only perform the part solo. Golden Harvest refused, and Li returned to the Bruceploitation grind.

Working as a director on some of his own pictures, Li's Bruceploitation movies are mostly Taiwanese co-productions made under the name Li Shao-lung (a transliteration of Bruce's screen name, Lee Siu-lung). His last movie was *Pink Trap* (1985). Today he teaches martial arts to children and the elderly.

Return of the Tiger (1978) co-stars the Dragon Lady—Angela Mao!

★ BRUCE LE (HUANG KIN-LUNG)

The least handsome of the bunch, but the best martial artist, Burma-born Huang Kin-lung got scouted for Shaw Brothers and became a regular contract player for the studio. He appeared in minor roles in classic Shaw productions like their contemporary gangster flick *The Teahouse* and their wild superhero movie *Super Inframan*. But in 1976 he met up with the Filipino-Chinese director Joseph Kong (real name, Joseph Velasco) for their first Bruceploitation movie, *Bruce's Fingers* (1976), co-starring Nora Miao, Bolo Yeung, and even Lo Lieh of *Five Fingers of Death* fame. Studded with sleazy sex scenes, the movie chronicles Le's low-budget quest to find Bruce Lee's Finger Book before the bad guys learn the secret of Bruce's iron finger technique.

Velasco and Le worked together on eight Bruceploitation flicks after *Bruce's Fingers*, including *Bruce's Secret Kung Fu* (1976), *Treasure of Bruce Le* (1977), *Bruce and the Shaolin Bronzemen* (1980), *The Clones of Bruce Lee* (1980), and *Bruce Strikes Back* (1982). All told, between 1976 and 1982, he made about 25 Bruceploitation movies, most of them shot for PT Insantra, a small-time Hong Kong company run by Robert Theh and Duncan Leong, who sold Le all across South America and Europe. Insantra later put together a package of 21 kung fu movies, 12 of them featuring Bruce Le, and made a deal with Roy Winnick of Best Film & Video to handle the worldwide marketing of this package. When the broadcast premiere of Bruce Le's *Enter the Game of Death* on Los Angeles' KTLA became the channel's highest-rated feature for the month of May 1981, it was suddenly easy for Winnick to find buyers. He sold 15 of the movies to Telepictures Corp. to form their "Masters of Fury" package and the remaining six were sold to another syndication outfit, Group Four. Some channels reported that the Bruceploitation movies drew a 100% increase in audience over other movies in the same time slot.

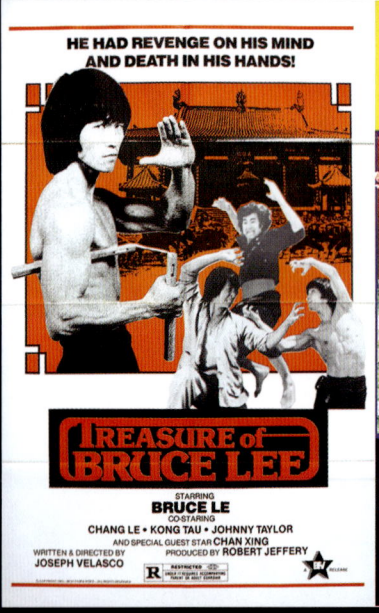

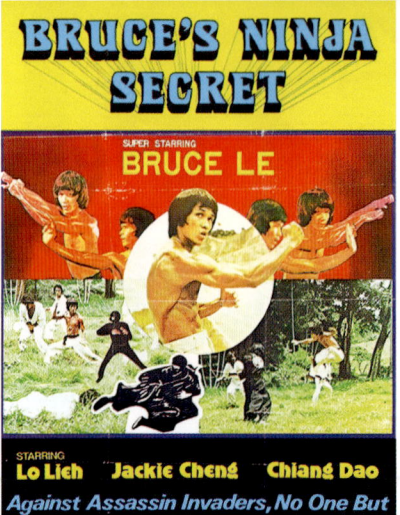

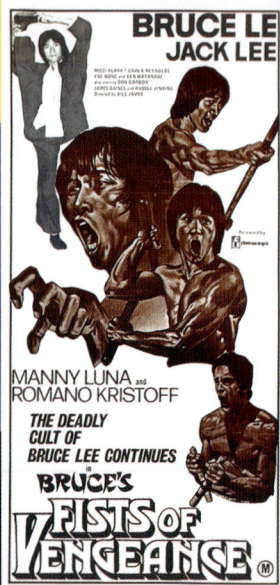

Le went to LA to shoot intros for KTLA's "Fist of Fury Week" and started directing and starring in Bruceploitation films for Dick Randall. In one of these, *Bruce Strikes Back*, Le gets out of prison and heads to Rome to get his head together, where he encounters "Chick Norris," played by Randall's wife, Corliss. Co-directed with Joseph Velasco, the film had a $50,000 budget, which was extremely low, even for a Bruceploitation movie.

At one point, Le had plans to go to India and make a movie called *Hare Krishna*, which would focus on how kung fu shows the power of mind over matter. "The story will show how the mind can put out a fire or lift a chair," he explained. It never happened.

He even shopped around a TVseries in America called *F.I.S.T.*, about a group of crimefighters who, for some reason, aren't allowed to use guns. A fast-talking hustler, Bruce Le loved to play the markets, and later in his life he reportedly even did a little jail time for financial chicanery in Mainland China. He's still in the movie business today.

(opposite page) *Treasure of Bruce Lee* (1979) is better known as *Treasure of Bruce Le* and was also released as *Kung Fu Streetfighter*. *Bruce's Ninja Secret* (ca. 1985) is mostly composed of footage from *Bruce and the Shaolin Bronzemen* (1982) and *Bruce's Deadly Fingers* (1976), and also called *Bruce's Last Battle* and *Bruce's Secret Kung Fu*. *Bruce's Fists of Vengeance* (1980) is a Filipino production starring Bruce Le and Romano Kristoff, a Spanish actor who worked in the Philippines.

(left) *Bruce vs. the Black Dragon* was the first US release of *Bruce and Shaolin Kung Fu*.

★ DRAGON LEE (MOON KYOUNG-SEOK, aka BRUCE LEI)

South Korea's Dragon Lee (billed as Bruce Lei in *Ways of Kung Fu*, 1978) trained in taekwondo with Kim Tai-Chung, who'd go on to double for Bruce Lee in *Game of Death*, and trained in hapkido with with superkicker Hwang In-Shik, who plays a Japanese fighter that Bruce takes out during the climax of *Way of the Dragon*. Despite these connections, Moon actually found his way into the movie business when the guy who painted the billboards at his local cinema told him he looked like Bruce Lee and introduced him to Hwacheon Film Co. The studio immediately threw their exciting new discovery into *The Last Fist of Fury* (1977), and shortly after, two of Hwacheon's Hong Kong partners came to visit their South Korean offices.

Tomas Tang and Joseph Lai got rich from international sales and often made fake Korean movies with Hwacheon to beat Korea's strict quota system, which limited the number of foreign films that could be shown in local cinemas. Co-productions were exempt, however, so many Hong Kong companies inserted fake Korean credits in their movies to make them appear to be locally shot co-productions. Tang and Lai liked the idea of shooting Bruceploitation flicks on the cheap in Korea, so Moon was rechristened Dragon Lee and the pair quickly got to work. Together, they made over twenty Bruceploitation movies with Dragon Lee between 1977 and 1983, but they had a habit of recycling footage, so it's hard to know the exact number.

Dragon Lee also became attached to a production called *Enter Another Dragon* alongside John Saxon and Ron Van Clief, but the project fell apart, leaving behind nothing but Neal Adams poster art, which was recycled for another Dragon Lee movie, *Enter Three Dragons* (see page 162). When Aquarius released *Kung Fu Fever* in 1982, they billed Lee as Bruce Rhee on the posters and ads. A savvy businessman, Lee once owned a chain of movie theaters and still works in television today.

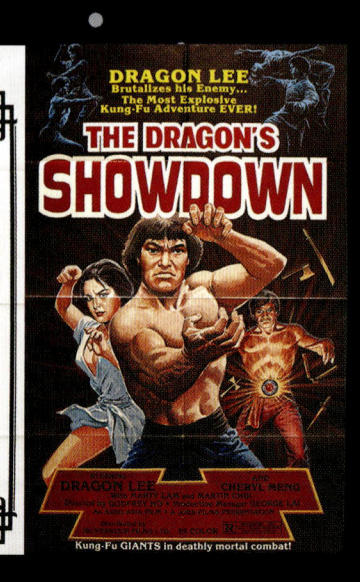

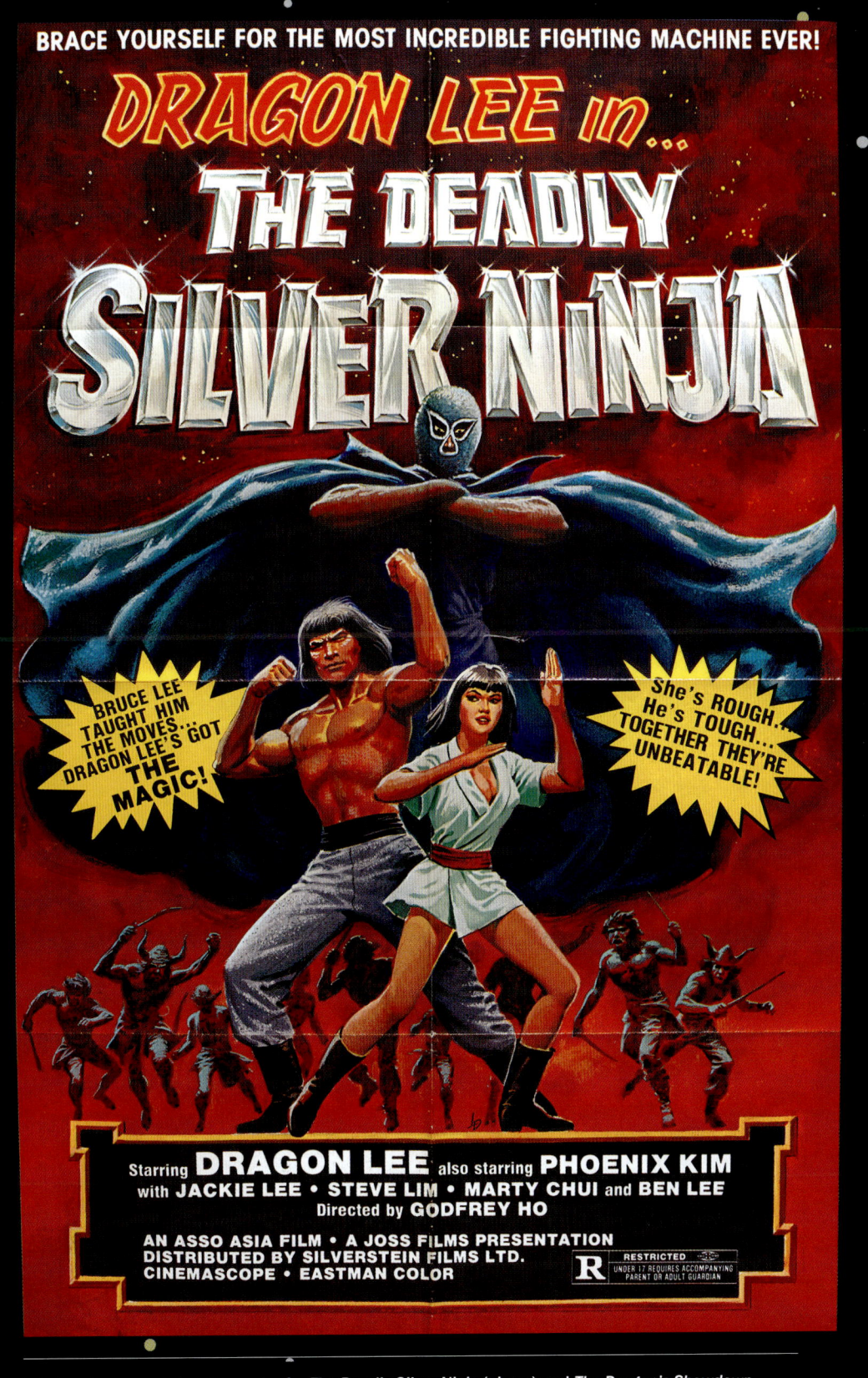

Luis Dominguez painted the poster for *The Deadly Silver Ninja* (above) and *The Dragon's Showdown* (1980, opposite page), while Marcus Boas painted *Dragon on Fire* (1978, opposite page) and *Rage of the Dragon* (1980, also opposite page). Larry Joachim spotted Boas selling art at a convention and hired him almost immediately, paying him $1,000 per one sheet. Boas would use lobby cards and stills for reference and had a few rules of thumb, such as "Don't put women on a poster." As he was told by one distributor, "Kung fu people don't like women."

★ BRUCE LEUNG (aka BRUCE LIANG)

Bruce Leung (sometimes known as Bruce Liang) was a serious street brawler trained in martial arts by his dad and uncle. He started doing stunts at 15 but was later discovered by producer-director Ng See-yuen while street fighting for cash. His English name at the time was David, but Ng changed it to Bruce for *Little Godfather from Hong Kong* (1974), which Cannon released in the US as *The Godfather Squad*. He'd go on to make several Bruceploitation movies, often handling action choreography duties as well, but he's most notorious for the Bruce-Lee-goes-to-Hell movie, *The Dragon Lives Again* (1977, see page 114). In 1983, he did a TV series that became a hit in Mainland China but got him banned from working in Taiwan for political reasons. In 1988 he disappeared completely from the screen and went into business but was rediscovered in 2004 when Stephen Chow cast him as a disarmingly disheveled bad guy known only as "The Beast" in *Kung Fu Hustle*. Chow, a Bruce Lee fanatic, considered Leung the best of the Bruceploitation imitators. Since then he's more than redeemed his name by appearing in award-winning pictures, like the retro-action crowd-pleaser *Gallants* (2010).

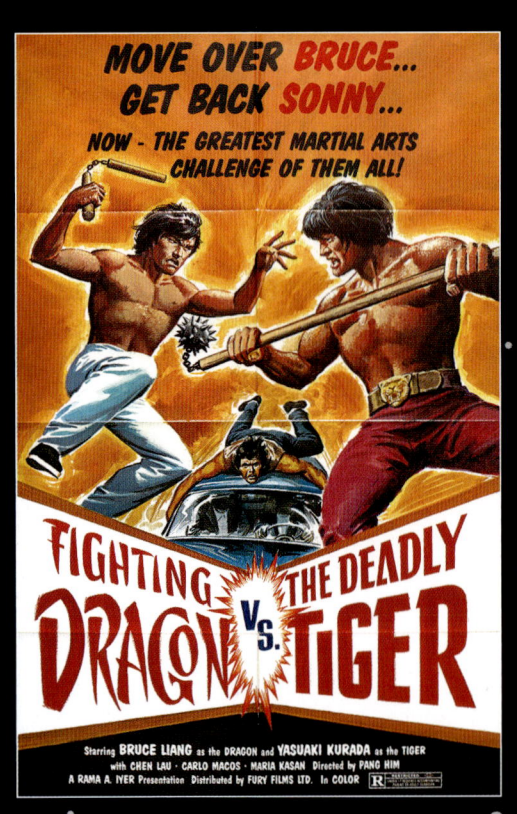

(left) *Fighting Dragon vs. The Deadly Tiger* (aka *Challenge Me Dragon*, 1975) is a feature composed of *Fight! Dragon* television episodes starring Yasuaki Kurata and Bruce Leung.

(right) *Lee Kicks Back* (aka *Fists, Kicks, and the Evils*, 1979) rewrites Muhammad Ali's famous quote that he will "float like a butterfly, sting like a bee."

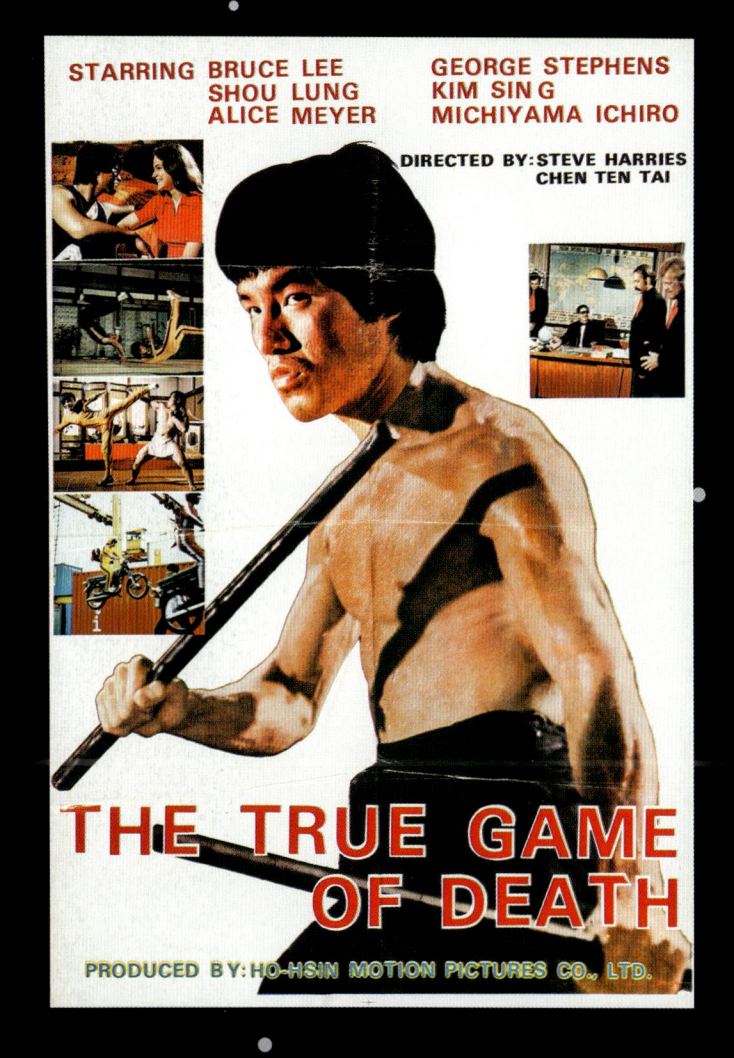

★ SHOU LUNG

Shou Lung, whose real name is Lung Tien-hsiang, is a Taiwanese TV actor and Shaw Brothers contract player scouted by Chang Cheh, who cast him in several movies. Shou Lung only made two Bruceploitation flicks, *True Game of Death* (1979) and *Bruce Against Snake in the Eagle's Shadow* (aka *Sea Girls*, 1979), which also happens to be a Chansploitation movie. But *True Game of Death* is a real freakshow. It begins with eerily slowed-down archival footage of Bruce Lee at a press conference while a dubbed voice continuously repeats, "You got the picture, I don't think I have anything else to say. Just put the drug in his drink like I told you." Cut to headlines of Lee's death and then the same footage of Lee's funeral we've seen a hundred times, but scored with a mournful trumpet solo. When Shou Lung makes love, the movie cuts to randomly assembled footage of the actual Bruce Lee overdubbed with disconcerting knuckle cracking sounds. Later, the same thing happens when he reads a magazine. The climax restages a cheapjack version of the *Game of Death* tower finale, in which Shou Lung battles a Dan Inosanto look-alike on the first floor, two underfed sumo wrestlers on the second, and a Black guy in shorts and a cape on the third.

★ BRONSON LEE

Bronson Lee is actually Japanese karate champion and 8th-degree black belt Tadashi Yamashita, who starred in the *Za Karate* trilogy from Toei Studios in which he played a Japanese karate champion and 8th-degree black belt named Tadashi Yamashita. An article in the spring 1977 issue of *Fighting Stars* mentioned that these movies were so successful in Tokyo, "awestruck mobs of curious citizens" followed Yamashita around from a distance, calling him "The Oriental Bronson." When the first film in the trilogy was picked up by New Line Cinema, editor Jack Sholder and dubbing supervisor Joe Ellison of August Films were put in charge of the American cut, and the result—*Bronson Lee, Champion* (1978)—gave Yamashita a new name and replaced his voice with a dubbed hick accent. The only film in which he's actually listed in the credits as Bronson Lee is the Hong Kong actioner *The Magnificent Three* (1979), co-starring Yasuaki Kurata (aka Bruce Lo and Sonny Bruce; see page 138). Yamashita claims to have taught Bruce Lee how to use the nunchuks and can be glimpsed in *Enter the Dragon* hitting Bob Wall with wooden sticks. He's a legitimate championship motorcycle racer back in his native Okinawa and originally moved to the US in 1964 to race but wound up opening a string of dojos instead. Later, he teamed up with Sonny Chiba and Sue Shihomi in *The Soul of Bruce Lee* (1977) and had supporting parts in American action fare like *Seven*, *The Octagon*, and *Gymkata*. *Sword of Heaven* (see page 315) was his ill-fated attempt to break into the US market as an action hero, at a time when he was playing guest villains on television shows like *Knight Rider* and *Gavilan*.

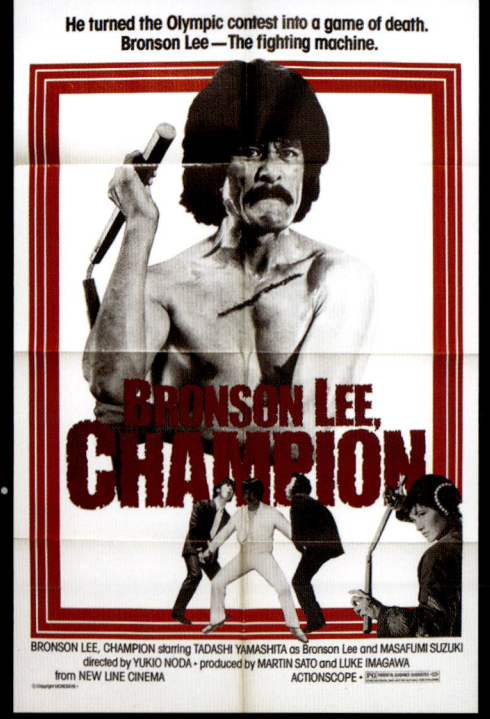

★ BRUCE CHEUNG

Bruce Cheung, a South Korean actor, never really played Bruce Lee in a single film. Instead, he often portrayed the bad guy in movies like *Fists of Bruce Lee*, *Bruce and Shaolin Kung Fu*, and *Dynamo*. He also appeared in a few Chansploitation flicks like *Shaolin Drunken Monkey* (1981), *Revenge of Drunken Master* (1981), and *Jackie and Bruce to the Rescue* (1982). His final performance was in John Woo's grindhouse Vietnam epic, *Heroes Shed No Tears* (1986), playing an evil general turned druglord who spends most of the movie locked in teeny tiny finger handcuffs.

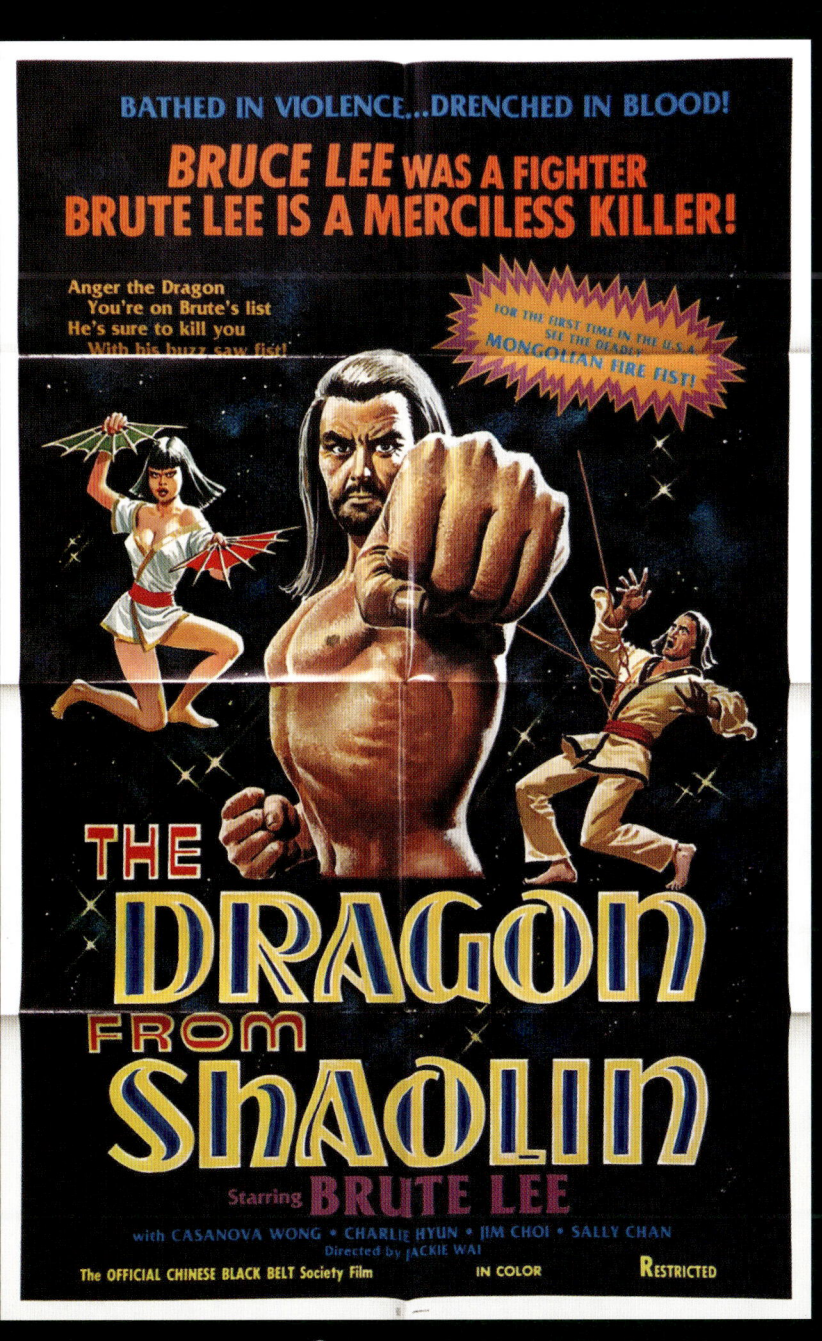

The Dragon from Shaolin was actually *Wonderman of Shaolin* (1979) in US theaters, but on home video, Master Arts slapped that title and some Luis Dominguez poster art onto a print of *Brawl Busters* instead.

★ BRUCE LO AND SONNY BRUCE

Bruce Lo and Sonny Bruce are both Japanese karate star Yasuaki Kurata, who's appeared alongside everyone from Jackie Chan and Sammo Hung to Jet Li and Chow Yun-fat. His father, an established master of Shito-ryu karate, owned a dojo and began instructing him as a youngster. Some visiting Chinese producers discovered him in 1970, and after appearing in numerous martial arts movies filmed in Hong Kong and Taiwan, he returned to Japan to star in the TV series *Fight! Dragon* and co-star with Sonny Chiba in *The Executioner* and with Etsuko Shihomi in *Sister Street Fighter: Hanging by a Thread* (all 1974). Meanwhile, New York distributor Larry Joachim had just signed a three-picture deal with Toei and was looking for a martial arts picture to launch his newly formed Trans-Continental Film Corp. During a screening of *The Executioner*, 14-year-old Marco Joachim whispered to his dad that Kurata looked like Bruce Lee and suggested they give him a new moniker for the trailer. "Witness Bruce Lo as he takes on a dozen skilled fighters, bare-handed!" was added to the narration over footage of Kurata in action. The second Toei title from Trans-Continental was *Which Is Stronger, Karate or Tiger?* (1976), which begins with Kurata karate-chopping live chickens and ends with him wrestling a Bengal tiger. In between, he plays a masked ring fighter called the Iron Man. Trans-Continental released it as *The Tigers Claw* in January 1979, with Kurata billed as Bruce Lo in the advertising. The same year, Howard Mahler Films reissued *Kung Fu—The Invisible Fist* under the title *The Real Dragon* with Kurata billed as Sonny Bruce.

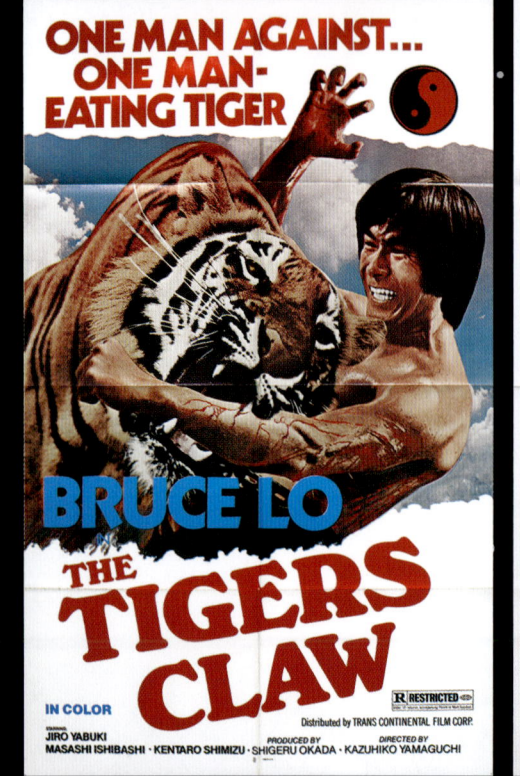

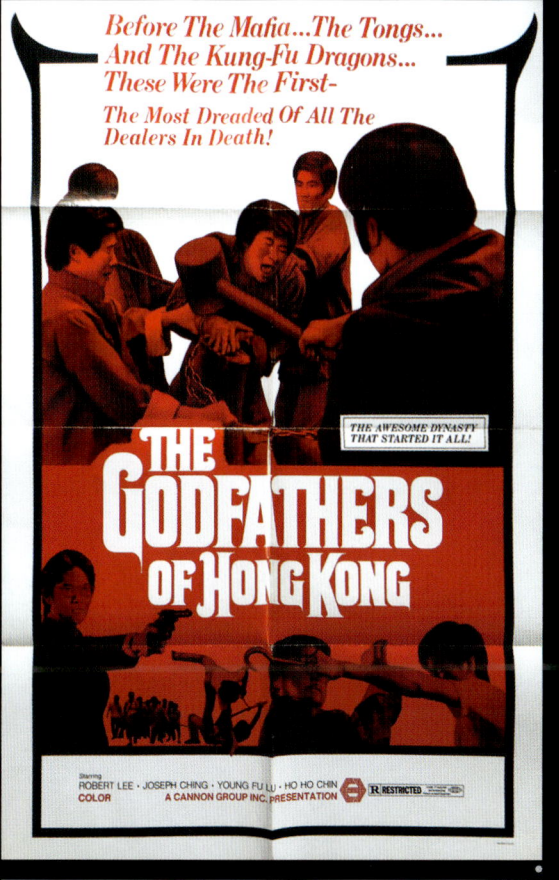

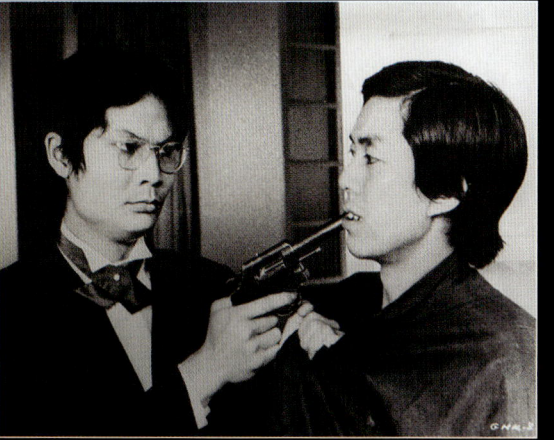

★ ROBERT LEE

The real Robert Lee is Bruce Lee's brother (see page 80), but the one who received billing on some American ads for *The Godfathers of Hong Kong* as "Bruce Lee's brother" is actually a gifted Korean martial artist, Kam Chun-Pak. Always managing to wind up on the wrong side of history, Kam backed Korea's General Park Chung Hee when he staged a military coup in 1961 and later became one of Park's bodyguards. A notorious authoritarian ruler, President Park was assassinated in 1979 by the head of his own intelligence services. Kam went to Vietnam in 1965, where he established a massive dojo in Saigon with over 1,000 students and taught the bodyguards of the notoriously corrupt and repressive prime minister, Nguyen Cao Ky, most famous for stealing elections and running a massive drug smuggling operation. As Vietnam crumbled, Kam moved to Hong Kong, where he enjoyed a brief career in movies before relocating to the United States where he

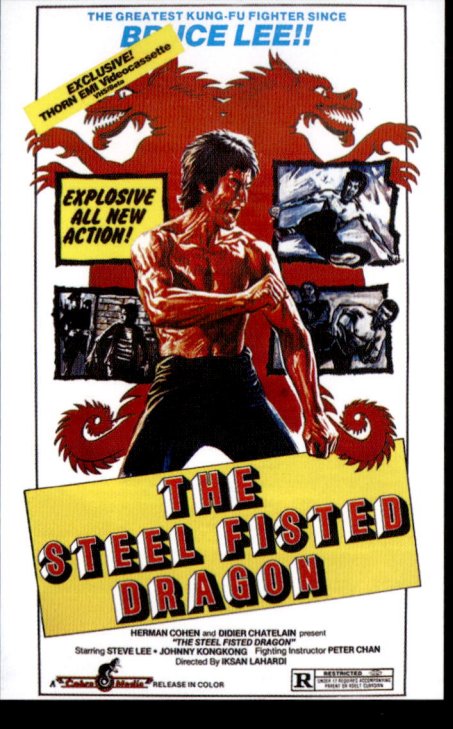

★ BRUCE LEI

Bruce Lei—aka Steve Lee, an Indonesian actor—was in *Cobra* (1977) and *The Steel Fisted Dragon*. Very little information is known about him.

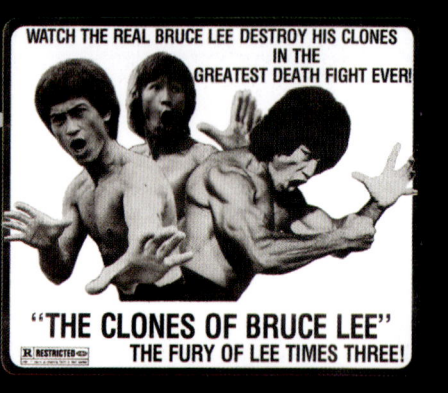

★ BRUCE TAI

Bruce Tai, sometimes billed as Bruce Thai, only appears in *The Clones of Bruce Lee* (see page 120) and the Bruce Le–choreographed Chansploitation flick *Little Master* (1979), both of which were shot in Thailand, leading

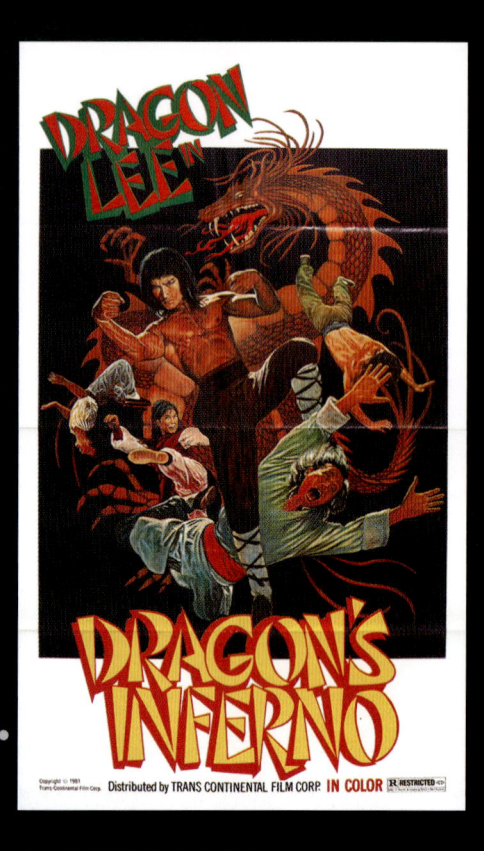

★ BRUCE LAI

Bruce Lai was born Chang Il-Do and became a South Korean martial arts instructor at the American Osan Airbase when he was 17 years old. Later he trained servicemen at the US 8th Army Headquarters before appearing in Dragon Lee movies like *Dragon on Fire* (1978) and *Dragon's Inferno* (aka *Bruce Lee's Ways of Kung Fu*, 1979). He passed away in 2014 at the age of 64.

★ BRUCE LY

Yung Henry Yu wasn't much of a Bruce Lee imitator, despite his billing in this movie, which is actually the poster for *From China with Death* (aka *Wits to Wits*, 1974) with a piece of paper bearing a new title slapped over the bottom. He would be billed as Bruce Ly in *Chinatown Connection* (1990) co-starring with Lee Majors II, and *Open Fire* (1989) in the role of Master Ly opposite David Carradine.

★ BRUCE PAK

Billed as Bruce Pak, Kwak Mu-Seong was a Korean actor who starred in *Return of the Fist of Fury* and later in the South Korean Bruceploitation film *Four Infernos to Cross* (1978).

★ BRUCE K.L. LEA

Bruce K.L. Lea is actually Jun Chong (see page 315), a respected taekwondo instructor, who never wanted to be a Bruce Lee clone. In 1976 he teamed up with action director Lee Doo-Yong to shoot *Visitor to America* on location in Los Angeles. Chong plays a Korean martial artist who comes to LA looking for his uncle, only to discover that he's been murdered by "a Japanese, a black man, a white man, a Mexican, and a cowboy," a witness named Susan explains.

Strapping his uncle's cremated remains around his neck, Lea heads to the nearest belly-dancing joint to drown his sorrows in scotch, then stumbles home, where he's ambushed by a bald-headed Black man in a cape. Lea kills him, gets arrested, gets released, and winds up seducing Susan with acupuncture. Eventually, he discovers that his uncle was mixed up with drug dealers and was probably a drug dealer himself. The movie ends with a desert confrontation that leaves Chong sadder and wiser about the ways of the world while leaving Susan dead.

Terry Levene of Aquarius Releasing acquired the film, which had nothing to do with Bruce Lee, and recruited his trailer editor, Jim Markovic, to turn it into a Bruceploitation movie. Markovic's neighbor let him borrow a tombstone he had lying around in his backyard, and Wayne Weil (see page 156) airbrushed Bruce Lee's name and birth/death dates onto it in gold. Accompanied by a high school student he'd found to play Lee, Markovic drove to a cemetery on Route 17 in Paramus, New Jersey, to find a new final resting place for Bruce. The duo barely had enough time to get a shot of the tombstone in a narrow trench they'd dug before the police arrived and detained them for illegally digging on cemetery property. Neither had criminal records so they were released with a warning, and the actual shot of the high schooler leaping out of a hole in the ground was filmed on the other side of the highway. Add in an optical effect of lightning and a shot of the movie poster and this 20-second prologue of Bruce Lee seemingly jumping out of his own grave becomes all the justification the movie needs to rechristen Jun Chong as Bruce K.L. Lea and to dub in the sound of Lee's cries and shrieks over the soundtrack. Voilà! A Bruceploitation movie is born! Markovic also created the trailer, in which Adolph Caesar reads incredible lies about Lee making a spiritual agreement with the invincible and unbeatable Black Angel of Death to free him from the torment of his grave.

Chong would go on to star in and produce *L.A. Streetfighters* (see page 316) before opening a couple of successful taekwondo schools in LA, while director Lee Doo-Yong would become one of Korea's action exploitation kings, shooting lower-body action films like *Left Foot of Wrath* and *One-Legged Man of Death*.

Aquarius' poster for *Bruce Lee Fights Back from the Grave* brazenly rips off Richard Corben's art for Meat Loaf's *Bat Out of Hell* album.

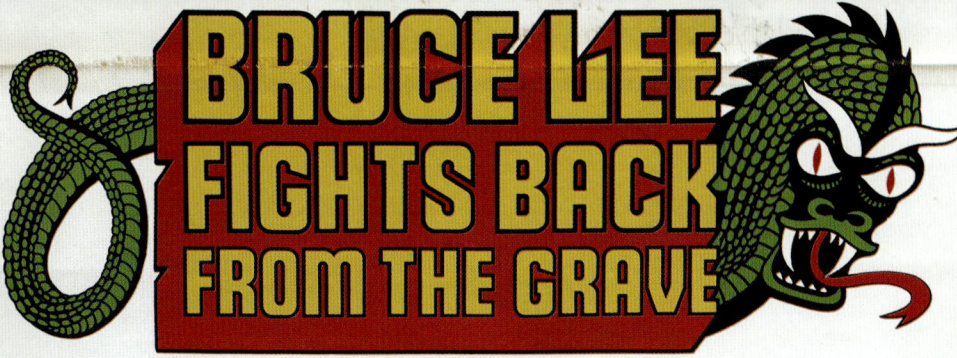

You Can't Keep a Good Man Down!

BRUCE LEE FIGHTS BACK FROM THE GRAVE

R RESTRICTED

also starring DEBORAH CHAPLIN ANTHONY BRONSON STEVE MACK
directed by BERT LENZI music by MAURICE SARLI HEAD GORILLA RELEASING, INC. © 1978 HEAD GORILLA INC.

★ MARTY AND ROCKY LEE

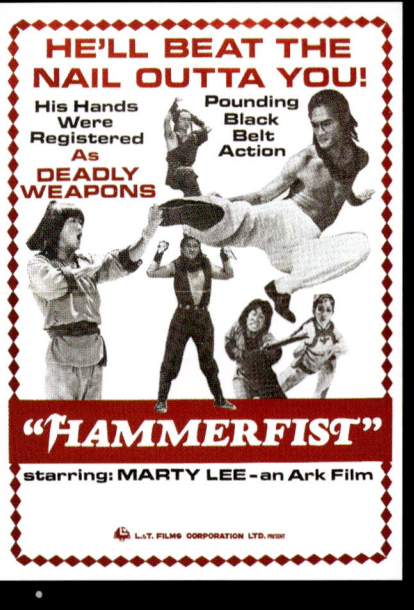

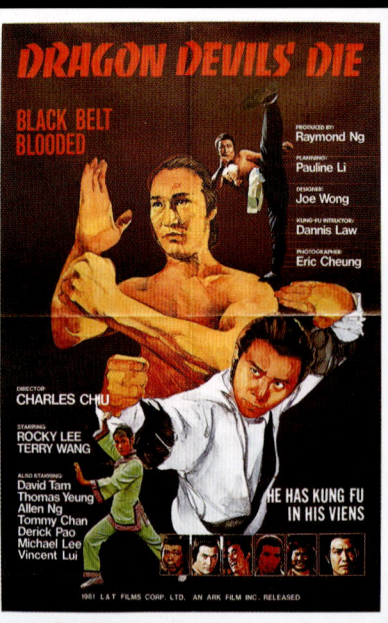

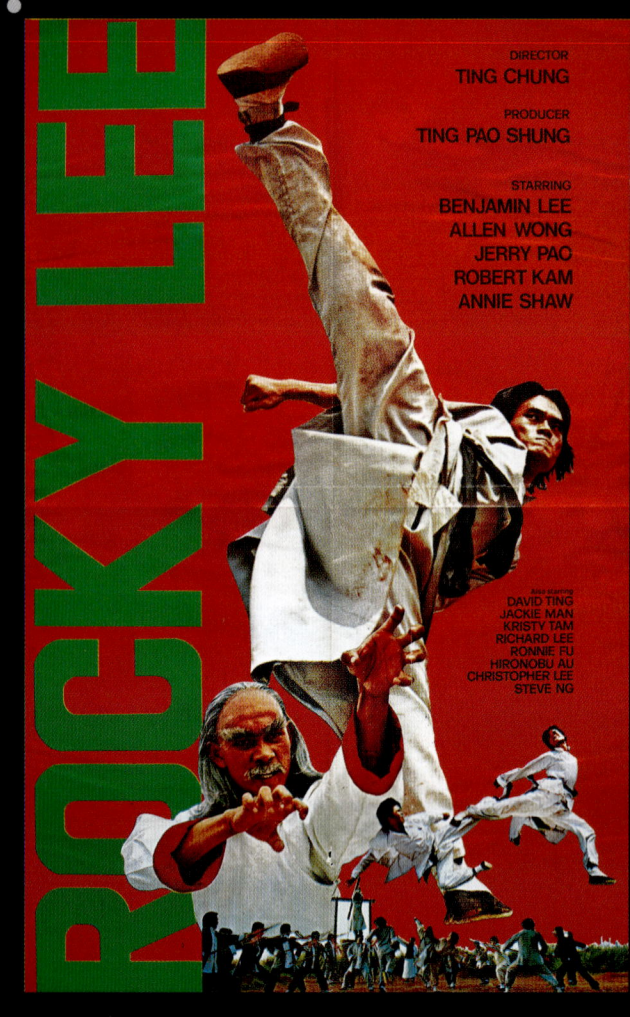

Both Marty and Rocky Lee are actually superkicker John Liu Chung-liang (see page 326). *Hammerfist* is usually called *Renegade Monk* (aka *Shaolin Ex-Monk*, 1978), while *Rocky Lee* is *The Mar's Villa* (1977), a rollicking old-school kung fu flick also known as *Wu Tang Magic Kick*. The Rocky Lee monicker also turns up on the one sheet for *Dragon Devils Die* (aka *Blooded Treasury Fight*, 1979) and seems to be used as a one-off name for another superkicker, Dorian Tan Tao-liang, nicknamed "Flash Legs" for his speedy footwork.

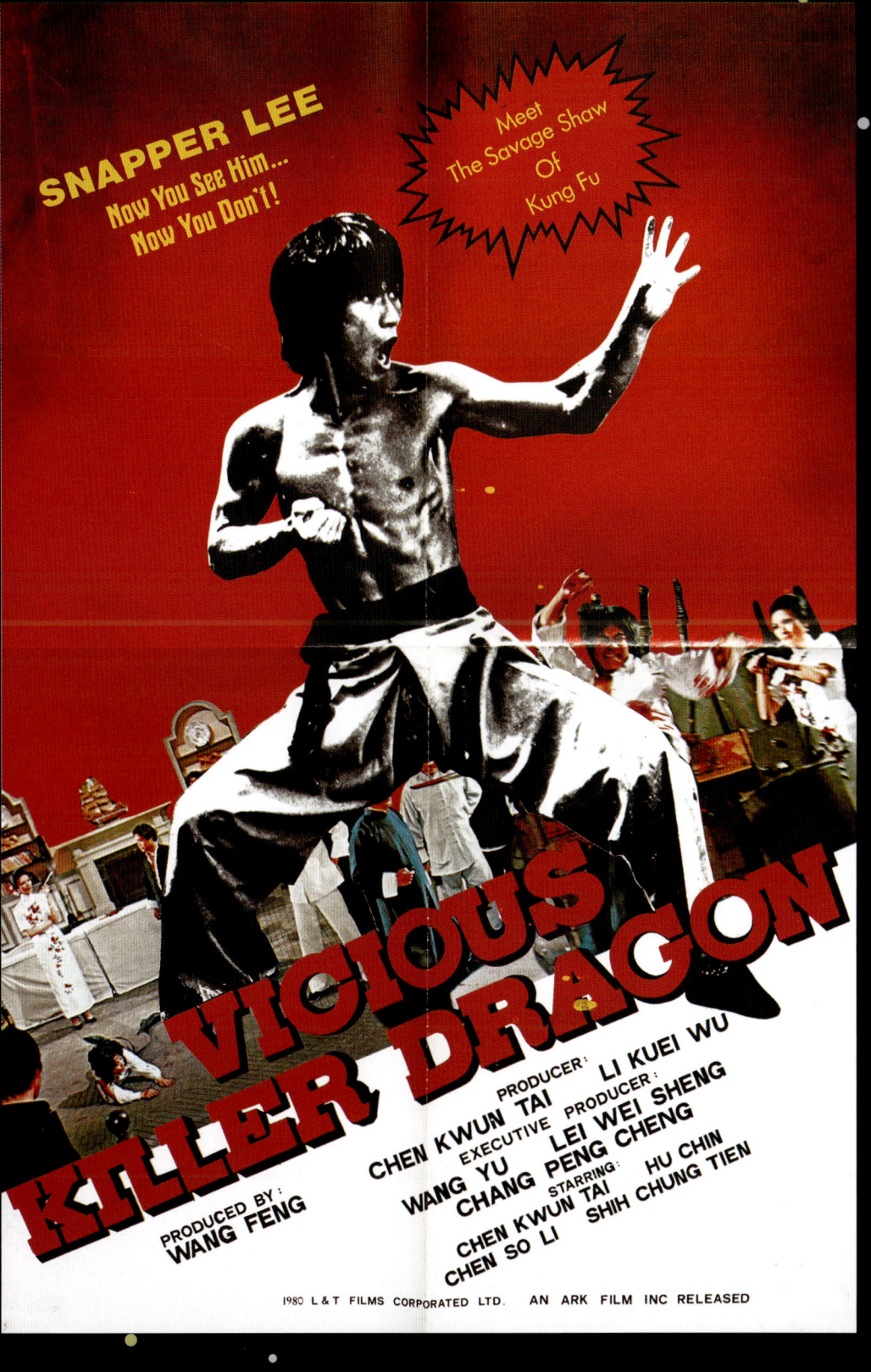

★ SNAPPER LEE

Snapper Lee only appears on this poster for *Vicious Killer Dragon* (aka *Hero from

★ JOHNNY YUNE

Then there was Korean-American Johnny Yune, who starred in the low-budget comedy hit *They Call Me Bruce?* (1982), also released as *A Fistful of Chopsticks*, about a cook named Bruce who is frequently mistaken for a certain kung fu hero and gets conned into becoming a drug smuggler. Yune first attracted attention in the States as a nightclub entertainer who could sing opera, along with other musical styles, in 15 different languages—*Ose Shalom* is his 1975 album of Hebrew tunes. He was also a popular but hokey standup comedian whose numerous appearances on *The Tonight Show Starring Johnny Carson* led to the failed NBC pilot *Sergeant T.K. Yu* (1979), a dramatic comedy in which he played a mild but karate-wise LA police detective from Korea who moonlights as a nightclub singer and comedian. After that, he appeared briefly with Jackie Chan and Michael Hui in the Golden Harvest co-production *The Cannonball Run* (1981) before making his biggest splash with *They Call Me Bruce?*, a video and cable TV staple during the '80s. The immediate followup was supposed to be *Inspector Bruce—Master of Disguise*, but that project fell apart, and by the time *They Still Call Me Bruce* (1987) hit a few dozen theaters on its way to video store shelves, no one seemed to be interested in Yune anymore.

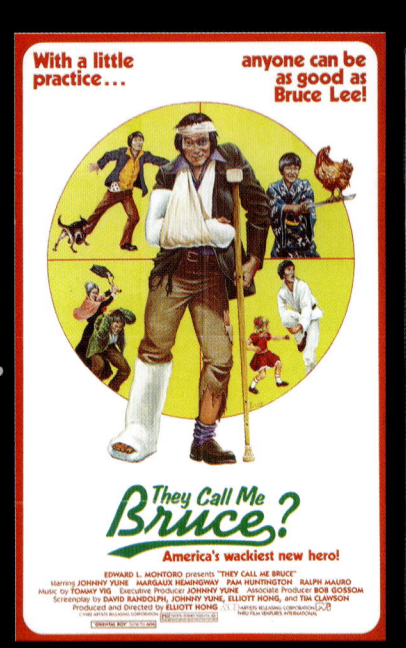

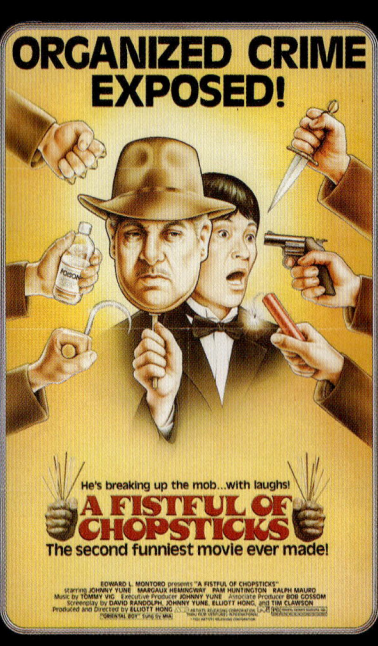

(above) *They Call Me Bruce?* and *A Fistful of Chopsticks* are both the same movie under different titles, released by Film Ventures International, a small-time distributor that would stumble into big bucks, and lots of lawsuits, after ripping off studio fare like *Jaws* and *The Exorcist* (see page 320).

★ EVAN KIM

It wasn't just China and Korea who manufactured artificial Bruces. In the States, Evan Kim did a great Bruce Lee imitation in "A Fistful of Yen," the hilarious 32-minute parody of *Enter the Dragon* and centerpiece of *The Kentucky Fried Movie* (1977), co-starring Master Bong Soo Han, his hapkido teacher. A taekwondo practitioner in real life, Kim showed off his fighting moves as Clint Eastwood's partner in the final Dirty Harry movie, *The Dead Pool* (1988), and worked with Ed Parker and Bong Soo Han on a screenplay for a martial arts movie that never got made. He also played "Suki" in the Golden Harvest–Fox co-production *Megaforce* (1982), a massive sci-fi flop in which the characters wear silver jumpsuits and headbands and ride around on science fiction motorcycles that can fly.

Irene Yah-Ling Sun, Evan Kim are featured in CBS' "Khan" opener Friday at 8 p.m.

★ MYRON BRUCE LEE

Myron Bruce Lee was an actor known as Myron Lee, whose one credit is playing a character named Li in director Al Adamson's second movie starring Jim Kelly, *Death Dimension* (1978; see page 222). Less than two weeks before *Death Dimension* was supposed to start shooting in Hawaii, producer Oscar Nichols needed a Bruce Lee type and remembered a letter that had been published in the local paper two years previously from a guy named Bill Lee who said he one day hoped to portray Bruce in a movie. Nichols ran a piece in the same paper asking Bill Lee to get in touch because he could make his dreams come true. Myron Lee, a karate practitioner and student at the University of Hawaii, responded instead and Nichols put him in the film. The press for *Death Dimension* took great pains to point out that Myron was born in Hong Kong "just like Bruce Lee" (who wasn't) and the local newspaper ads trumpeted, "Introducing Honolulu's Own Myron Bruce Lee. He's Mean Tough and Deadly."

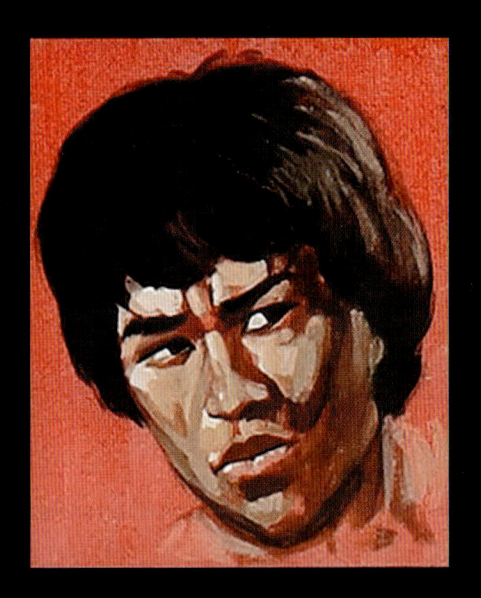

THE PHILIPPINES WERE KNOCKING OFF Bruce Lee movies before anyone. Producer and director Luis San Juan had been making wildly popular James Bond knock-offs back in the '60s like *We Only Live Was-Is* (1968) and *Dr. Yes* (1965), but in 1972 he noticed the popularity of Bruce Lee and cast Ramon Zamora in *The Pig, Boss* (1972).

Zamora had started as a stuntman and dancer before becoming a TV comedian on *Super Laff-In*, where one of his regular characters was a handicapped man possessed by the spirit of a Nazi who had a little Hitler mustache and spoke nonsense German, including his famous tagline, "Spraken-hayt!" But Ferdinand Marcos' television censorship made it hard for him to be funny on broadcast TV, so he moved over to film. In February 1973 he appeared in *The Radical Boxer Challenges the Big Boss*. *Fish of Fury* (1973) came next, then *The King Plaster* (a knock-off of *King Boxer*). A credible imitator, when Bruce Lee died he cemented his franchise with *Shadow of the Dragon* (1973), *Game of Death* (1974), *Return of the Dragon* (1977), and *Bruce Liit* (1978). In *They Call Me Chop Suey* (1975) he plays a kitchen worker haunted by the spirit of Bruce Lee whose secret chop suey ingredient sparks a gang war. Surprisingly, it was a big seller in the European market.

Next came Bruce Ly (Rey Malonzo), who started out in Ramon Zamora movies but quickly began making his own Lee vehicles. First billed as Bruce Ly in *Golden Chaku* (1977), in 1978 he appeared with Ramon Zamora in *Bruce Liit* (1978) a Niño Muhlach vehicle. Niño, a pudgy and wildly popular child star, played the "Bruce" character and Zamora played his dad, a fisherman who's murdered when an evil white landlord tries to take over the fishing trade in their town. Niño goes to train with the classic white-haired kung fu master, where he meets Bruce Ly, another one of his students,

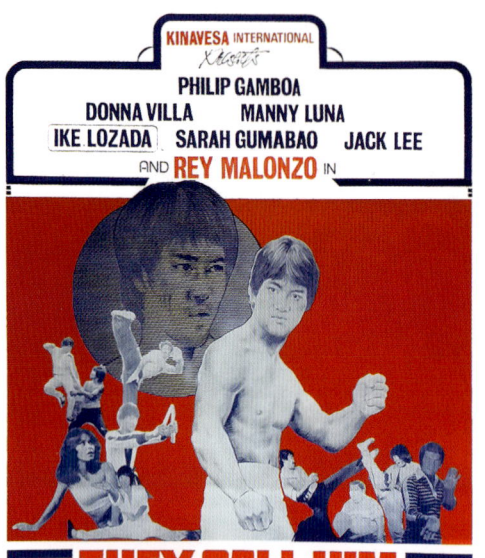

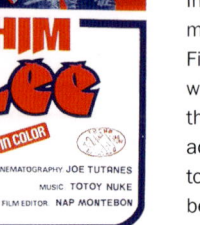

In 1972, President Marcos placed the Philippines under martial law, which would last for the next nine years. Films had to submit their scripts to a censorship board, which had the side effect of ensuring they had scripts in the first place. Action movies made few changes, simply adding an epilogue about how the carnage depicted took place under the old society and everything was all better now under President Marcos.

who reveals that Zamora is still alive. Then the three of them team up to take down the landlord. Ly later became the mayor of the city of Caloocan (the fourth-largest city in the Philippines) from 1995 to 2001, despite facing a recall election in 1996, which he won.

The last of the Filipino Bruce Lees was Trovador Ramos, who was shooting bit parts in Hong Kong movies in 1973 and says that he sparred with Bruce Lee one day at the gym and won. He came back to the Philippines and used that claim to fame to appear in films like *Red Belt Masters* (1974), which turned him into a small-time celebrity, even though he never actually imitated Bruce Lee onscreen.

Lasing Master

BUONG KASIYAHANG INIHAHANDOG NG EMPEROR FILMS International, Inc.

CHIQUITO
PANCHITO · TINTOY & NIDA BLANCA in

Akala nila sila'ng original, di nila alam, nasa atin ang genuine. Sa technique at style taob si Jacky Chan. Master sa lahat ng bagay bago sumabak, ubos, ang tagay!!!

LASING MASTER

MAX ALVARADO · TSING TONG TSAI
TONY CARRION · ELY ROQUE
introducing DEBRA LIZ featuring TATLONG PINOY

directed by JOSE 'Pepe' WENCESLAO

Fung Ku

R.V.Q. Productions, Inc. proudly presents

DOLPHY · LOTIS KEY

FUNG KU in COLOR

starring **CRISTINA REYES** and **EDDIE GARCIA**

co-starring JOAQUIN FAJARDO · ERNIE ORTEGA · CARLOS DIAZ · GOLA ER 'CANTON' SALAZAR · JAY GRAMA · PMP STUNTMEN and the SOS DAREDEVILS
featuring EDISON YU · POLO CHI

MUSIC: ERNANI CUENCO
CINEMATOGRAPHY: MANUEL BOLITANO
STORY & SCREENPLAY: ADDING FERNANDO
DIRECTION: JOSE 'Pepe' WENCESLAO

Pinoy Boxer

TETRA VISION FILMS presents

JACK LEE ★ CECILLE CASTILLO ★ BOY FERNANDEZ
AND **REY MALONZO**

PINOY BOXER

ERNIE ORTEGA · DON PEPOT
MATIMTIMAN CRUZ
PONS DE GUZMAN

INTRODUCING ALLAN SHISHIR · JET SAHARA
CINEMATOGRAPHY: POL CUENCO
SCREENPLAY: NANING ESTRELLA
DIRECTION: LEONARDO 'DING' PASCUAL

The Pig Boss

LUIS SAN JUAN PRODUCTIONS PRESENTS
A DAJ BROS. FILMS INITIAL OFFE[RING]

RAMON ZAMORA
VINA MORENA · JANE LAUREL

IN HIS BIGGEST AND MOST EXCITING R[OLE]

NEVER BEFORE!!!! IN LOCAL MOVIES HAVE YOU SEEN SUCH AN ASTONISHING, FANTASTIC AND AUTHENTIC ART OF SELF-DEFENSE

...AS MASTERED THE WRONG M[AN] IT'S FUNNI[ER] MORE HILARIO[US] WONDE[RFUL] FU[N] SIMI[LAR] O[NE] OF T[HE] WOR[LD] FASCINATI[NG] OUTRAGEO[US] DEVASTAT[ING] AND DEADLY

SPECIAL GUEST STAR **AMANDA SUAREZ**

THE PIG, BOSS

BEN PEREZ · SORAYA and VIC GAZA '72 KARATE CHAMPION
TANGE · BALOT · PABO · PEPOT GOLAY · PENGGOT · MENGGAY
JOANN GRIFFITH · RUDY EVANGELISTA · LARRY ESGUERRA · JESS SANTOS and the SOS DAREDEVILS
INTRODUCING MONINA ROJO and MENCHIE PALMA

STORY & SCREEN PLAY: JUN SAN JUAN
CINEMATOGRAPHY: SUSING M. CORPUS
MUSIC: PABLO VERGARA
DIRECTION: LUIS SAN JUAN

TO BE FILMED ABROAD IN FULL COLOR! DIRECTION LUIS SAN JUAN
THE FRIENDS CONNECTED

Lasing Master (1980) was a Filipino version of Jackie Chan's *Drunken Master*, while *Fung Ku* (1973) parodied David Carradine's *Kung Fu* TV show. *Pinoy Boxer* (1980) sent up *King Boxer*, the original title of *Five Fingers of Death*, while *The Pig, Boss* (1972) was *The Big Boss*. *The Dragon, the Lizard, the Boxer* (1977) mocked Shaw Brothers' *The Five Venoms*, *Iking Boxer* (1973) parodied *King Boxer*, and so did *King Plaster* (1972).

WAY OF THE DRAGON (1972) had cleaned up at the American box office when Bryanston released it as *Return of the Dragon* in 1974, with audiences lining up around the block to see the "new" Bruce Lee flick, so Raymond Chow knew a market still existed for Bruce Lee, and he knew where he could find some unseen footage. He'd dragged his feet for as long as possible, but he finally sucked it up and paid Linda Lee $200,000 for the rights to the 100 minutes of footage Lee had shot back in 1972 for his philosophical martial arts movie. Chow hired Robert Clouse to direct, and hired Korean actor Kim Tae-Jeong to play Bruce Lee, re-naming him "Tang Long," the name of Lee's character in *Way of the Dragon*.

A sequel to *Way*, *Game of Death* kicks off with recycled footage of the Bruce Lee / Chuck Norris fight from the end of *Way* being interrupted by a falling light that almost kills Lee, now portrayed by Tang Long and called Billy Lo. Turns out, Billy Lo's "accident" comes courtesy of the Mafia, who make their home on the upper floors of the Red Pepper Restaurant. They control the entertainment industry with an iron hand, but Billy Lo won't fight in their tournaments and they must quash his rebellion before the other celebrities under their thumb start getting ideas.

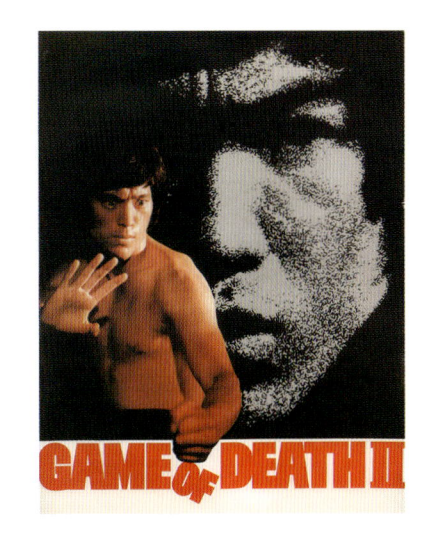

Tang Long is depicted as Bruce Lee via the jankiest techniques possible: shooting him through plants, slatted screens, from a long way away, or while he covers his face with hand towels, enormous sunglasses, or both at the same time. When he fights, he's doubled by Yuen Biao, one of Jackie Chan's Chinese Opera School brothers, and throughout the movie the camera keeps cutting to reaction shots of the actual Bruce Lee cobbled together from his movies—in one case, superimposing a photograph of Bruce Lee's face over Tang Long's reflection in a mirror.

This constant cutting to footage of Lee's actual face gives the impression that Tang Long is some kind of shapeshifting were-Bruce struggling against a rising full moon. Finally, he can no longer resist the urge and transforms completely into Bruce for the 11-minute climax, consisting of footage Lee actually shot and cut for *Game of Death*, as he advances through the upper floors of the Red Pepper Restaurant and battles his former student, Dan Inosato, Korean hapkido master Ji Han-Jae, and American basketball star Kareem Abdul-Jabbar.

Game made almost $10 million in the US alone. Golden Harvest promised hitmaker Ng See-yuen unseen footage of Bruce to use if he agreed to deliver a *Game* sequel. Reluctantly, Tang Long signed on, which is when Ng discovered that all that unseen footage didn't exist. Recruiting ace action choreographer Yuen Wo-ping (*The Matrix*; *Crouching Tiger, Hidden Dragon*), famous Korean super-kicker Hwang Jang-Lee, and a ton of Hong Kong's best stunt players (Yuen Biao, Corey Yuen), he delivered *Tower of Death*,(1981), an over-the-top remake of *Enter the Dragon*.

Tang returned to South Korea, where he made action hits like *Miss Please Be Patient* (1981) and *Jackie vs. Bruce to the Rescue* (1982) with Taiwanese Jackie Chan imitator Lee Siu-ming. Although he didn't want to imitate Bruce any more after doing *Tower of Death* he agreed to play the ghost of Bruce Lee in Ng See-yuen's American co-production, *No Retreat, No Surrender* (1986; see page 332).

Bruce Lee wasn't the first star to take martial arts movies into the American mainstream, but he was the one everyone wanted to be. An army of cheap knock-offs couldn't tarnish his legacy, and his shadow would loom over every kung fu movie for the rest of the decade.

TIMES SQUARE AND 42ND STREET are not the same thing. When it comes to movie exhibition 42nd Street, aka the Deuce, is a world unto itself. The ten theaters on the strip between 7th and 8th Avenues were built between 1900 and 1920 and were successful playhouses for legit stage productions until the the Great Depression, when, one by one, eight of the playhouses converted to motion picture exhibition under ownership of either Brandt Theaters or Cinema Circuit, and two became burlesque houses.

Studio-owned theater chains like Loew's and RKO had theaters around the corner and they didn't appreciate the sudden competition and either squeezed these exhibitors for more money per booking or denied them access to the newest movies. Left to fend for themselves, the 42nd Street grind theaters resorted to carny tactics to capture customers, constructing flashy fronts covered with stills and poster art, changing the titles of their movies to accentuate their racier elements, and even pulling a few dirty tricks along the way. The same day the RKO Palace in Times Square started running a film of the Primo Carnera vs. Max Baer title fight as an "exclusive Broadway showing," one of the 42nd Street grinders booked the year-old *The Prizefighter and the Lady*, which featured a staged bout between the fighters, and advertised it as *Baer vs. Carnera*. RKO "nearly burst a corporate blood vessel trying to stop the Brandts."

The public embraced the carnival atmosphere. In 1941 alone, 10 million patrons bought tickets to the eight movie theaters on 42nd Street, and in 1956 the theaters brought in $5 million in ticket sales. Pinball arcades, shooting galleries, Fascination game parlors, novelty shops, cafeterias, Automats, hot dog stands, and pizza joints filled the spaces between theaters and spilled over into Times Square.

Most of the theaters started grinding away at 8 or 9am, shutting down their projectors at 4 in the morning. Ticket prices varied from one theater to the next but were always cheaper than in the Broadway houses around the corner, and each theater had its own booking policy. The Apollo always showed foreign films, while the Times Square Theater next door specialized in westerns and action movies.

By the early '70s, hookers in hot pants pounded the pavement outside the cinemas, which were subjected to constant visits by cops looking for escaped cons and bail jumpers. The NYPD's Missing Persons Unit made regular visits to the grindhouses and the Port Authority Bus Terminal across 8th Avenue to search for runaways who'd step off Greyhounds from the Midwest directly into this intense slice of urban chaos.

"People that didn't know what to do with their time, didn't have a job—they'd waste their time away in a movie theater watching kung fu movies," remembers Taimak, star of *The Last Dragon* (see page 351), who frequented the 42nd Street theaters as a teenager. "They'd smoke weed, half of them, and it became a cultish environment that wasn't necessarily violent. It wasn't very safe either for a young guy to be in there. I was like 13, 14 years old. But I was just mesmerized by the martial arts."

In 1974, ABC decided to cancel *Kung Fu* after David Carradine ate some peyote, got naked, and wandered around his Laurel Canyon neighborhood, breaking a neighbor's window, bleeding all over the place, and accusing innocent bystanders of being witches. It wasn't a good look for a network television star. Prime time would be largely kung fu–free for the rest of the decade, but that's okay, because kung fu movies were all over the big screen, from Flagstaff to Fort Lauderdale.

The heart of this beast lay in Times Square, where most independent distributors made their homes. America's first indie distributors had been a loose-knit gang of grifters, carnies, and con artists known collectively as the Forty Thieves, who traveled the country in the '30s and '40s, showing full-frontal childbirth films and nightmare-inducing venereal disease reels in tents pitched outside the city limits.

By the '60s they'd ditched their tents and started shipping their prints from office suites in Times Square, but otherwise not much had changed. Bare-knuckle carnival barkers with too much confidence and not enough shame, distributors like William Mishkin paid off theater owners with cufflinks and cash to get the best bookings for his faded prints of recycled and recut movies ("These pictures were old enough to vote," one colleague said) while Joseph Brenner tried to re-release *Birth of a Nation* in 1970, sparking an NAACP protest.

Times Square also housed more corporate and upscale companies like Commonwealth United, a multimillion-dollar powerhouse formed after a real estate holding company with too much cash acquired a TV company, and then got into production and theatrical distribution of made-for-TV movies that never should've seen the light of a projector.

Commonwealth collapsed in 1970 and AIP bought the remains, offering jobs to many of its employees, but four of them chose to strike out on their own: Mel Maron, their sales manager in New York, formed Maron Films; Terry Levene, also in New York, formed Aquarius Releasing (see page 166); Richard Ellman, in LA, founded Ellman Film Enterprises (see page 66); and Wayne Weil, their advertising guru, went to work for the prestigious Shorlane-Benet advertising agency, located in the Selwyn Building, right upstairs from the Aquarius offices, where he'd create some of the most outrageous movie posters and ad campaigns of the day. These men became some of the kingpins of kung fu distribution, releasing everything from *Fearless Fighters* (see page 66) to *Queen Boxer* (see page 126) while desperately trying to fill the gap left by Bruce Lee.

> **EBONY FIST AWARD TO "TNT" STAR**
>
> Jeanne Bell, currently being praised as the new superstar in the black galaxy for her starring role in New World Pictures' TNT JACKSON, has been further honored with the coveted Ebony Fist Award, bestowed upon her by a nonpartisan panel of judges, martial arts experts and film industry figures. Jeanne was cited for her "expert form, flexibility and muscle tone" as demonstrated in the abundant action sequences of TNT JACKSON. Ms. Bell, who beat out such other contenders as Tamara Dobson, Pam Grier and Vonetta McGee for the career-boosting prize, stated "this is not only a great honor for myself, but for black women as a whole."

(left) When they awarded Jeanne Bell the fictitious Ebony Fist Award, the New World Pictures marketing department made sure to throw some shade on the competition.

(opposite page) However, when they declared Jillian Kesner winner of the North American Black Belt Olympics, they couldn't be bothered to spell her name correctly.

See
JILLIAN KESSNER
1981 Winner
North American
Black Belt Olympics
R. Croci
FIRECRACKER
She'll Blow You Away!
Starring JILLIAN KESNER • DARBY HINTON with KEN METCALFE • CHANDA ROMERO • TONY FERRER
VIC DIAZ • REYMOND KING • Screenplay by KEN METCALFE and CIRIO H. SANTIAGO • Produced by SYED KECHIK • Directed by CIRIO H. SANTIAGO
Additional Scenes Directed by ALAN HOLZMAN • A NEW WORLD PICTURE © NEW WORLD PICTURES 1981
R RESTRICTED UNDER 17 REQUIRES ACCOMPANYING PARENT OR ADULT GUARDIAN
NSS 810061

There are many ways to kill a man...

He knew them all!

THERE IS NO MATCH FOR

MACROMAN

Starring
ARAUJO (THE MASTER) • **ENYAW LIEW** • **JERRY RAGES** • Executive Producer **FRANK PRATT**
Directed by **TED KNIGHT** • Produced by **N.I. ROLF** • AN ede FILMS PRESENTATION

R RESTRICTED
Under 17 requires accompanying Parent or Adult Guardian

© COPYRIGHT 1980 ede FILMS / ALL RIGHTS RESERVED

DESIGN / CINEMA HORIZONS • NEW YORK

Distributors recycled and repurposed their prints for as long as possible. The 1974 Aquarius release, *Forced to Fight*, got edited into the middle of their *Fist of Fear, Touch of Death* (see page 108) in 1980, then reissued as *Kung Fu of the Five Hand Ninja Gang* in 1983, as *Butchers from Hell* in 1985, and as *Blood Kick* in 1988.

Dealing with relatively unknown Asian movies, no one could contradict whatever distributors plastered on their posters. When New World Pictures readied the release of *TNT Jackson* (1974), a kung fu *Cleopatra Jones* cash-in shot in the Philippines, someone quickly realized that if they hoped to gain any kind of credibility with the "Kiyah!" crowd, they'd better promote leading lady Jeanne Bell as something other than *Playboy*'s Miss October 1969. That's when their head of marketing and promotion, Jon Davison, decided to name her the winner of the non-existent Ebony Fist Award.

Making even less sense are the billing blocks, especially on the posters created by Shorlane-Benet's Cinema Horizons. They needed these blocks to make the movies look legit, but often the distributor had no idea who appeared in the movie. The credits on *Bruce Lee Fights Back from the Grave* were lifted from the same year's *Brutal Justice*, with Aquarius Releasing—the distributor of both—hiding behind the handle Head Gorilla Releasing. No one seems to know who was behind EDE Films, a company that put out three kung fu movies in 1980, but the billing blocks on the posters are total fabrications. There's an actor named Marshall Art in *Kung Fu of the 8 Drunkards*, and one of the stars of *The Lost Kung Fu Secret* is the typeface Helios Bold. Araujo, the credited star of *Machoman*, is the surname of Shorlane-Benet's bookkeeper. A freelance artist for the agency is listed as director for two of the movies. One of the producers, Enyaw Liew, is Wayne Weil spelled backwards.

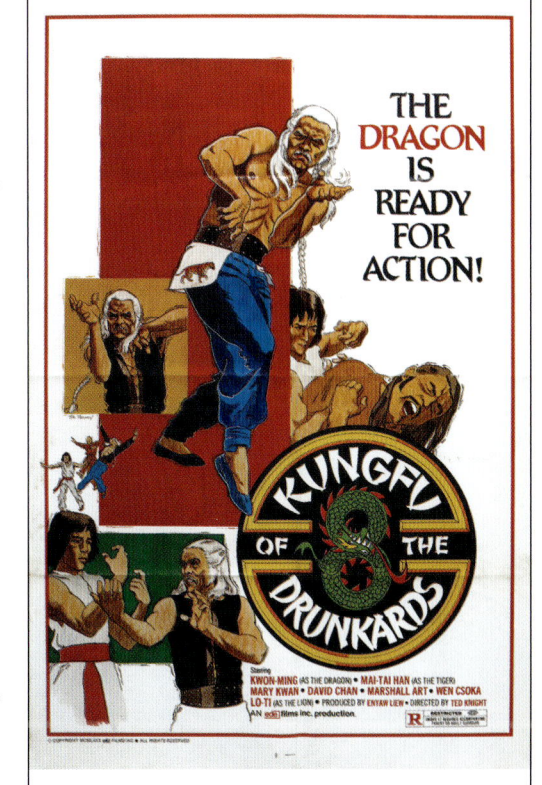

(opposite page and above, top) Tom Tierney painted the posters for *Machoman* and *Kung Fu of the 8 Drunkards*. For more on Tierney, see page 165.

(above, bottom) Graphic design humor: The stars of *The Lost Kung Fu Secret*, David Chiang and Paul Chang Chung, were renamed after typesetting fonts for the film's US release.

DEADLIER THAN CHIBA, QUICKER THAN "THE JUICE"
LOOK OUT BABY, CAUSE...

BRUCE is LOOSE

Starring
Lee Bruce
the only star who could
play the part written for
Bruce Lee!

"THE MOST VIOLENT, SPECTACULAR FIGHTING WE'VE EVER SEEN"
— KUNG FU EXPRESS

NEVER SHOWN BEFORE!

Starring LEE BRUCE with LO LIEH • YUEN HUA
and SHANG KUAN LING FUNG

COLOR AN OFFICIAL CHINESE BLACK BELT SOCIETY FILM
RESTRICTED ADMISSION NO ONE UNDER 17 WILL BE ADMITTED WITHOUT PARENT OR ADULT GUARDIAN

© 1980 WILLIAM MISHKIN MOTION PICTURES INC.

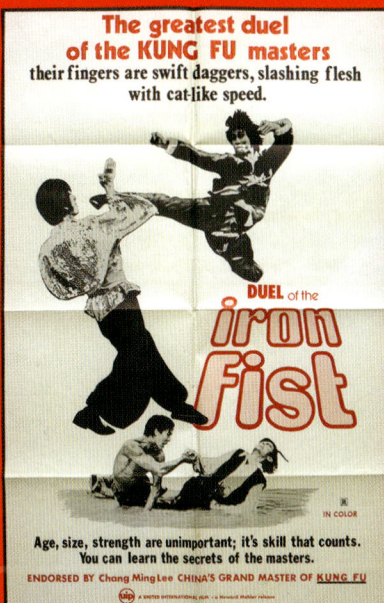

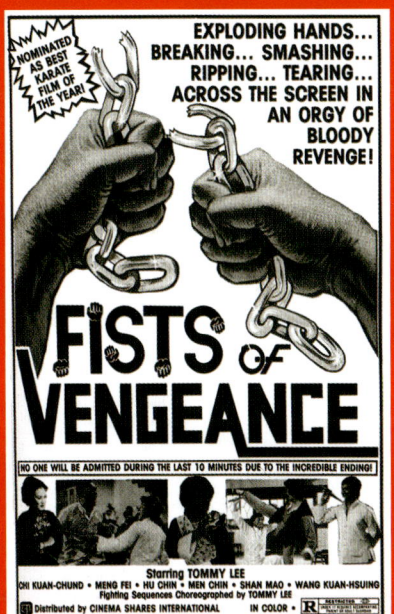

(opposite page, and this page top, left) *Bruce is Loose* (1977) and *Brawl Busters* (1978) were released by William Mishkin under his Extraordinary Films label. Best known today for producing nudies and Andy Milligan horror movies, Mishkin switched to action in the late '70s and was the New York subdistributor for Ark Films, Unifilm International, and other companies that dealt in kung fu movies.

(top, right) *Duel of the Iron Fist* was not endorsed by Chang Ming Lee, China's Grand Master of Kung Fu, because he doesn't exist. Similarly, *Fists of Vengeance* (1973) was never nominated as the Best Karate Film of the Year by anyone except its own distributor.

New World later made the Filipino co-production *Firecracker* with virtually the same script, only this time with blonde-haired Jillian Kesner in the lead and with a soundtrack stolen from 1980's *Shogun Assassin*. The poster misspells Kesner's name, but that's okay because it also calls her "1981 Winner, North American Black Belt Olympics," which didn't exist.

Several movies were endorsed by the fictitious "Official Chinese Black Belt Society," while *Fists of the Double K* received the approval of the even more exclusive "Royal K/K Society" and the ads for *Martial Monks* crowed that it had won "The Hong Kong Black Belt Award." No one is a grandmaster of kung fu unless you're talking about the mysterious and nonexistent Chang Ming Lee, who endorsed *Duel of the Iron Fist* on its poster, and the ad campaign for *Brawl Busters* features pull quotes from *Kung Fu Express*, a publication that has yet to publish a single issue. And then there's *Last Fist of Fury*, which was "Nominated Best Picture of '78 in Asia." It wasn't.

And independent distributors always announced more projects than they delivered. Harry Hope really meant to make *Enter Another Dragon* starring John Saxon, Ron Van Clief, and Bruce Le, and even commissioned revolutionary comic book artist Neal Adams to design a poster. When the project fell through, Cinematic Releasing used the artwork for their Dragon Lee movie, *Enter Three Dragons*. And there really were plans to make *Ilsa Meets Bruce Lee in the Devil's Triangle* in 1976, starring a TBD Bruce Lee impersonator and Dyanne Thorne of the unsavory Nazi sexploitation *Ilsa* movies. Thorne even began training for the movie, which ultimately fell apart before anyone even wrote the script, but not before someone designed an ad. Because, after all, the ad was the most important part of any movie.

(opposite page) The artwork for Serafim Karalexis's *Enter Three Dragons* is the only evidence this unproduced movie exists. It's often confused with Harry Hope's equally unproduced *Enter Another Dragon*. Tangentially, Hope was one of the few American producers who spoke Mandarin and he claimed to always hire Hong Kong stunt choreographers for his movies. "When the action in a film slows down," he said, "people get up and go to the restrooms and the snack bar. But the minute the action starts again, bam, they're back to watch the bam-bam!"

starring **DRAGON LEE** and **RON VAN CLIEF**

ENTER THREE DRAGONS

A MADISON WORLD FILM

SERAFIM KARALEXIS PRESENTS

starring DRAGON LEE • RON VAN CLIEF • ROY HORTON • LISA HAYS
co-starring JASON PAI POW • MENG FU • THOMSON KAO KAN   written by LOUIS FENG
photography by YUE CHAN   action directors YUEN PING & SHU HSIA   edited by JIM MARCOVIC
Produced by SERAFIM KARALEXIS   Co-Produced by YEO BAN YEE   Directed by ERIC LANGSTON
PG PARENTAL GUIDANCE SUGGESTED   CINEMASCOPE   IN COLOR   distributed by CINEMATIC RELEASING CORP.
©Copyright by S. Karalexis

LUIS DOMINGUEZ

"**On October 17, 1923,** an eerie-looking baby was born in the beautiful city of Cordoba, Argentina!" crowed an editorial in the December 1972 issue of *Eerie*. That baby was Luis Dominguez, an incredibly prolific artist who worked for a lot of the lower-tier comic book companies in the United States that often farmed out work to artists in South America and the Philippines to take advantage of lower page rates. After moving to the States in 1959, he worked for Charlton and Gold Key comics on dozens of western, war, and horror titles before hooking up with prestigious DC Comics in the '70s. His art for DC mostly consisted of covers for titles like *House of Mystery*, *House of Secrets*, *Weird War Tales*, *Weird Western Tales*, *Jonah Hex*, and *Ghosts*—in fact, he drew over half of the covers for *Ghosts*, which ran for 112 issues. He earned a place in cover artist Valhalla, however, for his work on *Unexpected* #202, which featured his fearsome, fanged Easter Bunny about to kill and eat three children on an Easter egg hunt.

Dominguez would also paint covers for Warren's *Vampirella* and *Eerie* magazines and two 1975 issues of Marvel's *Deadly Hands of Kung Fu* (#13, #16). In the '80s, he painted numerous movie posters for 21st Century Distribution, Silverstein Films, Bedford Entertainment, Almi Pictures, and other New York–based companies, most of them in the martial arts and horror genres. Dominguez passed away in Miami, Florida, on July 1, 2020, at 97 years old.

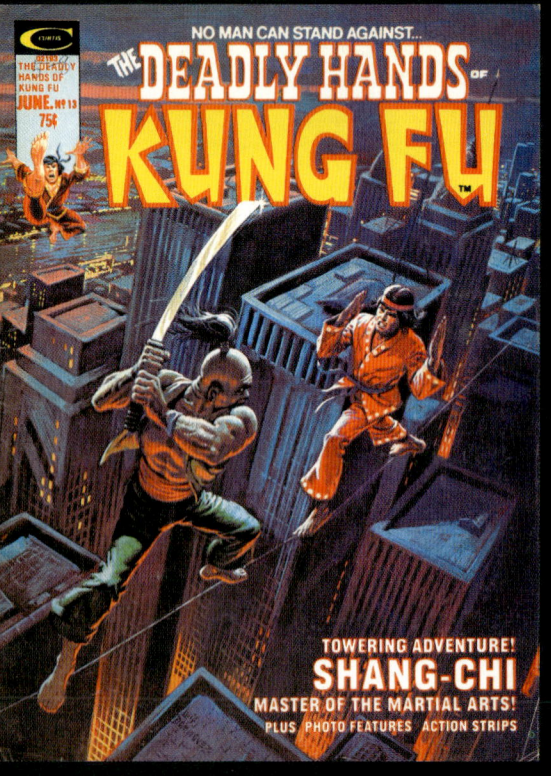

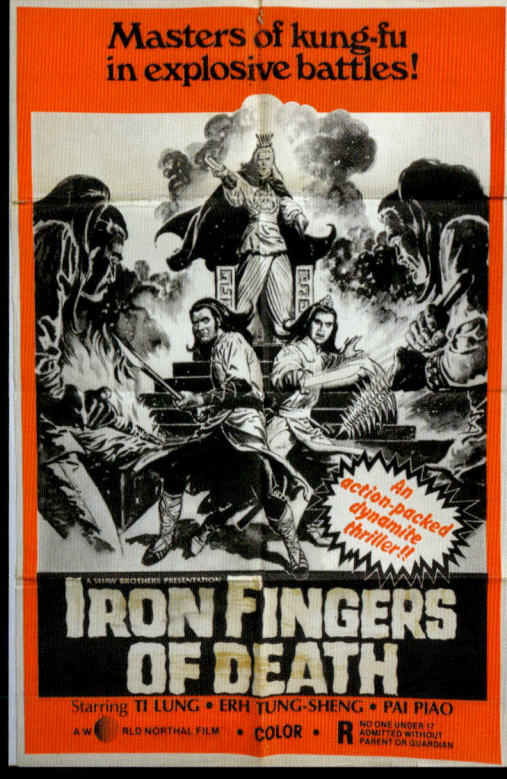

TOM TIERNEY

TOM TIERNEY PAINTED THE POSTER for *Machoman* and several other kung fu releases in the '70s and '80s, and his bold graphic style stood out from the pack. Born in Beaumont, Texas, he moved to New York City after getting out of the Army in 1953, determined to become a commercial artist. Although he joked about living off "ketchup soup," he actually landed on his feet quickly and became one of the most successful fashion illustrators of the '60s and '70s, with his work appearing in everything from *Reader's Digest* to *Playboy*.

In 1976, he created a book of paper dolls as a gift for his mother, containing images of her favorite movie stars of the '30s, like Clark Gable and Jean Harlow. A literary agent saw the one-of-a-kind creation and sold it to Dover, who published it as *Thirty from the '30s*. The book was so successful that it sparked a paper doll revival and Tierney went on to create at least 350 paper doll books, selling over four million copies.

He painted movie posters for the ad agency Shorlane-Benet and also illustrated numerous Barbie and Jem and the Holograms books for children. His final paper doll book was of Pope Francis, which was completed right before Tierney's death in 2014.

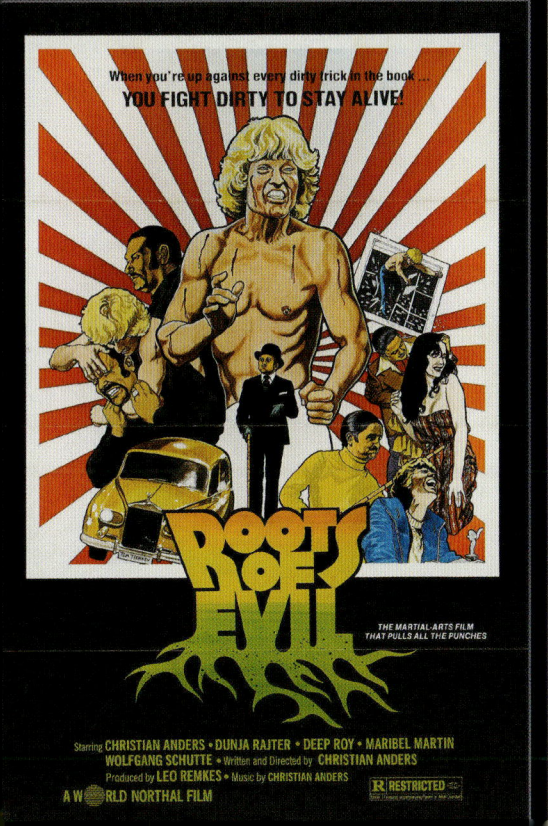

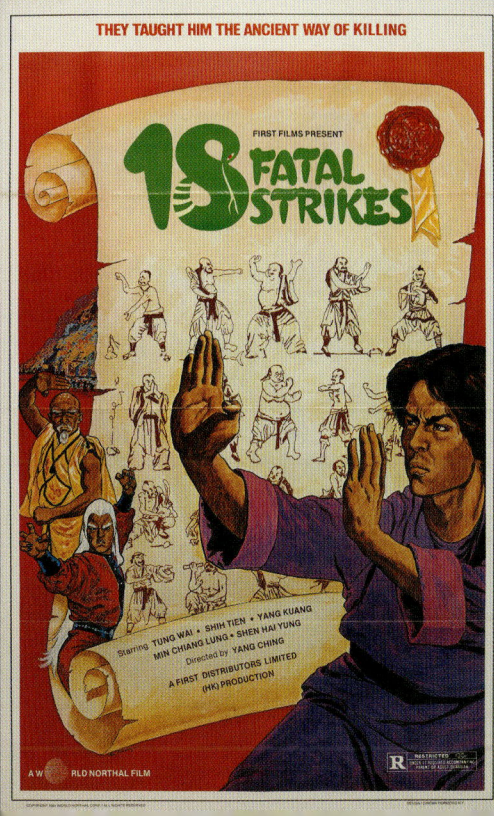

DIRECTORY OF DISTRIBUTORS

AQUARIUS RELEASING, INC.

The son of movie theater owners, Terry Levene worked for Fox and Columbia before joining Commonwealth United in 1968 as their Eastern Division sales manager, working under Mel Maron. When the company went bankrupt and AIP took over their library, Levene left to form his own company, Aquarius Releasing, in February 1970.

The general manager of Brandt's 42nd Street Theaters offered Levene a tiny office in the Selwyn Building rent-free until the company started making money, which didn't take long, since Aquarius quickly found its niche handling adult films for West Coast producer/distributors like David F. Friedman (*Thar She Blows*) and Bob Cresse (*Love Camp 7*) who wanted to see their softcore porn get wider play. Aquarius moved into suite 301 of the Selwyn, where the former dressing room of stars like Al Jolson and James Cagney became Levene's office.

Aquarius' "Adult Showcase" network of theaters grew to over 20 venues throughout New York's five boroughs, but hardcore came with big headaches, and after three years of costly, time-consuming, and downright harrowing legal issues—including a federal indictment for conspiracy and interstate transportation of an obscene film after he put a 35mm porn print of *Belinda* (1972) on a Greyhound bus that passed through New Jersey and Pennsylvania on its way to a booking in Buffalo—Levene had enough of the adult movie biz.

In the summer of '73, Levene moved on to Asian action movies. His first notable post-porno pic was, incredibly, a kiddie matinee called *Kung Fu Kids*, then came *Queen Boxer*, and after that the hits just kept coming: *Women in Cell Block 7*, *The Tongfather*, *Forced to Fight*, *Kung Fu Massacre*, *The Black Dragon vs. the Yellow Tiger*, *Mean Frank and Crazy Tony*—what Levene called "gorilla pix" and *Variety* defined as "outright exploitation fare offering graphic violence, softcore sex and mucho shock elements for the younger hordes."

For the next decade and a half Levene was the tri-state area's Head Gorilla. When the manager of the Selwyn claimed that *A Boy and His Dog* was flopping because people thought it was a kiddie picture, Levene advised him to retitle it *A Psycho Boy and His Killer Dog, Blood*. For the New York opening of *Doctor Butcher, MD* a flatbed truck was transformed into a "Butchermobile" that traveled throughout Manhattan and the outer boroughs, promoting the film's arrival.

Terry Levene was the king of an exploitation carnival minting money from martial arts, and he wasn't alone.

AQUARIUS RELEASING, INC.

More Murderous Than The MAFIA.
Gorier Than The GODFATHER.
It's The Kung-Fu Terror Of
The TONGFATHER!

TERRY LEVENE PRESENTS

THE TONGFATHER

The Most Ungodly Father Of Them All.

AN AQUARIUS FILMS RELEASE OF A SINO-AMERICAN CO-PRODUCTION
Prints by TECHNICOLOR

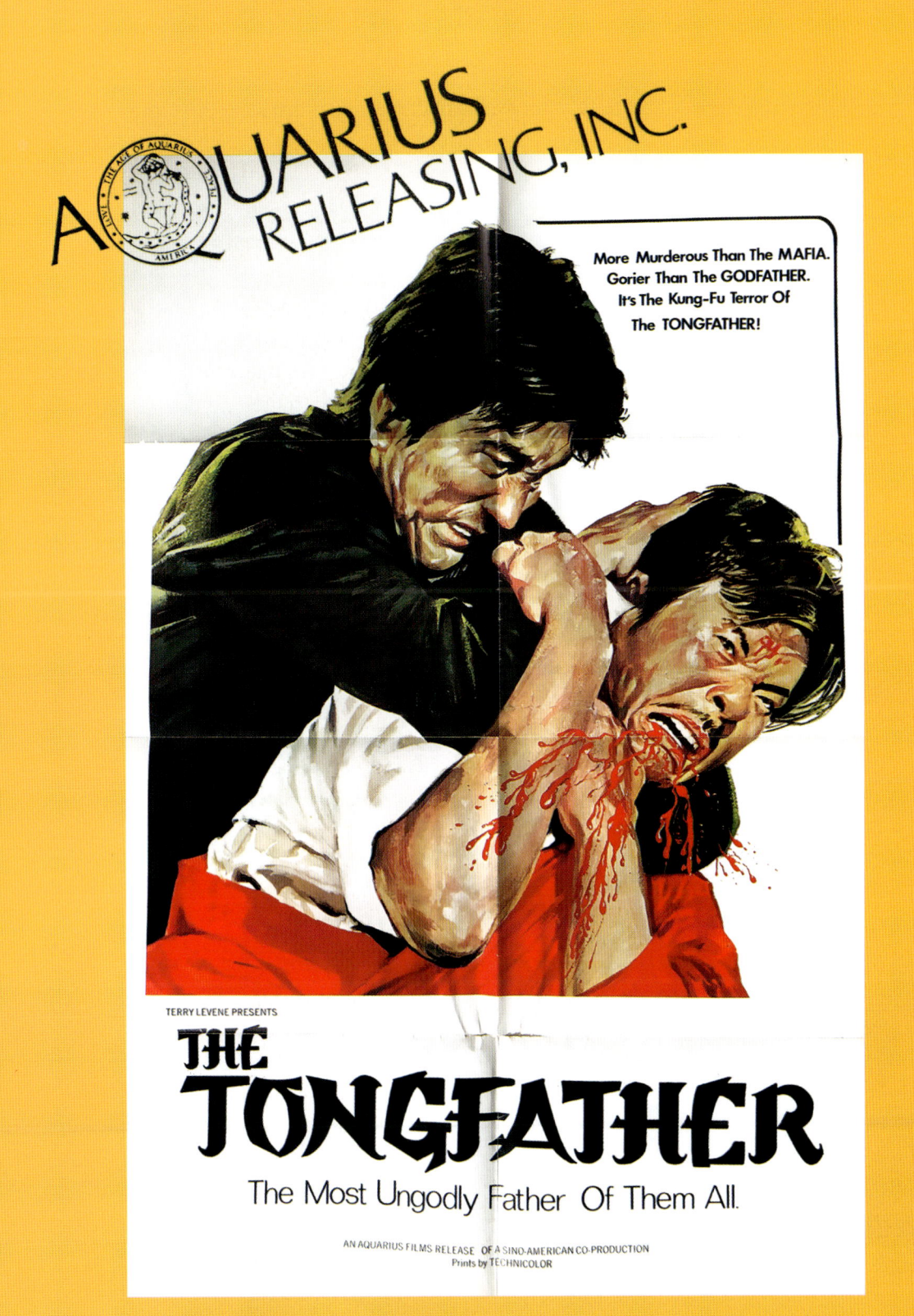

Aquarius' *Tongfather* was *The Notorious Bandit* (1974), a chunk of cheap Taiwanese gold about a secret agent tracking down drug-dealing Japanese low-lifes and busting their skulls wide open.

HOWARD MAHLER FILMS

Howard Mahler was a film booker for Columbia Pictures in the early '50s, then held similar positions at United Artists and MGM-TV before grabbing a gig as sales manager for George Waldman's film exchange office, which handled distribution in the New York City, Albany, and Buffalo areas for AIP, Realart, and Crown International. From there he became AIP's Eastern Division sales manager, then joined Allied Artists in August 1969 as their vice president in charge of the Eastern Sales Division, but resigned the following June and launched Howard Mahler Films two months later. His company's first client was the newly formed New World Pictures, and Mahler handled the East Coast promotion, merchandising, and sales for their debut releases, *Angels Die Hard* and *The Student Nurses*. As a sub-distributor for Serafim Karalexis, the VP of Boston-based United International Pictures, Mahler made a mint with *Duel of the Iron Fist* and was soon purchasing his own kung fu product for national distribution, including *The Mandarin Magician*, *The Bamboo Brotherhood*, and *The Chinese Mechanic*, as well as New York–made efforts like *Force Four*, *Devil's Express*, and *Velvet Smooth*, featuring a who's who of local Black and Latino martial artists and dojo owners. He even went to the Shaw Brothers for a pair of down 'n' dirty grindhouse shockers, *Killer Snakes* and *Killers on Wheels*. He phased out his operation in the early '80s and went to work for United Film Distribution as a sales manager, then moved to Tri-Star Pictures in 1985, where he was a vice president of the Eastern Sales Division until his death from a heart attack on April 26, 1990. He was 60.

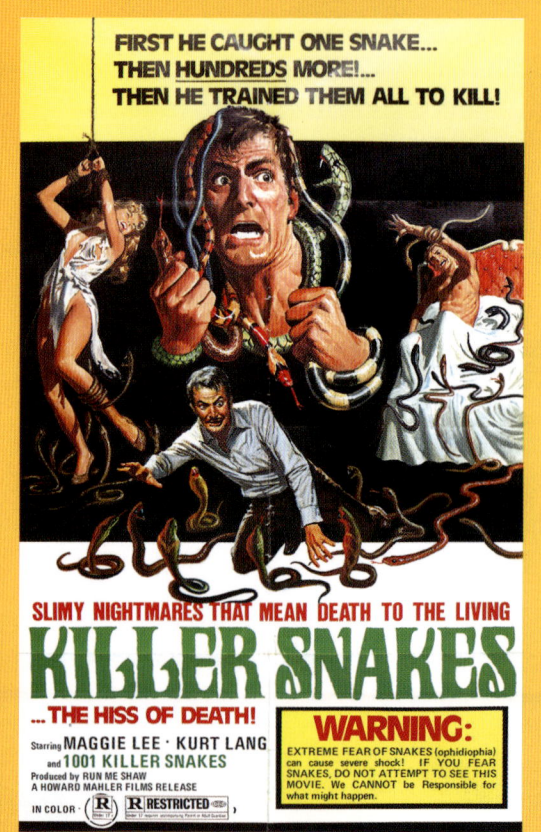

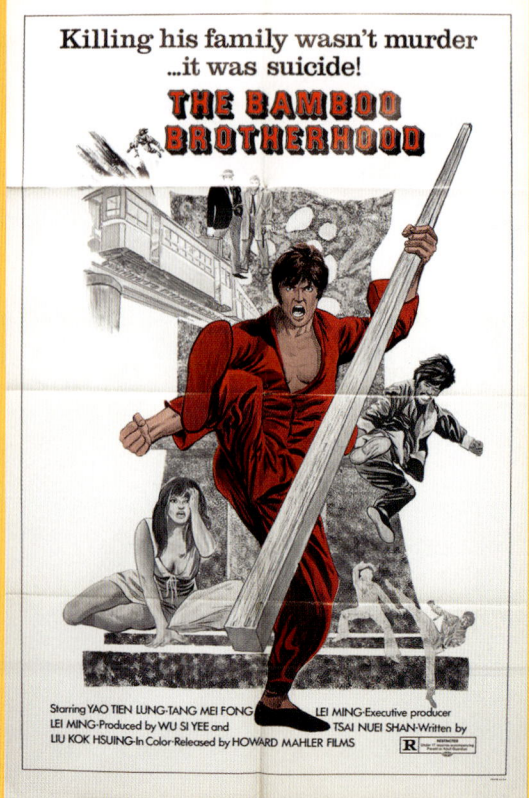

PACIFIC GROVE FILM ENTERPRISES

A restaurateur and former manager of Trader Vic's in San Francisco, Harry Ho ran Pacific Grove Film Enterprises out of the back room of a popular Tenderloin gay bar located at 45 Turk Street. A decade earlier, it had been the location of his successful Chinese eatery, Ho's Cuisine, but times had changed and so had the name, alternating between the Harry Ho Tavern, the Landmark Room, or simply The Landmark. Pacific Grove's first release was a double bill of *Warriors vs. Demons* (1971) and *The Bitter Flower* (1970) at one theater in Honolulu in 1972, but business picked up once the kung fu fad hit the following year. *Queen of Fist* did so well in San Francisco that Crown International Pictures bought it for national distribution, changed the title to *Kung Fu Mama*, and played it all over the country for the next 10 years. *Kung Fu Girl Fighter* ran in San Francisco as *Fist on the Waterfront* but went out nationally as *Shanghai Connection*. *Bruce Lee and I* was the Unicorn Chan movie *Fist of Unicorn*, while *Kung Fu Master: Bruce Lee Style* was really Joseph Velasco's *Tough Guy* with a lot of Isaac Hayes' "Theme from *Shaft*" in the trailer. After their initial releases, Ho sold all three of these plus *Kung Fu—The Brothers* (1972) to Goldstone Film Enterprises for national distribution. In the '80s, he switched to theater management, operating Pacific Grove Theatres out of the St. Francis I & II, one of the last remaining double-feature grindhouses on Market Street, before dropping out of the public eye in the early '90s.

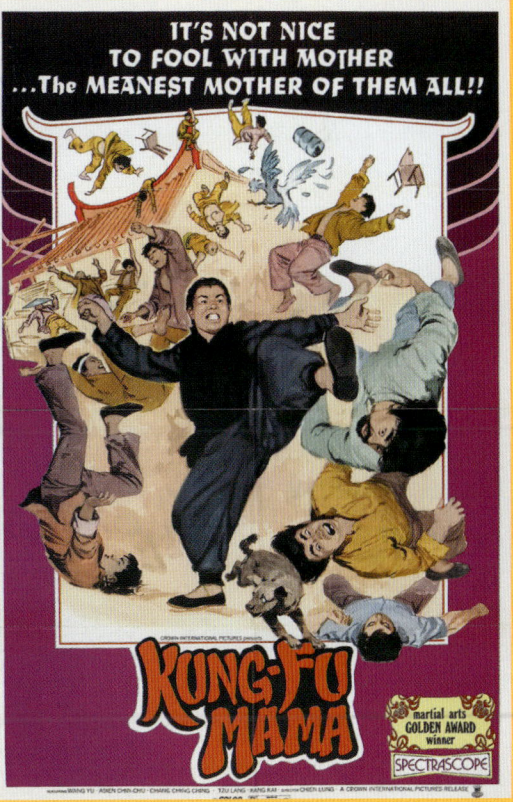

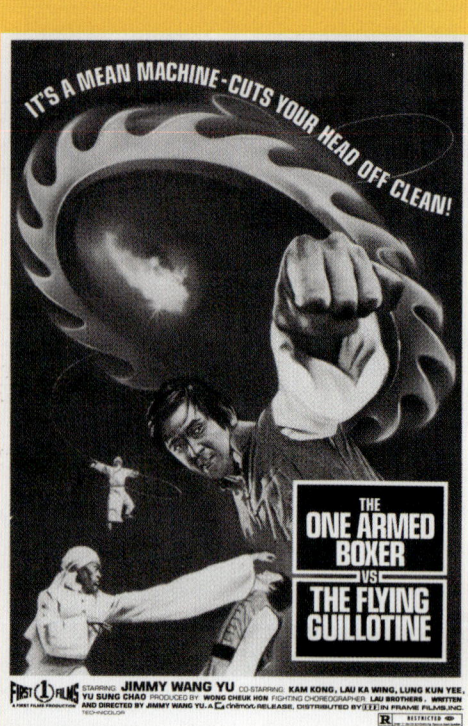

IN-FRAME FILMS

Arthur C. Webb was in charge of the Caribbean territories for Cinema International Corporation before he and his brother, Rodney R. Webb, formed In-Frame Films in Philadelphia in 1974. They had a relationship with First Films of Hong Kong and released several of their kung fu movies beginning with *The Dragon Squad* in December 1974 and ending with *The One-Armed Boxer vs. The Flying Guillotine* three years later. (Seymour Borde & Associates wound up taking over and distributing this film with a new campaign as *Master of the Flying Guillotine*.) Both movies starred Jimmy Wong Yu, whom Rodney cast in the ill-fated action spoof he was producing in Europe, *The New Spartans* (see page 195). The other First Films released by In-Frame were *Karate One by One*, *Return of the Panther*, *Super Dragon* (aka *Furious Slaughter*, also starring Jimmy Wong Yu), and *Thou Shall Not Kill but Once*. In 1976, the Webbs snagged *How Funny Can Sex Be*, an Italian comedy starring Giancarlo Giannini, which became their biggest hit. It wasn't big enough, however, and by 1978 In-Frame was out of business.

L&T FILMS / ARK FILMS

L&T Films was a Hong Kong holding company run by a shipping magnate named Tan Siu-Lin, who seemingly had his hands in everything: textiles, currency trading, video arcades, mahogany, and kung fu movies. L&T opened an office in Guam so they could ship their goods around the world using the cheaper US Postal Service. Naturally, this included 35mm kung fu movie prints. L&T's films were distributed in the States by Ark Films, a partnership between Tan, his sons Henry and Willie, and southern sub-distributors Harry and Belton Clark of the Jacksonville-based Clark Film Releasing. A couple of good ol' boys who started their business in the early '60s, the Clarks had already released a number of kung fu movies on their own, including two starring Chan Wai-Man, *The Chinese Mack* and *The Chinese Godfather*, the latter including a short documentary called "The Last Days of Bruce Lee," which included footage from Lee's funeral. The Clarks expanded their distribution territory during the '80s to include most of the South and remained in business long after their competitors had evaporated, keeping a client list that included Tyler Perry, Miramax Films, and the Weinstein Company. (See also Unifilm International Company, page 179.)

HEADLINER PRODUCTIONS

Born in 1892, Roy Reid was one of the original Forty Thieves, who specialized in selling sizzle rather than steak. A former vaudeville theater manager, Reid learned the ins and outs of the business from fellow Thieves Louis Sonney and Dwain Esper while working for their company, Roadshow Attractions. He booked the featurette *Birth of Triplets by Caesarian Delivery* from the 1940s into the '70s, and also managed to resurrect other mothballed items like *Mom and Dad* at the dawn of the Me Decade. In the '50s he founded Headliner Productions with drive-in owner Dale Gasteiger and the pair produced three Ed Wood films—*The Violent Years* (1956), *The Sinister Urge* (1960), and *Married Too Young* (1962)—before abandoning sexploitation for kung fu in the mid-'70s. Approximately 83 years old by that point, Reid was singularly out of step with the times and approved bizarrely anachronistic advertising campaigns. The ads for his early '80s release *Succubare* makes the Asian horror-action import look like an Italian mondo movie from two decades earlier, while the poster for the 3D kung fu movie *Tiger Man* (1983; see page 276) prominently features a roller coaster, a big selling point for one of the first major studio 3D features, *Man in the Dark*, released way back in 1953. When Reid passed away in 1987 he was preparing to distribute a martial arts movie imported from Korea. Following his death, Headliner was dormant for a few years until Gasteiger and new partner, Gregory Hatanaka, revived it in the early '90s as Headliner Entertainment Group with theatrical releases including John Woo's *The Killer*, Yuen Wo-ping's *Tiger Cage 2*, and the Toho production *Tokyo: The Last Megalopolis*.

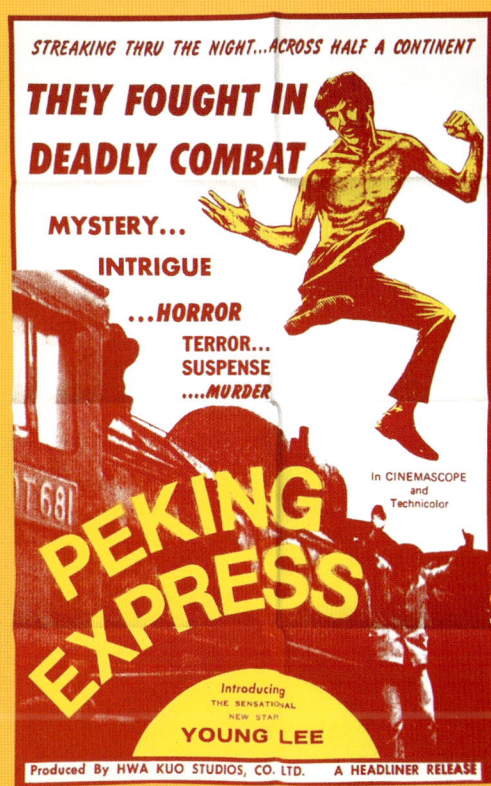

The artwork for *Peking Express*, *Duel of the Masters*, and *Korean Connection* all feature the same sickly-looking martial arts master striking an awkward pose. Presumably, Reid believed in getting his money's worth out of the few pieces of advertising art he paid for.

CINEMA SHARES / WORLD NORTHAL

Mel Maron spent the '50s and '60s running roadshows for MGM's biggest films. While studio execs scratched their heads over Stanley Kubrick's *2001: A Space Odyssey*, Maron grabbed a pull quote from the *Christian Science Monitor* and turned it into a psychedelic hit as "The Ultimate Trip."

In 1975 he took his marketing moxie to Cinema Shares, which had entered the overcrowded martial arts market a year earlier with four kung fu quickies, all starring Japanese martial artist Yasuaki Kurata. He launched their television syndication department, creating TV-friendly versions of their theatrical releases, like *The Killing Machine*. But whereas English-dubbed Japanese movies had no problem on American television, programmers still resisted Chinese kung fu flicks.

"Everybody thought I was a nut, because nobody was able to get television to accept dubbed kung fu movies," Maron says.

Maron left Cinema Shares for the World Northal Corporation. Founded in 1976 to distribute foreign films, World Northal was so classy it played "Promenade" from Mussorgsky's "Pictures at an Exhibition" over its company logo. And it was here that Maron decided to unleash the beast. Before he'd left Cinema Shares he'd licensed 12 kung fu movies from Wolfe Cohen, the sales agent for Globe Films, which owned the North American rights to the Shaw Brothers' library. He brought that contract with him to World Northal and beefed up his slate with six movies from Golden Harvest. Ready or not, World Northal was in the kung fu business.

The first of their Shaw Brothers acquisitions, *The Chinatown Kid*, landed in April 1979 at the New Amsterdam and was followed by a double bill of *Master Killer* and *Duel of the Iron Fist* at the Lyric, then *5 Masters of Death*, *Savage 5*, *Executioners of Death* (aka *Executioners of Shaolin*), *Queen Hustler*, *Black Magic*, *Five Deadly Venoms*, *The Deadly Angels*—approximately one a month for the next six years. Shaw had been shy about theatrical distribution in the States, but Maron won them over, and their movies made bank at the box office.

And just a few years down the road, in the early 1980s, Maron would brainstorm the next evolutionary leap for kung fu movies in America—syndicated packages for commercial TV—making both Shaw and World Northal a lot of money in the process.

A SHAW BROTHERS
PRESENTATION
MORTAL
COMBAT
WHERE THE BETTER MAN STAYS ALIVE!
Starring
TO-LUNG THE TIGER OF THE SOUTHERN SKY • Produced by RUNME SHAW
Directed by CHANG CHEH
A WORLD NORTHAL FILM
R RESTRICTED
UNDER 17 REQUIRES ACCOMPANYING PARENT OR ADULT GUARDIAN

She's Unstoppable!
She's Unbeatable!
She's Incredible!
She's the new superstar
of Karate/Kung-Fu!
She'll shatter
your senses with her
violent revenge!
A
Girl
Called
Tigress
Starring SHANG KUAN - LING FU - KAM KANG - YASUKI KURATA
Directed by WANG HUN-CHANG
Screenplay by CHU HSIANG-KEN
IN COLOR
R

FIVE SINISTER DISCIPLES
DEALING IN DEATH!
THEY STRIKE
SWIFTLY...
SURELY...
FATALLY!
The 5
Deadly
Venoms
A SHAW BROTHERS PRESENTATION OF A
DORCHESTER PRODUCTIONS LIMITED RELEASE PRODUCED BY RUNME SHAW
STARRING SUN CHIEN • KUO CHUE • LO MENG • WEI PAI • LU FENG
DISTRIBUTED BY WORLD NORTHAL CORPORATION R RESTRICTED

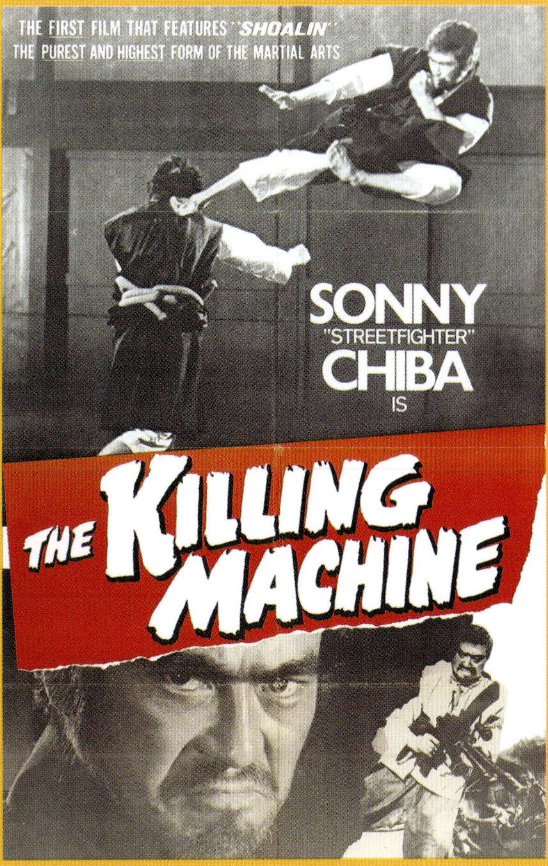
THE FIRST FILM THAT FEATURES "SHOALIN"
THE PUREST AND HIGHEST FORM OF THE MARTIAL ARTS
SONNY
"STREETFIGHTER"
CHIBA
IS
THE KILLING
MACHINE

21ST CENTURY DISTRIBUTION

Founded by Tom Ward and Art Schweitzer sometime in the mid-'70s, they released kung fu flicks as well as low-budget Italian and American horror movies. Academy Award nominee Adolph Caesar did the voiceovers for most of their trailers and Luis Dominguez painted the majority of their posters. During the bankruptcy of Dimension Pictures in 1981, they acquired Dimension's library, which included *Dolemite* and its sequel, *The Human Tornado*, as well as *Exit the Dragon, Enter the Tiger*. Later, Ward got voted out of the company and started Saturn Productions, which mostly put out kung fu movies on videocassette. In 1989, the company got gobbled up by securities fraudster Giancarlo Parretti, who also purchased MGM, the Cannon Group, and French studio Pathé. He tried to mash them all together but wound up making a giant mess when he fired all the accountants, put his 21-year-old daughter in a senior position, and eventually got sentenced to four years in prison for misuse of corporate funds. Rebranded 21st Century Film Corporation, the company was awarded to former Cannon co-head Menahem Golan as part of his severance package and managed to survive into the mid-'90s with lackluster offerings like Albert Pyun's *Captain America* movie, *Bloodmatch*, *Desert Kickboxer*, and *Death Wish V: The Face of Death*.

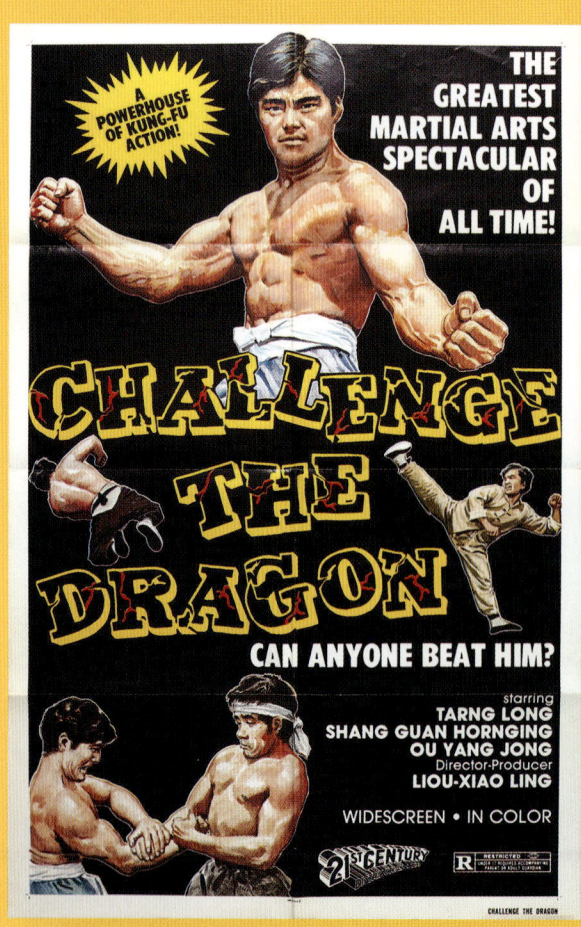

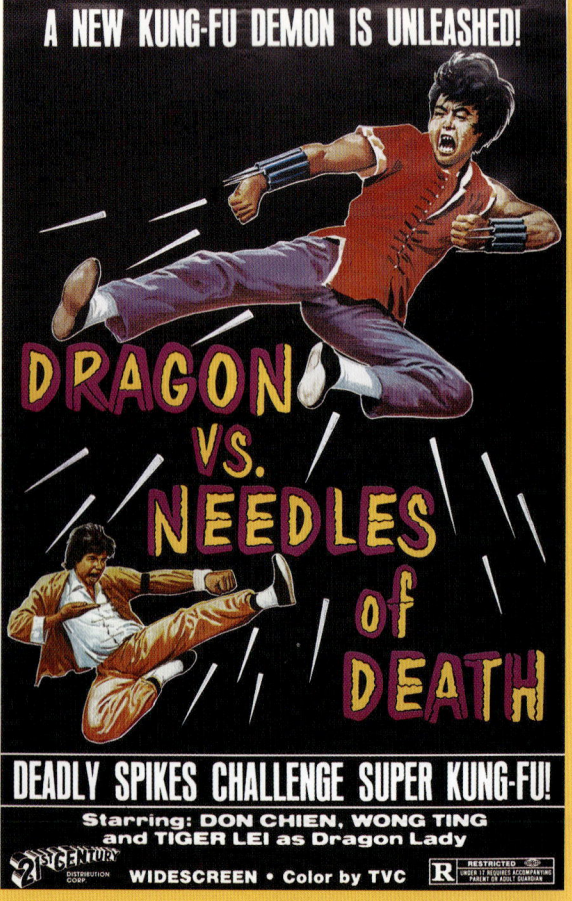

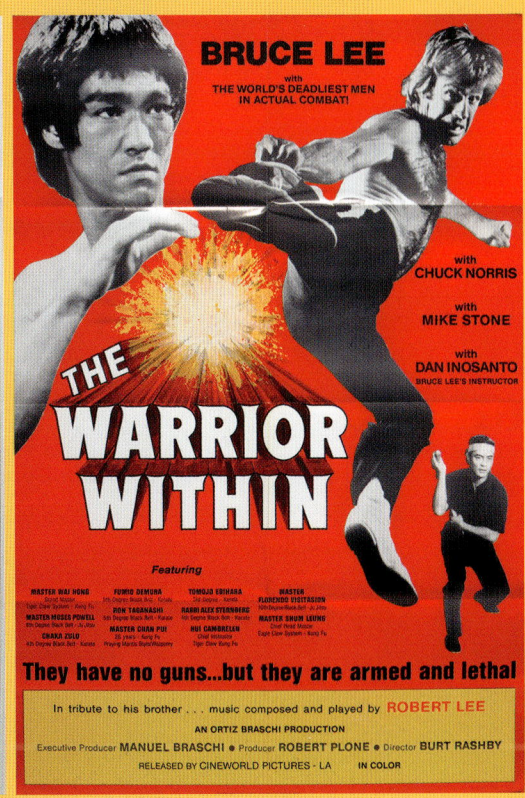

CINEWORLD PICTURES

Marcia Silen and her partner, Joan DeAnda, started out making 16mm softcore porn features like *Orgy in the Ozarks*, *Psychodrama*, and *Purse Snatch*, which they produced as MJ Productions and released as MarJon Film Distributors. Silen produced and cast the films and DeAnda wrote and directed them, the notable exception being Ed Wood's *Take It Out in Trade*, which they just produced and distributed. Most of their films were shot in a day, and Silen's politics were informed by the bottom line. As she said in an interview, "Even our sexually oriented films don't denigrate women . . . you don't need to in order to make money." As the cops cracked down on hardcore in the early '70s, FBI agents wearing wires started showing up at their offices, trying to bully them into going hardcore so they could make an arrest. Recognizing the fuzz because they always offered way too much money for movies, Silen and DeAnda got out of the business. The duo took over the former Bijou porno theater in Los Angeles, screening classic films starring strong women like Mae West and Rosalind Russell alongside contemporary works by female filmmakers. For a while they booked non-theatrical venues and ran a company called Newomen Releasing, which specialized in movies by and about women, before opening Cineworld Pictures in 1977. Because they couldn't get a bank loan, their first movies were bottom-of-the-barrel kung fu flicks, blaxploitation retitles like *Black Agent Lucky King*, and 35mm blowups of their own 16mm softcore films. Some of their kung fu releases were *The Dragon Lives Again*, *Kill the Golden Goose*, *The Last Challenge of the Dragon*, and the documentary *The Warrior Within*. In the late '80s Silen and DeAnda got into children's home video.

TRANSMEDIA DISTRIBUTION

When Golden Harvest announced that Jackie Chan would be traveling to Texas in 1980 to star in a Warner Bros. co-production from the makers of *Enter the Dragon* and Lo Wei and Ng See-yuen put a $300,000 price tag on the US rights to their back catalog Jackie Chan films, Pal Ming of Hong Kong's Eternal Film Company had a brainstorm: Why not establish a distribution company in the United States and start promoting her newest star, Indonesian martial artist Willy Dozan, as Billy Chong, the next best thing to Jackie Chan? The result was Transmedia Distribution, which operated out of the Holmdel, New Jersey, home of Eternal's US rep, Alice Hsia. Transmedia released six Billy Chong movies designed to cash in on the early-'80s Jackie Chan craze that never happened: *A Hard Way to Die* and *Superpower* in 1980; *Kung Fu Executioner* and *Jade Claw* in 1981; *Kung Fu Zombie* in 1982; and *A Fist Full of Talons* in 1983. *Han Bo Warrior*, a Chong-less Transmedia release from '82, turned out to be a retitling of Eternal's very first production, *Rage of the Wind* (1973), starring Yasuaki Kurata. After both Chan and Chong failed to take America by storm, Transmedia called it quits and sold off six of their films to World Northal for inclusion in the Black Belt Theatre 2 television package, and they were never heard from again.

UNIFILM INTERNATIONAL COMPANY

Neva Friedenn entered the film business as the director of project development at Bryanston Releasing during the time when *Return of the Dragon* and *The Texas Chain Saw Massacre* were bringing in big bucks, and then wrote three independently produced exploitation movies in quick succession—*SuperVan* (1977), *Sweater Girls* (1978), and *The Toolbox Murders* (1978)—before learning the ins and outs of theatrical distribution at Condor Films. There she worked as L&T's West Coast booker until a clash with an incompetent sales agent led to her untimely departure. Shortly thereafter, at 4:30am an executive from L&T in the Philippines called and told her he wanted her to start a second company for them to distribute a stockpile of films that the Clark brothers didn't know anything about. He sent her $5,000 and a few weeks later Unifilm International was in business and 35mm prints of the company's inaugural release, a John Liu movie titled *Assignment to Kill*, arrived from L&T Films' office in Guam via the USPS. At the same time she was starting Unifilm, Neva was the consulting editor for *Martial Arts Movies* magazine and a writer for other publications, including *Kick Illustrated*, which ran her early and exhaustive three-part interview with Jackie Chan in their March–May 1981 issues. Unifilm released almost 200 movies theatrically in nine years, licensing many of them to cable and broadcast as part of their three "Masters of Kung Fu" packages as well as to home video, and also produced one of cult auteur Andy Milligan's low-budget final features, *The Weirdo* (1989).

ROCKET PICTURES

Larry Joachim's main booking agent for many years was Ray Wells (whose real name was Raphael Arguelles), a playwright and screenwriter who managed a Spanish-language movie theater in New York and also handled Larry's Spanish-speaking territories. Wells wrote the first draft of the *Black Samurai* screenplay for Larry and traveled throughout South America selling *The Green Hornet* country by country.

"First time he called me," Joachim remembers, "he said, 'I got an offer here, Larry. It's $10,000 for Venezuela, and it's a great offer! You're never gonna get a better offer!' I said, 'Ray, shut your fuckin' mouth! Come back here to New York right now! I'm not using you anymore!' [Pause] 'Well, let me talk to the guy again.' So he called me a day later: 'He's up to $12,000.' I said, 'Fuck you!' Next day it's 'Okay, I got you $25,000.' I said, 'I'll take it!' Every single country in South America we went through just like that."

When the two had a falling-out in the early '80s, Wells left to form his own distribution company, Rocket Pictures, which put out *Revenge of the Deadly Dragons* and *Duel of the 7 Tigers* in 1982. Rocket's third release was going to be a reissue of the 1975 Filipino actioner *Bamboo Trap*, starring Ron Van Clief and Leo Fong. New artwork was created, the title was changed to *Devil's Dragons,* and there were plans to shoot new wraparound footage with Van Clief, but Wells died before a deal could be made, and the company folded before the re-release could happen.

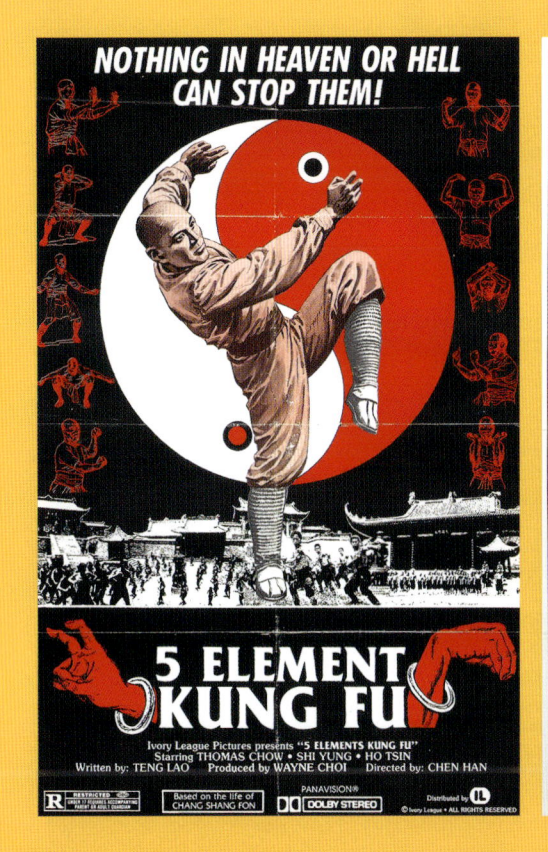

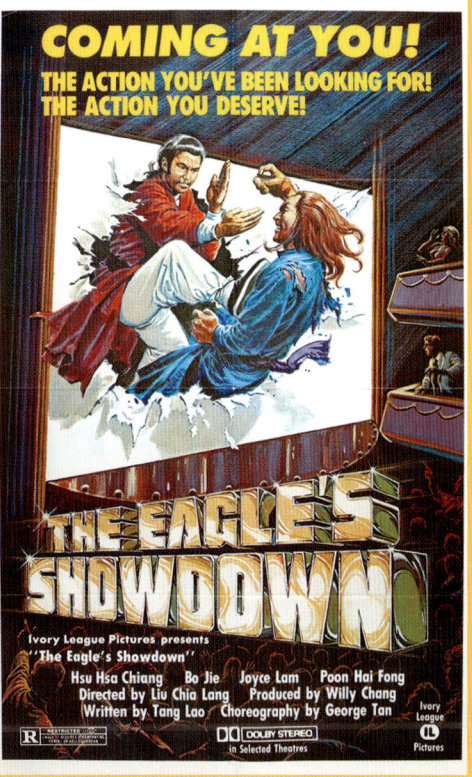

IVORY LEAGUE PICTURES

One of the few African-American distributors in the business (see also page 199), Ivory Lee Harris examined and shipped prints for Avco Embassy before becoming one of their film bookers. In 1972, he was hired by Jerry Gross' Cinemation Industries as their national print controller not long after the company released its massive, industry-changing success, *Sweet Sweetback's Badasssss Song* (1971). While at Cinemation he handled such films as *Attack of the Kung Fu Girls*, *Sting of the Dragon Masters*, and *The Dynamite Brothers* (see page 76) before the company went belly-up in 1976. Harris landed at Peppercorn-Wormser for the next year, helping them release the Shaw Brothers film *Heroes Two* under the title *Bloody Fists* and was then hired by Mel Maron at Cinema Shares as his right-hand man and print controller. This was in 1978, the same year Maron made a deal with Shaw Brothers through their sales agent, Wolfe Cohen, to bring their movies to American screens on a regular basis. Maron then moved to World Northal, taking the Shaw Brothers deal—and Harris—with him. "Wherever I went, Ivory went," Maron says. At World Northal, Maron theatrically distributed Shaw favorites like *Master Killer*, *Five Deadly Venoms*, *Black Magic*, and many more. The pair moved to Almi Pictures in 1982, and it was during this time that Harris established his own company, Ivory League Pictures, and started distributing kung fu movies on the side while still working for Maron. League was also involved with the aborted Taimak film *The Black Ninja* in 1987. By then, the Maron-Harris team had made one final move—to Castle Hill Productions, in 1985—where Harris remained until succumbing to kidney failure on March 12, 2001, four days shy of his 49th birthday.

In Color — English Titles

TRAIL OF BLOOD

U.S. PREMIERE
First Showing IN HAWAII

TOHO THEATRE
KAPIOLANI BLVD.   PH. 949-5578
6:30–8:30 p.m.
Sat. Mat. 2:30
Sun. 12:30 cont.

•••• STARRING ••••
Yoshio Harada • Atsuo Nakamura
Kayo Matsuo • Ryohei Uchida

SPECIAL TICKET
Any 4 Programs
Good Any Night

SUN – MON Oct
Kurosawa's
MEN WHO TREA[D ON]
THE TIGER'S T[AIL]
7:15 and 10:40
Teshigahara's
WOMAN IN THE [DUNES]
8:30

TUES – THURS O[ct]
Shinoda's
SCANDALOUS A[DVENTURES OF]
BURAIKAN (104)
Kurosawa's
SANJURO (96)

FRI – SUN Oct 15
Inagaki's
SAMURAI TRILO[GY]
7 & 10:45
Kurosawa's
YOJIMBO (110)

COLOR — ENGLISH SUBTITLES

TOHO THEATRE
KAPIOLANI BLVD.   PH. 949-5578
SHOW TIME 6:30–8:30
SAT. MAT. 2:30
SUN. 12:30 CONT.

U.S. PREMIERE
FIRST SHOWING IN HAWAII

starring
★ MEIKO KAJI
★ TOSHIO KUROSAWA
★ EIJI OKADA

A WOMAN BORN THROUGH RESENTMENT,
DOOMED FOR VENGEANCE
MEN CALLED HER...

SNOW BLOOD

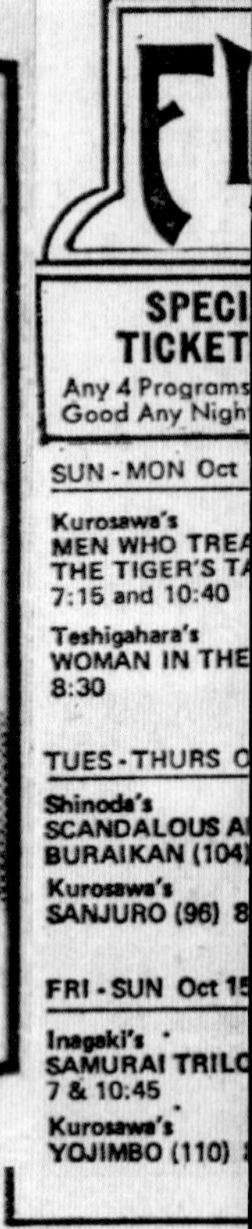

Flashin[g]
the ulti[mate]
weapon
vengea[nce]

COLUMBIA PICTURES P[RESENTS]
"LIGHTNING SWOR[D]"
YUKO HAMA • Exec[utive]
GOYU KOJIMA
COLUMBIA PICTURES/A D[IVISION]

Samurai pictures swept the country thanks to screenings at arthouses, college campuses, art galleries, community centers, and even public libraries, often bundled together as touring packages. 1971's "Films of Japan" stormed several cities with a combination of samurai mayhem *(Sword of Doom, Kill!)* and Akira Kurosawa. The Elgin Cinema in New York hosted "The New Japanese Cinema" in the summer of '73, and a few weeks later the New Yorker Theater unveiled "The Magnificent 19"—19 movies starring Toshiro Mifune. But the biggest line-up was the legendary 10-week Cinema East series at the Regency Theatre on Broadway at 67th Street. The ads promised "Over 50 films from Japan featuring the samurai, classic, contemporary, and the first showing of the yakuza."

...MS OF JAPAN

MON - TUES Oct 18 - 19
SAMURAI TRILOGY PART II (100)
6:45 & 10:40
Okamoto's
SWORD OF DOOM (122) 8:35

WED - FRI Oct 20 - 22
SAMURAI TRILOGY PART III (100)
7 & 10:30
Shindo's
ONIBABA (104) 9 PM

SAT - TUES Oct 22 - 26
Inagaki's
CHUSHINGURA (210)
Sat and Tues 8 PM;
Sun & Mon 4 & 8 PM

GERMANTOWN'S BANDBOX
30 ARMAT ST.
VI 4-3511 VI 4-8844

CLIP AND SAVE THIS AD!

TOYO
COLLEGE WALK at BERETANIA
Phone 538-1654

STARTS TONIGHT ● 6:30 PM Cont.
Adult Japanese Film/English Titles
No One Under 18 Admitted Without Parent

★★ FIRST HAWAII SHOWING ★★

EXPLOSIVE!
"YAKUZA" Means Danger!
—A TRUE STORY—
Violence Was Their Outlet!
★★ ALL STAR CAST ★★
● SHINICHI CHIBA
● BUNTA SUGAWARA
● NOBUO KANEKO
● HIROSHI NAWA
AND KINYA KITAOJI
as Yamanaka

— PLUS CO-FEATURE —
WANG YU
WILD! EXPLOSIVE!
THE HAMMER OF GOD

LIGHTNING SWORDS OF DEATH

...SU Production In Cooperation With TOHO COMPANY LTD.
" • Starring TOMISABURO WAKAYAMA • GOH KATO
SHINTARO KATSU • Original Story by KAZUO KOIKE
by KAZUO KOIKE • Directed by KENJI MISUMI
...MBIA PICTURES INDUSTRIES, INC.   **R** RESTRICTED

---

10 Week Samurai Festival

NOW through SATURDAY
THE BLIND SWORDSMAN in
ZATOICHI'S CONSPIRACY
NEW YORK PREMIERE
Complete Schedule Available At Box Office or By Mail • SERIES TICKETS: 4 Shows — $6.00

REGENCY THEATRE
BROADWAY & 67TH STREET (One Block from Lincoln Center) 595-0012

BRACE YOURSELF!

KEN-DO
IS HERE!

THE FORBIDDEN ART OF INSTANT DEATH!

THE STEEL EDGE OF REVENGE

KELLY-JORDAN DISTRIBUTION Presents a FUJI TELECASTING CO. and TOKYO ELGA CO. Production in association with TOHO INTERNATIONAL CO., LTD. "THE STEEL EDGE OF REVENGE" Starring TATSUYA NAKADAI · TETSURO TAMBA · RURIKO ASAOKA · Executive Producers SANEZUMI FUJIMOTO · HIDEO FUKUDA · Screenplay by KEI TAZAKA · HIDEO GOSHA · Photography by KOZO OKAZAKI · Music by MASARU SATO Directed by HIDEO GOSHA KELLY-JORDAN DISTRIBUTION/A SUBSIDIARY OF KELLY-JORDAN ENTERPRISES, INC. WIDESCREEN/IN COLOR

PG PARENTAL GUIDANCE SUGGESTED
Some material may not be suitable for pre-teenagers

AFTER 1973, EVERY DISTRIBUTOR WANTED to find the next Bruce Lee. They'd created plenty of clones, but audiences craved a brand-new, real-life, actual superstar, and for a while it looked like he might be Japanese.

In early 1974, Ken Takakura, Japan's iconic tough guy, appeared on the cover of highbrow movie magazine *Film Comment*, headlining that issue's 10-page article, "Yakuza-Eiga: A Primer" written by Paul Schrader, author of *Transcendental Style in Film: Ozu, Bresson, Dreyer*. Schrader defined yakuza-eiga as "the Japanese gangster film" and claimed they had replaced Japan's dying chambara "period samurai films," which is pretty surprising, considering chambara were at the peak of their popularity in the States.

Samurai movies had caught fire in the '50s when *Rashomon*, *Gate of Hell*, and *Samurai, The Legend of Musashi* took home the Academy Award for Best Foreign Language films in 1951, 1954, and 1955. Three of Akira Kurosawa's best films had been remade as westerns in the first half of the '60s—*Seven Samurai* as the box-office sensation *The Magnificent Seven* (1960), *Rashomon* as the Paul Newman vehicle *The Outrage* (1964), and *Yojimbo* as Sergio Leone's groundbreaking Italian western *A Fistful of Dollars* (1964)—and Kenji Misumi's *Sword of Vengeance* films (aka the Lone Wolf and Cub series) were such huge hits at the Toho theaters in Los Angeles and San Francisco in '72 and '73 that they caught the attention of Columbia Pictures. Eager to tap into the same urban demographic that was fueling the Chinese kung fu craze, the studio snatched up the US rights to the third film in the series, *Baby Cart to Hades* (1972), and released an English-dubbed version in March 1974 under the title *Lightning Swords of Death*. A few months later, Hideo Gosha's epic *Goyokin* (1969), hailed as "a film of stunning beauty and power" by Kevin Thomas of the *Los Angeles Times*, was acquired by indie distributors Kelly-Jordan Enterprises, who cut the film by nearly 40 minutes, dubbed it into English, and sent it out on the action circuit under the title *The Steel Edge of Revenge*. Tom Laughlin (see page 35) bought the remake rights and turned it into *The Master Gunfighter*, which relocated the story from Japan to California.

Schrader's *Film Comment* article not only hyped the filmmaker's favorite Toei yakuza films but also included a page from his screenplay *The Yakuza*, which was in production at Warner Bros. and starring Robert Mitchum and Ken Takakura. "Yakuza-Eiga: A Primer" wasn't just an article—it was a promotional piece for a Hollywood movie.

One person who was willing to gamble on Schrader's yakuza-eiga hype was Robert Shaye, president of New Line Cinema. The small Manhattan-based distribution company had made a name for itself with an eclectic slate of releases ranging from rock films (*Jimi Plays Berkeley*) to arthouse oddities (*Pink Flamingos*), but it hadn't had a breakout hit . . . yet. They'd come close. At the Cannes Film Festival in 1972, Shaye had been so impressed by the audience reaction to *The Big Boss* that Shaye immediately tried to secure the US distribution rights to that film as well as *Fist of Fury* but couldn't come up with the required $50,000. After reading Schrader's article, he was convinced

SENSATIONAL NEW YORK OPENING!
CINERAMA, RKO 86th ST. TWIN #2, RKO 59th ST. TWIN #2

$80,250
FIRST 7 DAYS

THE FIRST ⓧ-RATED FIGHT SCENES IN SCREEN HISTORY!

"CHIBA is the natural successor to Bruce Lee!"
—PLAYBOY MAGAZINE

THE STREET FIGHTER

INTRODUCING THE INCREDIBLE **SONNY CHIBA**

CONTACT: STANLEY E. DUDELSON at **NEW LINE CINEMA**
853 Broadway, New York, N.Y. 10003   Tel. (212) 674-7460
or your local distributor.

that an English-dubbed yakuza movie released ahead of the eagerly anticipated *The Godfather: Part II*, as well as the big-budget Warner Bros. film *The Yakuza*, might kick off the next big trend. He immediately called Toei and arranged for a shopping visit.

After a couple of days in the Toei screening rooms in Tokyo, he felt like he'd made a mistake. Nothing clicked. Then he spotted a poster for a recent karate movie, *Gekitotsu! Satsujin-ken*, featuring a guy who'd starred in a couple of sci-fi schlockers that kept showing up on late-night TV. Shaye requested a screening. His translator spent most of the movie covering her eyes.

"It was pretty far out," Shaye remembered.

The star was Shinichi Chiba, who didn't particularly like the movie.

"After I saw the final film, it wasn't okay with me," the actor said. "I didn't like ripping out vocal cords."

Chiba had planned to be an Olympic gymnast, but an injury sent him into film. He was a Toei contract player while studying Kyokushin karate under sensei Masutatsu "Mas" Oyama and later founded the Japan Action Club, a stunt training school for martial artists and actors.

Back in New York, Shaye showed *Gekitotsu! Satsujin-ken* to his friend Jack Sholder, an editor who created nearly all of New Line's trailers. Sholder gave the leading actors and actresses American names but it was Shaye who famously renamed the leading man: Sonny Chiba.

The title became *The Street Fighter*. Sholder created the film's title sequence and cut and scripted the trailer, while Shaye came up with the tagline "6 feet 6" of half-breed fury," to introduce the purely Japanese, 5'10" Chiba to American audiences.

Playboy called Chiba "the natural successor to Bruce Lee," but *Street Fighter* earned an X from the MPAA and a "C" (for Condemned) from the Catholic Church. *Boxoffice* magazine predicted that it "should cause a sensation," and it did. Critics went into convulsions of revulsion.

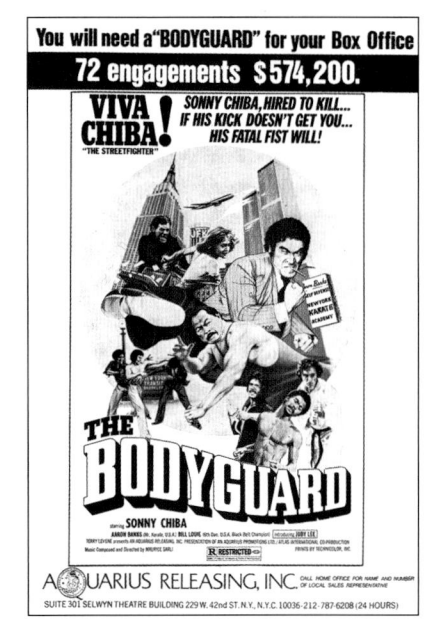

(opposite page) New Line's trade ad trumpeting *The Street Fighter* grosses.

(above) Trade ad from Terry Levene's Aquarius shills the success of *The Bodyguard*, while Larry Joachim's Trans-Continental Films brags about the gross of *The Executioner*.

The *New York Daily News* called it "a mess of faked blood, faked vomit and faked anatomical parts ripped from his opponents," the *Los Angeles Times* labeled it "sickening and slick," and inexplicably Lynn Minton, a writer for *McCall's* magazine, sent her 16-year-old daughter and 17-year-old son to cover it for her column "Movie Guide for Puzzled Parents."

But by carefully cataloging the movie's over-the-top mayhem ("nonstop eye-gouging, throat-ripping, skull-crushing and body-breaking . . . Chiba castrates a rapist and tears the throat out of another enemy . . . muscled hands ripping out eyes, necks and even a pair of testicles . . ."), every horrified review served as an ad.

Everyone attempted to cash in on the controversy. *The Dragon Squad*, a Chinese martial arts movie starring Wong Yu, showed up in theaters a few weeks later with a tagline boasting: "The 4 top living kung fu street fighters all in one motion picture." In February 1975, a movie titled *Bogard*, about an African-American bare-knuckle fighter named Leroy Fisk ("The meanest, baddest streetfighter in town," according to the ads), opened alongside *The Street Fighter*. *Bogard* was also rated X for violence but failed to attract the same attention as the Chiba film and disappeared. A year and a half later, New Line acquired it from the producers and reissued it as *The Black Street Fighter*.

Less than seven months later, New Line had their sequel, *Return of the Streetfighter*, ready to rumble. They paired it with a re-release of *The Street Fighter*, calling the double bill "Back to Back and Twice as Mean!" Both movies had now been edited to avoid extreme gore, which ensured more bookings, but the films felt toothless.

The next year saw four more Chiba films reach American shores, beginning with *Shorinji Kempo* (1975), in which he plays Doshin So, a military intelligence agent who escapes Manchuria during the Soviet invasion and returns home to the grim realities of post-war Japan, where he hopes to restore a sense of national pride by creating the titular martial art. Cinema Shares International released it stateside as *The Killing Machine*.

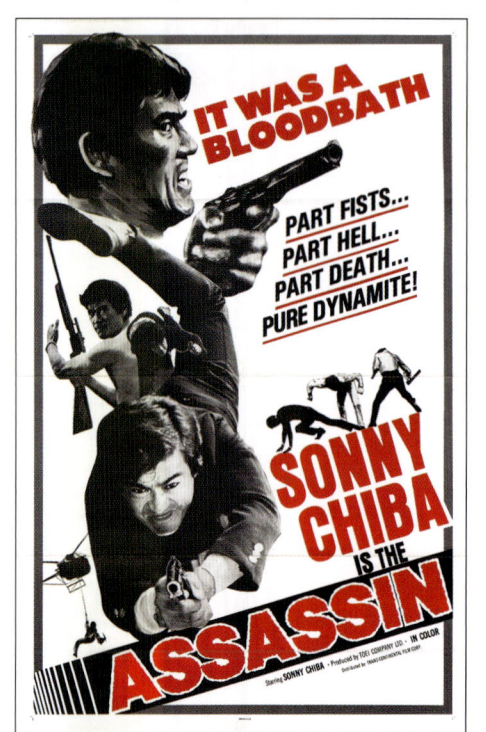

Next came *Karate Bull Fighter* (1975), the first of three films based on the life of master Mas Oyama, founder of Kyokushin Karate. United Artists released it as *Champion of Death* in October '76, smack in the middle of the same period when the company was collecting Best Picture Academy Awards for *One Flew Over the Cuckoo's Nest* (1975), *Rocky* (1976), and *Annie Hall* (1977).

Aquarius Releasing picked up *Bodyguard Kiba* (1973), and Terry Levene hired Simon Nuchtern and Joseph Ellison of August Films not only to dub and reedit the film, but also "Americanize" it with a seven-minute opener shot around New York City. This new footage consisted of newspaper headlines reacting to a Mafia rubout, karate practitioners chanting, "Vi-va, Chi-ba!", a training scene between special guests Bill Louie and Aaron Banks (filmed inside the latter's New York Karate Academy in Times Square), and an opening crawl of Ezekiel 25:17, which may feel familiar to fans of *Pulp Fiction* (1994). It begins:

> *The path of the righteous man and defender is beset on all sides by the inequities of the selfish, and the tyranny of evil men . . .*

The Bodyguard premiered in Chicago on September 3, 1976, and became one of Aquarius' greatest successes, thanks to an action-packed trailer narrated once again by Adolph Caesar. "Faster than Ali! Meaner than Bruce Lee! Sonny Chiba, the *Street Fighter*, is back as the meanest, bloodiest, most violent ass-kicking and arm-ripping mother yet!"

Caesar also narrated the trailer for *Sister Street Fighter* (1974), which New Line sold as the second sequel to *The Street Fighter* but was actually the first film in a separate trilogy. The star of all three movies was Etsuko Shihomi, a supporting actress in the *Street Fighter* films and a member of Chiba's stunt training school. She was renamed "Sue Shiomi" for one of the best New Line ad campaigns of the '70s with Caesar's hype man trailer narration: "She's a one-woman death squad! He's a one-man army! They won't be hard to find—there'll be a trail of bodies leading right to them! Karate's deadliest team in *Sister Street Fighter*!"

Even after the trend slowed, the term "street fighter" still had some exploitation value: Etonic added a "Sister Street Fighter" sneaker to their "Street Fighter" line of footwear, L&T/Ark had a Bruce Le movie called *Kung Fu Streetfighter* in circulation, and late '79 saw the release of *Lady Street Fighter*, a James Bryan cheapie starring Renee Harmon and someone calling himself Trace Carradine.

Distributors were trying anything to get audiences to come to martial arts movies as the '70s came to an end, but more and more the genre was losing blood and limping along, like one of the pathetic punks who tried to get in the way of Sonny Chiba's *Street Fighter*.

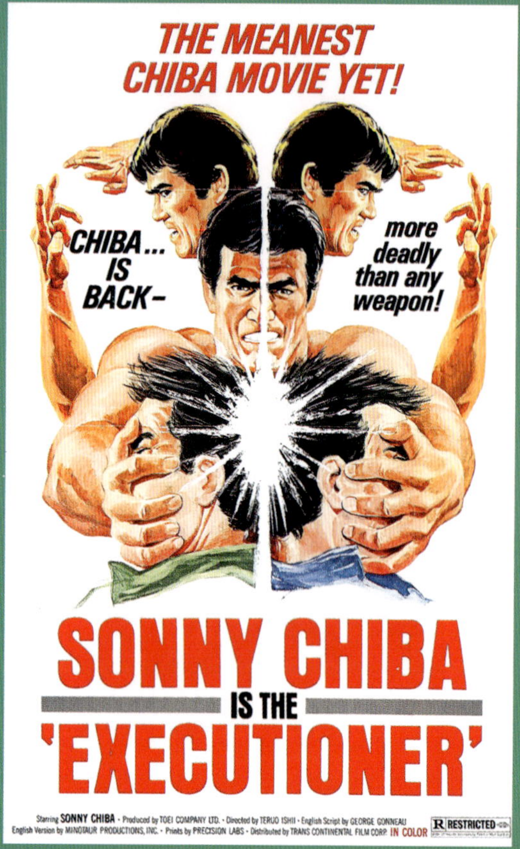
THE MEANEST
CHIBA MOVIE YET!
CHIBA... IS BACK–
more deadly than any weapon!
SONNY CHIBA
IS THE
'EXECUTIONER'
Starring SONNY CHIBA • Produced by TOEI COMPANY LTD. • Directed by TERUO ISHII • English Script by GEORGE GONNEAU
English Version by MINOTAUR PRODUCTIONS, INC. • Prints by PRECISION LABS • Distributed by TRANS CONTINENTAL FILM CORP. IN COLOR
R RESTRICTED

ALL-NEW ACTION! A Brand New Adventure!
Sonny Chiba THE STREETFIGHTER Is Back!
The DRAGON Died! But His Spirit Never Rested! Now! Sonny Chiba In A Rampage Of Destruction Against The Evil Foes That Slew The Dragon To Release...
"SOUL of CHIBA"
Starring: SONNY CHIBA
JAMES YAMASHITA • ETSUKO SHIOMI
R
L.T. FILMS CORPORATION LTD. PRESENT

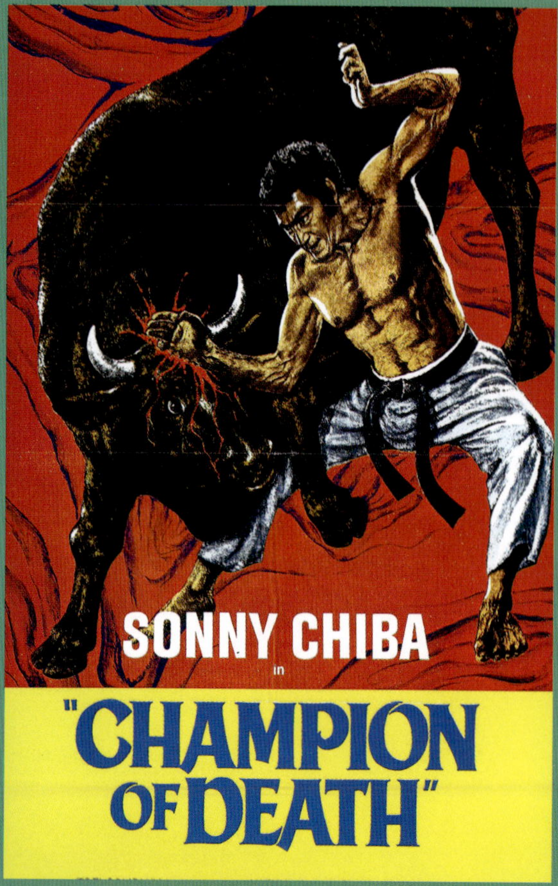
SONNY CHIBA
in
"CHAMPION OF DEATH"

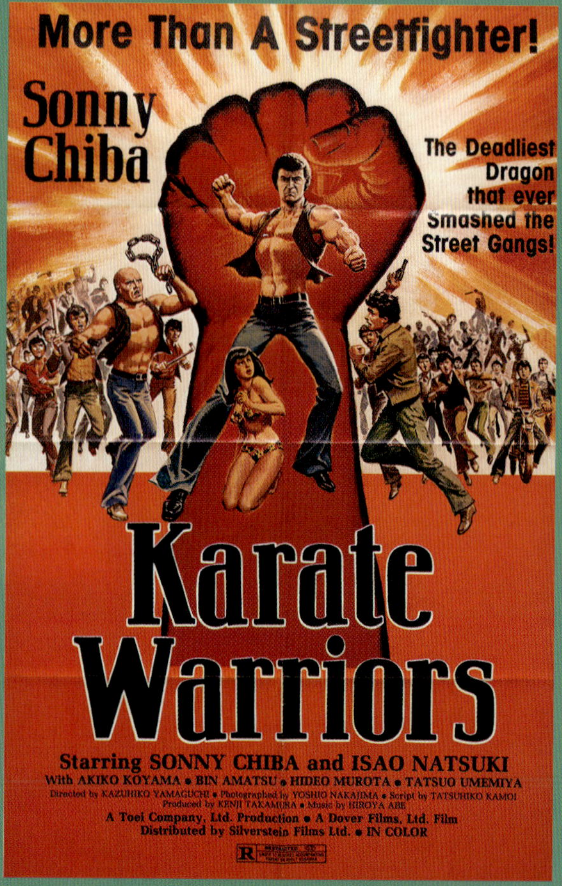
More Than A Streetfighter!
Sonny Chiba
The Deadliest Dragon that ever Smashed the Street Gangs!
Karate Warriors
Starring SONNY CHIBA and ISAO NATSUKI
With AKIKO KOYAMA • BIN AMATSU • HIDEO MUROTA • TATSUO UMEMIYA
Directed by KAZUHIKO YAMAGUCHI • Photographed by YOSHIO NAKAJIMA • Script by TATSUHIKO KAMOI
Produced by KENJI TAKAMURA • Music by HIROYA ABE
A Toei Company, Ltd. Production • A Dover Films, Ltd. Film
Distributed by Silverstein Films Ltd. • IN COLOR
R

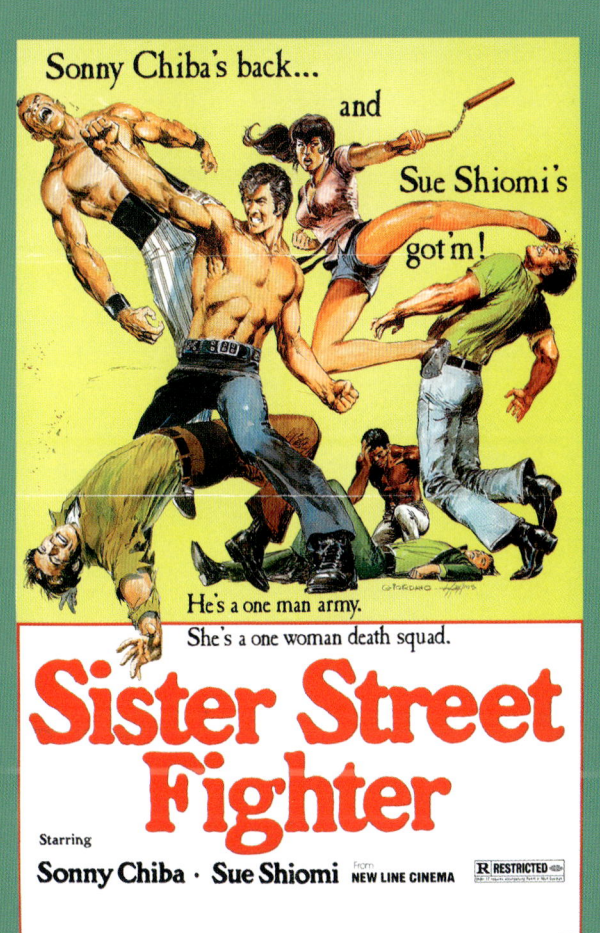

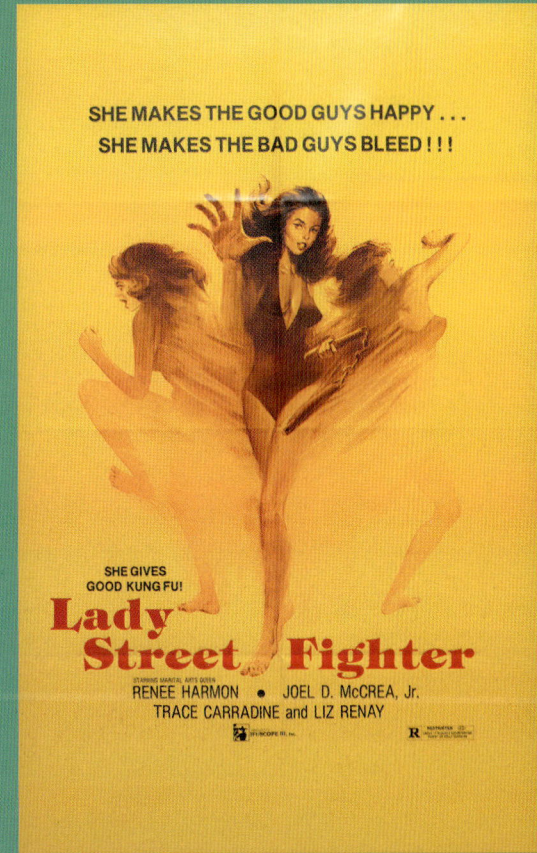

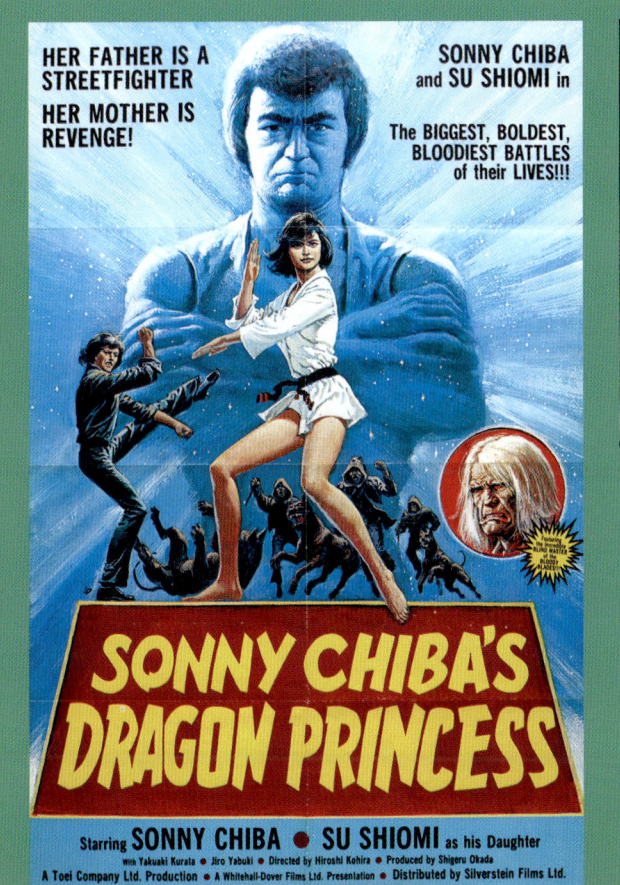

Sonny Chiba's back... and **Sue Shiomi's got 'm!**

He's a one man army. She's a one woman death squad.

Sister Street Fighter

Starring **Sonny Chiba • Sue Shiomi** From **NEW LINE CINEMA**

SHE MAKES THE GOOD GUYS HAPPY...
SHE MAKES THE BAD GUYS BLEED!!!

SHE GIVES GOOD KUNG FU!

Lady Street Fighter

STARRING MARTIAL ARTS QUEEN
RENEE HARMON • JOEL D. McCREA, Jr.
TRACE CARRADINE and LIZ RENAY

HER FATHER IS A STREETFIGHTER
HER MOTHER IS REVENGE!

SONNY CHIBA and SU SHIOMI in
The BIGGEST, BOLDEST, BLOODIEST BATTLES of their LIVES!!!

SONNY CHIBA'S DRAGON PRINCESS

Starring **SONNY CHIBA • SU SHIOMI** as his Daughter
With Yakuki Kurata • Jiro Yabuki • Directed by Hiroshi Kohira • Produced by Shigeru Okada
A Toei Company Ltd. Production • A Whitehall-Dover Films Ltd. Presentation • Distributed by Silverstein Films Ltd.
CINEMASCOPE • COLOR BY DELUXE

Etonic

Etonic Lady Street Fighter Running Shoe
Heel/arch support, 3 layer insole, with flared elevated heel...

32.99

Several comic book artists were responsible for the martial arts poster art on these pages. Luis Dominguez painted *Karate Warriors* and *Dragon Princess*, while Neal Adams and Dick Giordano co-signed *Sister Street Fighter*. *Lady Street Fighter* is unsigned, but all indicators suggest it was drawn by Roger LaManna.

(bottom, right): Etonic's line of Street Fighter sneakers were designed by renowned sports podiatrist Dr. Rob Roy McGregor, author of *EEVeTeC: The McGregor Solution for Managing the Pains of Fitness*.

AS THE '70S PROGRESSED, kung fu movies feasted on their own corpse, and every day there was less meat on the bones. The genre needed new blood. As early as 1974, Samuel Z. Arkoff, producer, trend-hunter, and co-founder of AIP, had predicted in an interview, "The standard kung fu feature will be dead by summer. To be successful, kung fu will have to be grafted onto other genres."

In 1973, the spaghetti western *My Name Is Shanghai Joe* starred a Japanese man, reportedly a hairdresser from Rome who'd never acted before, playing a Chinese immigrant in the Wild West, tangling with the worst America had to offer. A threadbare crowd-pleaser, spiced up with spurts of graphic violence and a cynical eye for star-spangled hypocrisy, it hit US screens in 1975 as both *The Dragon Strikes Back* and *Shanghai Joe*. No one showed up to see it under either title.

In 1974, Shaw Brothers not only co-produced its own spaghetti western, *The Stranger and the Gunfighter*, starring Lee Van Cleef and Lo Lieh, but it also turned out a caged-women-vs.-depraved-pirates picture with German co-director Ernst Hofbauer (the "Titan of Teen Libido") called *Virgins of the Seven Seas*. In the US, distributors retitled it *The Bod Squad* and Gene Siskel dubbed it his Dog of the Week (see page 317).

Warner Bros. also approached Shaw about co-producing a sequel to their fighting female blaxploitation flick, *Cleopatra Jones*, starring 6'2" Tamara Dobson. Looking for a hit, Shaw leapt at the opportunity, and in 1975 the two studios released *Cleopatra Jones and the Casino of Gold*. The *New York Times* called Dobson "one of nature's androgynous wonders . . . a large, beautiful, overwhelming presence." They called the movie "trashy."

Golden Harvest didn't fare any better. Bruce Lee had almost worked with the bargain basement Bond, George Lazenby, on *Stoner*, but after his death they recast the part, pairing Angela Mao with Lazenby in the sleepy sex film instead. Now it was Jimmy Wong Yu's turn.

Approached by the inexperienced but optimistic Australian Brian Trenchard-Smith, Golden Harvest sent Wong Yu to Australia to make an international cop picture with Hong Kong action, *The Man from Hong Kong* (aka *The Dragon Flies*, 1975). The most '70s of all '70s action movies, with car chases that won't quit, head-cracking action by Sammo Hung, and an earworm of a theme song ("Sky High" by Jigsaw, which became a bigger global hit than the movie), it feels like a high point that international co-productions wouldn't reach again.

THE GREATEST FIGHTING MACHINE THE WEST HAS EVER KNOWN

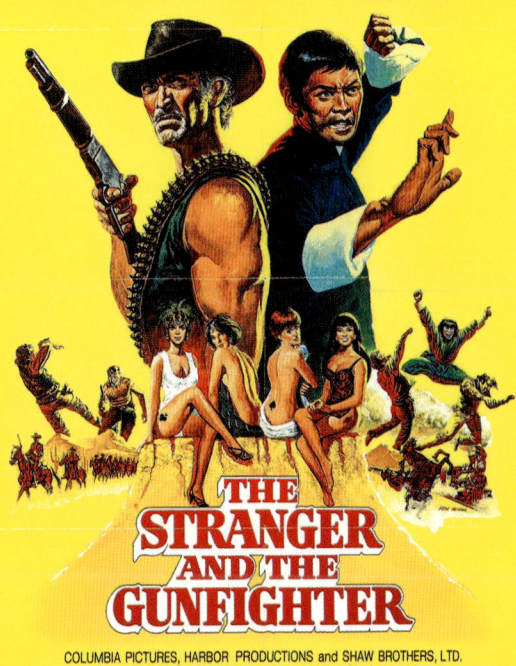

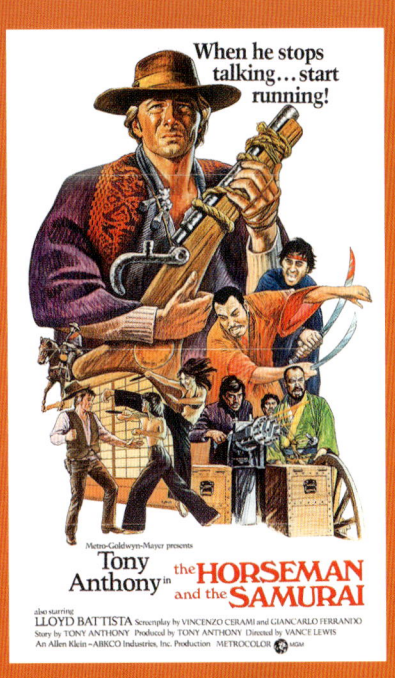

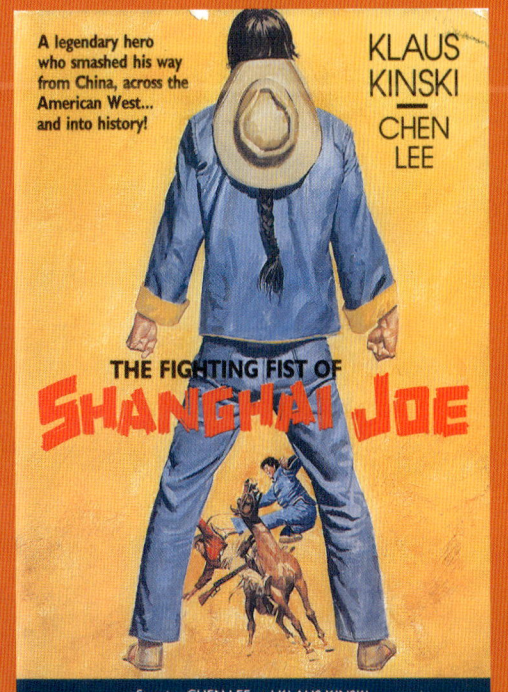

Spaghetti Westerns, horror movies—distributors tried every martial arts mash-up they could think of. Whether it was *Red Sun* (1971, opposite page) with Toshiro Mifune and Charles Bronson, *The Stranger and the Gunfighter* (1974) with Lee Van Cleef and Lo Lieh, or *The 7 Brothers Meet Dracula* (aka *Legend of the Seven Golden Vampires*, 1974).

THE DRAGON! HE'S THE ULTIMATE WEAPON
IN THE ULTIMATE ADVENTURE!
The Dragon flies...The Dragon stings...The Dragon kills like no man alive!
THE DRAGON FLIES
Get ready for Jimmy Wang Yu– The new King of Kung Fu!
20th Century-Fox Presents A GOLDEN HARVEST—MOVIE COMPANY CO-PRODUCTION
Starring
JIMMY WANG YU · GEORGE LAZENBY
in "THE DRAGON FLIES"
Produced by RAYMOND CHOW and JOHN FRASER Written and Directed by BRIAN TRENCHARD-SMITH
Music NOEL QUINLAN COLOR BY DE LUXE®
R RESTRICTED

In 1975, Wong Yu was also cast alongside Patrick Wayne (John Wayne's son), Fred Williamson, Toshiro Mifune, and Oliver Reed in a *Blazing Saddles*–style spoof of men on a mission films called *The New Spartans*. The scattershot plot involved a retired Scottish general and his daughter setting out to right the world's wrongs by forming an elite five-man fighting team composed of the aforementioned actors, plus Jimmy Wong Yu as Wang Fu, kung fu expert and martial arts movie star. Production shut down after nine days when its financing collapsed, but not before Wong Yu got into a fistfight with Oliver Reed in the hotel bar one night.

Back in Taiwan, Wong Yu continued to cash in on his stardom in movies like *A Cookbook of Birth Control* (1975) and *My Wacky, Wacky World* (1975). "I don't think any of my films are good," he says. "I'll take the money and then it's already done. Film producers offered me a lot of money, they'd say 'Hey, Jimmy!' and they would offer me one million dollars, which was a lot of money. Shaw only paid me a few hundred dollars each month, and here they are offering me a hundred times more for one movie. Of course, I would take the job. You would, too." However, a new Hong Kong star appeared at the end of the '70s who would split Asian and American audiences for martial arts films and send them on their separate ways.

(opposite page) *The Dragon Flies* was the original title of Wong Yu's *The Man from Hong Kong*.

(above, top) Australia didn't "do" action, so *The Man from Hong Kong* took the censors by surprise. Director Brian Trenchard-Smith "went for a lot of outrageous crotch-kicking and testicle squeezing" and had to sweet talk the censor, claiming it was "Tom and Jerry, Chinese style, with a bit of red paint!" It didn't crack the box office top 10 in Australia, however, but it did break the box office record in Pakistan, previously held by Elizabeth Taylor's *Cleopatra*.

(above, bottom) A behind-the-scenes publicity shot from the never-completed *The New Spartans*. Jimmy Wong Yu isn't in the picture, so maybe he's the one holding the camera?

IN THE LATE '70S, a Bruce Lee impersonator named Jackie Chan (*New Fist of Fury*, 1976) found himself trapped in a terrible contract with Lo Wei, who paid him $400 per month with an additional $400 for each completed film. Unable to make his big-nosed Bruce Lee click at the box office, Lo Wei loaned him out to the savvy producer Ng See-yuen, who immediately paired him with action choreographer Yuen Wo-ping and their two kung fu comedies, *Snake in the Eagle's Shadow* and *Drunken Master* (both 1978), blew the doors off the Hong Kong box office. Chan was suddenly the biggest hometown star since Bruce Lee.

Trading Bruce Lee's intensity for shaggy, low-key charm, these flicks pioneered the kung fu comedy wave that was about to swamp Hong Kong, and because he was looking for the next big thing, Raymond Chow made it clear he wanted to bring Jackie to Golden Harvest and give him a huge salary, big budgets, and creative freedom.

The second he smelled cash, Lo Wei locked down Chan's contract and doubled his salary, but Chan still pulled less than $1,000 per month. Finally, in late 1979, Jackie defied Lo Wei and shot *Young Master* (1980) for Golden Harvest. War broke out between Lo Wei, Golden Harvest, and the Sun Yee On triad, who were secretly Lo Wei's financial backers. Jackie, and his manager Willie Chan, realized that there was a very good chance these negotiations might wind up leaving Chan dead.

Golden Harvest turned to the only actor rumored to be enough of a badass to sit down for dinner with the triads: Jimmy Wong Yu. Willie told Jackie, "Jimmy is going to try to broker a peace agreement . . . If he succeeds, we're off the hook. If he fails, it really doesn't matter because you won't be around to find out."

The first peace meeting ended on an ambiguous note when the police were summoned to break it up, but Wong Yu eventually worked everything out, Lo Wei got paid, the triad backed off, and Golden Harvest was happy enough to pay Wong Yu $250,000 for his trouble.

Thanks to the second-biggest star of the previous generation, the biggest star of the next generation had been born. But it would be a long time before America got a clue because at this point, Asian and American kung fu movies parted ways. In America, kung fu movies raced for the bottom, the rails greased with an endless supply of shoddy

Bruceploitation schlock. In Hong Kong, an upwardly mobile population partying under a non-stop money shower thanks to a booming economy, wanted contemporary dramas and their kung fu served with a side of laughs.

Fewer and fewer foreign films seemed right for American audiences, and distributors despaired. Which is when the Black audience rode to the rescue. At least for a little while.

(top, left) A sure sign that no one knew how to make him a star, this trade ad for Jackie Chan's *New Fist of Fury* gives lots of room to Bruce Lee and Lo Wei's names but hardly mentions Chan's. It also sports plenty of pictures of boobs but barely one of its star.

(top, right) A Bruce Lee–inspired poster for Chan's Bruce Lee-inspired *New Fist of Fury*.

(bottom, right) It wasn't just the United States. Hong Kong kung fu found big audiences across Canada, as indicated by this flier for the Golden Harvest Theatre in Toronto, advertising Jackie Chan's *Drunken Master*.

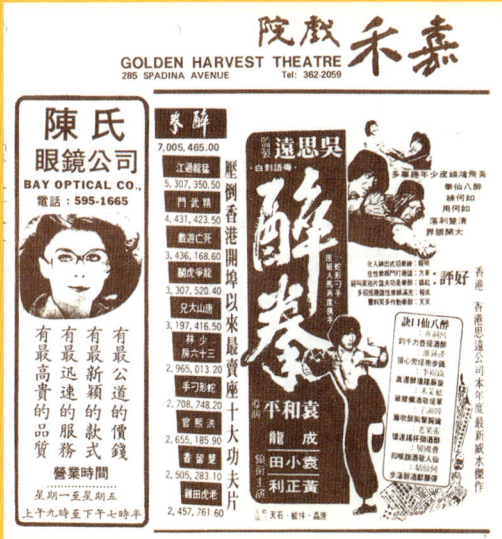

197

MARTIAL MUSIC

MUSICIANS WERE AS CRAZY FOR kung fu as everyone else. Elvis got his black belt in karate from German Shotokan instructor, Juergen Seydel, in 1958 while stationed overseas. During his midnight show at the Las Vegas Hilton on February 18, 1973, he and his bodyguards traded karate chops and kicks with four drunken rowdies from Peru who jumped onstage. They claimed later they only wanted to shake the King's hand, and the King declined to press charges. Presley also financed the Tennessee Karate Institute and footed the bill for the 1974 US Karate Team's European tour.

Bunny Sigler, the absolutely ferocious Philly R&B artist with a voice like a calloused fist, had his crank yanked so hard by *Five Fingers of Death* that he recorded "Theme for Five Fingers of Death" in which he threatened to chop John Shaft and Super Fly in half, then instructed his students in the ways of kung fu amid a barrage of grunts, yells, and a sweet bass line. A few months later, James Brown assured listeners of his #1 R&B hit "The Payback" that he didn't know karate, but he knew ka-razor.

In the spring of 1974, Carl Douglas, a Jamaican singer living in London, finished the recording session for his sure-to-be-a-hit single "I Want to Give You My Everything" with 10 minutes of studio time left on the clock, so he banged out "Kung Fu Fighting" for the B-side. The song immediately sold two million copies (to date, it's sold about 11 million) and became an unstoppable earworm on FM radio after becoming a dance hit in clubs.

Long before composer Alan Silvestri was famous for his frequent collaborations with director Robert Zemeckis and his scores for the *Predator* and *Avengers* franchises, the two-time Oscar nominee provided a very '70s soundtrack for a 3D kung fu movie called *Tiger Man* (see page 276) that started filming in September 1976 but didn't get completed until 1983. Silvestri later called the movie "dumb" and said, "I never got paid for that one." In fact, no one who worked on *Tiger Man* received any kind of compensation except leading man Wong Tao. He got a leather jacket.

The *National Lampoon* put out a single called "Kung Fu Christmas," featuring the voices of Gilda Radner and Bill Murray, in

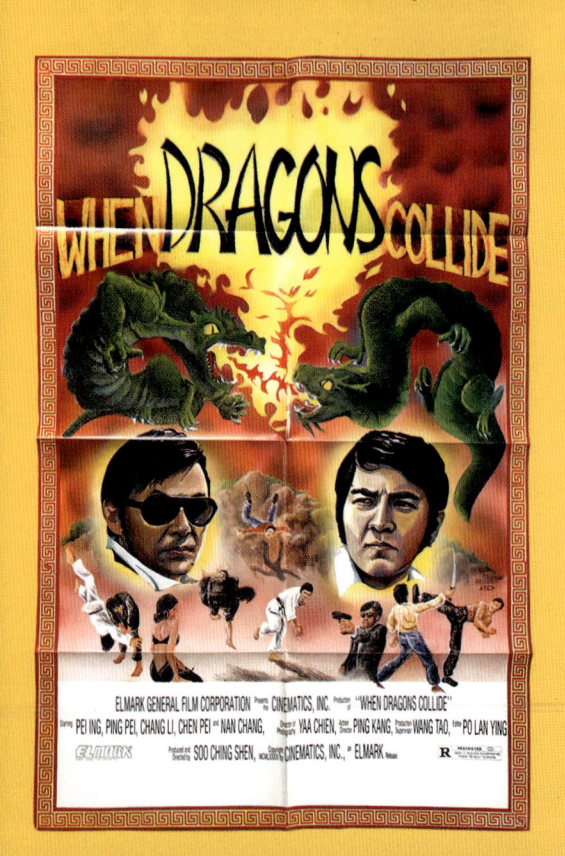

1974. Disco vocalist Kandy sang "King of Kung Fu" in 1975, co-written by 16-year-old aspiring actress Rebecca De Mornay (*Risky Business*, *The Hand That Rocks the Cradle*), for the Bruce Li flick *Goodbye Bruce Lee: His Last Game of Death*. Synthesizer wizard and massive Hindi hitmaker Bappi Lahiri wrote and sang "Let's Dance for the Great Guy Bruce Lee" for the Bollywood film *Morchha* in 1980. And plenty of people have pointed out that the title of Neil Diamond's 1976 song "Don't Think, Feel" might be lifted from a Bruce Lee line in *Enter the Dragon*. It's probably not, but that's the power of Bruce: you hear him everywhere. Even where he's not.

THUNDERFIST

MARTIAL ARTS EXECUTIONER

An Emperor International Film (H.K.) — Produced by **Jimmy L. Pascual**
Starring **ALEX LUNG, STEVE YU, YUKIO SOMENO,** and **JENNY JONES**
Directed by **Teddy Yip** — Music by the **LaMont Johnson Quintette and Orchestra**
In Eastman Color and Emperorscope — Distributed by **Artisan Releasing Corporation**
Executive Producer   Harry Hope

PG PARENTAL GUIDANCE SUGGESTED — SOME MATERIAL MAY NOT BE SUITABLE FOR PRE-TEENAGERS

J. LaMont Johnson, a funky keyboard player for jazz greats like Jackie McLean, landed a day job with a movie distributor called Futurama International. He ordered a kung fu picture for them to release, *Death Blow*, but before the deal closed and after the film elements arrived, Futurama shuttered. Hungry for a slice of the kung fu pie, Johnson retitled the movie *Thunderfist* (1973), added a sweet jazz soundtrack, and formed Artisan Releasing to put it out, becoming the first Black man to start a film distribution company in 40 years. Artisan folded before its second kung fu release, *The Cobra Knows No Mercy*, could play, but Johnson later formed Elmark General, which released *When Dragons Collide* (1983, opposite page) a vehicle for Betty Ting Pei.

IN THE '70S, AFRICAN-AMERICAN COLLEGE ENROLLMENT grew by 370%, African-American median family income doubled, and so did the percentage of African Americans holding white-collar jobs. Minority business ownership quadrupled. And on August 11, 1973, at 1520 Sedgwick Avenue, DJ Kool Herc made history when he set up his turntables in the building's rec room and spun for the very first time.

Other DJs had spun at other parties, but Herc's sound system shattered spines. Growing up in Jamaica, he'd heard the epic outdoor sound systems operated by pioneers like Tom Wong, a Chinese-Jamaican record dealer who spun R&B LPs by Black artists imported from the States and banned on the radio. Herc knew how to make his speakers boom.

Herc's system was loud, but clear, with a heavy bass, and he liked to dance. He'd spent a lot of time watching people on the floor and seen how the serious ones waited for the instrumental breaks to let the sweat fly. Herc took two turntables and played the break on one, then smoothly slid into the break on the other, starting with James Brown's breakdown on "Give It Up or Turnit a Loose," then sliding into "Bongo Rock" before dropping down on Babe Ruth's "The Mexican," stretching out the breaks into an endless party that never stopped.

As he played, his buddy Coke La Roc, who was mostly there to sell pot, hid on the side of the room, out of sight of the crowd, and rapped into the mic, toasting his friends on the dance floor, letting folks know who was holding and who was selling ("We got my man Easy Al from 26th Street, Double Green Mean Machine Black Tape, come get it!") or throwing out phrases like "If a freak is unique, then that's the freak you seek!"; "You rock and you don't stop!"; and "Hotel, motel, you don't tell, we don't tell!"

The kids who danced to the breaks—break-boys—went wild. Eventually they'd be called b-boys or breakdancers, but right now they were just young Black and Latino kids who'd had their futures stolen, their horizons shortened, and their life expectancies limited. All they wanted to do was meet some girls, kiss some boys, dress fly, show off their moves on the dance floor, and get their buzz on, like kids everywhere.

The original invitation to the first party where DJ Kool Herc spun. He booked the rec room for $25, charged 50 cents for soda, 75 cents for hot dogs, and a dollar for beer. The proceeds went to benefit his sister, who needed back-to-school clothes.

But living in the Bronx—savagely sliced in half by the Cross Bronx Expressway, with federal funding brutally yanked by President Nixon, city funding drastically slashed by a bankrupt municipality, and with government figures like Robert Moses writing public epitaphs like "You must concede that this Bronx slum and others in Brooklyn and Manhattan are unrepairable. They are beyond rebuilding, tinkering, and restoring. They must be leveled to the ground"—these kids had no access to public culture, and so they made their own.

Without art museums, they painted graffiti. Kept from the ballet, they invented b-boying. With no access to the philharmonic, they created hip hop. And they built their world from what they got out of music and the movies. Martial arts movies, to be exact.

Ark Films aimed many of their ad campaigns at Black audiences, including the one for *Black Kung Fu Dragon* (aka *Mysterious Footworks of Kung Fu*, 1978). Third-billed "Betty Tin" is actress Betty Ting Pei, who's not in this movie but did produce it, and was married to star Charles Heung at the time. Unifilm International re-released it as *Kung Fu Mystery Kicker* in 1983.

IN THE '60S AND '70S, a network of martial arts schools and dojos blanketed America, connected by magazines and tournaments. Many of the teachers came from working-class backgrounds, most of them discovered martial arts in the military, and they all lived in a country that didn't care very much about their sport. They weren't rich, many of them weren't white, and they knew that if they wanted something, they'd have to fight for it.

Charles Bonet's family had emigrated from Puerto Rico when he was two and his dad never learned English, so even though he was a nurse back home, in the States he worked as a hospital janitor. A small Puerto Rican kid in a tough Italian neighborhood, Bonet fought to survive, soaking up free karate and judo lessons from the Police Athletic League whenever they brought in a guest teacher.

At a party, he hooked up with another karate enthusiast, Eddie Reyes, after noticing his calloused knuckles, and the two of them began working out in Washington Heights Park. Even in the winter, they'd practice in their gis in knee-high snow. Eventually the superintendent of a nearby building gave them a "roach-infested, rat-infested basement with a dirt floor" to use. It was cold, it was shabby, it didn't have any lights, and at first Bonet was scared to even go down the stairs, but it was better than the park.

When Bonet returned from Vietnam, he opened his Bronx Buddakai and hung a sign over the door: "We're not fancy, we're for real."

"My students were rough kids from a tough neighborhood, a drug-infested hood," he said. "A lot of parents used to question how tough I was and I told them, 'We don't live in the Taj Mahal, we live in the damn South Bronx.' I taught them how to survive and the most important lesson: how to kick some ass."

In DC, Dennis Brown spotted a tiny sign reading "Kung Fu and Tai Chi" in the window of a Tracy's Karate school, ran inside, and signed up with Mr. Lin. A few years later, they had their own place and Brown ran Lin's Kung Fu. "No disrespect to my old neighborhood," Brown says, "but it was THE drug neighborhood in DC." He kept the door locked and buzzed in his students. Occasionally he'd find a bullet hole in the window. "There was a drive-by in front of the school and we dragged the guy in and tried to save him," he said. "We found bodies in the alley out back."

Owen Wat-son strikes a pose.

But it was better than the park. Besides, some of his top black belts came from that neighborhood and the way Brown saw it, "They needed it. There were no rec centers. There was no YMCA."

Owen Wat-son taught at the University of the Streets, a school he founded in the East Village. Nicknamed "The Priest," he grew up in South Bronx gangs, doing a few years in the Royal Knights before graduating to the Young Sinners. He dropped out of high school, became a Navy SEAL, served in Vietnam, then came back to New York and founded the University of the Streets, where he let kids who couldn't afford lessons pay for them by cleaning up around the studio. Sly and the Family Stone wound up studying with him, and his ambition was to open a monastery.

Teachers attracted students by winning tournaments, which got you on the covers of the magazines like *Black Belt* and *Inside Kung-Fu*, and tournaments were everywhere. Students would drive 12 hours and sleep packed into motel rooms or in the backs of vans to fight each other for titles and publicity at the Battle of Atlanta, the Warrior's Cup out of Chicago, the Long Beach National, the Diamond National, and if you were in New York City there was Aaron Banks' circus: the long-running Oriental World of Self-Defense at Madison Square Garden. In 1974, Banks sold 18,000 tickets to his gonzo line-up of fights: karate vs. kung fu, judo vs. wrestling, a male karateka vs. a female karateka. He had Joseph Greenstein, a 93-year-old vegetarian billed as the Mighty Atom, who punched spikes through wood with his bare hands. Newspapers panted over Joe Mystic, a "48 year old West Orange, NJ carpenter [who] burns himself alive, spreading Sunoco 220 on parts of his body, then enflaming it. Through

Competitions lived and died by their special guests, who ranged from movie stars like Tadashi Yamashita to Ted Vollrath, a legless karate champion and 3rd-degree black belt.

203

his martial arts internal powers he avoids being affected by the flames. He also eats razor blades." Ralf Bialla of Germany caught bullets in his teeth. Moses Powell balanced himself on one finger. Ernest Hyman broke 2,000 pounds of ice with his bare hands.

Wat-son, and many others, taught at the widespread Jerome Mackey Schools, which Mackey started in the '60s and ran in a relatively hands-off manner except to count his cash. Called the Colonel Sanders of judo, because of his love of franchising, his company went public in 1968, airing television ads encouraging viewers to "call Jerome Mackey and be the wrong guy to attack." In 1975, a US attorney charged Mackey and seven stockbrokers with mail fraud for manipulating its stock in a pump-and-dump scheme. Eventually, New York's Department of Consumer Affairs sued Mackey's schools into oblivion.

But there were always more.

Scouts from various schools showed up at other teachers' dojos and asked to train with the instructor. This was a coded challenge to fight. Some dojos designated enforcers to take on the challenge so their teacher didn't have to.

A lot of the people involved in the scene were Vietnam vets, some grew up in gangs, others in violent households, and drug and alcohol abuse sometimes took the place of therapy. Owen Wat-son returned to NYC after his tour in Vietnam only to discover that his entire SEAL team had been killed in action after he left. "I was out of my mind," he said. "I was a bum. Crazy. Drunk in the gutter."

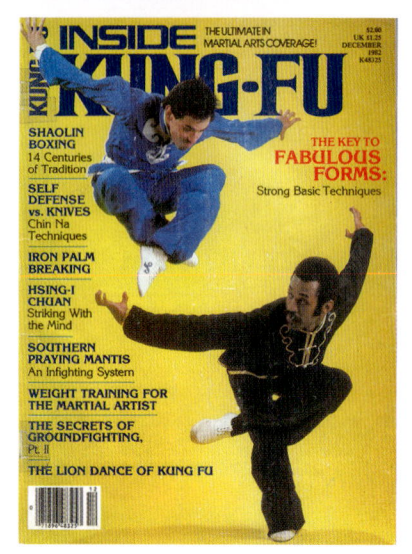

(top) Dennis Brown appeared on this cover of *Inside Kung-Fu* as he was going to China to train, causing his profile to explode internationally.

(bottom) Owen Wat-son in action.

These were hurt men, troubled men, men who'd been knocked around by their fathers, veterans with trauma and PTSD, but they loved karate and kung fu in all of its infinite variations: Vee-jitsu, Sanuces, Chinese Shotokan, US Kodokan, Okinawan Kenpo, Tang So Doo, Hung Gar. Martial arts saved their souls and inspired them to do great things. Luis Fernandez, one of Bonet's students, worked an after-school program so violent, all its previous teachers had quit. Some of Owen Wat-son's students bluntly declared that his teaching had saved their lives. Bonet devoted himself to the Martial Arts for the Handicapped Society.

As kung fu movies faded from mainstream movie theaters, distributors realized that, thanks to its link with martial arts, the Black community contained the motherload of kung fu fans. Warner Bros. began double-booking their blaxploitation movies with kung fu films throughout the early '70s before finally co-producing *Cleopatra Jones and the Casino of Gold* (1975) with Shaw Brothers. Theaters that catered to Black audiences were almost evenly split in their programming, half blaxploitation and half kung fu.

So distributors thought it made sense to look for a Bruce Lee replacement among the audience who loved martial arts the most: the Black and Latino audience. And the obvious place to start was with someone who'd been touched by Lee himself: Jim Kelly.

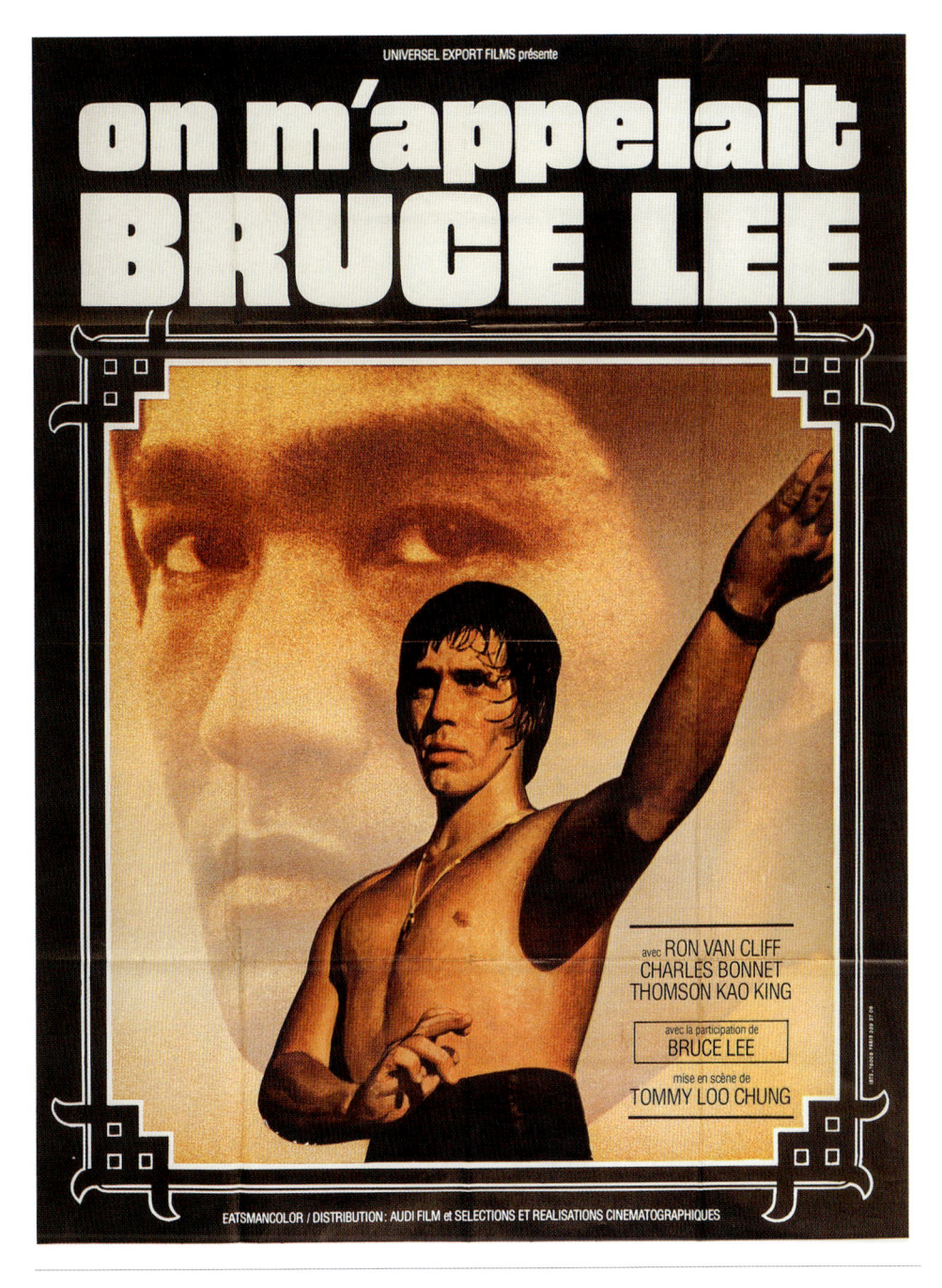

A French poster for Charles Bonet's *Black Dragon's Revenge* (1975).

THE FIRST BLACK MARTIAL ARTIST to break big should have been Rockne Tarkington, who didn't even know martial arts. A stage actor who'd moved most successfully to television, Tarkington had the dubious honor of being the first Black actor to appear on *The Andy Griffith Show* and the only Black actor to speak a single line on any of the show's 249 episodes. Tarkington became famous playing the shipwrecked merchant marine, Elihu Morgan, on "Danger Island" a treasure-hunting, globe-trotting, shot-in-Mexico, cliffhanger that aired in 10-minute bursts on the Saturday morning *Banana Splits Adventure Hour*. For a solid season in 1968, playgrounds echoed with his catchphrase, "Uh-oh, Chongo!"

(Badass Breakdown: Chongo was Tarkington's sidekick, played by Kim Kahana, a Hawaiian-Japanese martial artist and third-grade dropout who hitchhiked to LA at 13, became a paratrooper in the Korean War, was unsuccessfully executed by a North Korean firing squad, dug himself out of a mass grave, spent two years completely blind after a hand grenade went off in his face, walked away from a plane crash that killed 35 other passengers, and finally became a stuntman because, honestly, nothing seemed to kill him. He choreographed all the action on "Danger Island," doubled for Charles Bronson for 20 years, and opened his own dojo in LA during the '60s.)

Hired to play Williams in *Enter the Dragon*, Tarkington didn't love his low salary but figured he'd wait until three days before departing for Hong Kong and demand a raise. Rather than negotiate, the producers recast. Kelly's agent sent him on the audition, saying, "You won't get the part, but I want you to go out there and meet the producers."

He got the part.

A shoe salesman who'd parlayed some 1971 karate championships into his own dojo called Kelly's Karate Studio, Jim Kelly viewed karate as "a stepping stone to get on the screen," as he said in an interview. A former football star from Kentucky, he'd torn up his scholarship to the University of Louisville when the coach called one of his Black teammates a racial slur. Assessing his options, Kelly decided to become an actor because "acting would give me everything I needed out of life to be successful. And those things were to make a lot of money, become very popular, and be very influential and motivational to young Black kids."

> **"THE MOVIE BUSINESS IS A TOY. IT DOESN'T MATTER TO ME."**
> —JIM KELLY

A last-minute gig coaching Calvin Lockhart in karate for the neo-noir *Melinda* (1972) turned into a small role as a karate coach in the film that put Kelly on deck when *Enter the Dragon* needed a new actor. And watching his performance, it's easy to see why his agent wanted him to meet Fred Weintraub and Co.

Generating lethal doses of charisma, Kelly struts onstage in *Enter the Dragon* wearing a burgundy suit with a yellow turtleneck, gets stopped by two racist white cops,

(top, left) French one sheet for *Black Belt Jones*.

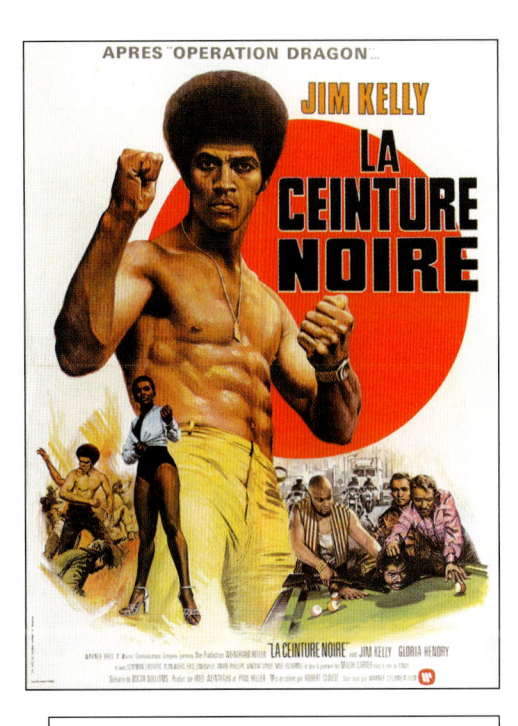

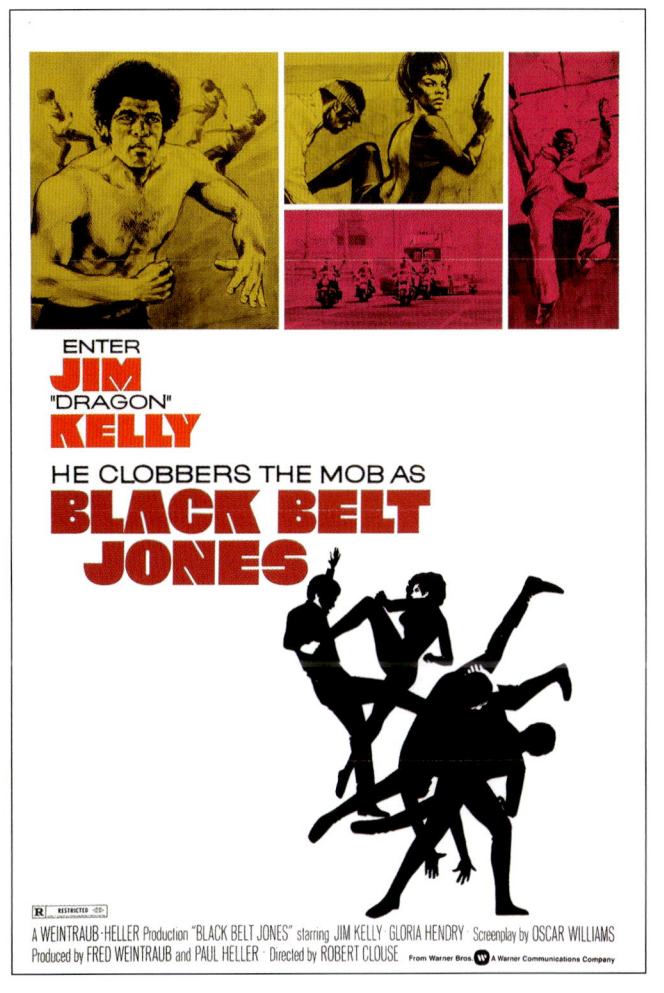

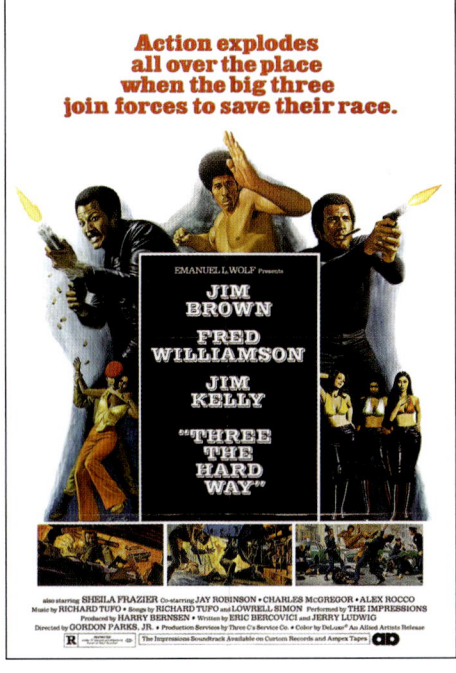

(top, right) One sheet for *Black Belt Jones*. Marvel's martial arts magazine, *The Deadly Hands of Kung Fu*, raved of the movie, "There is also precisely the right touch of brooding, emerging Third World anger inherent in *Black Belt*'s style, deftly underplayed by Kelly."

(bottom, left) One sheet for *Three the Hard Way,* the biggest hit Kelly had after *Enter the Dragon*.

(bottom, right) Everyone was ready for Kelly to be as big as Bruce Lee, and the studio pulled out all the stops to promote him hard, even making stickers and posters for fans.

Jim Kelly was a star, but distributors still paired *Black Samurai* with a Bruce Lee re-release to remind audiences of their association in *Enter the Dragon*.

kicks their asses with karate, then steals their cruiser and drives himself to the airport. It's one of cinema's greatest entrances. With his iconic Afro and laid-back cool, Kelly beds chicks, zings one-liners, and generally steals the show before being beaten to death by the bad guy.

For years, Kelly groused about getting killed halfway through the movie, claiming he should have survived to the end because he had more martial arts experience than co-star John Saxon, ("I am not very happy about that," Kelly has said on numerous occasions. "But he had more screen credits, so he stayed alive.") Nevertheless, *Enter the Dragon* made him a star.

Back in the States, producer Fred Weintraub convinced Warner Bros. to back him in signing Kelly to a three-picture deal and rolled cameras on *Black Belt Jones* (1974), which Kelly described as "an incredible experience. It was my first film where I was the star. I'm the man." But the most exciting discovery of 1974 turned out to be Richard Pryor, who co-wrote the year's box office smash, *Blazing Saddles*, and won a Grammy for his standup comedy album. Suddenly, everyone wanted funny, not kung fu.

Directed by *Dragon*'s Robert Clouse, *Black Belt Jones* tries to get hip to the lighter tone of '74 by showcasing Kelly's penchant for punching people in the balls alongside a climax that sees him lead an all-girl trampoline team in the heist of a Mafia-owned winery, followed by a silly showdown in a car wash, slopping over with soap suds. *Black Belt Jones* bombed.

Kelly didn't worry, because three months later he appeared in the lavish blaxploitation spectacle, *Three the Hard Way*, alongside two of the genre's greatest stars, Fred Williamson and Jim Brown. James Bond on a budget, with a comic book plot about white supremacists trying to eliminate Black people by poisoning the water supply, it hit pay dirt, which helped take some of the sting out of *Golden Needles*, released one month later, and the second of Kelly's Weintraub films. A Joe Don Baker action vehicle that gave Kelly a small part and a single action scene, it bombed, too.

Kelly couldn't connect. He looked stiff onscreen and his cocky cool had curdled into an enormous ego. In interviews he talked about himself in the third person, publicly challenging respected boxers like George Foreman and Muhammad Ali to fights ("I could beat Frazier, Ali, and George Foreman all in one night") and bragging about injuring his own stuntmen, claiming that on *Black Belt Jones* "I split one guy's skull and broke up another guy's face because they were unqualified to fight me." He claimed to have seen less than five movies in his lifetime because there were no Black characters he identified with and he dismissed the karate tournament scene as "a bunch of bull."

In 1975, Kelly proclaimed, "After this year, I will be the number one Black star, and in three years, I'll be the number one world-wide box office champion—Black or white."

That same year he co-starred with Williamson and Brown in *Take a Hard Ride*, a spaghetti western in which his character didn't have any lines. It bombed. Kelly's last film on his Weintraub contract was *Hot Potato* (1976), a slapdash sequel to *Black Belt Jones* showcasing Kelly's Bruce Lee imitation. Reviewers said it wasn't a disappointment because "no one really expected it to be any good in the first place." Exhibitors saw it at an advanced screening and refused to play the movie unless Warner Bros. paired it with a re-release of *Enter the Dragon*, a guaranteed hit.

Jim Kelly's career looked to be cooked, but back on the East Coast, a cool dude in platform shoes walked into Serafim Karalexis' office.

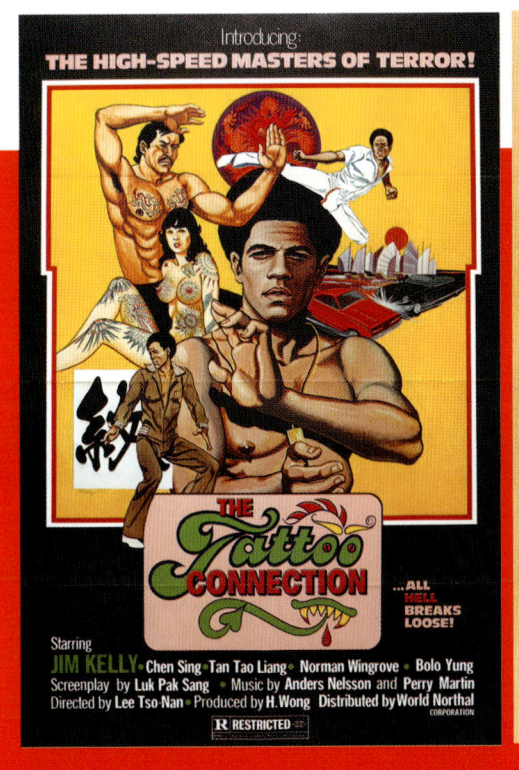

(left) Kelly claimed that *The Tattoo Connection* was "the best martial arts film since *Enter the Dragon*," but it was virtually ignored in the US.

(right) A poster promoting the double bill of *Enter the Dragon* and *Hot Potato*, a movie exhibitors refused to screen on its own. By the time it came out, Jim Kelly couldn't carry a solo movie at the box office and they wouldn't screen it if it wasn't paired with his Bruce Lee picture, *Enter the Dragon*.

AS EARLY AS THE MIDDLE OF 1973, Serafim Karalexis realized that the typical film audience for kung fu movies had changed. Even with *Duel of the Iron Fist*, Angela Mao's films, and the national success of Bruce Lee's *Enter the Dragon*, the kung fu trend was fading from the mainstream fast.

As he put it, the remaining audience was made up of "Blacks, Puerto Ricans, Chicanos, and Orientals . . . The whites were no longer there."

He needed to stay ahead of the curve to stay on top of the box office, and to do that he needed a martial arts movie with a Black hero.

"And since no Hong Kong film would have a Black hero, I realized that I was going to have to produce the film myself," he said. His partners at United International told him he was crazy. "This time I'm so crazy I'm leaving," he told them, then sold his shares in their partnership and moved to New York, called up casting agents and asked for a Black actor who could do kung fu.

Actors came from as far away as Chicago, Detroit, and Miami, but none of them were right. After almost 200 dead-end auditions, a big dude in platform shoes strolled into Karalexis' office.

"Let me see your kick," Karalexis said. "You can take off your shoes if you want."

"I don't have to," the dude answered, and unleashed a kick that practically scraped the ceiling.

His name was Ron Van Clief, 31 years old, a transit cop and a bouncer looking to do something new with his life. He'd studied stunt work under Alex Stevens, Frank Sinatra's stand-in, and done some work on *Shaft* and *The Anderson Tapes*, but after seeing a screening of the Shaw Brothers' angry young man movie, *The Boxer from Shantung* (1972), at the newly opened Music Palace theater in Chinatown, he started thinking that maybe he had a future in film. Karalexis thought he might, too. He'd studied shotokan karate, Hakkoryu jiu-jitsu, and kendo. He could kick, he was handsome, and he was built like he could crush bricks with his bare hands.

Born and raised in Brooklyn, Van Clief had joined the Marines and done boot camp at Camp Lejeune in Jacksonville, North Carolina, where he claims the constant racism culminated in his being arrested for refusing to sit in the back of a bus, followed by a failed lynching that left him with 20 broken bones. A friend in the Corps broke him out of the local hospital because he and Van Clief feared the white doctors might try to give him an overdose to tie up the failed lynching's loose ends.

Throughout the '50s, Van Clief had studied martial arts with Moses Powell, Frank Ruiz, and Peter Urban, and now, not sure what to do with himself, he'd wandered into the Music Palace and seen the light, flickering through a 35mm print of *The Boxer from Shantung*. Karalexis signed him up and sent him to the Philippines to appear in a co-production with his Hong Kong business partner, Yeo Ban-yee, of Yangtze films.

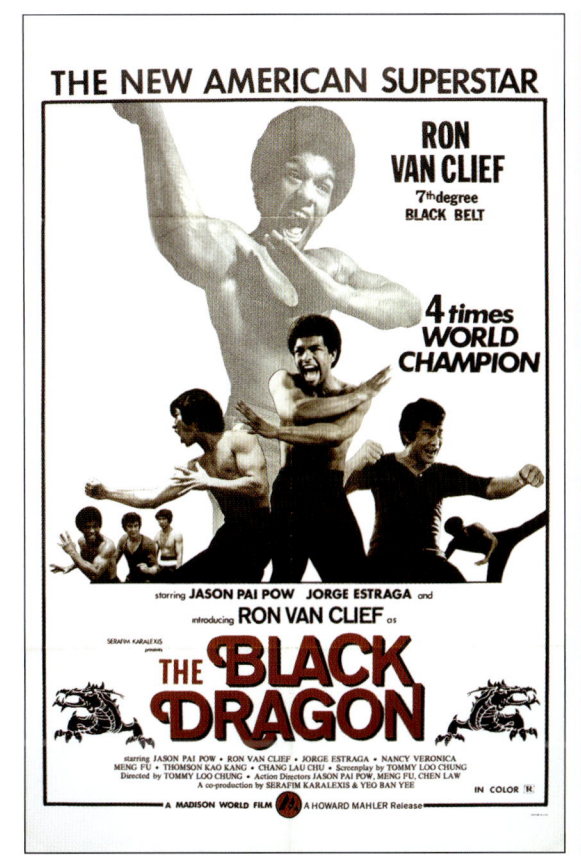

One sheets for *The Black Dragon*, shot in the Philippines with a budget of about $150,000. In a later interview, Van Clief said, "These superhero types of movies are made for children. The kids love them but the scripts are usually bad." Nevertheless, he thought the boom would continue. "I'm glad Chuck Norris is doing well. He's the prototype of the American martial artist. Me, Bill Wallace, Joe Lewis, we'll all catch up—all the good martial artists will get into films as the boom continues." Unfortunately, it didn't.

The problem was that Karalexis needed to stay in New York to handle the legal fallout of his separation from his partners, and Yeo Ban-yee needed a movie that appealed to Chinese audiences, so his Chinese hero had to save the day. Van Clief came back from the eight-week shoot with a movie called *Tough Guy* starring Jason Pai Piao. The movie had plenty of action, and the entire cast seemed to be allergic to shirts, so it was packed with wall-to-wall eye candy for the ladies, but Van Clief appeared in only about 14 minutes of the 90-minute film.

Karalexis didn't bat an eye. He retitled the movie *The Black Dragon*, put Van Clief front and center in the advertising, and hired smooth-voiced R&B disc jockey Gerry Bledsoe of WWRL in New York to narrate the trailer, which promised "none of that jumping around and flying through the air, 'cause this is the real shit!" The film opened in Detroit in late 1974 and hit big, hopping on and off *Variety*'s list of top 50 grossers for the rest of the year, and eventually earning over $6 million at the box office and a write-up about Karalexis and his sudden success in the *New Yorker*. Karalexis signed Van Clief up for three more movies.

starring
RON VAN CLIEF
THE 4 TIMES WORLD CHAMPION!
with
CHARLES La Pantera **BONET**

THE BLACK DRAGON REVENGES

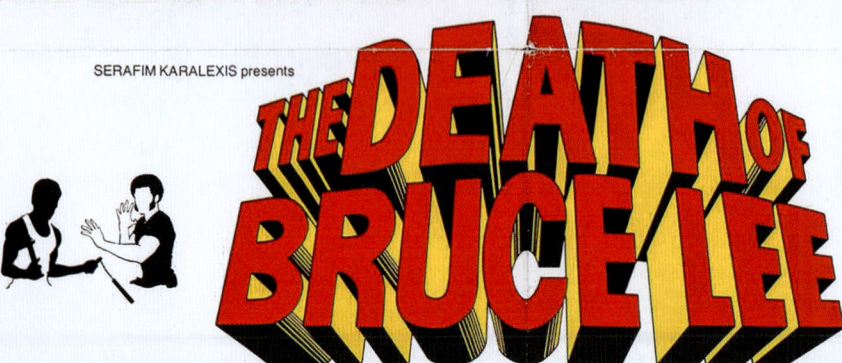

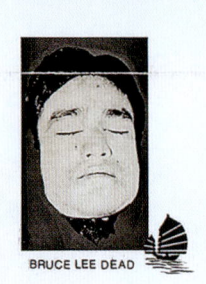

SERAFIM KARALEXIS presents

THE DEATH OF BRUCE LEE

BRUCE LEE DEAD

R RESTRICTED   IN COLOR

starring RON VAN CLIEF • CHARLES BONET • JASON PAI POW • THOMSON KAO KAN • MENG FU • MAYBLE • LINDA HO • TONY PA SAN • Written by NORBERT ALBERTSON
Directed by TOMMY FOO CHING • Action Directors RON VAN CLIEF • CHARLES BONET • PETER MENG FU • TONY PA SAN
Produced by SERAFIM KARALEXIS in association with HOWARD MAHLER • A MADISON WORLD FILM • A HOWARD MAHLER RELEASE

"**COME ON, RON,**" **CHARLES BONET SAID.** "You're jiving me."

He figured it was a Hollywood thing.

"You get a card from a Hollywood producer, you think it's a joke, man. It's too far-fetched."

But Ron Van Clief insisted. A real movie producer wanted to send Charles and Ron to Hong Kong to make a movie. Serafim Karalexis knew that Bruce Lee was more popular dead than he'd ever been alive, so he wanted to do another *Black Dragon* movie with Ron and this time he had two fresh angles: make it about Bruce Lee, and team his Black martial artist with a Latino one.

He'd shot a kung fu and karate documentary in New York in 1975 called *The Super Weapon* and part of it had focused on Charles Bonet, a lightning-fast Puerto Rican fighter and former Marine with the precision of a drill instructor and great rhythm, ending a lot of his strikes with a tiny, whipcrack flourish. Karalexis showed him the script for the new *Black Dragon* movie, signed him up, renamed him "La Pantera: The Puerto Rican Panther," and stuck him on a plane with Van Clief to Hong Kong: the Black Dragon and the Puerto Rican Panther, like Bing Crosby and Bob Hope, hitting the road.

This time, Karalexis supervised the shoot himself. Bonet had never acted before, and on his first take a stuntman came running at him with a knife, letting out a bloodcurdling scream. Reflexively, Bonet knocked him out cold with a single kick.

"I'm sorry, I'm sorry," he kept saying. "I thought he was going to kill me."

Only extensive apologies convinced the rest of the stuntmen that Bonet could control himself.

The plot of *The Black Dragon's Revenge* is about what you'd expect. Hired by a mysterious benefactor, Van Clief heads to Hong Kong to solve the mystery of Bruce Lee's death with the help of Bonet, improbably named Charlie Woodcock. Van Clief's character is named "Ron Van Clief" and struts into fights wearing a T-shirt stretched across his bulging pecs that reads, "Ronnie Van Clief, Master Instructor." With the feel of a movie assembled in the editing room and a shooting style set to "haphazard," the first hour coasts by on choppy editing and the easygoing charm of Van Clief and Bonet's genuine chemistry. It has all the hallmarks of a Bruceploitation movie: a photo of Bruce Lee's corpse in its coffin, henchmen jumping out of nowhere to attack the heroes unprompted, and someone in blackface.

But the last 30 minutes snap into B-movie overdrive with a series of vigorous fights, long displays of Bonet and Van Clief's savage styles, a plot that almost gels into coherence, and a finale that features Bonet getting a poison dart to the neck, a cackling villainess throwing poisonous snakes at everyone, and Van Clief twisting a bad guy's head off like a chicken while wielding a lightning fast pair of golden sais and calling someone a jive turkey.

As for the answer to the question of who killed Bruce Lee? Eventually the old master sits down and explains, "You ask a difficult question, my son, thus I can only answer you with the words of my teacher . . . and his teacher's teacher. In my search for the truth, I was told that the sky has unexpected clouds and storms. A man has sudden fortune and misfortune. . . . As you know, there's only one way to be born, a hundred to die. On the path of death walk men of all ages, and you find out the universe is ruled by letting things alone." THE END.

Sorry, who killed Bruce Lee?

Like a lot of martial arts teachers, Ron Van Clief performed demonstrations to attract students, often with Owen Wat-son. Their demos quickly became legendary, with one magazine calling them "slick, stagy, and among the best shows in New York." When one of Van Clief's movies opened, people would line up for the pre-show demonstrations and mob him for pictures and autographs after.

Van Clief taught at both open- and closed-door dojos, the closed-door dojos tucked away in the basements of grocery stores or deep in the basement of the Empire State Building. Its classes were full contact and the language was rough. Van Clief, being a movie star, had people showing up to "train" with him constantly and he reveled in knocking them out. As one student said, "Our dojo was a circle of crazy."

Van Clief had served in Vietnam and fought constantly with his father growing up, as did Bonet. To Van Clief, the tougher way was the only way, which is what passed for normal among a lot of the teachers at the time who often rode their students hard. When Ron Van Clief did a theater demo for *The Black Dragon's Revenge*, he insisted his best student perform, even though the kid had walking pneumonia. The demo had been advertised heavily and a crowd came out. The student did a perfect kata that ended with a back somersault. When he came down he heard his ankle snap. It wobbled from side to side on the end of his leg as he performed his courtesy bow, stepped back into formation, waited for the demo to finish, then went to the hospital.

The next day, Van Clief came to visit.

"A broken leg is nothing," he told the student. "I've broken so many of my bones. Which leg is it?"

"Right leg."

"Perfect," Van Clief said. "We need to build up your left leg anyway."

(above) *The Black Dragon's Revenge* was a success, but not *The Super Weapon* (opposite page) despite Karalexis loving it. "This was probably the film I liked the most," he said in an interview. "People didn't want to see reality. They wanted fantasy, they wanted breaking walls, tables, all the fakery, gimmickry, and special effects."

starring RON VAN CLIEF
THE 4 TIMES KARATE WORLD CHAMPION

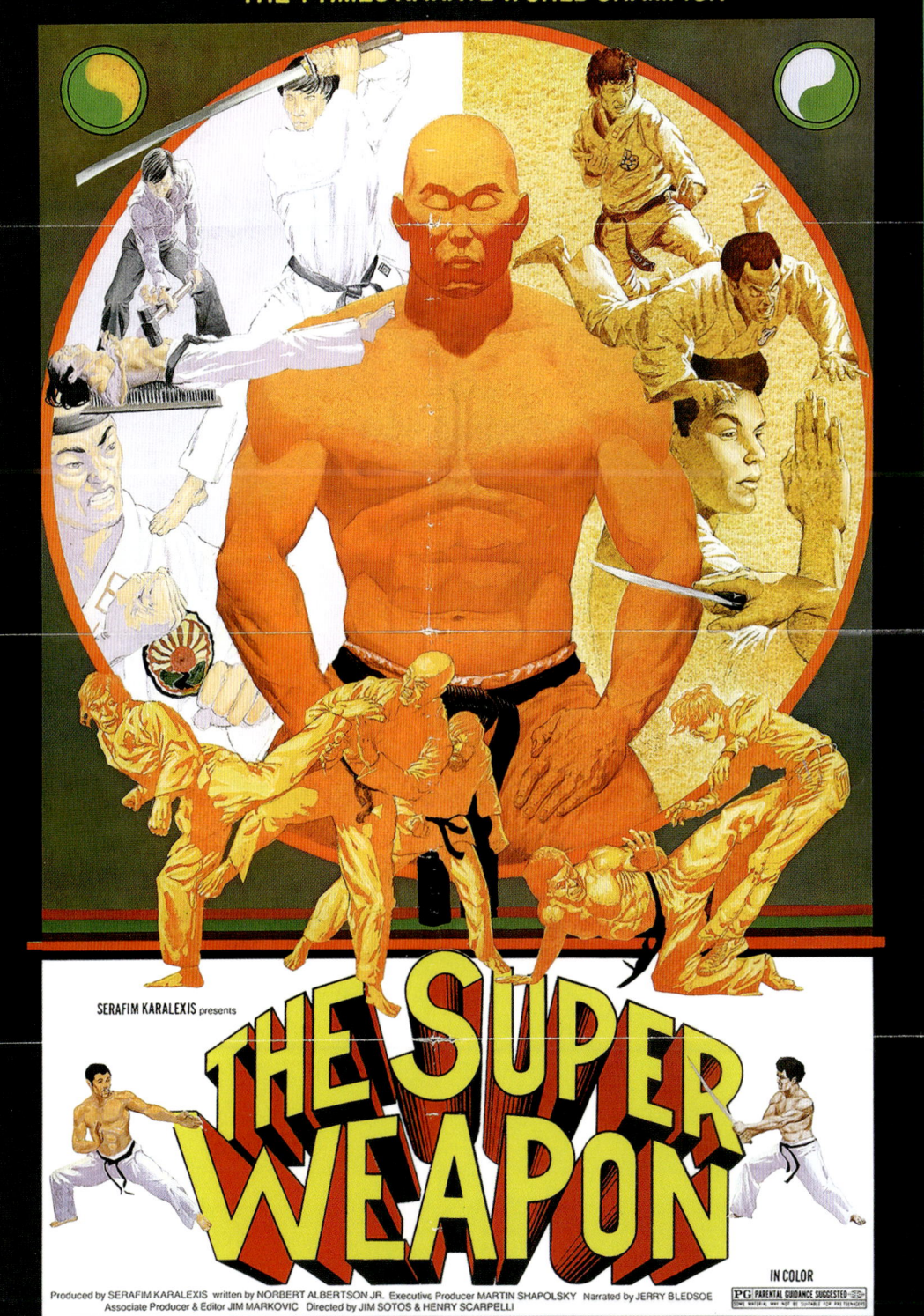

SERAFIM KARALEXIS presents

THE SUPER WEAPON

IN COLOR

PG PARENTAL GUIDANCE SUGGESTED

Produced by SERAFIM KARALEXIS   written by NORBERT ALBERTSON JR.   Executive Producer MARTIN SHAPOLSKY   Narrated by JERRY BLEDSOE
Associate Producer & Editor JIM MARKOVIC   Directed by JIM SOTOS & HENRY SCARPELLI

A MADISON WORLD FILM   A HOWARD MAHLER RELEASE

THEN CHARLES BONET LOST HIS DOJO. The result of a rent dispute with his landlord, he had to close his doors and move from the Bronx to the Ridgefield Self Defense Academy. It ticked him off and became the basis for Serafim Karalexis' next movie, *The Slum Lords* (1977).

"I think it's the last of my karate pictures," Karalexis said at the time. "If this one doesn't do what I think it should, then I will drop the whole business."

Budgeted at $250,000, it was directed by Robert Warmflash, who had no directing experience, and starred Bonet, essentially playing himself, alongside Bill Louie and Speedy Leacock, a tough, scrappy karate kid who was one of George Cofield's infamous "Gunners."

Working out of the Tong Dojo in Flatbush, Cofield's school produced champions like the Walder Twins and Thomas LaPuppet, but he was described as "a tough man to work under, a tough man to know, and a tough man to learn from." Cofield smacked his students with a bamboo stick when they made a mistake, drove them hard, and coached them from the sidelines of their tournaments. "He was a street guy," one student said. "A hustler-type guy. And viewed by most as being very, very mean." But Tong Dojo was the center of Black karate in Brooklyn, and Speedy Leacock was one of its best.

The Slums Lords wasn't anyone's best. Goofy and slipshod, it begins with its own theme song ("That's a promise! / I'm gonna get ya!") before narrator Gerry Bledsoe sums up the entire movie: "When you can't afford to move, even a rat-infested tenement can be called home. But when landlords turn off your heat, water, gas, and electricity, there's only one thing to do: fight."

And after a multiethnic cabal of evil landlords murder Bonet's dad to drive him from his building, Bonet and Leacock do fight! Dummies fly from tenement rooftops, throwing stars embed themselves in faces, Bonet sneaks across a nighttime lawn in a bright yellow blouse, and people scream. A lot. For a very long time.

The Slum Lords becomes more and more deranged as it progresses, with cackling landlords dreaming of the payday that will allow them to "get the hell out of this crummy city and live like a human being." Actors accidentally refer to each other by their real names, somehow the yakuza happens, and the shadow of the boom mic hangs over it all.

When Warmflash turned in the finished product, Karalexis got in the editing room.

"Now that I look at it," he said in an interview, "I'm beginning to have second thoughts . . . Which is why I'm staying here every day supervising the editing."

Whether in its ads or in its dialogue, *Death Promise* declared class warfare like no other martial arts movie, hoping to tap into urban audience's real-life frustrations. As the opening voiceover grimly stated, "In large US cities, millions of people live a life of poverty in old run-down apartment dwellings. The poor tenants trapped in these buildings must put up with constant harassment by greedy landlords who want to throw them out for higher rents." But apparently audiences didn't want the reality of their lives to follow them into the movie theater, and *Death Promise* wasn't nearly as successful as the *Black Dragon* movies.

FILTHY RICH LANDLORDS GET AWAY WITH MURDER.
IT'S TIME THEY PAY FOR IT.
SERAFIM KARALEXIS presents
DEATH PROMISE
starring
CHARLES BONET
IN COLOR
R
starring CHARLES BONET SPEEDY LEACOCK BILL LOUIE THOMPSON KAO KANG VINCENT VAN LYNN THOM KENDELL ABE HENDY DAVID KIRK BOB LONG
ROCKY CREVICE MONICA GERMAINE TONY DE CAPRIO ANTHONY LAU PETE RICHARDSON STUART WARMFLASH JASON LAU JERRY NG VAN GOLDY DAN DOYLE
written by NORBERT ALBERTSON JR. directed by ROBERT WARMFLASH edited by JIM MARKOVIC
MUSIC & SONGS PERFORMED BY OPUS ORIGINAL MUSIC BY MIKE FELDER & BILL DANIELS POST PRODUCTION RAINBOW PRO. COLOR BY PRECISION DE LUXE
produced by SERAFIM KARALEXIS associate producers HOWARD MAHLER & HANK STERN
A MADISON WORLD FILM A HOWARD MAHLER Release

The advertising billed it as a movie in the tradition of Charles Bronson's *Death Wish*, claiming it was about "the poor against the rich," which shows a deep misunderstanding of *Death Wish*. Renamed *Speedy & the Panther*, after its stars, Karalexis eventually changed its name to *Death Promise*, which sounds much more definite than a mere *Death Wish*.

The movie didn't bomb. It disappeared. Robert Warmflash became a post-production supervisor and never directed again. Karalexis didn't "drop the whole business" as promised. Instead he released the South African crime pic *Death of a Snowman* under the titles *Black Trash* and *Soul Patrol*, but mostly stuck with Bruceploitation—*They Call Me Bruce Lee*, *The Young Dragon*, *The Real Bruce Lee*, *The King of Kung Fu*, *Enter Three Dragons*—until a deal with Roy Horan and Seasonal Film led to him presenting Jackie Chan's *Eagle's Shadow* in 1982 and *Ninja Warriors* (aka *Ninja in the Dragon's Den*) in 1984. Only then did he abandon martial arts movies, producing a biopic about the Russian ballerina Anna Pavlova alongside Michael Powell and Martin Scorsese. Bonet went on to appear in a few more films, including the pyromaniac disco slasher *Don't Go in the House* (1979), but *Death Promise* represented his last leading role.

For all its lo-fi silliness, *Death Promise* might have had more meaning for Bonet than for anyone else. When he moved to New York, his family lived on San Juan Hill in Manhattan, a neighborhood packed with Italian, Black, and Puerto Rican families. In the '50s, the city slated it for demolition to make way for Lincoln Center. Robert Moses took charge of the project and evicted 7,000 families to make way for his opera house, the Bonets among them.*

Relocation funds for the families never materialized, and, like the South Bronx, San Juan Hill became yet another New York City neighborhood destroyed by the city's master planner. *Death Promise* declared, "Filthy-rich landlords have been getting away long enough. It's time they paid for it!"

In the real world, they never do.

By 1977, audiences cared very little about kung fu, and even Jim Kelly couldn't find work. His contract with Weintraub and Warners had concluded, and they showed zero interest in renewing.

Then he got a phone call from Larry Joachim.

*You can see the wreckage of post-condemnation San Juan Hill as it's demolished in the background of *West Side Story* (1961).

(opposite page) Like a lot of movies, distributors designed one ad campaign for white audiences and another for Black viewers.

(above) The original title of *Death Promise* was *Speedy and the Panther* to capitalize on the local fame of Speedy Leacock, Charles Bonet's co-star and founder of New York City's Black Magic Dojo.

THE SUCCESS OF THE GREEN HORNET and its sequel, *Fury of the Dragon*, gave Larry Joachim the cash to produce his own martial arts epic. He'd divorced Barbara Loden and married Barbara Holden and the newlyweds purchased the rights to a novel entitled *The Warlock*, the sixth in the Black Samurai series of men's adventure paperbacks by African-American author and martial artist Marc Olden. For the role of the Black Samurai himself, Larry and Barbara hired Ron Van Clief, and as director, they secured respected actor, D'Urville Martin, whose directorial debut, *Dolemite*, was making big bucks at theaters around the country.

Shortly before filming began, Van Clief had a disagreement with Larry over pay and left the project. The director, crew, and co-stars all decamped in solidarity and suddenly Joachim didn't have a movie. He turned to his friend, Sam Sherman, who helped him secure Al Adamson as the new director, but they still needed their Black Samurai. Marco, then 13, had an idea.

"Jim Kelly?!" Larry exploded at him. "We can't afford Jim Kelly!"

"Why don't you ask him how much he wants," Marco replied.

"He'll turn us down!"

"You'll never know unless you ask."

Marco had been right before, so Larry called Jim Kelly's agent, and it turned out that after *Hot Potato* they could secure his services for $30,000—the same amount Van Clief had tried to get out of Larry, but Kelly had been in *Enter the Dragon*.

While his stepmother dashed out the screenplay (she's credited as "B. Readick" on the film), Marco read a handful of Olden's *Black Samurai* paperbacks and was unimpressed with the idea of the titular hero taking orders from a former president of the United States.

"I grew up watching '60s spy stuff and thought it would be cooler if he worked for a secret counterintelligence agency that was an acronym, like U.N.C.L.E. or SPECTRE," Marco explains, "and I also wanted something that referenced Jim Kelly being in *Enter the Dragon*, so I made the character an agent for D.R.A.G.O.N., which is short for Defense Reserve Agency, Guardian of Nations."

It wasn't Marco's only creative input. After a few days of filming, he received a panicked call from Larry on the West Coast. (Marco was home in Manhattan.)

"My dad said that they had filmed the whole script and only had enough footage for a 50-minute movie," Marco says. "He wanted more ideas . . . but nothing that would cost too much. I had just watched *Thunderball*, which has James Bond using a jet pack, so I told him 'Have the Black Samurai fly around in a jet pack!' After they filmed that, he'd call every night for more ideas. I'd say 'Give him a pen that shoots flames' or 'Get more midgets.'"

The *Black Samurai* poster was a copy of the cover from the original Signet paperback, executed by an artist for the Brill & Waldstein agency.

JIM KELLY AS THE BLACK SAMURAI
AGENT FOR DRAGON

JIM KELLY as the **BLACK SAMURAI**, Produced by BARBARA HOLDEN, Executive Producer LAURENCE JOACHIM, Directed by AL ADAMSON
A BJLJ International Corp. Production, Screenplay by B. READICK, Based on the novel by MARC OLDEN

The Center Theater, an all-night porno fleapit on Market Street in downtown Philadelphia, changed its name to the Bruce Lee Center in February 1981 and programmed only martial arts double features for the next 14 months, yet never showed an actual Bruce Lee movie during that entire time.

The budget came in at $75,000—not much, considering 40% of it went to Kelly. The resulting movie is unsurprisingly decrepit, with Larry Joachim himself dubbing at least four characters on the soundtrack, one of them a woman. Because of language, violence, and nudity the film was given an R by the MPAA, but Larry prepared an edited version that could play on double features with his two *Green Hornet* films and, surprisingly, *Black Samurai* became a box-office success that stayed in theatrical release for almost 10 years.

For Kelly, it was a $30,000 payday that didn't do much to burnish his image or raise his rate. He decamped for Hong Kong, where he made *The Tattoo Connection* (1978), which did well in Hong Kong but almost zero business in the US, despite being marketed as *Black Belt Jones 2: The Tattoo Connection* and despite Kelly's claims that "it's the best martial arts film since *Enter the Dragon*."

American audiences might have stayed away from the December 1979 release of *The Tattoo Connection* because it had been preceded by the summer 1978 release of *Death Dimension*, a bottom-of-the-barrel Dick Randall production starring Kelly. Joachim was friends with Randall and had put him in touch with Kelly and Al Adamson to make what they described in the press as a Bond-ian Italian-American co-production in 3D. A year later it plopped onto screens, courtesy of Richard Ellman's Movietime Films, introducing "Honolulu's own Myron Bruce Lee," a student from the University of Hawaii who answered a newspaper ad looking for a Bruce Lee impersonator less than two weeks before filming began. It wasn't even in 3D.

Death Dimension tells that age-old story of a scientist who invents a freeze bomb to aid mankind only to have it fall into the wrong hands. Myron Bruce Lee doesn't even show up until the 30-minute mark, after which he disappears for another half hour. And while Jim Kelly's karate is tighter and faster than normal, it doesn't really matter anymore. The movie is mostly a tax shelter for its investors, and the fact that it's one of the few movies to shoot at the Mustang Ranch, America's most famous brothel, only makes it feel sadder. Kelly isn't even pictured in the advertising for the 1980 reissue as *Freeze Bomb*, which gives him third billing below James Bond one-shot George Lazenby and *Goldfinger* henchman Harold "Odd Job" Sakata.

After that, Kelly started focusing on tennis and moving away from movies.

"White America just was not and is not ready for a Black hero," he said. "It's the worst it's been for a Black actor for a long time."

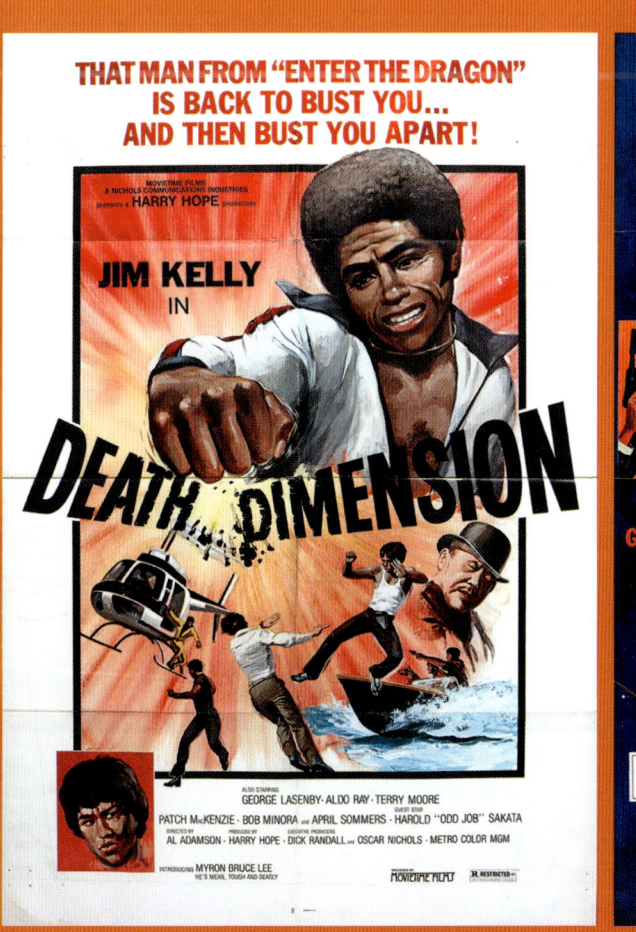

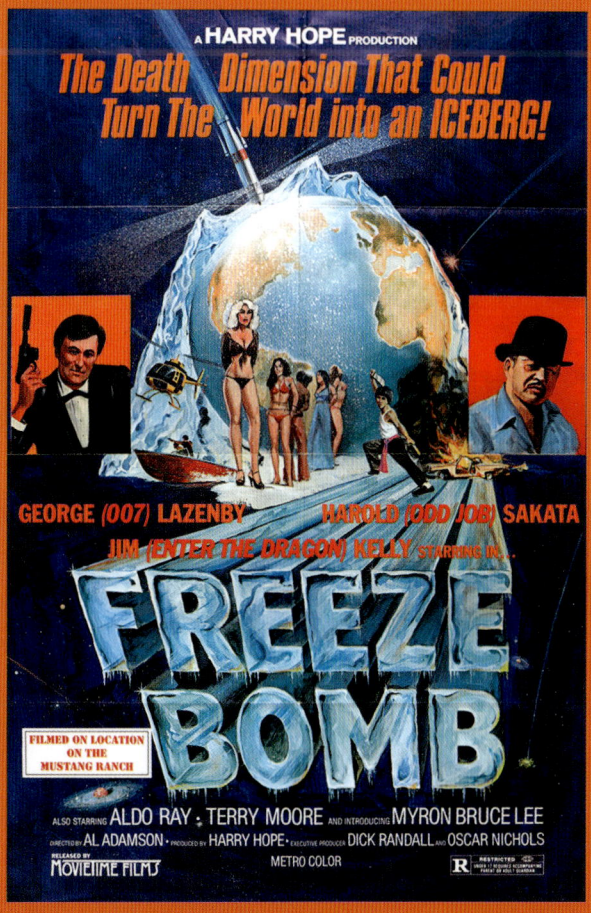

Death Dimension (1978) was re-released in 1980 as *Freeze Bomb*. Both were released by Movietime, a venture by our friend Richard Ellman (*Fearless Fighters*; see page 66), who had opened his company as a video store, but discovered not enough people owned VCRs and got back into theatrical distribution.

NDEPENDENT DISTRIBUTORS KEPT LOOKING FOR a Black star who could click. In the silly Cirio Santiago–produced Filipino movie *Bamboo Gods & Iron Men*, released by AIP in 1974, James Iglehart and his wife (played by former Miss Black America Shirley Washington) accidentally buy an antique that inspires shenanigans, including an attack by bees, which sends them running naked across their lawn shouting, "Bees! Bees! Bees! Bees! Bees!"

Also revolving around the theft of an antique, *Force Four* (1975) is a lethargic vehicle for a fistful of the city's martial artists: Owen Wat-son; Warhawk Tanzania with his mighty mustache, awesome Afro, and superhuman sideburns; and Malachi Lee, a teacher with a dojo on 23rd Street who would die unexpectedly the following year. Mostly it's a slipshod travelogue of NYC neighborhoods and a fashion show of bell bottoms and platform shoes.

Warhawk Tanzania went on to make *Devil's Express* (1976), which, despite ending with Warhawk in a pair of skintight golden overalls, fighting screaming ghosts and a grotty monster in New York's subway system, has its most exciting moment in the opening credits as the camera prowls 42nd Street, revealing a Karalexis-Mahler–distributed double bill of *Kung Fu Cops* and *The Black Dragon* at the Liberty Theater.

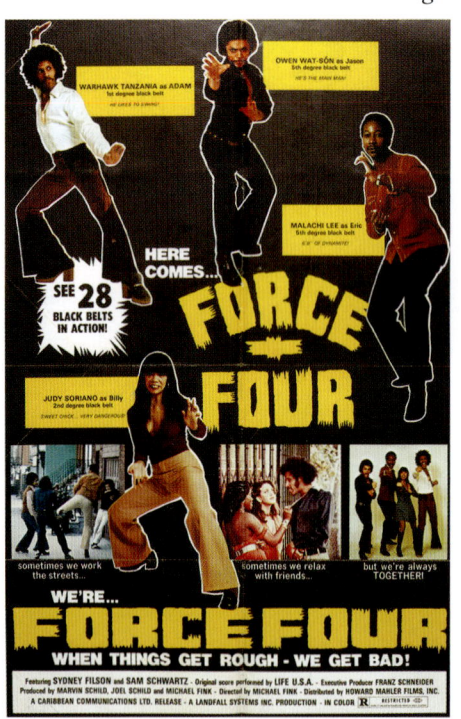

As the '70s limped to their end, kung fu met the one killer it couldn't conquer: comedy. Richard Pryor held the box office heavyweight belt, and Rudy Ray Moore's pimp-fu hit, *Dolemite* (1975), made it impossible to take these rickety productions seriously anymore. Moore's sequel was *The Human Tornado* (1976), which dared to send up *Enter the Dragon*'s mirror-shattering climax in its riotous opening credits. World karate champion (and Chuck Norris' future trainer) Howard Jackson was on hand to provide histrionics and action choreography, but mostly Rudy Ray Moore's pimp-fu was exactly the kind of combat you expected from a tubby middle-aged man who'd seen too many kung fu flicks.

Ron Van Clief worked harder than ever, taking a Cadillac from theater to theater, doing demonstrations, and signing autographs for Terry Levene, even when he wasn't in the movie being premiered. When reporters asked why he did it, he answered honestly: It's the money.

"There is nothing else," he said.

His business cards proclaimed him a "zenpsychotherapist," he endorsed a vitamin line, put together a T-shirt deal with Warner Bros., and even considered signing with

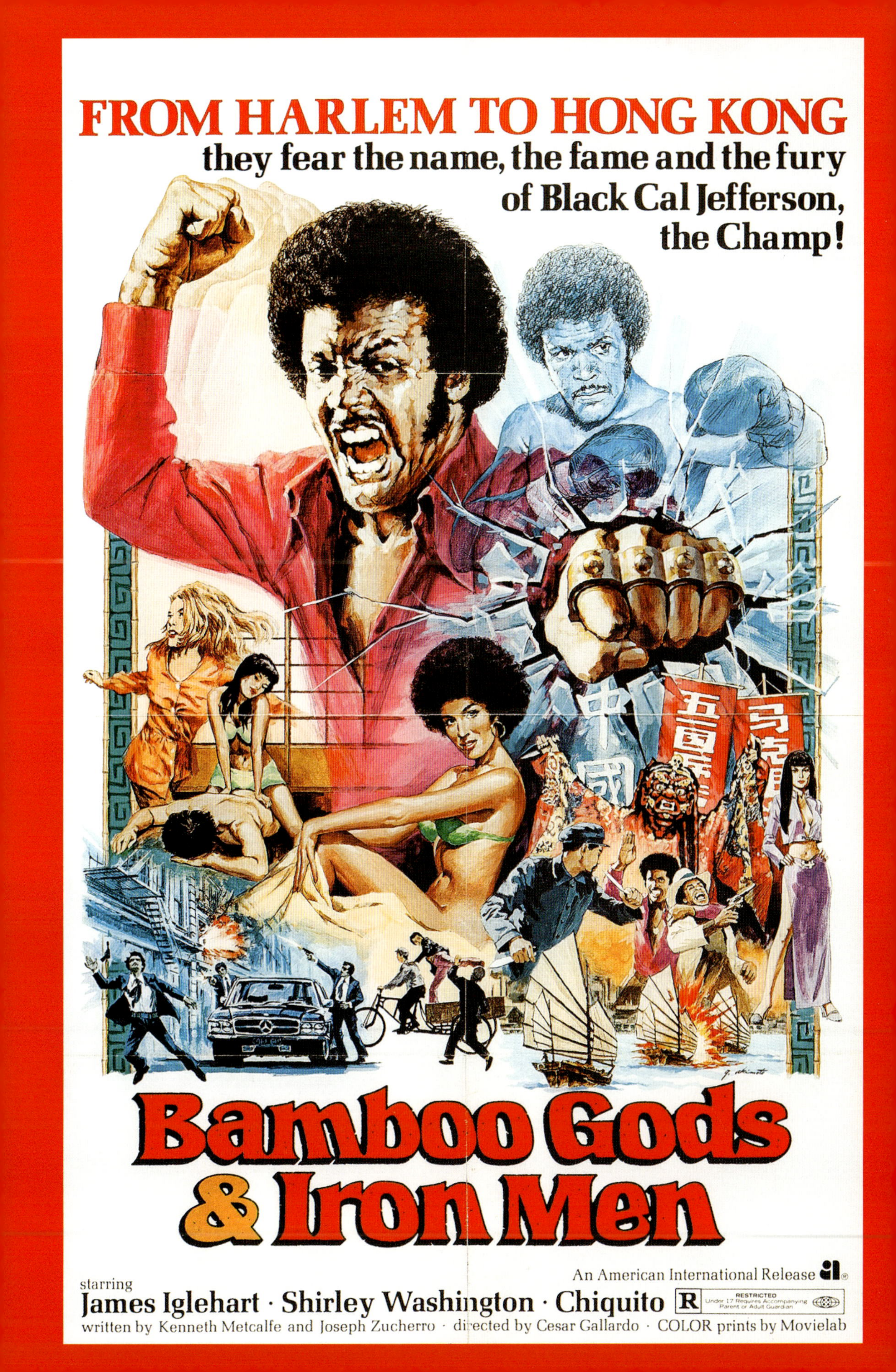
FROM HARLEM TO HONG KONG
they fear the name, the fame and the fury
of Black Cal Jefferson,
the Champ!
Bamboo Gods
& Iron Men
An American International Release
starring
James Iglehart · Shirley Washington · Chiquito
R
RESTRICTED
Under 17 Requires Accompanying Parent or Adult Guardian
written by Kenneth Metcalfe and Joseph Zucherro · directed by Cesar Gallardo · COLOR prints by Movielab

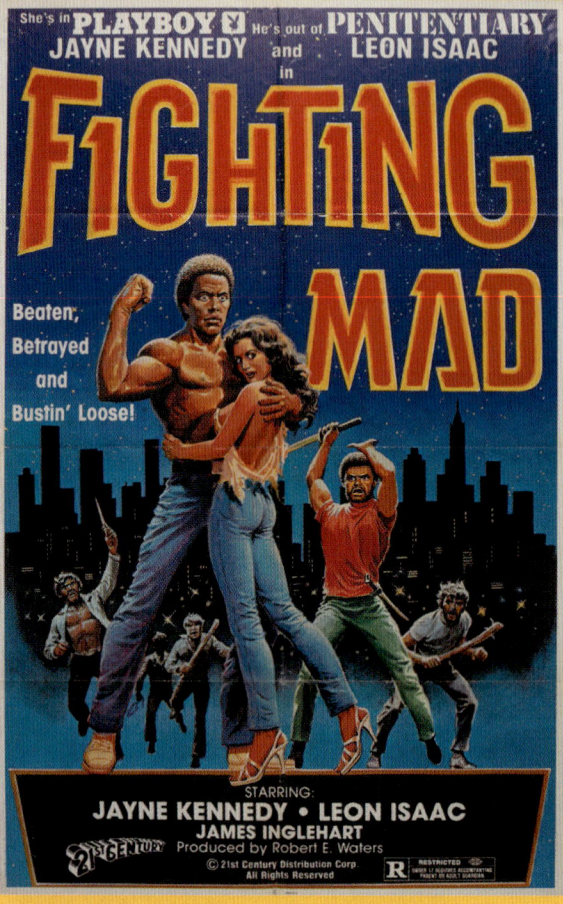

The last of three Filipino action movies James Iglehart starred in for filmmaker Cirio H. Santiago, *Vengeance Is Mine* was trimmed by 20 minutes ahead of its US release in 1978 as *Death Force*. When co-stars Leon Isaac Kennedy (*Penitentiary*) and Jayne Kennedy (*The NFL Today*) became more famous in the early '80s, it was reissued as *Fighting Mad*.

Casablanca Records to cut a "soft jazz" album, but the bulk of his living came from teaching.

Ron Van Clief never achieved his fullest potential as an action star, and Hollywood never came calling. In fact, almost every single one of his movies is a foreign co-production. But for a while he was as big a star as a Black martial artist could be. As one of his students pointed out, "No one believed in him. He was just a Black kid from Brooklyn, and people were waiting to see him fail."

In 1977, 15-year-old Carl Scott made his motion picture debut in *Soul Brothers of Kung Fu*, and he's probably the best big-screen Black martial artist of the bunch. Discovered as an extra in Ng See-yuen's *Bruce Lee: The Man, the Myth*, he'd studied under Sijo Saabir Quwi Muhammad (born Steve Sanders; see page 17) and come up through the Black Karate Federation. Ng's producer, Pau Ming, cast him in a Hong Kong movie with Bruce Li, and Carl's mom gave permission for him to go as long as they shot in the summer so he could be home in time to start 10th grade. *Soul Brothers of Kung Fu* wasn't a huge hit but it's a fantastic showcase for Scott, a lanky, limber, baby-faced fighter whose supporting role takes over the movie with his energy, going out like a champ in his final fight playing possum, headbutting his opponent, and throwing rocks.

Scott fought fast, with great rhythm, dropping low and popping high, snapping out kicks and flicking his fists, occasionally breaking into a grin in the middle of a rumble like he's having the time of his life. His onscreen elegance came from his proficiency in multiple forms of kung fu, which emphasized speed and grace, rather than karate which wanted you to put your opponent on the floor, fast. Production company Eternal Films snapped him up and produced a few more flicks with him, pairing Scott with Jackie Chan imitator Billy Chong and shooting their movies for million-dollar budgets in Phoenix, Arizona. He seemed to be going places, but time wasn't on his side.

As the '70s rolled on, martial arts dojos closed all over the country, with each year's survey of big-city martial arts academies listing fewer names than the year before. After a 70-year-old woman was stabbed to death with a butter knife, the New York papers took the trouble to note that "the three defendants escaped with a small amount of money that they spent at a neighborhood theater where the movie starred the late Bruce Lee . . ."

More and more, the press linked kung fu to violence. Principals in Queens high schools complained to the papers about gang violence, blaming it on the diet of blaxploitation and kung fu movies the kids consumed. By 1975, New York's police and firefighter unions, irritated at the way they were being treated by the city in contract negotiations, put together a pamphlet called *Welcome to Fear City* featuring a hooded, grinning skull on the cover, and gave it out to tourists at airports and hotels. It depicted the city as a crime-ridden hellhole, advised tourists not to take the subway for any reason whatsover, and not to leave their hotels after dark.

The economy was weak, crime was rising alongside unemployment. Kung fu movies had gone from being the toast of Hollywood to something distributors threw into run-down urban movie theaters with one hand while pinching their noses shut with the other.

Then, in July 1977, a pair of lightning strikes shut down the power grid, leaving NYC dark. Looters rampaged, shattering shop windows and setting fires. Roughly 4,500 people were arrested. Jason Lau, a Wing Chun teacher and friend of Ron Van Clief's who sometimes joined him at his movie theater demos, did his best to hold down his part of Flatbush, taking out looters with strikes to the throat, but despite the actions of hundreds of citizens like him, the image the country took away was of New York City as a crime-infested madhouse.

But the blackout had an upside. Among the looters were a bunch of DJs, like Casanova Fly, who stole the equipment they needed to launch their careers. Hip hop had lain dormant for much of the '70s, retreating to nightclubs and catering to a more upscale crowd, losing some of its street energy in the process. 1977 saw Kool Herc get stabbed multiple times in a club, and he retreated from the scene. But that same year, Afrika Bambaata founded his Zulu Nation and started to spin, and when Grand Wizard Theodore's mom came upstairs to see what all that noise was coming out of his room, he grabbed his turntable to stop the record, accidentally inventing scratching, which became one of hip hop's key techniques.

Grandmaster Flash and the Furious Five started true syncopated rapping over their songs as Flash caught the beat and perfected Theodore's scratching technique, organizing freestyle battles where MCs faced off, one on one, armed only with their skills, not for money, but for respect, like something out of a kung fu movie.

B-boying had become a backwater, dismissed as kiddie stuff performed on a playground, but Richard Colón aka Crazy Legs wasn't going to quit. Inspired by the kung fu movies he soaked up on the Deuce, Crazy Legs traveled through the five boroughs tracking down each great b-boy artist he could find, challenging them to a competition and studying their skills. In 1977, juiced by the experience, he helped form the Rocksteady Crew, who'd take b-boying international, starting with a performance at a Bronx library whose flyer bragged that they would demonstrate, "Breaking, Rapping & Graffiti, an original blend of dancing, acrobatics, and martial arts."

Down on the Lower East Side, a filmmaker named Charlie Ahearn started going to the Alfred E. Smith projects, where a karate student named Nathan Ingram asked him to shoot a movie improvised by him and his fellow students. It blossomed into *The Deadly Art of Survival* (1979), a no wave 8mm movie, barely one hour long, full of street noise, actors losing track of their conversations in the middle, terrible ninjas, and a bad guy who operates out of Handsome Harry's Disco Dojo. But it also features uncomfortably raw moments, like a battered and bleeding Ingram flopped across his bed, expressionless, while his mom berates him for getting beaten up yet again. Over him hangs a Bruce Lee poster, and nowhere is the gulf between dream and reality made more painfully clear than the contrast between his battered and humiliated body and the gleaming and invulnerable Bruce Lee.

When the artist's collective, Colab, organized a show in an abandoned building uptown called "The Times Square Show" in the summer of 1980, Ahearn included one of the posters from *The Deadly Art of Survival,* since it had been inspired by the kung fu flicks he'd seen on the Deuce. It caught the eye of a graffiti artist named

(left) The star of *Devil's Express* (1976) is Warhawk Tanzania (born Warren Hawkins), an anomaly among the Big Apple–based martial arts movie stars of the 1970s in that he had prior acting experience, having appeared on stage in productions of Black-authored plays like *Ceremonies in Dark Old Men* by Lonne Elder III, *Sometimes a Hard Head Makes a Soft Behind* by Sonny Jim Gaines, and *Don't Bother Me, I Can't Cope* by Vinnette Carroll. A Chinese Goju black belt, trained by Ron Van Clief, he starred in only two New York–lensed low-budget kung fu flicks—the other was *Force Four* (1975)—before fading into obscurity.

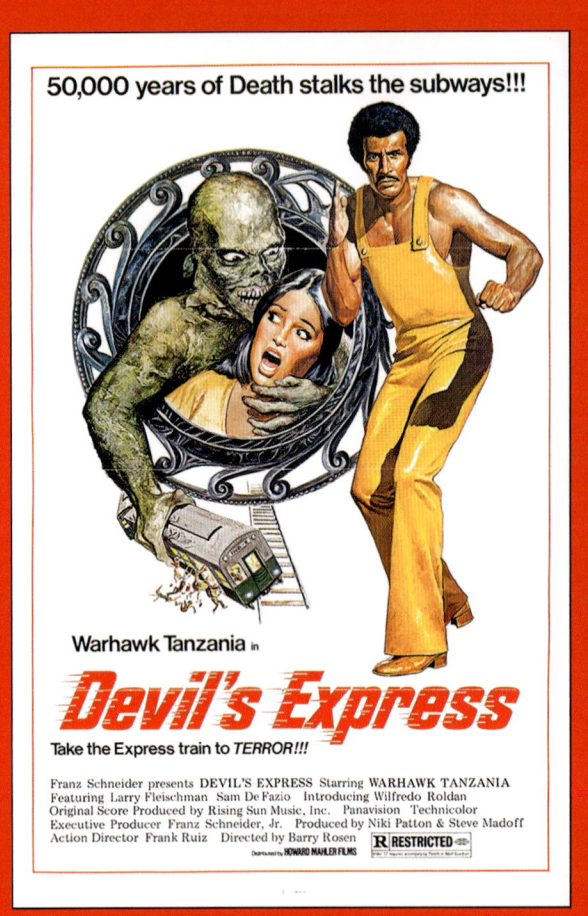

(right) Cinematic Releasing sent *Devil's Express* back to grindhouses in 1980 as *Gang Wars*, with an ad campaign that downplayed the horror element while trying to capitalize on *Star Wars* and *The Warriors*.

(left) Nathan Ingram, pictured here, was no chump. He's the one who pushed Charlie Ahearn into shooting his crew, who called their school "The Deadly Art of Survival." In 1981, he single-handedly stopped a bank robbery, earning praise from New York City's mayor. Ingram worked in community centers and taught martial arts for most of his life.

(right) A 1983 newspaper ad for a preview of Ahearn's *Wild Style* in Times Square. Samples from the movie would show up on albums by everyone from Cypress Hill to MF Doom.

Fab 5 Freddy, and the two of them would collaborate on *Wild Style* (1983), the movie that would help take hip hop global.

Around the same time, Robert Fitzgerald Diggs' older cousin started bringing him to 42nd Street, where they'd soak up kung fu movies. Diggs kept coming back throughout the '80s, learning when the lineups changed so he could get six different movies for the price of one. In the late '80s he'd change his name to RZA and found the Wu-Tang Clan.

The Black experience in martial arts movies may have missed its shot at the big time, but its energy migrated into music, giving new life to hip hop, and when "Rapper's Delight" became its first big single in 1979, it sent b-boys sailing across the dance floor on their shoulders, their backs, and their heads. Black music, dance, graffiti, and street culture was ready to take off and fly. But a Black martial artist hadn't gone mainstream. No one had replaced Bruce Lee. But toward the end of the decade, David Carradine decided it was time for one more try.

NUNCHUKS

WHETHER THEY'RE SPELLED "NUNCHUKS," "numchucks," "ninja chucks," or "nunchakus," clearly two sticks linked by a bit of string are the most deadly weapons ever created. Even Supreme Court justice Sonia Sotomayor fears and loathes them.

Bruce Lee made nunchuks sexy in *Enter the Dragon,* but two months after the movie came out *Newsweek* published an article called "Killer Sticks" (October 15, 1973) about how an expert could use nunchuks to "bash or strangle his victim" and claimed they were used to attack the police in Baltimore. The very next day, the Philadelphia police commissioner ordered that anyone found with nunchuks would be arrested on sight. In California, the *Newsweek* article got cited when a bill was introduced for a nunchuk ban, and New York state banned them that same year. (They stayed banned until 2018.) But despite the claim that they were used by gang members, few if any police officers admitted that they had actually witnessed any nunchuk attacks, and *Newsweek* never revealed the author of the scare piece. Nevertheless, the fear persisted, with newspaper articles citing them being "twirled" ominously in the "dingy headquarters" of Lyndon LaRouche's National Caucus of Labor Committees, a student group that had reportedly kidnapped and tortured its own members and planned to overthrow the government of the United States.

Martial arts magazines offered nunchuks and all kinds of fun weapons for sale, while at the same time it was completely illegal to own them in certain states. In New York City, you could only carry them down the street if you were on the way to surrender them at your local precinct house (and then only after giving the police 24 hours' written notice) and in California you could own a shotgun or a .45, but owning nunchuks or a shuriken (throwing star) was a felony offense that came with a five-year sentence.

The laws led to arrests despite the fact that the weapons only ever actually seemed to be a menace in movies. As one 15-year veteran of the LAPD's gang unit said, "Gang members, and a lot of other young people, carry the nunchaku a lot, but I personally have never heard of an incident of violence using them . . . The most common gang weapon is the sawed-off shotgun."

In 2000, James Maloney of Long Island was peering through a telescope when a telephone repairman mistook it for a rifle and called the police. Their search of his home turned up no weapons except for a pair of nunchuks tucked under his mattress. Maloney explained their presence, saying, "A pair of nunchaku I can leave tucked under my mattress 24/7 with very low risk that my kids are going to pick them up and blow their brains out." The police charged Maloney with possession of a dangerous weapon, and he eventually pled guilty to one count of disorderly conduct and agreed to destroy the nunchuks. However, on further consideration, he filed an appeal stating that this violated his Second Amendment right to bear arms, and it wound its way to the Second Circuit, where future Supreme Court justice Sonia Sotomayor ruled that the Second Amendment wasn't binding on the New York State government. Maloney's case was dismissed, but Sotomayor's decision was used against her during her nomination hearings when Senator Orrin Hatch (R-UT) asked her about her ruling. "Sir," Sotomayor replied, "these are martial arts sticks . . . and when the sticks are swung . . . if there's anybody near you, you're going to be seriously injured . . . [I]t can bust someone's skull."

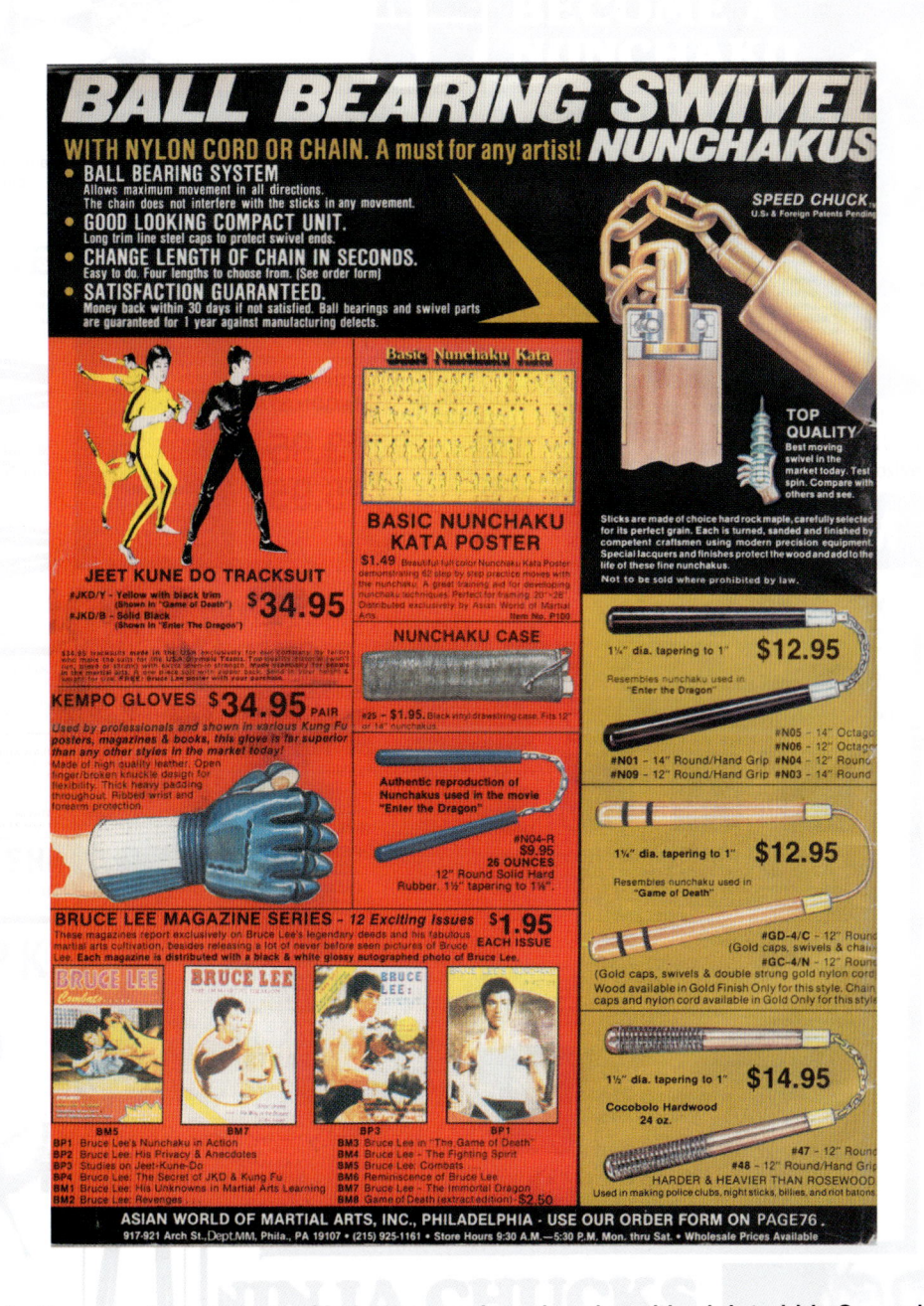

Marking the first and only time in American history that nunchuks entered the Senate record.

COUNT DANTE, AKA THE MOST DANGEROUS MAN ALIVE, and founder of the Black Dragon Society, was born John Timothy Keehan in Chicago on February 2, 1939. His father, Jack, was a physician and director of the Ashland State Bank, and his mother, Dorothy, occasionally appeared on the *Tribune*'s society pages. In his teens Keehan attended Mount Carmel High School and boxed at Johnny Coulon's 63rd Street gym. After graduation he joined the Marine reserves and later the Army, where he learned hand-to-hand combat and jiu-jitsu.

By 1962, Keehan was teaching at Gene Wyka's Judo and Karate Center in Brighton Park and making occasional trips to Phoenix, Arizona, to study under Robert Trias, founder of the United States Karate Association (see page 12). Training full-time, Keehan quickly earned his second-degree black belt and was appointed the USKA's Midwest representative.

Wanting to reach the mainstream, Keehan organized tournaments that emphasized the flashier aspects of the martial arts; a savvy publicist, he appeared on the cover of one tournament program smashing eight rows of bricks with his elbow. His early tournaments attracted a host of martial arts luminaries—like Ed Parker, Jhoon Rhee, and a pre–*Enter the Dragon* Bruce Lee. One of his former students, James Jones, remembers him as an ideal instructor. "John was a person who focused on basics and fundamentals," he says. Keehan was one of the few men who could punch a brick in half, though at one event it took three strikes and Keehan wound up breaking five bones in his hand. Still, he showed up at the dojo the next day, his hand in a cast.

Keehan also gained a reputation for being one of the first white senseis in the country to accept non-white students. "Race never played a part in John's teaching," says Jones, who is Black. In December 1964, Trias expelled Keehan from the

USKA. He later said that Keehan "was given too much power too young and too fast." The future Count Dante did seem to be drifting off course. On July 22, 1965, Keehan and Doug Dwyer, a longtime friend and fellow instructor, were arrested after a drunken attempt to blow out a window at Gene Wyka's martial arts school with a dynamite cap. He got two years' probation. Around the same time, Keehan bought a lion cub, which he kept at his dojo on Ashland and walked around town like a dog. In the summer of 1967, he promoted an audacious exhibition in which a bull would be killed with a single blow. Keehan purchased a bull from the Chicago stockyards and drove it around town on the back of a flatbed truck festooned with signs announcing the event. After the seats were filled, Keehan announced that the event had been shut down by the Chicago SPCA. The bull lived.

That year Keehan legally changed his name to Juan Raphael Dante, telling people that he wanted to reclaim the royal title he lost after his parents immigrated to the US in 1936, during the Spanish Civil War. It's never been clear why a South Side Irish guy like Keehan decided he was a Spanish count, or how he chose his new name (though Mount Carmel High School is located on Dante Avenue). Regardless, his new name and background came with a flashier image. At a 1967 tournament, he arrived wearing a flowing cape and brandishing a cane capped by a lion's head; he'd dyed his hair jet-black and sported a neatly trimmed beard, reflecting his new side gig in cosmetology. That same year he opened a salon, the House of Dante.

Inspired by kung fu dim mak, or "poison hand," strikes, which emphasize thumbing out eyes, flaying skin, and fish-hooking lips, the freshly minted Count Dante assembled the *World's Deadliest Fighting Secrets* pamphlet and advertised it heavily in comic books.

By 1969, Keehan had opened three new Imperial Academies of Fighting Arts in the city and continued to hold full-contact tournaments. Keehan claimed to have taught 60% of Chicago's karate instructors, to which *Black Belt* managing editor D. David Dreis replied, "Which is one reason why *Black Belt* didn't cover Chicago." One instructor described a Dante tournament he judged as an "amateur boxing match" and said he'd never judge another.

On April 24, 1970, Keehan assembled a gang of former students to settle a beef with the Green Dragon Society's Black Cobra Hall of Gun-Fu and Kenpo. According to news reports, Keehan and his crew broke down the rival dojo's front door and found six Green Dragons inside. In the melee, one of the Green Dragon students grabbed a sword from the wall and stabbed one of Keehan's crew. The 26-year-old staggered outside and died on the sidewalk. Keehan, 31, was charged with aggravated battery and impersonating a police officer. (No explanation was given for the latter charge.)

The judge dismissed all charges but not before upbraiding both sides: "You're each as guilty as the other," he bellowed. Though Keehan was acquitted, his name was blackened. He tried to offer a mea culpa in an *Official Karate* article. "My days of fighting at the drop of a hat have come to an end," he wrote. "And challenges I will accept no more unless first attacked." His vow was short-lived: his lawyer recalls him beating up two men in a liquor store parking lot after they laughed at the bogus Spanish coat of arms on the door of his brown Caddy and assaulting another guy in a bar who called him a "fruit."

By 1974, Keehan had a acquired a financial interest in a chain of adult bookstores and a car dealership. He eventually ran afoul of South Side mob boss Jimmy "the Bomber" Catuara and had to pay him $25,000 in apology money. In the fall of 1974, Keehan was subpoenaed by the state's attorney and given a lie detector test about his possible role in the heist of more than $4 million from the headquarters of Purolator Security. The experience seemed to shake Keehan, and by 1975, he was clearly unwell—one friend recalls him stumbling through a conversation before admitting that he was mixing booze and painkillers.

Keehan died on May 25, 1975, in his Edgewater condo from a bleeding peptic ulcer, probably brought on by years of stress and hard living. He was all of 36.

And yet . . .

"He's dead and we're still talking about him," says James Jones. "He did what he set out to accomplish."

SHORTLY AFTER HE SNUCK INTO a showing of *Enter the Dragon* at Mann's Chinese Theatre in Hollywood, David Carradine was visited at his home by John Barrymore Jr., the deeply troubled fourth generation member of the Barrymore acting dynasty. He handed Carradine a 70-page manuscript to read, but Carradine had to read it fast so that Barrymore could return it to James Coburn's private library before the *Our Man Flint* actor returned on Monday morning. Intrigued, Carradine flipped open the manuscript to the title page and saw: "A film by James Coburn, Bruce Lee, Stirling Silliphant, THE SILENT FLUTE."

Set in a time and place never identified, where a contest is held every 10 years to select a martial artist who will be the Keeper of the Book, it tells the tale of Cord the Seeker, determined to survive the Three Trials so he can get his hands on the Book and become the greatest martial arts master who ever lived. Along the way he encounters Ah Sahm the Blind Man, and the Three Trials, which are represented by the Monkey Man, the Rhythm Man, and the Panther Man (aka Death). The production notes explained that Coburn was to direct, co-produce, and act in the film as Cord; Lee would've staged and directed all of the combat sequences and also appeared in the film as the Monkey Man, the Rhythm Man, the Panther Man, and Ah Sahm the Blind Man.

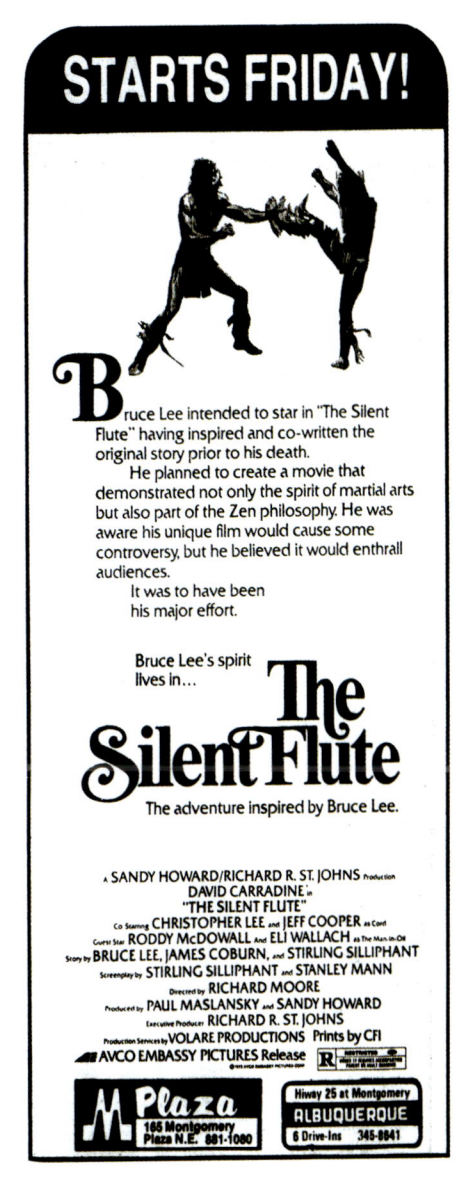

Lee and Silliphant had originally tried to get Steve McQueen to play Cord back in 1968, but when that didn't work out they approached another of Lee's celebrity students, James Coburn, who jumped at the chance once he found out he would also get to direct. The three men brought it to Ted Ashley at Warner Bros., who was only willing to give them the green light if they shot the film in India. After an unsuccessful three weeks scouting locations, Coburn nixed the deal, which infuriated Lee and was one of the deciding factors in his move to Hong Kong. Coburn and Silliphant eventually set it up at 20th Century Fox in 1973, but by then Lee was famous and told them he no longer wanted to be involved. He died soon after, and for a while it seemed like the project had died with him.

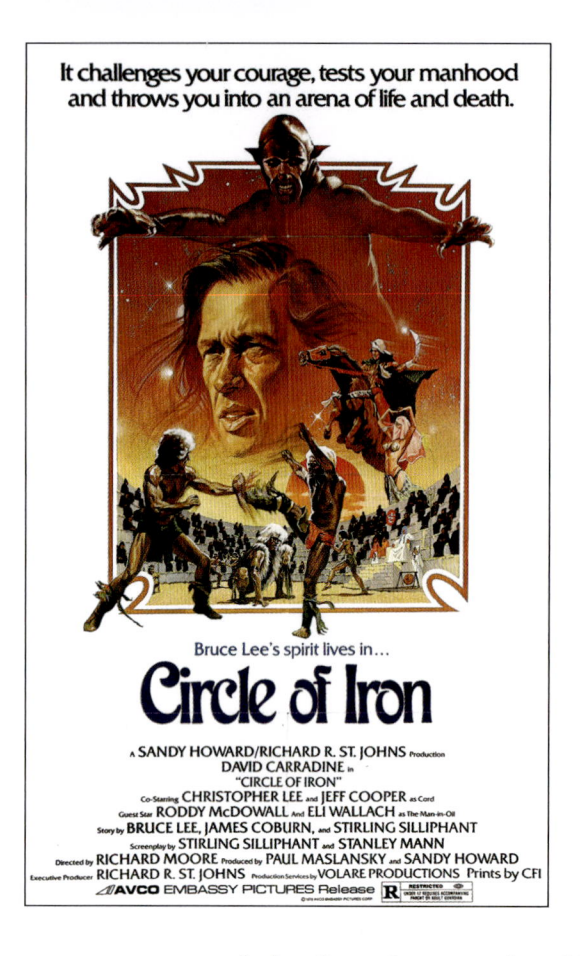

Carradine fell in love with the story and spent the next few years not only thinking about it but telling anyone who'd listen that he was possessed by the spirit of Bruce Lee, beginning with *TV Guide* in January 1974. "That Bruce Lee, I get a thing from him, man, a spiritual essence. It's like you take from Nureyev, Valentino, Jesus Christ and Wilt Chamberlain. You look at them and see what they can do and you say, 'Man, there's hope for me.'" When the writer reminded him that Bruce Lee was dead and he was referring to him in the present tense, Carradine responded disdainfully, "You just don't understand the spiritual essence, man."

Sometimes he would mix it up a bit, saying in one interview, "I created this Kung Fu monster. I'm the spirit who got everyone interested in the martial arts—even before Bruce Lee came along." But most of the time his claims were more along the lines of "When Bruce died, his spirit went into me."

Carradine expressed interest in the project as soon as he learned that Silliphant and Coburn had made a deal with producer Sandy Howard. After wasting a couple of months trying to get Carradine to play Cord the Seeker, a part Carradine felt he had already done on *Kung Fu* for three seasons, Howard decided it would be a good role for Joe Lewis (see page 280), who Bruce Lee himself had considered "the greatest karate fighter of all time." But the kickboxing champ had already turned down the role back in 1973 out of respect to his friend Lee. Now he said no for a different reason: he didn't want to work with Carradine.

Carradine already had someone else in mind for the role, anyways: his best friend, Canadian actor Jeff Cooper. Filming began October 28, 1977. On the second day, Carradine missed a cue and elbowed Cooper in the face, driving his teeth through his cheek, an injury that required nine stitches to close. Carradine's nose got broken twice in four days, once by action choreographer Kam Yuen and the second time by Cooper.

"They're the best martial arts fights ever put on film," Howard told *Boxoffice* after the shoot wrapped in February '78, right around the time he offered Joe Lewis $1,500 to help fix them. Lewis really didn't want to, but he also didn't want to say no to the producer who'd just signed him to a four-picture deal. Sets resembling the Israeli locations were constructed on a Hollywood soundstage, and Lewis had one week to choreograph inserts between Carradine and Cooper that the editors then had to cut into every fight scene. Filming went smoothly until the day Mike Stone arrived on the set in full Monkey Man makeup, and Carradine, realizing the 10th-degree black belt was there to double him, got into a heated argument with Howard, kicked Lewis, and tore apart the cave walls. As Stone walked off the set, he said to Lewis, "That guy's crazy. I'm not working with him."

Howard boasted to *Boxoffice* that the film had already been sold all over the world except for two countries—one of those being the United States. Finally, Avco Embassy picked up American rights to *The Silent Flute* in late August 1978, announced its tentative release date as February 1979, and immediately went into panic mode when they realized they now had to market a Bruce Lee movie that had even less Bruce Lee in it than *Game of Death*.

As they tested the movie in various cities, Carradine started up again with his "possessed by Bruce" nonsense, telling one popular columnist, "When Bruce died his spirit possessed me . . . I felt it happen . . . I was being guided by the master."

Unfortunately, the master guided very few ticket buyers toward *Circle of Iron* when it opened three months later, barely bringing $1 million in rentals back to Avco Embassy. It was the last gasp of Bruceploitation, and the end of the '70s.

As for Black martial arts movie stars, Carl Scott would make a few more movies with Billy Chong in the early '80s, and Ron Van Clief had a couple of movies left in him, but the era of the great Black Hollywood hope was over. It ended not through lack of trying, but because in 1977 Paragon Films decided to cash in on the CB radio craze with a movie called *Cindy Jo and the Texas Turnaround*, starring a karate champion named Carlos Ray Norris.

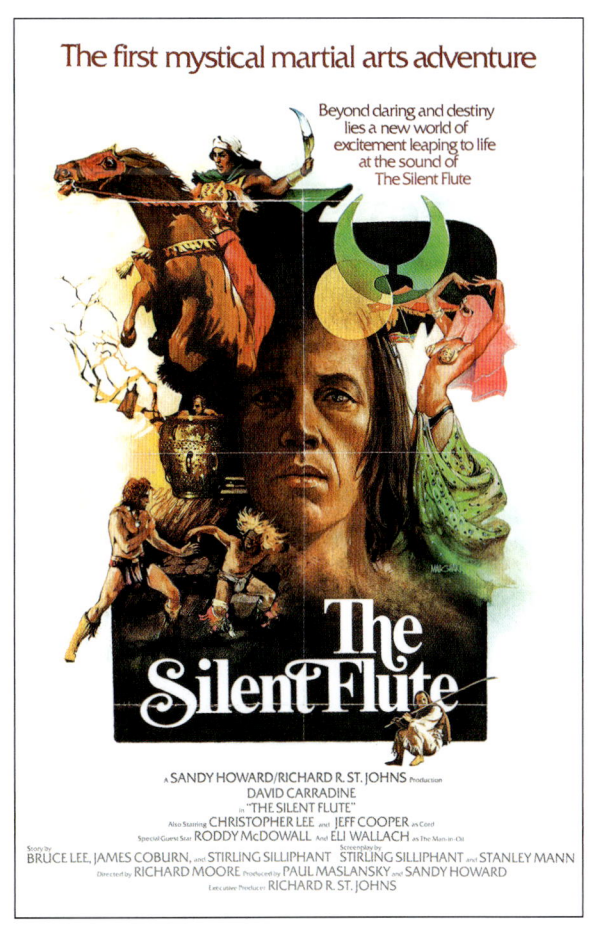

Avco Embassy changed *The Silent Flute*'s title to *Circle of Iron* (opposite page), before changing it to *Death to the Fourth Degree*, before changing it back to *The Silent Flute* (above) in some theaters while leaving it *Circle of Iron* for general release. Carradine said of the title, "I never could figure out what the hell it means."

THE '70S OIL CRISIS PROMPTED the federal government to mandate a 55mph speed limit, which hit long haul truckers hard. Gas shortages and speed traps meant that quick communication between 18-wheelers became a matter of survival and suddenly no big rig could roll without a citizen's band radio connecting it to a network of fellow truckers. Almost overnight, CB radio became cool.

The pop and country charts teemed with story songs that could be turned into movies and in October 1976 Sam Peckinpah announced that his next movie would be *Convoy*, based on C.W. McCall's #1 Hot Country hit song. Burt Reynolds read his friend Hal Needham's script for a trucker movie called *Smokey and the Bandit*, told him it was the worst thing he'd ever seen, and agreed to star.

Suddenly, truckers were hot.

Larry Joachim convinced his friend, former TV producer Bernard Tabakin, to ditch the expensive star he had on board his trucker movie and sign a karate champ named Carlos Ray Norris—his friends called him Chuck. They shot a chunk of the movie and took it to Sam Arkoff at AIP, who couldn't care less about karate but loved CB radio. He threw in $100,000 so the producers could finish their $240,000 picture, and history was made. But not all at once.

Chuck Norris was a nice guy from Oklahoma who said things like "gosh" and "sonuvagun." He'd dedicated his life to Christ when he was 12 and dedicated himself to karate while stationed in Korea. He started fighting in tournaments to promote his California karate studios and eventually started teaching. He got interested in acting when the parent of one of his students, Steve McQueen, told him that movie work "could be profitable for you."

Norris started shopping around a script called *Good Guys Wear Black,* but everywhere he went producers told him he was a karate champion, not an action star. When Tabakin called to offer him the lead in *Cindy Jo and the Texas Turnaround*, Norris

(above) An early ad for Chuck Norris' karate studio.

(opposite page) *Slaughter in San Francisco* was the US title of a film that began as a Lo Wei / Bruce Lee project called *Yellow-Faced Tiger*. But when Lee walked, it mutated into a Don Wong Tao vehicle in which Wong Tao battles Chuck Norris' shirtless crime lord. The poster was painted by comic book legend Neal Adams.

set his *Good Guys* script aside and agreed to take a salary of $5,000. He put together his own team of black belts he trusted enough to "go hard," and they shot the picture in 11 days. Retitled *Breaker! Breaker!* (1977), it premiered at an Atlanta drive-in, beating *Smokey and the Bandit* to theaters by a month and beating Peckinpah's *Convoy* to screens by a year.

Breaker! made millions. Norris wanted to make *Good Guys Wear Black* next, his passion project about a special ops unit from Vietnam who get picked off one by one after returning home. But producers told him *Breaker!* was a fluke. "Chuck," they said. "You're an athlete. You're not an actor."

He finally convinced producer Al Belkin to put up $700,000 by telling him, "There's four million karate people in America. They all know who I am. And if only half of them go to the movie, that's a $6 million gross on a $1 million budget."

Belkin's company, American Cinema Productions, had never produced a movie, they were just a financing company for tax shelter films. Every year, between Christmas Day and January 1, they crisscrossed the country on the owner's private jet convincing rich people with end-of-year tax problems to write them a check they'd funnel into a film.

Belkin signed onto *Good Guys Wear Black* (1978), telling his staff that if it didn't work out they'd all be out of a job. It didn't work out. No one would release *Good Guys*, so Belkin rented out theaters and distributed it himself. They made millions, then repeated this massive success with *A Force of One* (1979) the following year.

Norris wanted to make *Devil Turf* next, about a warrior priest punching out sinners, but Belkin convinced him to enter *The Octagon* (1980), America's first big ninja movie. In it, Norris fought Tadashi Yamashita (Bronson Lee himself; see page 136), American Cinema Releasing four-walled the finished film again, and the result was another $18 million box office bonanza.

Nothing could stop this money train, yet American Cinema Releasing inexplicably told Norris they wouldn't be making any more movies together. Some executives said that was crazy. They got fired. The Chuck Norris movies had grown ACR from five employees to 240. Within a few years of his moving on, they were back down to five again. Norris, however, thrived. No one could understand why.

Jim Kelly said of Norris, "You take Chuck Norris, and just change the color of his skin, he'd be lucky to get a job." Then again, no one was listening to anything Jim Kelly had to say by the late '70s, which is too bad, because he comes closer than anyone else to putting his finger on Norris' appeal.

"I've seen Oriental films which are 10 times better than the Norris films," Kelly pointed out. "The action is 20 times better. Bruce Li has better karate, more charisma, style, class and presence than Norris. But Norris is the great white hope, which white America is always looking for. He's the all-American guy, the friendly personality, always smiling and grinning. He's part of the establishment."

Exactly.

Norris is a soft-spoken, suburban dad who happens to be able to kick your butt. Few people will say anything bad about him because there's not much bad to say. He's genuinely nice, even if that makes him a little bit boring. He often appealed his movie's R ratings to have them reduced to PG so kids can see them. He got his script ideas from *Reader's Digest*. He walked out on his big, multipicture MGM deal after only one movie because he thought they wanted him to sell senseless violence.

The '70s saw Black, Latino, and Asian stars take kung fu mainstream, kicking and punching on the grimy streets of New York and Hong Kong. But the country was sick of the gritty city. They wanted to move to a brighter, cleaner city that sat shining on a hill. They no longer wanted to fight the power. They wanted to *be* the power.

By 1979, unemployment ran high, the country had been humiliated by a failed attempt to rescue hostages in Iran that left eight American soldiers dead in the Middle Eastern desert, inflation was spiraling out of control, and Black unemployment stood at 14%, its highest ever. America wanted to turn away from the defeat in Vietnam and look toward Europe, where we were convinced we could beat the Soviet menace. We wanted a New Morning in America, and we had a new president who would take us there. He even talked like an action movie star, full of quips and one-liners.

"A recession is when your neighbor loses his job," the new president said in 1980. "A depression is when you lose yours. And recovery is when Jimmy Carter loses his."

Welcome to the Reagan years.

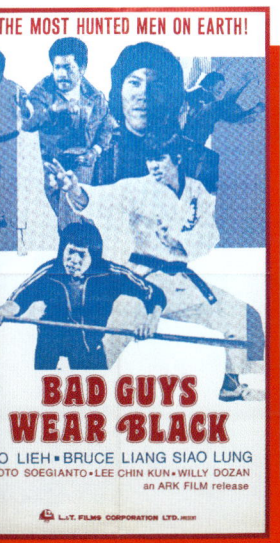

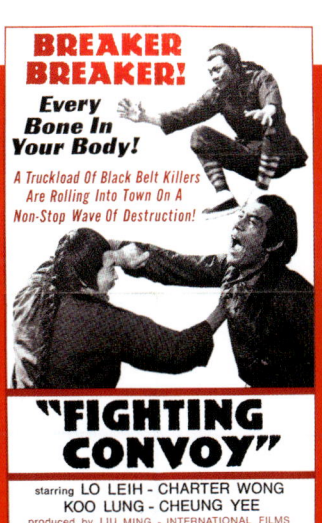

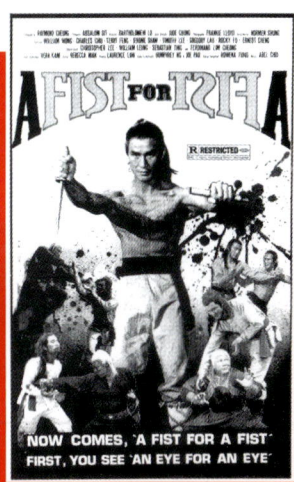

(opposite page) Newspaper ad for the *Breaker! Breaker!* world premiere promising live karate demonstrations at four drive-ins. They worked! *Breaker!* grossed $12 million.

(above) Chuck Norris was the biggest thing at the box office since Bruce Lee, so excited distributors tweaked the titles of his movies for their own flicks, like *Good Guys Wear Black* and *The Octagon*, or tweaked his titles into taglines for cheapies like *Fighting Convoy* and *A Fist for a Fist*.

THE EIGHTIES

THE MOST EXCITING KUNG FU ADVENTURE

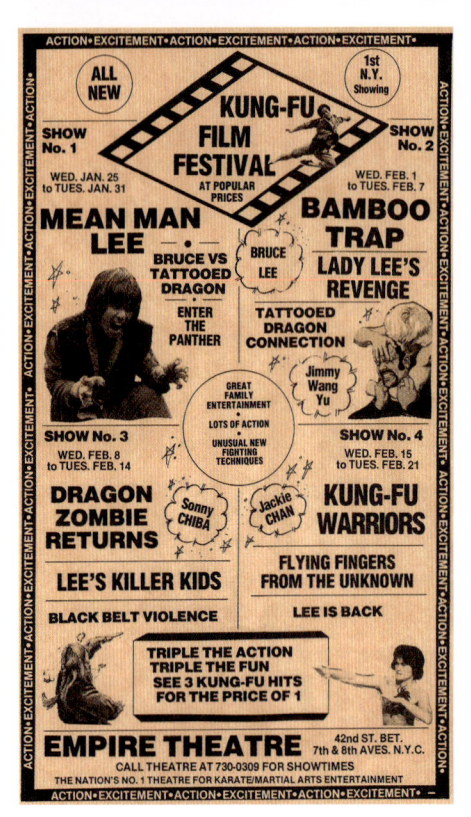

BY THE EARLY '80S, EVERYONE identified 42nd Street with two things: kung fu and crime. Grindhouse projectionists taped up the edges of their projection booth windows to avoid getting stoned on the non-stop pot smoke seeping in from the auditoriums. The New Amsterdam was about to open a double feature of Steve McQueen's *The Getaway* and *Velvet Smooth*, a follow-up to *Force Four* featuring the same cast and crew (Owen Wat-son, Frank Ruiz, Sidney Filson), when masked gunmen tried to hijack the armored car picking up the box office receipts. They held 19 employees hostage for two hours, killed two security guards, left the New Amsterdam's lobby riddled with bullet holes, and fled without any loot.

Opened in July 1974 next door to the New Amsterdam theater, the Cine 42 discovered its destiny when Sonny Chiba's *The Executioner* debuted in the summer of 1978. Larry Joachim had picked up *Chokugeki! Jigoku-ken* (1974), retitling it *The Executioner*, and it was his son Marco's idea to have the image of Sonny Chiba smashing two heads together appear on its posters and newspaper ads. "The meanest Chiba movie yet!" reportedly did so well at the Cine 42 that it single-handedly established the theater's reputation as the premier showcase for martial arts movies on the East Coast throughout the '80s. It was twinned soon after and immediately began running kung fu double and triple bills, sometimes in both auditoriums at once.

Flicks like *Shaolin and Wu Tang* and *Shaolin vs. Lama* made the Cine 42 such a kung fu hotspot that the Globe, a porn theater on Broadway near 42nd Street, changed its name to the Cine 43 and started showing kung fu double bills, too. The Cine 42

responded by leasing the Rialto I & II across the street and showing kung fu triple features there, even renting subtitled Shaw Brothers prints of *My Young Auntie* and *Bastard Swordsman* from Chinatown's Music Palace. Another exhibitor, John Colacenti, converted the Roxy Burlesk porno joint into a 24-hour video grindhouse that ran kung fu movies on big-screen televisions before opening the Roxy Tri-plex next door to the New Amsterdam. Both venues raised the admission price to $5.00 at 11pm to discourage people from using the theater as a crash pad.

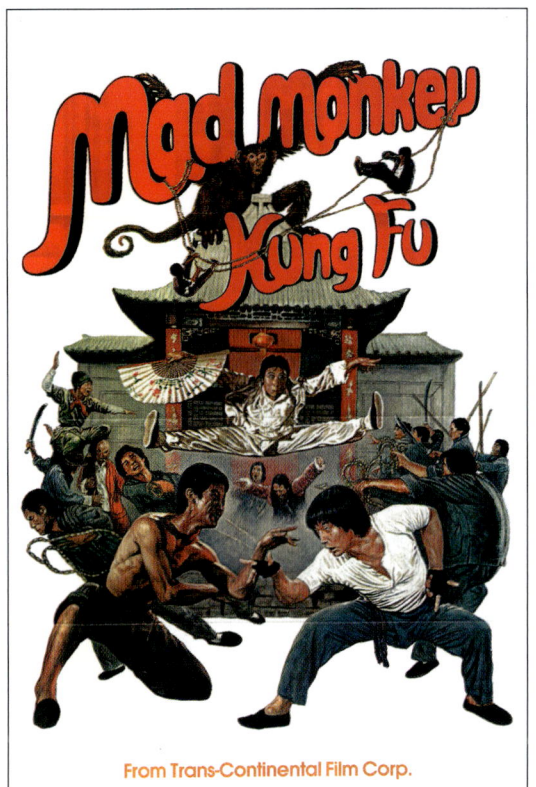

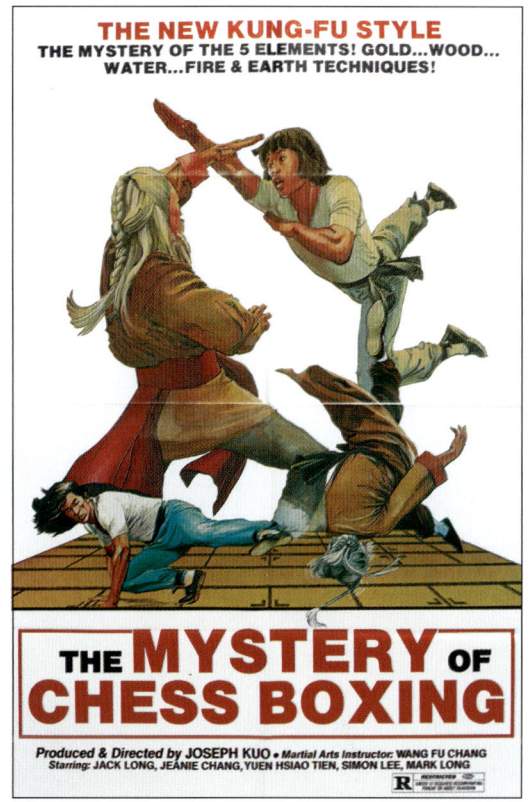

Kung fu movies played inner-city theaters on The Loop in Chicago, in Boston's Combat Zone, on Market Street in San Francisco, and on Broadway in downtown LA, and again and again the same scenario played out in homes across the country: suburban (read: white) kids wanted to go see the good stuff at the inner city (read: Black) movie theaters and their parents told them: "Hell no!" From the Bruce Lee Center in Philadelphia to the Scrumpy Dump in Cleveland, kung fu played almost exclusively to Black and Latino audiences, but more and more kids in the vanilla suburbs wanted in on the action.

It would be up to a middle-aged arthouse movie distributor named Mel Maron to realize that if the kids couldn't come to the grindhouse, he'd beam the grindhouse into their living rooms.

(opposite page) The Empire printed flyers advertising "kung fu festivals" and even installed two wooden ninjas on top of their marquee for a ninja triple bill. One remained there for years after the Empire closed.

(above) Two stalwarts on the grindhouse circuit: Lau Kar-leung's *Mad Monkey Kung Fu* and Joseph Kuo's *The Mystery of Chess Boxing* (both 1979) grossed big bucks whenever they played the Cine 42.

BYONG YU

KOREAN TAEKWONDO EXPERT BYONG YU arrived in the States in the late 1960s and quickly gained recognition as one of the oldest and fiercest fighters on the tournament circuit. After retirement, he ran a chain of martial arts studios in the San Francisco Bay Area while breaking bricks with his elbows, hands, and head at exhibitions and on TV shows like *Thrillseekers* and *The Tonight Show Starring Johnny Carson*, which convinced producer Raymond Chow that he might be star material. Yu made only one movie—Golden Harvest's ultra-sleazy *The Association*, in which he co-stars with Angela Mao (in a dual role)—but he's often credited with appearing in 30 other movies he had nothing to do with, including Sammo Hung's *The Victim*. So how exactly did *that* happen?

In the mid-'80s, when kung fu movies were everywhere on TV and independent stations were buying up syndication packages with titles like *Kung Fu Justice* (Cinema Shares) and *Masters of Fury* (Telepictures Corp.), a company called Acama Films decided their "Martial Arts Theater" package of 39 movies needed something special to make it stand apart from the competition: a real karate champ to appear in videotaped intros for 30 of the movies. Yu got the gig, but instead of just crediting him as the host, Acama also listed him as the star of all 30 movies in the programming notes that were sent to the stations.

From that point on, every time one of those stations aired *The Guy with Secret Kung Fu* or *Deadly Snail vs. Kung Fu Killer*, Yu's name showed up in the local television listings as the film's star. This went on for years, resulting in a lot of these movies being added to Yu's filmography during the early days of the Internet Movie Database. Even today, you can google his name and find site after site listing Yu as one of the hardest-working men in show business.

BYONG YU

俞炳龍
（陳　旭攝）

"**K**UNG FU MOVIES WERE REALLY enjoying their biggest success with downtown urban audiences, primarily the African-American audiences," Mel Maron explained. "A lot of kids were hungry to see those pictures, but they couldn't because their parents felt uncomfortable letting them go to the downtown theaters."

If the kids wouldn't come to Times Square, Maron would bring Times Square to them. After he moved from Cinema Shares to World Northal and established himself as the exclusive distributor of Shaw Brothers films, Maron enlisted Larry Bensky and John Keogh, his editorial team from Cinema Shares, to prepare TV versions for his first "Black Belt Theater" package. Maron believed that audiences would accept dubbed kung fu movies on TV, and in February 1981 *Bruce Lee: His Last Days, His Last Nights* and *Master Killer* made their commercial TV debuts on KCOP 13 Los Angeles and earned killer ratings.

On Saturday, May 2, 1981, as part of a program called Drive-In Movie, New York's WNEW 5 ran their first "Black Belt Theater" film, which was also *Bruce Lee: His Last Days, His Last Nights*. The ratings were strong, and when they aired *The Chinatown Kid* on August 8, to quote a trade ad in *Broadcasting* magazine, it "aced a tennis match, beat out a grand prix, sliced up a golf tournament, outran a track meet and clobbered two other movies."

The first two "Black Belt Theater" packages generated $6 million in gross sales, and two more packages containing an army of 40 more films were in the works. By late 1983, World Northal had so many Shaw Brothers movies on their release schedule that the Movieland on Broadway had to run a five-week "Sir Run Run Shaw Kung-Fu Festival" to help clear the slate so the films could be included in the company's upcoming TV syndication package.

Suddenly, everyone needed a kung fu television package of their own.

Unifilm International had three "Masters of Kung Fu" packages with 13 films in each. 21st Century called theirs "Tribute to Bruce Lee," while Performance Advertising Services named theirs "Tribute to Fists of Fury" with four of the 15 starring Bruce Li. "Masters of Fury" from Telepictures Corp. focused on Bruce Le.

(above) An illustration from Aquarius' television package, which bragged about bringing stars like Sonny Chiba and Ron Van Clief into living rooms everywhere. Karate films, their sales brochure explained to station managers, "invariably adhere to a strict morality that stresses love of family, respect for elders, and punishment for wrong-doing." Also, eye-gouging and testicle-crunching.

Station managers hated foreign films with the passion of a thousand burning suns, but while the Moral Majority were putting heat on television stations to show less sex, they hadn't gotten around to crusading against violence . . . yet. George Hankoff, the head of World Northal's TV division, knew the stations had to screen *something*, and kung fu movies turned out to be the answer.

Television packages erupted like molten lava: "Kung Fu Theatre" (Golden West Television), "Karate Connection" (Mediacast Television), "Kung Fu Features" (Harmony Gold), "Golden Dragon Kung Fu Package" (Pete Rodgers), and "Martial Arts Theater" (Cineworld). Dubbed kung fu movies on TV became a Saturday afternoon ritual for Americans everywhere, so why did they need to go to the movie theaters anymore?

Trade ads for Black Belt Theater's TV packages and a sales sheet (bottom, right) for National Telefilm Associates' "Kung Fu Gold" package that mostly included films from Larry Joachim's company, Trans-Continental.

FLYOVER FIGHTERS

MIAMI-BASED MOC KAN-SENT DIDN'T MAKE the first martial arts movie on American soil—that distinction probably belongs to Paul Kyriazi, whose samurai shorts *Trapped*, *Blade of Doom*, and *The Tournament* were shot in California several years earlier—but his sole filmmaking effort, *The Deadly Touch*, was most certainly the first feature-length kung fu movie stamped "Made in the USA."

Kan-Sent, a Cuban-Chinese sensei, not only produced and directed but also starred in the PG-rated regional rarity, which played in three Miami theaters for two weeks in November 1974 and was never seen again. Kyriazi, on the other hand, went on to make a handful of higher-profile martial arts actioners like *Death Machines*, *Weapons of Death*, and *Ninja Busters*.

Meanwhile, former Green Beret and Ohio native Don Bendell returned home from Vietnam in 1970 with judo and jiu-jitsu training and an interest in adding karate and taekwondo to the mix. When kung fu movies became the rage, he wrote a screenplay called *The Instructor* and spent the next four years trying to get it made, finally succeeding in 1980 with his own Pro-Am instructor, Bob Chaney, in the title role. After four-walling the Civic Theatre in Akron for an attention-getting world premiere in 1983, Bendell landed a distribution deal with Shapiro Entertainment that came with an extra $5,000 to shoot additional scenes for the beginning of the movie. He also cut a 10-minute preview that helped Shapiro sell the film to 164 countries and land a domestic home video deal with Vestron Video. Bendell never made another film but has since written numerous novels and nonfiction books.

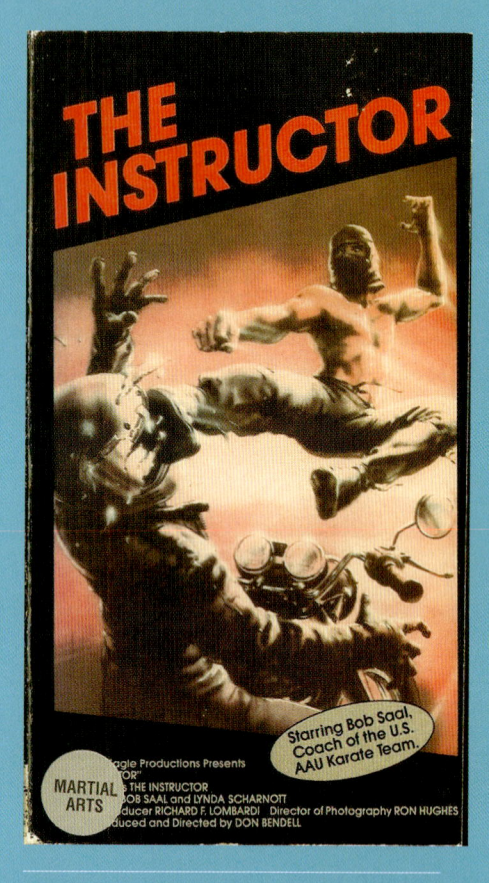

The promotional art for *The Instructor* was drawn by none other than visionary filmmaker James Cameron, who was working for Saturn International Pictures while they were readying the release of his feature directorial debut, *Piranha II: The Spawning*, circa 1983.

Schlock distributor Saturn International Pictures (run by the same guys who fired Neva Friedenn from their Condor Films a couple of years earlier—see page 179), got the Cine 42 in New York City to screen *The Instructor* for a few days as *The Ninja Instructor* ahead of its video release in 1985, making it one of several flyover films to ride the trendy ninja wave.

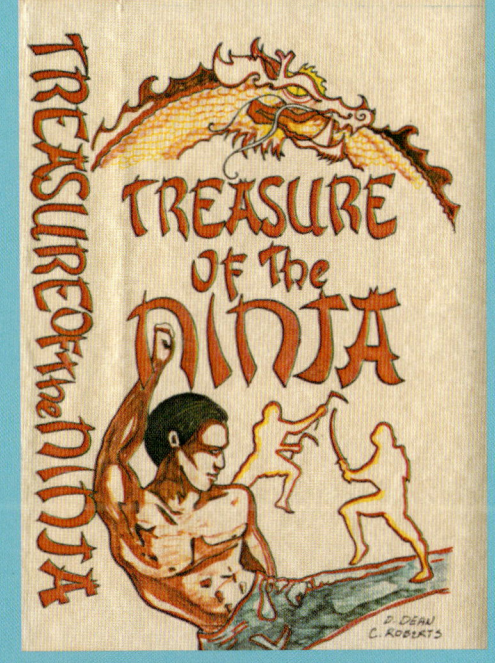

After *Miami Connection* (see page 316) and *Justice, Ninja Style* (see page 315) came *Pushed Too Far*, filmed around Indianapolis and Greenfield, Indiana, in 1987 and featuring a ninja on horseback who appears in the dreams of a karate instructor (three-time USKA world champ Herb Johnson) whose wife is one of the victims of The Bear, a psychotic ex-pro wrestler who's terrorizing the town. Hoosier-bred character actor and AAMCO pitchman Claude Akins stars as the local sheriff and attended the world premiere (in two Greenfield theaters) in February 1988.

Next, real-life ninja Stephen K. Hayes appeared as himself in *Black and White*, providing ninjutsu guidance to a blond-haired ninja student (Craig Boyett) whose motorcycle breaks down en route to a ninja seminar in Houston and he waits out the repair time by wiping out the redneck town's local KKK chapter. Filmed in Sealy, Texas, in 1988, it went unreleased until Menahem Golan's rebranded 21st Century Film Corporation sent it straight to video as *Ninja Vengeance* in 1993.

But the undisputed master of regional martial arts moviemaking is William Lee, who wrote, produced, and directed the incredible *Treasure of the Ninja* while finishing his graduate degree in film at Ohio State University. He also starred in the 106-minute Super 8 production (as a character named Magneta Faze) and choreographed the fighting; and when he failed to find distribution, he took on that responsibility as well, holding the world premiere in a Columbus, Ohio, theater in 1987 and selling VHS copies through the mail. The 2021 Blu-ray from AGFA / Bleeding Skull contains another of his movies, the Super 8 feature *Dragon vs. Ninja* (1984), plus a commentary and short films by Lee.

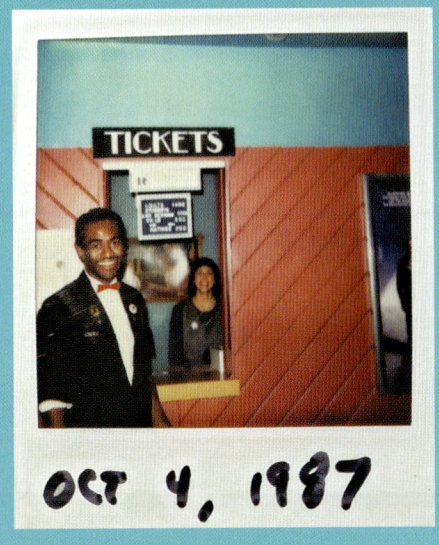

William Lee at the premiere of his feature film *Treasure of the Ninja*.

ALEXANDER FU SHENG

THE NINTH AND LEAST ACADEMICALLY INCLINED of eleven children, Cheung Fu-sheng dropped out of school at 15, got tired of the dead-end construction jobs he picked up, and enrolled in the Shaw Brothers' year-long training program to become an actor. His star potential was immediately recognized by Chang Cheh, and he quickly moved from nonspeaking background parts to leading roles by his sixth film. Billed as Alexander Fu Sheng, he spent the next five years working exclusively for Chang Cheh in his Shaolin kung fu sagas and wu xia spectacles. He married pop singing sensation Jenny Tseng in 1976, the same year a *Variety* critic—underwhelmed by *Shaolin Avengers*—referred to a "local Fu Sheng craze" he doubted would catch on elsewhere. Actually, Shaw Brothers had been trying for years to stir up enthusiasm for the charismatic young actor in Hawaii, calling him "Shaw's super star" in the newspaper ads for every single one of his movies that opened at the Shaw-owned Empress Theatre in Honolulu.

Daily News reporter Peter Coutros was strolling through New York's Chinatown one day in December 1975 when he noticed a long line of people in front of the Music Palace box office—not only Chinese, but African-American and Latino moviegoers as well. He asked the cinema's hip young manager, Kevin Kam, what was

A SHAW BROTHERS PRESENTATION **5 MASTERS OF DEATH** DISTRIBUTED BY WORLD NORTHAL

drawing this crowd and was told "Alexander Fu Sheng... the hottest kung fu star since Bruce Lee." Intrigued, Coutros got in line, bought a ticket, and ended up giving *Disciples of Shaolin* and Fu Sheng a fairly positive write-up in the following day's paper.

An English-dubbed version of *Heroes Two*, the actor's first starring role, was released on the US action circuit under two different titles (*Bloody Fists* and *Blood Brothers*) in 1977, but Fu Sheng made his biggest mark on American audiences after the Black Belt Theatre packages premiered on television in early 1981. Similar to Jackie Chan, Fu Sheng possessed considerable comic skills that were often ignored in the push to present him in the States as the next Bruce Lee. Like both Lee and Chan, he also wanted to direct, and after he was sidelined by two serious injuries in the late '70s—a concussion sustained during rehearsals for Sun Chung's *The Deadly Breaking Sword* and a broken leg one year later on the set of Chor Yuen's *Heroes Shed No Tears*—he started thinking more about moving behind the camera. Action ace Lau Kar-leung and his brother Lau Kar-wing enlisted him for their latest projects, as did newcomer Wong Jing, while Fu Sheng began work on his own directorial debut, *Wits of the Brats*. Any talk of his career being over were put to rest when *Legendary Weapons of China* came out and pulled in almost $10 million HK, making it Fu Sheng's top moneymaker and the ninth highest-grossing film of 1982 at the Hong Kong box office.

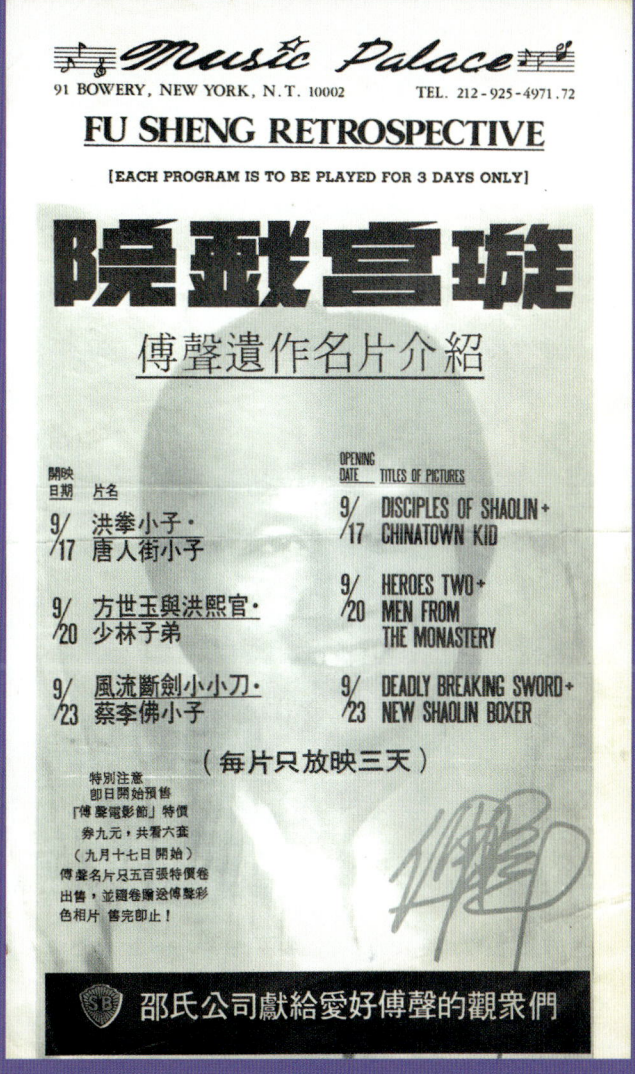

Wong Jing's *Hong Kong Playboys* became Fu Sheng's second biggest box office hit a year and a half later, banking over $7 million HK in 19 days before leaving theaters on July 6, 1983. Shortly after 10pm that same evening, Fu Sheng climbed into his Porsche 911. Since his license had been suspended for reckless driving, he was in the passenger seat and his older brother, Horatio Chun-sing, was behind the wheel to shuttle him to a midnight location shoot 45 minutes away. Speeding through the bends and twists of Tai Au Mun Road, Horatio lost control of the Porsche, which crashed into a concrete post and flipped over. Both brothers were rushed to the hospital, but five hours later it was Fu Sheng who was pronounced dead from massive head and chest injuries. He was 29 years old.

Nearly three thousand people showed up for his funeral. So many wreaths were sent to the funeral home that they lined the sidewalk outside and across the street. One woman who had never even seen a Fu Sheng movie told a reporter for the *South China Morning Post* that she had left her three small children in the care of her husband so she could pay her respects to the late actor. When asked why, she replied, "Ten years ago I attended the funeral service of another kung fu star, Bruce Lee."

During the month he died, six Fu Sheng movies could be watched on TV in different parts of the United States thanks to World Northal's Black Belt Theatre packages—*The Avenging Eagle*, *Bloody Avengers*, *The Chinatown Kid*, *5 Masters of Death*, *Master of Disaster*, and *Ten Tigers from Kwangtung*—though the company never acknowledged his passing. Sometime in 1984, Ron Van Clief memorialized the late actor in a minute-long intro to *The Chinatown Kid* for WNEW 5's Drive-In Movie, but it didn't air until April of the following year.

Karen Shaub, co-editor of the fanzines *Fangraphic* and *The Jade Screen*, was an early stateside supporter who once made a three-hour round trip to see Fu Sheng's *The Chinatown Kid* in a run-down suburban Tampa drive-in. She had planned to dedicate most of *The Jade Screen* #4 to him. When she learned of his death, she was so overcome that she scrapped the issue and ceased publishing the fanzine. Shaw Brothers produced a short subject called *A Tribute to Fu Sheng*, which was sent to all of their Chinatown theaters to play before *Hong Kong Playboys* and during Fu Sheng Film Festivals. Two years after his death, the Empress Theatre in Honolulu was still handing out 8x10 color photos of him for return engagements of *The Proud Twins* and *Na Cha the Great*, and when the theater closed for good in February 1986, the last films shown were *A Tribute to Fu Sheng*, followed by *5 Shaolin Masters*.

DISTRIBUTORS WERE DESPERATE TO LURE audiences back into their seats. At first they thought the answer would be Jackie Chan. In Hong Kong, audiences had been introduced to Chan's comedy kung fu revolution in 1978, but the ground had been laid by Sammo Hung, the portly martial artist who takes on Bruce Lee at the beginning of *Enter the Dragon* and a graduate of the same harsh Chinese Opera school as Chan, and a host of other '80s kung fu talent, known collectively as the Seven Little Fortunes. Hung delivered very fast, very furious, very funny kung fu movies, starting with *The Iron-Fisted Monk* (1977) before roasting the Bruceploitation genre with *Enter the Fat Dragon* (1978), in which his overweight, pig-raising, kung fu savant beats the tar out of a Bruce Lee impersonator on the set of a Bruceploitation film.

Sammo's "little brother," Jackie took his "big brother's" instincts for comedy kung fu, mixed them with his physical genius, and became a Bruce Lee–sized star with *Snake in the Eagle's Shadow* and *Drunken Master* (both 1978). In them, Chan plays a hapless kid who isn't very good at kung fu because he's either too stupid (*Snake*) or too lazy (*Drunken*) to study, but he rises to the occasion under the tutelage of a hard-drinking, pipe-puffing, degenerate bum who happens to be a great kung fu master, played with screen-burning charisma and jaw-dropping flexibility in both films by Simon Yuen, the 66-year-old father of director Yuen Wo-ping.

The movies didn't just turn Chan into a box office sensation, they also turned Yuen's Beggar So character into a star, and with great success came great opportunities. Before he died one year later in January 1979, Yuen managed to reprise his Beggar So role in 15 movies with names that included variations on "Drunken" and "Master" (*Dance of the Drunk Mantis*, *Story of the Drunken Master*, *World of the Drunken Master*, *An Old Kung Fu Master*).

Then the Jackie Chan imitators started coming out of the woodwork.

Willy Dozan, an Indonesian martial artist, found success in Hong Kong under the Jackie Chan–ish name Billy Chong, sporting the same floppy haircut as Chan, the same acrobatic style of kung fu, and the same co-star (Simon Yuen) in *Crystal Fist* (1979), his *Snake in the Eagle's Shadow* knock-off. Picked up and promoted by Eternal Films, their reps positioned him to the press as a relief from Bruceploitation movies that had "trashed the market," which must have stung a bit for the other big star in their stable, Bruce Li. Chong never quite took off in Hong Kong or the US, but he left behind a tiny treasure trove of movies sporting his charismatic, ultra-athletic performances before he found true fame back in Indonesia starring in and directing two huge hit TV series in the '90s.

Ulysses Tzan (born Romeo Santiago) became the "Jackie Chan of the Philippines" with his *Drunken Master* clone, *Mantis Boxer* (1979), and *Superhand: Shadow of the Dancing Master* (1980), in which he plays the "Dancing Master," a knock-off of Chan's

Serafim Karalexis took the promotion of *Eagle's Shadow* (*Snake in the Eagle's Shadow*, 1978) extremely personally, dictating to Neal Adams exactly what he should paint on the poster. His press book recommended holding free screenings for local martial arts schools, and that "the exhibitor should arrange for a van or a car (with a loud speaker system playing the various radio spots and popular music) to go through the various populated neighborhoods 3 days prior to opening."

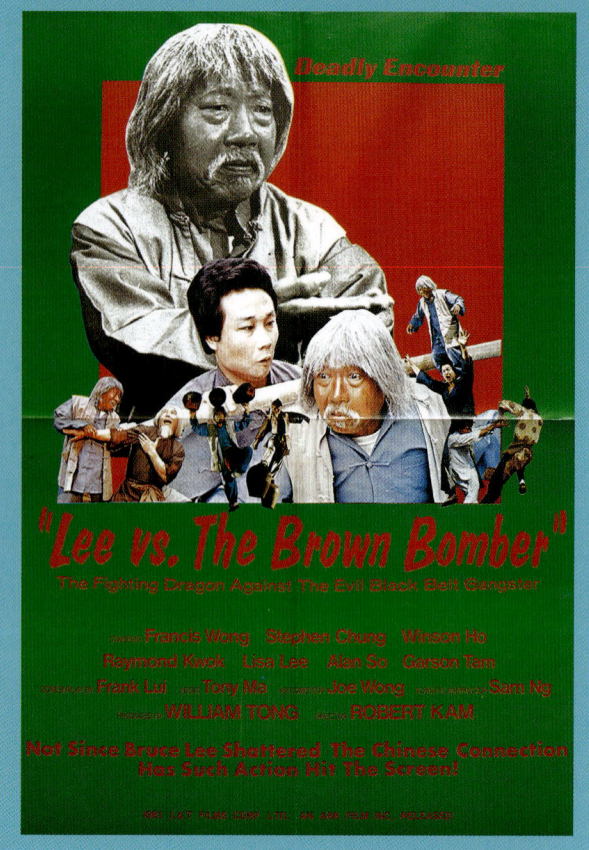

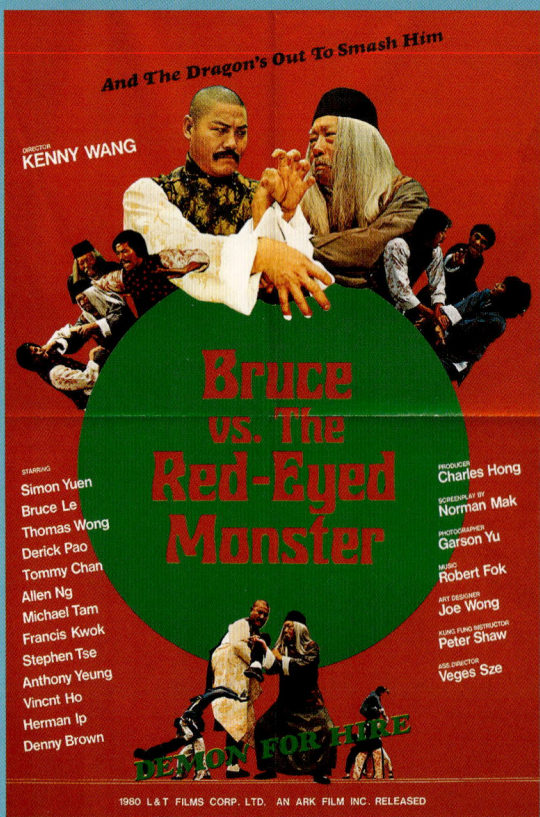

Jackie Chan was the first new thing to hit Hong Kong action movies since Bruce Lee in 1972, so excited distributors could be excused for mugging audiences with as many knock-offs and copycats as they could, and for spinning off Simon Yuen's Beggar So character into as many "Drunken" movies as possible.

260

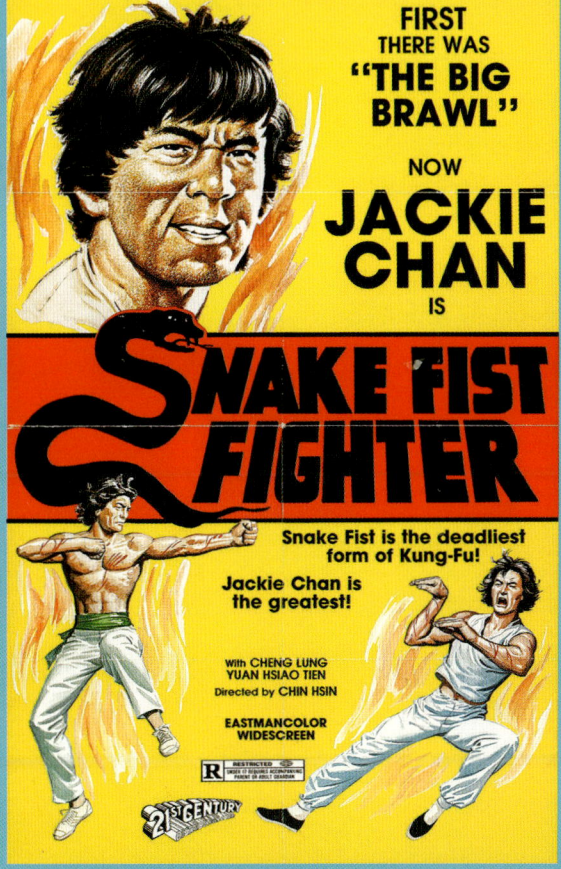

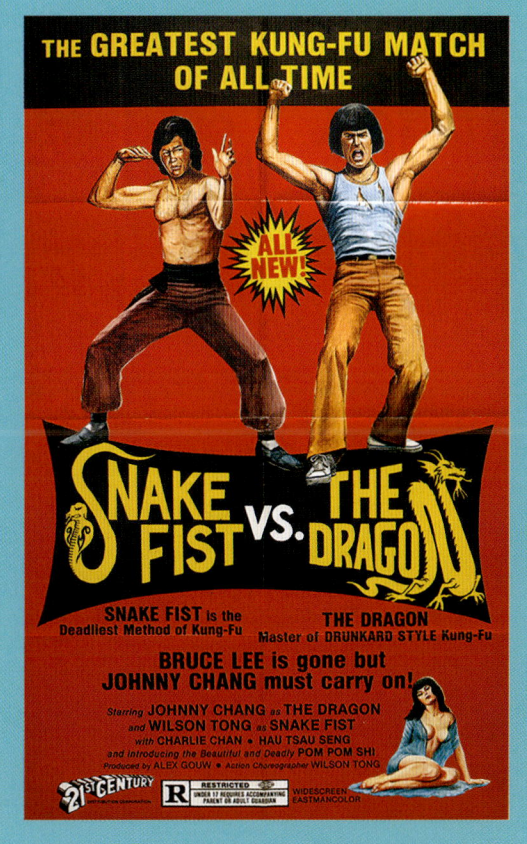

(top, left) *The Jade Warriors* is actually Hung's *Knockabout* (1979), a Golden Harvest production picked up by World Northal. Juan Biao is not a Latino superstar but Hung and Chan's ultra-flexible "little brother" from Chinese Opera school, Yuen Biao.

(top, right) *Snake Fist vs. The Dragon* was actually *Snake in the Monkey's Shadow* (1979), which was a knock-off of *Snake in Eagle's Shadow* starring John Cheung, who'd later appear in a bunch of American martial arts movies like *Dragon: The Bruce Lee Story*.

(bottom, left) The evil genius responsible for unearthing Jackie Chan's first film and reissuing it as *Snake Fist Fighter* was Dick Randall, who also dug up Bruce Lee's early, non–martial arts movies and helped Serafim Karalexis repackage them as a "new" Bruce Lee film (see page 107).

Drunken Master. Elton Chong appeared with Jackie Chan's haircut, costume, and plot points in a handful of Korean Jackie Chansploitation flicks like *Fist of Golden Monkey*, directed by Godfrey Ho. Shing Lung appeared in a Thai Jackie Chan knock-off, *Little Master* (1979), while Bruce Li teamed up with *Drunken Master* co-star Simon Yuen for *Blind Fist of Bruce* (1979), which is a mash-up of both *Drunken Master* and *Snake in the Eagle's Shadow*.

In 1979, Neva Friedenn was working as a booker for LA-based Condor Films when a martial artist and actor named John Ladalski wandered in, introduced himself, and explained that he had just arrived from Hong Kong. As Ladalski perused a pile of posters and ad sheets, Friedenn casually asked what was happening over there. He told her comedy kung fu was the big new thing, Jackie Chan was the hottest star of the moment, and she should seek out *Fearless Hyena*, *Snake in the Eagle's Shadow*, and *Drunken Master* at the Kim Sing theater in LA's Chinatown. She took his advice, became an instant Chan fan, and set out on a mission to acquire the US rights to his early films.

After the phenomenal success of Chan's kung fu comedies, Golden Harvest lured the actor away from Seasonal with the promise of bigger budgets, more creative freedom, and international co-productions with Hollywood studios like Warner Bros. "America is a big market—everybody wants to get in," Chan told *Fighting Stars* magazine. "I am trying to get in and I hope American audiences will like me." Maybe they would have if Raymond Chow hadn't pushed him as the next Bruce Lee and saddled him with the usual *Enter the Dragon* production team for *The Big Brawl* (aka *Battle Creek Brawl*, 1980), a tired 1920s gangster romp directed by Robert Clouse that featured all the thrills and blistering fight choreography of a sack of dead cats. Warner Bros. opened the film wide and it tanked everywhere but New York, where the studio hedged its bets *Hot Potato*–style by pairing it with *Enter the Dragon*. The $5.5 million production ended up bringing Warner Bros. only $3 million in rentals, less than half of what *Kill or Be Killed* pulled in for Film Ventures and a third of what American Cinema pocketed for *The Octagon*.

The Jade Claw is actually *Crystal Fist* (1979), which teamed Billy Chong up with Simon Yuen.

Invisible Kung Fu Dragon (aka *Monkey Fist, Floating Snake*, 1980) is a Jackie Chan–inspired comedy starring Mu-Chuan Chen and featuring Riz Ortolani music from *Day of Anger*.

Hands of Lightning (aka *Hard Bastard*, 1981) was a showcase for Chan's opponent at the end of *Drunken Master*, Hwang Jang-Lee, a Korean super-kicker.

Mean Drunken Master (aka *Iron Bridge Kung Fu*, 1979) was yet another Simon Yuen cash-in project.

THE MOST DANGEROUS
ANIMAL ALIVE!
TRANSMEDIA PRESENTS
JADE
CLAW
Starring
BILLY CHONG • YUEN SIU TIN
Directed by HWA I HUNG
Produced by PAL MING
AN ETERNAL FILM (H.K.) CO. LIMITED PRODUCTION
A TRAMSMEDIA DISTRIBUTION CORPORATION RELEASE
R RESTRICTED
UNDER 17 REQUIRES ACCOMPANYING PARENT OR ADULT GUARDIAN

INVISIBLE
KUNG FU
DRAGON
SEE HOW GREAT 'MONKEY STYLE' IS!!!
THE FASTEST FISTS EVER! Lightning Quick! Faster Than The Speed Of Sight!
FLASH KING and KASPER LEE
A MAGNIFICENT PRESENTATION OF SUPER MONKEY KUNG FU
STARRING: CHEN XING YUEN HUA CHANG YI JACKY CHANG
EXECUTIVE PRODUCER: C.P. CHIN PRODUCTION MANAGER: P.C. TSAI
MUSIC CONDUCTED AND ARRANGED BY: JAMES LEE & C.S. CHAN
L & T FILMS CORPORATED LTD. AN ARK FILM INC RELEASED

The Incredible JACKY LEE,
the World's Fastest...
HANDS OF
LIGHTNING
Co-starring WONG CHENG LI
SAM YUEN AND BOBBY MAH
Directed by GODFREY HO
R RESTRICTED

SEE JACKY CHAN´S DEADLIEST ENEMY
HE KILLS WITHOUT WARNING!
"MEAN DRUNKEN MASTER"
MEAN
DRUNKEN MASTER
CAST David Li Eddy Chung Charles Chiu Dannis Law Terry Lo
PRODUCER Eric Cheng KUNG FUNG INSTRUCTOR Rocky Fu DESIGN CONSULTANT Joe Wong
R RESTRICTED

When Jackie came to the United States to promote *The Big Brawl*, he stopped by the LA offices of *Inside Kung-Fu* on a day when no writers were around, so his first-ever English-language interview was conducted by the magazine's merchandising manager, James Lew. Not so coincidentally, that's when Neva Friedenn called their offices looking for someone who could connect her with Jackie's Hong Kong producer. In the interest of etiquette, Friedenn wanted the magazine's publisher, Curtis Wong, to make the introduction. Wong, realizing Friedenn knew more about Jackie than he did, was only too happy.

The result, in Friedenn's own words, was "a three-and-a-half-hour interview during which I tried to figure out which of the '70s Chan films would perform best in our domestic market while Jackie Chan himself hilariously pantomimed the fight scenes from them." *Kick Illustrated* spread their lively conversation across three issues (March–May 1981) and Friedenn wrote more articles about Jackie for *Martial Arts Movies* and *Official Karate* before starting her successful kung fu movie distribution outfit, Unifilm International, that year (see page 179). "By that point, neither Lo Wei nor Seasonal Films boss Ng See-yuen was willing to sell US domestic rights to a Jackie Chan title for less than $300,000," Friedenn said. "Needless to say, I never acquired any of the '70s Chan product."

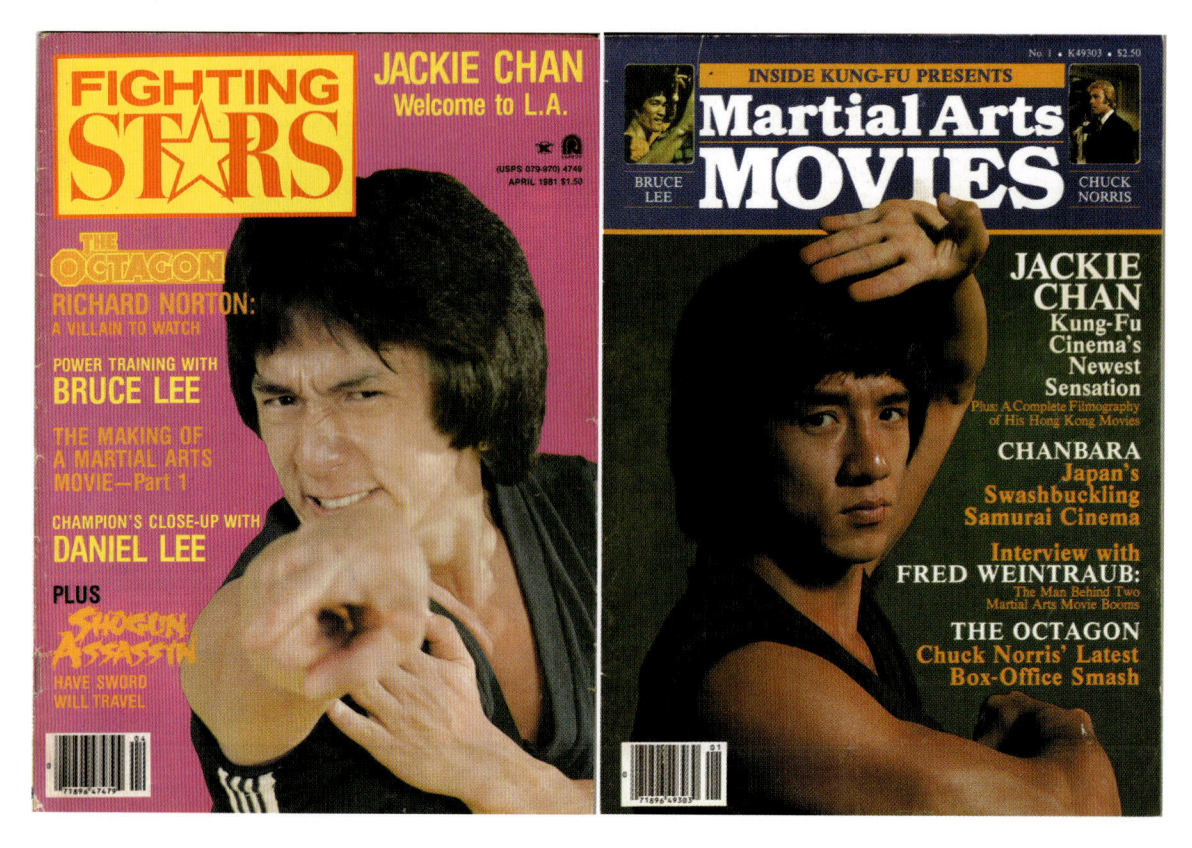

The first distributor to actually offer the $300,000 asking price for *Snake in the Eagle's Shadow* was Serafim Karalexis, but he was flatly rejected by Seasonal's US representative, Roy Horan (see page 331). Months later, at the 1981 Cannes Film Festival, Karalexis upped the ante to $500,000 and was turned down a second time. Meanwhile, knock-off Jackie movies like *Jade Claw*, *World of Drunken Master*, and *Mean Drunken Master* were hitting stateside grindhouses, damaging the Chan brand while siphoning away profits.

A Hollywood film investor joined forces with Karalexis and added another $250,000 to the pot, but when Horan declined that staggering sum as well, it became obvious that *no* amount of money from an independent distributor would be enough for Ng See-yuen, who was just looking to start a relationship with a major studio. When no one in Hollywood showed interest in what Seasonal was selling, Horan went back to Karalexis and agreed to a straight percentage deal with no advance, going from $750,000 to bupkes in a matter of months. *The Eagle's Shadow* finally opened in regional US release in October 1982, two full years after Karalexis had made his initial offer. Although it performed well, especially in the New York area (where it opened on April Fools' Day in 1983), "it didn't do anywhere as well as it could have because it was two years too late and too many rip-offs were released prior to the original," Karalexis said.

One of these was *Snake Fist vs. the Dragon*, a cheapjack ripoff of *Snake in the Eagle's Shadow* starring a Jackie imitator billed as Johnny Chang, which managed to make $1.4 million in regional release from 21st Century Distribution. Flush with success from this "Chansploitation" surprise hit, 21st Century released an "all new" Chan movie in 1981, *Snake Fist Fighter*, and their trailer did its best to hype Chan as the new Bruce Lee, adding quotes from young Chan fans to the usual Adolph

Caesar–voiced hyperbole. "He's definitely the greatest I've seen since Bruce Lee!" one voice enthuses. "Snake Fist is the method they use to kill people!" another cries. "That Jackie Chan is a mean motherfuc[BLEEP]!" An article in *Martial Arts Movies* revealed that *Snake Fist Fighter* was actually the first movie Chan ever starred in. Made in 1971, it was released in 1973 under the title *The Cub Tiger from Kwantung*, then got re-edited with new footage of Simon Yuen and released again in 1979 as *Master with Cracked Fingers* before re-appearing in '81 as *Snake Fist Fighter*. Another Chan scam, *Jackie Chan and the 36 Crazy Fists*, was a 1977 cheapie that Chan had worked on as the fight choreographer. An eight-minute behind-the-scenes featurette showing "kung fu director" Jackie at work was tacked on to the beginning, enabling the distributor to give him "special appearance by" and "directed by" credits in the advertising.

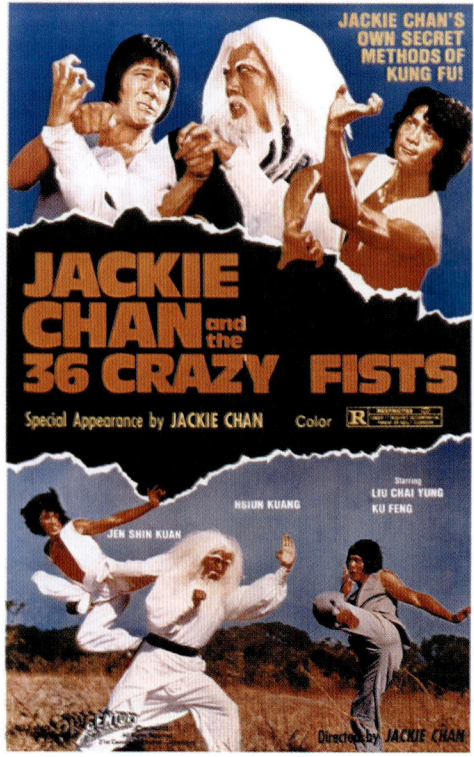

The Jackie Chan Invasion was faltering, and by now distributors were already looking for the next big thing. Mainland China, eager to bolster tourism after the Cultural Revolution (1966–1976), authorized the production of a kung fu movie to be shot at the historic Shaolin Temple. When the crew arrived, the temple was a wreck, with only three remaining monks. Nevertheless, an authentic cast of real-life martial artists spent a year shooting *Shaolin Temple* (1982) there, which showcased its teenaged star, a national wu shu champion named Li Lian-je. Distributed globally, it became a massive hit, especially in China where it attracted tens of millions of ticket buyers and turned the ailing Shaolin Temple into a major tourist destination. Distributors pressured Li Lian-je to change his name to something that would look better on a poster. The name he picked? Jet Li.

In May 1984, Golden Harvest announced that it was sending Jackie Chan to America *again*, this time to New York City for *The Protector*, a cop film written and directed by James Glickenhaus (*The Exterminator*). That summer, Larry Joachim got the cheaper Spanish-language rights to *The Fearless Hyena* and opened an English print on 42nd Street, where it cleaned up before anyone realized it was an unauthorized release. A few months later, another distributor showed his disdain for Ng See-yuen by renting a subtitled print of *Drunken Master* from a Chinatown theater and booking it into the same 42nd Street theater while brazenly running ads in the New York newspapers proclaiming it "Jacky Chan's greatest classic." This pirated run killed its theatrical prospects in the States. "At the time, you could gross $80,000 to $100,000 on 42nd Street, sometimes more, so that took out a big chunk of potential earnings," said Serafim Karalexis, who passed on *Drunken Master* and let his distributor, Cinematic Releasing, acquire Seasonal's *Dance of the Drunk Mantis* instead.

That same year, despite having only been paid around two bucks a day to appear in *Shaolin Temple*, Jet Li agreed to make another Mainland martial arts picture with the same producers, this one called *Kids from Shaolin* (1984). Reuniting virtually the same cast and crew, the writers based the script on personal stories told to them by Jet Li and other members of his wu shu team, and it feels like a lighter-than-air kung fu version of *The Sound of Music*. That's not to say making it was easy. Like *Shaolin Temple*, *Kids from Shaolin* took almost a year to shoot, and during the summer months temperatures approached 105 degrees; the crew passed the time by cracking eggs on the ground and watching them fry. The strenuous conditions barely show, however, as Jet Li is, once again, so charming that he occasionally ignores gravity entirely, performing more of the wu shu feats that made *Shaolin Temple* such a jaw-dropper.

LIVING/ARTS

TV & Radio 67

LIVES IN THE ARTS

Boston's own karate kid

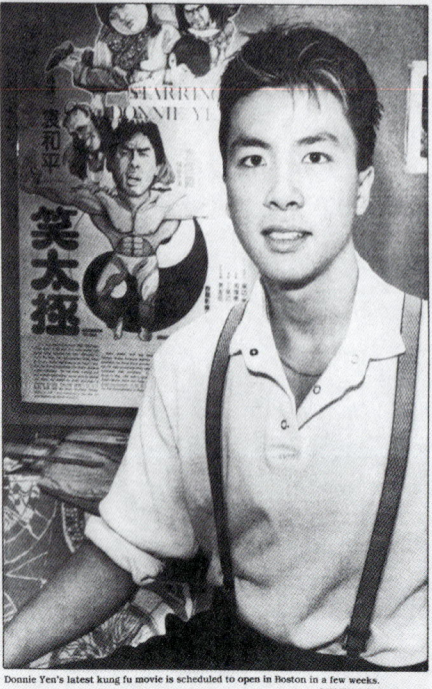

By Jay Carr
Globe Staff

Donnie Yen leads a life in the arts – the martial arts. Yen, 21, of Newton, is a kung fu movie star. "Drunken Tai Chi," which he filmed in Hong Kong last year, is a hit both in theaters and on videocassette. In a few weeks, the Pagoda Theater in Chinatown will present the Boston premiere of "Mismatched Couples," Yen's second kung fu film.

The genre has come a long way since the Bruce Lee days, Yen says. "The standard keeps getting tougher. The audience expects new things, more daring stunts. In this kind of film you do your own stunts. Usually there's just one take, so you've got to get it right."

Yen, with his spiked hair and up-to-date looks, is at the forefront of a new kind of kung fu movie. Call it new wave crossover kung fu, aimed at the youth market. In addition to the usual leaps, twists, kicks and flips, "Drunken Tai Chi" contains comedy and a break-dancing scene. Yen also does trick riding on a bike, and swivelhips his way through a firecracker and rocket trap on a narrow street. "In 'Mismatched Couples,' there's a teen-age break-dancing party. Kids in Hong Kong like break-dancing. I also have a tennis match with my opponent. He plays tennis with kung fu moves. I play on a BMX bicycle. I use the back wheel to hit the ball back."

The plot of "Drunken Tai Chi," Yen says, is stereotyped. His father and brother are murdered. He studies with a kung fu master and gets revenge. "Mismatched Couples," he says, is more modern. The speed and peppiness of the acrobatic action in "Drunken Tai Chi" make Western action movies look like a field of rusting tanks. Part of what makes martial arts movies exciting, Yen says, is the fact that they're dangerous. "This mark on my arm is where I got a 9,000-degree burn during the firecracker scene. I went to the hospital three times on 'Mismatched Couples.' See this finger? Five stitches. I had to karatechop a beer bottle, and they forgot to use a fake one. I lost two fingernails, too.

"In another scene, I'm fighting a guy in a boxing ring. I get kicked in the face, and had to fly out of the ring, bounce back off the wall, and land on the floor. There's no mat on the floor. That turned out OK – just a nail cut through my palm. Another time, a guy picks me up and throws me down. I dive away from the camera and bounce three times – boom, boom, boom. On the third bounce I landed on my shoulder. I hurt a ligament and some nerves. The doctor said I had to rest. I said, 'Just put pain-killers in my shoulder. I have to finish.' My right hand wasn't working very well that day, so we changed that fight scene. I used left-hand punches. I think the stunt stuff has reached a peak. Most kung fu stars burn out in their 30s."

Yen, born in Hong Kong, came to Boston with his family in 1975, when he was 11. His father, Klyster

LIVES, Page 63

Donnie Yen's latest kung fu movie is scheduled to open in Boston in a few weeks.
GLOBE STAFF PHOTO BY GEORGE RIZER

This was around the same time a Hong Kong expat who'd moved to Boston when he was 11 years old finally came home. Donnie Yen's father managed Boston's Chinese daily paper, *Sing Tao*, while his mother was Bow Sim Mark, a wu shu champion. She trained her son at her Boston school until the coach of the Beijing wu shu team (where Jet Li had gotten his start) told him he should study in China. And so, at 17, Yen moved to China for two years. On his way home, he stopped in Hong Kong to audition for Yuen Wo-ping, who was looking for a new protégé to shape into a star after he'd done so well with Jackie.

Thrown into the deep end, Yen worked as Yuen's stuntman for eight months, then starred in *Drunken Tai Chi* (1984), which took a year to shoot, followed by the breakdance-inflenced *Mismatched Couples*. Yuen and Yen shared a bunk bed but the shoots were trials by fire. Over the course of the films, Yen burned his arm, got five stitches in his finger, injured the ligaments in his shoulder, and went to the hospital three times.

Mismatched Couples came out in 1985 and flopped. Fed up with working so hard for seemingly no reward, Yen returned to the States, tail between his legs, too embarrassed to even say goodbye to Yuen in person. He might have

268

passed Jackie in midair, flying home to Hong Kong after *The Protector* flopped, making less than $1 million against its $7 million budget. Chan's second attempt to break into Hollywood had failed, and he turned his back on the American market, seemingly for good.

In Boston, Donnie Yen gave interviews bragging about breaking into Hollywood and shooting a movie with Shaw Brothers, but Shaw was having problems of their own. Eager to cash in on Jet Li's massive profile, they teamed him up with their ace martial arts director, Lau Kar-leung, and sent a Hong Kong crew to Mainland China to shoot the epic *Martial Arts of Shaolin* in 1986. However, Li hated the way Lau and his Hong Kong crew talked down to the Mainland talent, and the two clashed repeatedly. Shaw, meanwhile, went out of business, shutting down all film production so abruptly that, reportedly, when *Martial Arts of Shaolin* wrapped, their Hong Kong crew found themselves stranded on the Mainland with no tickets home.

Ironically, *Martial Arts of Shaolin* still did well at the box office, but Li felt burned and would soon move to the United States and leave his wife to marry an actress, prompting a full-scale tabloid scandal. He'd make a few films, like the San Francisco–set *Dragon Fight* (1989), but largely lived in limbo. Back in Hong Kong, the back-to-back releases of John Woo's *A Better Tomorrow* (1986) and Ringo Lam's *City on Fire* (1987) made Chow Yun-fat a superstar and saw two-fisted blazing Berettas replace bare-fisted kung fu as the onscreen weapon of choice. In 1988, Michelle Yeoh gave up her action career to marry luxury brand magnate Dickson Poon, one of the heads of D&B Films, the company that had produced her movies. Around the same time, Cynthia Rothrock (see page 333) made a bid for international stardom, leaving Hong Kong behind.

Alexander Fu Sheng was dead, Donnie Yen was a teaching assistant at his mother's school, and Jet Li was lying low in San Francisco. Jackie Chan might have been the new Bruce Lee, but who was going to be the next Jackie Chan? By the time the late '80s rolled around, the answer was "Nobody."

The 'WALKING DEAD' are the most DEADLY!

THE SHAW BROTHERS PRESENT

REVENGE OF THE ZOMBIES

One of the most shocking and bizarre films of the year!

Starring LOIS LEE / LINDA WEIT and TAMMY
Produced by RUN RUN SHAW / Directed by HORACE MENGA

A WORLD NORTHAL FILM

R — RESTRICTED

CREEPY FU

SINCE 1973, DISTRIBUTORS HAD BEEN trying to cross-pollinate kung fu with horror in order to shoot some juice into both genres. Horror wasn't foreign to Chinese movies. The very first sound adaptation of *The Phantom of the Opera* was also the very first Chinese horror movie, *Song at Midnight* (1937), a sophisticated gothic that owed a lot to the atmosphere of James Whale's movies, like *Bride of Frankenstein*. *Midnight* became a big hit, inspiring director Ma-Xu Weibang to crank out horror flicks like *Walking Corpse in an Old House* (1938) and *The Leper Girl* (1939), but his 1941 sequel to *Song at Midnight* flopped, and he wound up making movies for the occupying Japanese army, which got him branded as a collaborator and sent him fleeing to Hong Kong, where he was eventually run over by a streetcar.

Shaw Brothers turned out some classy horror flicks in the '50s and '60s, mostly from their premier director of elegant historical films, Li Han-hsiang, but in October 1975, Shaw director Ho Meng-hua struck gonzo gold with *Black Magic*, which took folk magic, true crime stories, and a dose of xenophobia and stirred it all into a chunky porridge about a Chinese woman living in Malaysia who hires a local wizard to brew up a love potion. Unfortunately, the potion involves involuntary tongue removal and human bodies boiled down for oil. That was just a warm-up for *Black Magic 2* (1976), which featured immortality serums made from breast milk and pubic hair, and worms wriggling out of open sores.

For almost 10 years, Shaw hemorrhaged films about "civilized" Hong Kongers traveling to "primitive" foreign countries (read: anywhere not Hong Kong) where filthy local wizards doled out blood curses like branded T-shirts at a wellness conference. Kuei Chih-hung took Ho Meng-hua's brand of horror and made a series of films—*Hex* (1980), *Hex Versus Witchcraft* (1980), *Hex After Hex* (1982), and *The Boxer's Omen* (1983)—that made audiences barf in their popcorn. *Boxer's Omen* in particular is nothing more than a 90-minute freak-out that looks like the last 10 minutes of *2001: A Space Odyssey* if you replaced the flashing colors and swirling stars with writhing maggots and bright green pus. Shaw's run came to a truly traumatic end with *Seeding of a Ghost* (1983), in which the titular

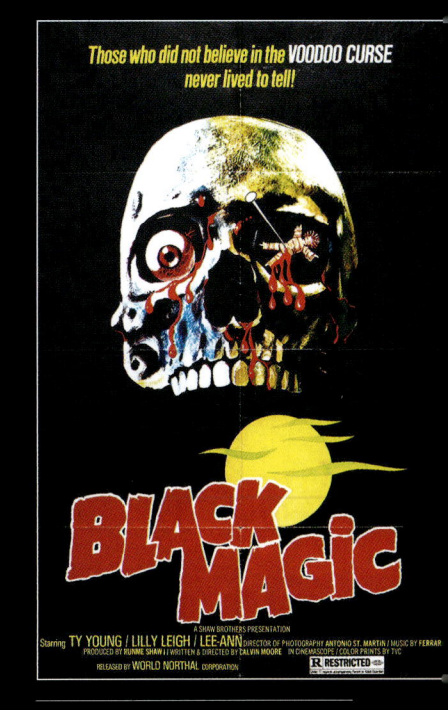

Shaw's formula was simple. Scary foreigners + xenophobia + goopy black magic rituals + sex + gross-out special effects + Scream Queen Tanny = *Black Magic* movies

ghost of the title, actually a rotten corpse, does, indeed, get seeded. Graphically.

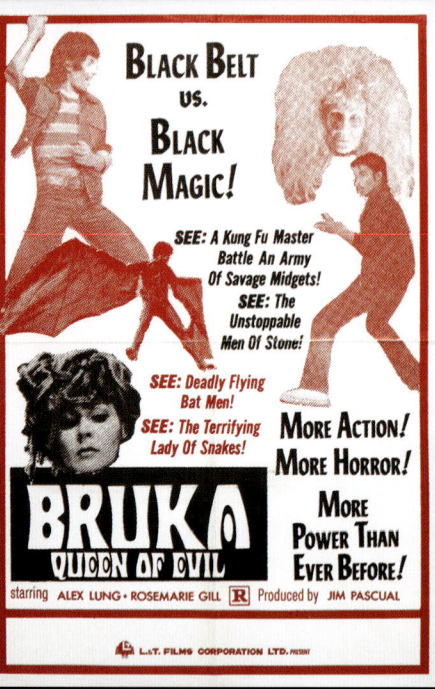

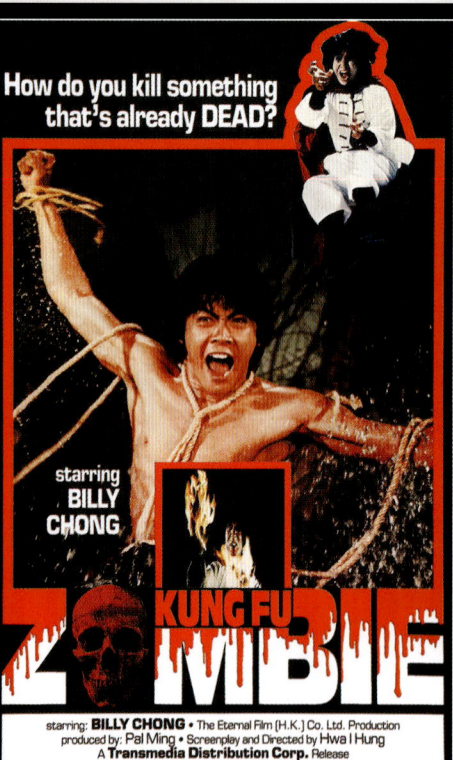

Independent American distributors tried to cash in on these movies, retitling *Black Magic 2* as *Revenge of the Zombies* and unleashing it in 1982, with Lo Lieh credited as "Lois Lieh." But usually they just scoured martial arts movies looking for weird elements that could justify a spooky title and poster. Polly Shang Kuan appeared in *The Ghostly Face* (1971), wherein a bad guy wore a spooky rubber mask, and *Dragon Zombies Return* (aka *The Zodiac Fighters*, 1978), which sported fighters using zodiac kung fu. Judy Lee (see page 126) was billed as "Kathy Leen" in *Kung Fu Exorcist* (1977), which is actually *Shaolin Monk* but is sometimes called *Killer Priest*, and also starred in *Kung Fu Halloween* (aka *Fist of Dragon* and *The Fighter with Two Faces*, 1977), which featured a brief scene of people dancing in fright masks that figured prominently in the trailer.

In the early '80s, Sammo Hung conquered the Hong Kong box office again with *Encounter of the Spooky Kind* and *Mr. Vampire* (which spawned 31 sequels, spin-offs, and copycat films), combining hopping vampires, black magic, and martial arts. Meanwhile, Yuen Wo-ping and his brothers turned out berserk kung fu hoedowns featuring demons, serial killers, talking fish, and fire-breathing monsters in *Dreadnaught* (1981), *The Miracle Fighters* (1982), and *Taoism Drunkard* (1983). But by then, American distributors had lost their interest in importing martial arts movies from Hong Kong, and these clearly superior movies played the Chinatown circuit instead of Western grindhouses.

(top) *Bruka, Queen of Evil* (1975) was another Jimmy L. Pascual quickie shot in the Philippines.

(bottom) Jackie Chan imitator Billy Chong starred in one of the best kung fu horror movies of them all,

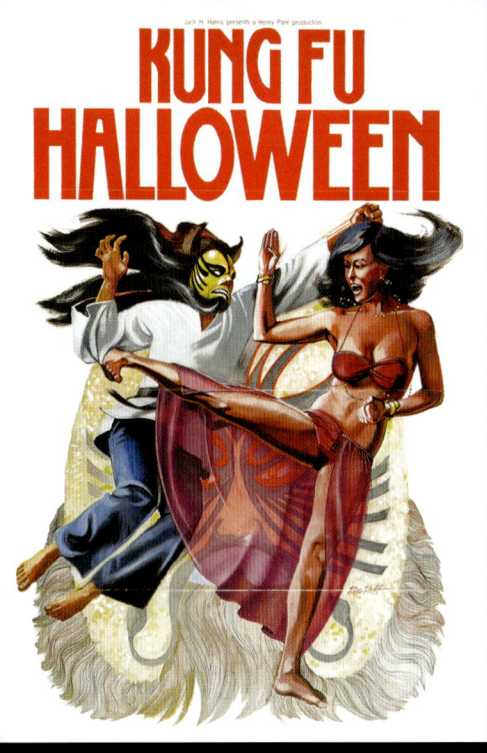

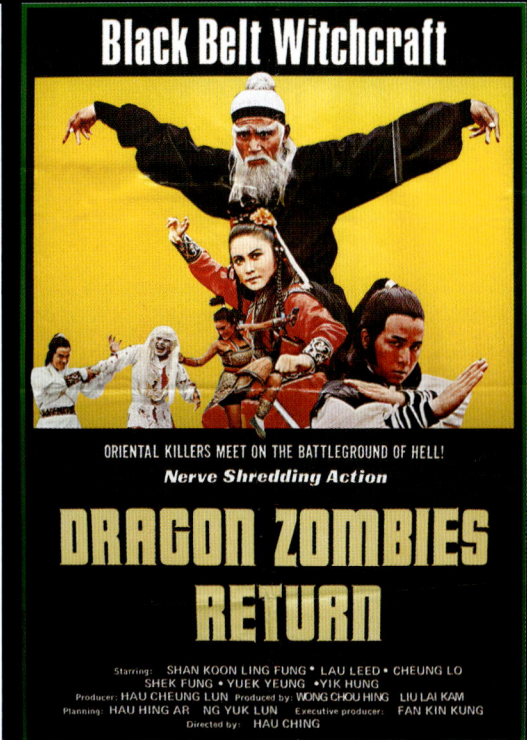

Kung Fu Halloween (aka *Fist of Dragon*, 1977) stars Lo Lieh and Judy Lee; *Dragon Zombies Return* (aka *The Zodiac Fighters*, 1978) stars Lo Lieh and Polly Shang Kuan; *Dragon vs. Dracula* (aka *The Golden Mask*, 1977) is a star vehicle for ace action choreographer Stephen Tung Wai that later got re-released as *Bad Ninjas Wear Gold*; and *The Ghostly Face* (1973) is another horror fu flick starring Polly Shang Kuan.

MASTER OF MASTERS

HONG KONG MANUFACTURED MANY MASTERS, thanks to two big hits. The first was Jimmy Wong Yu's *Master of the Flying Guillotine* (aka *One-Armed Boxer vs. the Flying Guillotine*, 1976). One long fight scene set at a martial-arts competition, it exerted a stealth influence on fighting video games from *Street Fighter* to *Mortal Kombat*. With an Indian fighter who comes complete with an attack owl and stretchy arms, a blind assassin disguised as a Buddhist monk, and a heavy Krautrock soundtrack, it's wonderfully doom-laden, with a finale set in a coffin shop featuring spring-loaded axes and a finishing move that rockets the loser through the air to land in his own coffin.

Next came *Master Killer* (aka *The 36th Chamber of Shaolin*, 1978), which made Gordon Liu's bald head an international icon. Directed by his godbrother, Lau Kar-leung, the groundbreaking Shaw Brothers action choreographer (see page 22). *Master Killer* stars Liu as a young idiot who seeks sanctuary inside the Shaolin monastery after his family are wiped out by government officials. The movie's centerpiece is a training sequence transforming him from a hotheaded blockhead into an unbeatable martial monk, and it's essentially an hour-long cinematic tone poem celebrating the virtues of discipline and commitment. Not just a box office hit, *Master Killer* influenced every training montage to come in the '80s and set the formula for a whole lot of retitled kung fu films.

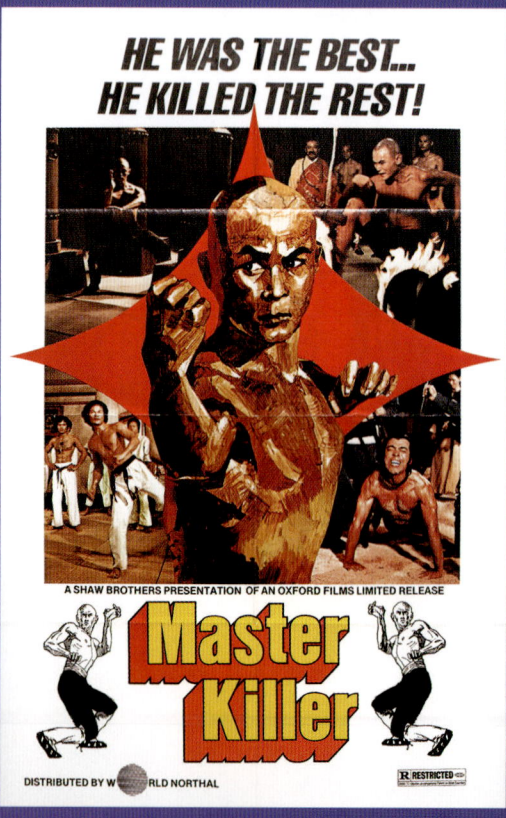

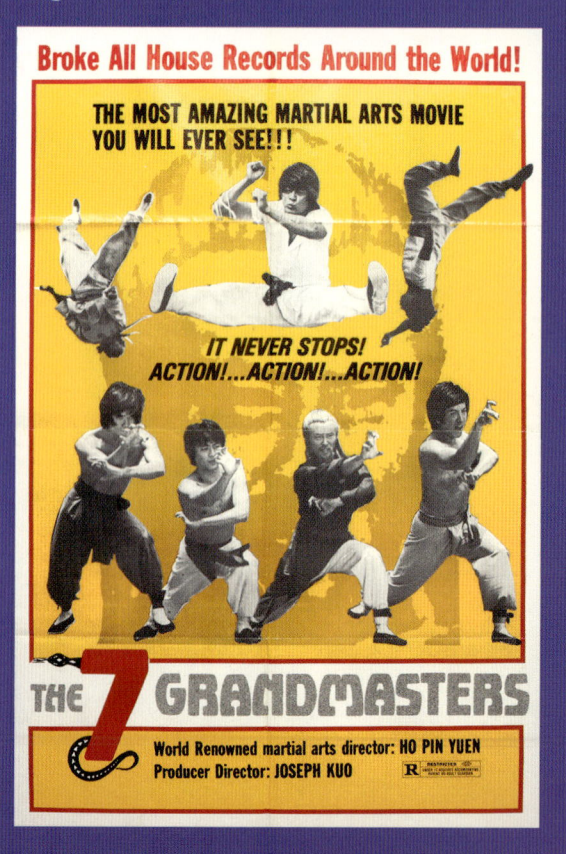

Armed with the Most Gruesome Weapon ever Conceived...
He Challenged the Warriors from Beyond Time!
Master of the Flying Guillotine
A CINEMARC RELEASE DISTRIBUTED BY SEYMOUR BORDE & ASSOC.
SPECIAL VISUAL EFFECTS
SUPER-CINE VISION®
R RESTRICTED

STARRING:
TAN TAO LIANG
KU FENG
HAN KUO TSAI
LI TANG MING
LI HAI SHENG
LIU I FAN
PAN YAO KUN
HSIUNG PING CHUNG
planning
CHIANG CHIEH
SU HSIU HSING
LIU NI
director
TU LU PO
INCREDIBLE MASTER BEGGARS
UIC

YOU AIN'T SEEN MEAN... TILL YOU CROSS HIS PATH!
THE SAVAGE SULTAN OF KUNG FU
MASTER OF VIOLENCE
starring
CHI KUN KWAN
LUNG KWAN YEE
directed by HO CHUN
produced by
KEUNG CHUN PING
and HENRY TAN
an Ark Film release

HEROES OF THE 3RD DIMENSION

SINCE THEY COULDN'T FIND a new star, and they couldn't reinvigorate the kung fu genre by mixing it with horror, distributors turned to technical tricks. The first 3D kung fu movie was almost made in 1974 by John Lawrence, the producer of *The Incredible Two-Headed Transplant* and *The Thing with Two Heads*, who shot a single 3D scene but never raised the funds necessary to complete his film. In September 1976, Matt Cimber started production on a 3D kung fu movie titled *Fist of Don Won*, starring Wong Tao, with porno/exploitation cinematographer Ken Gibb handling the 3D. They shot a fight on top of a speeding cable car in San Francisco and a scene on the Giant Dipper roller coaster at the Santa Cruz Beach Boardwalk before moving on to Taiwan, Hong Kong, and the Philippines. The movie was retitled *Tiger Man* shortly before Bond director Terence Young shot additional 3D sequences, and then Chris Condon shot more in his StereoVision 3D format a couple of years later. The final version was screened for Paramount in the summer of 1981 for a possible domestic release, but the studio passed and the film eventually came out in 1983 through Roy Reid's bargain basement Headliner Productions.

In the mid-'70s, porno filmmaker Michael Findlay developed a 3D system called Super Depth in which two lenses attached to the front of a camera recorded the left and right eye images directly to the negative in an over-under 2.35:1 format. A deal was made for two Taiwanese 3D kung fu movies, *Dynasty* and *13 Nuns*, to be filmed using the system and Findlay was on location during the production of both as a consultant. *Dynasty* was released in Hong Kong in April 1977 and topped $1 million in a mere

LEAPING OUT OF AN ERA OF SPECTACLE COMES...
THE MOST SENSATIONAL ENTERTAINMENT EXPERIENCE OF A LIFETIME!
DYNASTY
IN
SUPER 3-D
AND
QUADROPHONIC SOUND
Introducing
BOBBY MING
Director CHANG MEI CHUN
An Eastern Media Production (H.K.) Presentation-1977
Produced by FRANK WONG • A JAD FILMS INTERNATIONAL Release
R RESTRICTED
UNDER 17 REQUIRES ACCOMPANYING PARENT OR ADULT GUARDIAN
DISTRIBUTED BY
CINEMA SHARES INTERNATIONAL DISTRIBUTION CORPORATION

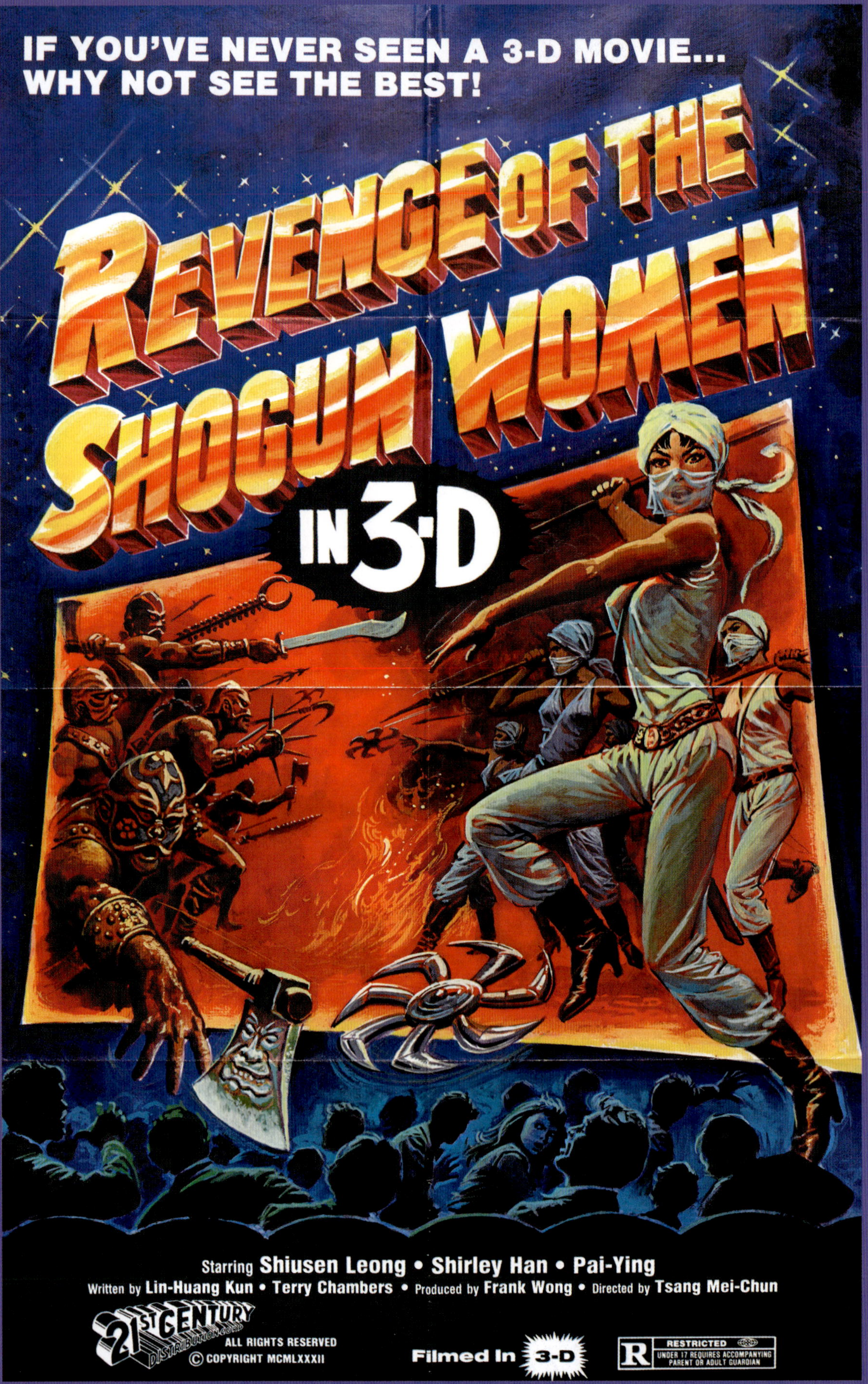
IF YOU'VE NEVER SEEN A 3-D MOVIE...
WHY NOT SEE THE BEST!
REVENGE OF THE SHOGUN WOMEN
IN 3-D
Starring Shiusen Leong • Shirley Han • Pai-Ying
Written by Lin-Huang Kun • Terry Chambers • Produced by Frank Wong • Directed by Tsang Mei-Chun
21ST CENTURY DISTRIBUTION CORP.
ALL RIGHTS RESERVED
© COPYRIGHT MCMLXXXII
Filmed In 3-D
R
RESTRICTED
UNDER 17 REQUIRES ACCOMPANYING PARENT OR ADULT GUARDIAN

five days. The US premiere was set for the Budco 1 in downtown Philadelphia on August 3, 1977, but unfortunately on May 16, 1977, while Findlay was boarding a helicopter on top of the Pan Am building, its front landing gear collapsed and its 20-foot long rotor scythed through the passengers, killing Findlay and three others. *13 Nuns* got picked up by 21st Century Distribution, the title was changed to *Revenge of the Shogun Women*, and it was released in New York City on January 15, 1982.

Jackie Chan sustained a broken hip during the making of *Magnificent Bodyguards*, a 3D movie shot in dual Techniscope and printed over-under, which throws everything at its viewers, including darts, poles, swords, feet, fists, boulders, snakes, spears, and lots of visible wires. It opened at the Pagoda Palace in San Francisco on July 19, 1978, but didn't get many other North American show dates apart from a week or two in Vancouver in 1981. 21st Century announced a summer 1982 release, but it never materialized. Another Chinese production, *The North and South Chivalry*, is rumored to have been shot in 3D but doesn't seem to have played anywhere in that format.

In early 1983, veteran producer Albert Band told his son, exploitation king Charles Band, about *The Far Arena*, a novel he had just read by the co-creator of the *Destroyer* paperback series, Richard Sapir. In it, the premier gladiator of ancient Rome is found preserved in Arctic ice 16 centuries later by oil rig workers, thawed out, and brought back to life. The younger Band thought the same idea, done in 3D with a samurai instead of a gladiator, would make a great movie, and hired Alan J. Adler, who had written *Parasite* and *Metalstorm: The Destruction of Jared-Syn*, the Bands' previous 3D productions, to write a treatment called *Frozen Shogun*. By the time it went into production, interest in 3D was fading fast and the resulting film was shot flat as *Swordkill* and eventually released in 1985 as *Ghost Warrior*.

AFTER HIS FOUR-WALLED MOVIES MADE millions, Chuck Norris had a couple of moderate hits with the big studios that cemented his place as America's leading martial arts movie star. With no better ideas, producers searched for more blond, Anglo karate champions. Enter Joe Lewis. The Golden Boy of Karate, preternaturally gifted in the ring, Lewis moved fast, hit hard, and displayed a light-speed tactical genius in the middle of even the most punishing bouts. A former Marine, world heavyweight karate and kickboxing champion, and the eventual inspiration for Ken Masters in the *Street Fighter* video games, Lewis even impressed himself.

"I really believe that I can hit the screen and give something to the audience like they haven't seen since Marlon Brando," he said in an interview. "I really feel I have that power."

Producer Sandy Howard tried to bottle the Lewis lightning in *Jaguar Lives!* (1979). The supposed launching pad for a whole series of international adventures starring Lewis, Howard wanted to give audiences a Bondgasm, packing the cast with Donald Pleasence (Blofeld in *You Only Live Twice*), Christopher Lee (Scaramanga in *The Man with the Golden Gun*), Joseph Wiseman (Dr. No in *Dr. No*), and Bond Girl Barbara Bach (*The Spy Who Loved Me*), even throwing in John Huston (M in *Casino Royale*) as a finishing move.

Despite all that talent, *Jaguar* fizzled. Loathing failure, Lewis made sure to trash the movie in public.

"I've had a couple of very competent directors see the film," he told reporters. "They weren't pleased with the script, they weren't pleased with the direction, nor were they pleased with my acting."

Were they pleased with anything?

"They were pleased with what I had going for me."

Fred Weintraub and Robert Clouse tried to make Lewis work with *Force: Five!* (1981), this time augmenting him with a lineup of martial artists, like full-contact powerhouse Benny "the Jet" Urquidez, long-limbed Australian Richard Norton (both of whom would later find work fighting Jackie Chan), and karate champ Sonny Barnes. A knock-off of *Enter the Dragon* mixed with fears around the Jonestown Massacre and the rise of the Moonies, it sends five martial arts masters to a remote island to rescue a young girl from a cult. But despite the presence of hapkido grandmaster Bong Soo Han (dubbed by James Hong) as the Reverend Rhee, and the Schlitz Malt Liquor bull as an agent of death, the movie barely did any business.

Lewis would rewrite his failed Hollywood projects, portraying himself as the victim of Hollywood liars who "knew nothing about working with actors" in long interviews during which he namedropped Willie Nelson, Elvis Presley, Marlon Brando, Bruce Lee, Kareem Abdul-Jabbar, Jesus Christ, and Adolf Hitler. Hollywood, in turn, kept looking for a new hero.

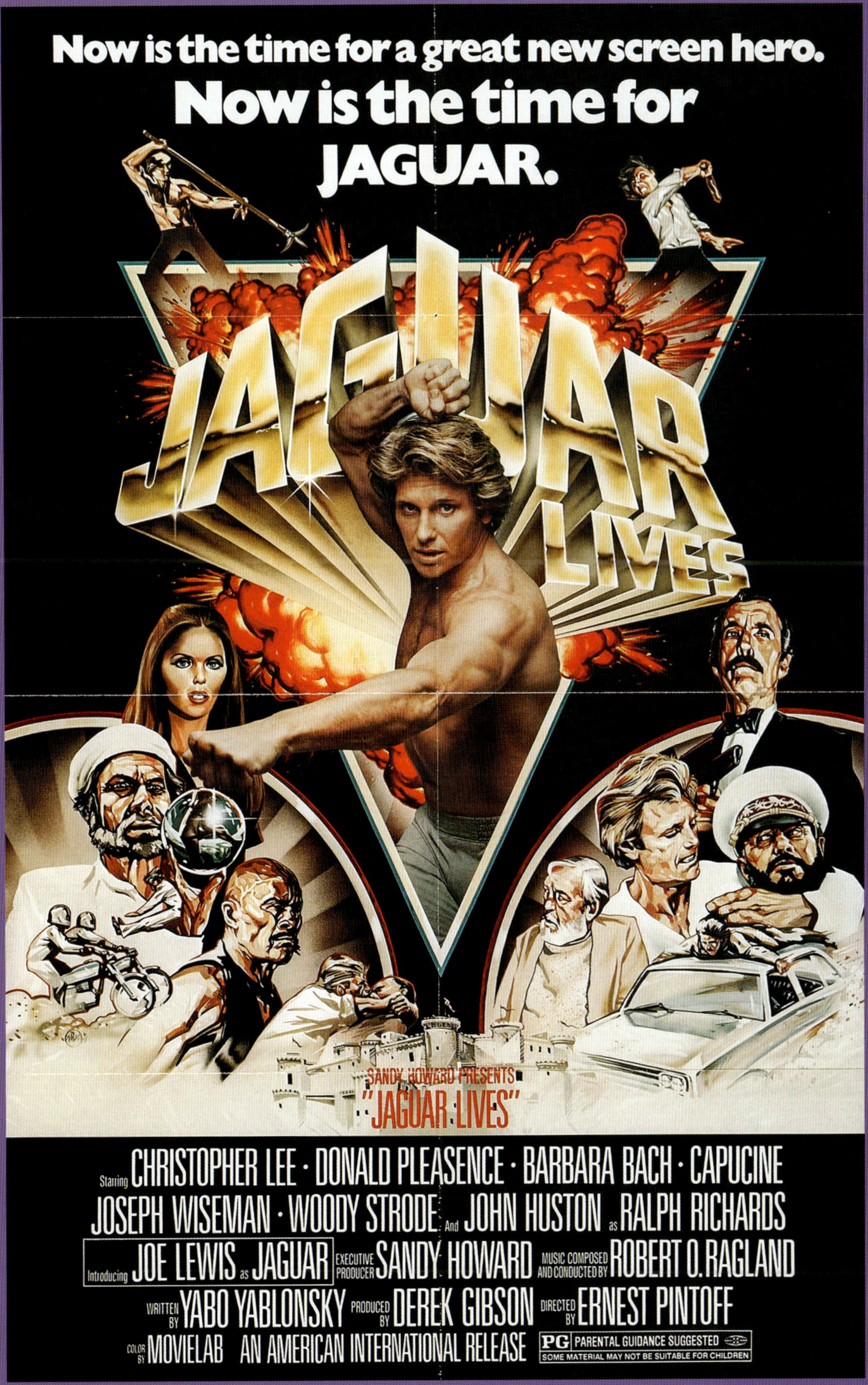
Now is the time for a great new screen hero.
Now is the time for
JAGUAR.
JAGUAR
LIVES
SANDY HOWARD PRESENTS
"JAGUAR LIVES"
Starring CHRISTOPHER LEE · DONALD PLEASENCE · BARBARA BACH · CAPUCINE
JOSEPH WISEMAN · WOODY STRODE And JOHN HUSTON as RALPH RICHARDS
Introducing JOE LEWIS as JAGUAR
EXECUTIVE PRODUCER SANDY HOWARD
MUSIC COMPOSED AND CONDUCTED BY ROBERT O. RAGLAND
WRITTEN BY YABO YABLONSKY
PRODUCED BY DEREK GIBSON
DIRECTED BY ERNEST PINTOFF
COLOR BY MOVIELAB
AN AMERICAN INTERNATIONAL RELEASE
PG PARENTAL GUIDANCE SUGGESTED
SOME MATERIAL MAY NOT BE SUITABLE FOR CHILDREN

Maybe martial arts movies were over? Audiences, after all, seemed to be uncomfortable with all that barehanded brutality. Not an interview went by when Chuck Norris didn't have to uncork his canned answer about not promoting violence. Reporters with columns to fill often headed to a "seedy downtown theatre" and took in a kung fu flick, then reported back to their readers like someone filing copy from a war zone.

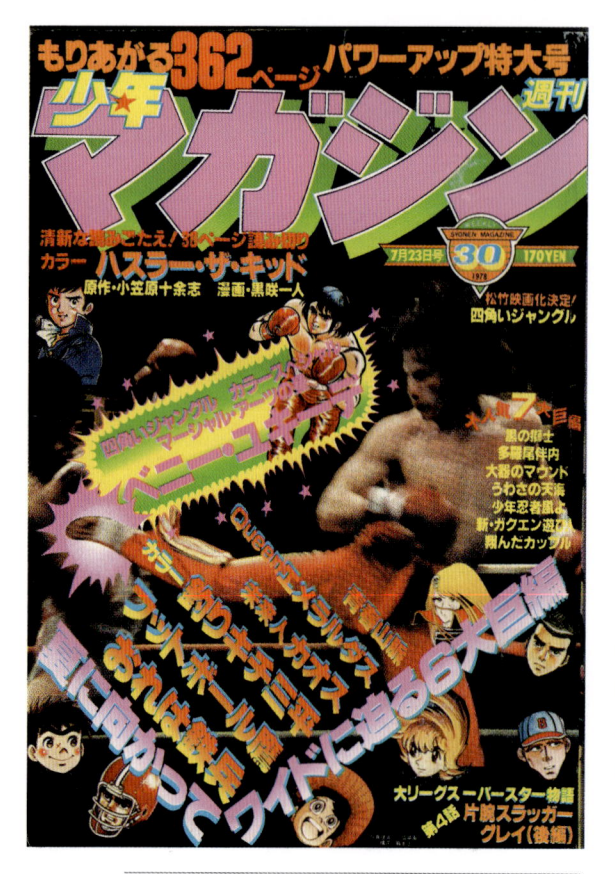

"During the kung fu film, I jotted down every line of audience commentary," Matt Seiden scribbled in the *Baltimore Sun*. "When I read over the dialogue I had scribbled down in the darkness, I felt as if I had been taking dictation from the Devil himself."

Everyone making martial arts movies felt a need to disavow martial arts movies, too.

"It is not a martial arts film," one of the actors declared in an interview promoting *Jaguar Lives!* "It is an action/adventure film."

After they optioned a bestselling ninja novel called *The Ninja*, producers Richard Zanuck and David Brown were even touchier as they developed it for the big screen.

"This is a world class film, and therefore we're a little touchy about it being labeled a martial arts movie," Brown said, touchily, in an interview about their martial arts movie.

Clouse took the tactic a lot of people did, implying that the bloody, violent martial arts movies on inner-city screens weren't American, but "Oriental."

By the time he appeared in *Force: Five!* Benny "the Jet" Urquidez was already so famous on the international kickboxing circuit that there were Japanese manga about him.

"Unlike Oriental audiences, who seem to want as much blood and gore as you can give them," Clouse said, "American audiences will tire of that rather quickly."

Unironically, he then revealed the title of the Jackie Chan picture he was currently writing: *The Bloodrun*.

FIVE AGAINST A THOUSAND... THE ODDS ARE EVEN.

FORCE: FIVE

AMERICAN CINEMA PRODUCTIONS PRESENTS A FRED WEINTRAUB PRODUCTION "FORCE: FIVE"
Starring: JOE LEWIS · MASTER BONG SOO HAN · RICHARD NORTON · BENNY URQUIDEZ · SONNY BARNES · PAM HUNTINGTON · RON HAYDEN
Directed By ROBERT CLOUSE   Produced By FRED WEINTRAUB   Screenplay By ROBERT CLOUSE
Based On A Screenplay By EMIL FARKAS And GEORGE GOLDSMITH   Music By BILL GOLDSTEIN   AN AMERICAN CINEMA RELEASE

© 1981 American Communications Industries, Inc. All rights reserved.

IF MARTIAL ARTS HAD FADED from the big screen, they were alive and well on TV thanks to James Clavell, whose life changed when he read the following sentence in one of his daughter's schoolbooks, "In 1600, an Englishman went to Japan and became a Samurai."

It sent him researching the life of 17th-century English navigator William Adams and his experiences in Japan, and the result was the 800-page bestselling novel, *Shōgun*. A screenplay adaptation by *Lawrence of Arabia* scribe Robert Bolt drew Richard Attenborough on board as director and landed Sean Connery in the lead role, but when that deal fell apart, Clavell reluctantly agreed to let it be produced as a television mini-series. The five-part, 12-hour event cost $22 million and aired on NBC the week of September 15, 1980. It became the second-highest-rated mini-series of all time after *Roots* and sparked what journalists dubbed "Samurai Night Fever."

"Liquor stores were reporting strong sake sales," *Broadcasting* magazine wrote. "Boutiques were running out of kimonos and Japanese words like hai (yes), domo (thank you) and dozo (please) were creeping into the American vernacular."

The mini-series also intensified the public's interest in ninjas, which had started five months earlier with the publication of Eric Van Lustbader's bestseller *The Ninja*.

Ninjas crawled all over "Force Seven," the 1982 season finale of NBC's motorcycle

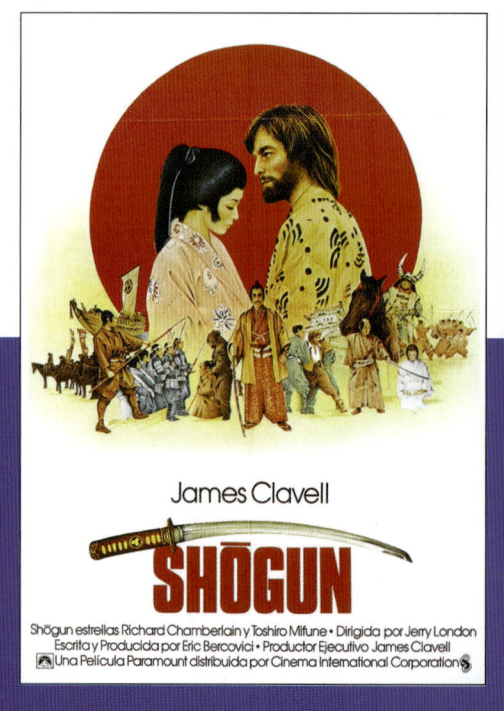

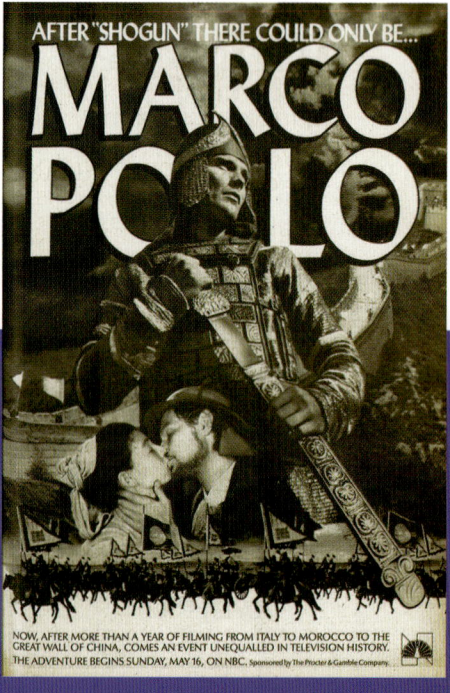

(left) *Shōgun* sold seven million copies and became a Broadway musical. It's the third in Clavell's six-volume "Asian Saga" inspired by the time he spent in a Japanese POW camp after being shot in the face during World War II.

(right) *Marco Polo*'s cast included Burt Lancaster, John Gielgud, Anne Bancroft, John Houseman, and Leonard Nimoy.

THE NINJA

A NOVEL BY ERIC VAN LUSTBADER

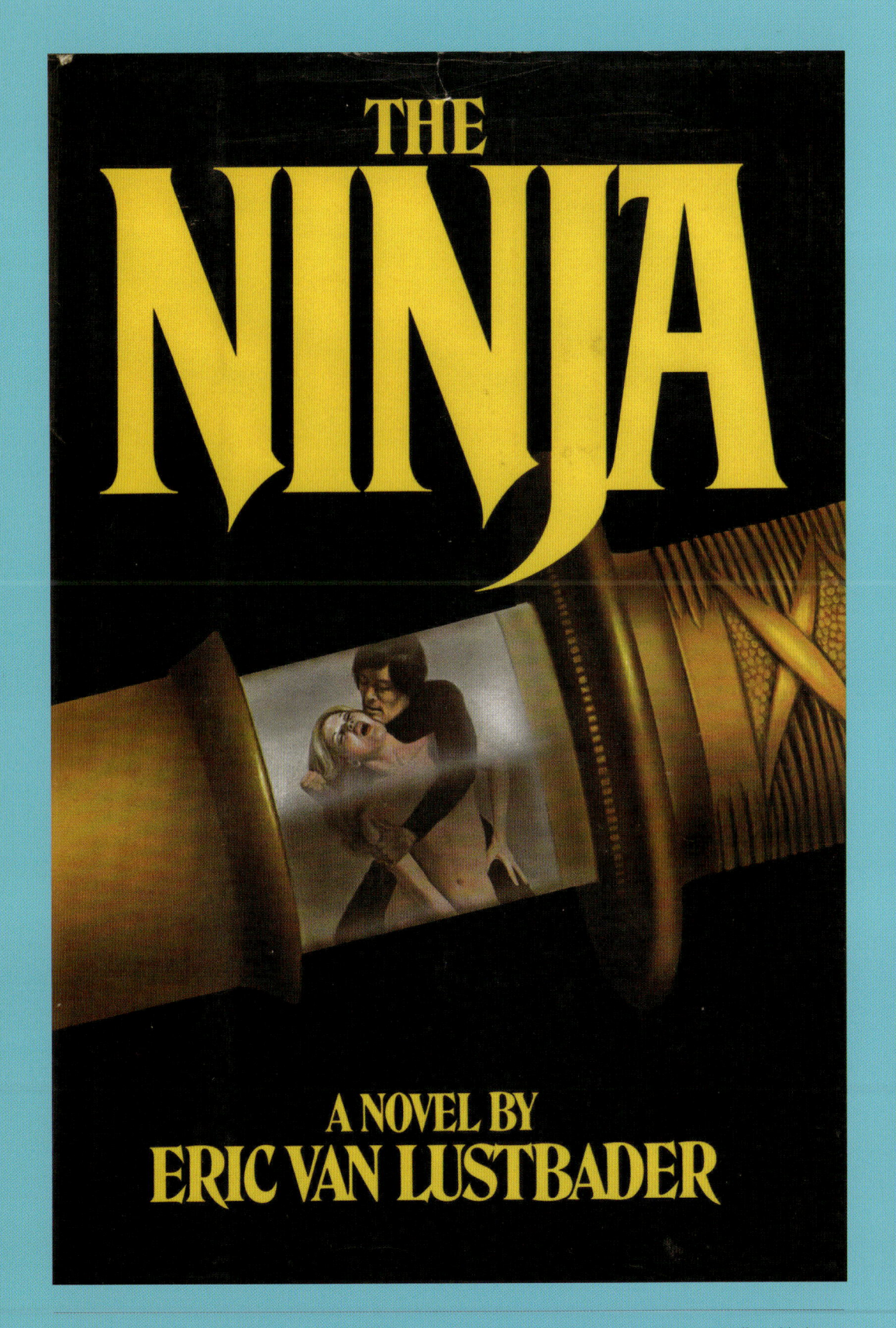

The Ninja would spawn five sequels between 1984 and 1995 featuring its hero, Nicholas Linnear, tangling with the mafia, the yakuza, psychic warriors, and so many ninjas.

patrol program *CHiPs*. Force Seven was the name of a secret police unit of martial artists led by eyepatch-wearing Lt. John Le Garre (Fred Dryer), who must stop his nemesis Nakura (John Rhys-Davies) from using a hijacked missile to detonate nerve gas over Los Angeles. All of the actors wear hoods during the climactic action scene except Dan Inosanto, evidently the only cast member who didn't need a fight double.

Neither *Beach Patrol* nor *Samurai* made it past shooting their pilots, which were eventually screened as a TV movie double feature.

This backdoor pilot for a *Force Seven* series that never happened followed hot on the heels of "A Threat of War," the second karate-themed *CHiPs* episode with guest star Danny Bonaduce as the nunchuk-swinging gang member Billy Rogers.

ABC's attempt to ride this wave was *Samurai*, sometimes referred to as "Samurai District Attorney" by people who aren't 100% convinced that it actually exists. It does. Joe Penny plays a half-Japanese city prosecutor who "uses the code of the Samurai and his skills in Oriental martial arts to move against crime a little faster than more conventional police procedures." In other words, DA by day, samurai by night. ABC was so proud of *Samurai* that they premiered it as the second half of a Monday Night Movie "Action Double Feature" alongside *Beach Patrol*.

Then came *Shōgun*'s successor, *Marco Polo*, with an 800-page screenplay that scared off the first two actors hired to play the titular explorer. Michael Ontkean vanished one week before filming began in the fall of 1980 and was replaced by Mandy Patinkin, who fled the scene a week after shooting started, leaving the role to newcomer Ken Marshall. The nine-month shoot stretched to 13 months as the budget ballooned from $12.5 million to somewhere around $30 million. The 10-hour miniseries aired over four nights during the week of May 16, 1982, and was successful, but not *Shōgun*-level successful.

By 1986, Kwai Chang Caine was ready to return to the airwaves with a new two-hour TV movie, this time on CBS. In an interview with the New York *Daily News* to promote *Kung Fu: The Movie*, David Carradine revealed that the story for the telefilm dated back to December 1980, when he was in New York to host *Saturday Night Live* and met with actor Radames Pera, who had played Young Caine on the original series. The two traded ideas between helium hits from balloons floating around them in the Manhattan nightspot Maxwell's Plum, and the next day Carradine began writing it on NBC napkins in the Peacock Commissary. Set in 1885, Caine is now 10 years older and happily settled in Northern California, but that changes when he's falsely accused of

Robert Clouse and Fred Weintraub recruited gymnastics champion Kurt Thomas to star in *Gymkata*. So famous he has three gymnastic moves named after him, Thomas' 1979 record for most gold medals won at a world championship (six) stood until Simone Biles beat it in 2018. He died of a stroke in 2020.

killing a missionary in an opium den and goes on the run again. This time he's pursued not only by the law but by a vengeful Manchu lord (Mako) and his young assistant, Chang Fung (Brandon Lee). It aired as a CBS Saturday Night Movie on February 1, 1986—Brandon Lee's 21st birthday.

Eighteen months later, another attempt was made to restart *Kung Fu*, this time as a contemporary series. The hour-long pilot *Kung Fu: The Next Generation* aired as part of the CBS Summer Playhouse on June 19, 1987. David Carradine is nowhere to be found, but Brandon Lee is back, this time as Johnny Caine, the rebellious great-great-grandson of Kwai Chang Caine, who's always getting into trouble with the law. After the pilot was over, viewers could call a 900-prefix "yes" or "no" number to vote on whether or not it went to series. It didn't. Five years later another attempt, *Kung Fu: The Legend Continues*—with Carradine again returning—did click with audiences and ran for four seasons in syndication.

MOTION PICTURE PRODUCERS HAD MOVED through their five stages of grief over the death of Bruce Lee and finally, a decade later, reached acceptance and finally stopped trying to find his replacement. Now it fell to the ultimate average American, Chuck Norris, to re-capture the zeitgeist.

Like America, Norris had been traumatized by the Vietnam War. In 1970, during a karate tournament, he'd been called to the phone and learned that his little brother, Wieland Norris, had been killed in Vietnam, one month shy of his 28th birthday. It hung over Norris for the rest of his life.

"He was very, very close to me," Norris said in an interview. "Real close as a brother. He was a friend and everything else. He was my top black belt, one of my first black belts . . . He was really a good boy."

Always tight with his family (Chuck's brother, Aaron, choreographed most of his films), Norris publicly struggled with Wieland's death, which seemed to bleed over into his films. *Breaker! Breaker!* saw his character investigate his little brother's disappearance, his script for *Good Guys Wear Black* wrestled with the aftermath of Vietnam, and he dedicated his 1988 autobiography to his little brother, but it still wasn't enough. In 1982, after walking out on his big MGM contract because he felt like it required him to be too violent, he met Mexican-American screenwriter Lance Hool, who had written a script about American POWs left behind in 'Nam. Norris realized it was time for him to confront the war directly.

Once again, no one agreed. Norris finally found a home for his Vietnam project with the low-rent Israeli exploitation merchants Menahem Golan and Yoram Globus, two cousins who'd bought the nearly bankrupt Cannon Films from Friedland and Dewey (see page 68) for the bargain basement price of $500,000. Their enthusiasm for Norris' Vietnam movie earned them his undying loyalty.

"Menahem gave me a break when I really needed one," Norris said in interviews. "I've been courted by other studios, sure, but Cannon helped me when I needed it."

Chuck Norris was a real-life karate champion recruited to star in movies and also to sell these jeans, called either Action, or Karate, Jeans. Catalogs focused on Norris's denim-clad crotch and breathed heavily about his pants' "unique hidden gusset" that didn't bind the wearer's, um, "legs."

CHUCK NORRIS

WILDFORCE

WILDFORCE PRODUCTIONS in association with AEI, MAN and GUN and TWE Presents CHUCK NORRIS in "WILDFORCE"
Director of Photography PERTTI MUTANEN Music by ROB WALSH Assistant Director LAURI HARJOLA
Written by JAMES BOOTH Associate Producer MOSHE DIAMANT
Executive Producers RONNIE HADAR and SID CAPLAN Produced by MARK COHEN and MARKUS SELIN
Directed by JERRY JAMESON

Wildforce was an original screenplay co-written by Finnish filmmaker Renny Harlin that was rewritten by actor-screenwriter James Booth (*Pray for Death*) for director Jerry Jameson (*Airport '77*) with Chuck Norris cast in the lead. Norris backed out after this sales sheet was printed, and his son, Mike Norris, took over the role. Harlin's directorial debut, it came out in 1986 as *Born American*, got banned in Finland and Sweden, and served as Harlin's calling card to Hollywood, where he'd direct *Nightmare on Elm Street IV: The Dream Master* and *Die Hard 2*.

He went on to make eight more movies with them (plus the *Walker, Texas Ranger* two-hour pilot), but his first two were based on Hool's script, *Missing in Action* (1984) and *Missing in Action II: The Beginning* (1985). Huge hits that rocketed his salary to almost $2 million per picture, a far cry from the $5,000 he got for *Breaker! Breaker!* The reason they hit big? Americans needed a sequel to Vietnam, and this time they wanted to win.

The Vietnam War: Part II had commenced with *First Blood* (1982), which gave America the Passion of the Vietnam Vet. John Rambo (Sylvester Stallone), a veteran looking for a little peace and quiet, is ultimately crucified for the sins of his high command. A surprisingly nuanced portrayal of a vet returning home, and a huge hit that sent Stallone's career supernova, it opened barely three weeks before 1982's other big Vietnam-related opening: the unveiling of the Vietnam Memorial in Washington, DC. Designed by Maya Lin, a Chinese-American from Ohio, its somber look had politicians decrying it as "the black gash of shame," but its opening ceremony became a five-day event attended by President Reagan and thousands of veterans who wept openly and forced America to at least briefly face the cost of the War.

Vietnam had previously been background noise, but now it was in the foreground, and filmmakers saw an opportunity to cash in. Within 11 months, Gene Hackman

---

(above) Trade ad for Lance Hool's *Missing in Action*, Norris' first movie with Cannon, which is actually its own sequel. Hool shot *MIA 2* back-to-back with Joseph Zito's *MIA*, but during editing everyone realized part 2 was the superior film, so it was released first, while Hool's movie covering Norris' backstory was released less than four months later.

headed back to Vietnam to bring home our POWs in *Uncommon Valor* (1983), leading a no-name cast, and directed by Ted Kotcheff of *First Blood* fame. Based on a failed real-life mission to bring American POWs home, headed by Bo Gritz and financed by Clint Eastwood (*Dirty Harry*), the movie's funereal ad campaign got tossed at the last minute and replaced by posters bearing the tagline, "C'mon, buddy, we're going home." It became the surprise hit of 1983, with audiences cheering to reporters on their way out of theaters, "We get to the win the Vietnam War."

That same fall, America invaded the tiny island of Grenada, a hapless, pointless invasion rewritten as a proxy Vietnam victory. The following year, Norris starred in *Missing in Action*, and one year later, John Rambo returned to Vietnam, this time in hero mode, to win the war again in the dumber and more fun *Rambo: First Blood Part II*.

America was back—bigger, better, and more of a bully than ever. Even Bruce Springsteen got in on the game with the mega–smash hit song "Born in the U.S.A," which sounded like patriotism's soundtrack if you didn't listen too hard to the lyrics.

But there was one enemy from the East even America couldn't defeat. Hollywood had finally found its next major martial arts trend.

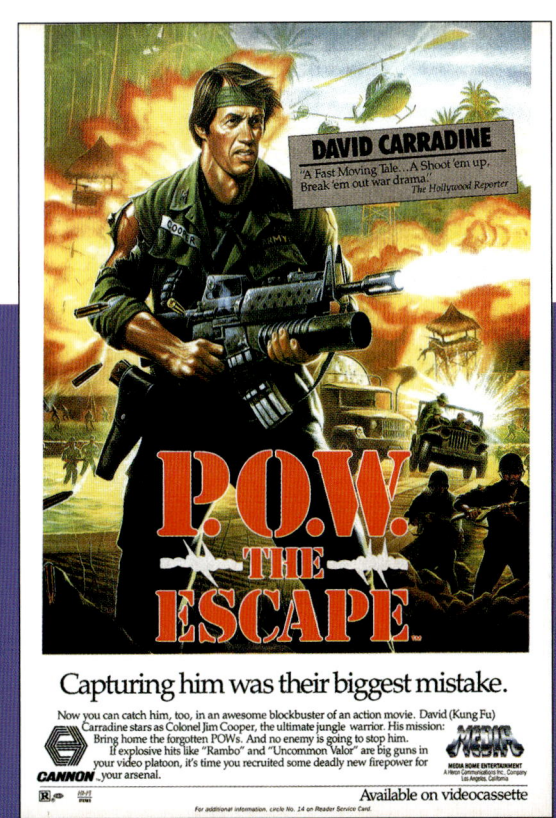

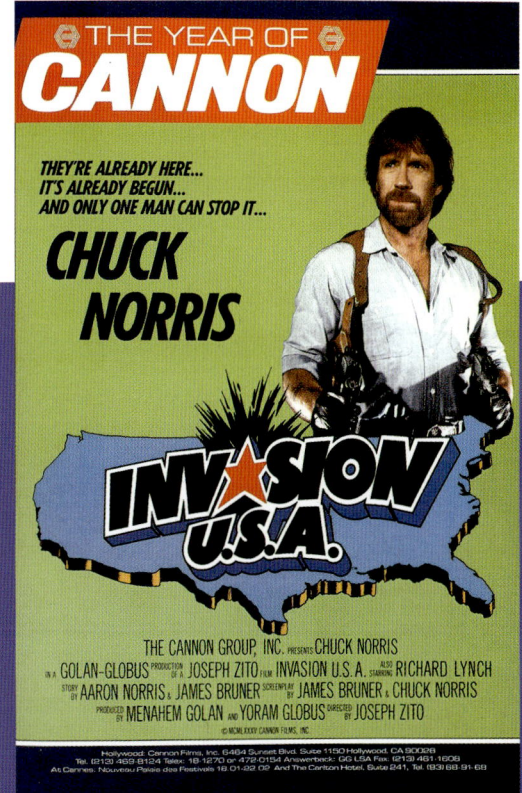

(left) One of the *Missing in Action* producers, Gideon Amir, co-wrote and directed Cannon's *P.O.W. The Escape* (1986), which recycles music from *Revenge of the Ninja* and *The Delta Force* and literally drapes an American flag over the shoulder of star David Carradine for one battle sequence.

(right) Soon, Americans would stop refighting the Vietnam War and start fighting the War on Terror. Chuck Norris brought it all home with *Invasion U.S.A.* (see page 301).

N THE '80S, NINJAS WERE everywhere. With their roots in the battlefields of 14th-century Japan, ninjas were assassins who practiced the art of . . . oh, who cares? All you need to know is that ninjas can totally kill you without even thinking about it. In fact, you are only alive right this minute because a ninja is trying very hard not to shoot a blow dart through your neck.

Despite statements to the contrary, the first person to teach the actual martial art of ninjutsu in America was Ronald Duncan, a Black man from Panama who'd emigrated to the States in 1954 and started teaching private ninjutsu classes after hours at his Brooklyn dojo in 1964. Even before the ninja boom, he ninja-ed on TV, catching arrows on shows like ABC's *Wide World of Sports*.

In 1964, Ian Fleming wrote his last Bond book, *You Only Live Twice*, which concludes with 007 turning Japanese and forgetting his life as a white man. The 1967 movie version featured Japanese actor Tetsuro Tamba, as Tiger Tanaka, a super-macho Japanese spy who trains Bond as a ninja. Another box office bonanza, this movie marked the entry of the ninja into mainstream Western pop culture.

In 1976, David Parks, son of director Gordon Parks (*Shaft*), announced that he was about to start shooting a movie called *Ninja* in Austin, Texas, which would make America's first ninja movie the work of a Black director. Starring Peter Harrell, who'd recently appeared in Gordon Parks' movie *Leadbelly* (1976), Harrell claimed that *Ninja* "has the political overtones of *Z*," an Academy Award-winning political thriller from Algeria. "It involves social problems, assassination, covert operations, and espionage," Harrell said, while Parks claimed it was "aimed at removing the stereotype identification of races or ethnic groups." After that, silence. Except for a few newspaper announcements, no one ever heard from *Ninja* again.

In 1980, author Eric Van Lustbader's thriller *The Ninja* dominated the *New York Times* bestseller list for five months and got optioned by 20th Century Fox, who pledged a $20 million budget and lined up super-producers Richard Zanuck and David Brown (*The Sting*, *Jaws*) to adapt. Menahem Golan and Yoram Globus instantly had brain embolisms. A longtime collaborator, Mike Stone, had recently pitched them a ninja project starring himself and there was no way they were letting some Hollywood big shots beat them to the box office.

And so *Enter the Ninja* (1981) was born. Cannon cast Franco Nero, the hunky Italian star of spaghetti western

Ronald Duncan (front row) with one of his classes. He taught ninjutsu after his regular class hours, usually 7pm–midnight, or even later.

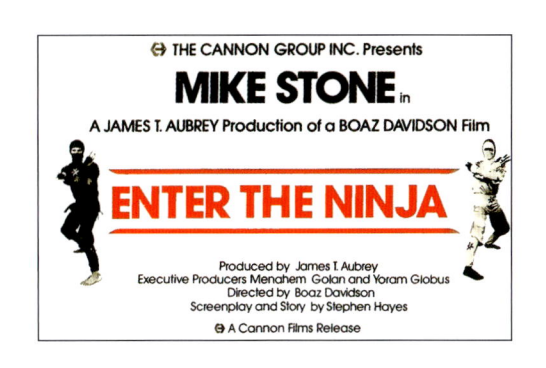

Django, as a ninja whom we first meet dressed in white, stabbing, slashing, and shooting arrows at a bunch of red-suited ninjas (extra-spicy flavored ninjas), before fighting a black-clad ninja (extra-deadly flavored ninja), jumping off a waterfall and cutting off an old dude's head—but it turns out that it's a fake head and this is the ninja equivalent of graduating magna cum laude from ninja college.

Like many recent college graduates, Nero has no idea what to do with himself, so he bums around the Philippines, where his old buddy Frank runs a farm, but has two problems: alcoholism and Mr. Venarius, an evil rich guy who wants his farm. Nero can't cure Frank's alcoholism, but he does cure his Mr. Venarius problem by murdering him with throwing stars, although by that point Frank is dead, too, but no one cares because he's not a ninja. *Enter* made big bank in Europe before Cannon successfully rolled it out in Arizona and other regional markets, but its success left a trail of dead bodies in its wake. The *Enter the Ninja* press kit describes the first few weeks of production as "a period of adjustment"—which is a polite way of saying Menahem Golan arrived on set, hated what he saw, fired director Emmett Alston and everyone else in the crew except the sound man, and replaced star and writer Mike Stone with Franco Nero, who happened to be attending the nearby Manila Film Festival. He paid Stone to stay on as the fight choreographer, but it was another stuntman who stole the show.

Sho Kosugi had impressed Stone at an impromptu audition and been hired as a stunt ninja. His gymnastic and martial arts skills saw his part grow bigger and bigger until he was doubling almost every single actor, finally landing a featured role as the silent killer who answers the call when Mr. Venarius shrieks, "I want my black ninja and I want him now!"

Convinced that their black ninja was made of money, Golan and Globus signed Kosugi up for their next ninja movie, *Revenge of the Ninja*. Stone's next movie? *Raw Force*.

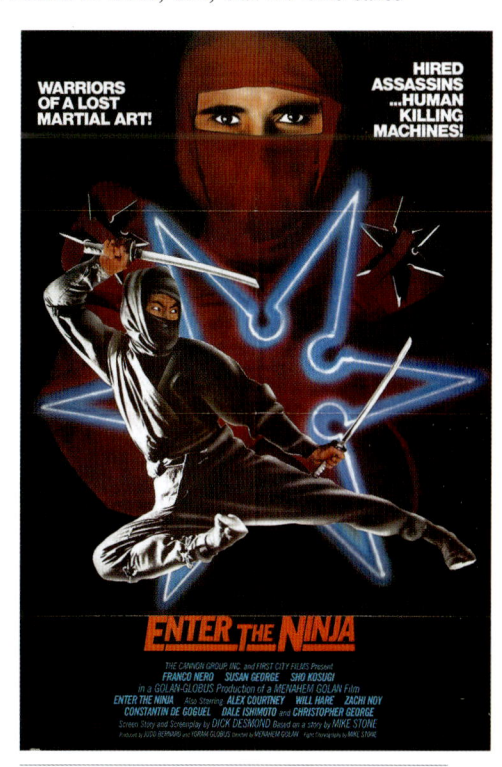

(top) The original trade announcement for *Enter the Ninja* when Cannon journeyman Boaz Davidson was slated to direct, Mike Stone starred, and martial artist Stephen Hayes was credited as writer.

(bottom) *Enter the Ninja*'s one sheet showed a deft grasp of ninja knowledge: make sure everyone has a mask on so it doesn't matter who you cast in the parts, and have a neon-edged throwing star so 12-year-old boys can't resist buying a ticket.

RAW FARCE

DESPITE A STRING OF SUCCESSFUL exploitation releases including, *Dolemite*, *The Muthers*, and *Exit the Dragon, Enter the Tiger*, Dimension Pictures was on the verge of bankruptcy when aspiring director Edward Murphy wandered into their Sunset Strip offices for a meeting with company president Larry Woolner. Although Murphy's directing experience consisted entirely of community theater in the Philippines, where he'd settled down after his military service, low-budget producers will often choose enthusiasm over experience because it's cheaper, so Woolner sent Murphy home to write a script based on the following criteria: kung fu, zombies, girls in cages.

Starring Cameron Mitchell (*Carousel*) as a drunk sea captain and his real-life girlfriend, the musical comedy star Hope Holiday, as his movie girlfriend, *Raw Force* featured Vic Diaz, who plays a bad guy in pretty much every movie shot in the Philippines, as a cannibal monk, with local Bruce Lee imitator Rey Malonzo (see page 148), and Mike Stone doing the action. Stone described the 1982 shoot succinctly:

"It was horrible."

Actors passed out from the heat. Zombie extras had their heads sliced open. Co-star Jillian Kesner fractured a toe. John Dresden twisted his ankle. Rey Malonzo had to get stitches in his scalp after being dropped on his head. When a bridge exploded it turned out to have been built of the wrong materials, causing it to collapse too quickly. Crew members raced to the wreckage as the dust settled, saying, "I thought we had a bunch of dead people on our hands."

Containing as many shots of San Miguel beer as it does of Jillian Kesner, thanks to the fact that the brewery bailed them out of a financial hole midway through production in exchange for product placement, *Raw Force* was released in the New York area by Aquarius' Terry Levene, who promoted the film by hiring a flatbed truck to drive around Manhattan carrying bikini-clad girls inside a bamboo cage. Critics called the finished film "a travesty," "bizarre," "inept," "preposterous," "poorly photographed," "unfunny," "cheapo," and "technically inferior."

They're not wrong, but it's also a perfect sampler platter of everything you could expect from a shot-in-the-Philippines exploitation movie: guns, gangs, girls, kung fu, and a man with a Hitler mustache wielding a rocket launcher.

Raw Force was produced by Larry Woolner, who started out owning a chain of theaters in Louisiana with his brothers. He went on to co-found Roger Corman's New World Pictures, then left and opened his Dimension Pictures literally right across the street. It collapsed after 10 years, and Woolner produced *Raw Force* independently. He would never produce another movie again.

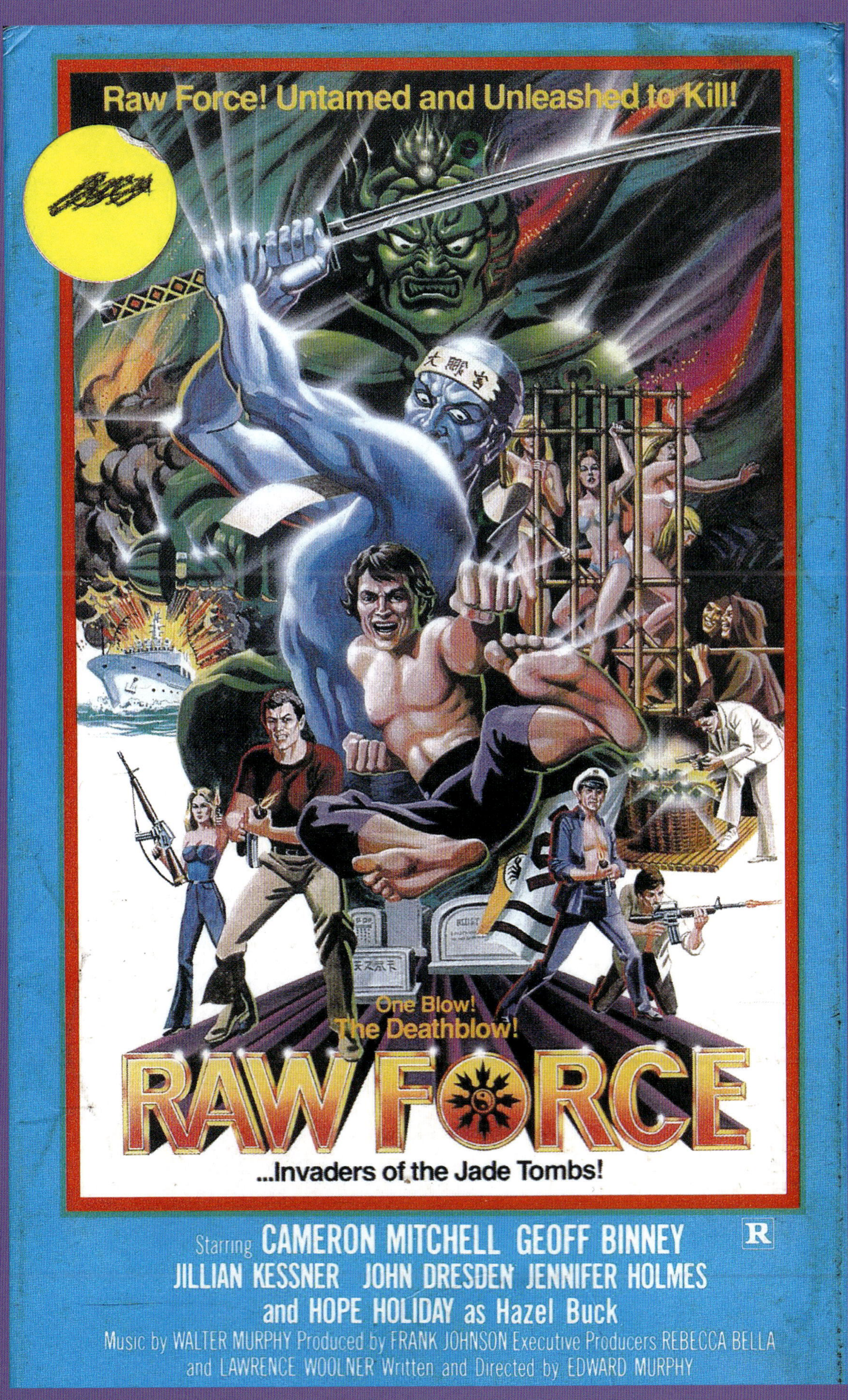
Raw Force! Untamed and Unleashed to Kill!
One Blow!
The Deathblow!
RAW FORCE
...Invaders of the Jade Tombs!
R
Starring CAMERON MITCHELL GEOFF BINNEY
JILLIAN KESSNER JOHN DRESDEN JENNIFER HOLMES
and HOPE HOLIDAY as Hazel Buck
Music by WALTER MURPHY Produced by FRANK JOHNSON Executive Producers REBECCA BELLA
and LAWRENCE WOOLNER Written and Directed by EDWARD MURPHY

BORN IN JAPAN, SHO KOSUGI'S sisters bullied him into studying martial arts because they thought he was tall and weak. He took up kendo and judo and in later interviews claims to have studied ninjutsu with an elderly ninja master living incognito in his neighborhood named "Uncle Yamamoto" who mysteriously disappeared before he could be contacted by any fact checkers.

After failing his university entrance exam, Kosugi's sisters told him he should go immediately to America, where it was easier to get into college. Used to doing what his sisters said, Kosugi arrived in LA speaking no English. All he had were two suitcases and $500, which three muggers tried to steal before he took them out with a couple of kicks.

He worked his way through California State University teaching martial arts and planned to become an accountant. Instead, he wound up opening two martial arts dojos and appeared in minor roles in *Bruce Lee Fights Back from the Grave* (1976; see page 142), and *The Bad News Bears Go to Japan* (1978), but after impressing Golan and Globus on *Enter the Ninja* (1981) Kosugi was only too eager to star in its sequel, *Revenge of the Ninja*, even though, as he himself said, "I am not the great actor."

The first American action movie with a Japanese star pretty much ever, *Revenge of the Ninja* was directed by Sam Firstenberg and shot in Salt Lake City because LA was too expensive. It opens with a rowdy band of ninjas showing up at Kosugi's Japanese home and redecorating it in wall-to-wall dead family members. As Kosugi's pal Keith Vitali growls, "Ninjas are the worst bastards the world has ever known!"

Sho moves to America and works in an art gallery, but soon his business partner, Braden, is slipping into bathrooms, putting on a silver mask and ninja suit, and getting into the heroin business with Mafia guys who could not be more stereotypical if they were made out of linguini. Everything ends in a shocking explosion of ninja-on-ninja rooftop violence that feels like the '80s stabbing you in both eyes at the same time: Jacuzzis, smoke bombs, ninjas posing against the skyline, scythes, swords, and a flamethrower. Audiences threw money at the film, and it ultimately earned over $13 million.

Golan believed he would earn even more loot with its sequel, *Ninja III: The Domination*, because it would include ninjas plus every trend possible. Kosugi felt otherwise.

"It doesn't work," he said in an interview. "He was believing in ninja mystery, plus breakdancing, and also trying to make psychic concept."

Which is a pretty fair description of *Ninja III: The Domination*. Firstenberg helmed again, and Kosugi played an evil ninja in what's essentially *The Exorcist vs. the Ninja in Flashdance* with a part-time aerobics instructor (Lucinda Dickey) possessed by the spirit of an evil ninja and Kosugi, sporting a jaunty eye patch, in the Max Von Sydow

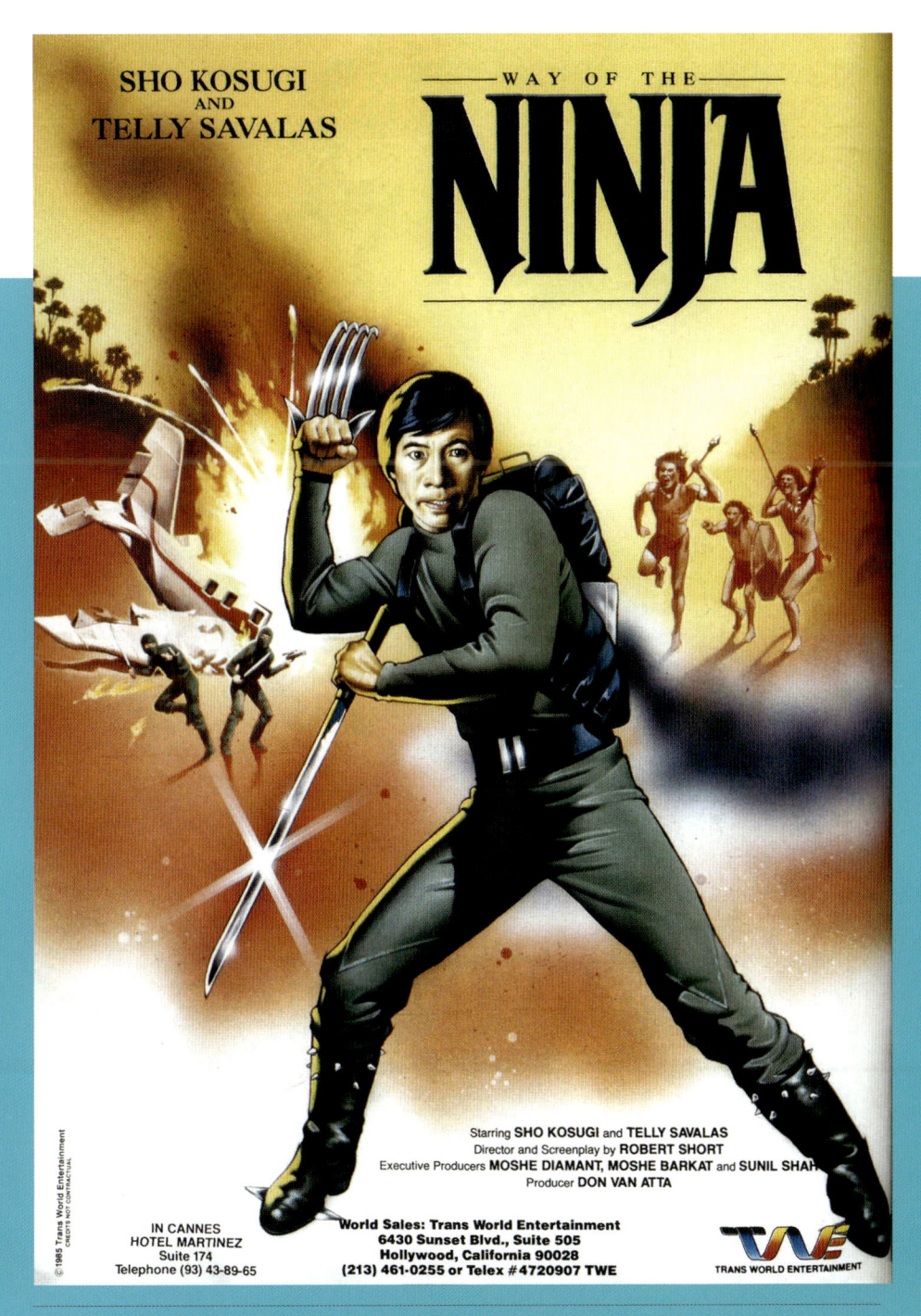

Way of the Ninja was supposed to be Kosugi's follow-up to *Pray for Death*. Co-starring television's Telly Savalas (*Kojak*), it was set to be written and directed by Academy Award–winning makeup artist Robert Short. Neither of those things happened, however, and it mutated into *Rage of Honor*, based on Short's screenplay.

Kosugi spent months in 1985 prepping *The Devil's Odds* and *Pray for Death 2* for Trans World. The latter was never made, but the former was rewritten to become the buddy cop comedy *The Wild Pair* (1987) starring Beau Bridges and Bubba Smith.

role. Featuring lots of dry ice, aerobics, a flying ninja sword, and berserk editing, Kosugi was right, it doesn't work, and it made less money than its predecessors. But Cannon had faith in the ninjas = money equation and planned to make *American Ninja* with Kosugi until he left, partly because he had great offers elsewhere, partly because he was miffed Golan had cut one of his big action scenes from *Ninja III: The Domination*.

Kosugi teamed up with the hapless Emmett Alston, the director fired from *Enter the Ninja*, for another movie shot in the Philippines, *9 Deaths of the Ninja*.

"My last film was terrible," Kosugi said about it in a later interview. "I had no control or input over anything."

Next, he co-starred with veteran tough guy Lee Van Cleef in NBC's ninja series, *The Master*. Van Cleef played an American ninja returning to America to search for the daughter he never knew. There he meets a young drifter named Max and his pet hamster, Henry, and the three of them travel around in Max's customized van, with evil ninja Okasa (Kosugi) in pursuit. The series was canceled after 13 episodes, and Kosugi vowed he'd never do television again. Not only did he consider the show "corny" but television's hectic production schedule meant he couldn't deliver the impressive action and intricate ninja weapons his fans demanded.

Kosugi needed a post-Cannon hit to prove he could make it on his own. He'd already sold one of his martial arts schools and turned the other into the headquarters for Sho Kosugi Ninja Enterprises, selling ninja weapons and memorabilia. He was playing to win.

"I just don't want to be a movie star," he told a reporter. "The next two years are very critical for me. I want to make good pictures."

Signing up with Cannon's competitor, Trans World Entertainment, Kosugi found his new ninja home with *Pray for Death* (1985), which was so violent the MPAA gave it an X rating and, after selling close to 100,000 VHS units, it turned Kosugi into a huge international star. He tried to hang up his ninja suit and become a more typical '80s action hero in Trans World's *Rage of Honor* (1987), but it didn't do as well in theaters even though it became another big hit on home video.

THE SHO KOSUGI PLASTIC NINJA SWORD SET
A realistic plastic ninja sword with rubber square guard, hand-wrapped cloth handle, sliver blade and black sheath. 24" long with a 14" blade. Set includes 3 foam ninja stars, exploding distractions, Sho Kosugi Ninja poster, Sword Guard eyepatch.
WA5500A **$9.95**
Although all precautions have been taken to insure that every item is safe, we recommend that parental supervision be exercised.

Kosugi scouted his own locations, consulted on casting, choreographed his own fights, even sat in the editing room while his movies got put together. He ran his own mail-order business, shilled for Honda when they came out with their Hurricane motorcycle, and just said no by founding Ninjas Against Drugs.

Kosugi gave it his all onscreen. *Rage of Honor* sent him to the hospital with serious burns due to a mistimed pyrotechnic. Only a quick-witted stuntman saved him from a 36-story fall while shooting the climax of *Revenge of the Ninja*. Doing his own stunts broke his shoulder and dislocated his heel and most of his toes, but he couldn't slow down.

"I don't expect this to last forever," Kosugi commented on the ninja craze.

In the '90s, Kosugi saw which way the wind was blowing and returned to Japan, where his career continued to burn hot on television.

Maybe it was because his older sisters pushed him hard, maybe it was his background in economics, but Sho Kosugi always knew his value and had no problem asking for what he was worth. Cannon transformed him from a faceless extra inside a ninja suit to the first Japanese star of an American action movie, but when they wouldn't pay his price, he left without hesitation.

Not 50 years earlier, Japanese actors like Miki Morita were relegated to roles as houseboys and sinister Orientals, while judo masters like Sego Murakami and Ken Kuniyuki got put in concentration camps. Sho Kosugi was a Japanese movie star making American movies and using his Japanese heritage to put the box office in a headlock. Revenge had rarely tasted so sweet or looked so cool.

IN 1985, AMERICA REACHED PEAK NINJA. Ninjas conquered comic books: Storm Shadow shredded spinner racks in *G.I. Joe*, and the Teenage Mutant Ninja Turtles shot out of the sewers and straight into stardom. The ubiquitous Japanese-American actor Mako, a frequent face on *M*A*S*H* and *McHale's Navy*, played a ninja on an episode of *Magnum P.I.* ("The Arrow That Is Not Aimed"), in *The Greatest American Hero* ("30 Seconds over Little Tokyo"), and in a TV pilot that aired on ABC (*The Last Ninja*).

Remco released ninja action figures both small (their "Ninja Strike Force" line) and large (the "Secret of the Ninja" line, which generously included not just ninjas, but Shaolin monks, judo kings, commandos, karate black belts, taekwondo warriors, and Thai kickboxers). *Dungeons & Dragons* added ninjas as a character class. Kawasaki's new Ninja 900 and Ninja 600 motorcycles outsold all their other bikes. Parfums de Couer racked up $20 million with their Ninja cosmetic line, which included perfume, body spray, and lotion. The company's president said of the ninja name, "It's short, pronounceable and Oriental ... Most Americans don't really know what the word means."

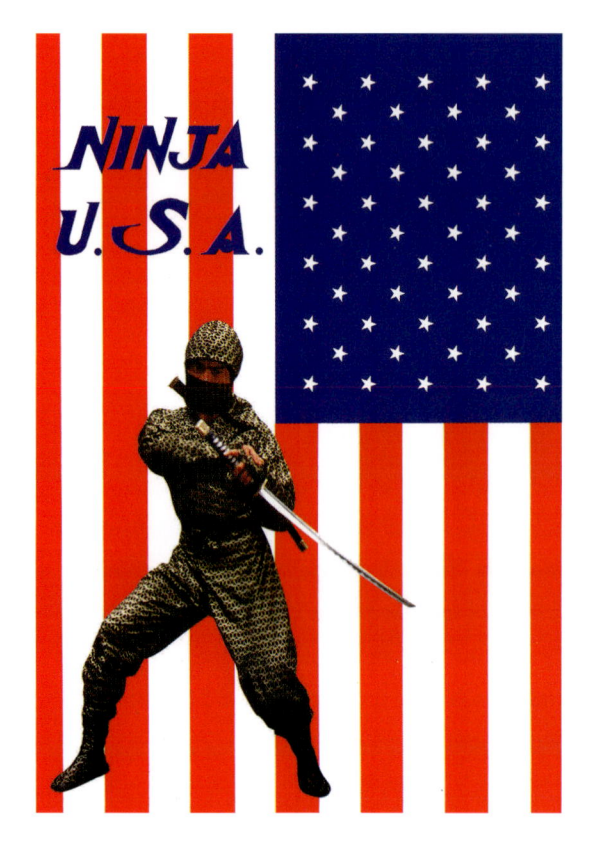

But everyone knew it meant money. One Halloween, a New Jersey costume shop sold 250 ninja costumes and claimed they could have sold 2,500 more. Constant calls forced them to record a terse message on their phone: "We are out of Ninja costumes." When a surprise order of ninja costumes arrived two days before October 31, they sold all 40 of them in under three hours. In Tampa, Master Jhoon Rhee opened his latest taekwondo school with an ad promoting a two-for-one discount and "Halloween NINJA costumes ON SALE!"

At $39.95 with an additional $6.95 for the hood ($10 extra to come in camouflage), ninja costumes became the affordable badass fashion choice for criminals everywhere. The criminal ninjapocalypse began in 1984 when two teenagers dressed in ninja suits and armed with samurai swords invaded the home of *Laverne & Shirley* actress Penny Marshall, holding her hostage and stealing several hundred dollars. Despite claiming they were just "out to have fun" they received three years in juvie.

Over the next few years, people dressed as ninjas stole Halloween candy from children, slashed motorcycle seats on vandalism sprees, knocked over gas stations, blew blowdarts into the doors of Chinese restaurants, robbed nightclubs, took hostages, and committed murder. Disgruntled former employees, ex-boyfriends, and sometimes total strangers showed up on college campuses, in backyards, and in houses carrying swords, Uzis, and crossbows. Some of these fake ninjas racked up real body counts, like serial killer Charles Ng, who murdered over 11 women while engaged in an elaborate fantasy that he was a ninja warrior.

"It's getting to be a hassle in the streets . . . Most everybody tries to put it under the rug, but it's an ongoing problem," one karate instructor in Buffalo said. Cops set stakeouts for marauding gangs of neighborhood ninjas. A delegate to the Maryland General Assembly, Nancy Murphy, co-sponsored a bill to classify throwing stars as deadly weapons, saying she wanted to fight the "kung fu epidemic."

INTERNATIONAL NINJA SOCIETY

At last! The *International Ninja Society* is now open for NEW membership. You can become an official member of the INS. New members will:

- Become an approved member of the INS.
- Receive an official certificate of membership.
- Receive an approved membership card.
- Receive an INS members only patch.
- Receive your own individual INS registration number.

To enroll in the *International Ninja Society*, send your name and complete mailing address along with a money order or personal check for $20.00 to

INS
P.O. Box 171221
Dublin, OH 43017

Cannon craved a piece of the action, but they'd lost their in-house ninja, Sho Kosugi, to his own success. However, they had a terrific title, *American Ninja*, and so they pre-sold it as the latest from the team behind *Missing in Action*: star Chuck Norris, director Joseph Zito, and writer James Bruner. It didn't matter that none of them wanted to make a ninja movie. Norris had recently read an article in *Reader's Digest* about terrorists in America, so Bruner wrote him a ninja-free script about terrorists. Their concession to Cannon? Chuck's codename: American Ninja. Golan realized this was a waste of a good title, so he sent the *MIA* crew to make *Invasion U.S.A.* and got Sam Firstenberg to direct *American Ninja* based on an uncredited rewrite by Bruner. Model turned actor Michael Dudikoff took over the Chuck Norris role and Mike Stone choreographed the action of what became one of the greatest bar mitzvah films ever made.

Meet Joe Armstrong (Dudikoff), an American soldier with amnesia. When his convoy is attacked by horny ninjas who want to kidnap the colonel's daughter for sexual intercourse, he instinctively defeats them using his previously unknown ninja skills. Treated with suspicion because of a few ninja rituals he clings to that remind him of his lost past, it's not until an elderly ninja teaches Dudikoff the great traditions

Ninja Crimes Spreading Across U.S., Puzzle Police

By DAN NAKASO
Knight Ridder Newspapers

A man dressed as a ninja warrior blasts the University of Kentucky campus with gunfire and wounds two people. The same day in Southern California, B-movie queen Susan Cabot-Roman is beaten to death in her Encino home. Her son, a rabid martial-arts fan who told investigators the killer was a ninja, is later arrested on murder charges.

An elderly couple in Fayetteville, N.C., are discovered in their home with their throats slashed and their bodies stabbed repeatedly. Two U.S. Army soldiers charged in the killings later are found with a black ninja outfit, knives, darts and a blowgun.

Two men dressed in ninja clothes gun down an elderly Jewish couple in their car as they return to their home in the Brentwood area of Los Angeles from services during Yom Kippur

robes, hood and armory of nasty-looking weapons became the stuff of folklore and grew into a market for American-made chop-and-block movies.

What's happening off the screen is much more frightening, psychiatrists say.

Sometimes the fantasy visions get blurred with the real-life ideas of the audience — especially viewers with identity problems, said Dr. Alfred Coodley,

Police Seeking 'Ninja Robber'

HALTOM CITY

'Ninjas' crime ring smashed, police repo[rt]

JOSEPH PALMER
Herald Staff Writer

Bradenton police say they smashed a major burglary ring with the arrests of five members of a gang accused of terrorizing East Bradenton

Most of the members are juveniles, Abrams said. But an adult who was arrested a week ago is also allegedly a member of the group, he said.

Daryl Mays Colbert, 18, of 304 12th St. E., was charged with aggravated assault after a

needed the money to buy drugs, said A[brams]. All the burglaries were carried out at night the strong-arm robberies were done at all of the day, he added.

Several of the victims of strong-arm r[obberies]

Five teens pretending to be ninja warriors are charged in var[ious]

By Mary Holleran and Todd Lighty
Democrat and Chronicle

Five teen-agers who told police they were acting out roles as ancient Japanese warriors were charged yesterday with 45 counts of criminal mischief after a vandalism spree on two separate nights in Scottsville.

The 13- to 15-year-olds, whom Wheatland police would not identify, were released to their parents and referred to Monroe County Family Court. The charges include felony counts of criminal mischief and misdemeanor counts of fourth-degree criminal mischief.

"They told us they did this as part of a fantasy of ninja warriors, which they had watched on television," said Officer Donald A. Tubman, patrol supervisor for the Wheatland police.

"The kids wore dark clothing when they went out and sneaked around the town. They were pretending to be the silent warrior and went about doing their thing in Scottsvil[le."]

In 12th- and 1[3th-century Japan,] draped ninja war[ri]ers and spies wit[h]

martial arts. The warriors were featured in the 1983 MGM movie *Revenge of Ninja* and a made-for-television movie called *The Last Ninja*.

Tubman said the first acts of vandalism occurred between midnight and 6 a.m. on July 31. During the night, four of the five juveniles charged in the two-day spree scratched the paint on a car with a knife and damaged above-ground swim[ming pools] at 16 E. Grenadier Road, 19[...] and 25 Diana Drive. The [...]

'Ninja warrior' attacker given a life sentence

Associated Press

AUSTIN — A 20-year-old man was sentenced to life in prison Thursday for stabbing and beating a woman while he was dressed in a black "ninja warrior" costume.

Jurors deliberated for two hours before recommending the life sentence for Tony Wigley, 20, in the aggravated robbery of Ellen Duwe, 43.

Wigley, described as a drifter from Ohio, was convicted Wednesday of the Aug. 29 attack on Duwe in her home.

Duwe was hit in the head several times with a hammer and was stabbed in the chest and twice in the neck after being confronted in her bathroom by a man dressed in a black ninja costume.

The attacker also tried to hammer the knife into Duwe's skull and checked her pulse bef[ore leaving] the house.

In closing arguments Assistant District Att[orney] Wommack described D[uwe's injuries] as "murderous and de[...] indeed."

Before reaching its [verdict the] jury asked to see all [evidence,] which included doze[ns of photo]graphs.

Wigley is believ[ed to have] watched the house fr[om a vantage] across the street and [waited for] up to two days in Duw[e's house before] the attack.

Authorities said [...] Duwe to write a $6[...] name. He was arre[sted the next] day trying to cash t[...]

Prosecutors said [...]

Questions [...] Virginia 'N[inja']

PORTSMOUTH, Va. (UPI) — Police may turn to a psychi[atrist] for clues on why a man obs[essed] with the movie "Revenge o[f the] Ninja" donned the garb o[f an] oriental warrior and murd[ered] two people before turning his [own] machine gun on himself.

Police say Gregory Eley[...] dressed in his black "Ninja"[...] and armed with an arsen[al of] weapons, gunned down Ar[...] Jones, 47, and Wayne Massey, [a] friend, Friday night at Jones' [fash]ionable Dutch colonial home.

Two boys hiding upstairs h[eard] Eley cry out for God's forgive[ness] before he pressed the Israeli-m[ade] Uzi submachine gun to his c[hest] and pulled the trigger, hitting [him]self twice, said police detec[tive] Sylvia Kaiser.

Kaiser said Jones was [shot] "numerous times," while Ma[ssey] was shot "a couple of times" in [the] neck. All three were dead w[hen] police arrived.

Authorities who found El[ey's] body said he was armed with [a] submachine gun, two crossbo[ws, a] .45 automatic pistol and th[ree] oriental battle stars. He [had] blackened his face and pulle[d a] mask over it.

Teen held as Ninja gang thug

A man suspected of being involved in several robberies attributed to a youth gang known as Ninja was arrested by Bradenton police detectives Tuesday.

Keith J. Henderson, 18, of 214 10th Ave. E., was being held in the Manatee County Jail Wednesday. He is accused of burglary and failure to appear in court on a previous prowling charge. Bail is set at $4,023.

"He [is] one of the main sources of the gang," said Detective Steve

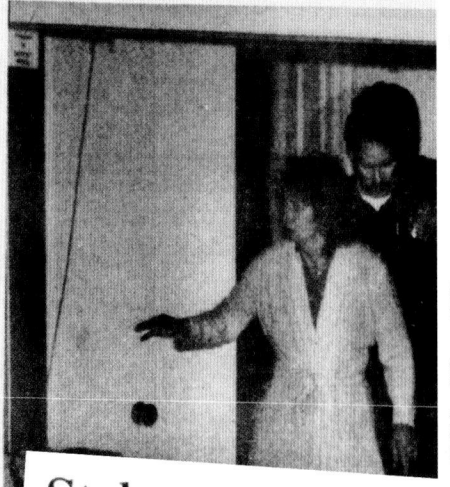

The ninja crime wave was real. In 1985, a 17-year-old kid playing "ninja warrior" on a power transformer was in critical condition after getting 34,500 volts through his body, causing 1,800 New Jersey residents to lose power for 30 minutes. In 1987, in Chicago, three men dressed as ninjas robbed a nightclub of $35,000 after beating and terrorizing 20 patrons at gunpoint. They were caught when they used the money to buy cars and put a down payment on a house. One of the suspects suffered a heart attack while being questioned by the police. A 17-year-old Massachusetts resident terrorized his former girlfriend's family with an axe while dressed as a ninja. He was later discovered living inside the walls of her home. As the *St. Louis Post Dispatch* said in 1985, "Police, community leaders, psychologists and professional karate instructors are trying to deal with the problem."

CHUCK NORRIS
ASSASSINATION!
RANDOM MURDER!
TERRORISM!
ONLY ONE POWER
CAN STOP IT...
AMERICAN NINJA™
THE CANNON GROUP, INC. PRESENTS CHUCK NORRIS
IN A GOLAN-GLOBUS PRODUCTION AMERICAN NINJA WRITTEN BY CHUCK NORRIS AND JAMES BRUNER
PRODUCED BY MENAHEM GOLAN AND YORAM GLOBUS DIRECTED BY JOSEPH ZITO © MCMLXXXIV CANNON FILMS, INC.

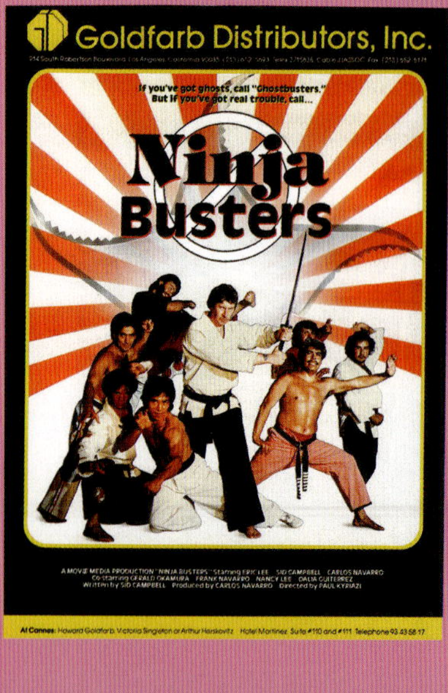
Goldfarb Distributors, Inc.
If you've got ghosts, call "Ghostbusters."
But if you've got real trouble, call...
Ninja Busters
A MOVIE MEDIA PRODUCTION "NINJA BUSTERS" Starring ERIC LEE SID CAMPBELL CARLOS NAVARRO
Co-starring GERALD OKAMURA FRANK NAVARRO NANCY LEE DALIA GUITERREZ
Written by SID CAMPBELL Produced by CARLOS NAVARRO Directed by PAUL KYRIAZI
At Cannes: Howard Goldfarb, Victoria Singleton or Arthur Herskovitz Hotel Martinez Suite #110 and #111 Telephone 93 43 58 17

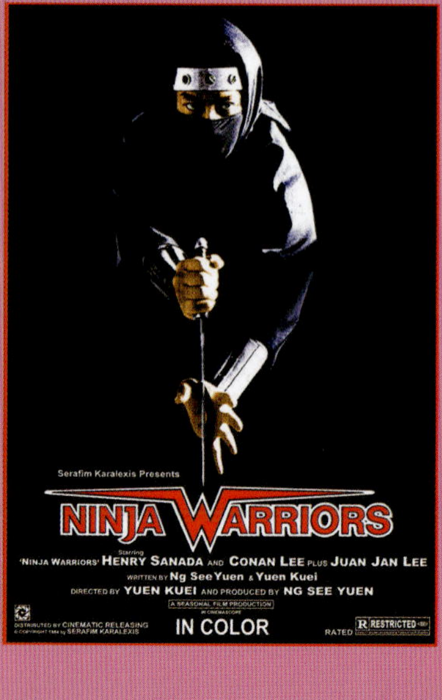
Serafim Karalexis Presents
NINJA WARRIORS
Starring
'NINJA WARRIORS' HENRY SANADA AND CONAN LEE PLUS JUAN JAN LEE
WRITTEN BY Ng See Yuen & Yuen Kuei
DIRECTED BY YUEN KUEI AND PRODUCED BY NG SEE YUEN
A SEASONAL FILM PRODUCTION
DISTRIBUTED BY CINEMATIC RELEASING
IN COLOR
RATED R RESTRICTED

KUNG FU AT ITS BEST!
MAFIA VS NINJA
THE "MOB" FINALLY MEETS ITS MATCH!
Starring:
ALEXANDER LOU SILVIO AZZOLINI WANG HSIA
CHARLEMA HSU EUGENE TRAMMEL

of his people (ninjas) that he is able to embrace his heritage and become a man. A ninja man who destroys orange, red, blue, and yellow ninjas sporting wrist lasers. This celebration of manhood climaxes when, instead of reading the Torah, he jumps out of an exploding helicopter. Mazel tov!

American Ninja 2: The Confrontation (1987) reunited Stone and Firstenberg with co-stars Dudikoff and the inimitable Steve James, as two Army Rangers/ninjas investigating a series of missing Marines on an island so anti-American that soldiers have to wear jams and muscle shirts instead of their uniforms so they don't antagonize the locals and also so Cannon can save money on costumes. Eventually it's revealed that the Marines are being kidnapped and turned into genetically engineered ninja warriors to protect powerful drug dealers.

There would be three more *American Ninja* movies released in 1988, 1989, and 1993, each of declining quality and each featuring declining quantities of Steve James and Michael Dudikoff, but despite ending with a whimper and not a bang, the *American Ninja* movies are the only Cannon movies with licensed merchandise like action figures, suction cup throwing stars, and plastic ninja swords.

Cannon's ninja boom taught audiences that ninjas came in every color of the rainbow, they were comfortable killing us with lasers and flamethrowers as well as with their bare hands, and they were very, very lucrative. Pity poor Eric Van Lustbader, whose hit book launched the wave but whose prestige motion picture adaptation died in development hell, while Golan and Globus made bank not just at the box office but also on home video, where *Ninja III: The Domination* and *American Ninja* sold at least 70,000 units each. Ninjas moved the needle when it came to home video.

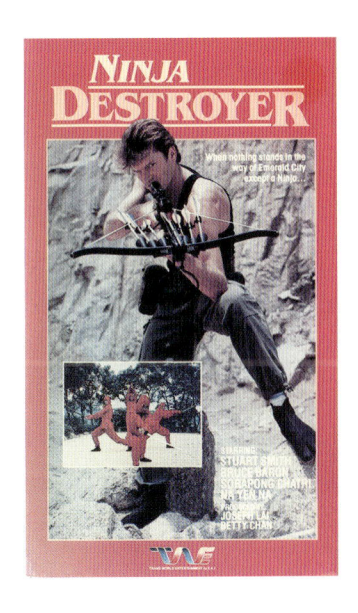

"The joke is you put 'ninja' in the title and you can sell a couple thousand extra copies," the vice president of Master Arts Video, Rod Hurley, said in an interview.

Enter three men determined to double down on that formula.

(opposite page, top) Chuck Norris made a sales sheet, but not an actual movie, of *American Ninja*.

(opposite page, bottom) Paul Kyriazi's *Ninja Busters* only saw the light of a few test screenings before the distributor put it on the shelf. It didn't get a release until a print was discovered in a warehouse sale in 2014. *Ninja Warriors* (aka *Ninja in the Dragon's Den*, 1982) is a starring vehicle for the Japanese actor Hiroyuki "Henry" Sanada, directed by one of the Seven Little Fortunes, Corey Yuen Kwai. *Mafia vs. Ninja* (1984) opened at the 42nd Street Empire in December 1985, headlining a ninja triple bill with the Shaw Brothers productions *Super Ninjas* and *Challenge of the Ninja*.

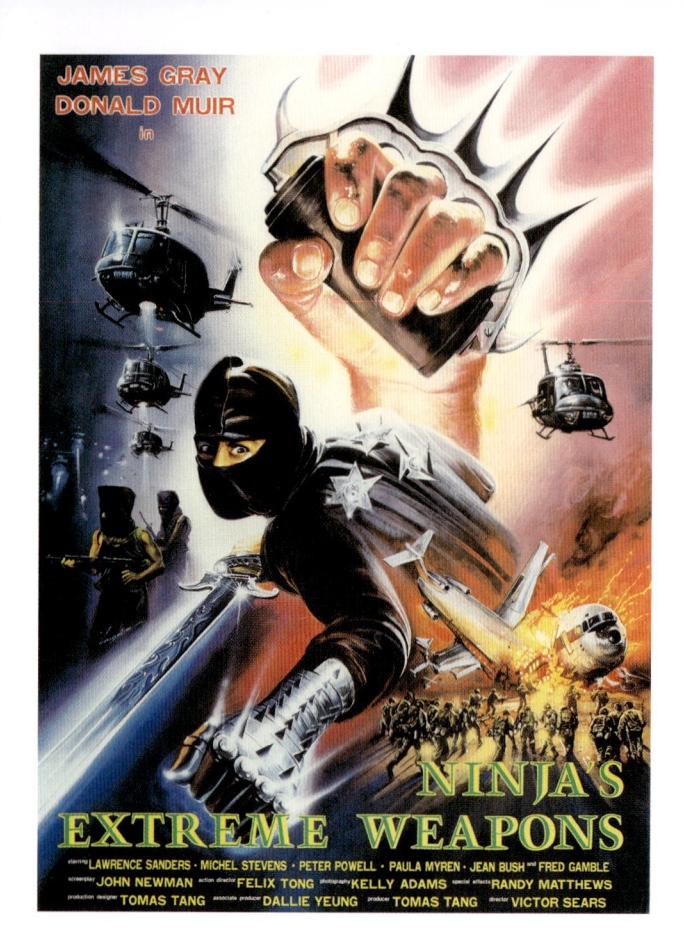

IN 1969, TERRY LAI SAW an opportunity: few Hong Kong filmmakers sold their movies overseas, so she started Intercontinental Film Distributors (IFD), a company that would take ninja movies into fifth gear. But in the beginning, they simply dubbed Hong Kong product into English for international sales. She made so much money, she soon started producing Hong Kong movies with foreign talent like Chris Mitchum (Robert Mitchum's son) and Tony Ferrer (the Filipino James Bond) and hired her little brother, Joseph Lai, to help out.

Terry eventually realized it was more lucrative to distribute foreign movies in China, and today she's made hundreds of millions distributing everything from Disney to Dreamworks, but Joseph liked the old business model just fine and decided to team up with his college buddy, Tomas Tang, to form IFD Films & Arts to make super-cheap movies in Korea, selling them as fake Korean co-productions to get around Korea's screen quota system. Together they made close to 20 Bruceploitation movies featuring Dragon Lee, usually directed or co-directed by a guy named Godfrey Ho, often opening with a title card reading, "A Masterpiece Presented by Joseph Lai & Tomas Tang."

Ho got into the masterpiece business after rising through the ranks at Shaw Brothers, eventually becoming Chang Cheh's assistant director. After getting fired from Shaw when one of his scripts bombed at the box office, Ho made *Paris Killer* (1974) and sold it to Lai for distribution. Ho directed his first "Masterpiece" for Lai and Tang in 1978, and after that the three of them became the Clouse/Weintraub of Asia, only faster, cheaper, and more out of control.

(above) *Ninja's Extreme Weapons* (1987) is a Thai movie that Filmark inserted ninja footage into. It features a pack of multicolored ninjas and a climax with a fire-breathing dragon suit. The dragon is not on the poster, nor is anything on the poster actually in the movie.

(opposite page) *Ninja Demon's Massacre* (1987) is another Thai crime film, this one starring Sorapong Chatree, who was Thailand's biggest male star of the '70s, with ninja scenes courtesy of Filmark.

Exploiting the fact that Hong Kong distributors didn't aggressively chase international sales, IFD was one of the few Chinese companies to regularly attend the American and Cannes Film Markets, where Lai would knock out 30 to 40 contracts for foreign sales while keeping an eye on global trends. It was there that he spotted Cannon's *Enter the Ninja* and came back to Hong Kong, where he told Ho the new plan: ninjas! They didn't quite understand what ninjas were but they knew one thing: they could double all their lead actors with actual martial artists because no one knew who was actually under those ninja hoods.

With an eye on the international market, Ho remembered meeting Richard Harrison on the Shaw Brothers production *Marco Polo* (1975) and gave him a call. An affable actor who'd passed up the Clint Eastwood part in *A Fistful of Dollars*, Harrison found most of his fame in foreign genre pictures, and he signed on for a few IFD ninja flicks. Shooting without sound because the movies would be dubbed anyways, Ho started cranking out movies in two weeks, with another three weeks for all the dubbing and post-production.

The global market loved it.

Harrison appeared in *Scorpion Thunderbolt* (1984), *Ninja Thunderbolt* (1984), and *Golden Ninja Warrior* (1985), which became famous for their use of souvenir shop–quality swords, men in eyeliner, Garfield phones, and juicy, meme-ready dubbed dialogue about the ninja empire. Ultimately, it's impossible to know how many movies Harrison made for IFD because, much to his dismay, the footage he shot got recycled endlessly. Harrison footage appears in *Ninja the Protector* (1985), *Diamond Ninja Force* (1985), *Ninja Terminator* (1985), six *Ninja Operation* movies (all 1986), *Hitman the Cobra* (1986), *Cobra Against Ninja* (1986), *Ninja Champion* (1986), *Ninja Commandments* (1986), *Ninja Hunt* (1986), and *Ninja Kill* (1986).

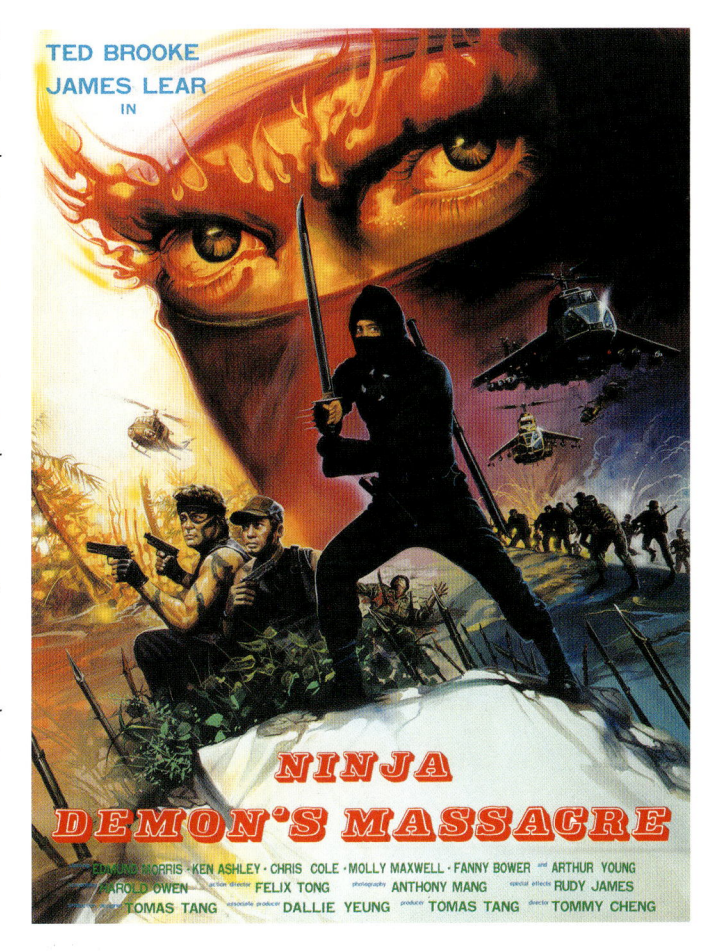

TONY GABLE
JUDY CAINE
AND
ROD PENN
IN
TOUGH NINJA
THE SHADOW WARRIOR
Starring PHILIP KO · RAYMOND CHAN · ROGER LOCKHART · LILY CHEN · KEN KURODA
and JUNE HACK Directed By LARRY HUTTON Written By JOSEPH KONG
Production Designed By TOLO PORE Special Effects SAMMY LOUIS MIKE WONG
Producer TOMAS TANG Associate Producer DALLIE YEUNG

JOHN WILFORD
IN
NINJA,
PHANTOM HEROS
U.S.A.

BIONIC NINJA
THOUGHT, WORD, DEED AND ART OF KILLING
OF THE BIONIC WARRIOR
IN THE WAYS OF THE NINJA
KELLY STEVE · ALAN HEMMINGS · RICK WILSON in a TIM ASHBY film BIONIC NINJA
STARRING PETER CHAN · ANDY MAN · JACK YOUNG · PAULINE CHAO · ALEX BAKER
ALAN JACKSON HART HOPE TOLO PORE KEN SHO
DALLIE YEUNG TOMAS TANG TIM ASHBY

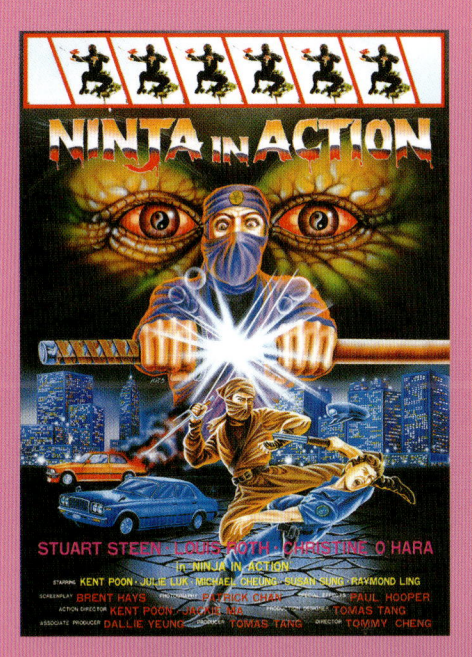

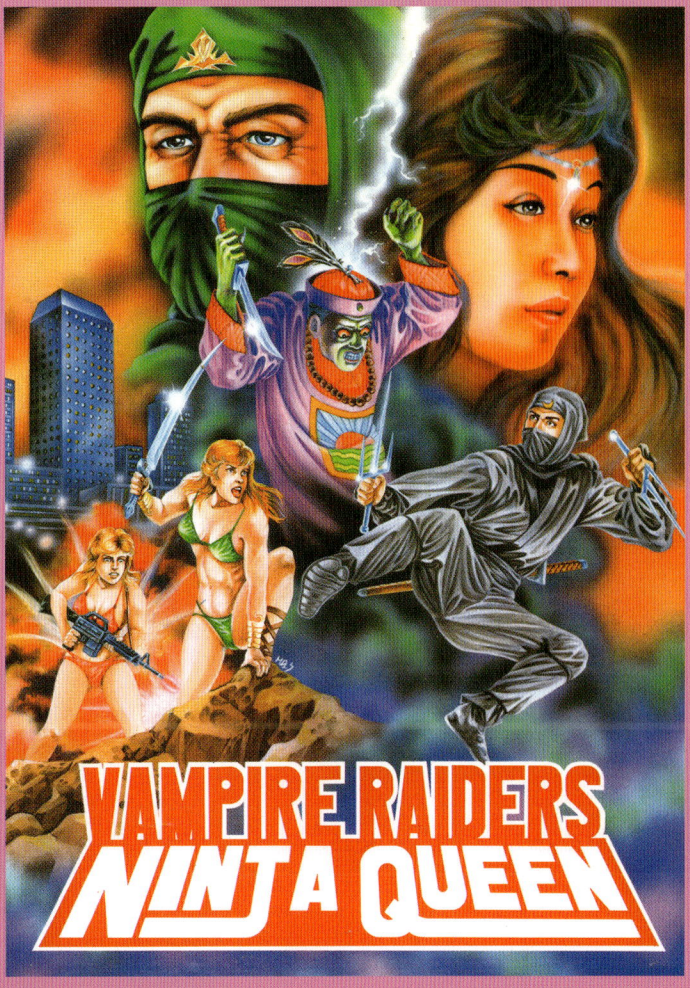

IFD and Filmark were exploitation geniuses who did it faster, weirder, and for less. Godfrey Ho had one direction for actors on set: "I can't see your acting—more acting!" When they pivoted from ninja movies to kickboxing films, Filmark took one of their foreign actors, Paulo Tocha, fresh from fighting Jean-Claude Van Damme in *Bloodsport* and re-named him "Bruce Stallion," a mash-up of Bruce Lee and Sylvester Stallone. Their sales sheets and posters were always instantly recognizable at film markets, whether they were ultra-realistic (*Robo Vampire*) or airbrushed fever dreams that incorporated every action movie trope, all at the same time (*Twinkle Ninja Fantasy*).

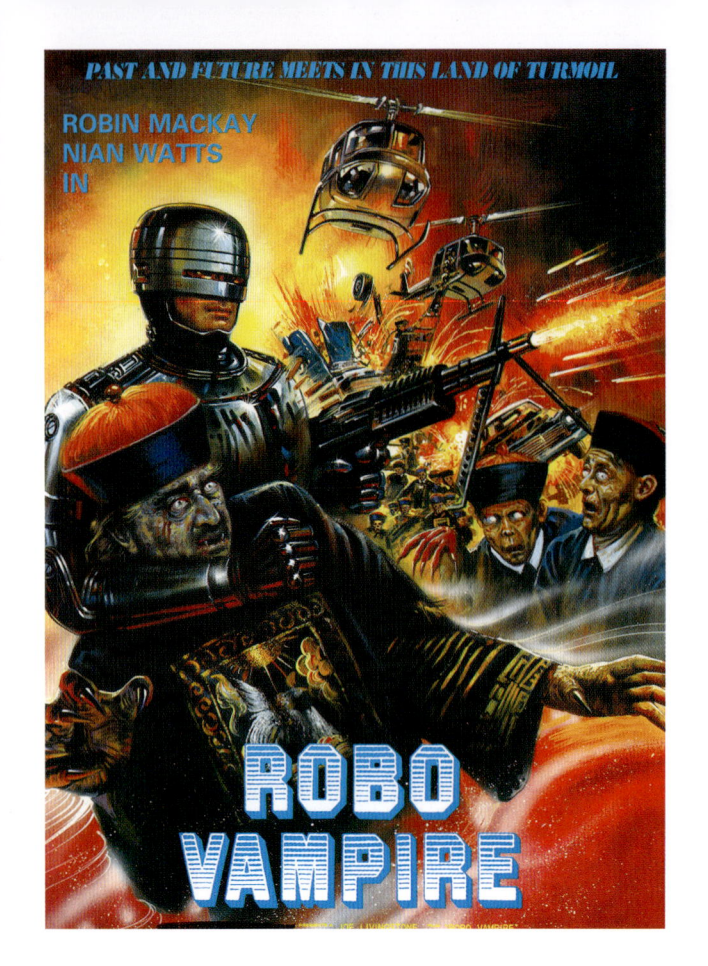

Demand for ninja movies outstripped supply, and soon IFD was buying Taiwanese Black movies, Thai action movies, Filipino and Korean martial arts movies and chopping them up to make more ninja movies. They bought Korean war movies like Shin Sang-ok's *The Last Flight to Pyongyang* (1971) and released it in 1983 as *Sky Risk Commandos* after slashing it from 130 minutes to 85.

When IFD ran out of Richard Harrison footage, they sent assistants to hostels in Hong Kong, recruiting any Westerner they saw. Martial artists like Mark Houghton and Steve Tartalia began stopping by their offices and showing up on their sets, while English-speaking dubbers worked overtime, sometimes sleeping in their studios. Eventually, IFD started skipping a step and cast their dubbers like Pierre Tremblay and Stuart Onslow-Smyth in their movies.

Business boomed, and IFD were so busy that when a young martial artist from Belgium named Jean-Claude Van Varenberg came by their offices in the Garley Building to drop off his headshot, Lai told him they would be only too happy to make a movie featuring him but they had eight or nine they needed to make first. That near-miss didn't stop IFD from turning on a dime after the now-rechristened Jean-Claude Van Damme made *Bloodsport* (1988) for Cannon, which became a huge hit. Suddenly, IFD was turning out kickboxing tournament movies for international buyers. IFD would do anything for their international buyers. Alphonse Beni, a thoughtful, soft-spoken film distributor from Cameroon, went to France and became a sexploitation star before returning to Cameroon, where he helped kickstart its film industry. He met the IFD team at the Cannes market and made them an offer they couldn't refuse (actually, IFD never refused any offers): he'd buy the Cameroonian rights to any movie in which he was the star. That's how they made *Ninja Operation: Knight and Warrior*, which would get repurposed into *Fire Operation* (1987) and *Top Mission* (1987).

Time, space, and facts warp around IFD. Some say that Ho, Tang, and Lai fell out and broke up, founding competing companies (Filmark, Asso) in Hong Kong. Other people noticed that all these companies were on different floors of the Garley Building and wondered if it was all just a complicated tax scam. Some people wondered if Tomas Tang and Godfrey Ho were the same person. The fact that Ho said whatever he felt like in interviews, that he used several aliases on his films, and that Tang died in a massive 1996 fire that destroyed his company's business records, all add to the cloud of confusion.

Whatever the truth, Ho and Lai did eventually part ways, with Ho founding Filmswell, where he made some movies with Cynthia Rothrock (*Undefeatable*) and directed the indefensible *Laboratory of the Devil* (1992), which was supposedly about Japan's wartime atrocities but was actually a lurid shocker featuring real autopsy footage of actual corpses.

Ho, Tang, and Lai (and Lai's wife, producer Betty Chan) achieved a lunatic alchemy at IFD, but what made their productions possible was the VHS boom.

STARTING IN 1982, AMERICAN SALES of VCRs and pre-recorded videotapes doubled every year, and suddenly there weren't enough movies in the world to feed all the hungry VCRs. If you had something resembling a film, you were in business. If it had ninjas in it, you could sell it by the pound.

Hong Kong's legendary action choreographer, Tong Kai, made his directorial debut with *Shaolin Prince* (1983), a star-studded Shaw Brothers comedy that became *Death Mask of the Ninja* on American video store shelves. *Devil Rider!* a dime-store shot-in-Florida biker flick from 1970 featuring the Sunshine State's karate legend, Johnny Pachivas, got totally tubular cover art when it was reissued as *Master's Revenge*.

Video stores became a United Nations of ninjas. The so-called only ninja in Sweden, Bo F. Munthe, teamed up with director Mats Helge, fresh out of prison for financial misdeeds on his previous movie, to make *Ninja Mission*, a make-it-up-as-we-go-along, Soviet-hating action flick with an unbelievably violent ending and very few ninjas. It became a video hit, sold to 54 countries, and paved the way for Helge to make eight more movies for the international home video market, including three with David Carradine (*Animal Protector*, *Fatal Secret*, *The Mad Bunch*), even though it's rumored that Carradine thought he was only shooting one. Helge disappeared in the early '90s in a puff of rumors about more financial chicanery.

If you couldn't afford to shoot a movie with a star, you got one to introduce a cheap acquisition for you. Sho Kosugi's new home after Cannon, Trans World Entertainment, put together *Ninja Theater Hosted by Sho Kosugi*, which saw Kosugi demonstrate a different ninja weapon in every episode before standing in front of his trophies to introduce any number of Godfrey Ho ninja pictures. Exploitation queen Sybil Danning (*Panther Squad*) shot intros and outros for 26 movies in USA Home Video's *Sybil Danning Adventure Video*, featuring Aquarius titles like *Fist of Fear, Touch of Death*, as well as Bobby Kim's *Kill the Ninja*. The American Ninja himself, Michael Dudikoff, fulfilled his contractual obligations to Cannon by hosting *Michael Dudikoff Presents Action Adventure Theater*.

Tadashi Yamashita (see page 136) had toplined a trio of Japanese karate films for Toei, which led to supporting roles in American productions like the ninja flick *The Octagon* (1980) starring Chuck Norris, but he wanted another shot at action stardom and hoped *The Shinobi Ninja* would be it. Slated to be shot in London, where Yamashita knew an Arab prince willing to provide funding, everything was going great until his arriving film crew was turned back at the airport because no one had bothered with minor details such as getting them work permits.

A year later, Yamashita turned up in LA with a finished cut of the movie and hosted a buyer's screening. Unfortunately, the entire cast had been dubbed into English by the same two voice actors and the only purchase offer was from a distributor who wanted

The Master Executioner...
The Dragon of Death!
DEATH MASK OF THE NINJA

Master's Revenge
Bad-ass bikers.....
.....they ride for blood!
a LOU TILMAN presentation
Produced by BRAD F. GRINTER and CHARLES G. WARD
Starring SHARON MAHON • RIDGELY ABELE • JOHNNY PACHIVAS
Screenplay by CARON McGOWAN, B. F. GRINTER and C.G. WARD

NOT SUITABLE FOR AUDIENCES UNDER 17 YEARS OF AGE
SYBIL DANNING'S ADVENTURE VIDEO
ONE MAN FACES AN ARMY OF DEATH!
NINJA WARRIORS
AVID Home Entertainment

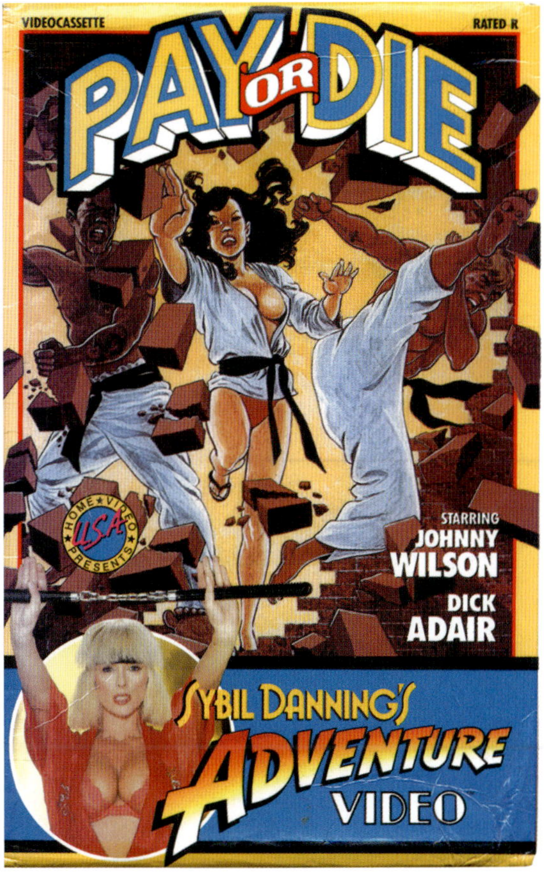

VIDEOCASSETTE
RATED R
PAY OR DIE
USA HOME VIDEO PRESENTS
STARRING
JOHNNY WILSON
DICK ADAIR
SYBIL DANNING'S ADVENTURE VIDEO

THE JAPANESE WARRIOR SOUGHT PEACE IN AMERICA. FATE HANDED HIM THE

SWORD OF HEAVEN

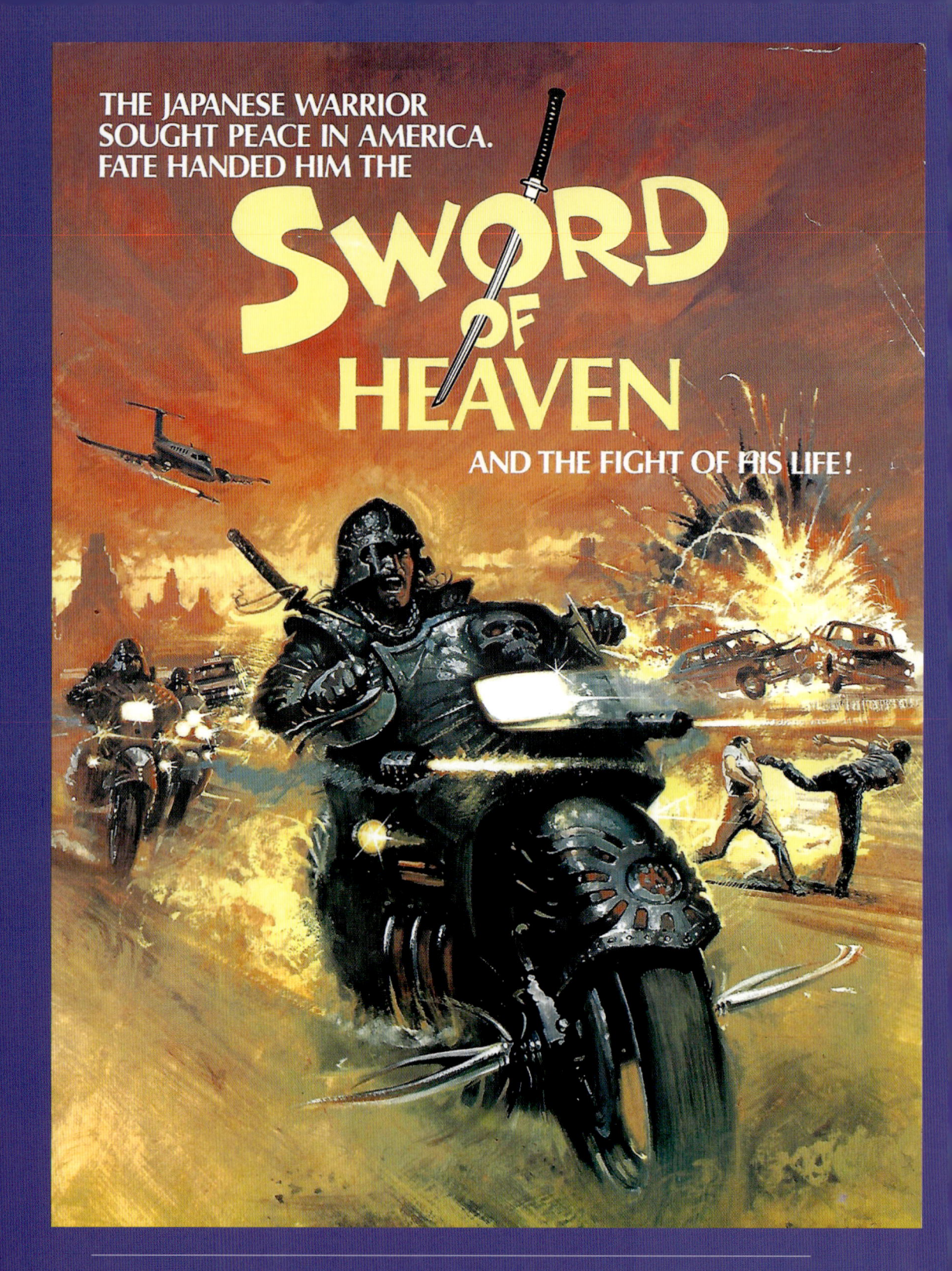

AND THE FIGHT OF HIS LIFE!

(above) A sales tool for *Sword of Heaven*. Regular Chuck Norris screenwriter James Bruner (*Eye for an Eye*, *Missing in Action*, *Invasion U.S.A.*, *The Delta Force*), was a friend of Yamashita's and wrote *Sword* as a vehicle for himself to direct before it got hijacked by Yamashita's student.

(opposite page) The far less stimulating Trans World VHS cover featuring an image of a bloody sword waiting for the bus.

to shoot new footage and turn it into a comedy. Offended, Yamashita took his movie and went home. It didn't see the light of day again until Burbank Video issued it on videocassette in 1991.

Sword of Heaven was his second attempt at a star vehicle. One of Yamashita's students, Joe Randazzo, convinced a relative to put money into the production, ousted the director, and rewrote the script to make his own role more substantial. The resulting film could charitably be called a mess.

Everyone, everywhere, wanted in on the ninja game. Ron White was a private detective and author of the book *So You Want to Be a Private Detective*, holder of two Guinness world records for lying on a bed of nails, and the chief instructor of the Cobra Karate System in St. Louis, Missouri, but he really wanted to make a ninja movie called *Ninja, the Ultimate Warrior*.

He convinced a local modeling and talent agency to put up $12,589.43 of the budget, including $2,500 for a special appearance by Bill "Superfoot" Wallace. The agency expected to make their money back by sharing "the profits from selling Ninja movie posters," but when White abandoned that movie to make *Justice, Ninja Style* without cutting in the talent agency, they sued him despite the fact that White claimed it was a totally different movie. He wasn't worried, however, claiming that he expected to make $50,000 on his $15,000 investment from home video sales alone.

Shot on video in De Soto, Missouri, recruiting local extras for $1 a day, *Justice, Ninja Style* tells the story of a man framed for a murder he didn't commit, and the lone ninja in that Midwestern town of 6,500 who believes he didn't do it. Running 70 minutes, the only place renters could find the finished film were mom-and-pop video shops in the St. Louis area, or overseas, where its video distributor added 10 minutes of footage and billed White as "Liberty King, the Ninja."

In 1985, Jun Chong (star of *Bruce Lee Fights Back from the Grave*; see page 142) started his own production company in LA, Action Brothers, and made a film with Phillip Rhee, one of his former students. To direct, they hired Richard Park Woo-Sung, a Korean filmmaker who'd spent seven years as assistant director to Korea's master filmmaker, Im Kwon-Taek, before breaking out on his own. He'd directed Bobby Kim (see page 324) in *Mortal Battle* (aka *Kill the Ninja*, 1975) and *Blazing Fists* (1977) before running afoul of the authoritarian President Park's strict censorship laws and doing some jail time. Then he moved to St. Louis, Missouri, in 1977.

After the assassination of President Park he returned to Korea to shoot *Return of the Great Fighter* (1980), then went back to America and made several movies about

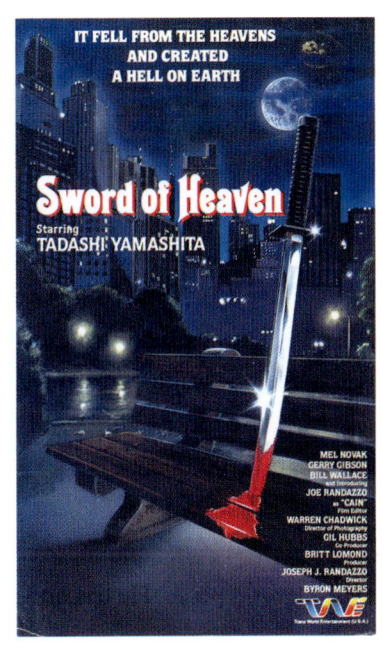

Jun Chong's real mission was to teach taekwondo, so even screenings of *Ninja Turf* became promotional opportunities for his classes. In 1990, he stopped appearing in films but returned 15 years later to play small parts and cameos.

the immigrant experience, the first of which was *L.A. Streetfighters* (aka *Ninja Turf*, 1985). Featuring Phillip Rhee as Tony, the new kid in school, and Jun Chong (then 41) as leader of a high school gang, there's also poor Mark, who never had a birthday cake, a ferocious cameo from Bill "Superfoot" Wallace, and a total lack of familiarity with authentic human behavior. It also doesn't actually have any ninjas. *Variety* called it "a poorly lit, poorly staged and crudely made film," while *Boxoffice* asked, "This is a joke, right?"

Nevertheless, the $200,000 production was licensed to RCA Columbia Pictures Home Video and wound up on the shelves of every video store in the country. Jun Chong's Action Brothers would team up with Lee Doo-Young again for *Silent Assassins* (1988) starring Linda Blair, while Richard W.S. Park would head to Miami, where he made the ninja-packed *Miami Connection* (1987) with Master Y.K. Kim, a Korean immigrant who'd moved to Orlando in 1978 after buying a friend's taekwondo school, which turned out to be 10 students, a tiny room, and a single mat.

Undeterred, Kim worked as a janitor, passed out handbills, and relentlessly promoted his taekwondo schools until he had 2,000 students, which is when he mortgaged his schools to raise the $1 million needed to co-star in a Bobby Kim movie directed by Richard W.S. Park. Bobby Kim dropped out, and the movie became a star vehicle for Master Y.K. Kim and his belief that taekwondo could bring about world peace. Kim wasn't happy with the results. After viewing the film, he walked out of the screening and went home, where he slept for 48 hours.

"I was physically and mentally exhausted," he said in an interview. "Financially, I was dead. Morally, I was dead. I just wanted to forget the movie."

But he refused to give up. He bought out his partners and went to Hollywood, where helpful distributors told him to "throw it in the trash." He went to Cannes, but no one wanted it there, either. Teaching himself filmmaking from books, he rewrote the script, re-edited and reshot the picture, and finally sold the international rights for $100,000.

"I know I lost money," he said. "But I do not regret it at all."

He then announced plans to make another movie about taekwondo as a force for world peace. He has not yet made this film.

DOG OF THE WEEK

FOR NEARLY 25 YEARS, Gene Siskel and Roger Ebert were America's national film critics, thanks to their syndicated television shows that ran collectively from 1975 to 1999 on hundreds of stations. In the early years of their PBS show, *Sneak Previews*, they'd each throw a bone to the "Dog of the Week," the worst movie they'd seen. They even had a canine mascot who would join them in the balcony for the segment. At first it was Spot the Wonder Dog, but when his owner got into a pay dispute with the producers, he was replaced by Sparky the Wonder Dog, an unpredictable prima donna who ended up dying of kidney failure. When the pair left *Sneak Previews* in 1982 for their syndicated series *At the Movies*, the segment was renamed Stinker-of-the-Week and the mascot became Aroma the Educated Skunk. By then, the theaters they frequented to find their dogs and stinkers—Loop grindhouses like the McVickers and Oriental as well as suburban drive-ins—were shutting down, making their choices more mainstream and less interesting.

Once, Ebert's dog was *Invincible Devil*, which he described as "Another interchangeable kung fu movie with one new twist: at one point, the hero is attacked by six guys who clang cymbals together in his ears."

After suffering through *The Tongfather* he complained, "Sometimes I wonder if they didn't just make one lousy kung fu movie a long time ago and release it under a hundred different titles. The battles always look the same, the plots are always the same and the karate chops always sound like somebody's attacking a Naugahyde sofa with a Ping Pong paddle."

But at heart, the two critics seemed to be rooting for the genre, covering it with far more open minds than the *New York Times*, which stopped reviewing kung fu movies altogether after 1973. As Siskel explained after thrashing *Last Fist of Fury*, "Why should we spend all this time, week after week, knocking inferior kung fu films? Because the people who go to see these movies are truly among the most loyal of filmgoers and they're getting mightily ripped off."

One sheets for *L.A. Streetfighters* and *Ninja Turf*, which are actually the exact same movie with exactly the same number of ninjas in it: none.

...FORCED TO BECOME DEADLY WARRIORS

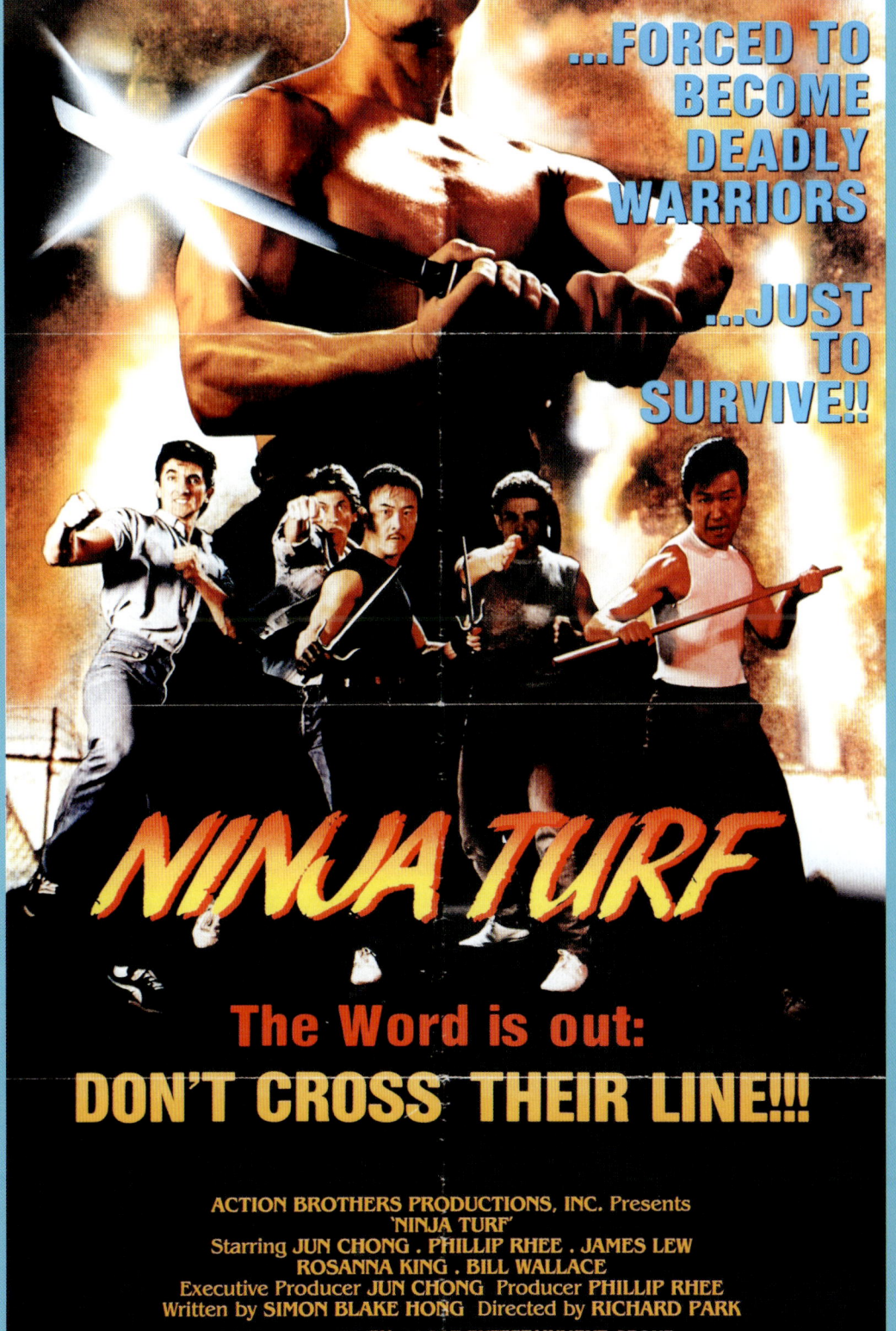

...JUST TO SURVIVE!!

NINJA TURF

The Word is out:
DON'T CROSS THEIR LINE!!!

ACTION BROTHERS PRODUCTIONS, INC. Presents
'NINJA TURF'
Starring JUN CHONG . PHILLIP RHEE . JAMES LEW
ROSANNA KING . BILL WALLACE
Executive Producer JUN CHONG   Producer PHILLIP RHEE
Written by SIMON BLAKE HONG   Directed by RICHARD PARK
RELEASED BY ASCOT ENTERTAINMENT GROUP
© 1986 ASCOT ENTERTAINMENT GROUP

R RESTRICTED
UNDER 17 REQUIRES ACCOMPANYING PARENT OR ADULT GUARDIAN

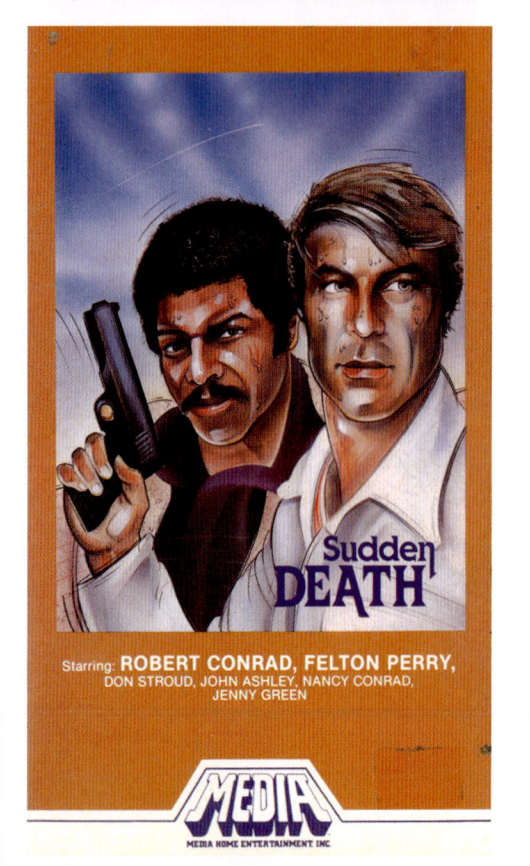

THE VHS MARKET IN THE '80s was a repeat of the independent distribution game in the '70s, with distributors staging a race to the bottom, turning out increasingly terrible movies as they tried to cash in on the audience before it wised up. Companies like AIP and Dimension that had played the low-budget quickie game were gone, replaced by outfits like Cannon and Trans World who were willing to endure the razor-thin profit margins of home video. The most infamous of the bunch was Film Ventures International, the brainchild of Edward L. Montoro, who'd built his company into an exploitation powerhouse with *Beyond the Door*, an Italian *Exorcist* knock-off that earned him a ton of money as well as a lawsuit from Warner Bros. that ultimately went nowhere.

Montoro picked up a three-year-old South African martial arts movie, *Kill or Be Killed*, about a local boy, James Ryan, competing in a karate tournament run by a Nazi. It became such a big hit that Montoro dispatched his producer, Igo Kantor, to South Africa with instructions to round up the original cast and shoot a sequel. Most American companies wouldn't shoot in South Africa due to apartheid, but . . . money! *Kill and Kill Again* (1981) was written by the son of the *New York Times*' powerful film critic, Bosley Crowther, and was such a success that Film Ventures planned a third James Ryan actioner. *The Most Dangerous Man Alive* was announced as a gadget-heavy 007-type adventure pairing Ryan with Sybil Danning, to be directed in Mexico by John "Bud" Cardos. However, a massive lawsuit from Universal over FVI's *Jaws* rip-off, *Great White* (1981), knocked the wind out of the company. Montoro, reeling from a recent divorce and making increasingly erratic business decisions (like dumping tens of thousands into "fixing" the US-Filipino actioner *Alley Cat*, 1984) took $1 million from the company coffers and disappeared in a puff of ninja smoke, never to be seen again.

Filipino filmmakers repackaged old films like 1975's *Hustler Squad* ("You pay for the pleasure. The killing is free") and a Robert Conrad–Don Stroud display of Kajukenbo titled *Sudden Death*. Written by Oscar Williams, the scribe behind *Hot Potato* and *Black Belt Jones*, the movie was to co-star Jim Kelly as Conrad's sidekick until he dropped out and was replaced by Felton Perry. The same year Bryanston acquired *Sudden Death*, the company's president, Lou Peraino, son of mobster Anthony Peraino, was sentenced to prison for interstate shipment of obscene materials and the film got dumped into theaters like a corpse, only to pop up on video a few years later.

Video store buyers followed a strict hierarchy. At the top of the heap were movies that convinced a star (loosely defined) to show up on set for a few days. Filipino director Teddy Page turned out cinematic concoctions that made Godfrey Ho seem sane, but both men shared a taste for Richard Harrison, who appeared in Page's *Blood Debts* and *Fireback* wielding cartoonishly large firearms. Cameron Mitchell appeared in the original Broadway production of *Death of a Salesman*, but did Willy Loman take on 12 hands, 12 feet, and 24 reasons to die? Mitchell did in *Kill Squad*.

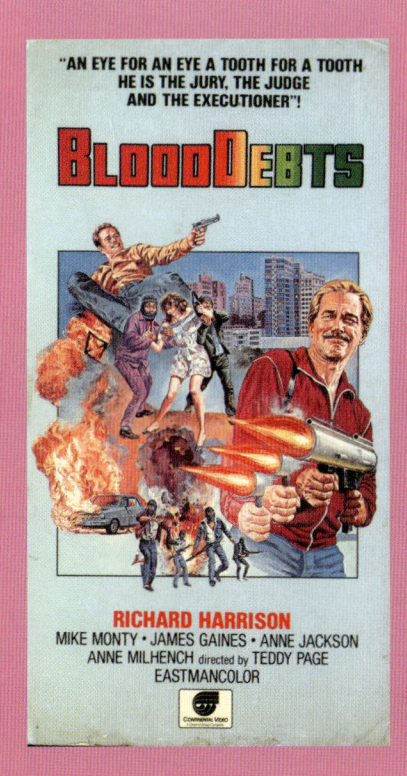

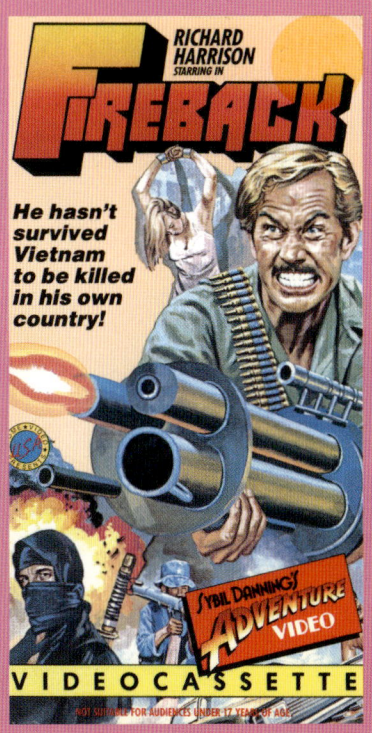

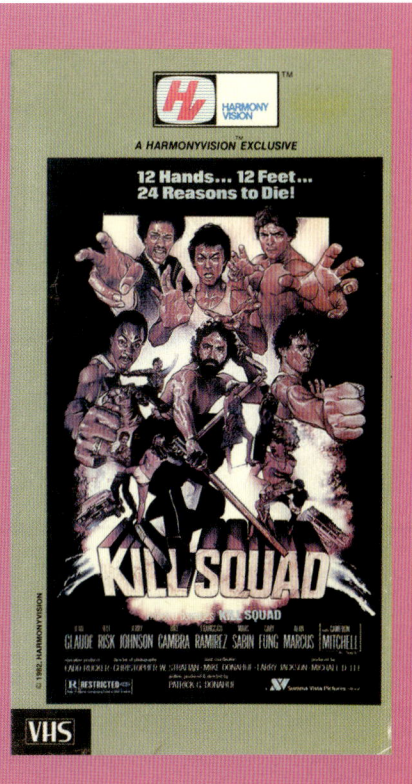

1971 BRUCE LEE SHOOK THE WORLD!
1987 BRANDON LEE CONTINUES THE LEGEND.....

SCREENINGS AT CANNES
MAY 9 SAT. PALAIS H 3:30 PM
MAY 11 MON. PALAIS H 3:30 PM
MAY 15 FRI. PALAIS G 5:30 PM

BRANDON LEE
LEGACY OF RAGE

ASIAN FILMS B.V. PRESENTS A D & B FILMS PRODUCTION "LEGACY OF RAGE"
STARRING BRANDON LEE MICHAEL WONG REGINA KENT ALSO STARRING ONNO BOELEE TANYA GEORGE
WRITTEN BY CLIFTON COLE AND RAYMOND FUNG ASSOCIATE PRODUCERS CLIFTON COLE AND RAYMOND FUNG
CINEMATOGRAPHER JIMMY BOSCO SPECIAL EFFECTS SUPERVISOR ALAN S. WHIBERY ACTION COORDINATOR RANDY MANG
EXECUTIVE PRODUCER DICKSON POON PRODUCED BY JOHN SHUM AND LINDA KUK DIRECTED BY RONNY YU

If they couldn't land a big star, producers tried to lure one of their kids onto their sets instead. In fact, it felt like they'd been waiting all their lives for a chance to cast Bruce Lee's son, Brandon, last seen on the big screen at eight years old, turning his back on the cameras filming his father's funeral. As a teenager, Brandon had given up martial arts for soccer, weirded out by the dojos featuring giant photos of his dad on their walls. After a casting agent cajoled him into appearing in 1986's *Kung Fu: The Movie*, he thought his acting career might take off, but no other offers came, except one from Hong Kong to star in a revenge flick called *Legacy of Rage* (1986).

Legacy garnered Brandon a Best New Performer nomination at the Hong Kong Film Awards, and the producers wanted to shoot a sequel but, allegedly, only if Brandon imitated his father. Instead, Brandon packed up and headed back to Hollywood, where he spent years as a script reader, doing stage work and a bit of television before he got an agent, put together a reel of scenes from *Rage*, and landed a role opposite Dolph Lundgren in *Showdown in Little Tokyo* (1991). He followed it up with *Rapid Fire* (1992) and then was approached about playing his father in the big-budget Hollywood biopic *Dragon: The Bruce Lee Story* (1993), which he rejected. His big break seemed to arrive when he beat out Christian Slater and Johnny Depp to land the lead role in *The Crow* (1994), a big-budget supernatural action movie based on a comic book. A month into shooting, Lee was accidentally killed by a prop gun.

But Brandon Lee was merely the best known of the bunch. Robert Mitchum had found fame in Hollywood classics like *Night of the Hunter*, but his son, Chris, wound up in *Eyes of the Dragon* and Golden Harvest co-productions like *H-Bomb*. Chuck Norris spent the '80s getting bigger and bigger, but you could still get his son, Mike, at a discount rate for *Survival Game* (1987). Later, Mike would appear in *Death Ring* (1992) alongside the son of superstar Steve McQueen, Chad McQueen, who'd played one of the bullies in *The Karate Kid* (1984). He'd also played a cop partnered with Cynthia Rothrock in *Martial Law* (1990). Also playing a cop was Lee Majors II, son of Lee Majors of *The Six Million Dollar Man* fame, who co-starred with Yung Henry Yu (aka Bruce Ly) as a cop in the drug-busting flick, *The Chinatown Connection* (1990). Not only was its investor, John A. Esseff, under the impression that Yung was Bruce Lee's actual protégé, but Esseff also contributed many packages of mozzarella cheese to the production, thanks to another of his money-making schemes, which stood in onscreen as packages of drugs.

Some folks, tired of waiting around for famous people to need cash or have kids, transformed themselves into their own home-video heroes. Few people worked harder to be a star than Leo Fong. When some Filipino producers cold-called him one night at 5am to offer him a Bruceploitation movie, he turned them down, choosing to go it alone. This boxing champion from Arkansas had studied with Bruce Lee after seeing him perform in a backyard luau early in his career, then wrote, starred in, and sometimes directed his own movies like *Kill Factor*, *Tiger's Revenge*, and *Enforcer from Death Row*, which were all the same movie under different titles. In the '80s, he turned out a string of movies like *Killpoint* and *Bionic Ninja* that were surprisingly violent fare for a former Methodist minister and that made most of their money on video. In *Low Blow* (1986), Fong takes on a cult controlled by an unnaturally tight-faced Cameron Mitchell, but he can't order a meal, park his car, or even cross the street without having to stomp a thug's head into jelly, blast some sicko out of his socks, or chop open a cretin's Mercedes with a power saw (carefully putting on his safety goggles first).

Fong's lawless America comes to its biggest, bloodiest life in *Killpoint* (1984), about an enormously violent street gang that robs supermarkets by massacring all the customers with military grade hardware, the theft of which is being investigated by an ATF agent played by Richard "Shaft" Roundtree. On its opening weekend in New York City it made $1 million, probably because of Roundtree, since Fong, the star and producer of the picture, isn't mentioned anywhere in its trailer or ads.

"These movies get no advertising budget," Fong lamented to the press. "They're released in between the big movies, when a theater needs a film for a short run. That's not really fair. We put everything we've got into our movies. People get hurt trying to make the scenes real."

Fong wasn't alone.

In Colorado, Bobby Kim labeled himself "the Oriental Charles Bronson" and boasted of an unexplained connection to Bruce Lee, making a handful of action movies with his brother, Hok Kim, whom he said was a popular screenwriter in Korea. He probably wasn't. Running three taekwondo schools, Kim had had a brief career doing action back in Hong Kong and he managed to convince folks like Joe Lewis and Bill "Superfoot" Wallace to appear in his American films. Touchingly, he told one journalist, "I am also trying to contact Rocky."

Bobby Kim starred in *Kill Line,* which he may have directed and definitely produced. Completed in 1989, it wasn't released until 1991.

KILLPOINT

1 AM
ASSAULT ON A POLICE ARSENAL.

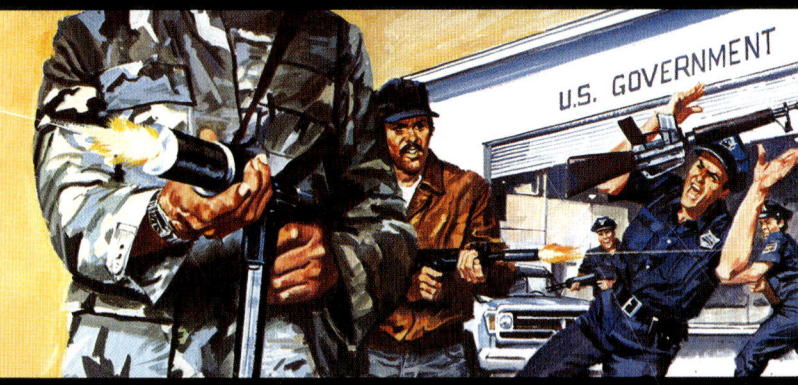

2 AM
THE GUNS ARE ON THE STREETS.

3 AM
INNOCENT VICTIMS SLAUGHTERED.

KillPoint
...WHEN VIOLENCE IS OUT OF CONTROL!

"KILLPOINT" STARRING LEO FONG · RICHARD ROUNDTREE · CAMERON MITCHELL · STACK PIERCE · HOPE HOLIDAY · DIANA LEIGH
PRODUCED BY FRANK HARRIS AND DIANE STEVENETT · EXECUTIVE PRODUCERS ROGER JACOBSON AND DANA J. WELCH · WRITTEN AND DIRECTED BY FRANK HARRIS · MUSIC COMPOSED BY SCOTT DALEY
TECHNICAL ADVISOR: SPECIAL AGENT RONALD J. ADAMS, RIVERSIDE POLICE DEPT.

A CROWN INTERNATIONAL PICTURES RELEASE
© 1983 CROWN INTERNATIONAL PICTURES, INC.

Manchurian Avenger was only one of nine movies Bobby Kim made in four years.

The ferociously flexible superkicker John Liu went from starring in second-tier Taiwanese movies to writing, producing, and directing his own second-tier international co-productions: a shot-in-Paris John Liu biopic mixed with a shot-in-backyards spy movie (*Zen Kwun Do Strikes in Paris*, 1979), a shot-in-backyards spy movie (*Ninja in the Claws of the CIA*, 1981), a shot-in-Spain western (*Dragon Blood*, 1982), and a shot-in-New York ninja movie (*New York Ninja*). *Ninja in the Claws of the CIA* sees Liu recruited by the CIA, then he has a lot of sex, goes on the run, and restrains himself from achieving orgasm via his incredible powers of tai chi while the American military studies his sex drive. In *New York Ninja*, he plays a TV news cameraman who puts his ninja skills to use tracking down the gang that killed his fiancée and a psycho known as the Plutonium Killer. Shot in the fall of 1984 and produced by 21st Century Distribution, it became a casualty of the company's bankruptcy sale and remained unedited and unreleased until a box of 35mm picture negative (but no soundtrack) turned up in the film archive of Vinegar Syndrome 35 years later. One of their editors, Kurtis Spieler, transferred all of the footage, pieced the film together, wrote a new script, hired a new cast of actors to dub the voices (including Don "the Dragon" Wilson and Cynthia Rothrock), and enlisted the band Voyag3r to create an original and very '80s-sounding score. The finished film came out on Blu-ray from Vinegar Syndrome in 2021, along with a soundtrack album and, later, a comic book sequel. As for Liu, he gave up on the film business after shooting his vanity productions to concentrate on teaching his own martial art, Zen Kwun Do.

Actor Ulli Lommel found fame appearing in movies directed by Germany's arthouse prince, Rainer Werner Fassbinder, and American pop art king Andy Warhol before directing around 40 of his own flicks, including *Overkill* (1987), a buddy movie about a wild man American cop with a mullet, played by three-time *Playgirl* centerfold Steve Rally, teaming up with a straightlaced Japanese cop toting a samurai sword, played by John Nishio, who wasn't in anything else ever again. Arriving when Americans were getting sweaty about Japan overtaking them economically, there's not a lot to distinguish it from other low-budget movies shot around borrowed backyard swim-

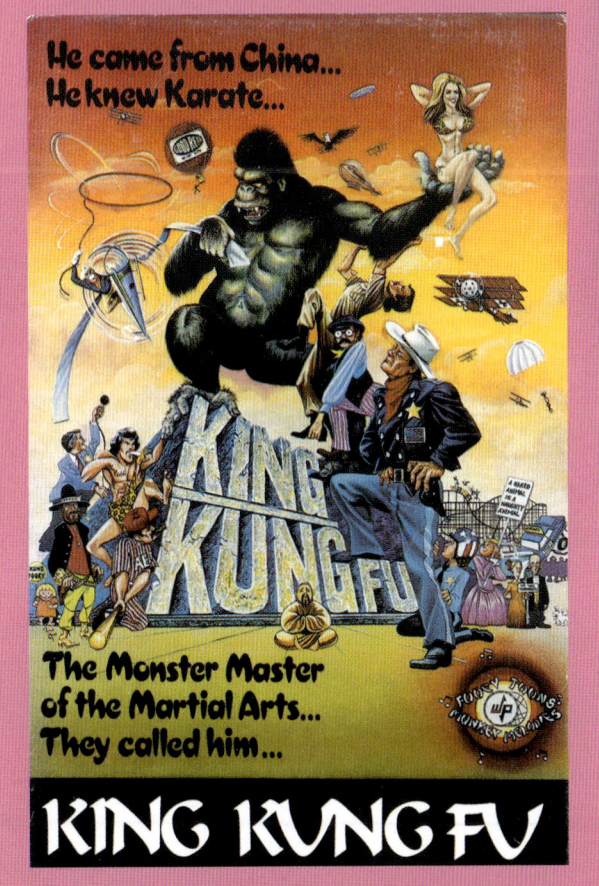

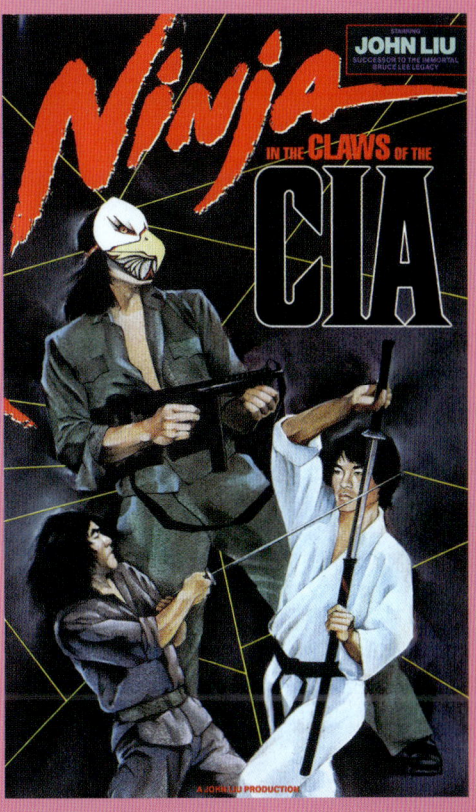

(top) An ad for John Liu's *New York Ninja*, which boasted the tagline "When you back a tiger into a corner . . . he comes out fighting." Beside it is the VHS cover of *Ninja in the Claws of the CIA*.

(bottom, left) *King Kung Fu*'s VHS cover.

(bottom, right) A plaintive ad looking for someone, anyone, to distribute *King Kung Fu*.

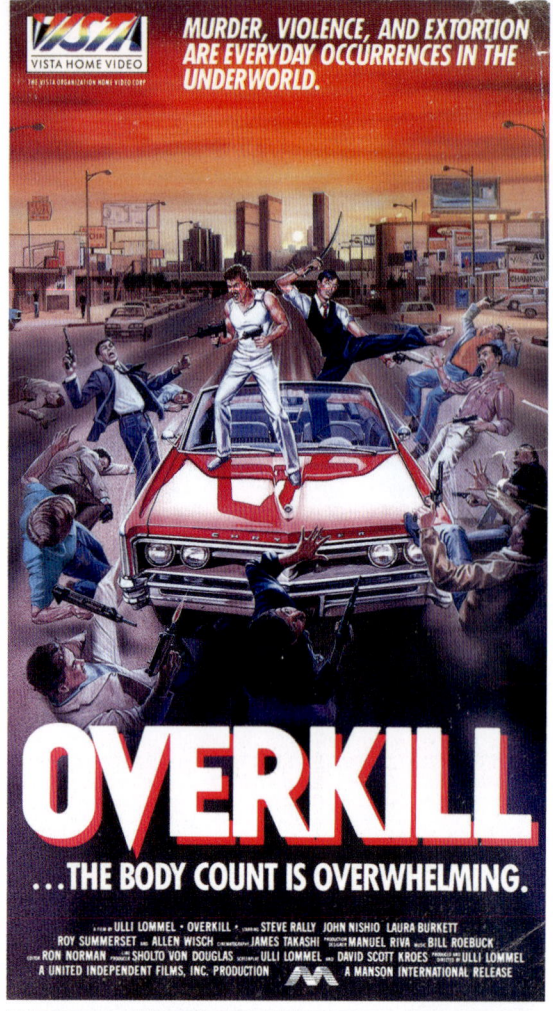

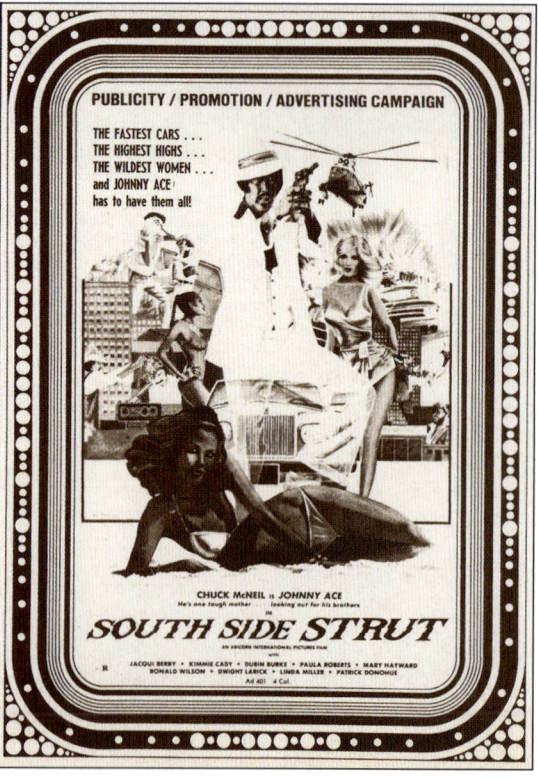

ming pools except for Nishio's relaxed, understated performance and the movie's deep anti-Japanese xenophobia.

Wichita native Lance Hayes always wanted to make a movie, and in 1974 he started shooting *King Kung Fu* about a gorilla trained in kung fu who escapes in Kansas while en route to New York City. After roundhouse kicking a bunch of people in the face, the gorilla abducts a Pizza Hut waitress and scales a Holiday Inn, the tallest building in Wichita. It took two years to shoot and 11 years to edit, finally getting released in a handful of theaters and on home video in 1987.

At least they actually made a movie. UCLA grad Chuck McNeil founded his Nyeusi Cinema to produce movies like *Ice Cream Charlie* back in 1974, whose wrap party was attended by such luminaries as Flip Wilson and the Jackson 5, according to a press release written by Chuck McNeil himself. He'd go on to make a blaxploitation private eye film, *Dragonspade*, and a Bruceploitation movie, *Dragon from the East* (1982) with Nguyen Ly, billed as Jimbo Lee, after which he planned to make *Dojo,* which he said would bring "more of a Japanese slant to the genre."

McNeil claimed *Dragon* cost $1 million, which, if you've ever seen the footage, is very, very hard to believe. It's also unclear if *Dragon from the East* was ever actually released. Just as unclear are how many of McNeil's movies, with titles like *South Side Strut*, *Disco-DynoMite*, and *Angel Dust–Devil Drugs*, even existed. What is clear is that around the same time he made *Dragon*, McNeil (who often cast himself in his films as a character named Johnny Ace) went to Miami to shoot a movie called *Miami Summer* and put out ads through a local agency looking for talent. Wannabe actors paid $67.50 to make a one-minute videotaped screen test, but instead of getting callbacks, McNeil returned to California without shooting an inch of *Miami Summer* footage. When contacted about the scam, he claimed to know nothing about it and said he would still shoot *Miami Summer* but not in Miami, claiming that it was "a bad scene." Miami police considered pressing charges, but ultimately, what could they do when someone disappeared like a ninja holding everyone's cash?

Some people say McNeil's movies exist, others claim they were never released. One thing is sure, however: their finished footage looks sparse. As McNeil said of *Dragon from the East*, "We started out to do a good movie—I mean, nobody deliberately sinks their time and money and effort into something they know from the beginning is going to be bad . . . I tried."

FAST AND FURIOUS

LIKE MOST USC FILM SCHOOL GRADUATES, Tim Everitt and Tom Sartori wanted to make a feature film. Unlike other USC Film School grads, they wanted to at least break even on their investment, so they asked a distributor what would make money "no matter how bad it is, as long as it's 90 minutes long and in focus." Make a kung fu movie, the distributor said.

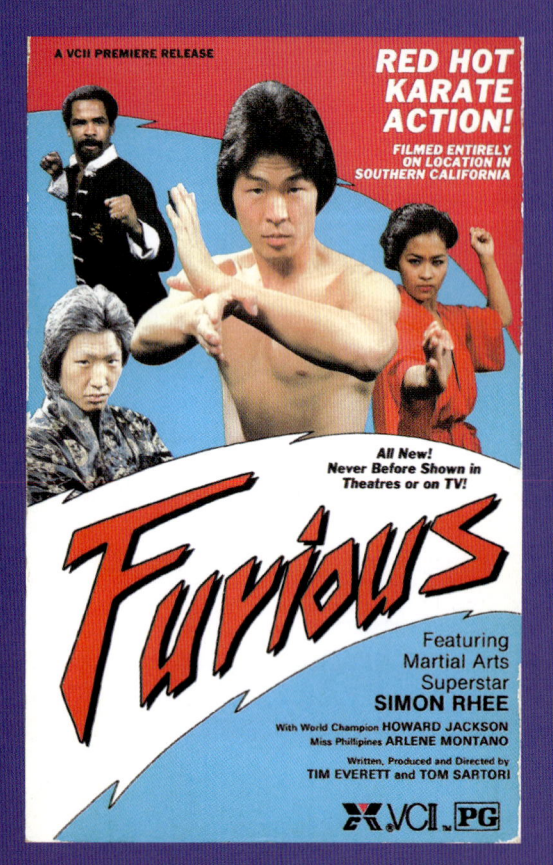

So they did.

Furious (1984) had no script and very little dialogue so they could easily dub it for the international market. They wanted to shoot for seven days, but on the seventh day their two stars went drinking in Tijuana, so, okay, they shot for six. Total budget? $18,000. The stars were the Rhee brothers, Phillip and Simon, local taekwondo instructors who would go on to become accomplished actors and stunt choreographers, and most of the cast were their students and friends, like Howard Jackson of *The Human Tornado* fame.

The Rhees had their own Los Angeles dojos and they wanted to pull off choreography they'd never seen onscreen before, so the action is relatively accomplished, but the movie itself is a sort of surrealist symphony that does for kung fu movies what Alejandro Jodorowsky's *El Topo* did for westerns, only with more chickens. There are chickens all over this movie. Chickens are cradled, roasted, eaten, and shot from fingers. Sometimes people are turned into chickens. Toward the end of the movie a helpful magician explains why there are all these chickens, then Simon Rhee kicks him, he turns into a farting pig, and dies.

Everitt and Sartori wanted to make sure *Furious* looked like a real movie, so they shot it in 35mm and hid the fact that their crew consisted of two people by padding its end credits with the slightly altered closing credits of *Star Trek II: The Wrath of Khan*. It ran for six days, four-walled at the Pickfair, a Hindi movie theater in LA, and even got a blurb in the *Los Angeles Times*. But it would be a bit player in *Furious* (and also *L.A. Streetfighters*) who would become the next big martial arts star.

ROY HORAN

ON OCTOBER 12, 2021, Roy Horan died while hiking in the hills near his home in Los Angeles. An important Westerner in Hong Kong film, Horan had lived as a hunter-trapper among the Indigenous peoples of the Northwest Territories for two years after university before moving to Japan, then to Taiwan, where he got tangled up in the film business through his friendship with Korean superkicker Hwang Jang-Lee. Horan would appear in two movies featuring Hwang (the Bruceploitation flick *The Story of the Dragon* and the John Liu–Hwang Jang-Lee showcase *The Snuff Bottle Connection*) before going on to play the killer Russian priest in Jackie Chan's breakthrough film, *Snake in the Eagle's Shadow* (1978), and the evil, island-owning, deer-blood-drinking knock-off Mr. Han in *Game of Death II* (1981).

But Horan played a bigger part in Hong Kong film history behind the camera than in front of it. When he entered the industry, foreign markets outside Taiwan, Malaysia, Thailand, and maybe Japan weren't regarded as profitable. But Horan, speaking fluent Chinese (we cannot confirm if it was Mandarin, Cantonese, or both), befriended super-producer Ng See-yuen, and convinced him he could sell Seasonal's films to Western territories. Learning the ropes as he went along, asking for higher and higher fees to figure out where the ceiling was, Horan became a huge source of revenue for Ng.

Thanks to Horan's hard-charging expansion westward, Seasonal took Jackie Chan's *Snake in the Eagle's Shadow* around the world and later opened US offices, making it the first Hong Kong company besides Golden Harvest to do so. Horan also helped produce what became the *No Retreat, No Surrender* trilogy of films, which put Hong Kong and Western talent on the same screen, gave Jean-Claude Van Damme his first major role, and became huge hits in theaters and especially on home video. After leaving the movie industry in 1991, Horan served as an adjunct professor at Hong Kong Polytechnic University and his self-help book *Vigilance of the Heart* was published in 2018.

THE LAST MAJOR WESTERN ACTOR to make movies in Hong Kong had been Ron Van Clief. A martial artist named Vincent Lyn had gone to Hong Kong briefly in 1980. After his wife encouraged him to take his modeling portfolio to Shaw Brothers, he met Mona Fong's right-hand woman, Virginia Lok. She gave him a screen test and offered him a three-picture deal. However, his wife had second thoughts about Lyn appearing onscreen in a movie where he'd romance another woman, so she ultimately convinced him to stay home.

When Dennis Brown began appearing on the cover of *Inside Kung-Fu* magazine, the Huangs, who owned the American Theater in Washington, DC, suddenly asked if he'd be interested in shooting a movie in Taiwan. Financing much of this production was the owner of New York City's Sun Sing theater.

They sent Brown to Taiwan, where he appeared in a Chang Cheh movie called *The Dancing Warrior* (1985). All of Chang Cheh's stars had recently made a movie to raise a retirement fund for their master (*Shanghai Thirteen*, 1984), but instead of taking the money and going on vacation, the 61-year-old director poured the profits into *The Dancing Warrior*, which combined interpretive dance with martial arts.

Ricky Cheng plays a dancer who comes to America to appear on Broadway but instead winds up competing in underground kung fu fights to the death, ("He's got style but he's no ninja material," one character observes.) There he gets into two elaborate fights with Brown, who plays a local New York kung fu master. The two become friends, Brown gets murdered in an underground tournament, and Cheng seeks revenge in an elaborate combat-dance finale. It may not be the best movie Chang Cheh ever directed, but it's certainly one of the most unique, and Brown has so much screen presence, it's a pity he never made another movie.

Actors and martial artists kept up with every new movie from Hong Kong, while Hong Kong producers and directors kept looking for ways into the lucrative American market. When Corey Yuen Kwai went to Seattle to visit his sister, he saw *The Karate Kid* and immediately called Ng See-yuen, telling him *The Karate Kid* was *Drunken Master* only with no drinking and worse action. Ng decided to make a Hong Kong version with Chinese stuntmen and Western actors.

Ng hired Keith Strandberg to work on the script. Strandberg, a Mandarin-speaking tour guide and martial artist, had cold-called him a few years earlier and they'd spent the afternoon together talking movies. When they parted, Ng told him if he ever made an English-language film, Strandberg could write it. That time was now.

Ng and Yuen set up auditions with American karate kids like Cynthia Rothrock, Karen Shepherd, Peter Cunningham, and Ernie Reyes Jr. There they found Kurt McKinney, their star, and also Jean-Claude Van Damme, who'd play Ivan the Russian, the movie's heel. Sales fell to Roy Horan, Seasonal's foreign sales agent, who had to figure out what to do with this remake of *The Karate Kid*, only cornier and with bet-

DENNIS BROWN WEEK!

U. S. CAPITOL CLASSICS
martial arts tournament

Presented by
Dennis Brown Shaolin Wu-Shu Academy

The Greatest Display
of Martial Arts
Talent Ever
Assembled.

SATURDAY
AUGUST 10, 1985
Washington
Convention
Center

Tournament
Information:
882-4435

See Dennis Brown's
first Kung-Fu Spectacular
THE DANCING WARRIOR
directed by Chang Chieh

STARTS TODAY
Exclusively at

American Theater
L'Enfant Plaza
D & 10th Sts., S.W.
Show times; check listing
Information Call 554-2111

An ad proclaiming opening weekend of *The Dancing Warrior* as "Dennis Brown Week" at the American Theater, the Chinatown theater in Washington, DC.

ter action. But it did have a 15-minute sequence in the middle where *Game of Death*'s Tang Long reprised his Bruce Lee impersonation to teach McKinney kung fu, and a gorgeously athletic finale where McKinney powers up to defeat Van Damme when someone shouts the title of the film at him. *No Retreat, No Surrender* came out in spring 1986 in 371 American theaters and grossed $4 million, before going on to become a huge hit on video. Seasonal's gamble had succeeded, and they immediately went to work on a sequel. Meanwhile, that same year, after being spotted in her Seasonal audition, Cynthia Rothrock went to Hong Kong and starred in Corey Yuen's *Yes, Madam* (1985) opposite first-time actor Michelle Yeoh. It made Rothrock the biggest Western star in Hong Kong and Seasonal quickly signed her up for *No Retreat, No Surrender 2: Raging Thunder*.

Abandoning *The Karate Kid* to riff on Chuck Norris' Vietnam movies, then in vogue (see page 288), this one would send McKinney to Thailand, where his girlfriend would be abducted and he'd have to rescue her from a paramilitary camp of crooks. Production had already started in Thailand when a cable arrived from Van Damme's lawyer saying the star wouldn't shoot in Thailand due to safety concerns. Van Damme managed to convince McKinney to drop out of the movie, too, which wasn't too hard, since the star had a sweet deal to appear in an American soap opera. With the meter ticking and a cast and crew already in Thailand, Roy Horan scoured Los Angeles for replacements. He happened to call Jun Chong's dojo and got Loren Avedon on the phone.

Avedon had appeared in one scene in *Furious* because one of his teacher's students, Phillip Rhee, was in the film, then he'd appeared with his teacher, Jun Chong, as a gang member getting whacked with a wooden sword in *L.A. Streetfighters*. Raised mostly by his mom, a commercial director, Avedon grew up on film sets and saw his first Bruce Lee movie in England when he was 11. He'd fallen in love with martial arts, and when his family moved back to the States he searched LA both for a teacher and for more martial arts flicks, watching a ton of them on KCOP's "Kung Fu Theater." He was working days at a Dodge dealership and working out at Jun Chong's dojo by night when he got Horan's call. The sales agent said he needed a 23-year-old actor, about six feet tall, who knew martial arts and could get to a three-month shoot in Thailand. "You're talking to him," Avedon said. A week later he'd signed a three-picture deal and was on a plane to Thailand. After an audition with Matthias Hues in the parking lot of Bangkok's Ambassador Hotel, he was hired on *No Retreat, No Surrender 2* for $1,000/day.

He'd done some stuntwork before but on day one of the shoot, Yuen asked him to climb across a cable strung 30 feet off the ground.

"You've got three languages going on and nobody telling me how to balance on this cable," Avedon remembers. "I got stuck in the middle and looked down at these jagged rocks 30 feet below and I thought, 'Okay, this is it. The film's over. I'm over. Cut. Find another piece of white meat for your movie.' But you either get it or you don't. The bottom line is that it's your butt up there onscreen."

He stayed in the picture.

The pyrotechnic-stuffed finale of the movie got shot first, and after the Hollywood special effects technician was fired for almost blowing a hole in an actor with an improperly rigged squib, a new team of Thai guys came in. They believed in making pyrotechnic effects with C-4 plastic explosives and gallons of diesel fuel, and gave actors machine guns that fired live rounds because blanks were too expensive. It's a miracle no one died.

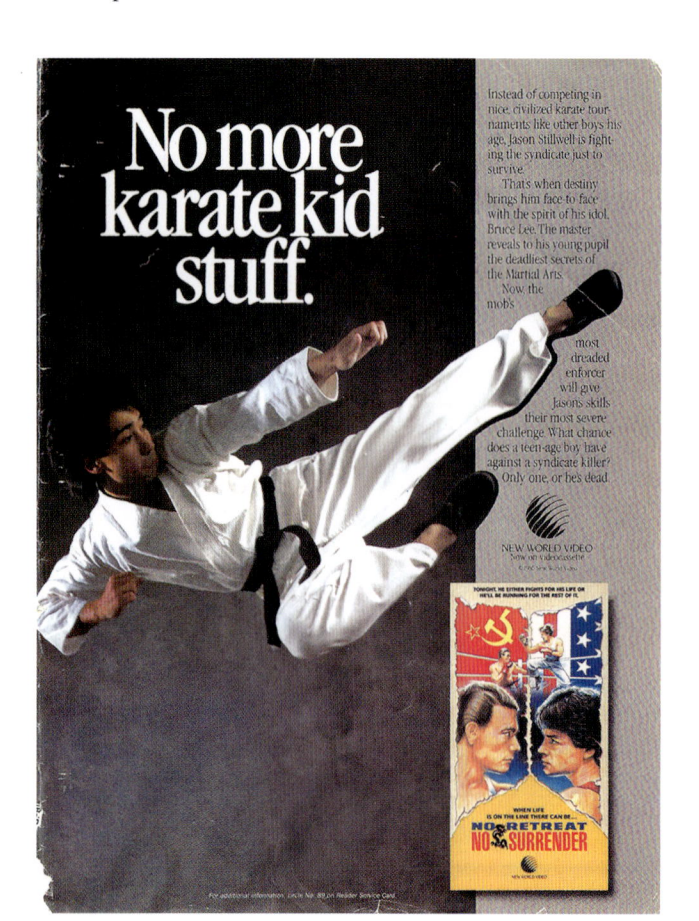

The movie got picked up by the B-movie home video maven Shapiro-Glickenhaus Entertainment, who released it in theaters opposite its Dolph Lundgren vehicle *Red Scorpion*, which it beat at the box office like a rented mule. Avedon came back to America to await offers, and . . . nothing happened.

**When they stand together...
No one else stands a chance.**

NO RETREAT NO SURRENDER II

Meanwhile, in Hong Kong, foreign fighters were being imported by the dozen. Vincent Lyn finally came back and made movies with Cynthia Rothrock (*Blonde Fury*), Yuen Wo-ping (*Tiger Cage*), and Jackie Chan (*Armour of God II: Operation Condor*). Action ace Michiko Nishiwaki left Japan because she couldn't find roles in her home country that let women kick butt. Michael Woods hailed from Rhode Island, Mark Houghton came from the UK, the ripped actress Agnes Aurelio came from the Philippines. The kickboxing champion Benny "the Jet" Urquidez had already proven such a popular fighter in Japan, he'd inspired a pop song and a manga about his exploits in the ring, and he wound up taking on Jackie Chan in the climax of *Wheels on Meals* (1984) and *Dragons Forever* (1988).

IN THE RING OF DEATH,
ONLY ONE MAN CAN BE KING!
LOREN AVEDON
BILLY BLANKS
RICHARD JAECKEL
DON STROUD
THE KING OF THE KICKBOXERS

Finally, in the spring of '89, Avedon got the call that *No Retreat, No Surrender 3: Blood Brothers* was happening. He headed down to Clearwater, Florida, where legendary karate black belt, Keith Vitali, had been cast as his brother. Inspired by Joe Lewis and Bruce Lee, Vitali had already appeared in *Wheels on Meals* with Jackie Chan and opposite Sho Kosugi in *Revenge of the Ninja*, and Avedon was in awe, which turned to terror when Vitali fractured his wrist. The producers wanted to replace him, but Avedon threatened to quit without his co-star. They rewrote the script to include Vitali's cast, but he remained in excruciating pain throughout the shoot.

NR, NS 3: BB scored serious production value when the producers learned that President George H.W. Bush was landing at a nearby airbase in Air Force One. Telling the Secret Service they were a Hong Kong news team shooting footage of life in America, they grabbed their shots of the president getting off the plane, took the footage back to Hong Kong, and painted a rifle's crosshairs over his face. Suddenly *NR, NS 3: BB* had become a movie about a presidential assassination attempt.

The last movie Avedon made for Seasonal was *King of the Kickboxers* (1990), a Thai-set film about a martial arts snuff movie ring that features blistering karate work from Keith Cooke, a karate champ making his first onscreen appearance as Avedon's Mr. Miyagi–style mentor. Billy Blanks (see page 341) gives a fabulously committed and deeply demented performance. Without using a single wire assist, he seems to defy gravity, hovering in midair while unleashing ferocious kicks. While shooting the climax, he accidentally clipped Avedon in the back with his heel and knocked the wind out of him for a full five minutes.

King of the Kickboxers was huge around the world, although it only had a limited theatrical release in the States, but it didn't matter anymore. Blanks and Avedon delivered a demo at the Video Sales Distribution Association convention in Las Vegas that helped *Kickboxers* do big business on home video. Theatrical didn't count. As the '80s drew to a close, the money was in home video.

IN 1982, JANE FONDA, then 45 years old and at the height of her fame, released the *Jane Fonda Workout* video based on her bestselling *Jane Fonda Workout Book*. The very first exercise videotape, it moved millions of units and launched a worldwide workout video boom. Martial artists weren't shy about following her into the ring.

Sho Kosugi and Trans World Entertainment quickly put together *Master Class* in which Kosugi and his son, Kane, demonstrate self-defense techniques on dudes in gray ninja suits. It wasn't so much a workout video as a promotional stunt since it featured scenes from *Pray for Death*, scheduled to come out the following month. Kosugi would fully embrace the workout trend with his 1996 *Ninjaerobics* where he gets in shape with "six beautiful ladies in glamorous costumes." Then, in the 2000s, he created another workout program, *Towelcise*, which had a weird obsession with towels and anchored his Japanese TV series, *Anytime Anywhere! Sho Kosugi's Towel Exercise*, in which he frantically sang, danced, and used a towel.

The next challenger to enter the Octagon: Tiana Alexandra, a Vietnamese-American martial artist determined to make the most of her limited gifts. The daughter of an official in the South Vietnamese government who had fled to Washington, DC, after the assassination of South Vietnam's President Diem in 1963, she studied taekwondo with Master Jhoon Rhee, then ran away to LA the second she turned 16. Bruce Lee, a friend of Rhee's, kept an eye on her, and two years later, on the Fourth of July, she married his student, Academy Award–winning screenwriter Stirling Silliphant, then 56.

Soon, Alexandra was appearing on talk shows and game shows with Silliphant, in movies like *The Killer Elite* with James Caan (becoming the first Vietnamese-American to get a Screen Actors Guild card), and promoting her singing career with expensive videos shot around the world. In 1986 she started making her *Karatecize* fitness videos, which Trans World issued on video as *Karatix*. They looked like the kind of nightmares Cyndi Lauper might have after

A sales sheet for Sho Kosugi's *Master Class*, which was also an ad for his upcoming *Pray for Death*.

338

sniffing glue and nodding off in front of a Jane Fonda workout tape. Spiked with ninjas doing flips in front of its neon color scheme, aggressively large hair, eye-melting video toaster effects, and scored to Tiana's pop songs, these tapes hypnotized viewers with Tiana's always-on, 5,000-degree intensity.

Trans World also produced *Catch the Heat*, which Silliphant wrote as an action showcase for his wife's fighting skills and offbeat sense of humor. As *Variety* noted, "Alexandra is a real looker, solid martial arts practitioner and the only reason to sit through this weak programmer." She plays DEA agent Checkers Goldberg, who goes undercover as the sing-song-speaking ding-a-ling dancer Cinderella Pu, to investigate crime lord Jason Hannibal (a bemused, watery-eyed Rod Steiger), whose talent agency in Brazil is actually a front for a narcotics smuggling operation. It turns out the agency's female clients are unknowing mules carrying uncut heroin into the States inside their chests after undergoing what they were told was breast enlargement surgery, and Checkers/Cinderella is the next to go under the knife. Originally titled *Feel the Heat*, this asinine actioner, helmed by *Breakin'* and *Rappin'* director Joel Silberg, reunited *In the Heat of the Night* Oscar winners Silliphant and Steiger, but it failed to generate much heat.

Unpredictably, in 1988, Alexandra began working on a documentary about her Vietnamese roots, executive produced by Oliver Stone. *From Hollywood to Hanoi* hit theaters and HBO in 1995, with the *Los Angeles Times* calling it "extraordinarily moving" and the *New York Times* calling it "intense, personal, supremely self-confident" before comparing Alexandra to Michael Moore. Later she'd produce David Cronenberg's Sigmund Freud biopic, *A Dangerous Method* (2011).

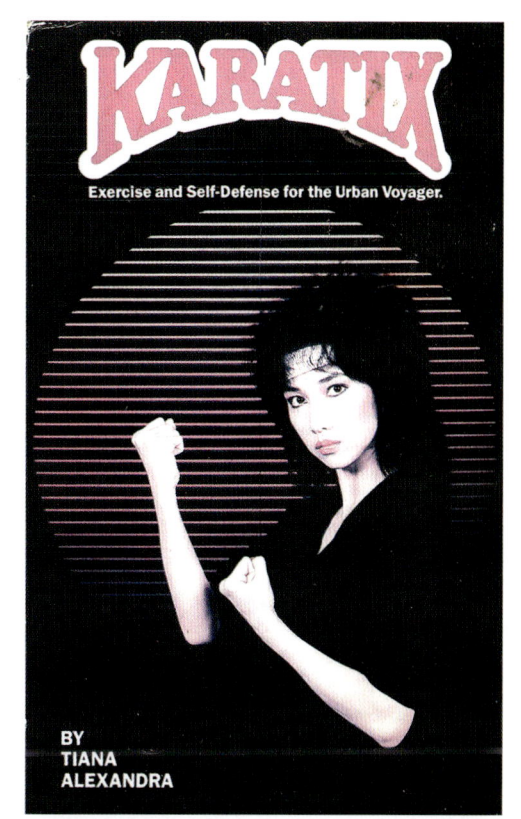

(top) The video box for Tiana Alexandra's exercise tape, *Karatix*. (bottom) A trade ad for her 1987 action movie, *Catch the Heat*, under its original title.

ROD STEIGER HAS THE HANDS OF A SURGEON AND THE MIND OF A SMUGGLER

This sizzling action-adventure features Oscar winner Rod Steiger ("In The Heat of The Night") as a drug kingpin who uses his surgeon's skills in an exotic smuggling scheme. And beautiful Tiana Alexandra, the only woman trained in martial arts by the master Bruce Lee.

"Catch The Heat" has it all: fast action; big stars; sex; and a plot that won't let your customers down for a second. No wonder—it's written by Academy Award winner Sterling Silliphant ("Towering Inferno"; "Poseidon Adventure").

So heat up your sales. Look for your traffic stopping 3-D counter cards, and order by January 7.

An ad for video store buyers for Alexandra's *Catch the Heat*, a film that reunited *In the Heat of the Night* Oscar winners Sterling Silliphant and Rod Steiger through serendipity when the latter replaced Robert Loggia, who then went on to play the bad guy in an even worse Silliphant-scripted stinker, *Over the Top*, the same year.

Incredibly, she remained married to Silliphant until his death in 1996 at the age of 78.

In 1987, David Carradine became a workout video hustler with his *Tai Chi Workout* and *Kung Fu Workout*, the latter of which is notable for making Carradine and his class wear padded uniforms that look like they came from a direct-to-video *Star Trek* knock-off. After introducing both workouts from the front yard of Yamashiro Restaurant in LA, the camera spends just a few minutes shooting a visibly unsteady Carradine teaching slow moves until he slips to the back of the class and another teacher takes over.

But the king of karate workouts was undeniably Billy Blanks. Growing up dirt poor, he was inspired to take karate after seeing Bruce Lee play Kato on *The Green Hornet*. Blanks made his motion picture debut in Leo Fong's cult classic, *Low Blow* (1986), then worked as Catherine Bach's bodyguard in the Philippines while she filmed the direct-to-video *Driving Force* (1989) co-starring Patrick Swayze's brother, Don. After one of the cast was fired, Blanks was asked to fill in and had a blast.

Next, he appeared in the Hong Kong movie *King of the Kickboxers* (1990; see page 337) and *The Master* (1992), wearing an outrageous wig and fighting Jet Li on a Los Angeles city bus, but all along he was developing an aerobics cardio program that incorporated martial arts. At first he called it *Karobics*, but in 1992, he registered the name Tae Bo, and in 1998, he began a series of late-night infomercials that rocketed his tapes and DVDs to $80 million in sales. To date, Blanks has taught thousands of Tae Bo routines, some specifically targeted at couples, children, and Christians.

Throughout the history of martial arts movies, Black and Hispanic actors struggled to get paid what they were worth. Traumatized by a long history of being ripped off, they distrusted the wrong people and trusted people who were even worse. So a story like Billy Blanks', of a Black man who came from nothing and built a martial arts empire that he actually owned, and that actually made him rich, feels like some kind of justice.

Tough and Deadly (1995) was one of two buddy pictures Blanks made with the professional wrestler Rowdy Roddy Piper, the other being *Back in Action* (1994). Both movies were powered entirely by the charismatic chemistry of their two leads.

VIDEO COMPANIES

ALL SEASONS ENTERTAINMENT

In August 1985, the national sales manager for All Seasons Entertainment, Kathleen Clinton, made a $260,000 deal with Alpha Film and Lo Wei Productions for the home video rights to 13 Jackie Chan movies—$20,000 per title as an advance against 20% royalties—with plans to put out two productions per month. *Spiritual Kung Fu* and *Fearless Hyena* were the first pair released, followed by *Snake & Crane Arts of Shaolin* and *Dragon Fist*, but only 11 of the 13 came out before All Seasons called it a day.

CINEMA GROUP HOME VIDEO

Andre Blay, the former head of Embassy Home Entertainment, teamed up with movie producer Elliott Kastner and bought out half of Cinema Group Entertainment in 1987, just as the company's home video label was inking a deal with Golden Harvest for the rights to 44 of their films. Within six months, Blay and Kastner were sued by the parent company and so they bought out the other half of the company in the settlement, then changed the name to Palisades Entertainment. Six months after that, the show was over with fewer than a quarter of the Golden Harvest titles released: *The Association*, *The Big Bet*, *Dragon Lord*, *Dreadnaught*, *The Fate of Lee Khan*, *Game of Death II*, *H-Bomb*, *The Invincible Sword*, *Jackie Chan's Police Force*, and *My Lucky Stars*.

DRAGON VIDEO

After the plug was pulled on his Taimak film, *The Black Ninja*, George Tan moved into an office at 701 7th Avenue in Times Square and launched Dragon Video, running two-page ads in *Black Belt* magazine offering "the finest in martial arts entertainment" on VHS. He also claimed to be writing a 10-volume encyclopedia of Bruce Lee titled *Tracking the Dragon* that promised to be "the most detailed biography ever written on the man" and would "leave no stone unturned." The first five volumes were due to be published by November 27, 1990—"in time for [Bruce's] 50th birthday"—but the tome remains unpublished to this day. Dragon Video faded away sometime in the '90s as Tan relocated to Southeast Asia and got involved in filmmaking and other home video enterprises overseas.

EMBASSY HOME ENTERTAINMENT

In 1985, the Coca-Cola Co. paid $485 million for Embassy Communications, then turned around a year later and sold their very successful home video entity, Embassy Home Entertainment (EHE), to Nelson Entertainment for $85 million. During this time, EHE put out a package of martial arts movies they had acquired from World Northal—*Dynamo*, *Golgo 13: Kowloon Assignment*, *A Man Called Tiger*, *Master Killer*, *Slaughter in San Francisco*, *The Tattoo Connection*, *The Tattooed Dragon*, *The Three Avengers*, and *When Taekwondo Strikes*—which contributed to the estimated $172 million in sales the company made during those two years.

FAR EAST FLIX

John Gainfort, who loved kung fu movies ever since his father took him to see *Fists of Fury* and *The Chinese Connection* on 42nd Street, started Far East Flix in 1992 and still operates the business to this day. Early on, he sold tapes at New York–area comic shows and through mail order, running ads in *Fangoria* magazine. His best-selling titles back then were *Godzilla vs. Mechagodzilla II*, John Woo's *The Killer* and *Hard Boiled*, and *The Five Deadly Venoms*. These days, he sells through his website, and the Japanese TV series *The Yagyu Conspiracy* is one of his most popular sellers.

GOODTIMES HOME VIDEO

If you ever wondered why there were always racks of Goodtimes videos taking up space in record stores and the music departments of retailers like Kmart, Ames, Woolworth, and McCrory, there's a very good explanation: Goodtimes was a division of Cayre Industries, which owned numerous record labels and was one of the first companies to get into the mass marketing of cheap public domain videotapes. *How* cheap was Goodtimes? you ask. So cheap, they let the buyers write the titles on the tapes rather than paying to print labels for each movie. Goodtimes was also one of many public domain companies to put out *Fists of Fury* and *The Chinese Connection* on video, and most of their subsequent martial arts releases had either "Bruce" or "ninja" in the title, with *Bruce Lee vs. Ninja* earning special mention for including both. (See also: VIDEO TREASURES on page 346.)

JARS VIDEO COLLECTIBLES

Founded in 1987 by Joseph Ragus Sr., JARS Video Collectibles was a mail-order sales and rental service that carried martial arts movies from all the major companies and was widely regarded as one of the most reliable sellers in the business. Ragus also took orders over the phone, which often led to hours-long conversations with fans about their favorite kung fu stars and movies. He passed away on January 25, 2022, at age 67.

MASTER ARTS VIDEO

Joseph A. Pershes started Master Arts Video in Northridge, California, in 1984 and quickly won over kung fu fans with a wide range of titles including *Dragon Lee vs. The Five Brothers*, *Duel of Ultimate Weapons*, *Invincible Obsessed Fighter*, *7 Star Grand Mantis*, *The True Game of Death*, and a couple of surprises like *Lightning Kung Fu*, which had been the name of Sammo Hung's *The Victim* in US theaters but turned out to be Shaw Brothers' *Shaolin Prince* on the Master Arts tape. Some of their titles are still highly sought after today by video collectors.

OCEAN SHORES VIDEO LTD.

Formed by Garrie J. Roman in 1980 as a subsidiary of the Ocean Shores Group, a Hong Kong company that specialized in investment and gold trading, Ocean Shores Video was run by a former bullion dealer named Jackson Hung and quickly established itself as "the leader in Chinese kung fu" with a catalog boasting "hundreds of the best kung fu movies in English." Business was so strong that, in 1984, they opened a US branch called Ocean Video in North Hollywood, California.

RAINBOW AUDIO & VIDEO INCORPORATION

Based in San Francisco, Rainbow Audio & Video distributed Hong Kong television programs and movies on videocassette, including many martial arts and heroic bloodshed movies from big studios like Shaw Brothers and Golden Harvest. Throughout the 1980s, their tapes were available in Asian video stores across the United States, as well as specialty video shops like Kim's Video in New York City. Rainbow changed its name to Pan-Asia Video, Inc., in the early '90s and eventually became Tai Seng Video.

REGAL VIDEO

The shadiest of all '80s video companies that dealt in martial arts movies, Regal Video regularly released movies without the inconvenience of acquiring their rights. It was located somewhere in New York City and run by someone who operated under the pseudonym Jay Davison. Regal's kung fu releases include *Survival of a Dragon*, *Snake Fist of a Buddhist Dragon*, *Kung Fu Rebels*, *Rivals of the Silver Fox*, and others.

SATURN PRODUCTIONS

Shortly after Tom Ward resigned as the president and CFO of 21st Century Distribution in 1983, he started Saturn Productions, a video label mostly devoted to English-dubbed kung fu movies. Since he already knew the theater owners on 42nd Street, the 35mm prints of many Saturn releases would play exclusively on the block after being transferred to video, including *5 Pattern Dragon Claws*, *Incredible Shaolin Thunderkick*, *Mantis Under Falcon Claws*, *Raiders of Buddhist Kung Fu*, *Silver Hermit from Shaolin Temple*, and others. Saturn videocassettes were also sold at the concession stands of a couple of the 42nd Street theaters.

SOUTH GATE ENTERTAINMENT

Run by Yoram Pelman, the former head of Trans World Entertainment, South Gate is best remembered by kung fu fans for putting out a handful of Shaw Brothers films on video circa 1990, including letterboxed editions of *The Chinatown Kid* and *The Bells of Death*. The other releases were *Two Champions of Shaolin*, *Challenge of the Masters*, *Duel of Fists*, and *King Boxer*. South Gate was dissolved in May 1992.

UNICORN VIDEO

Formed in Chatsworth, California, in 1981 by Edward Goldstein (CEO) and his son Keith (VP of sales), Unicorn made a name for itself early on with a catalog of Spanish-language movies, blaxploitation, and action-adventure films, including martial arts movies like *Against the Drunken Cat Paws*, *Dance of Death*, *Death Duel of Mantis*, *The Eighteen Jade Arhats*, *Return of the Chinese Boxer*, and many others. Edward Goldstein died of a heart attack in May 1990 at the age of 67, and Unicorn vanished from the home video field a short time later.

VIDEO GEMS

When husband-and-wife owners Joseph and Vivienne Infante started Video Gems in Los Angeles in 1979, their output mostly consisted of children's films and violent martial arts movies. Some of the many titles they released from the latter genre include *Bruce Le in New Guinea*, *Enter the Panther*, *Fist of Fury II*, *Incredible Master Beggars*, *Kill the Golden Goose*, *Ninja Massacre*, *The Real Bruce Lee*, and *Two Graves to Kung-Fu*. The couple filed Chapter 11 bankruptcy in April 1987, and Video Gems was history by the time Joseph died of cancer in September 1992 at age 59.

VIDEO TREASURES

Owned and operated by Pete Hyman and Jack Rose of Surplus Record and Tape Distributors and Stan Sirote of Countrywide Tape and Record Distributors, Video Treasures was another company that specialized in discount mass market and public domain video releases, including martial arts fight compilations and double features recorded at the lowest-quality SLP speed—but, unlike Goodtimes, they at least printed the titles of the movies on their tapes.

VISTA HOME VIDEO

A subsidiary of the Vista Organization Ltd., Vista Home Video was formed in July 1986 and headed by Nicholas Santrizos, the former president of Thorn EMI/HBO Video. In 1987 they released five Shaw Brothers movies on VHS: *Fists of the White Lotus*, *Shaolin Executioner*, *Shaolin Challenges Ninja*, *Super Ninjas*, and *Ten Tigers of Kwangtung*.

OCEAN SHORES ®️ VIDEO LIMITED   ®️ OMNI VIDEO CASSETTE

OCEAN SHORES
THE LEADER IN CHINESE KUNG FU

Enjoy Your Movie At Home

We have hundreds of best Kung-Fu Movies in English Version for exclusive world video rights (except South East Asia) which are available for sale.

Other film titles for theatrical and T.V. rights for U.S.A., Canada, Europe, Latin America and Africa also available.

Further information, please contact: Mr. Jackson Hung, Managing Director, Ocean Shores Video Ltd.

OCEAN SHORES VIDEO LTD.
(A MEMBER OF OCEAN SHORES GROUP)

Suite 1711, Hang Lung Centre, Paterson Street, Hong Kong. Tel: 5-779325 (4 Lines) Cable: "OCEAN SHORE" Telex 65806 SHORE HX
Banker: American Express Bank H.K.

AT THE MANILA INTERNATIONAL FILM FESTIVAL CONTACT: Mr. Jackson Hung, Hilton Hotel, Manila, Jan. 18-23rd, 1982
P.S. WE ARE ALSO INTERESTED IN BUYING THEATRICAL/35MM AND VIDEO RIGHTS

DIGITAL DOJO

KARATE CHAMP APPEARED IN 1984, one year after the Great Video Game Crash, when too many developers flooded the market with too much substandard product, causing the closure of mall arcades and home computer stores across the country. Despite the slump, Data East's *Karate Champ* instantly began sucking up quarters with its innovative one-on-one battles, voice acting, "hold-back-to-block" mechanic, and bonus training round in which players fought a bull, Mas Oyama-style.

Home computer gaming made a comeback in 1984 as well with yet another game featuring martial artists with bull heads (another Oyama tribute?): Jordan Mechner's *Karateka*, developed in his dorm room for the Apple II. There had been martial arts games for home computers before, like the Atari 2600's *Karate* (1982), which the Digital Press voted "one of the worst games of all time," and *Attack of the Phantom Karate Devils* (1983), featuring a final level that intentionally and confusingly looked like the game had malfunctioned, but Broderbund snapped up *Karateka* and released it for the ultra-affordable Commodore 64, where it became one of their all-time bestsellers alongside *Where in the World is Carmen San Diego?*

In December 1984, *Kung-Fu Master* debuted in Japan, sending players through five levels of a pagoda, fighting a different martial arts master on each one, *Game of Death*–style. At the last minute, Data East changed its title to *Spartan-X*, the name of the latest Jackie Chan hit (aka *Wheels on Meals*, 1984) and renamed its main characters Thomas and Sylvia after Jackie and his girlfriend in the movie. There would also be a released-in-Japan-only *Spartan X 2* in 1991, and an NES game called *Jackie Chan's Action Kung Fu*, released in 1990.

In 1984, Bruce Lee got a by-the-numbers platform jumper called *Bruce Lee* for the Atari 400 and 800. It would be 1989 before he got another fighting game, *Bruce Lee Lives: The Fall of Hong Kong Palace*, that came complete with a book written by his widow, Linda Lee.

1985 saw *Shanghai Kid* and *Yie Ar Kung Fu* hit arcades, with *Yie Ar* taking the genre forward with its 11 playable characters. *36th Chamber of Shaolin* got its due in the 1989 Amiga game *Chambers of Shaolin*, and ninjas inevitably appeared in *Dragon Ninja* (1988), but the next big fighting game was Capcom's *Street Fighter* (1987).

It would be *Street Fighter II* (1991), a slicker, more sophisticated iteration, that became a mega hit, but *Street Fighter* still managed to be ranked one of the top dedicated arcade games of 1988 and hooked plenty of players. And its only playable characters came straight out of the '70s: blond, Caucasian champ Ken Masters, based on Joe Lewis (see 280), and the intense, dark-haired Ryu, based on the original bullfighter himself, Mas Oyama.

(bottom) *Cyber Ninja* (1988) tied a movie to a video game, courtesy of game company Namco and its creator, Keita Amemiya, who would go on to direct the popular home video hit *Zeiram* (1991). The movie version of *Cyber Ninja* eventually landed on American shores in 1995, but the game, a side-scrolling ninja adventure, never arrived in the West.

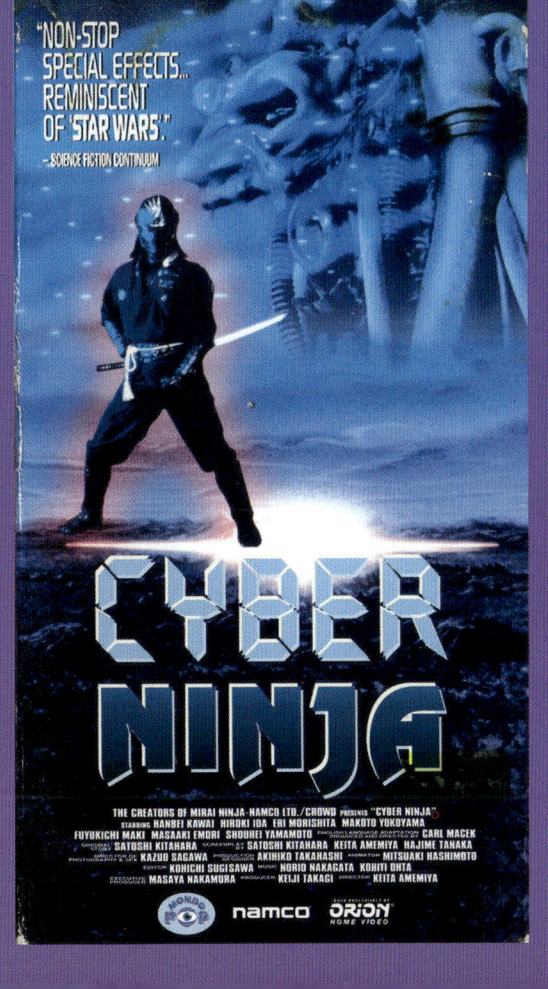

He's a martial arts master who refuses to fight.
He's a Bruce Lee fan who's so sure he's Oriental that
he eats popcorn with chopsticks.
His friends think he's too serious.
His family thinks he's crazy.
His enemies think he's no challenge.
But she knows he's
THE LAST DRAGON.
ALL THE POWER, GLAMOUR,
AND EXCITEMENT OF MOTOWN
FEATURING THE MUSIC OF
STEVIE WONDER, SMOKEY ROBINSON,
THE TEMPTATIONS, SYREETA, ROCKWELL,
CHARLENE, WILLIE HUTCH, ALFIE, VANITY
AND
DeBARGE
BERRY GORDY'S
THE LAST DRAGON
TRI-STAR PICTURES PRESENTS "BERRY GORDY'S THE LAST DRAGON" A MOTOWN PRODUCTIONS PICTURE
Starring TAIMAK JULIUS J. CARRY III CHRIS MURNEY LEO O'BRIEN FAITH PRINCE GLEN EATON and VANITY
Director of Photography JAMES A. CONTNER Executive Producer BERRY GORDY Written by LOUIS VENOSTA
Produced by RUPERT HITZIG Directed by MICHAEL SCHULTZ
PG-13 Parents Are Strongly Cautioned to Give Special Guidance for Attendance of Children Under 13
Some Material May Be Inappropriate for Young Children
ORIGINAL SOUNDTRACK ALBUM AVAILABLE ON MOTOWN RECORDS AND CASSETTES
DOLBY STEREO
IN SELECTED THEATRES
A TRI-STAR RELEASE
©1985 Tri-Star Pictures.
All Rights Reserved.
TRI STAR PICTURES

Teen-Agers Rampage in Center City

Rampage in Midcity

Shops are v 20 Seized as Youths Battle, Loot Shops
in rampage along Chestnut Street

EVEN THOUGH AUDIENCES HAD MOSTLY moved to home video, there were still people going to movie theaters and watching either threadbare American martial arts flicks or re-releases of old-school kung fu. It seemed like someone could make some money from that audience and so Motown's Berry Gordy decided it would be him.

Depending on how you look at it, *The Last Dragon* (1985) was either a corrective to *The Karate Kid*, which had come out the year before and managed to completely scrub the Black experience from American martial arts, or it was one of the biggest-budgeted Bruceploitation flicks ever made. The brainchild of Gordy, a man with an eye for talent, it starred Prince protégé Vanity, who had just left the Purple One to record her *Wild Animal* album. Gordy may have come late to the kung fu party, but he thought combining music and martial arts made sense.

The movie's main character, Leroy Green, a young, Black martial artist, took forever to cast. The filmmakers finally settled on Taimak Guarriello, a student of Ron Van Clief's, who wasn't the greatest actor ever born but whose martial arts skills were fierce and who had a terrific energy the filmmakers thought they could harness. A few days into shooting, Vanity walked off the set as a ploy to renegotiate her deal, but instead of sitting down at the table, the producers replaced her with Laura Carrington, best known at the time as "the Blind Girl" from Lionel Richie's video for "Hello." Realizing she held a weak hand, Vanity agreed to come back after they acquiesced to a few face-saving concessions. Taimak tried the same thing, maybe thinking that as the star he had more leverage, but the second he didn't show up on set, the producers re-cast the part with Clayton Prince, an actor who had almost landed the role in the first place. Taimak came back fast.

Helmed by Michael Schultz, an African-American director best known for comedies like *Car Wash* (1976) and *Which Way Is Up?* (1977), *The Last Dragon* is a cut and paste

---

(opposite page) A weirdly family-friendly film, *The Last Dragon* featured Taimak as a sweet, virginal martial artist who could catch bullets in his teeth and glowed with power when he took on the bragging bad guy, Sho Nuff.

(above) Headlines breathlessly covering *The Last Dragon* Easter Sunday disturbance in Philadelphia.

of the entire legacy of kung fu cinema, from the wisecracking old master of *Snake in Eagle's Shadow* to a scene shot inside the Victory theater on the Deuce. There are outbreaks of b-boying, a small scene-stealing part by Ernie Reyes Jr. (who would soon shoot to fame in the Golden Harvest co-production *Teenage Mutant Ninja Turtles*, 1990), more mugging than you'd find at midnight in Central Park, and Ron Van Clief, the Black Dragon himself, choreographing the action.

Bursting with music, shot on a tight schedule and even tighter budget, *The Last Dragon* got terrible reviews but did well enough for people to talk sequel. The plan was to do three movies and a clothing line, but Taimak had interest from other investors for a film called *The Black Ninja*, and if Berry Gordy wanted him for another *Dragon* movie, he felt he had a good negotiating position. But Gordy, uninterested in dealing with temperamental actors again, scrapped the film. When *The Black Ninja* fell apart soon after, Taimak was left without a franchise.

The Last Dragon proved to be a gift, however, for people who liked to link kung fu movies to violence. On Easter Sunday 1985 in Philadelphia, *Friday the 13th Part V* and *The Last Dragon* were screening at the Duke and Duchess on Chestnut Street. Thousands of kids, fresh out of church, were told the afternoon screenings were sold out, so they hung around the block, going to arcades and talking to their friends. When the doors opened at 4pm to let the audiences out, a group of kids rushed the doors to get in, and it devolved into a riot. Five thousand kids spent two hours fighting, breaking windows, and looting at least three stores. Police in riot gear appeared, made arrests, and shut down the arcades.

Police Commissioner Gregore Sambor blamed *The Last Dragon*.

"As far as I could tell, it started there," he told the press. "They come out and all want to be kung fu masters. We've had this happen before."

Despite people on the scene saying it was kids wanting to get into the next movie who started the disturbance, and the theater owner pointing out *The Last Dragon* was rated PG-13 and had been playing for two and a half weeks without incident, the cops used the riot as an excuse to start cracking down on kung fu. They wanted theater managers to

MAN DIES IN KARATE ATTACK AT KUNG FU MOVIE

(above) A headline commemorating the August 1985 murder of an audience member at the 42nd Street Apollo Theater during *The Last Dragon*.

(opposite page) *The Last Dragon* put Taimak on the cover of magazines, shilled soundtrack albums, and ran cross-promotions with hair product companies. Anything to sell tickets! The casting call notice is for Taimak's *Black Ninja* movie that never came to fruition.

INSIDE KARATE

K48667
August 1985
$2.00 £1.50 DGS

The Last Dragon's
TAIMAK!
The Next Master of Martial Arts Movies?

STREET SURVIVAL
The Science of Staying Alive

DEADLY DEFENSE
Break Your Opponent's Body

Gogen "The Cat" Yamaguchi:
Karate's Last Warrior

HARA-KIRI
Death Before Dishonor

BLACK HAIR IS in cooperation with TRI-STAR PICTURES celebrates the release of BERRY GORDY'S **THE LAST DRAGON**
Written by LOUIS VENOSTA Directed by MICHAEL SCHULTZ
starring **VANITY**

WIN! INVITATIONS TO A SPECIAL SCREENING MARCH 20TH. PLUS MANY OTHER PRIZES FROM THE FILM.

BHI COUPON
BLACK HAIR IS
$7.50 OFF RELAXER

OFFICIAL ENTRY
I want to see the special screening of Berry Gordy's 'The Last Dragon'.
Name
Address
Phone _____ Age ___
Mail or bring to BLACK HAIR IS
137 E. 62nd St. New York, NY 10021
No purchase necessary. Drawing to be held 12 noon, March 19, 1985 at the salon. Winners will be notified by phone.

Get the Glow March 22nd at a theater near you!

ATTENTION OPEN CASTING CALL
For The New Movie Starring
TAIMAK
Hero of "The Last Dragon"
Saturday, April 11, 1987

8:00 a.m. until 12:30 p.m. at
Movie Center Five
235 Westr 125 Street (bet. 7 & 8 Aves.)
**RAPPERS • DANCERS
ACTORS • ACTRESSES
• MARTIAL ARTISTS •**
Ivory League Pictures and Taimak
Hope To See You
(212) 996-4102 (24 hr Hot Line)

inform them in advance when these ultra-violent kung fu movies would be shown so they could arrange for mounted officers and extra cops to be stationed outside the theaters to control crowds.

That August, at the Apollo Theater on 42nd Street, an argument broke out between two middle-aged patrons during a screening of *The Last Dragon*, and one beat the other to death. He seemed to be deeply unbalanced, and the other man may have died of a heart attack rather than what the papers called "a barrage of karate chops," but it didn't matter. Reporters dragged out the Easter Sunday riot in Philadelphia again and declared *The Last Dragon* "a movie likely to draw an audience of fanatics aroused by it." It didn't help that a murder and rape suspect had been arrested in the same Deuce theater a few months before, also during a screening of *The Last Dragon*.

The Last Dragon blame game started an ugly trend that saw theater owners and managers target Black films as sites of potential violence, and it would be the last big American martial arts movie where Black martial artists took center stage.

A few years later, Jean-Claude Van Damme minted box office gold with Cannon's *Bloodsport* (1988) and tournament movies became all the rage. The Rhee brothers turned in *Best of the Best* (1989), Don "the Dragon" Wilson rocketed to straight-to-video fame with *Bloodfist* (1989), and the whole trend culminated in the birth of the multimedia *Mortal Kombat* franchise and its 1995 blockbuster Hollywood film.

Except for the Roxy's programming and the Saturn Productions videotapes sold at the Lyric's concession stand, kung fu movies disappeared from the Deuce completely after October 1987, the same month WNEW 5 stopped showing "Black Belt Theater" movies on Saturday afternoons. The Deuce remained kung fu–free for two years, until Jean-Claude Van Damme's *Kickboxer* kicked its way onto both screens of the Cine 42 in October 1989, with two old house favorites as its co-features: *The Mystery of Chess Boxing* in one theater and *Mad Monkey Kung Fu* in the other.

The idea of working hard to develop your skills fell out of favor in the get-rich-quick fever of the '80s, when years of training could be condensed into a single action montage set to a snappy song, and Ivy League grads became overnight successes on Wall Street. Run DMC took hip hop mainstream, eliminating smooth flow for battle rhymes and embracing the American mainstream with their chart-shattering Aerosmith duet "Walk This Way." As early as 1983, graffiti, once seen as urban blight, was the centerpiece of a show at the blue chip Sidney Janis Gallery on the Upper West Side. Fab 5 Freddy sold one of his spray-painted canvases to European-American Bank. He sold another to Chase Manhattan.

Chinatown theaters across America had long battled racial violence. The Ritz in Minneapolis closed in 1980 and re-opened as a Chinese theater run by a man named Sy Soo before it was firebombed less than a year later. The arsonists sprayed "White Power" across its front doors. In LA, an unknown thug smashed the Kuo Hwa's glass front doors every Friday night for 12 weeks. But what finally shut down the Chinese theaters was home video.

The Pagoda in New York died first. In an interview with the *Daily News*, an usher at the Music Palace said, "People don't need us anymore. They can rent the new movies before we show them here." In Los Angeles, one theater manager said, "Most of our customers are older immigrants . . . We get very few teen-agers . . . they don't come unless the parents bring them." In the lobby, a customer said his teenaged children refused to come with him on his weekly trek to the Garfield. Then he pointed to his three-year-old son and said, "When he grows up, he won't watch Chinese movies either."

It wasn't just the Chinese theaters. In 1984, Leonard Clark and Robert Brandt claimed their grindhouses on the Deuce were still drawing up to 10,000 paying customers every day, but the arrival of crack cocaine changed everything. Suddenly the dealers, who used to trail alongside pedestrians hawking everything from switchblade knives to photo IDs, were shouting, "Crack it up, jumbo, jumbo" to passersby, who felt empty vials crunching underfoot. Transactions went down in the open or under the cover of the marquees. Raging, fist-swinging freak-outs spilled over into the Broadway theater district.

In one sweep of 42nd Street, the NYPD arrested 32 crack dealers. Cash-strapped families stopped attending movies on the Deuce, intimidated by the violence. Soon, Clark reported to *Variety* that ticket sales were down by a third in his theaters, and the Brandt houses were taking a similar hit. Something had to be done. The two theater owners joined forces and enlisted the help of the Guardian Angels, New York City's unofficial vigilante gang of amateur law enforcers, offering them a rent-free office on the fourth floor of the Selwyn Theatre Building in exchange for their help cleaning up the street. They strung "Crack Down on Crack" banners outside their theaters and became a constant presence, confronting dealers and chasing them from the block, but audiences still wouldn't come back. (In a strange coincidence, one of the Angels helping clean up the Deuce was Clayton Prince, who had almost replaced Taimak in *The Last Dragon*.) Crack broke New York City, rocketing the homicide rate to an all-time high of 2,245 murders in 1990 and giving the mayor the justification he needed to unleash the police on Black and brown communities, ready to bust skulls in the name of law and order.

Behind the scenes, the wheels of the 42nd Street Urban Development Corporation were turning, and the Deuce's days were numbered. Claiming concern for the neighborhood's well-being, civic leaders wanted to "clean up" the street, but it was really all about the Benjamins. The Corporation's 1984 redevelopment proposal promised the city $776 million in real estate taxes over the next 20 years, as opposed to only $123 million if the block was left in its current condition. To New York City, this was a no-brainer.

Business owners filed 42 lawsuits to stop the demolition of the Deuce, but even though it took 56 lawyers, six years, and $300 million in compensation, the city ultimately demolished all three blocks of the Deuce, condemning 34 buildings and moving 236 tenants. It wasn't over until 1996, but in the end, three city blocks of businesses and restaurants used by a majority minority population were replaced by Broadway theaters showing *The Lion King* and offices for the whitest of white-collar workers. Similar scenes took place all over the country, wherever grindhouse theaters occupied potentially valuable real estate.

World Northal went into a tailspin during the latter half of the '80s after the Metromedia channels that had been such good customers were sold to Rupert Murdoch's News Corporation and 20th Century Fox, neither of which wanted to continue kung fu programming. As a result, the fifth and final "Black Belt Theater" package—which contained 12 titles, including *Disciples of the Master Killer* (aka *Disciples of the 36th Chamber*), *Fangs of the Tigress* (aka *My Young Auntie*), and *The Invincible Pole Fighter* (aka *The 8 Diagram Pole Fighter*)—was a complete no-show in New York City, although four channels elsewhere picked it up. The films ran in LA, Atlanta, Houston, and Miami from spring 1987 into 1989, then World Northal dissolved.

While crack and real estate taxes killed kung fu movies on the ground, another enemy helped take them off the airwaves. In 1984, President Reagan's FCC removed the requirement that you could only broadcast 12 minutes of advertising for every hour of programming. The airwaves were suddenly for sale to the highest bidder, and the first modern infomercial appeared in 1985. By 1988, they generated $350 million in sales, ramping up to $900 million by 1993, filling Saturday mornings and late-night slots with come-ons for Cher's Aquasentials, Richard Simmons' Deal-a-Meal, Victoria Jackson's Beauty Breakthroughs, and the Bacon Wave. Dionne Warwick and her Psychic Friends hoovered money from the pockets of lonely suckers, while Ronald Reagan's son Michael shilled the Euro Trym Diet Patch, which turned out to be a scam that resulted in big fines.

Everyone hated infomercials, but everyone watched them.

"What do you want me to say?" barked Martin Blair, a spokesman for New York's WCBS to the *New York Times*. "Yeah, we run them. So what?"

CHINATOWN'S LAST THEATER

93 BOWERY, NEW YORK, NY
BOX OFFICE HOTLINE 212-925-1079

(opposite page) New York's Sun Sing tried to lure customers with fliers adertising their latest movies.

(above) Maybe the saddest newspaper ad of all time.

TIGER YANG & ABFLEX

THE CLAIMS PUT FORTH in late-night infomercials eventually came to the attention of the Federal Trade Commission, which launched investigations with names like Project Workout and Operation Waistline. One product that invited scrutiny, and helped usher in the end of the era, was the AbFlex, a device that guaranteed its users "a flat, sexy stomach in just three minutes a day!" and resembled "a small Stealth fighter that you aim at your stomach," according to one TV critic. The celebrity spokesman for AbFlex was martial arts legend Tiger Yang, a star of over 30 kung fu movies, including *Game of Death II*, *Blind Fist of Bruce*, and *Little Mad Guy*. A Korean martial artist and creator of Moo Yea-Do—a combination of karate, kung fu, aikido, and taekwondo—Yang's achievements included training Muhammad Ali for his 1976 War of the World fight in Tokyo against professional wrestler Antonio Inoki, teaching martial arts to police officers in Chicago and CIA agents in Washington, DC, breaking blocks of ice with his bare hands on *The Tonight Show Starring Johnny Carson*, and pulling an eight-ton truck with his mouth on the ABC reality series *That's Incredible!*

Yang signed with a new talent agency in 1980 and was cast in the upcoming *Cleopatra Jones and the Cambodian Connection* as the martial arts expert in a team of mercenary specialists who join forces with Cleo (Tamara Dobson) to wipe out a heroin processing plant in Cambodia. Ted Post (*Good Guys Wear Black*) was set to direct, but the talent agency went belly-up and the film never got beyond a synopsis. Yang opened a Moo Yea-Do school in California to make ends meet, where schlock filmmaker Ted V. Mikels of *Astro-Zombies* and *Blood Orgy of the She-Devils* infamy hired him for a quickie action vehicle that began filming in May 1982 as *Operation Overkill* and promptly wrapped eight years later as *Mission: Killfast*. By the time it was released, Yang's name was in the international news for challenging heavyweight champs Mike Tyson and Leon Spinks to fights in Seoul (the Spinks fight *almost* happened), and within a few years he was on TV, taking a sledgehammer to cinderblocks balanced on the six-pack abdominals of AbFlex president Martin Van Der Hoeven, to the astonishment of late-night viewers nationwide.

By 1996, AbFlex was one of several abdominal crunching devices causing a frenzy on late-night TV. The Ab Roller, Perfect Abs, the Ab Trainer, the Ab Coach, the Ab Answer, Abs Only, and the Ab Machine battled it out for viewer dollars, suing each other, and sparking the federal investigations that, in particular, saw the AbFlex legally barred from making spot-reduction claims. By the time the fighting was over, $1 billion in ab devices had been sold, but the battle for eyeballs between the ab device peddlers had pushed the price for television airtime beyond what an independent investor could afford. By 1999, thanks to Tiger Yang and the Ab Device Apocalypse, late-night airtime was too expensive for lone wolves with a dream, like Billy Blanks, to afford and it became the almost exclusive property of enormous direct marketing firms.

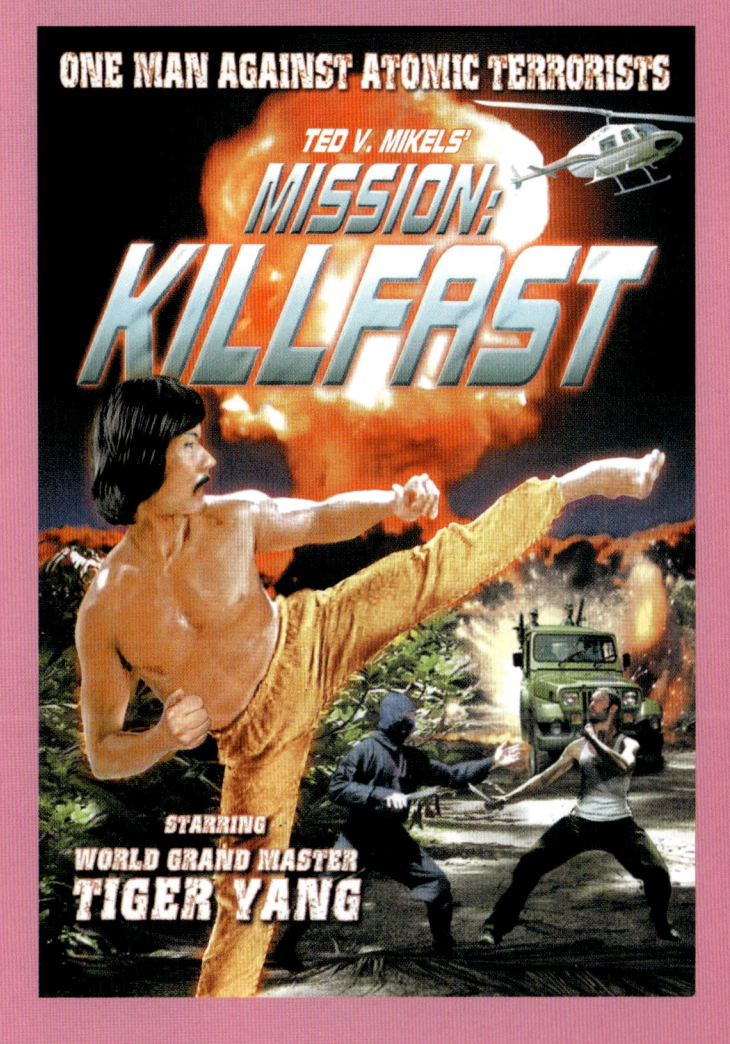

The dragons had finally been defeated by the most powerful enemy of all: cold, hard cash.

PEG MURCHIE PRODUCTIONS
PROUDLY PRESENTS
TED V. MIKELS'
MOTION PICTURE SEMINAR
An electrifying 1 day excursion into the magic of movie-making. Twice World Champion Martial-Arts Master Tiger Yang on panel.
SUNDAY, APRIL 27th
10:00 A.M.-5:30 P.M.
WESTLAKE PLAZA HOTEL
880 Westlake Blvd.
Luncheon included
$65 (student discount $10)

ENTER THE VIDEO KID

WORLD NORTHAL STOPPED RELEASING Shaw Brothers movies in the late '80s, but fans still wanted product and bootleggers were there to meet their needs. 79th Street Video in Chicago boasted a selection of 30,000 movies and once rented 5,000 videos in a single day. "The most profitable thing going on for me is karate films," owner Russ Pine told the *Chicago Tribune* in 1994. "Over the last 10 years, I've had to replace *Chinese Super Ninjas*, *Five Fingers of Death*, and *Five Deadly Venoms* between 200 and 300 times."

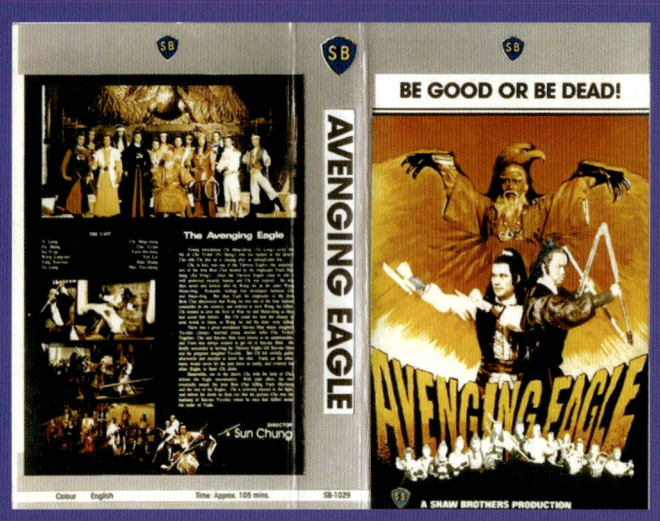

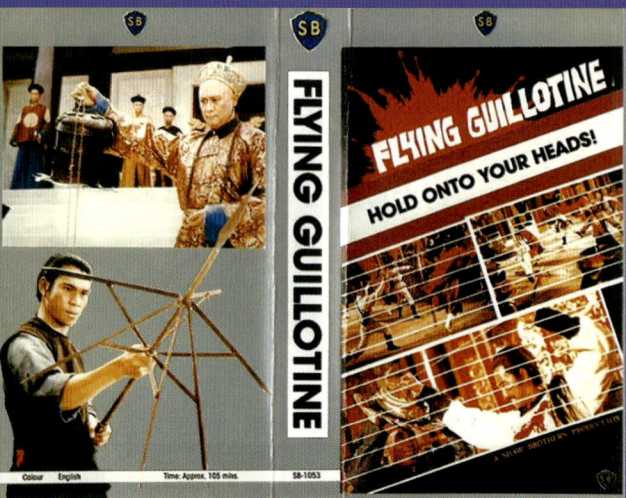

Coincidentally or not, those were also the first three kung fu movies released by the notorious bootleg outfit SB Video when it was launched in the fall of 1985 by a 16-year-old who was known around 42nd Street as the Video Kid but who was actually Johnnyray Gasca, a Puerto Rican kid from the Bronx. Deuce denizens gave him that nickname because he was the only person they knew who had two VCRs and a video camera. After ingratiating himself with theater managers and projectionists by plying them with videotapes, Gasca was given carte blanche to record whatever movies he wanted directly off the grindhouse screens, usually from balconies that were closed to the public. He also ingratiated himself with editor Larry Bensky and his assistant, John Keogh, who cut trailers and TV spots for World Northal. Gasca was soon dropping by the editing suite whenever Bensky wasn't there to run off VHS copies directly from the ¾-inch masters. Word spread quickly and the teenage entrepreneur was soon making deals with sub-distributors, enlisting professional duplicators to fill orders, and taking on a business partner he refers to as Ralph who helped create box art for the SB releases. "I made $97,000 from '87 to late '88, and about $40,000 in '89," Gasca states.

Everything went smoothly until a wheeler-dealer who called himself George Tan entered the picture. His last name sure as hell wasn't Tan; he'd appropriated that from Larry Tan, an actor, fight choreographer, and martial arts instructor who had trained celebrities like Billy Idol and Joel Grey. An associate of Ralph's—the two supplied kung fu programming for the Roxy video grindhouses—the mustached and mulleted Tan had gotten $8,000 from Ralph to shoot fight scenes for *The Black Ninja*, which was set to star Taimak of the *The Last Dragon*. *Black Ninja* was written by Tan and Keogh as a remake of Shaw's *8 Diagram Pole Fighter* with an African-American gang in place of the Yang Clan, but Tan's bootleg version of the original *Pole Fighter* hit stores before Gasca's SB version, and Gasca blew a gasket when he found out his bootleg had been bootlegged. He literally ran Tan off the Deuce.

Around that time, someone at World Northal showed up for work one day with a tape of *8 Diagram Pole Fighter* they'd spotted in a store window, and within a minute of popping it into a VCR and pressing "play," the salespeople in the TV division recognized the film as one of their own. This pan-and-scan transfer of the top title in their upcoming "Black Belt Theater 5" package could only have come from their own editing suite. Bensky and Keogh were immediately fired.

"They walked me out of the building—threw me out with all my personal stuff," Bensky remembers. "It was my fault because I didn't watch [Keogh] closely enough."

And Gasca?

"The last title I put out was *Stroke of Death* aka *Monkey Kung Fu*," he said. "Then I went to California to try to get in the film business with Cannon." When he arrived and saw SB Videos on the shelves in some LA video stores, he realized his bootlegs had arrived in Hollywood before he did.

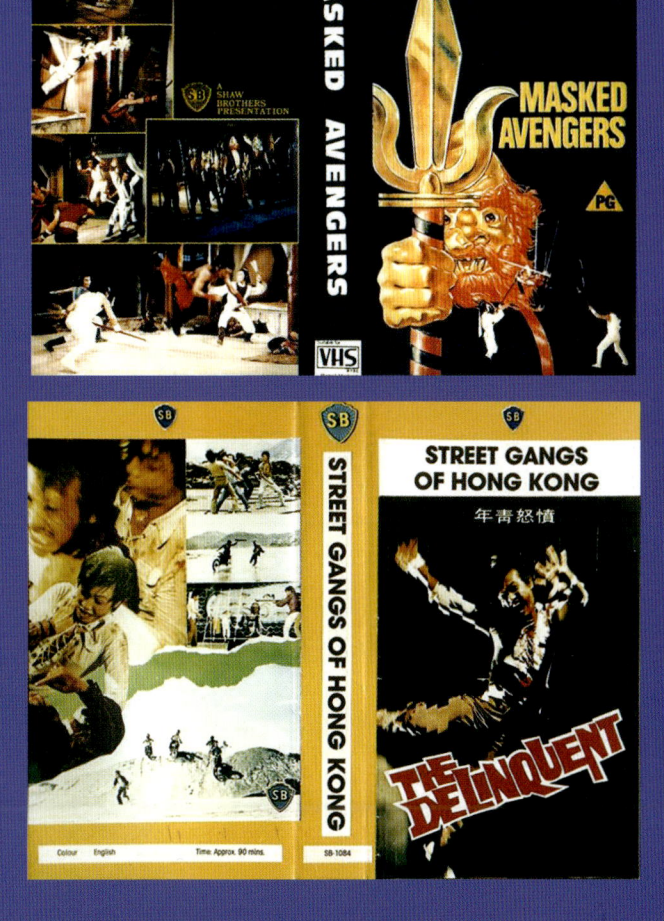

(top) A 1986 ad for Brooklyn and Queens video stores like Crazy Mary's Video Asylum that sold Johnnyray Gasca's SB Videos.

(bottom) Taiwanese actress Pearl Chang Ling, star of the most popular TV series in Taiwan during the 1974-1975 season, *The Bodyguards*, managed to parlay her small-screen fame (even Chiang Kai-shek was a fan) into a career as an action heroine in wu xia films like *China Armed Escort* (1976), *Invincible Swordswoman* (1977), and *My Blade, My Life* (1978). She stepped behind the camera in the early '80s to write, produce, and direct a handful of increasingly strange vanity projects, including the insane wu xia fantasy *Wolf Devil Woman* (1982), her best-known film in the US thanks to its home video release through Ocean Shores.

Martial arts movies hit the bargain bin. Oscar-winning editor and Grindhouse Releasing co-founder Bob Murawski designed this "Karate Classics" flyer in 1987 while working for Detroit-based sub-distributor Mason Releasing Corp. with the goal of squeezing a few more flat-rate bookings out of the 35mm prints that MRC still had in storage.

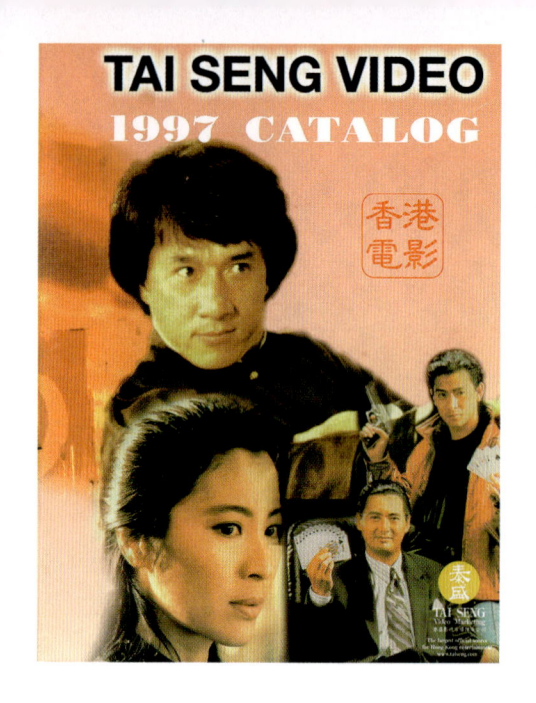

NOTHING EVER ENDS. IN 1993, Bruceploitation returned to the big time when Jason Scott Lee played Bruce in *Dragon: The Bruce Lee Story*. Approved by Linda Lee, it featured scenes of Lee fighting a demon, perpetuated the myth that Warner Bros. stole his idea for the *Kung Fu* TV show, and earned $35 million at the box office.

In 1995, Jackie Chan tried to break into Hollywood . . . again. Only this time it worked. He starred, choreographed the action, and handpicked his director and co-stars for *Rumble in the Bronx*, which grossed $32 million. The following year, he dusted off his 1992 movie, *Police Story 3: Supercop*, dubbed it into English, and watched as it picked up a cool $16 million in the States. One year later, Sammo Hung directed the Wong Fei-hung movie *Once Upon a Time in China and America* (1997), down in Texas, which became a huge hit. Suddenly, Hong Kong movies were cool.

Sammo took meetings with Lucasfilm and landed a network television show, *Martial Law* (1998–2000). Yuen Wo-ping became an international superstar choreographing the action on *The Matrix* (1999). Chinese producers became cinema sherpas, shepherding Anglo executives to Chinatown theaters around the Los Angeles area, like the Garfield and the Kuo Hwa, to see Hong Kong films.

Times were changing, but history kept repeating itself. When Antoine Fuqua directed Hong Kong star Chow Yun-fat in his debut Hollywood film, *The Replacement Killers* (1998), the studio notes came fast and furious, some of them plainly racist, like the injunction that Chow could not kiss his Anglo co-star, Mira Sorvino. Fuqua, who was Black, did his best but figured he'd get fired until Chow called a meeting with the executives.

"He's the director," Chow said, pointing to Fuqua. "Back off and let him direct, or fire him, and I'll quit."

They backed off. The movie became a hit. Like W.E.B. Du Bois said, "China is colored, and knows to what the colored skin in this modern world subjects its owner."

Tai Seng, a San Francisco–based Chinese video distributor, started an English Department in 1996 due to popular demand from fans. They put out letterboxed, subtitled, uncut versions of Hong Kong movies, some with special features. Immediately, other video distributors pushed back, stealing their sales materials at trade shows and telling them their movies would fail even as their titles climbed the charts.

"They're not used to seeing these films distributed by Asians, and they're not used to seeing them treated with respect," Frank Djeng, the head of the English Department,

ROM THE GENIUS BEHIND THE *A CHINESE GHOST STORY* SERIES

A DEMONIC FORCE GRIPS THE CITY IN TERROR. ALL ARE DEFENSELESS AGAINST ITS POWER. ALL BUT THREE... THREE WOMEN WARRIORS.

the Heroic Trio

ANITA MUI
THE MADONNA OF ASIA

MAGGIE CHEUNG
FORMER MISS HONG KONG

MICHELLE YEOH
ASIA'S TOP ACTION ACTRESS

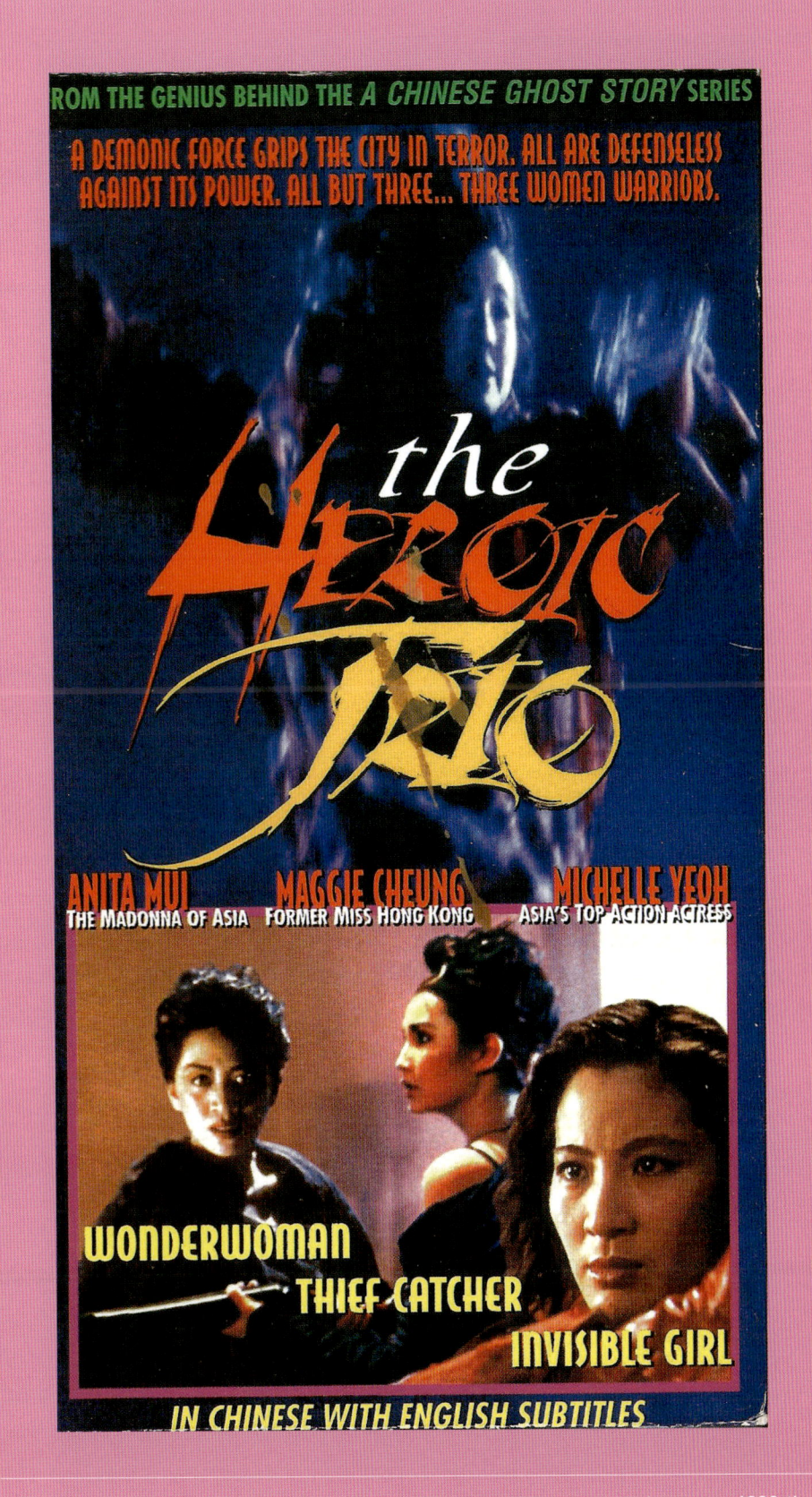

WONDERWOMAN
THIEF CATCHER
INVISIBLE GIRL

IN CHINESE WITH ENGLISH SUBTITLES

Tai Seng's movies earned respect from eager fans, and their sales were massive. In summer 1996, their tape of the Michelle Yeoh, Maggie Cheung, Anita Mui fantasy kung fu flick *The Heroic Trio* became the number one bestselling video in Virgin Megastores across America, prompting one competitor to gripe, "Who the hell is this Tai Seng?"

says. "They felt threatened, and they should have been. Because we ate into their profit margins."

By the late '90s, Netflix, Blockbuster, and Wal-Mart were putting in orders for tens of thousands of Tai Seng's tapes and DVDs. Tape traders and fanzines popped up everywhere. Kung fu movies had once inspired Black and Latino kids and now those same kids kept the flame alive. Barry Long, a clerk at Kim's Video, an ultrahip New York City video superstore popular with filmmakers, punks, and punk filmmakers, began going to Chinatown and buying Hong Kong movies on VHS and writing English language synopses on Post-it notes he taped to the back. He preached the Hong Kong gospel, constantly making new converts, and eventually co-wrote the pivotal book *Hong Kong Babylon*, which, in the mid-'90s, was excerpted in the prestigious *New Yorker* magazine.

Up in Times Square, Charles Woods opened the 43rd Chamber, selling legit and bootleg kung fu movies, which became a pilgrimage site for fans from the suburbs and a social club for Black martial artists and film fans in the city.

In 1993, RZA and the Wu-Tang Clan released their album *Enter the Wu-Tang (36 Chambers)*. It went platinum, returned New York City to prominence in hip hop after the scene had shifted to the West Coast and set the template for hardcore hip hop throughout the '90s. It also featured samples from *Shaolin vs. Wu Tang*, *Executioners from Shaolin*, *Five Deadly Venoms*, and *Ten Tigers of Kwantung*. RZA had seen them all in 42nd Street grindhouses.

Clayton Prince, who almost replaced Taimak in *The Last Dragon*, wound up playing the martial arts sidekick on the CBS series *Dark Justice* from 1991 to 1993. In a weird twist, he bought the *Black Ninja* title and released his own version direct to video in 2003. Bobby Samuels started studying martial arts after seeing *Five Fingers of Death* in Times Square. He learned Hung Gar kung fu from Maurice Turnstall in Philadelphia, but his other teacher was the movies.

(top) Fan magazines were essential to keep the fires burning. Author/actress/black belt Sidney Filson became the first female editor of an American martial arts magazine in 1977 with the publication *Dragon*.

(bottom) In 1985, the authors of *Martial Arts Movies from Bruce Lee to the Ninjas*—Ric Meyers and Bill and Karen Palmer—and *Spaghetti Cinema* editor William Connolly created M.A.M.A. (Martial Arts Movie Associates), which ran for 20 years and 55 issues.

"My VCR broke freeze framing on David Chiang, trying to learn moves from him," he said.

He got a job with an airline for the free tickets and used his vacation time to return to Hong Kong again and again until he got hired as a stuntman on *Gambling Ghost* (1991). When the airline pink-slipped him, he called Sammo Hung and asked for a job.

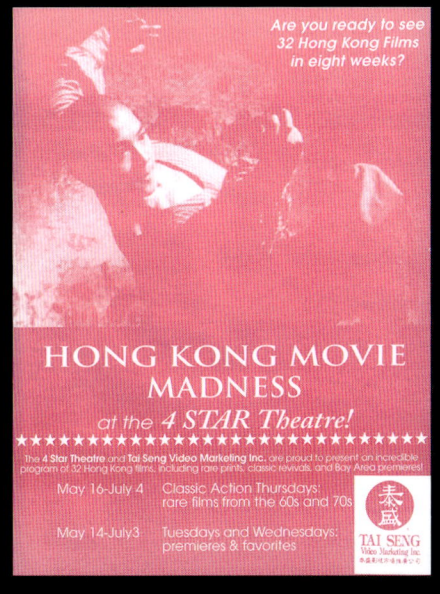

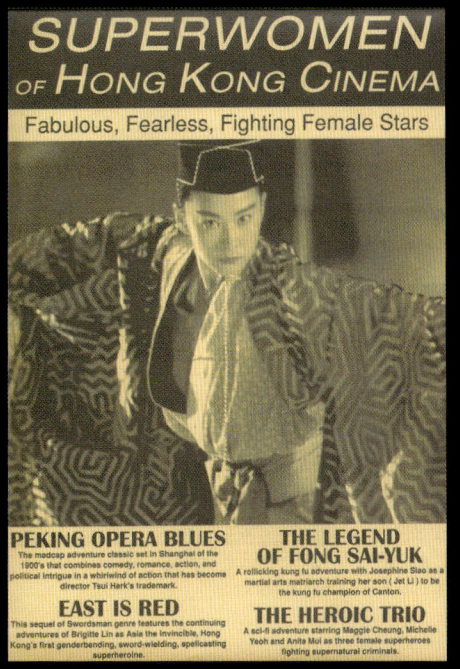

(top row) Floridians Wanda Butts, Karen Shaub, and Rebecca Hall started *Fangraphic* in 1976, producing 12 issues before Shaub and Hall changed the name to *The Jade Screen* and published three more issues as a duo, ending in 1983.

(bottom row) As Chinatown cinemas closed, fans and savvy programmers would book prints from Golden Harvest and Tai Seng directly, scheduling Hong Kong marathons and showcases at the 4 Star in San Francisco and Cinema Village in NYC.

For the next several years he worked as a stuntman and assistant for Hung, becoming the first Black American member of the Hong Kong Stuntman's Association.

And what about the old-school heroes? The ones who started it all?

Angela Mao retired from the movies, relocated to the US, and opened several restaurants in Queens. In 1994, at the age of 51, Ron Van Clief returned to the ring to fight in the UFC. Although he was defeated by Royce Gracie, he went on to serve as commissioner of the UFC. Dennis Brown is still teaching kung fu in DC. Loren Avedon produced some of his own movies before working as a stuntman and action choreographer on film and TV. Jim Kelly passed away in 2013. Jimmy Wong Yu had mostly retired from acting before he suffered a debilitating stroke in 2011. However, he threw himself into his physical therapy and appeared in an action role in the 2011 movie, *Wu Xia* for which he was nominated for two film awards, and won Best Actor at the Taipei Film Awards in 2013 for his performance in *Soul*. Sadly, he passed away in 2022. Charles Bonet died while this book was being written. La Pantera had seen his home taken from him as a kid, had his dojo seized as an adult, played a guy fighting to save his home in *Death Promise*, and at the end of his life he had become actually homeless.

The '80s had left Bonet feeling unmoored, and he'd abandoned New York City, ("I started to feel like doors were closing in on me," he said.) For years, he wrestled with drug addiction and eventually wound up on the streets. When his former students discovered their beloved teacher was homeless, they picked him up, put a roof over his head, and helped him get sober. When we interviewed him for this book, he was living in Arizona, running an informal street ministry. One of the last things he said in an interview was that he'd recently received another call from Ron Van Clief.

"He said, 'Pantera?'" Bonet told us. "'You ready to come out of retirement?' He said a company wanted to do a sequel to *The Death of Bruce Lee* and they wanted us. I said, 'I'm ready whenever you are.' I'm just as good, just as mean, and just as fast as I used to be."

And he was. They all were. They all are.

Bonet joins Sonny Chiba, Leo Fong, and Corey Yuen, who all left us too soon. But wherever light passes through a projector, they live again. Young, angry, men and women, Black and white, Asian and Latino. Standing up to the Man with nothing but their empty hands. And they win. Over and over again they win. You can tear down their neighborhoods, make them walk through doors marked "Colored Only," rig their fights, dump their films, stack the odds, but when one goes down, another steps into their place, fighting with kung fu, karate, hapkido, hip hop, nunchuks, windmills, head spins, two turntables, a can of spray paint.

They can never be defeated, their spirit cannot be broken, they'll never retreat, they'll never surrender, because they're an unstoppable army—an Army of Bruce.

Maybe the Bruceploitation movies got it right after all?

Because this dragon never dies. This dragon can't be killed. This dragon goes on and on.

This dragon lives forever.

(opposite page) San Francisco's Sun Sing became a movie theater in 1949. It appeared as a location in Orson Welles' *Lady from Shanghai* that same year. It closed in 1986 and is now a retail space.

(above) The last double feature to play at the Music Palace was *City Hunter* (1993) and *Liu Jai: Home for the Intimate Ghosts* (1991) on Friday, June 30, 2000. It is now the Wyndham Garden Hotel. The hundreds of 35mm film prints found in its basement, stretching back to the glory days of the Hong Kong film industry, wound up in a dumpster.

THIS STORY NEVER ENDS

"THE BEST MARTIAL ARTS ON EARTH COME FROM SATURN

THE CRIPPLED MASTERS vs. SONNY CHIBA

There's always more to this story. We haven't even talked about the late '80s craze for girls-with-guns movies that introduced the world to hard-hitting, high-kicking action actresses like Yukari Oshima and Moon Lee. We completely skipped any mention of the legion of talented disabled martial artists who made their way to the silver screen, too, like Ted Vollrath, a veteran who lost both his legs in the Korean War and went on to be a champion on the tournament circuit, dishing out karate beatdowns from his wheelchair. He starred in *Mr. No Legs* (1978), a wild exploitation film from the mind of director Ricou Browning, the stuntman who played the creature in the first *Creature from the Black Lagoon* and who created the lovable TV dolphin Flipper.

Then there was Thomas Hong Chiu-ming, a victim of thalidomide poisoning who was born with no arms, and Frankie Shun Chung-chuen, who didn't have the use of his legs. Together, between 1979 and 1983, these two wildly accomplished martial artists starred in three kung fu movies, including *Crippled Masters* (1979) and *Fighting Life* (1981), demonstrating their jaw-dropping abilities, even if the films themselves are pretty threadbare.

These movies are a journey with no end, full of an uncountable number of heroes, and this book is barely the first step along a road that will take you to places you never dreamed. Never stop! Wild treasures await you!

ACKNOWLEDGMENTS

We couldn't have written this book without the help and participation of the following individuals. They all went above and beyond by sharing their time, their memories, and their photographs, even diving back into family albums and financial records to make sure that this book is as accurate as possible. Any errors are entirely ours, not theirs.

Bill Ackerman
Loren Avedon
Maryam Aziz
Jason Bailey
Brian Bankston
John Blyth Barrymore
Don Bendell
Larry Bensky
Joshua Bilmes
Marcus Boas
Charles Bonet
Joe Bob Briggs
Dennis and Andrena Brown
James Bruner
Brian Camp
Zack Carlson
John Charles
Dennis Coffey
William Connolly
Gary Crutcher
Mike Decker
Sebastian del Castillo
Grant Delin
Michael Dennis
Matt Desiderio
John W. Donaldson
John Dvi-Vardhana
Jesse Easley
Richard Ellman
Ryan Emerson
Luis Fernandez
Tim Ferrante
Sidney Filson
Alice Fraser
Neva Friedenn
Veronica Fury
Johnnyray Gasca
Colin Geddes
Michael Gingold

Teel James Glenn
Jeff Goodhartz
John Grace
David Gregory
Daniel Griffith
Donald Guarisco
Harry Guerro
Larry Hama
Jon Hatton
Lance D. Hayes
Jim Healy
Gary Hertz
Marc Edward Heuck
Bruce Holecheck
Alice Hsia
Judge Sandra Ikuta
Ed Ikuta
Carey Ishizuka
Wanda Iola
Kier-La Janisse
Laird Jimenez
Larry Joachim
Marco Joachim
C. Courtney Joyner
Jonathan Kaplan
Larry Karaszewski
Serafim Karalexis
Scott Kaufman
Paul Kazee
Dan Kelly
Erik Knutsen
David Anthony Kraft
Paul Kyriazi
Tim League
Andrew Leavold
Sarai Berenstein Levene
Terry Levene
Vincent Lyn
Jim Markovic
Mel Maron

Paul Maslak
Kelli McAdams
Ric Meyers
Steve Mitchell
Carl Morano
Bob Murawski
Devin Murphy
Simon Nuchtern
Craig Oldham
Kathy O'Tierney
Danny Opatoshu
Serge Ou
Danny Peary
Glenn Perry
Clayton Prince
Steve Puchalski
Joe Rubin
Robert Samuels
Edwin Samuelson
John Sandstrom
Ryo Sandstrom
Josh Schafer
Karen Shaub
Sam Sherman
Jack Sholder
Jason Simos
Taimak
Brad Tierney
Goran Topalovic
Curtis Tsui
Brandon Upson
Marc Walkow
Julie Webber
Wayne Weil
Michael J. Weldon
William Wilson
Michael Worth
Joe Ziemba

IMAGE CREDITS

FEATURED ARTISTS

Hisham Abed: page 198 * **Neal Adams**: 113 (*Bruce Lee The Man, The Myth*), 141 (*They Call Me Bruce Lee [From China with Death]*), 163, 211-219, 241, 247 (*The Mystery of Chess Boxing*), 259* **Neal Adams and Dick Giordano**: 191 (*Sister Street Fighter*) * **George Akimoto**: 225 * **Ken Barr**: 87 (*Kung Fu Avengers*), 193 (*The Stranger and the Gunfighter*) * **Marcus Boas**: 95 (*Dragon Lee vs. the 5 Brothers*), 132 (*Dragon on Fire* and *Rage of the Dragon*), 140 (*Dragon's Inferno*), 180, 247 (*Mad Monkey Kung Fu*), 251 (NTA ad) * **James Cameron**: 252 (*The Instructor*) * **Nick Cardy**: 186 * **Chet Collom**: 67, 147 (Myron Bruce Lee painting), 223 * **Jim Craig**: 91 (*Hands of the Dragon*) * **Ron Croci**: 157 * **Luis Dominguez**: 122-123 (*Dynamite Dragon*), 129, 132 (*The Dragon's Showdown*), 133, 134 (*Fighting Dragon vs. The Deadly Tiger*), 137 (*The Dragon from Shaolin*), 164, 181 (*The Eagle's Showdown*), 190 (*Karate Warriors*), 191 (*Dragon Princess*), 226 (*Fighting Mad*), 276 (*Magnificent Bodyguard*), 278, 313 (*Death Mask of the Ninja*) * **B. Emmett**: 143, 187 (*The Bodyguard*) * **Fritz**: 73 * **Paul Fung, Jr.**: 90 (*Hong Kong Phooey*) * **Charles Gehm**: 84 (*Judo Boy*) * **Bob Gleason**: 152 * **Mike Grell**: 91 (*Karate Kid #1*) * **Larry Hama and Ralph Reese**: 183 (*Zatoichi*) * **"Hary"**: 12-13 * **Richard Hescox**: 146 (*They Call Me Bruce?*) * **H.**: 287 * **Ken Hoff**: 273 (*Kung Fu Halloween*) * **Carey Ishizuka**: 367 (*Fangraphic*) * **Jim Janes**: 103 * **David Jarvis**: 193 (*The Horseman and the Samurai*) * **Michael Kanarek**: 189 * **Dick Knipe**: 175 (*5 Deadly Venoms*) * **Mort Künstler**: 207 (*Three the Hard Way*) * **Roger LaManna**: 191 (*Lady Street Fighter*) * **Bob Larkin**: 87 (*Mondo*) * **Lyall**: 326 * **M.V.**: 281 * **Fran Matera**: 83 (Bruce Lee comic) * **Maughan**: 238-239 * **Frank McLaughlin**: 88 (*Judomaster* and *The Charlton Bullseye #3*) * **Gray Morrow** 76-77 (*The Dynamite Brothers* and *Main Street Women*) * **Joseph Musso**: 327 (*King Kung Fu*) * **Tim Passey**: 295 * **Bob Peak**: 80 (*Enter the Dragon*) * **Barye Phillips**: 84 (*Kill Me in Tokyo* and *Kill Me in Shunjuku*) * **Warren Sattler**: 88 (*Yang #5*), 89 (*House of Yang #5*) * **Barry Smith**: 85 (*K'ing Kung Fu #1: Son of the Flying Tiger*) * **John Solie**: 78 (*Seven Blows of the Dragon*), 156 * **Robert Tanenbaum**: 209 (*Hot Potato*) * **Tom Tierney**: 109, 121 (*Chinese Hercules*), 158, 159 (*Kung Fu of the 8 Drunkards*), 165, 174, 209 (*The Tattoo Connection*), 263 (*Jade Claw*), 313 (*Pay or Die*) * **J. Van Tamelen**: 146 (*A Fistful of Chopsticks*) * **C.W. Taylor**: 283 * **Al Weiss**: 90 (*Richard Dragon, Kung Fu Fighter #2*) * **Honi Werner**: 285 * **Wil**: 289 * **Phyllis Williams**: 366 (*M.A.M.A.*) * **Greg Winters**: 291 (*P.O.W. the Escape*) * **Mike Zeck**: 89 (*Master of Kung Fu*) * Credits for all other illustrations are unknown.

ART AND PHOTO CREDITS

8-11 (Jack Sergel material): courtesy **Julie Webber**; 15: courtesy **Johnson Publishing Company**; 16, 292: courtesy the **Glenn Perry Collection**; 17: courtesy **Sijo Steve Muhammad and the Black Karate Federation**; 21, 23, 54: courtesy **Brian Bankston/Cool Ass Cinema**; 28: courtesy the **Jack Tillmany Collection**; 29 (The Pagoda photo): courtesy **The Lee Family/Museum of Chinese in America (MOCA) Collection**; 29 (Sun Sing photo): courtesy **Corky Lee**; 29 (Music Palace photo); 255, 369 (Music Palace photo): courtesy **Goran Topalovic**; 31: courtesy **Heritage Auctions**; 48-49, 106-107, 120 (*The Young Dragon*), 121 (*The King of Kung Fu*), 141 (*They Call Me Bruce Lee [From China with Death]*), 161 (*Duel of the Iron Fist*), 163, 211-219, 259, 304 (*Ninja Warriors*): courtesy **Serafim Karalexis**; 65: courtesy **Dan Kelly**; 67, 147 (Myron Bruce Lee painting), 223: courtesy **Richard Ellman**; 70 (Super 8 film boxes): courtesy **Paul Kazee**; 76-77 (*The Dynamite Brothers* and *Main Street Women*): courtesy **Samuel Sherman**; 80 (Robert Lee photo); 111, 208 (Jim Kelly photo), 235-236, 353 (*Inside Karate*): courtesy **Ed Ikuta**; 98-99, 103, 116, 128 (*Call Me Dragon*), 132 (*Dragon on Fire* and *Rage of the Dragon*), 138 (*The Tigers Claw*), 140 (*The Steel Fisted Dragon* and *Dragon's Inferno*), 188, 190 (*The Executioner*), 221, 247 (*Mad Monkey Kung Fu*): courtesy **Televentures Corporation**; 102 (New Amsterdam photo): courtesy **Richard Baron**; 105 (*Fist Like Lee Part II*): courtesy **happiestkidfinds.com**; 108 (Adolph Caesar and Fred Williamson photo), 109, 143, 167, 250: courtesy **Terry Levene/Aquarius Releasing**; 128 (*Wanted! Bruce Li, Dead or Alive* and *Bruce Li's Magnum Fist*), 130 (*Bruce's Ninja Secret*), 179, 243 (*Octagon Force* and *A Fist for a Fist*), 263 (*Mean Drunken Master*): courtesy **Neva Friedenn**; 148-151 (Pinoy Collection and Filipino ads): courtesy **Simon Santos**; 155 (Empire Theater photo): courtesy **American Classic Images**; 164 (*The Deadly Hands of Kung Fu #13*): courtesy **Charles Damiano**; 164 (*Iron Fingers of Death*), 256: courtesy **Skeme Richards**; 197 (Golden Harvest Theatre flyer): courtesy **Colin Geddes**; 202, 229, 366 (*Dragon*): courtesy **Sidney Filson/*Dragon* magazine**; 204 (*Inside Kung-Fu*): courtesy **Dennis and Andrena Brown**; 208 (Cine 42 photo): courtesy **Fred Holt**; 246 (Empire Theatre flyer): courtesy the **Gary Hertz Collection**; 246 (Empire Theatre photo): courtesy **Matt Weber**; 253: courtesy **William Lee**; 265 (Bella Union photo): courtesy **Greg Mancuso**; 269: courtesy **Jared King**; 314: courtesy **James Bruner**; 356: courtesy **John W. Donaldson**; 360-361: courtesy **Tom Fardy/Venom Video**; 363: courtesy **Bob Murawski**; 366 (*M.A.M.A.*), 367 (*The Jade Screen*): courtesy **John Grace**; 368: courtesy **Gundi Vigfusson**; all other images courtesy **Grady Hendrix and Chris Poggiali**.

ABOUT THE AUTHORS

GRADY HENDRIX is an award-winning *New York Times* bestselling author and one of the founders of the New York Asian Film Festival. He's covered the Asian film industry for *Variety*, *Sight & Sound*, and *Film Comment*, among others. He lives in NYC.

CHRIS POGGIALI is a librarian, writer, and film historian who edited the fanzine *Temple of Schlock* from 1987 to 1991 and brought it back as a blog in 2008. He has written about film for numerous magazines, websites, and DVDs/Blu-rays.